New Wave of British Heavy Metal
The Bands of the NWOBHM (1978–1982)

Contents

1 Introduction to NWOBHM   **1**
- 1.1 New Wave of British Heavy Metal 1
  - 1.1.1 Background 1
  - 1.1.2 Identity and style 3
  - 1.1.3 Music and lyrics 4
  - 1.1.4 History 5
  - 1.1.5 Influences and legacy 10
  - 1.1.6 See also 11
  - 1.1.7 Notes 11
  - 1.1.8 References 18

2 NWOBHM BANDS (in Alphabetical Order)   **20**
- 2.1 A II Z 20
  - 2.1.1 Career 20
  - 2.1.2 Discography 20
  - 2.1.3 See also 20
  - 2.1.4 References 20
  - 2.1.5 External links 20
- 2.2 Angel Witch 21
  - 2.2.1 Biography 21
  - 2.2.2 Influence 21
  - 2.2.3 Band members 22
  - 2.2.4 Timeline 22
  - 2.2.5 Discography 22
  - 2.2.6 See also 23
  - 2.2.7 References 23
  - 2.2.8 External links 23
- 2.3 Atomkraft 23
  - 2.3.1 History 23
  - 2.3.2 Discography 25

	2.3.3	Personnel	25
	2.3.4	See also	25
	2.3.5	Bibliography	25
	2.3.6	External links	25
2.4	Avenger (British band)		25
	2.4.1	History	26
	2.4.2	Members	26
	2.4.3	Discography	26
	2.4.4	See also	26
	2.4.5	References	26
	2.4.6	External links	27
2.5	Baby Tuckoo		27
	2.5.1	Discography[5]	27
	2.5.2	See also	27
	2.5.3	References	27
2.6	Battleaxe (band)		27
	2.6.1	Cover art	27
	2.6.2	Changing of "Ians"	28
	2.6.3	Personnel changes	28
	2.6.4	Latest developments	28
	2.6.5	Members *For Burn This Town*	28
	2.6.6	Members For *Power from the Universe*	28
	2.6.7	Post *Universe* Lineup 1	29
	2.6.8	Post *Universe* Lineup 2	29
	2.6.9	*Nightmare Zone* Lineup	29
	2.6.10	Current Lineup	29
	2.6.11	Discography	29
	2.6.12	Discography compilations	29
	2.6.13	See also	29
	2.6.14	External links	29
2.7	Black Rose (UK band)		29
	2.7.1	History	30
	2.7.2	Discography	30
	2.7.3	Band Members	31
	2.7.4	See also	31
	2.7.5	References	31
	2.7.6	External links	31
2.8	Blitzkrieg (band)		31

- 2.8.1 History . . . 31
- 2.8.2 Members . . . 31
- 2.8.3 Former members . . . 31
- 2.8.4 Discography . . . 32
- 2.8.5 See also . . . 32
- 2.8.6 References . . . 32
- 2.8.7 External links . . . 32
- 2.9 Bronz . . . 32
  - 2.9.1 Career . . . 33
  - 2.9.2 Albums . . . 33
  - 2.9.3 See also . . . 33
  - 2.9.4 References . . . 33
  - 2.9.5 External links . . . 34
- 2.10 Budgie (band) . . . 34
  - 2.10.1 Career . . . 34
  - 2.10.2 Musical style and legacy . . . 35
  - 2.10.3 Members . . . 35
  - 2.10.4 Discography . . . 35
  - 2.10.5 References . . . 35
  - 2.10.6 Notes . . . 36
  - 2.10.7 External links . . . 36
- 2.11 Chateaux (band) . . . 36
  - 2.11.1 Biography . . . 36
  - 2.11.2 Line-up . . . 37
  - 2.11.3 Discography . . . 37
  - 2.11.4 See also . . . 37
  - 2.11.5 References . . . 37
  - 2.11.6 External links . . . 37
- 2.12 Chrome Molly . . . 37
  - 2.12.1 History . . . 37
  - 2.12.2 Discography . . . 38
  - 2.12.3 See also . . . 38
  - 2.12.4 References . . . 38
  - 2.12.5 External links . . . 38
- 2.13 Cloven Hoof (band) . . . 38
  - 2.13.1 Biography . . . 38
  - 2.13.2 Discography . . . 39
  - 2.13.3 Line-up . . . 40

- 2.13.4 Former members (those featured on albums) ... 40
- 2.13.5 See also ... 40
- 2.13.6 References ... 40
- 2.13.7 External links ... 40
- 2.14 Dedringer ... 40
  - 2.14.1 History ... 40
  - 2.14.2 Line-up ... 41
  - 2.14.3 Discography ... 41
  - 2.14.4 See also ... 41
  - 2.14.5 References ... 41
  - 2.14.6 External links ... 41
- 2.15 Def Leppard ... 41
  - 2.15.1 History ... 42
  - 2.15.2 Musical style and legacy ... 48
  - 2.15.3 Band members ... 49
  - 2.15.4 Side projects ... 49
  - 2.15.5 Discography ... 49
  - 2.15.6 Awards and nominations ... 49
  - 2.15.7 See also ... 50
  - 2.15.8 References ... 50
  - 2.15.9 External links ... 52
- 2.16 Demon (band) ... 52
  - 2.16.1 Early years ... 52
  - 2.16.2 1985-1992 ... 52
  - 2.16.3 Reunion 2001-present ... 52
  - 2.16.4 Members ... 53
  - 2.16.5 Discography ... 53
  - 2.16.6 See also ... 54
  - 2.16.7 References ... 54
  - 2.16.8 External links ... 54
- 2.17 Diamond Head (band) ... 54
  - 2.17.1 Band history ... 54
  - 2.17.2 Influences ... 57
  - 2.17.3 Lack of success ... 57
  - 2.17.4 Influence on Metallica ... 57
  - 2.17.5 Band members ... 58
  - 2.17.6 Discography ... 58
  - 2.17.7 See also ... 59

2.17.8	References	59
2.17.9	External links	59
2.18	Dumpy's Rusty Nuts	60
2.18.1	See also	60
2.18.2	References	60
2.18.3	External links	60
2.19	E. F. Band	60
2.19.1	Discography	61
2.19.2	See also	61
2.19.3	External links	61
2.20	Elixir (band)	61
2.20.1	History	61
2.20.2	Discography	62
2.20.3	See also	62
2.20.4	References	62
2.20.5	External links	62
2.21	Eric Bell	62
2.21.1	Career	62
2.21.2	Discography	64
2.21.3	References	64
2.21.4	External links	64
2.22	Ethel the Frog (band)	64
2.22.1	Career	65
2.22.2	Post Ethel	65
2.22.3	Line-up	65
2.22.4	Discography	65
2.22.5	See also	65
2.22.6	References	65
2.22.7	External links	65
2.23	Fist (band)	65
2.23.1	Discography	66
2.23.2	See also	66
2.23.3	References	66
2.23.4	External links	66
2.24	Geoff Barton	66
2.24.1	References	67
2.25	Girl (band)	67
2.25.1	History	67

- 2.25.2 Members 67
- 2.25.3 Discography 67
- 2.25.4 Videography 68
- 2.25.5 See also 68
- 2.25.6 References 68
- 2.25.7 External links 68
- 2.25.8 Sources 68
- 2.26 Girlschool 68
  - 2.26.1 History 68
  - 2.26.2 Music and style 74
  - 2.26.3 Reception 75
  - 2.26.4 Legacy 75
  - 2.26.5 Band members 76
  - 2.26.6 Discography 76
  - 2.26.7 Videography 76
  - 2.26.8 See also 76
  - 2.26.9 References 76
  - 2.26.10 External links 80
- 2.27 Grim Reaper (band) 80
  - 2.27.1 History 80
  - 2.27.2 Band members 81
  - 2.27.3 Discography 81
  - 2.27.4 In popular culture 81
  - 2.27.5 See also 81
  - 2.27.6 References 82
  - 2.27.7 External links 82
- 2.28 Haze (band) 82
  - 2.28.1 History 82
  - 2.28.2 Images 82
  - 2.28.3 Discography 82
  - 2.28.4 References 83
  - 2.28.5 External links 83
- 2.29 Hell (band) 83
  - 2.29.1 Biography 83
  - 2.29.2 Musical style 84
  - 2.29.3 Band members 84
  - 2.29.4 Discography 85
  - 2.29.5 References 85

- 2.29.6 External links . . . 85
- 2.30 HellsBelles . . . 85
  - 2.30.1 1980s - Hell's Belles . . . 85
  - 2.30.2 2000s - HellsBelles . . . 86
  - 2.30.3 Current members . . . 86
  - 2.30.4 Original members . . . 86
  - 2.30.5 Other members . . . 87
  - 2.30.6 See also . . . 87
  - 2.30.7 References . . . 87
  - 2.30.8 External links . . . 87
- 2.31 Hollow Ground (band) . . . 87
  - 2.31.1 Biography . . . 87
  - 2.31.2 Members . . . 87
  - 2.31.3 Discography . . . 87
  - 2.31.4 See also . . . 88
  - 2.31.5 References . . . 88
  - 2.31.6 External links . . . 88
- 2.32 Holocaust (band) . . . 88
  - 2.32.1 Discography . . . 88
  - 2.32.2 Cover versions . . . 89
  - 2.32.3 See also . . . 89
  - 2.32.4 References . . . 89
  - 2.32.5 External links . . . 89
- 2.33 Iron Maiden . . . 89
  - 2.33.1 History . . . 89
  - 2.33.2 Image and legacy . . . 97
  - 2.33.3 Musical style and influences . . . 99
  - 2.33.4 Awards . . . 100
  - 2.33.5 Band members . . . 100
  - 2.33.6 Discography . . . 100
  - 2.33.7 Concert tours . . . 100
  - 2.33.8 See also . . . 100
  - 2.33.9 Notes . . . 100
  - 2.33.10 References . . . 104
  - 2.33.11 External links . . . 111
- 2.34 Jaguar (band) . . . 111
  - 2.34.1 History . . . 112
  - 2.34.2 Music style . . . 113

- 2.34.3 Discography ... 113
  - 2.34.4 Present band members ... 114
  - 2.34.5 Past band members ... 114
  - 2.34.6 See also ... 114
  - 2.34.7 References ... 114
  - 2.34.8 External links ... 114
- 2.35 Jameson Raid (band) ... 114
  - 2.35.1 Career ... 114
  - 2.35.2 Members ... 115
  - 2.35.3 Discography ... 116
  - 2.35.4 See also ... 116
  - 2.35.5 References ... 116
  - 2.35.6 External links ... 116
- 2.36 John McCoy (musician) ... 117
  - 2.36.1 Early career ... 117
  - 2.36.2 Career with Gillan ... 117
  - 2.36.3 Mammoth ... 117
  - 2.36.4 Equipment ... 117
  - 2.36.5 List of bands and artists worked with ... 117
  - 2.36.6 References ... 118
- 2.37 Judas Priest ... 118
  - 2.37.1 History ... 118
  - 2.37.2 Musical style and influence ... 124
  - 2.37.3 Personnel ... 125
  - 2.37.4 Discography ... 125
  - 2.37.5 Tours ... 125
  - 2.37.6 References ... 126
  - 2.37.7 External links ... 127
- 2.38 Lionheart (band) ... 127
  - 2.38.1 History ... 128
  - 2.38.2 Discography ... 128
  - 2.38.3 See also ... 128
  - 2.38.4 External links ... 128
- 2.39 List of New Wave of British Heavy Metal bands ... 128
  - 2.39.1 A ... 129
  - 2.39.2 B ... 129
  - 2.39.3 C ... 130
  - 2.39.4 D ... 131

2.39.5 E	131
2.39.6 F	132
2.39.7 G	132
2.39.8 H	133
2.39.9 I	133
2.39.10 J	134
2.39.11 K	134
2.39.12 L	134
2.39.13 M	134
2.39.14 N	135
2.39.15 O	135
2.39.16 P	135
2.39.17 Q	136
2.39.18 R	136
2.39.19 S	136
2.39.20 T	138
2.39.21 U	139
2.39.22 V	139
2.39.23 W	139
2.39.24 X	140
2.39.25 Y	140
2.39.26 Z	140
2.39.27 Notes	140
2.39.28 References	144
2.40 Magnum (band)	144
2.40.1 History	144
2.40.2 Band members	147
2.40.3 Discography	147
2.40.4 References	147
2.40.5 External links	147
2.41 Mama's Boys	148
2.41.1 Biography	148
2.41.2 Band members	149
2.41.3 Discography	149
2.41.4 See also	149
2.41.5 References	149
2.41.6 External links	149
2.42 Marseille (band)	149

- 2.42.1 History . . . 149
- 2.42.2 Band members . . . 150
- 2.42.3 Discography . . . 150
- 2.42.4 See also . . . 151
- 2.42.5 References . . . 151
- 2.42.6 External links . . . 151
- 2.43 Mirage (metal band) . . . 151
  - 2.43.1 References . . . 151
- 2.44 More (British band) . . . 151
  - 2.44.1 Line-ups . . . 152
  - 2.44.2 Discography . . . 153
  - 2.44.3 See also . . . 153
  - 2.44.4 References . . . 153
  - 2.44.5 External links . . . 153
- 2.45 Motörhead . . . 154
  - 2.45.1 History . . . 154
  - 2.45.2 Style . . . 164
  - 2.45.3 Cover art . . . 165
  - 2.45.4 Members . . . 166
  - 2.45.5 Discography . . . 166
  - 2.45.6 Filmography . . . 166
  - 2.45.7 Notes . . . 167
  - 2.45.8 References . . . 167
  - 2.45.9 Sources . . . 169
  - 2.45.10 Further reading . . . 170
  - 2.45.11 External links . . . 170
- 2.46 Nicky Moore . . . 170
  - 2.46.1 Discography . . . 170
  - 2.46.2 See also . . . 171
  - 2.46.3 References . . . 171
  - 2.46.4 External links . . . 172
- 2.47 Nightwing (band) . . . 172
  - 2.47.1 Formation, Something In The Air and Black Summer . . . 172
  - 2.47.2 Max Bacon, Stand Up and Be Counted and My Kingdom Come . . . 172
  - 2.47.3 Dave Evans, Glynn Porrino, Night of Mystery - Alive! Alive! and Nightwing VI . . . 172
  - 2.47.4 1996 Reunion, Natural Survivors, 2006 reunion and 8472 . . . 172
  - 2.47.5 Personnel . . . 173
  - 2.47.6 Discography . . . 173

- 2.47.7 See also . . . 173
- 2.47.8 References . . . 173
- 2.47.9 External links . . . 173
- 2.48 Pagan Altar . . . 174
  - 2.48.1 Biography . . . 174
  - 2.48.2 Line-up . . . 174
  - 2.48.3 Discography . . . 174
  - 2.48.4 See also . . . 174
  - 2.48.5 References . . . 174
  - 2.48.6 External links . . . 174
- 2.49 Paul Di'Anno . . . 175
  - 2.49.1 Career . . . 175
  - 2.49.2 The Beast . . . 179
  - 2.49.3 Singing style . . . 179
  - 2.49.4 Other interests . . . 179
  - 2.49.5 Personal life . . . 179
  - 2.49.6 Band timeline . . . 179
  - 2.49.7 Discography . . . 180
  - 2.49.8 See also . . . 182
  - 2.49.9 References . . . 182
  - 2.49.10 External links . . . 182
- 2.50 Persian Risk . . . 182
  - 2.50.1 History . . . 183
  - 2.50.2 Post break-up activities . . . 183
  - 2.50.3 Discography . . . 184
  - 2.50.4 See also . . . 184
  - 2.50.5 References . . . 184
  - 2.50.6 External links . . . 184
- 2.51 Pet Hate . . . 185
  - 2.51.1 See also . . . 185
- 2.52 Praying Mantis (band) . . . 185
  - 2.52.1 Career . . . 185
  - 2.52.2 Discography . . . 185
  - 2.52.3 Compilations . . . 186
  - 2.52.4 Lineups . . . 186
  - 2.52.5 See also . . . 186
  - 2.52.6 References . . . 186
  - 2.52.7 External links . . . 186

- 2.53 Quartz (metal band) 186
  - 2.53.1 History 186
  - 2.53.2 Members 187
  - 2.53.3 Discography 187
  - 2.53.4 See also 187
  - 2.53.5 References 187
  - 2.53.6 External links 187
- 2.54 Rainbow (rock band) 187
  - 2.54.1 History 188
  - 2.54.2 Band members 191
  - 2.54.3 Lineups 191
  - 2.54.4 Discography 191
  - 2.54.5 References 191
  - 2.54.6 Bibliography 192
  - 2.54.7 External links 192
- 2.55 Raven (British band) 192
  - 2.55.1 History 192
  - 2.55.2 Members 194
  - 2.55.3 Discography 194
  - 2.55.4 See also 195
  - 2.55.5 References 195
  - 2.55.6 External links 195
- 2.56 Rock Goddess 195
  - 2.56.1 History 195
  - 2.56.2 Discography 195
  - 2.56.3 See also 196
  - 2.56.4 References 196
  - 2.56.5 External links 196
- 2.57 Rogue Male (band) 196
  - 2.57.1 Discography 196
  - 2.57.2 See also 197
  - 2.57.3 External links 197
- 2.58 Ronnie James Dio 197
  - 2.58.1 Early years, education and musical training 197
  - 2.58.2 Career 197
  - 2.58.3 Personal life 200
  - 2.58.4 Legacy 200
  - 2.58.5 Band timeline 201

- 2.58.6 Discography ... 201
- 2.58.7 References ... 201
- 2.58.8 Sources ... 202
- 2.58.9 External links ... 202

2.59 Salem (UK band) ... 202
- 2.59.1 Career ... 202
- 2.59.2 Line-up ... 203
- 2.59.3 Discography ... 204
- 2.59.4 See also ... 204
- 2.59.5 References ... 204
- 2.59.6 External links ... 205

2.60 Samson (band) ... 205
- 2.60.1 Career ... 205
- 2.60.2 Discography ... 206
- 2.60.3 Members ... 206
- 2.60.4 Lineups ... 206
- 2.60.5 See also ... 206
- 2.60.6 References ... 206
- 2.60.7 External links ... 206

2.61 Satan (band) ... 206
- 2.61.1 Members ... 207
- 2.61.2 Discography ... 207
- 2.61.3 See also ... 207
- 2.61.4 References ... 207
- 2.61.5 External links ... 207

2.62 Savage (band) ... 207
- 2.62.1 Discography ... 208
- 2.62.2 See also ... 208
- 2.62.3 References ... 208

2.63 Saxon (band) ... 208
- 2.63.1 History ... 209
- 2.63.2 Personnel ... 212
- 2.63.3 Discography ... 212
- 2.63.4 See also ... 213
- 2.63.5 References ... 213
- 2.63.6 External links ... 213

2.64 Shy (band) ... 213
- 2.64.1 Biography ... 213

- 2.64.2 Discography . . . 214
- 2.64.3 Current members . . . 214
- 2.64.4 Previous members . . . 214
- 2.64.5 See also . . . 214
- 2.64.6 References . . . 214
- 2.64.7 External links . . . 214
- 2.65 Spider (British band) . . . 215
  - 2.65.1 Career . . . 215
  - 2.65.2 Band members . . . 215
  - 2.65.3 Discography . . . 215
  - 2.65.4 See also . . . 215
  - 2.65.5 References . . . 215
  - 2.65.6 External links . . . 216
- 2.66 Stampede (band) . . . 216
  - 2.66.1 History . . . 216
  - 2.66.2 Disbandment . . . 217
  - 2.66.3 Reunion . . . 217
  - 2.66.4 Current members . . . 217
  - 2.66.5 Discography . . . 217
  - 2.66.6 See also . . . 218
  - 2.66.7 References . . . 218
  - 2.66.8 External links . . . 219
- 2.67 Starfighters (band) . . . 219
  - 2.67.1 Career . . . 219
  - 2.67.2 Discography . . . 219
  - 2.67.3 See also . . . 219
  - 2.67.4 References . . . 219
  - 2.67.5 External links . . . 219
- 2.68 Stratus (English band) . . . 220
  - 2.68.1 Discography . . . 220
  - 2.68.2 Line-up . . . 220
  - 2.68.3 See also . . . 220
  - 2.68.4 References . . . 220
- 2.69 Sweet Savage . . . 220
  - 2.69.1 History . . . 220
  - 2.69.2 Band members . . . 221
  - 2.69.3 Discography . . . 222
  - 2.69.4 See also . . . 223

CONTENTS

- 2.69.5 References ... 223
- 2.69.6 External links ... 223
- 2.70 Tank (band) ... 224
  - 2.70.1 History ... 224
  - 2.70.2 Discography ... 224
  - 2.70.3 Members ... 224
  - 2.70.4 See also ... 224
  - 2.70.5 References ... 224
  - 2.70.6 External links ... 224
- 2.71 Terraplane (band) ... 225
  - 2.71.1 Biography ... 225
  - 2.71.2 Discography ... 225
  - 2.71.3 See also ... 225
  - 2.71.4 References ... 225
- 2.72 The Handsome Beasts ... 225
  - 2.72.1 Career ... 225
  - 2.72.2 Discography ... 225
  - 2.72.3 See also ... 226
  - 2.72.4 References ... 226
  - 2.72.5 External links ... 226
- 2.73 Thin Lizzy ... 226
  - 2.73.1 History ... 226
  - 2.73.2 Other Thin Lizzy releases and tributes ... 234
  - 2.73.3 Origin of the band name ... 234
  - 2.73.4 Style and legacy ... 234
  - 2.73.5 Band members ... 235
  - 2.73.6 Discography ... 235
  - 2.73.7 References ... 235
  - 2.73.8 External links ... 236
- 2.74 Thunderstick ... 237
  - 2.74.1 Early days and Iron Maiden ... 237
  - 2.74.2 Self-named band and beyond ... 237
  - 2.74.3 Thunderstick band line-ups ... 237
  - 2.74.4 Discography ... 238
- 2.75 Tobruk (band) ... 238
  - 2.75.1 Discography ... 238
  - 2.75.2 See also ... 238
  - 2.75.3 References ... 239

- 2.75.4 External links . . . 239
- 2.76 Tokyo Blade . . . 239
  - 2.76.1 History . . . 239
  - 2.76.2 Members . . . 240
  - 2.76.3 Discography . . . 241
  - 2.76.4 Related releases . . . 241
  - 2.76.5 See also . . . 241
  - 2.76.6 References . . . 241
  - 2.76.7 External links . . . 242
- 2.77 Tredegar (band) . . . 242
  - 2.77.1 History . . . 242
  - 2.77.2 Discography . . . 242
  - 2.77.3 Former members . . . 242
  - 2.77.4 See also . . . 242
  - 2.77.5 External links . . . 242
- 2.78 Trespass (band) . . . 243
  - 2.78.1 Lineup . . . 243
  - 2.78.2 Recording Sessions[5] . . . 243
  - 2.78.3 See also . . . 244
  - 2.78.4 References . . . 245
- 2.79 Tygers of Pan Tang . . . 245
  - 2.79.1 Biography . . . 245
  - 2.79.2 Members . . . 246
  - 2.79.3 Discography . . . 246
  - 2.79.4 See also . . . 247
  - 2.79.5 References . . . 247
  - 2.79.6 External links . . . 248
- 2.80 Tytan . . . 248
  - 2.80.1 History . . . 248
  - 2.80.2 Discography . . . 248
  - 2.80.3 See also . . . 248
  - 2.80.4 References . . . 248
  - 2.80.5 External links . . . 248
- 2.81 UFO (band) . . . 249
  - 2.81.1 History . . . 249
  - 2.81.2 Band members . . . 251
  - 2.81.3 Discography . . . 252
  - 2.81.4 Videography . . . 252

- 2.81.5 References . . . 252
- 2.81.6 External links . . . 253
- 2.82 Urchin (band) . . . 253
  - 2.82.1 Early years . . . 253
  - 2.82.2 Line-up changes . . . 253
  - 2.82.3 Reunions . . . 253
  - 2.82.4 Discography . . . 253
  - 2.82.5 Members . . . 254
  - 2.82.6 See also . . . 255
  - 2.82.7 References . . . 255
  - 2.82.8 External links . . . 255
- 2.83 Vardis . . . 255
  - 2.83.1 Discography . . . 255
  - 2.83.2 See also . . . 256
  - 2.83.3 References . . . 256
  - 2.83.4 External links . . . 256
- 2.84 Venom (band) . . . 256
  - 2.84.1 Band history . . . 256
  - 2.84.2 Genre . . . 258
  - 2.84.3 Legacy and influence . . . 258
  - 2.84.4 Criticism . . . 258
  - 2.84.5 Members . . . 258
  - 2.84.6 Discography . . . 259
  - 2.84.7 See also . . . 259
  - 2.84.8 References . . . 259
  - 2.84.9 External links . . . 259
- 2.85 White Spirit (band) . . . 259
  - 2.85.1 History . . . 259
  - 2.85.2 Members . . . 260
  - 2.85.3 Discography . . . 260
  - 2.85.4 See also . . . 260
  - 2.85.5 References . . . 260
  - 2.85.6 External links . . . 261
- 2.86 Whitesnake . . . 261
  - 2.86.1 History . . . 261
  - 2.86.2 Discography . . . 266
  - 2.86.3 Members . . . 266
  - 2.86.4 In other media . . . 267

	2.86.5	Tours	267
	2.86.6	Notes	268
	2.86.7	References and further reading	269
	2.86.8	External links	269
2.87	Wild Horses (British band)		269
	2.87.1	History	269
	2.87.2	Members	270
	2.87.3	Discography	270
	2.87.4	See also	270
	2.87.5	References	270
	2.87.6	External links	271
2.88	Witchfinder General (band)		271
	2.88.1	Biography	271
	2.88.2	Members	271
	2.88.3	Discography	271
	2.88.4	See also	271
	2.88.5	References	271
	2.88.6	External links	271
2.89	Witchfynde		271
	2.89.1	Early days	271
	2.89.2	Second album and change of musical direction	272
	2.89.3	Departure with Rondelet Records	272
	2.89.4	Mausoleum Records, fourth album and split	272
	2.89.5	Reunion, 1999-present	272
	2.89.6	Line-up	272
	2.89.7	Discography	273
	2.89.8	See also	273
	2.89.9	References	273
	2.89.10	External links	273
2.90	Wrathchild		273
	2.90.1	History	273
	2.90.2	Line-ups	275
	2.90.3	Discography	275
	2.90.4	Members	275
	2.90.5	See also	275
	2.90.6	References	275
	2.90.7	External links	275

3 Related Topics & Heavy Metal Magazines   **276**

3.1	Heavy metal fashion		276
	3.1.1	Origins	276
	3.1.2	Other influences	276
	3.1.3	References	277
	3.1.4	External links	278
3.2	Heavy metal subculture		278
	3.2.1	Nomenclature	278
	3.2.2	Subculture	278
	3.2.3	Social aspects	279
	3.2.4	Intolerance to other music	279
	3.2.5	Attire	280
	3.2.6	International variations	280
	3.2.7	References	281
3.3	Kerrang!		282
	3.3.1	History	282
	3.3.2	Website	282
	3.3.3	Kerrang! Awards	282
	3.3.4	Kerrang! Radio	282
	3.3.5	Kerrang! TV	283
	3.3.6	Kerrang! Tour	283
	3.3.7	The Official Kerrang! Rock Chart	283
	3.3.8	International editions	283
	3.3.9	References	283
	3.3.10	External links	284
3.4	Metal Forces		284
	3.4.1	Background	284
	3.4.2	*Metal Forces* Official Website	284
	3.4.3	*Metal Forces presents: Demolition - Scream Your Brains Out!*	285
	3.4.4	Notes	285
	3.4.5	External links	285
3.5	Metal Hammer		285
	3.5.1	History	285
	3.5.2	Metal Hammer Golden Gods Awards	286
	3.5.3	MetalHammer.co.uk	286
	3.5.4	Publishers	286
	3.5.5	See also	287
	3.5.6	References	287
	3.5.7	External links	287

		3.6	Raw Power (TV series)	287
		3.6.1	Origins	287
		3.6.2	Presenters	287
		3.6.3	References	288
		3.6.4	External links	288
	3.7		Terrorizer (magazine)	288
		3.7.1	History	288
		3.7.2	Genre Specials	289
		3.7.3	Terrorizer Online	291
		3.7.4	John Peel	291
		3.7.5	Writers	291
		3.7.6	References	291
		3.7.7	External links	291
	3.8		Zero Tolerance (magazine)	291
		3.8.1	External links	292
4	**Text and image sources, contributors, and licenses**			**293**
	4.1		Text	293
	4.2		Images	311
	4.3		Content license	317

Chapter 1

Introduction to NWOBHM

1.1 New Wave of British Heavy Metal

The **New Wave of British Heavy Metal** (commonly abbreviated in **NWOBHM**) was a nationwide musical movement that started in the late 1970s in the United Kingdom and achieved international attention by the early 1980s. The term was first used by journalist Geoff Barton in the May 1979 issue of the British music newspaper *Sounds*, as a way of describing the emergence of new heavy metal bands in the late 1970s, during the period of punk rock's decline and the dominance of new wave music.

The New Wave of British Heavy Metal began as an underground phenomenon parallel to punk and largely ignored by the media, which, only through the promotion of rock DJ Neal Kay and *Sounds'* campaigning, reached the public conscience and gained radio coverage, recognition and success in the UK. The movement involved mostly young, white, male and working class musicians and fans, who suffered the hardships of the diffuse unemployment condition that hit Great Britain in the late 70s and early 80s. As a reaction, they created a community separated from mainstream society where to enjoy each other's company and their favourite loud music. It evolved in a new subculture with its own behavioural and visual codes and a shared set of values, which were quickly accepted by metal fans worldwide following the almost immediate diffusion of the music in the US, Europe and Japan.

Although fragmented in a collection of different styles, the music of the New Wave of British Heavy Metal is best remembered for drawing from the heavy metal of the 70s and fusing it with the intensity of punk rock, producing fast and aggressive songs. The DIY attitude of the new metal bands caused the diffusion of raw-sounding self-produced recordings and the proliferation of independent record labels. The song lyrics were usually about typically escapist themes, like mythology, fantasy, horror and rock lifestyle.

The movement spawned about a thousand metal bands, but only a few survived the advent of MTV and the rise of the more commercial glam metal in the second half of the 80s. Among them, only Iron Maiden and Def Leppard became international stars, although Motörhead and Saxon had also considerable success. Other groups, like Diamond Head, Venom and Raven, remained underground acts, but were a major influence for the very successful extreme metal subgenres of the late-80s and 90s. Many bands from the New Wave of British Heavy Metal reformed in the 2000s and are still active with live performances and new studio albums.

1.1.1 Background

Social unrest

For more details on this topic, see 1973–75 recession.

The United Kingdom in the second part of the 70s was

A miners' strike rally in 1984.

in a state of social unrest and diffused poverty.[1] The percentage of unemployed, especially among young people of the working class, was exceptionally high after a three-year-long period of economic recession,[2] when the politics of both Conservative and Labour Party governments had failed to find solutions for the social distress of large parts of the population.[3][4] As consequence of the progressive deindustrialization of the country, the rate of unemployment continued to rise in the early 80s and reached the record of 3,224,715 people in February 1983.[5] The discontent of so many people caused widespread social unrest, frequent strikes and culminated with a series of riots in 1981 (see 1981 Brixton riot, 1981 Toxteth riots).[6] The explosion of new bands and new musical styles coming from Great Britain in the late 70s is considered by most observers a consequence of the economic depression that hit the country before the governments of Prime Minister Margaret Thatcher, when the crowd of young people, deprived of the prospect of a job as factory workers or clerks that had befallen the previous generations, searched for different ways of earning money in the musical and entertainment business.[7]

New groups seem to be popping up every five minutes formed by guys who aren't dedicated to the music, but who think it's an easy way to make a fast buck...

"

"

Phil Lewis (Girl)[8]

The desperation and the violent reaction of a generation robbed of a safe future are well represented by the British punk movement of 1977–78, whose rebellion against the establishment continued diluted in new wave and post-punk music of the 80s.[9] Punks were politically militant, relished their anarchic attitude and stage practices like pogo, sported short and spiked hairstyles or shaved heads, wore safety pins and ripped clothes[10][11] and considered musical prowess unimportant as long as their music was simple and loud.[2] However, not all the working class male youths were taken by the punk movement, because some preferred to escape from their grim reality in heavy metal, which provided fun, stress relief and the companionship of their peers, all things stripped away from them because of their unemployment.[6][12]

Heavy Rock in the UK

The United Kingdom had been one of the cradles of the first heavy metal movement, born at the end of the 60s and flowered in the early 70s.[13] Of the many British bands that came to prominence in that period, Led Zeppelin, Black Sabbath and Deep Purple reached worldwide success and critical acclaim.[14][15] The success of the music genre, usually called heavy rock at the time,[16] generated a community of fans in Great Britain with strong ties to psychedelia, hippie doctrines and biker subculture.[17][18] All three bands cited above were in crisis in the last part of the 70s: Led Zeppelin were plagued by discord and personal tragedies and reduced drastically their activities,[14][19] Black Sabbath fired their charismatic but unreliable frontman Ozzy Osbourne[20] and Deep Purple disbanded.[21] As consequence, the whole movement lost much of its momentum and the interest of the media, focused on "the more fashionable or lucrative markets of the day such as disco, glam, mod, new wave and electronic music"[22] Just like progressive rock acts and other mainstream music groups of the 70s, heavy rock bands were viewed as "lumbering dinosaurs" by the music press infatuated with punk rock and new wave,[23][24] despite the fact that the major labels rushing to put punk bands under contract were the same that had supported the objects of their rage in the recent past.[19][25] Some writers even declared the premature demise of heavy metal altogether.[26][27]

The crisis of British heavy rock giants left space in the second half of the 70s to the rise of other bands,[28] like Queen,[29] Slade,[30] Sweet,[31] Wishbone Ash,[32] Status Quo,[33] Nazareth,[34] and Uriah Heep,[35] all of which had multiple chart entries in the UK and successful international tours.[22] The British chart results of the period show that there was still a vast audience for heavy metal in the country and also upcoming bands Thin Lizzy,[36] UFO[37] and Judas Priest,[38] had tangible success and media coverage in the late 70s.[22][39] Foreign hard rock acts, such as Blue Öyster Cult[40] and Ted Nugent[41] from the US, Rush[42] from Canada, Scorpions[43] from Germany and especially AC/DC[44] from Australia, climbed the British charts in the same period.[22]

Motörhead

Main article: Motörhead

Motörhead are a band founded in 1975 by already experienced musicians (their leader Ian 'Lemmy' Kilmister came from the space rock band Hawkwind,[46] Larry Wallis from Pink Fairies,[47] Eddie Clarke from Curtis Knight's Zeus[48]), which divides the critics about its belonging to the New Wave of British Heavy Metal. Some of them think that the band should be considered a precursor and inspirer of the movement but not part of it, because they gained recording contracts, toured the country and reached chart success way before any NWOBHM band stepped out of their local club scene.[22][49][50][51] Motörhead were also the only metal band of the period recording songs with veteran BBC radio DJ John Peel for his "Peel Sessions" program[52] and the first to reach No. 1 in the UK Albums Chart, with the live album *No Sleep 'til Hammersmith* in June 1981.[51] Lemmy himself said that "the NWOBHM (...) didn't do us much good", because Motörhead "came along a bit too early for it."[53]

1.1. NEW WAVE OF BRITISH HEAVY METAL

Lemmy of Motörhead was a reference figure for the whole movement.[45]

Other critics see Motörhead as chronologically the first significant exponent of the movement[54][55][56] and the first band to fully implement a crossover between punk rock and heavy metal.[57] Their fast music, the renunciation to technical virtuosity in favour of sheer loudness and their uncompromising attitude were equally welcomed by punks and heavy metal fans.[57] Motörhead were supported by many NWOBHM bands on tour,[19][58] but they also shared the stage with the punk band The Damned, of which Lemmy was a friend.[59] Motörhead's musical style became very popular during the New Wave of British Heavy Metal, making them a fundamental reference for the nascent movement and for musicians of various metal subgenres in the following decades.[60]

1.1.2 Identity and style

Main article: Heavy metal subculture

The New Wave of British Heavy Metal was a musical movement that involved both musicians and fans, linked by young age, prevalent male sex and white skin, class origin, ethic and aesthetic values.[61] According to American sociologist Deena Weinstein, the rise and growth of the movement meant the achievement of maturity for heavy metal, before branching out into various subgenres.[62][63] British heavy metal fans, commonly known as muthas, metalheads or headbangers for the typical movement of their head while listening to metal music,[64] dismissed the simplistic image of rebellious youth inherited from the counterculture of the 1960s[65] and the psychedelic attachments characteristic of heavy rock in the 70s,[12] creating a subculture separated from mainstream society,[66] with shared principles and codes for both artists and themselves.[67]

Patches with band logos and cover art are usually sewn on the denim jackets of metalheads.[64]

In the last part of the 70s, British metalheads coalesced in a closed community of peers that exalted power and celebrated masculinity in all its forms.[12][68][69] Weinstein wrote that "British heavy metal is neither misogynistic nor an expression of machismo; for the most part women are of no concern."[70] At the same time, it "is not racist, despite its uniformly white performers, and its lyrics are devoid of racial references",[70] though the movement appears strongly homophobic.[71][72][73] Headbangers showed scarce interest for political and social problems, finding in each other's company, in the consumption of beer and in the music the means to escape their bleak reality,[74] and for this reason they were often accused of nihilism[69][75] or escapism.[23][76] In contrast with punks, they loved musicianship and made idols of guitar virtuosos and singers,[77] with the live show viewed as the epiphany of their status.[78] Michael Schenker and Eddie Van Halen were the most celebrated young guitar heroes of the time.[79][80] The fans were very loyal to the music, to each other and to the bands, with which they shared the same origins and from which required coherence with their values, authenticity and continuous accessibility.[81][82] To depart from this strict code meant being marked as 'sell out' or 'poseur' and being somewhat excluded from the community.[83] The lyrics of the song "Denim and Leather" by Saxon reflect precisely the condition of British metalheads in those years of great enthusiasm.[84] Access to this male-dominated world for female musicians and fans was not easy, and only women who adapted to their male counterparts' standards and codes were accepted,[71] as attested by Girlschool[19][85] and Rock Goddess,[86] the only notable all-girl metal bands of that age.

The music, philosophy and lifestyle of heavy metal bands and fans were often panned by both left-wing critics and conservative public opinion,[87] described as senseless, ridiculous to the limit of self-parody[88] and even dangerous for the young generations.[69][87] The 1984 successful mockumentary *This Is Spinal Tap* addressed many idiosyncrasies of British metal bands, showing comic sides of that world which external observers would judge absurd.[19][89] Instead metal musicians regarded the movie's content as much too real.[19][90]

Visual aspects

Main article: Heavy metal fashion

The dress code of the British headbangers reflected the newly-found cohesion of the movement and recalls the look of 60s' rockers and American bikers.[91] The common threads were to sport long hair and wear jeans, black or white T-shirts with band logos and cover art, leather jackets or denim vests adorned with patches.[64] Following the example of Judas Priest, elements of S&M fashion were introduced in the metal wardrobe of the 80s and it became typical to show off metallic studs and ornaments or to see spandex and leather trousers worn by heavy metal musicians.[91][92] Elements of militaria, like bullet belts and insignia, were also introduced at this time.[93] This style of dress quickly became the uniform of metalheads worldwide.[94]

Most bands of the New Wave of British Heavy Metal had the same look of their fans and produced typical rock shows, loud and noisy but without special effects. A relevant exception was Iron Maiden, which created the character Eddie the Head to enrich their performances very early in their career.[54][95] Other exceptions were Demon,[96] Cloven Hoof[97] and Samson,[98] which used various props, costumes and tricks in their shows, while Pagan Altar[99] and Venom became well known for their elaborated scenography inspired by shock rock and satanism.[88][100][101]

1.1.3 Music and lyrics

People say Rush is heavy metal and so is Motörhead. They are worlds apart, yet they come under the same heading.

"
"

– Kelly Johnson (Girlschool)[102]

The marketing of record labels and the general media of the 80s dubbed all rock music with loud guitars of that period with the umbrella term heavy metal, reducing the New Wave of British Heavy Metal to a single music genre,[103][104][105] when the movement actually comprised bands with very different influences and styles.[106][107][108] Especially in the first years of the movement, what characterized the flood of heavy metal music was its raw sound, due in large part to low-budget productions, but also to the amateurish talents of many young bands.[109][110] Those young musicians were largely inspired by the works of the aforementioned successful bands of the 70s and by other minor groups like Budgie,[111] representing a sort of continuity with those heavy rock acts, whose music had gone temporarily out of fashion but was still vital underground.[39][112]

In a semi-conscious way, many new bands fused classic heavy metal with the immediacy of pub rock and the intensity of punk rock, implementing to various degrees the crossover of genres started by Motörhead;[107] in general they shunned ballads, reduced harmonies and produced shorter songs with sped up tempos and a very aggressive sound based on riffs and power chords, which featured vocals ranging from high pitch wails to gruff and low tuned.[113] Iron Maiden,[114] Angel Witch,[115][116] Saxon,[117] Holocaust,[118] Tygers of Pan Tang,[119] Girlschool,[120] Tank[115][121] and More[122] are notable performers of this style, which bands like Atomkraft,[123] Jaguar,[124] Raven[64][125] and Venom[88][100][126] stretched to even more extreme solutions. This new approach to heavy metal is considered by critics the greatest musical accomplishment of the New Wave of British Heavy Metal and a giant evolutionary step for the genre.[10][127]

Iron Maiden's Eddie in a horror/sci-fi setting. Horror and science fiction were recurring themes in both lyrics, show scenography and cover art for NWOBHM bands.[128]

However, a style more melodic and more akin to the hard

rock of bands like Rainbow, Magnum, UFO, Thin Lizzy and Whitesnake was equally represented during the New Wave of British Heavy Metal.[129] The music of Def Leppard,[130] Praying Mantis,[131] White Spirit,[132] Demon,[96] Shy,[133] Gaskin,[134] Dedringer[135] and many others contained hooks as much as riffs, often retained a closer link with blues rock,[136][137] included power ballads and featured keyboards, acoustic instruments, melodic and soaring vocals. In particular after the peak of the movement in 1981, this style more similar to that of mainstream American acts was favoured by the media and found a larger consensus in the British audience, becoming prevalent when also bands of the first group adopted it.[138][139][140] These changes of musical direction disoriented the less compromising fans and brought to the rejection of the bands which, to their eyes, had lost their coherence to pursue an elusive success.[138][141]

The two said styles do not exhaust all the musical influences found in the British metal music of the early 80s, because many bands were also inspired by progressive rock (Iron Maiden,[114] Diamond Head,[137] Blitzkrieg,[142] Demon,[96] Saracen,[143] Shiva,[144] Witchfynde[145]), boogie rock (Saxon,[146] Vardis,[147] Spider,[148][149] Le Griffe[150]) and glam rock (Girl,[151] Wrathchild[152]). Doom metal bands Pagan Altar and Witchfinder General were also part of the New Wave of British Heavy Metal and their albums are considered among the best examples of that already established subgenre.[99][149]

British writer John Tucker wrote that NWOBHM bands "were in general fuelled by 'first pints, first shags and first horror films' and their lyrics rolled everything into one big youthful fantasy".[110] In fact, they usually avoided social and political themes in their lyrics[153] or treated them in a shallow "street level" way,[154] using instead more frequently topics taken from mythology, the occult, fantasy, science fiction and horror films.[76][128][155][156] Songs about romance and lust were rare,[157] but the frequent lyrics about male bonding and rock lifestyle contain many sexist allusions.[158] Christian symbolism is often present in the lyrics and cover art,[159] as is the figure of Satan, used more as a shocking and macabre subject than as the antireligious device of 90s' black metal subculture.[88][126]

1.1.4 History

An underground movement (1975–78)

Thin Lizzy, UFO and Judas Priest were already playing international arenas,[160][161][162] when new heavy metal bands, composed by very young people, debuted in small venues in many cities of Great Britain.[10] The larger venues of the country were usually reserved for the chart-topping

Paul Di'Anno and Steve Harris of Iron Maiden. Di'Anno's appearance and personality made him look more like a punk singer than a metalhead.[109][114]

disco music, as "the concept of a rock club was pretty much unconceivable around 1978–79".[163] Just like most British bands in the past, the new groups spent their formative years playing live in clubs, pubs, dance halls and social circles for low wages; this training honed their skills, created a local fan base and enabled them to come in contact with managers and agents of record labels.[164]

Angel Witch, Iron Maiden, Praying Mantis and Samson from London,[165][166][167][168] Son of a Bitch (later Saxon) from Barnsley,[146] Diamond Head from Stourbridge,[169] Marseille from Liverpool,[170] White Spirit from Hartlepool,[171] Witchfynde from Derbyshire,[172] Vardis from Wakefield,[173] Def Leppard from Sheffield,[174] Raven and Tygers of Pan Tang from around Newcastle,[175][176] and Holocaust from Edinburgh[177] were the most important metal bands founded between 1975 and 1977 that animated the club scene of their respective cities and towns.[178] The first bands of the new-born musical movement contended space in the venues to punk outfits, causing often the specialization of clubs, which proposed only punk or only rock and hard rock.[179] Differences in ideology, attitude and looks caused also heated rivalries between the two audiences.[10][179] What punk and heavy metal musicians had in common was their DIY attitude towards the music business and the consequent practice of self-production and self-distribution of recorded material, in the form of audio cassette demos and privately pressed singles, initially addressed only to local supporters.[6] It caused also the birth and diffusion of small independent record labels, often an extension of record shops and independent recording studios, which sometimes produced both punk and metal releases.[180] Indie labels are considered very important for the movement's evolution, because they removed the intrusion of corporate business which had hindered rock music in the late-70s, giving local bands the chance to experiment with more extreme forms of music.[181]

NWOBHM was a fiction, really, an invention of Geoff Barton and *Sounds*. It was a cunning ruse to boost circulation. Having said that, it did represent a lot of bands that were utterly ignored by the mainstream media. Because of that it became real and people got behind it.

"

"

Bruce Dickinson[19]

While punk was intensely covered by the British and international media, the new grassroots metal movement remained underground until 1978, largely ignored by popular music magazines such as *New Musical Express*, *The Face* and *Melody Maker* and by radio stations.[5] The transmission of the news concerning bands and music happened by word-of-mouth and fanzines,[83][182] or through interested DJs, who travelled the country from club to club. Neal Kay was one of those DJs, who started to work in 1975 at a disco club called the Bandwagon in Kingsbury, North West London, housed in the back-room of the Prince of Wales pub and equipped with a massive sound system.[183][184] He transformed his nights at the Bandwagon in The Heavy Metal Soundhouse, a spot specialized in hard rock and heavy metal music and a place to listen to albums of established acts and to demos of new bands,[183][185] which circulated among fans through cassette trading.[186] Besides participating in air guitar competitions[187] and watching live shows,[183] the audience could also vote for the selections made by Kay.[188] The DJ made a weekly Heavy Metal Top 100 list of the most requested songs at The Soundhouse by both newcomers and established bands, and sent it to record shops and to the music journal *Sounds*, the only paper showing interest in the developing heavy metal scene.[188] Many young musicians realized that they were not alone in playing metal only through that weekly list, which included bands from all over the country.[189][190] At the time, Geoff Barton was a staffer at *Sounds* who wrote features on the new up-and-coming metal bands and was pivotal in directing the developing subculture of metalheads with his keen articles.[19][191] Under suggestion from his editor Alan Lewis and in an attempt to find a common stylistic element out of the bands' music, he used for the first time the term 'New Wave of British Heavy Metal' in his review of a gig of the *Metal Crusade* tour, featuring Angel Witch, Iron Maiden and Samson, at The Music Machine in London, on 8 May 1979.[10][192] That newly coined term became soon the identifier of the whole movement.[193]

The late Steve 'Steaming' Clark, lead guitarist of Def Leppard. Long and fast guitar solos were a characteristic of heavy metal music in the 80s.[194]

The first wave (1979–81)

Compilation albums featuring bands from the nascent movement started to circulate, issued by Neat Records, Heavy Metal Records and Ebony Records, which would become leaders in the market of independent metal labels during the 80s.[181][195][196] The fresh outlet of the Neal Key's chart, the attention of *Sounds* and the many compilations issued by indie labels focused the efforts of the new bands in producing demos and singles.[197] Iron Maiden's *The Sound-*

1.1. NEW WAVE OF BRITISH HEAVY METAL

house Tapes is one of the best known collection of such demos.[109] As Barton recalls: "There were hundreds of these bands. Maybe even thousands. Barely a day would go by without a clutch of new NWOBHM singles arriving in the *Sounds* office."[19]

Tommy Vance, a BBC radio host, took notice of the phenomenon and played singles of the new metal bands at his late night *Friday Rock Show* on BBC Radio 1.[19] Along with John Peel's broadcast,[19][198] Vance's was the only corporate radio show to feature songs from underground metal acts, many of which were invited to play live at BBC studios under supervision of long-time collaborator and producer Tony Wilson.[199] Alice's Restaurant Rock Radio, a pirate FM radio station of the capital,[200] also championed the new bands on air and with their own 'roadshow' in rock pubs and clubs.[201]

Despite the transition of the young bands from being local attractions to touring extensively the UK, A&R agents of the major record labels were still unable to ascertain the rising new trend.[202][203] Thus, most new bands signed contracts with small indie labels, which could only afford limited printings of singles and albums and usually offered only national distribution.[195][196] Many other bands, including Iron Maiden, Def Leppard and Diamond Head, self-produced their first releases and sold them through mail order or at concerts.[204][205][206][207] Saxon were the first to sign with an internationally distributed label, the French Carrere Records,[208] followed by Def Leppard with Phonogram in August 1979[209] and Iron Maiden with EMI in December 1979.[210] In early-1980, EMI tested the market with the Neal Kay-compiled album *Metal for Muthas* and with a UK tour of the bands that had contributed to the compilation,[211] eventually signing Angel Witch and Ethel the Frog[212] (Angel Witch were dropped after the release of their first single[213]).

Metal for Muthas was put down by *Sounds*, but was a commercial success[214] and may have been instrumental in urging major labels to sign more bands; A II Z went to Polydor,[215] Tygers of Pan Tang, Fist and White Spirit to MCA,[195] More to Atlantic,[122] Samson to RCA,[216] Demon to Carrere,[217] Girlschool to Bronze[218] and Praying Mantis to Arista.[219] The new releases by those bands were produced better and, together with intensive tours in the UK and Europe,[220] promoted definitely the movement to relevant national phenomenon, as evidenced by the good chart results of many of those first albums.[221][222][223] The best chart performances of that period were for Iron Maiden's debut album and for *Wheels of Steel* by Saxon, which reached No. 4 and No. 5 in the UK Albums Chart respectively, while their singles "Running Free", "Wheels of Steel" and "747 (Strangers in the Night)" entered the UK Singles Chart Top 50.[224][225] The immediate consequence of that success was increased media coverage for metal bands, which included appearances on the British music TV shows *Top of the Pops*[226][227][228] and *The Old Grey Whistle Test*.[229] Another remarkable effect of the expansion of the movement was the emergence of many new bands in the period between 1978 and 1980, the most notable of which were Savage,[230] Girlschool,[231] Trespass,[232] Demon,[233] Mama's Boys,[234] Fist,[235] Witchfinder General,[236] Satan,[237] Grim Reaper,[238] Venom,[239] Persian Risk,[240] Sweet Savage,[241] Blitzkrieg,[242] Jaguar[243] and Tank.[244]

The New Wave of British Heavy Metal was also beneficial to already established bands, which reclaimed the spotlight with new and acclaimed releases.[245][246] Ex-Deep Purple singer Ian Gillan returned to sing heavy metal with the album *Mr. Universe* in 1979[247] and was on the forefront of the British metal scene with his band Gillan in the following years.[248][249] His former band mate in Deep Purple Ritchie Blackmore also climbed the UK charts with his hard rock group Rainbow's releases *Down to Earth* (1979) and *Difficult to Cure* (1981).[250][251][252] Black Sabbath got back in shape and returned to success with the albums *Heaven and Hell* (1980) and *Mob Rules* (1981),[253][254] featuring the ex-Rainbow singer Ronnie James Dio.[255] 1980 stands out as a memorable year for hard rock and heavy metal in the British charts, with many other entries in the top 10: MSG's first album peaked at No. 8,[256] Whitesnake's *Ready an' Willing* at No. 6,[257] Judas Priest's best-seller *British Steel*[38] and Motörhead's *Ace of Spades* at No. 4,[51] while *Back in Black* by AC/DC reached number one.[44]

As proof of the successful revival of the British hard rock and metal scene, tours and gigs of old and new acts went sold out, both in the UK and in other European countries, where the movement had spread out.[136][138][139] World tours were no longer precluded to the groups generated from the NWOBHM, which were chosen as opening acts for major bands in arenas and stadiums: Iron Maiden supported Kiss in Europe in 1980[258] and embarked in their first world tour as headliners in 1981,[259] besides opening for Judas Priest and UFO in the US;[260] Def Leppard visited the US for the first time in 1980 for a three-month trek supporting Pat Travers, Judas Priest, Ted Nugent, AC/DC and Sammy Hagar;[261] Saxon opened for Judas Priest in Europe and for Rush and AC/DC in the US in 1981.[262][263] NWOBHM bands were present in the roster of the famous Reading Festival already in 1980[264][265] and were quickly promoted to headliners in the editions of 1981[266] and 1982.[267] The 1980 edition was remarkable also for the violent protest against Def Leppard, whose declared interest for the American market was badly received by British fans.[268][269] In addition to Reading, a new festival called Monsters of Rock was created in 1980 at Castle Donington, England, to showcase only hard rock and heavy metal acts.[64][270]

Into the mainstream (1982–83)

Iron Maiden's The Number of the Beast *was the first album of a band from the New Wave of British Heavy Metal to reach No.1 in the UK Albums Chart and many view it as a classic rock recording.*[271]

The New Wave of British Heavy Metal eventually found space on newspapers and music magazines different from *Sounds*, as journalists caught up with the "next big thing" happening in the UK.[272][273] *Melody Maker* even published a weekly heavy metal chart based on the sales of record shops.[274] *Sounds* publisher cashed in for his support to the movement issuing in June 1981 the first number of *Kerrang!*, a colour magazine directed by Geoff Barton, exclusively devoted to hard rock and heavy metal.[6][275] *Kerrang!* was a huge success and soon became the magazine of reference for metalheads worldwide,[275] followed shortly by the American *Circus* and *Hit Parader*, the German *Metal Hammer* and the British *Metal Forces*.[276][277] The attention of international media meant more sales of records and more world tours for NWOBHM bands, whose albums entered in many foreign charts.[278][279][280][281][282] Their assault to the British charts culminated with Iron Maiden's *The Number of the Beast* topping the UK Albums Chart on 10 April 1982 and staying at number 1 for two weeks.[283][284]

The success of the music produced by the movement and its passage from underground phenomenon to mainstream genre induced its main promoter Geoff Barton to declare finished the New Wave of British Heavy Metal in 1981,[285][286] in coincidence with the closure of the Bandwagon and subsequent demolition of the Prince of Wales pub to build a restaurant.[287] Although the movement had lost some of its appeal for the diehard fans, as evidenced by the increased popularity of "American influenced AOR releases" on national polls,[288] it retained enough vitality to launch a second wave of bands, which rose up from the underground and released their first albums in the period 1982–1983.[289] Avenger,[290] Rock Goddess,[86] Tysondog,[291] Tokyo Blade,[292] Elixir,[293] Atomkraft[294] and Rogue Male[295] are some of the bands that came to the spotlight after 1981.

NWOBHM bands had been steadily touring in the United States, but had not yet received enough FM radio airplay in that country to make a significant impression on American charts.[296] Def Leppard remedied to that, releasing at the beginning of 1983 *Pyromania*, an album which renounced to much of the aggressive sound of their older music for a more melodic and FM-friendly approach.[297][298][299] The band's goal of reaching a wider international audience, which included many female fans, was attained completely in the US,[269][300] where *Pyromania* peaked at No. 2 on the *Billboard* 200 chart behind Michael Jackson's *Thriller*.[301] Thanks to a string of hit singles and the smart use of music videos on the recently born MTV, the album had sold more than six millions copies in the US by 1984 and made Def Leppard superstars.[302] The overwhelming international success of *Pyromania* induced both American and British bands to follow Def Leppard's example,[303][304][305] giving a decisive boost to the more commercial and melodic glam metal and delivering a fatal blow to the New Wave of British Heavy Metal.[138]

Decline

Great Britain had been a pioneer of music videos, which suddenly stepped up from occasional promotional fancy to indispensable means to reach the audience when MTV started its broadcasting service in 1982.[306] The new TV broadcaster filled its programs with many hard rock and heavy metal videos,[307] too expensive for bands without a recording contract or signed to small independent labels.[308] Moreover, music videos exalted the visual side of a band, a department where British metal groups were often deficient.[309][310][311] So the New Wave of British Heavy Metal suffered the same decline as other musical movements based on low-budget productions and an underground following.[312] Many of its leaders, like Diamond Head, Tygers of Pan Tang, Angel Witch and Samson, were unable to follow up on their initial success and their attempts to update their sound and look to the new standards expected by the wider audience failed, alienating also the favours of fans of the first hour.[136][313][314] By the mid-1980s, image-driven and sex-celebrating glam metal emanating from Hollywood Sunset Strip, spearheaded by Van Halen and followed by bands such as Mötley Crüe, Quiet

Riot, Dokken, Great White, Ratt and W.A.S.P., quickly replaced other styles of metal in the tastes of many British rock fans.[138] New Jersey act Bon Jovi and the Swedish Europe, thanks to their successful fusion of hard rock and romantic pop,[315] became also very popular in the UK, with the first arriving even to headline the Monsters of Rock Festival in 1987.[316] Record companies latched onto the more sophisticated glam metal subgenre over the NWOBHM bands, which maintained a fan base in Europe, but found the home and US markets closed by American groups.[138]

Blitzkrieg are one of the NWOBHM bands which reformed in the 2000s.[317]

In addition, new but much less mainstream metal subgenres emerged around the same time and attracted many British metalheads. Power metal and thrash metal, both stemming from the New Wave of British Heavy Metal and maintaining much of its ethos,[318] were even faster and heavier and obtained good sale results and critical acclaim in the second half of the 80s,[108][319] with bands like Helloween,[320] Savatage,[321] Metallica,[322] Slayer,[323] Megadeth[324] and Anthrax.[325]

The New Wave of British Heavy Metal Encyclopedia by Malc Macmillan lists more than 500 recording bands established in the decade between 1975 and 1985 and related to the movement,[274] the last notable ones being Baby Tuckoo,[326] Chrome Molly,[327] Tredegar[328] and Battlezone.[329] Probably as many bands were born in the same time interval, but never emerged from their local club scene or recorded nothing more than demos or limited pressings of self-produced singles.[104][207] The disinterest of record labels, bad management, internal struggles and wrong musical choices that turned off much of their original fan base won the tenacity of almost all of those bands, which disbanded and disappeared by the end of the decade.[136][138][287] A few of the best known groups survived on foreign markets, like Praying Mantis in Japan[131] and Saxon, Demon and Tokyo Blade in Europe.[139][305][330] Some others, namely Raven,[331][332] Girlschool[333] and Grim Reaper,[334] tried to break through in the US market signing with American labels, but their attempts got no lasting results.

Two of the more popular bands of the movement, however, went on to considerable, lasting success. Iron Maiden has since then become one of the most commercially successful and influential heavy metal bands of all time,[335] even after adopting a more progressive style.[114] Def Leppard became even more successful, targeting the American mainstream rock market with their more refined hard rock sound.[298]

Revival

The widespread popularity of the Internet in the late 1990s/early 2000s helped NWOBHM fans and musicians to communicate again.[207] So the New Wave of British Heavy Metal experienced a minor revival, highlighted by the good sales of old vinyl and collectibles and by the demand of new performances.[336] The statements of appreciation by metal bands of the 90s,[337][338][339] the success of tribute bands, the re-issues of old albums and the production of new thoroughly edited compilations renewed the attention of the media and encouraged many of the original groups to reform for festival appearances and tours.[340] Probably the most important of those compilation albums, entitled *New Wave of British Heavy Metal '79 Revisited*, was compiled by Metallica's drummer Lars Ulrich and former *Sounds* and *Kerrang!* journalist Geoff Barton and released in 1990 as a double CD, featuring bands as obscure as Hollow Ground right through to the major acts of the era.[104]

A new publication called *Classic Rock*, featuring Barton and many of the writers from *Kerrang!*'s first run, championed the NWOBHM revival and continues to focus much of its attention on rock acts from the 80s.[341] Starting in the 2000s, many reformed bands recorded new albums and revisited their original styles, abandoned in the second half of the 80s.[342][343] Their presence at metal festivals and in the international rock club circuit has been constant ever since.[19]

1.1.5 Influences and legacy

Cronos of Venom. Venom are considered precursors of both black metal and thrash metal.[88][344]

The New Wave of British Heavy Metal re-ignited the creativity of a stagnant genre, but was heavily criticized for the excessive hype generated by local media in favour of mostly talentless musicians who, unlike the preceding decades, were unoriginal[345] and created no classic rock recording.[97][105][346] Nonetheless, the music produced during the New Wave of British Heavy Metal was very influential for their contemporaries in every part of the Western world;[108][347] today that hodgepodge of styles is seen as a nodal point for the diversification of heavy metal and an incubator of various subgenres, which developed in the second half of the 80s and became predominant in the 90s.[104][106][348] In fact, the great success of Def Leppard in the US was very important for the growth of glam metal,[138][349] just as the music, lyrics, cover art and attitude of bands like Angel Witch, Witchfynde, Cloven Hoof and especially Venom are regarded as fundamental for the development of black metal in its various forms in Europe and America.[88][350][351] The name attributed to that subgenre comes from Venom's album *Black Metal* of 1982.[88] Motörhead, Iron Maiden, Raven, Tank, Venom and other minor groups are viewed as precursors of speed metal and thrash metal, two subgenres which carried forward the crossover with punk, incorporating elements of hardcore and amplifying velocity of execution, aggression and loudness.[344][352][353][354] Starting around 1982, North America,[355] West Germany,[356] and Brazil[357] became the principal hotbeds for thrash metal outfits, giving birth to clearly defined regional scenes (see Bay Area thrash metal, Teutonic thrash metal, Brazilian thrash metal). Lars Ulrich, in particular, was an active fan and avid collector of NWOBHM recordings and memorabilia and, under his influence, the set lists of Metallica's early shows were filled with covers of British metal groups.[358][359]

The birth of speed metal in the early 80s was also decisive for the evolution of power metal in the second half of the decade,[361] with most notable exponents the German Helloween[319] and the American Manowar,[362] Savatage[321] and Virgin Steele.[363]

Since the beginning of the NWOBHM, North American bands like Anvil,[364] Riot,[364] Twisted Sister,[365] Manowar,[364] Virgin Steele,[366] The Rods,[367][368] Hellion,[369] Cirith Ungol[370] and Exciter[371] had a continuous exchange with the other side of the pond, where their music was appreciated by British metalheads.[139] In this climate of reciprocity, Manowar and Virgin Steele initially signed with the British indie label Music for Nations, while Twisted Sister recorded their first two albums in London.[365]

The sound of Japanese bands Earthshaker, Loudness, Anthem and other minor groups was also influenced by the New Wave of British Heavy Metal, whose British sound engineers they used for their early albums.[138][139][364] The Japanese band Bow Wow even transferred to England to be part of the British metal scene.[372]

Germany, Sweden, Denmark, Belgium, Netherlands, France and Spain were the first European countries which welcomed the new British bands and spawned imitators almost immediately.[139] Acts like Accept, Grave Digger, Sinner and Warlock from Germany,[373][374][375][376] E. F. Band from Sweden,[377] Mercyful Fate from Denmark,[378] Picture and Bodine from the Netherlands,[379][380] Trust and Nightmare from France,[381][382] Barón Rojo and Ángeles del Infierno from Spain,[383][384] were born between 1978 and 1982 and were heavily influenced by the sound of the New Wave of British Heavy Metal. Many of those bands signed with the Dutch Roadrunner Records or with the Belgian Mausoleum Records, indie labels which published also recordings of British NWOBHM acts.[385][386]

1.1.6 See also

- List of New Wave of British Heavy Metal bands
- Second British Invasion

1.1.7 Notes

[1] Zarnowitz, Victor; Moore, Geoffrey H. (October 1977). "The Recession and Recovery of 1973–1976". *Explorations in Economic Research, Volume 4, number 4* (PDF). National Bureau of Economic Research. pp. 1–87. Retrieved 26 October 2015.

[2] Christe: p.30

[3] "1974 Feb: Hung parliament looms". BBC News. 5 April 2005.

[4] "1974 Oct: Wilson makes it four". BBC News. 5 April 2005.

[5] Tucker: p.22

[6] Macmillan: p.21

[7] Tucker: pp.24–25

[8] Barton, Geoff (July 1980). "Phil Lewis Interview". *Sounds*.

[9] "British Punk". AllMusic. Retrieved 17 June 2015.

[10] Barton, Geoff (16 August 2005). "HM Soundhouse Special Features: The New Wave of British Heavy Metal". HMsoundhouse.com. Retrieved 18 March 2015.

[11] Weston Thomas, Pauline. "1970s Punk Fashion History Development". Fashion Era.com. Retrieved 21 April 2015.

[12] Ryan M. Moore in Bayer: p. 145–146

[13] Weinstein: pp.14–18

[14] Erlewine, Stephen Thomas. "Led Zeppelin Biography". AllMusic. Retrieved 26 April 2015.

[15] Welch, Chris (1988). "Come to the Sabbath". *Black Sabbath*. Bobcat Books. ISBN 0-7119-1738-8.

[16] Hatch, David; Millward, Stephen (1987). "After the Flood". *From Blues to Rock: An Analytical History of Pop Music*. Manchester, UK: Manchester University Press. pp. 167–168. ISBN 0-7190-1489-1. Retrieved 17 October 2015.

[17] Weinstein: p.18

[18] Walser: p.3

[19] Mitchell, Ben (13 April 2014). "Inside the World of New Wave of British Heavy Metal". *Esquire*. Retrieved 3 May 2015.

[20] Welch, Chris (1988). "Ozzy, Bloody Ozzy". *Black Sabbath*. Bobcat Books. ISBN 0-7119-1738-8.

[21] Thompson: p.191

[22] Macmillan: p.19

[23] Bushell & Halfin: p. 24

[24] "When Dinosaurs Roamed The Earth...". Punk77.co.uk. Retrieved 2 May 2015.

[25] Christe: p.28

[26] Smith, Richard (11 May 1978). "Will Heavy Metal Survive the Seventies?". *Circus* (181): 17–30.

[27] Johnson, Rick (October 1979). "Is Heavy Metal Dead? Last Drum Solo at the Power Chord Corral". *Creem* II (5): 42.

[28] Thompson: p.201

[29] "Queen – Official Charts". Official Charts Company. Retrieved 21 April 2015.

[30] "Slade – Official Charts". Official Charts Company. Retrieved 21 April 2015.

[31] "Sweet – Official Charts". Official Charts Company. Retrieved 21 April 2015.

[32] "Wishbone Ash – Official Charts". Official Charts Company. Retrieved 21 April 2015.

[33] "Status Quo – Official Charts". Official Charts Company. Retrieved 21 April 2015.

[34] "Nazareth – Official Charts". Official Charts Company. Retrieved 21 April 2015.

[35] "Uriah Heep Official Cahrts". Official Charts Company. Retrieved 17 May 2015.

[36] "Thin Lizzy – Official Charts". Official Charts Company. Retrieved 21 April 2015.

[37] "UFO – Official Charts". Official Charts Company. Retrieved 21 April 2015.

[38] "Judas Priest – Official Charts". Official Charts Company. Retrieved 21 April 2015.

[39] Tucker: p.36

[40] "Blue Oyster Cult – Official Charts". Official Charts Company. Retrieved 21 April 2015.

[41] "Ted Nugent – Official Charts". Official Charts Company. Retrieved 21 April 2015.

[42] "Rush – Official Charts". Official Charts Company. Retrieved 21 April 2015.

[43] "Scorpions – Official Charts". Official Charts Company. Retrieved 21 April 2015.

[44] "AC/DC – Official Charts". Official Charts Company. Retrieved 21 April 2015.

[45] Prato, Greg. "Lemmy – Biography". AllMusic. Retrieved 28 August 2015.

[46] Kilmister & Garza: pp.69–95

[47] Kilmister & Garza: p.98

[48] Erlewine, Stephen Thomas. "Curtis Knight Biography". AllMusic. Retrieved 4 May 2015.

[49] Tucker: p.47

[50] Iron Maiden and the New Wave of British Heavy Metal – Jerry Ewing – 94:00

[51] "Motorhead Official Charts". Official Charts Company. Retrieved 17 May 2015.

[52] "Keeping It Peel – Peel Sessions". BBC. Retrieved 28 April 2015.

[53] Kilmister & Garza: p.150

[54] Christe: p.35

[55] Dunn, McFadyen & Wise – 12:00

[56] "New Wave of British Heavy Metal". AllMusic. Retrieved 18 July 2015.

[57] Waksman: pp.170–171

[58] Millar, Robbi (1 March 1980). "The Dinosaur's Daughters". Sounds. Retrieved 30 December 2010.

[59] Kilmister & Garza: pp.119–120

[60] Kilmister & Garza: p.181, 197, 211, 252

[61] Weinstein: pp.101–102

[62] Weinstein: p.8

[63] Deena Weinstein in Bayer: p.21

[64] Christe: p.37

[65] Weinstein: p.110

[66] Weinstein: p.139

[67] Weinstein: pp.97–98

[68] Weinstein in Bayer: pp.24–25

[69] Moynihan & Søderlind: p. X

[70] Weinstein in Bayer: p.18

[71] Weinstein: p.105

[72] Walser: pp.128–130

[73] "Homophobia in Metal? Shamefully, It Still Exists". NME. 20 December 2010. Retrieved 27 June 2015.

[74] Weinstein: p.135

[75] Walser: p. 112

[76] Benjamin Earle in Bayer: p.37

[77] Waksman: p. 178, 219–220

[78] Weinstein: pp.217–218

[79] Weinstein: p.59

[80] Prato, Greg. "Eddie Van Halen Biography". AllMusic. Retrieved 26 June 2015.

[81] Magnus Nilsson in Bayer: p. 163–165

[82] Dunn, McFadyen – 30:18

[83] Weinstein: p.137

[84] Weinstein in Bayer: p.19

[85] Makowski, Pete (9 August 1980). "Back to Schooldays". Sounds. Retrieved 3 January 2011.

[86] MacMillan: pp.484–485

[87] Weinstein: pp.237–239

[88] Moynihan & Søderlind: pp. 11–14

[89] "This Is Spinal Tap". Rotten Tomatoes. Retrieved 21 April 2015.

[90] Yabroff, Jennie (2009). *The Real Spinal Tap*. Newsweek.

[91] Weinstein: p.30

[92] Daniels: pp.72–74

[93] Kilmister & Garza: p.224

[94] Weinstein in Bayer: p.27

[95] Bushell & Halfin: pp.13–16

[96] Rivadavia, Eduardo. "Demon biography". AllMusic. Retrieved 10 February 2012.

[97] Miller, Paul (1986). "UK Dekay?". *Mega Metal Kerrang!* (1): 30–31.

[98] Christe: p.39

[99] Rivadavia, Eduardo. "Pagan Altar Biography". AllMusic. Retrieved 22 March 2015.

[100] Christe: p.42

[101] "Kwotes of the Year". *Kerrang!* (32): 13. 30 December 1982. We don't do gigs, we do shows. It's fucking massive. If you stand at the front of the stage you're gonna get your head blown off!

[102] "Kelly Johnson – Making Music in a Man's World" (JPG). *Guitar World*: 20. March 1984. Retrieved 17 February 2015.

[103] Tucker: pp.33–34

[104] Rivadavia, Eduardo. "New Wave of British Heavy Metal '79 Revisited review". AllMusic. Retrieved 24 March 2015.

[105] Shore, Robert (January 2009). "NWOBHM: 30 Years On". Planetrock.com. Retrieved 3 May 2015.

[106] Weinstein: p.44

[107] Waksman: p.209

[108] Bowar, Chad. "What Is New Wave of British Heavy Metal?". *Heavy Metal 101*. About.com. Retrieved 30 March 2015.

[109] Christe: p.34

[110] Tucker: p.173

[111] Prato, Greg. "Budgie biography". AllMusic. Retrieved 4 April 2015.

[112] Bushell & Halfin: p. 32

[113] Christe: pp.34–36

[114] Waksman: pp.197–202

[115] Tucker: p. 65

[116] Christe: pp.40–42

[117] Dunn, McFadyen – 14:40

[118] MacMillan: pp.294–295

[119] Rivadavia, Eduardo. "Tygers of Pan Tang – Wild Cat review". AllMusic. Retrieved 17 June 2015.

[120] Corich, Robert M. (1998). *The Collection* (CD booklet). Girlschool. England: Sanctuary Records (CMDD014).

[121] Rivadavia, Eduardo. "Tank Biography". AllMusic. Retrieved 17 June 2015.

[122] Rivadavia, Eduardo. "More biography". AllMusic. Retrieved 10 February 2012.

[123] Rivadavia, Eduardo. "Atomkraft Biography". AllMusic. Retrieved 24 June 2015.

[124] Tucker: p.178

[125] Waksman: pp.189–192

[126] Waksman: pp. 192–195

[127] Tucker: p.100

[128] Bryan A. Bardine in Bayer: pp.127–133

[129] Earle in Bayer: pp.39–41

[130] Erlewine, Stephen Thomas. "Def Leppard biography". AllMusic. Retrieved 10 February 2012.

[131] Rivadavia, Eduardo. "Praying Mantis biography". AllMusic. Retrieved 10 February 2012.

[132] Rivadavia, Eduardo. "White Spirit biography". AllMusic. Retrieved 10 February 2012.

[133] "Shy biography". AllMusic. Retrieved 10 March 2015.

[134] Rivadavia, Eduardo. "Gaskin biography". AllMusic. Retrieved 10 March 2015.

[135] Rivadavia, Eduardo. "Dedringer biography". AllMusic. Retrieved 13 February 2012.

[136] Sinclair, David (5 April 1984). "Only the Strong Survive". *Kerrang!* (65): 29.

[137] Popoff: pp.96–97

[138] Tucker: pp.129–154

[139] Macmillan: p.22

[140] Dunn, McFadyen – 36:30

[141] Watts, Chris (19 November 1988). "Once Bitten... Twice Dry". *Kerrang!* (214): 28–29.

[142] Rivadavia, Eduardo. "Blitzkrieg biography". AllMusic. Retrieved 10 February 2012.

[143] Rivadavia, Eduardo. "Saracen Biography". AllMusic. Retrieved 10 March 2015.

[144] "Shiva Biography". AllMusic. Retrieved 10 March 2015.

[145] Rivadavia, Eduardo. "Witchfynde biography". AllMusic. Retrieved 10 February 2012.

[146] MacMillan: p.526

[147] Rivadavia, Eduardo. "Vardis biography". AllMusic. Retrieved 10 February 2012.

[148] "Spider Biography". AllMusic. Retrieved 10 March 2015.

[149] Christe: p.40

[150] "Le Griffe Biography". AllMusic. Retrieved 10 March 2015.

[151] Rivadavia, Eduardo. "Girl Biography". AllMusic. Retrieved 10 March 2015.

[152] "Wrathchild Biography". AllMusic. Retrieved 10 March 2015.

[153] Moore in Bayer: p.155

[154] Christe: p.36

[155] Weinstein: p.40

[156] Iain Campbell in Bayer: pp.110–122

[157] Weinstein in Bayer: p.25

[158] Weinstein: p.37

[159] Weinstein: p.39

[160] "Tour History". Thin Lizzy Guide.com. Retrieved 9 July 2015.

[161] "UFO Concert Setlists & Tour Dates". Set lIsts.fm. Retrieved 9 July 2015.

[162] "Judas Priest Concert Setlists & Tour Dates". Set lIsts.fm. Retrieved 9 July 2015.

[163] Iron Maiden and the New Wave of British Heavy Metal – Geoff Barton – 38:31

[164] Christe: p.32

[165] MacMillan: p.307

[166] MacMillan: p.446

[167] MacMillan: p.34

[168] MacMillan: pp.501–502

[169] MacMillan: p.169

[170] MacMillan: p.379

[171] MacMillan: pp.717–718

[172] MacMillan: p.732

[173] MacMillan: pp.680–681

[174] MacMillan: p.148

[175] MacMillan: p.467

[176] MacMillan: p.663

[177] MacMillan: p.294

[178] Iron Maiden and the New Wave of British Heavy Metal – 36:48

[179] Dunn, McFadyen – 5:48

[180] Dunn, McFadyen – 13:20

[181] Waksman: pp.186–189

[182] Tucker: p.89

[183] "The Soundhouse Story part 1". HMsoundhouse.com. Retrieved 18 July 2015.

[184] Iron Maiden and the New Wave of British Heavy Metal – 31:16

[185] Iron Maiden and the New Wave of British Heavy Metal – 32:53

[186] McGee, Hal (2 June 1992). "Cause and Effect". In James, Robin. *Cassette Mythos*. New York City: Autonomedia. ISBN 978-0-936756-69-1.

[187] Iron Maiden and the New Wave of British Heavy Metal – The Roots of Air Guitar with Neal Kay

[188] "The Soundhouse Story part 2". HMsoundhouse.com. Retrieved 18 July 2015.

[189] Dunn, McFadyen – 16:48

[190] Considine, J. D. (15 November 1990). "Metal Mania". *Rolling Stone* (591): 100–104.

[191] Waksman: pp.175–181

[192] Barton, Geoff (19 May 1979). "If You Want Blood (and Flashbombs and Dry Ice and Confetti) You Got It". *Sounds*: 28–29.

[193] Kirkby – 8:90

[194] Weinstein: p.24

[195] Tucker: pp. 95–102

[196] Roland, Paul (1984). "The State of Independents". *Extra Kerrang!* (1): 23, 24, 26, 46.

[197] Tucker: pp.81–88

[198] Fricke: pp.33–35

[199] Tucker: pp. 55–56

[200] "Alice's Restaurant". AMFM.org.uk. Retrieved 3 May 2015.

[201] Noble, Colin. "Colin Noble: ARfm - Our Presenters - Unsigned Show / Sunday Morning Show". ARfm. Retrieved 3 May 2015.

[202] Dunn, McFadyen – 13:18

[203] Tucker: p. 32

[204] Matthews – 33:20

[205] Fricke: pp.25–27

[206] Tucker: pp.120–121

[207] Macmillan: pp.24–27

[208] Tucker: p.29

[209] Fricke: p.39

[210] Bushell & Halfin: p.31

[211] Bushell & Halfin: p.67

[212] Rivadavia, Eduardo. "Ethel the Frog biography". AllMusic. Retrieved 10 February 2012.

[213] Rivadavia, Eduardo. "Angel Witch Biography". AllMusic. Retrieved 18 March 2015.

[214] Tucker: p.82

[215] Rivadavia, Eduardo. "A II Z biography". AllMusic. Retrieved 10 February 2012.

[216] "The Story of Samson". Book of Hours.net. Retrieved 1 July 2015.

[217] Barton, Geoff (September 1981). "The Night of the Demon". *Kerrang!* (3): 6–7.

[218] Ling, Dave (18 December 1999). "Interview with Gerry Bron". *Classic Rock* (9).

[219] MacMillan: p.448

[220] Tucker: pp.64–65, 69

[221] "Girlschool Official Charts". Official Charts Company. Retrieved 13 July 2015.

[222] "Def Leppard Official Charts". Official Charts Company. Retrieved 13 July 2015.

[223] "Tygers of Pan Tang Official Charts". Official Charts Company. Retrieved 13 July 2015.

[224] "Iron Maiden Official Charts". Official Charts Company. Retrieved 13 July 2015.

[225] "Saxon Official Charts". Official Charts Company. Retrieved 13 July 2015.

[226] "Iron maiden – Running Free Live in Top of the pops". YouTube. 25 March 2007. Retrieved 13 July 2015.

[227] "Saxon: 'Wheels of Steel', Top of the Pops 1980". YouTube. 1 May 2015. Retrieved 13 July 2015.

[228] "Motorhead and Girlschool – Please Don't Touch (Top of the Pops)". YouTube. 6 May 2013. Retrieved 13 July 2015.

[229] "Tygers of Pan Tang – Old Grey Whistle Test 1982". YouTube. 3 December 2010. Retrieved 13 July 2015.

[230] MacMillan: pp.520–521

[231] MacMillan: p.244

[232] MacMillan: p.647

[233] MacMillan: pp.155–156

[234] MacMillan: p.371

[235] MacMillan: p.220

[236] MacMillan: p.729

[237] MacMillan: pp.514–515

[238] MacMillan: p.261

[239] MacMillan: pp.684–685

[240] MacMillan: p.439

[241] MacMillan: p.601

[242] MacMillan: p.81

[243] MacMillan: pp.319–320

[244] MacMillan: p.608

[245] Tucker: pp.30–31

[246] Thompson: p.213

[247] Thompson: pp.217–219

[248] Charles, D. W. (December 1981). "Captain Gillan". *Kerrang!* (6): 10, 12.

[249] Popoff: pp.131–132

[250] "Rainbow – Official Charts". Official Charts Company. Retrieved 21 April 2015.

[251] Thompson: pp.221–222

[252] Popoff: p.279

[253] "Black Sabbath – Official Charts". Official Charts Company. Retrieved 21 April 2015.

[254] Popoff: pp.48–49

[255] Iommi, Tony; Lammers, T. J. (2011). "Bill goes to shits". *Iron Man: My Journey through Heaven and Hell with Black Sabbath*. Cambridge, Massachusets: Da Capo Press. ISBN 978-0-306-82054-0.

[256] "Michael Schenker Group – Official Charts". Official Charts Company. Retrieved 21 April 2015.

[257] "Whitesnake – Official Charts". Official Charts Company. Retrieved 21 April 2015.

[258] Bushell & Halfin: p.78

[259] Bushell & Halfin: p.89

[260] Bushell & Halfin: pp.92–93

[261] Fricke: pp. 50–55

[262] Sharpe-Young, Garry (2009). "Saxon". MusicMight. Retrieved 26 June 2015.

[263] MacMillan: p.527

[264] Tucker: pp. 62–64

[265] "The 20th Reading Rock Festival". UKRockfestivals.com. February 2011. Retrieved 4 May 2015.

[266] "The 21st Reading Rock Festival". UKRockfestivals.com. December 2011. Retrieved 21 June 2010.

[267] "The 22nd Reading Rock Festival". UKRockfestivals.com. January 2012. Retrieved 4 May 2015.

[268] Fricke: p.57

[269] Waksman: pp.202–206

[270] "Monsters of Rock 1980". UKRockfestivals.com. November 2013. Retrieved 4 May 2015.

[271] "Iron Maiden – The Number of the Beast". Acclaimed Music.net. Retrieved 29 March 2015.

[272] Bushell & Halfin: pp.77, 103

[273] Johnson, Howard (5 April 1984). "Don't Fear the Reaper...". *Kerrang!* (65): 11.

[274] Tucker: p.19

[275] Christe: p.38

[276] Christe: p.85

[277] Johnson, Howard (1984). "The Big Read". *Extra Kerrang!* (1): 38.

[278] "Iron Maiden – Killers (Album)". Swedishcharts.com. Retrieved 19 July 2015.

[279] "Infodisc.fr Note: You must select Iron Maiden". Infodisc.fr. Retrieved 19 July 2015.

[280] "Infodisc.fr Note: You must select Saxon". Infodisc.fr. Retrieved 19 July 2015.

[281] "Saxon – Denim and Leather (Album)". Swedishcharts.com. Retrieved 19 July 2015.

[282] "Def Leppard – High 'N' Dry awards". AllMusic. Retrieved 19 July 2015.

[283] "Official Albums Chart Results Matching: The Number Of The Beast". Official Charts Company. Retrieved 2 May 2015.

[284] Popoff: pp.170–171

[285] Barton, Geoff (4 October 1980). "Scrap Metal". *Sounds*: 39.

[286] Tucker: p.79

[287] Watts, Chris (19 December 1992). "Where Are They Now?". *Kerrang!* (423): 36–37.

[288] Crampton, Luke (30 December 1982). "Best Sellers of 1982". *Kerrang!* (32): 3.

[289] Tucker: p.81

[290] MacMillan: pp.51–52

[291] MacMillan: pp.672–673

[292] MacMillan: pp.627–628

[293] MacMillan: p.199

[294] MacMillan: p.46

[295] MacMillan: p.489

[296] Kirkby – 35:12

[297] Fricke: pp.83–84

[298] Earle in Bayer: p.44

[299] Popoff: p.92

[300] Fricke: p.50

[301] Fricke: p.12

[302] "RIAA Searchable Database: search for "Pyromania"". Recording Industry Association of America. Retrieved 22 June 2015.

[303] Earle in Bayer: p.47

[304] Rivadavia, Eduardo. "Black Rose – Boys Will Be Boys review". AllMusic. Retrieved 18 March 2015.

[305] MacMillan: p.528

[306] Konow, David (2 January 2003). *Bang Your Head: The Rise and Fall of Heavy Metal*. New York City: Three Rivers Press. pp. 133–134. ISBN 978-0-609-80732-3.

[307] Lane, Frederick S. (2006). *The Decency Wars: The Campaign to Cleanse American Culture*. Amherst, New York: Prometheus Books. p. 126. ISBN 1-59102-427-7.

[308] Dunn, McFadyen – 35:40

[309] Rivadavia, Eduardo. "Grim Reaper biography". AllMusic. Retrieved 10 February 2012.

[310] Rivadavia, Eduardo (20 August 2006). "Handsome Beasts Biography". AllMusic. Retrieved 25 June 2012.

[311] "Mammoth Biography". AllMusic. Retrieved 10 March 2015.

[312] Tucker: p.90

[313] Weinstein in Bayer: pp.22–23

[314] Tucker: pp.123–124

[315] Walser: pp. 120–121

[316] "Monsters of Rock 1987". UKRockfestivals.com. January 2012. Retrieved 4 May 2015.

[317] "Manowar, Diamond Head, Deicide, Others To Play Metal Meltdown IV". Blabbermouth.net. 18 January 2002. Retrieved 28 August 2015.

[318] Weinstein: pp.49–50

[319] Marsicano, Dan. "What Is Power Metal?". *Heavy Metal 101*. About.com. Retrieved 13 July 2015.

[320] Rivadavia, Eduardo. "Helloween Biography". AllMusic. Retrieved 8 August 2015.

1.1. NEW WAVE OF BRITISH HEAVY METAL

[321] Huey, Steve. "Savatage Biography". AllMusic. Retrieved 19 July 2015.

[322] Erlewine, Stephen Thomas. "Metallica Biography". AllMusic. Retrieved 2 July 2015.

[323] Huey, Steve. "Slayer Biography". AllMusic. Retrieved 2 July 2015.

[324] Erlewine, Stephen Thomas. "Megadeth Biography". AllMusic. Retrieved 2 July 2015.

[325] Erlewine, Stephen Thomas. "Anthrax Biography". AllMusic. Retrieved 2 July 2015.

[326] MacMillan: p.55

[327] MacMillan: pp.120–121

[328] MacMillan: pp.645–646

[329] MacMillan: p.63

[330] Rivadavia, Eduardo. "Saxon Biography". AllMusic. Retrieved 18 July 2015.

[331] Tucker: p.101

[332] Miller, Paul (1986). "The Madder They Come...". *Mega Metal Kerrang!* (4): 29.

[333] Johnson, Howard (30 October 1986). "Hear No Evil". *Kerrang!* (132): 10–11.

[334] MacMillan: pp.262–263

[335] Weber, Barry. "Iron Maiden Biography". AllMusic. Retrieved 20 March 2015.

[336] Tucker: pp.157–162, 167

[337] Macmillan: pp.22–23

[338] Tucker: pp.169–172

[339] "Kerrang! Iron Maiden Tribute Album". Metallica Official Website. 25 June 2008. Archived from the original on 28 June 2008. Retrieved 30 March 2015.

[340] Tucker: pp.163–169

[341] "Kerrang!'s Founding Editor To Head Up Classic Rock Magazine". Blabbermouth.net. 29 September 2004. Retrieved 14 April 2015.

[342] Rivadavia, Eduardo. "Jaguar biography". AllMusic. Retrieved 10 February 2012.

[343] Freeman, Phil. "Hell – Human Remains review". AllMusic. Retrieved 10 February 2012.

[344] McIver, Joel (1 October 2010). *The Bloody Reign of Slayer* (2 ed.). London, UK: Omnibus Press. pp. 20–21. ISBN 978-1-84938-386-8.

[345] Daniels: p.83

[346] McIver, Joel (9 January 2006). *Justice for All: The Truth About Metallica* (2 ed.). London, UK: Omnibus Press. p. 19. ISBN 978-1-84449-828-4. The New Wave of British Heavy Metal was crude, poorly produced and played by musicians with rudimentary talents

[347] Bayer: pp.190–191

[348] Dunn, McFadyen – 42:53

[349] Popoff, Martin (15 August 2014). *The Big Book of Hair Metal: The Illustrated Oral History of Heavy Metal's Debauched Decade*. Voyageur Press. p. 38. ISBN 978-0-7603-4546-7.

[350] Popoff: p. 74

[351] Popoff: p. 417

[352] "Speed/Thrash Metal". AllMusic. Retrieved 24 June 2015.

[353] McIver, Joel (9 January 2006). *Justice for All: The Truth About Metallica* (2 ed.). London, UK: Omnibus Press. pp. 18–22. ISBN 978-1-84449-828-4.

[354] Mustaine, Dave; Layden, Joe (2010). "Lars and Me, or What Am I Getting Myself Into?". *Mustaine – A Heavy Metal Memoire*. New York City: Harper Collins. ISBN 978-0-06-199703-7.

[355] Christe: pp.88, 92–93,108–111, 132–135

[356] Christe: pp.136–139

[357] Christe: p.106

[358] Tucker: pp.41–43

[359] McIver, Joel (9 January 2006). *Justice for All: The Truth About Metallica* (2 ed.). London, UK: Omnibus Press. pp. 23–25, 32. ISBN 978-1-84449-828-4.

[360] "Am I Evil? by Diamond Head". Setlists.fm. Retrieved 10 August 2015.

[361] "Power metal". AllMusic. Retrieved 17 July 2015.

[362] Monger, James Christopher. "Manowar Biography". AllMusic. Retrieved 19 July 2015.

[363] Reesman, Bryan. "Virgin Steele Biography". AllMusic. Retrieved 19 July 2015.

[364] Christe: p.44

[365] Christe: p.50

[366] DeFeis, David. "Virgin Steele Official Biography". virginsteele.com. Retrieved 9 May 2015.

[367] Rivadavia, Eduardo. "The Rods Biography". AllMusic. Retrieved 3 May 2015.

[368] Barton, Geoff (September 1981). "Armed & Ready". *Kerrang!* (3): 12.

[369] Rivadavia, Eduardo. "Hellion Biography". AllMusic. Retrieved 24 June 2015.

[370] Miller, Paul (1986). "The Men from Ungol". *Mega Metal Kerrang!* (4): 18–19.

[371] Hammonds, Steve (August 1983). "Exciter". *Metal Forces* (1): 33. Retrieved 3 July 2015.

[372] Johnson, Howard (19 May 1983). "Warning from Tokyo". *Kerrang!* (42): 24–26.

[373] Christe: p.43

[374] Norton, Justin M. (2010). "Grave Digger Interview". About.com. Retrieved 26 April 2015.

[375] Popoff: p.325

[376] Simmons, Sylvie (1986). "'Lock Jaw". *Mega Metal Kerrang!* (4): 8–11.

[377] Rivadavia, Eduardo. "EF Band biography". AllMusic. Retrieved 10 February 2012.

[378] "Decibel Hall of Fame – No. 74 -Mercyful Fate Melissa". *Decibel* (78): 48–54. April 2011. Retrieved 13 May 2014.

[379] "Picture Biography". Picture official Website. Retrieved 26 April 2015.

[380] "Bodine Biography". Regular Rocker.nl. Retrieved 26 April 2015.

[381] "Nicko McBrain Biography, Videos & Pictures". Drum Lessons.com. Retrieved 26 April 2015.

[382] Stein, Lior (9 April 2010). "Yves Campion (Nightmare) interview". Metal Express Radio. Retrieved 20 April 2010.

[383] AA.VV. "From el Rollo to Heavy Metal". In Martinez, Sìlvia; Fouce, Héctor. *Made in Spain: Studies in Popular Music*. New York City: Routledge. ISBN 978-0-203-12703-2. Retrieved 26 April 2015.

[384] "Explosion Heavy en el Norte" (JPG). *Heavy Rock* (in Spanish) (10): 18–22. 1982. Retrieved 26 April 2015.

[385] "About Roadrunner Records". Roadrunner Records. Retrieved 10 August 2015.

[386] Falckenbach, Alfie (March 2002). "Mausoleum: The story behind the legendary heavy metal label. Part I (1982–1986)". Music-Avenue.net. Archived from the original on 16 January 2011. Retrieved 22 March 2015.

1.1.8 References

Bibliography

- Bushell, Garry; Halfin, Ross (1984). *Iron Maiden – Running Free*. London, UK: Zomba Books. ISBN 978-0-946391-50-9.

- Christe, Ian (2004). *Sound of the Beast: The Complete Headbanging History of Heavy Metal*. !t Books (New York City: HarperCollins). ISBN 978-0-380-81127-4.

- Daniels, Neil (2010). *The Story of Judas Priest: Defenders of the Faith*. New York City: Omnibus Press. ISBN 978-1-84772-707-7.

- Fricke, David (1987). *Animal Instinct: The Def Leppard Story*. London, UK: Zomba Books. ISBN 0-946391-55-6.

- Kilmister, Ian; Garza, Janiss (2004). *White Line Fever*. New York City: Simon & Schuster. ISBN 0-684-85868-1.

- Macmillan, Malc (2012). *The New Wave of British Heavy Metal Encyclopedia*. Iron Pages Books (3 ed.) (Berlin, Germany: I.P. Verlag Jeske/Mader GbR). ISBN 978-3-931624-16-3.

- Moynihan, Michael; Søderlind, Difdrik (1998). *Lords of Chaos – The Bloody Rise of the Satanic Metal Underground*. Port Townsend, Washington, USA: Feral House. ISBN 0-922915-48-2.

- Popoff, Martin (1 November 2005). *The Collector's Guide to Heavy Metal: Volume 2: The Eighties*. Burlington, Ontario, Canada: Collector's Guide Publishing. ISBN 978-1-894959-31-5.

- Thompson, Dave (August 2004). *Smoke on the Water: The Deep Purple Story*. Toronto, Canada: ECW Press. ISBN 978-1-55022-618-8. Retrieved 25 December 2013.

- Tucker, John (2006). *Suzie Smiled... The New Wave of British Heavy Metal*. Shropshire, UK: Independent Music Press. ISBN 978-0-9549704-7-5.

- VV. AA. (2009). Gerd Bayer, eds. *Heavy Metal Music in Britain*. Farnham, Surrey, UK: Ashgate Publishing. ISBN 978-0-7546-6423-9.

- Waksman, Steve (2009). *This Ain't the Summer of Love: Conflict and Crossover in Heavy Metal and Punk*. Berkeley, California: University of California Press. ISBN 978-0-520-94388-9. Retrieved 8 January 2014.

- Walser, Robert (15 May 1993). *Running with the Devil: Power, Gender, and Madness in Heavy Metal Music*. Middletown, Connecticut: Wesleyan University. ISBN 978-0-8195-6260-9. Retrieved 6 April 2015.

- Weinstein, Deena (2000). *Heavy Metal: The Music and Its Culture*. Da Capo Press. ISBN 978-0-306-80970-5. Retrieved 8 January 2014.

Filmography

- Dunn, Sam; McFadyen, Scot; Wise, Jessica Joy (2005). *Metal: A Headbanger's Journey* (Documentary). Canada: Seville Pictures. ASIN B000EGEJIY.

- Dunn, Sam; McFadyen, Scot (10 December 2011). "New Wave of British Heavy Metal". *Metal Evolution* (Documentary). Toronto, Canada: Banger Films, Inc. ASIN B007GFYC0Q.

- *Iron Maiden and the New Wave of British Heavy Metal* (Documentary). New Malden, UK: Prism Films. 2008. ASIN B0016GLZ4M.

- Kirkby, Tim (26 November 2001). *Classic Albums: Iron Maiden – The Number of the Beast* (Documentary). London, UK: Isis Productions / Eagle Vision. ASIN B00005QJIA.

- Matthews, Amos (8 November 2004). *The History of Iron Maiden – Part 1: The Early Days* (Documentary). London, UK: EMI. ASIN B0006B29Z2.

Chapter 2

NWOBHM BANDS (in Alphabetical Order)

2.1 A II Z

A II Z were a heavy metal band founded in 1979 in Manchester, England by guitarist Gary Owens. The original lineup consisted of David Owens (vocals), Gary Owens (guitar), Cam Campbell (bass), Karl Reti (drums). For a short time they were one of the forerunners of the New Wave of British Heavy Metal movement. They disabanded in 1982.

2.1.1 Career

Manchester's A II Z (named after street-finder atlases) were the beneficiaries of fortuitous timing, being formed by brothers Dave (vocals) and Gary Owens (guitar), Cam Campbell (bass), and Karl Reti (drums), just in time (late 1979) to be swept up by the initial, deafening hubbub surrounding the New Wave of British Heavy Metal. Immediately signed by major label Polydor, the group, whose style bore resemblances to Motörhead, Sweet Savage and Weapon, recorded their 1980 debut album named *The Witch of Berkeley*, live at a hometown gig (actually the hall of Hazel Grove High School), then were sent out on the road in support of Girlschool and Black Sabbath. Neither of these experiences aided record sales, however, and following releases for Polydor 1981's "No Fun After Midnight" EP and "I'm the One Who Loves You", were dropped. Internal dissension had also taken root by this time and the Owens had in fact dispensed with their original rhythm section to work with new bassist Tony Backhouse and drummer Simon Wright (future AC/DC) on that final single. But the quartet's new and more commercial AOR direction failed to bear fruit and by the middle of 1982, A II Z dissolved. Guitarist Gary Owens joined the similarly ill-fated NWOBHM band; Tytan.

In 1993, Reborn Classics reissued *The Witch of Berkeley* as a bootleg CD which includes both singles as well as a four track demo from Jaguar. In 2006 Majestic Rock officially re-released *The Witch of Berkeley* and also included the two singles and their b-sides.

2.1.2 Discography

Studio Albums

- *The Witch of Berkeley* (live) LP (Polydor 1980)

Singles/EPs

- "No Fun After Midnight" 7"/12" (Polydor 1981)
- "I'm the One Who Loves You" 7" (Polydor 1981)

Reissue

- "The Witch of Berkeley" Bootleg CD (1993 Reborn Classics)
- "The Witch of Berkeley" CD (2006 Majestic Rock)

2.1.3 See also

- List of New Wave of British Heavy Metal bands

2.1.4 References

- Larkin, Colin; Ian Kenyon (1992). *The Guinness Who's who of Heavy Metal*. Guinness. p. 5. ISBN 0-85112-656-1.

2.1.5 External links

- MusicMight article, includes singles discography
- Entry in Allmusic
- VH-1 article entry
- NWOBHM.com entry

2.2 Angel Witch

Angel Witch are a British heavy metal band which formed in London, England in 1977 as part of the New Wave of British Heavy Metal movement. Despite critical acclaim in the music press, their only UK chart action consisted of a single week at No.75 (the lowest position in the charts) in 1980.[1]

2.2.1 Biography

The band was formed, originally under the name of Lucifer, and was initially composed of guitarist and vocalist Kevin Heybourne, guitarist Rob Downing, drummer Steve Jones, and bassist Barry Clements.[2] Lucifer split and Steve Jones joined up with Bruce Dickinson to form Speed. The remnants of Lucifer became Angel Witch, with the exceptions of Barry, who was replaced by Kevin Riddles, and Steve Jones, who was replaced by Dave Hogg. The following year Rob Downing left the band.

Angel Witch's first song to achieve mainstream popularity was "Baphomet", which was included on a compilation titled *Metal for Muthas*. This song drew a fair amount of attention to the band, and they eventually signed a recording deal with EMI. However, the deal was soon canceled, due to manager Ken Heybourne refusing to hand Angel Witch over to professional management, and bad performance of their first single released under the EMI label, which was entitled *Sweet Danger* and lasted a single week on British top charts.

In 1980, Bronze Records picked up the band and they soon proceeded to record and release their debut album, self-titled *Angel Witch*. This album is considered one of the most notable from the New Wave of British Heavy Metal, but subsequent to the album's release, the band's structure began to fall apart. The sacking of Dave Hogg, and Kevin Riddles leaving the band to join Tytan, and despite Heybourne's attempts to continue Angel Witch with other musicians, the end of the band was declared and he joined Deep Machine.

Angel Witch was brought back to activity on 1982, when Heybourne and two musicians from Deep Machine - namely vocalist Roger Marsden and drummer Ricky Bruce - left to assemble a new Angel Witch line-up together with bassist Jerry Cunningham. This line-up lasted a very short time, as Marsden's voice did not fit the style of the band very well. He was fired from the band and Heybourne assumed the vocals once more.

By 1983 the band had ceased its activities, and Heybourne moved to Blind Fury. In 1984, Angel Witch was once more brought to life, this time with the help of bassist Peter Gordelier (ex-Marquis De Sade), singer Dave Tattum and with Dave Hogg returning to the drums. This line-up recorded the album *Screamin' N' Bleedin'*. Dave Hogg was sacked yet again, but not without many snide remarks from the band's fans. He was replaced by Spencer Hollman. With the new drummer they recorded *Frontal Assault*, which deviated heavily from Angel Witch's previous albums, having many melodic elements.

Dave Tattum was sacked the same year and for a few years Angel Witch played as a trio on sporadic live performances. In 1989, they recorded a new live album, entitled simply *Live*.

Heybourne decided that it would be of the band's best interest to move to the USA, but the other members had no way of accomplishing that, having stable lives on their home country. Thus, an American incarnation of Angel Witch was born. It was composed of Heybourne, bassist Jon Torres (Lääz Rockit, Ulysses Siren), drummer Tom Hunting (Exodus) and guitarist Doug Piercy (Heathen, Anvil Chorus). This line-up functioned quite well, and soon the band had booked a fair amount of shows throughout the USA. However, it was found that Heybourne had some pending issues regarding immigration, and he was arrested one day before the first concert of the band. Without Heybourne, Angel Witch was soon dissolved.

After the release of the *Resurrection* compilation in 2000, the band intended to play together once more, but after a series of internal conflicts, Heybourne assembled yet another line-up, with new members.

They were on the bill for the traditional Orange Goblin Christmas show at The Camden Underworld, London, on Saturday 20 December 2008.

In 2009 their eponymous song "Angel Witch" was featured on the soundtrack of the action-adventure videogame, Brütal Legend.

In 2011 Angel Witch entered in the studio to record their fourth full-length studio album, entitled "As Above, So Below". It was recorded with Kevin Heybourne in guitar and vocals, Will Palmer on the bass guitar, Bill Steer on the guitar, and Andrew Prestidge on the drums. They also returned to playing live, with a second stage headline slot at Bloodstock Open Air in 2011.[3]

One-time Angel Witch bassist Jon Torres died on 3 September 2013 of a reported heart failure. He was 51 years old.[4]

2.2.2 Influence

Angel Witch have been claimed as an influence by many notable metal musicians, including Dave Mustaine (Megadeth) who graced the February 2010 cover of Decibel magazine wearing an Angel Witch shirt, Tom G. Warrior (Celtic Frost), and Chuck Schuldiner (Death). Bands that have covered Angel Witch songs in concert or on record include Trouble ("Confused" live), Six Feet Under ("Confused" on *Graveyard Classics*), Onslaught ("Confused" on *In Search of Sanity*), Skull Fist ("Angel Witch" live), Battle Ram ("Angel Witch" on the *Smash the Gates* EP), S.A.Slayer ("Dr. Phibes" & "Angel Witch" live) and Exodus ("Angel of Death" on *Blood In, Blood Out* as bonus track).

In 2007, German label Unbroken Records issued a "Tribute To Angel Witch" compilation album featuring 15 underground metal acts covering songs from the band's early singles and first 3 full-length releases.[5]

2.2.3 Band members

Current members

- **Kevin Heybourne** – lead vocals, guitar (1977–1982, 1984–1998, 2000–present)
- **Will Palmer** – bass guitar (2009–present)
- **Jimmy Martin** – guitar (2015–present)
- **Alan French** – drums (2015–present)

Former members

- **Roger Marsden** – lead vocals (1982) [6]
- **Dave Tattum** – lead vocals (1984–1986)
- **Rob Downing** – guitars (1978)
- **The German** – guitars (1979)
- **Grant Dennison** – guitars (1989–1990)
- **Doug Piercy** – guitars (1990–1992)
- **Lee Altus** – guitars (1993–1995)
- **Chris Fullard** – (2009 - 2010)
- **Myk Taylor** – guitars (1996–1998)
- **Keith Herzberg** – guitars (2000–2002)
- **Kevin Riddles** – bass guitar (1978–1981)
- **Jerry Cunningham** – bass guitar (1982)
- **Pete Gordelier** – bass guitar (1984–1987)
- **Jon Torres** – bass guitar (1989–1990)
- **Richie Wicks** – bass guitar (2000–2002)
- **Dave Hogg** – drums (1978–1980, 1984–1985)
- **Dave Dufort** – drums (1980–1981)
- **Ricky Bruce** – drums (1982)
- **Spencer Holman** – drums (1984–1986)
- **Tom Hunting** – drums (1990–1993)
- **Darren Minter** – drums (1994–1998)
- **Scott Higham** – drums (2000–2002)
- **Bill Steer** – guitars (2010–2014)
- **Andy Prestidge** – drums (2009–2015)
- **Tom Draper** – guitars (2013–2015)

2.2.4 Timeline

2.2.5 Discography

Studio Albums

- *Angel Witch* (1980)
- *Screamin' 'n' Bleedin'* (1985)
- *Frontal Assault* (1986)
- *As Above, So Below* (2012)

Live albums

- *Angel Witch Live* (1990)
- *2000: Live at the LA2* (2000)
- *Angel of Death: Live at East Anglia Rock Festival* (2006)
- *Burn the White Witch - Live in London* (2009)

Compilations

- *Doctor Phibes* (1986)
- *Screamin' Assault* (1988)
- *Resurrection* (1998)
- *Sinister History* (1999)

Extended plays & singles

- "Sweet Danger" [single] (1980)
- *Sweet Danger* [EP] (1980)
- "Angel Witch" [single] (1980)
- "Loser" [single] (1981)
- "Goodbye" [single] (1985)
- *They Wouldn't Dare* [EP] (2004)

2.2.6 See also

- List of New Wave of British Heavy Metal bands

2.2.7 References

[1] Official Singles Chart (UK) - Angelwitch

[2] Doomsday (10 October 2013). "Angel Witch". www.metal-archives.com. Retrieved 13 October 2013.

[3] Jennifer Coleman (16 November 2010). "First Sophie Lancaster Stage Bands Revealed". www.bloodstock.uk.com. Retrieved 13 October 2013.

[4] "Veteran San Francisco Bay Area Metal Musician JON TORRES Dies". www.blabbermouth.net. 4 September 2013. Retrieved 13 October 2013.

[5] "Emerald Working On Song For Upcoming ANGEL WITCH Tribute Album". www.bravewords.com. 11 June 2007. Retrieved 13 October 2013.

[6] http://www.metal-archives.com/bands/Angel_Witch/537

2.2.8 External links

- Angel Witch official Facebook page
- Angel Witch official MySpace page
- Angel Witch - Metal Blade Records artist page
- No Class fanzine interview 1981
- Angel Witch at NWOBHM.com

2.3 Atomkraft

Atomkraft are an English heavy/speed metal band who were part of the New Wave of British Heavy Metal movement. They formed in 1979 and disbanded 1988. Their "Total Metal" approach is somewhere between fellow NWOBHM bands such as Motörhead and Venom, punk rock bands such as The Dickies, and early Exodus or Slayer. The band subsequently reformed in 2005.

2.3.1 History

Moral Fibre

The roots of Atomkraft date back to the summer of 1979, when Tony 'Demolition' Dolan and Paul Spillett got together with the intention to form a band. Initially, going under the name of Moral Fibre and playing punk rock, they recruited guitarists Ian Legg and Chris Taylor. Ian Legg then left to be replaced by Sean Drew who also subsequently left. However the band continued to operate as a trio.

Atomkraft

On returning from a trip to Bremen, Germany, Chris presented his band mates with some button badges featuring the environmental slogan 'Atomkraft, Nein Danke!' (Nuclear Power, No Thanks!) They liked the way the word "Atomkraft" sounds and so adopted it as the band name, believing it suits the new "metal" sound they pursued. In the endeavour for something more metal and less punk they got rid of Chris.

After trying out a couple of guitarists they settled on Steve White, whom Tony knew from his art class at college. Another member of Tony's art class, Mark Irvine, joined on bass. With Tony on rhythm guitar and vocals and Paul on drums the new line-up played four shows. Unfortunately, Mark's parents disapproved of his heavy metal image and lifestyle and so persuaded him to quit the band. Tony switched back to bass and the band was able to continue.

Demon

In 1981 the band recorded the four song demo *Demon* at Impulse studios, this being funded by band member Paul Spillett who was the only one working at the time and with the help of Keith Nicol. It was their first "proper" demo, although, the limitation of time and a 2-track recorder gave results that were pretty bad. However, the band soldiered on, gaining experience by continuing to play live shows.

Total Metal

In early 1983, Atomkraft returned to Impulse studios to record another demo. Learning from their previous experience they opted to record only 2 tracks for the *Total Metal* demo, featuring the title track and "Death Valley". Steve passed a copy of the demo to Sam Kress, who ran a radio station and 'Whiplash' magazine. Sam liked the demo and promised to feature the band in his magazine. However, in late 1983, Steve left the band for personal reasons. Tony was left wondering what to do. By coincidence he was invited to stay with his sister in Canada to help out with her two kids, while she was studying. With Tony unemployed and the band effectively on hold, he decided to take her up on her offer.

Canada

In 1984 Paul Spillett joined Tony in Canada. Tony was further inspired when he got a copy of the magazine containing the write-up that Sam Kress promised. The write-up presented Atomkraft in a very positive light and also featured Venom, Raven, Metallica, Anthrax and Megadeth. Spurred on by this, Paul and Tony began writing material and returned to England in late 1984 to search for a guitarist. They later fell out over a girl and went their separate ways.

Pour the Metal In

While visiting Neat Records to see if anyone could recommend a drummer, Tony met Cronos of Venom who informed him that Ged Wolf (the brother of Venom's manager) was looking for a band having just left Tysondog. Tony and Ged got together and started auditioning for a guitarist, but initially did not have a lot of luck. Then a 16-year-old guitar player, Rob Mathew, was recommended as being a great guitar player and so they all met up. Fortunately they got on well and this became the new Atomkraft line-up. The band began working on the new material that Tony had been writing, and went on to record the *Pour the Metal In* demo at Neat Records studio. It featured 3 tracks, "Pour the Metal In", "Burn in Hell" and "Carousel". The demo is sent to various fanzines and received a good response. Dave Woods of Neat Records also hears the demo and offered them a deal, and so the band started work on the *Future Warriors* album.

Future Warriors

Recorded over a couple of weeks and produced by Keith Nichol, *Future Warriors* was released in September 1985. Despite getting a particularly poor review in Kerrang! magazine, other reviews were more positive and they got further requests for interviews. The band also opened for Slayer at The Marquee, where faulty equipment resulted in the band trashing the equipment in frustration after just three numbers. Despite this the band were asked to join the bill of the Venom/Exodus tour.

Queen of Death

After the end of the Venom/Exodus tour, Atomkraft prepared and recorded a new EP, with the tracks "Your Mentor" on the A-side and "Demolition", "Funeral Pyre" and "Mode III" on the B-side. Unfortunately, the EP did not get released in this form, as a rift developed in the band as a result of discussions over management.

Tony wanted to use the services of a London-based company, while Ged and Rob wanted to use Venom's management. The disagreement could not be resolved and so Tony left the band.

Neat then released the track "Your Mentor" as part of the Powertrax promotional cassette, while the vocal tracks on the rest of the "Your Mentor" sessions were re-recorded by Ian Davison-Swift from Avenger. D.C. Rage (Darren Cook of Avenger) was brought in as bassist and two new tracks were recorded, with the new four-piece, "Queen of Death" and "Protector" (although Alan Hunter of Tysondog had originally contributed vocals to "Protector"). In October 1986 the re-titled *Queen Of Death* EP was released with the title track and "Protector" on the A-side, and "Demolition", "Funeral Pyre" and "Mode III" on the B-side. The pictures on the back cover show the line-up of Ged, Rob, Ian and D.C. Rage although this line-up never played live. A re-recording of the track "Future Warriors", with Ian on vocals was also licensed for future inclusion in a compilation. However, it was not long before Tony was invited back in the band to replace D.C. Rage on bass, while retaining Ian on vocals.

Conductors of Noize

The new line-up records the mini-album *Conductors of Noize*, which was released in July 1987, and then promoted the record as part of support to Agent Steel and Nuclear Assault. The first date of the tour, at Hammersmith Odeon featured an expanded line-up of Max Penalty, Atomkraft, Onslaught, Nuclear Assault and Agent Steel, and was promoted as 'The Longest Day'. Atomkraft's performance was filmed for the *Live Conductors* video as well as being recorded for a live BBC radio broadcast. They also played Dynamo Festival alongside Testament, Destruction and Stryper with the show going out live on Dutch radio. With the tour at an end and the band preparing demos for the next album (to be titled *Atomized*), a thicker guitar sound was required, so simply re-recruiting D.C. Rage and Tony switching to guitar resolved this.

Disbandment

The expanded 5-piece embarked on a 1988 European tour with Nasty Savage and Exumer ultimately resulting in a 'unique' gig (for the time) in Katowice, Poland at Spodek Stadium. This show was recorded for live TV/video. On completion of the tour Ian left the band as did Tony (who was offered a position in Venom as replacement for Cronos), and despite Ged's attempts to recruit replacements the band folded in 1988.

Reformation

In 2004 Sanctuary Records (who have previously acquired the Neat Records back-catalogue) released an Atomkraft anthology. With renewed interest in the band, Tony reformed Atomkraft for live dates in 2005 and a possible new album. The 2005 line-up includes Payre Hulkoff (from Swedish industrial band Raubtier) on guitar and Steve Mason on drums. However, this line-up didn't release any new material.

Atomkraft didn't have real activities during the following years, despite of regular rumors about a possible new album. Finally, an EP of new material came out in 2011 on Austrian underground label W.A.R. Productions. This EP was called Cold Sweat and contents three unreleased tracks recorded with members of the 2005 line-up and session musicians plus a Thin Lizzy cover of the famous "Cold Sweat" track, featuring Australian guitar player Joe Matera on guitar solo.

Following the release of the Cold Sweat EP, Tony Dolan recruited a new line-up and did one date in London under the Atomkraft moniker in 2011, performing classic tracks and songs from the new EP. The 2011 line-up includes Kraen Maier and Rich Davenport on guitars, plus Paul Caffrey (from Gama Bomb) on drums.

This line-up of Atomkraft (minus Rich Davenport) performed the Future Warriors LP in its entirety in March 2014 at the second edition of the Brofest, a NWOBHM festival based in Newcastle upon Tyne. Former Venom guitarist Jeff Mantas appeared as a guest during the gig.

A new studio album, tentatively called "The Dark Angel", is still expected to be released.

2.3.2 Discography

Studio albums

- *Future Warriors* (1985)

EPs

- *Queen of Death* (1986)
- *Conductors of Noize* (1987)
- *Cold Sweat* (2011)

Compilation albums

- *Total Metal: The Neat Anthology* (2004)

Demos

- *Demon* (1981)
- *Total Metal* (1983)
- *Pour the Metal In* (1985)

2.3.3 Personnel

2.3.4 See also

- List of New Wave of British Heavy Metal bands

2.3.5 Bibliography

- Atomkraft Biography at tonydolan.net
- Tony Dolan Interview at The Metallist
- Tony Dolan Interview at Metal-Rules
- Tony Dolan Interview at Heavy Metal Radio

2.3.6 External links

- Tony 'Demolition' Dolan's Web Site
- Atomkraft at NWOBHM.com

2.4 Avenger (British band)

Avenger are a heavy metal band from Newcastle, England. Associated with the New Wave of British Heavy Metal scene, they released two albums in the 1980s before splitting up. The band reunited in 2005.

2.4.1 History

Brian Ross, Mick Moore and Gary Young founded Avenger late in 1982 after Ross and Moore's previous group, Blitzkrieg, split up.[1] the group began recording demos, "Hot 'n' Heavy Express", was their first appearance on record, included on a Neat Records compilation EP.[1] Their debut single for Neat, "Too Wild to Tame", followed in October 1983 after the addition of guitarist John Brownless.[2]

Shortly after this, lead singer Brian Ross left the group to join Satan; Satan's singer, Ian Swift, promptly joined Avenger as lead vocalist.[1] Adding guitarist Les Cheetham, they released their first LP, *Blood Sports*, in 1984. This began a period of the band playing regularly in western Europe at the time a hub of the emerging metal scene

A second album followed shortly after on Neat, entitled *Killer Elite* along with a three track accompanying video. The group toured the United States in 1986.[1] replacing Les Cheetam with Greg Reiter, The touring duty of the US tour fell to Darren Kurland as drummer . After 4 months returning to England the group broke up, blaming poor record label support preventing the band exploiting their potential in America. Ian Swift joining Atomkraft and Gary later joining Blitzkrieg.

The group's entire discography was released in 2002 by Sanctuary Records. As well as Brazilian Label Frontline Rock re releasing both albums in Latin America in 2003 In 2005 they reunited and toured across the UK and Europe with US group Y&T, among others.

The Avenger line-up changed again in 2007 with the departure of original bassist Mick Moore. The new line up of Avenger featuring Ian Swift on vocals, Gary Young, Liam Thompson (guitarist of Death in Blood), Sean Jefferies (guitarist of Fallen Skies, Earthrod) and Huw Holding (bass) have since toured with or played alongside bands such as Twisted Sister, Candlemass, Saxon, Rage, Raven, Sinner, Grim Reaper, UFO, Cradle of Filth, Skyclad and Diamond Head in 2007.[3]

The new album "The Slaughter Never Stops" was released December 2014.

2.4.2 Members

Current

- Ian Swift – vocals (1984-1986) (2005-2009) & (2013-present)
- Sean Jefferies – guitar (2006–2009; 2010–present)
- Liam Thompson – guitar and lead backing vocals (2005–present)
- Ian 'Fuzz' Fulton – bass and backing vocals (2010–present)
- Gary Young – drums and backing vocals (1982–1986; 2005–present)

Former

- Brian Ross – vocals (1982–1984)
- Andy Watson - vocals (2009-2011)
- Roddy B – vocals (2011-2013)
- Dean Thompson – guitar (2008–2011)
- Glenn S. Howes - guitar (2005)
- Les Cheetham – guitar (1984–1985)
- Greg Reiter – guitar (1985–1986)
- Mick Moore – bass (1982 1986 – 2005 – 2007)
- Huw Holding – bass (2006–2009)

2.4.3 Discography

- *One Take No Dubs...* – Live in the studio (Neat Records compilation, 1982)
- "Too Wild to Tame" / "On the Rocks" 7" (Neat Records, 1983)
- *Blood Sports* (Neat Records, 1984)
- *Killer Elite* (Neat Records, 1985)
- *Too Wild to Tame* (Sanctuary Records compilation, 2002)
- *The Slaughter Never Stops* Rocksector Records 2014

2.4.4 See also

- List of New Wave of British Heavy Metal bands

2.4.5 References

[1] Avenger at Allmusic

[2] Martin C. Strong. *The Great Metal Discography*. 2nd ed. Canongate, 2001, p. 45.

[3] "Avenger official myspace". Retrieved 2008-01-11.

2.4.6 External links

Official Facebook Page www.avenger-uk.com - Official Site https://soundcloud.com/avenger-uk/ - Soundcloud Pagehttps://twitter.com/AvengerUK1 - Official Twitter Page https://myspace.com/avengeruk - Official Myspace Page http://www.reverbnation.com/avengeruk4 - Official Reverbnation Page Official You Tube Channel

2.5 Baby Tuckoo

Baby Tuckoo was an English hard rock band, formed in Bradford, West Yorkshire, England in 1982. Their name is taken from the James Joyce novel *A Portrait of the Artist as a Young Man*.[1] They were generally considered a part of the New Wave of British Heavy Metal.

They released two albums with Rob Armitage (vocals), Neil Saxton (guitar), Andy Barrott (keyboards), Paul Smith (bass) and Tony Sugden (drums).[2] Prior to their recording career, Steve Holton (vocals) and Andy Tidswell (keyboards) were in the band.[3]

Armitage left to join Accept in 1987, but was replaced by the American David Reece in 1988 without having taken part in any releases from the band.[4] He later joined the UK outfit Jagged Edge, and founded a band named Passion.

2.5.1 Discography[5]

Albums

- 1984: *First Born* (Ultranoise)
- 1986: *Force Majeure* (Music for Nations)

Singles and EPs

- 1984: "Mony Mony" (Albion) - single
- 1986: "Rock (Rock)" (Music for Nations) - single and EP
- 1986: "The Tears of a Clown" (Fun After All) - EP (The A-side, a Smokey Robinson & the Miracles cover, was not included on any Baby Tuckoo album)

2.5.2 See also

- List of New Wave of British Heavy Metal bands

2.5.3 References

[1] Rockdetector's page about Baby Tuckoo

[2] *The New Wave Of British Heavy Metal Encyclopedia* by Malc Macmillan, Iron Pages, 2001, p. 57

[3] Rockdetector's page about Baby Tuckoo

[4] *The New Wave Of British Heavy Metal Encyclopedia* by Malc Macmillan, Iron Pages, 2001, p. 57

[5] *The New Wave Of British Heavy Metal Encyclopedia* by Malc Macmillan, Iron Pages, 2001, p. 57

2.6 Battleaxe (band)

For other uses, see Battleaxe (disambiguation).

Battleaxe is a heavy metal band from Sunderland, England. As one of the notable bands of the New Wave of British Heavy Metal scene, they started out with the name Warrior and morphed into **Battleaxe** sometime in early 1980. The band consisted of Dave King (vocals), Brian Smith (bass), Steve Hardy (guitar), and Ian Thompson (drums). After playing around the area and honing their chops, they entered the studio to make a demo called "Burn This Town". In doing so, they garnered the attention of Roadrunner Records and the result was their first album, *Burn This Town*.

2.6.1 Cover art

Once a deal had been struck with Roadrunner Records, the master tapes were sent to Roadrunner Records and the album title was agreed upon as *Burn this Town*. The record company asked the band for some concept ideas for the cover art work, so the guys asked a friend and local artist Arthur Ball if he could come up with anything. He then produced the first *Burn this Town* cover art work as it is now, but only as a rough proof drawing, and stated that, if it were approved by the record company, he would redraw the whole thing again to a much higher standard. However, when Roadrunner received the proof art work for approval, they went ahead and pressed 2000 units for a worldwide release without the band's consent. The rest is history. The original *Burn this Town* cover art work is one of the most talked-about album covers in heavy metal history. The graphic looked amateurish, and the band worried what it might do to their reputation. However, the music did the talking and the album sold well. The band began developing a reputation in the region as a solid heavy metal outfit.

2.6.2 Changing of "Ians"

Sometime after the recording of *Burn This Town*, maybe on tour, Ian Thompson either quit or was fired and another Ian, Ian McCormick, was brought in as their new drummer. This new dynamic added a different spark to the band and they continued building their reputation. Their efforts paid off when they entered the recording studio in Inverness, Scotland and did their second album, *Power From The Universe* for the Music For Nations label. This album showed a more refined and mature Battleaxe and contains the opening track "Chopper Attack."

2.6.3 Personnel changes

Success seemed to be on their doorstep as they tore up venues throughout England. On the eve of a major appearance at Hammersmith Odeon London in support of Saxon on their Crusader tour, some A&R guys from Atlantic Records were showing interest. After the show, they wanted the band to organise a showcase for them. It was then, for still unknown reasons to the band and fans, that Steve Hardy quit and they had to pull out of what could have been a major signing. It took almost two years before a new lineup was found that was somewhere near the quality and spirit to what they had. This was a severe blow to their career and put the band on hold until they could regain their ground. That happened when they toured the UK in support of Madam X, who had to pull out of the tour due to an illness, leaving Battleaxe to headline. They finished the tour at the Dominion theatre in London. The new lineup added Mick Percy and John Stormont. That lead and rhythm guitar combination put a new level and fuller sound to the band's performances live as well as in the studio. Soon after, they went into Neat Records studio to record the tracks Radio Thunder, Girl Crazee, and Killer woman. These tracks were added to their current EP release Nightmare Zone. John Stormont, one of the best lead guitarists around at the time, contributed a phenomenal lead break performance on the track Killer Woman. Sadly, John left the band for domestic reasons, and afterward, there was a rotating door of musicians until 1987 when they recruited Jason Holt on guitar and Stew Curtan on drums (after Ian McCormack hung up his sticks). During this period of instability, the band were lucky enough to have met drummer Paul Atkinson from Newcastle, filling in now and then, but not quite joining the band until a very later date (He is now a full-fledged member, recently recording the YouTube video to the band's fast and furious track Chopper Attack [from the PFTU album] see below). With this lineup, their sound had fattened, being made more powerful and adding much versatility that was not possible with one guitarist. The power and energy from this new lineup was sensational. Unfortunately again, as the way bands tend to do, this promising new lineup lasted only a short time before the lack of demand in the UK for good quality British rock died and a new wave of death metal and grunge appeared. This made it hard for Battleaxe to tour. Metallica, when first appearing on the metal scene, wanted to tour the UK and Europe with Battleaxe but because of strange politics within the band, changed their minds. However Battleaxe were added to a compilation album with Metallica, Manowar, and other big-named bands. This album is detailed on the band's web site. In 1995/6/7/8 the band hired another guitarist for a short while and did a spectacular gig at Klenal Hall Biker's Festival in (Northumberland. Plans were made to record a third album, and they went into the studio to record the demos that were to become the recently released *Nightmare Zone* EP. The third album was originally going to be called *Metal Edge*, but they were not able to secure interest from a record label back then, and the band began to lose interest. Touring and live gigs at the time were impossible due to the sheer lack of funding. The YouTube video recording was then done with just a four-piece lineup of Mick Percy Guitar, Paul Atkinson [Paul AT Kinson] from Skyclad on drums, and the two founding members, Brian Smith Bass, and Dave King Vocals (not the Fastaway vocalist Dave King, which many people get mixed up with).

2.6.4 Latest developments

2014 saw the re-mastering and re-release of the first two albums 'Burn This Town' and 'Power From The Universe' and the fresh release of their newest one 'Heavy Metal Sanctuary'.

Ricky Squires (ex Heavy Metal Kids etc) joined Battleaxe, replacing Kinson on drums, in May 2014 prior to their debut show at Bloodstock Open Air Festival.. With this new injection of energy and talent from Ricky the band plan to produce a new, even heavier, album over the coming months for release in 2016.

2.6.5 Members *For Burn This Town*

- Dave King - Vocals
- Brian Smith - Bass
- Steve Hardy - Guitar
- Ian Thompson - Drums

2.6.6 Members For *Power from the Universe*

- Dave King - Vocals

- Brian Smith - Bass
- Steve Hardy - Guitar
- Ian McCormick - Drums

2.6.7 Post *Universe* Lineup 1

- Dave King - Vocals
- Brian Smith - Bass
- Ian McCormick - Drums
- John Stormont - Guitar
- Mick Percy - Guitar

2.6.8 Post *Universe* Lineup 2

- Dave King - Vocals
- Brian Smith - Bass
- Mick Percy - Guitar
- Jason Holt - Guitar
- Stewart Curtin - Drums

2.6.9 *Nightmare Zone* Lineup

- Dave King - Vocals
- Brian Smith - Bass
- Mick Percy - Guitar
- John Stormont - Guitar
- Ian McCormack - Drums

2.6.10 Current Lineup

- Dave King - Vocals
- Brian Smith - Bass
- Mick Percy - Guitar
- Ricky Squires

2.6.11 Discography

- "Burn This Town" - Single - Burn This Town/Battleaxe (1981)
- *Burn This Town* - Album (Original Sleeve)(1983)
- *Burn This Town* - Album (Redesigned Sleeve) (1984)
- *Power from the Universe* - Album (1984)
- *Burn This Town* - CD Reissue (2005)
- *Power from the Universe* - CD Reissue (2005)
- *Nightmare Zone* - EP CD (Recorded 1987) (2005)
- "Heavy Metal Sanctuary" - Album (2014)

2.6.12 Discography compilations

- *Roxcalibur* - Burn This Town & Battleaxe (1982)
- *Hell on Earth* - Ready to Deliver (1983)
- *Metal Battle* - Ready to Deliver (1983)
- *Welcome to the Metal Zone* - Chopper Attack (1985)

2.6.13 See also

- List of New Wave of British Heavy Metal bands

2.6.14 External links

- Official website
- Battleaxe on Facebook

2.7 Black Rose (UK band)

Black Rose are an English heavy metal band from Teesside in the north east of England. They formed in 1976 under the name ICE but changed it to Black Rose in 1980 and were one of many British bands considered part of the New Wave of British Heavy Metal movement. The original line up was Steve Bardsley (lead vocals/guitar), Kenny Nicholson (guitar), Marty Rajn (bass) and Mark Eason (drums). Over the next nine years the band went through various line up changes and released quite a few records including two albums: *Boys Will Be Boys* (1984) and *Walk It How You Talk It* (1986) before splitting up in 1989. The band then reformed in 2006 and released their newest album *Cure for Your Disease* in 2010.

2.7.1 History

Black Rose started out as ICE back in 1978 when three friends from a School in Saltburn by the Sea decided to form a rock band. The three guys were Steve Bardsley, Marty Rajn and Mark Eason who soon became a four piece after they saw guitarist Kenny Nicholson playing in a local pub and asked him if he wanted to join up with them. Eason left the band citing musical differences and local drummer Charlie Mack was drafted in. As this line up they recorded their first demo tape at Impulse Studios in Wallsend Newcastle, the home of independent record label Neat Records, which consisted of 5 songs: Alright On The Night, Biker, Killer, Loveshock and Raising Hell. The demo was picked up by various Rock Disco play-lists and featured in the local charts section of UK Rock magazine Kerrang!.

Nicholson and Mack both left the band to pursue others ventures, Mack joined Emerson and then ended up in Samson and Nicholson went on to form both Holland[1] and Fast Kutz.[2] New guitarist Chris "wahwah" Watson and drummer Mal Smith then joined the band and they released their first single on the Teesbeat label called *No Point Runnin'* and this was the record that started getting people talking about this unknown little UK band. Unfortunately Rajn fell out with the rest of the band over various issues and departed, making way for young bass player Mick Thompson to step in. This went on to be probably the most stable line up of the band, recording and releasing an array of songs including their début album *Boys Will Be Boys* and featuring on a variety of compilation records. The band toured all over the UK and Europe playing alongside established bands including Raven, Terraplane, Budgie, Trust, Vardis, Atomic Rooster, Pretty Maids and Spider, and gathered a worldwide fanbase having fan clubs in Europe, Japan and the United States.

By the mid eighties they were also joined by guitar and keyboard player Gary Todd and major record labels Atlantic Records and Bronze Records both showed some interest in the band but neither signed them up to any deal so Watson got a bit disillusioned and left, making way for young guitarist Pat O'Neil. This line up recorded the band's second album *Walk It How You Talk It* released by Neat Records which saw them recording slightly more melodic songs which ultimately gained them some new fans but lost them some of the old. This album was also picked up by AJK, a subsidiary of K-tel in the USA where it was repackaged and ready to be released independently, but unfortunately never did because of a dispute over copyrights with a US band of the same name. This was to be the beginning of the end for the band and although they recorded some more material nothing was released and they split up in 1989.

In 2006 Bardsley, after speaking to Watson, decided to write some new material together and Black Rose were born again. British indie rock label Majestic Rock Records released a CD of the band's songs from 1980-89 called *Bright Lights Burnin'* and in 2010 the band released their third album *Cure for Your Disease* as an independent download-only release.

A new line up was put together and the band played their first gig in 25 years at the Cradle Will Rock festival in Shildon, County Durham. In 2012 they were invited to play at Hammerfest IV and also at the Headbangers Open Air festival in Germany. The band also released three new albums on German record labels.

2.7.2 Discography

Studio Albums

- *Boys Will Be Boys* (Bullet records 1984)
- *Walk It How You Talk It* (Neat records 1986)
- *Cure for Your Disease* (Metalizer records 2012)

EP's

- *Black Rose* EP (Bullet records 1984)
- *Nightmare* EP (Neat records 1985)

Compilations

- *Bright Lights Burnin'* (Majestic Rock records 2006)
- *The Early Years Remastered and More* (Hellion records 2012)
- *Loveshock* (High Roller records 2012)

Singles

- "No Point Runnin'" / "Sucker for Your Love" (Teesbeat 1982)
- "Boys Will Be Boys" / "Liar" (Bullet records 1984)

Featured on

- *One Take No Dubs* split EP (Neat records 1982)
- *Roxcalibur* (Guardian records 1982)
- *Metal Masters* (Castle records 1994)
- *The Flame Burns On* (Neat records 2002)

- *The Singles Collection Volumes 2 and 3' (Neat records 2002)*
- *Total Metal Attack* (Old School records 2004)

2.7.3 Band Members

Current members

- Steve Bardsley - lead vocals, guitar (1980-1989, 2006–present)
- Kenny Nicholson - guitar (1980-1982, 2011–present)
- Kiko Rivers - bass (2006–present)
- Chris Bennet - drums (2010–present)

Former members

- Marty Rajn - bass (1980-1982)
- Mark Eason - drums (1980-1982)
- Charlie Mack - drums (1982)
- Chris Watson - guitar (1982-1986, 2006-2011)
- Mal Smith - drums (1982-1986)
- Mick Thompson - bass (1982-1989)
- Gary Todd - guitar, keyboards (1985-1989)
- Pat O'Neil - guitar (1986-1989)
- Barry Youll - drums (1986-1987, 2006-2010)
- Davey Patterson - guitar (1989)
- Paul Fowler - drums (1987-1989)

2.7.4 See also

- List of New Wave of British Heavy Metal bands

2.7.5 References

[1]

[2] "Black Rose page on Encyclopaedia Metallum".

2.7.6 External links

- Official website
- Official Myspace website
- Official reverbnation website

2.8 Blitzkrieg (band)

Blitzkrieg are a heavy metal band initially from Leicester formed in 1980. The current line-up is Brian Ross (vocals), Ken Johnson (guitar), Alan Ross (guitar), Bill Baxter (bass) and Matt Graham (drums). Brian Ross is the only remaining member from the band's founding.

2.8.1 History

Blitzkrieg was formed in October 1980 after signing a record deal with Neat Records, a label that was signing many of the bands involved with the New Wave of British Heavy Metal (NWOBHM) movement. In the early stages of Blitzkrieg's career they regularly produced gigs in England, but then later split in 1981. Brian Ross most notably went on to join Satan, another metal band, along with stints in Avenger, Lone Wolf and Unter den Linden. In 1984 Ross and fellow founding member Jim Sirotto, along with guitarist Mick Proctor (ex-Tygers of Pan Tang), bass player Mick Moore (of Avenger) and drummer Sean Taylor (Satan/Blind Fury, ex-Raven) then decided that it was time to record the Blitzkrieg album that was originally planned to be released in 1981, *A Time of Changes*. It was later released in 1985.

Blitzkrieg released *10 Years of Blitzkrieg* in 1991. The released *Unholy Trinity* in 1995. The album *Ten* was released in 1997. *The Mists of Avalon* was released in 1998.

Ross was then involved in a car accident, which temporarily kept Blitzkrieg from playing. After he recovered, the band released the albums, *Absolute Power* (a studio album), *Absolutely Live* (a live album) and *Sins and Greed*. On 10 August 2007, Blitzkrieg released their album *Theatre of the Damned* through their record label Armageddon Music.

2.8.2 Members

- Brian Ross - vocals (1980–1981, 1984–91, 1992–94, 1996–99, 2001–present)
- Ken Johnson - guitars (2002–present)
- Alan Ross - guitars (2012–present)
- Bill Baxter - bass (2012–present)
- Matt Graham - drums (2015–present)

2.8.3 Former members

Guitars :

Brian Ross

- Ian Jones (1980–81)
- Jim Sirotto (1980–81, 1984–86) [born Jim Sieroto]
- John Antcliffe (1981)
- Mick Proctor (1984–86)
- J D Binnie (1986–87)
- Chris Beard (1986–87)
- Steve Robertson (1988–89)
- Glenn S. Howes (1988–90, 1996–99)
- Tony J. Liddle (1989–96, 2001–02)
- Phil Millar (1996)
- Martin Richardson (1996–98)
- Paul Nesbitt (1992, 1998–2006)
- Guy Laverick (2006-2011)
- Ken Johnson (2002–present)
- Alan Ross (2012–present)

Bass :

- Steve English (1980–81)
- Mick Moore (1981, 1984–86, 1991)
- Darren Parnaby (1986–87)
- Robbie Robertson (1988–89)
- Glenn Carey (1989–90)
- Dave Anderson (1992–94)
- Steve Ireland (1996)
- Gavin Gray (1996–99)
- Andy Galloway (2001–04)
- Bill Baxter (2012–present)

Drums :

- Steve Abbey (1980–81)
- Sean Taylor (1984–86, 1991–94)
- Sean Wilkinson (1986–87)
- Kyle Gibson (1988–89)
- Gary Young (1989–90)
- Paul Ward (1996)
- Paul White (1996)
- Neil Nattrass (1996)
- Mark Hancock (1996–98)
- Mark Wyndebank (1998–99)
- Mick Kerrigan (2012–2015)
- Matt Graham (2015-present)

2.8.4 Discography

2.8.5 See also

- List of New Wave of British Heavy Metal bands

2.8.6 References

2.8.7 External links

- Official Blitzkrieg website

2.9 Bronz

Bronz are an English hard rock band, formed in Bath in the mid-1970s. The band played mainly around the UK and at the 'free festivals' of the time. These included at Stonehenge in both 1977 and 1978, following an appearance at Glastonbury in 1976.

2.9.1 Career

After an early tie up with Dave Panton as their part-time manager in 1980, the band played many support slots at The Marquee and Music Machine with Angel Witch, More, Diamond Head, and Anvil. The band reappeared in 1983, with Chris Goulstone on guitar and keyboards, Shaun Kirkpatrick on guitar and backing vocals, Clive Deamer on drums, plus Paul Webb on bass guitar and vocals. They were signed to an independent record label, Bronze Records. The band recorded *Taken by Storm* with Ritchie Cordell and Glen Kolotkin, later helped by Gerry Bron and Mark Dearnly on production.[1]

They were launched onto the American market via a tie-in between Bronze Records and Island.[2] The line-up, then based in London, consisted of ex-Nightwing vocalist Max Bacon, Goulstone, Kirkpatrick, Webb and new drummer Carl Matthews. In 1998, an album of unreleased tracks from that time, entitled *Unfinished Business* was released.[2]

Following the demise of Bronze Records and the original line up in 1984, after a major US tour supporting Ratt, Kirkpatrick assembled a completely new line-up. With producer Max Norman they created their second album, *Carried by the Storm*,[3] which was recorded in London's Roundhouse and Power Plant recording studios. The band then comprised Kirkpatrick (guitars / Roland guitar synthesizer), Ian Baker (lead vocals), Mickey O'Donoghue (guitar), Clive Edwards (drums), and Lee Reddings (bass). Guest musicians included Phil Lanzon, Chris Thompson, Stevie Lange, Gary Barnacle and Charlie McCracken. During the final recording and completion of the album, the record label went into receivership, and until 2010 *Carried by the Storm* remained unreleased.

Bronz reformed briefly in 2000,[2] with the 1984 line-up including Paul Webb resuming lead vocal duties; plus Jake Kirkpatrick on bass guitar. The band played a number of shows together, and a deal was tied up with Sanctuary Records in 2003, with the release of live tracks from their 1984 US tour and some new material. This was released as *Bronz Live - Getting Higher*.

In 2005, Bronz with Goulstone, Thomas, and Scottish drummer Windsor McGilvray, appeared at the 25th anniversary of the beginning of the New Wave of British Heavy Metal, at the Astoria in London, along with Diamond Head and Jaguar.

In 2010 and 2011, the band line-up that recorded the second official studio album were promoting the belated release of *Carried by the Storm*. The tour incorporated the UK, Europe, and the US. Extensive dates for 2012 were undertaken, and the album received critical acclaim in the music press. The band led by Kirkpatrick appeared at the Hard Rock Hell Festival[4] in December 2011, with Max Bacon the band's original singer from the first album returning, and Paul Webb back on bass.

In July 2013, guitarist Shaun Kirkpatrick died. At the time, the band was working on a new album.[5]

2.9.2 Albums

- *Taken by Storm* (1984)
    - featuring the single "Send Down an Angel" b/w "Tiger" (1984)
- *Unfinished Business* (1998)
- *Bronz Live - Getting Higher* (2003)
- *Carried by the Storm* (2010)
    - "Can't Live Without Your Love" (Kirkpatrick)
    - "Carried by the Storm" (Kirkpatrick, O'Donoghue, Baker)
    - "There's a Reason" (Kirkpatrick, O'Donoghue, Baker)
    - "Man, Girl & Machine" (Kirkpatrick, O'Donoghue, Baker)
    - "When the Lights Die Down" (Kirkpatrick, O'Donoghue, Baker)
    - "You & Me" (Kirkpatrick, O'Donoghue, Baker)
    - "One More Time" (Kirkpatrick, O'Donoghue, Baker, Edwards, Reddings)
    - "Tell Her" (Kirkpatrick, O'Donoghue, Baker)
    - "Two Silhouettes" (Russ Ballard)
    - "Figure in the Dark" (Kirkpatrick, O'Donoghue, Baker)
    - "Dangerous Game" (Kirkpatrick, O'Donoghue, Baker)

2.9.3 See also

- List of New Wave of British Heavy Metal bands
- GTR

2.9.4 References

[1] "Taken by Storm - Bronz : Credits". AllMusic. Retrieved 2013-07-13.

[2] "Bronz - Music Biography, Credits and Discography". AllMusic. Retrieved 2013-07-13.

[3] "Tune Records c/o Your Tune Music Ltd". Yourtunerecords.com. Retrieved 2013-07-13.

[4] "Welcome To Hard Rock Hell VI - Fistful Of Rock". Hardrockhell.com. Retrieved 2013-07-13.

[5] "Bronz Guitarist Shaun Kirkpatrick Dies". Ultimateclassicrock.com. 2013-07-09. Retrieved 2013-07-13.

2.9.5 External links

- Bronz-music website
- Shaun Kirkpatrick's website
- Chrisgoulstone.co.uk
- Interview with Bronz from Hard Rock Hell Festival 2011

Ian Baker Photography

2.10 Budgie (band)

Budgie are a Welsh hard rock/heavy metal band from Cardiff. They are described by author Gary Sharpe-Young as one of the earliest heavy metal bands and a seminal influence to many acts of that scene,[2] with fast, heavy rock (an influence on the New Wave of British Heavy Metal (NWOBHM) and acts such as Metallica)[3] being played as early as 1971.[4] The band has been noted as "among the heaviest metal of its day".[5]

2.10.1 Career

Budgie formed in 1967 in Cardiff, Wales under the name Hills Contemporary Grass. Their original line-up consisted of Burke Shelley on vocals and bass, Tony Bourge on guitar and vocals, and Ray Phillips on drums.[6] After performing several gigs in 1968, the band changed their name to Budgie the following year and recorded their first demo.[2] The band originally formed under such names as Hills Contemporary Grass and Six Ton Budgie.[7] Burke Shelley has said that the band's name came from the fact that he, "loved the idea of playing noisy, heavy rock, but calling ourselves after something diametrically opposed to that".[8]

Their debut album in strong blues-oriented hard rock lines was recorded at Rockfield Studios with Black Sabbath producer Rodger Bain[9] and released in 1971, followed by *Squawk* in 1972. The third album, *Never Turn Your Back On a Friend* (1973), contained "Breadfan", which was covered by Metallica in 1988, the band having covered another Budgie song, "Crash Course In Brain Surgery" earlier in their career. Ray Philips left the band before the fourth album *In for the Kill!* was recorded and was replaced by Pete Boot (b. Peter Charles Boot, 30 September 1950, West Bromwich, Staffordshire).[10]

In late 1974, the band were joined by drummer Steve Williams for the album *Bandolier*, for live shows promoting this album and the follow-up, *If I Were Brittania I'd Waive the Rules*, the band were augmented by Welsh guitarist Myf Isaac, but both Bourge and Isaac left mid 1978 and were replaced by ex Trapeze guitarist Robert Kendrick. Music from the 1978 LP *Impeckable* was featured in the 1979 film *J-Men Forever* (shown frequently on the USA Network's "Night Flight" television series in the 1980s) which is now a cult classic. In late 1978, having been dropped by A&M and with no new recording contract, this line up floundered, and after 12 months Kendrick was replaced by "Big" John Thomas (b. 21 February 1952) in late 1979. This line up recorded two albums for Kingsley Wards 'Active' label: *Power Supply* (1980) and *Nightflight* (1981). 1982 saw them signed to RCA for *Deliver Us From Evil* their final recording for a "major label".

Burke Shelley and Steve Williams performing in 1981

The band continued to have success during the New Wave of British Heavy Metal scene, playing the Reading Festival in 1980 and then headlining the festival in 1982.[11] They built a particular following in Poland, where they played as the first heavy metal band behind the Iron Curtain, in 1982. Also notable was their tour support of Ozzy Osbourne's Blizzard of Ozz Tour.[12]

The band stopped gigging in 1988, members went into studio production, occasionally guesting on other projects; Thomas most notably worked on the *Phenomena* CD with Glenn Hughes[13][14] out of the Black Sabbath studios.

Although the group has had very little commercial success in America, they have enjoyed a strong fan following in Texas[15] and they have been known to receive radio airplay from Joe Anthony and Lou Roney on KMAC/KISS radio in San Antonio in the 1970s,[16] the band reformed using various drummers for one-off gigs in 1995, 1996 for outdoor festivals 'La Semana Alegre' in San Antonio, Texas. They toured in 2002-6, mostly in the United Kingdom, the NYC/NJ area, Dallas, and with a few shows in Europe including the Sweden Rock Festival and a return to post-Communist Poland. In 1999 the band reunited in Letchworth and officially reformed.

In 2006 Budgie undertook a thirty five date United Kingdom tour and a new album, titled *You're All Living In Cuckooland*, was released in the UK on 7 November that year. In 2007 they played dates in Sweden and Poland.

On 4 July 2007 Lees announced his departure from the band to concentrate on his teaching and solo career.

Following the departure of Lees, Dio lead guitarist and songwriter Craig Goldy offered his services while Ronnie James Dio was completing commitments with Heaven & Hell on their World Tour.

In February 2008 Craig Goldy accompanied Budgie on their first tour of Australia and has continued playing with Budgie as 'guest guitarist' for all of their shows.

Budgie's November 2010 tour of Eastern Europe had to be cancelled as Shelley was hospitalised on 9 November in Wejherowo, Poland with a 6 cm aortic aneurism. After surgery, he returned to Britain for recovery.[17] The band has since been on hiatus, as Shelley can't sing and play at the same time.

2.10.2 Musical style and legacy

Budgie's music is often described as a cross between the progressive textures of Rush and the heaviness of Black Sabbath.[1] Burke Shelley's vocals have been compared to Geddy Lee due to his similar approach of high-pitched banshee wails (incidentally, Shelley and Lee are also the bass players in their respective power-trio bands).[1] Although Budgie remained quite obscure during their early career, many future stars of hard rock/metal have cited them as an important influence and covered their songs, including Iron Maiden,[18] Metallica,[19] Van Halen,[20] Melvins,[21] Queens of the Stone Age, Alice in Chains,[22] and Soundgarden.[23]

2.10.3 Members

Timeline

2.10.4 Discography

Studio albums

Live albums

Compilation albums

EPs

- *If Swallowed, Do Not Induce Vomiting* (1980, Active BUDGE 1)

Singles (UK-exclusive unless stated otherwise)

- "Crash Course in Brain Surgery" / "Nude Disintegrating Parachutist Woman" (1971, MCA MK 5072)

- "Whiskey River" / "Guts" (1972, MCA MK 5085)

- "Whiskey River" / "Stranded" (1972, MCA 2185) - US-exclusive release

- "Zoom Club (Edit)" / "Wondering What Everyone Knows" (1974, MCA 133)

- "I Ain't No Mountain" / "Honey" (1975, MCA 175)

- "Smile Boy Smile" / "All at Sea" (1978, A&M AMS 7342)

- "Crime Against the World" / "Hellbender" (1980, Active BUDGE 2)

- "Keeping a Rendezvous" / "Apparatus" (1981, RCA BUDGE 3) - UK #71

- "I Turned to Stone (Part 1)" / "I Turned to Stone (Part 2)" (1981, RCA BUDGE 4)

- "I Turned to Stone" / "She Used Me Up" (1981, Tonpress S-445) - Polish release

- "Bored with Russia" / "Don't Cry" (1982, RCA 271)

2.10.5 References

- *The New Musical Express Book of Rock*, 1975, Star Books, ISBN 0-352-30074-4

- Sharpe-Young, Garry (2007). *Metal: The Definitive Guide*. London: Jawbone Press. ISBN 978-1-906002-01-5.

- Crocker, Chris (1993). *Metallica: The Frayed Ends of Metal*. New York: St. Martin's Press. ISBN 0-312-08635-0.

2.10.6 Notes

[1] "Artist-Budgie". AllMusic. Retrieved 28 September 2012.

[2] Sharpe-Young, Garry (2007), p. 30

[3] Archived July 1, 2015 at the Wayback Machine

[4] Album: Budgie, Track: Nude Disintegrating Parachutist Woman

[5] Crocker 1993, p. 106 *"Still recording into the eighties, Budgie was among the heaviest metal of its day."*

[6] UK. "Budgie's MySpace page". Myspace.com. Retrieved 2012-02-29.

[7] "Artists :: BUDGIE". MusicMight. Retrieved 2012-02-29.

[8] "Classic Rock » Blog Archive » The Top 14 Birds In Rock". Classicrockmagazine.com. 2009-02-24. Retrieved 2012-02-29.

[9] Henderson, Alex. "Budgie - Budgie". AllMusic. Retrieved 2012-02-29.

[10] Prato, Greg (2002-05-30). "Budgie". AllMusic. Retrieved 2012-02-29.

[11] A brief history of the Reading festival fatreg.com

[12] Archived June 6, 2011 at the Wayback Machine

[13] "Phonomena - Phonomena". AllMusic. Retrieved 2012-02-29.

[14] Phillip Hackney. "Whitesnake". Whitesnake.f9.co.uk. Retrieved 2012-02-29.

[15] Prato, Greg (2002-08-02). "Life in San Antonio - Budgie". AllMusic. Retrieved 2012-02-29.

[16] Mendiola, Jim. "San Antonio Current - SPECIAL ISSUES: Louder By Design". Sacurrent.com. Retrieved 2012-02-29.

[17] Shelley, Burke. "Latest update 20 November". Budgie.uk. Retrieved 11 December 2010.

[18] "Iron Maiden - Similar Artists, Megadeth,Influenced By, Followers". AllMusic. Retrieved 2013-02-15.

[19] "Metallica - Similar Artists, Influenced By, Followers". AllMusic. Retrieved 2013-02-15.

[20] Prato, Greg. "In for the Kill! - Budgie : Songs, Reviews, Credits, Awards". AllMusic. Retrieved 2013-02-15.

[21] "Melvins - Similar Artists, Influenced By, Followers". AllMusic. Retrieved 2013-02-15.

[22] "Alice in Chains - Similar Artists, Influenced By, Followers". AllMusic. Retrieved 2013-02-15.

[23] "Soundgarden - Similar Artists, Influenced By, Followers". AllMusic. Retrieved 2013-02-15.

2.10.7 External links

- Official website
- Budgie biography from BBC Wales
- Artist page at AllMusic

2.11 Chateaux (band)

Chateaux were a New Wave of British Heavy Metal band formed in 1981 in Cheltenham, Gloucestershire, United Kingdom. They released three albums during the 1980s through Ebony Records, then home to the likes of Grim Reaper and Savage. The band is notable for launching the career of Steve Grimmett, later of Grim Reaper and Onslaught.

2.11.1 Biography

The band were originally formed under the name of **Stealer**[1] circa 1981 by guitarist Tim Broughton, bassist Alex Houston and drummer Andre Baylis.[2] They were selected by the newly-started Ebony Records for inclusion on their 1982 *Metal Maniaxe* compilation, changing their name to Chateaux and contributing the track "Young Blood"; at the time, bassist Alex Houston was providing vocals, and the song was later released as a single by Ebony, backed with "Fight to the Last". 1983 saw the release of the band's debut album, *Chained and Desperate*, again on Ebony Records, produced by Daryl Johnson, and featuring vocals by ex-Medusa[3] and then-Grim Reaper man Steve Grimmett. For reasons unknown, the band insisted that Grimmett's appearance was simply that of a guest, allowing him to remain focussed on Grim Reaper.[4] The cover art was provided by MusicMight's Garry Sharpe-Young,[1] Martin Popoff, in his *Collector's Guide to Heavy Metal*, described the album as "riding the same mysterious mood as Reaper's first, Diamond Head, Savage, and Witchfinder General, *Chained and Desperate* combines integrity, songcraft, and grime in way rarely seen outside the confines of these early Brit masters. A swirling cauldron of glorious noise. 9/10."[5]

Only guitarist and chief songwriter Broughton remained by the release of Chateaux's second LP, *Fire Power* (Ebony, 1984). Replacing Baylis and Houston were bassist/vocalist Krys Mason (ex-Confessor) and drummer Chris Dadson (ex-Wolfbane, Sam Thunder and Aragorn). The second record was less well received than the debut, with Eduardo Rivadavia of Allmusic remarking that, "the second [record was] surprisingly plain and unremarkable by comparison"[6] and Popoff commenting that "songwriting focus is lost, the singular garage din of the debut heaving forth to both OTT excursions and flirtation with AOR rock structures."[7] The band saw a further deline with the release of their third album, *Highly Strung* (1985), and poor sales and the band's reluctance to tour outside their local region led to the band disbanding.[2] Nonetheless, Sanctuary Records re-released all three albums and the debut single as the *Fight to the Last* 2CD compilation in 2003.

2.11.2 Line-up

Last known line-up

- Tim Broughton (guitar)
- Chris Dadson (drums)
- Krys Mason (bass, vocals)

Previous members

- Steve Grimmett (vocals)
- Alex Houston (bass, vocals)
- Andre Baylis (drums)

2.11.3 Discography

- "Young Blood / Fight to the Last" 7" single (Ebony, 1982)
- *Chained and Desperate* LP (Ebony, 1983)
- *Fire Power* LP (Ebony, 1984)
- *Highly Strung* LP (Ebony, 1985)
- *Fight to the Last* compilation (Sanctuary, 2003)

2.11.4 See also

- List of New Wave of British Heavy Metal bands

2.11.5 References

[1] Sharpe-Young, Garry. "Chateaux biography". MusicMight. Retrieved 2012-02-10.

[2] Rivadavia, Eduardo. "Chateaux biography". Allmusic. Retrieved 2012-02-10.

[3] Sharpe-Young, Garry. "Medusa biography". MusicMight. Retrieved 2012-02-10.

[4] Rivadavia, Eduardo. *"Chained and Desperate* review". Allmusic. Retrieved 2012-02-10.

[5] Popoff, Martin (1997). *The Collector's Guide to Heavy Metal*, *Chained and Desperate* review, page 86, ISBN 1-896522-32-7.

[6] Rivadavia, Eduardo. *"Fire Power* review". Allmusic. Retrieved 2012-02-10.

[7] Popoff, Martin (1997). *The Collector's Guide to Heavy Metal*, *Fire Power* review, page 86, ISBN 1-896522-32-7.

2.11.6 External links

- Chateaux @ Allmusic
- Chateaux @ MusicMight

2.12 Chrome Molly

For the Die Monster Die album, see Chrome Molly (album).

Chrome Molly are a hard rock band from Leicester, England. They formed in 1984, releasing four albums before splitting up in 1991. They re-formed in 2009.

2.12.1 History

The band formed in 1981, and after an early demo settled on a line-up of singer Steve Hawkins, guitarist John Antcliffe, bass guitarist Nick Wastell and drummer Chris Green.[1][2] Mark Godfrey (Drums) replaced Chris Green after the release of the "You Said" EP (Bullet Becords, BOLT 10) in 1984 and prior to the recording of the band's debut album, *You Can't Have It All...or Can You?*, which was released in 1985.[1] After the second album *Stick It Out* (1987), Antcliffe was replaced by Tim Read, and the band signed to I.R.S. Records, their first release for the label a cover version of Squeeze's "Take Me I'm Yours".[2] IRS released the third album *Angst* in April 1988, which included the single "Shooting Me Down" which was written by Jim Lea and Noddy Holder of Slade and produced by Lea; The single received heavy airplay from BBC Radio 1 but suffered from a dispute between I.R.S. and distributors MCA Records.[1][3] They toured as support act with Alice Cooper on his Raise Your Fist And Yell tour in 1988, with guitarist Andrew Barrott added to the line-up.[1] They moved on to the Music for Nations label for fourth album *Slaphead* (1990).[1]

The band split up in 1991, although they played together as Van Halen tribute band Von Halen a few times.[3]

The band reformed in 2009 with members of the early line-up Hawkins, Antcliffe and Wastell joined by Greg Ellis, and announced a new album, *Gunpowder Diplomacy*.[3][4]

The band's first two albums were reissued by Cherry Red sublabel Lemon Recordings in 2010.[4]

The band returned to the studio with Toby Jepson from Little Angels in the producers chair, the album "Gunpowder Diplomacy" was released in 2013 by earMUSIC

Johnny Antcliffe left the band in December 2014 to be replaced in 2015 by John Foottit, the band return to the studio in August 2015 to record their sixth studio album with Toby Jepson again in the production role.

2.12.2 Discography

Albums

- *You Can't Have It All...or Can You?* (1985), Powerstation
- *Stick It Out* (1987), Powerstation
- *Angst* (1988), IRS
- *Slaphead* (1990), Music for Nations
- *Gunpowder Diplomacy* (2013) Edel

Compilations

- *You Can't Have It All...or Can You?/Stick It Out* (2010), Lemon

Singles

- "You Said" (1984), Bullet
- "Take It or Leave It" (1985), Powerstation
- "I Want to Find Out" (1986), Powerstation
- "Take Me I'm Yours" (1988), IRS
- "Thanx for the Angst" (1988), IRS
- "Shooting Me Down" (1988), IRS

2.12.3 See also

- List of New Wave of British Heavy Metal bands

2.12.4 References

[1] Larkin, Colin (1999) *The Virgin Encyclopedia of Heavy Rock*, Virgin Books, ISBN 0-7535-0257-7, p. 97

[2] Strong, Martin C. (2001) *The Great Metal Discography*, MOJO Books, ISBN 1-84195-185-4, p. 115

[3] "Rockers return", *Leicester Mercury*, 19 July 2010, retrieved 2012-05-02

[4] "Chrome Molly Return", *Classic Rock*, 24 June 2010, retrieved 2012-05-02

2.12.5 External links

- Official website

2.13 Cloven Hoof (band)

Cloven Hoof are a heavy metal band from Wolverhampton, United Kingdom, that was active from 1979 to 1990, and again from around 2000 onwards. The band was associated with the New Wave of British Heavy Metal movement, alongside bands such as Iron Maiden, Saxon and Diamond Head. Enduring many line-up changes, only founding bassist Lee Payne has remained present throughout the band's career.

2.13.1 Biography

Early Years: 1979-1987

Cloven Hoof went through a number of early line-up changes before settling on a steady line-up that would last for their first few recordings. Theatrical from the beginning, the four band members took up pseudonyms based on the four elements: David "Water" Potter, Steve "Fire" Rounds, Lee "Air" Payne and Kevin "Earth" Poutney.[1] This line-up recorded a successful demo tape in 1982, along with *The Opening Ritual* EP, and the debut *Cloven Hoof* album.

Following the release of their self-titled debut, David Potter left the band to be replaced by Rob Kendrick, who took up the "Water" pseudonym. This line-up only managed to record the live album *Fighting Back* before splitting up, leaving Lee Payne as the sole remaining band member.

1988-1990

Lee Payne reactivated the band in 1988, hiring vocalist Russ North and guitarist Andy Wood from Tredegar along with drummer Jon Brown.

With a whole new set of musicians in place, the band dropped the stage names and went on to record two more albums: 1988's *Dominator* and 1989's *A Sultan's Ransom*. Former member of Tredegar Lee Jones was brought into the band as a second guitarist soon after the release of these two albums, but contractual difficulties caused the band to split up again in 1990.

2001-2007

In the summer of 2001, Lee Payne began putting together a new line-up for the next incarnation of Cloven Hoof (following a telephone conversation with Andy Wood regarding the contractual difficulties which had caused the band's decade-long split.)

The band completed a live appearance at the *Keep It True II* Festival at the Tauberfrankenhalle in Lauda-Königshofen, Germany on 10 April 2004.

Eye of the Sun was recorded and released in 2006, with the help of musicians Matt Moreton on vocals, Andy Shortland on guitars, and Lynch Radinsky on drums. Tom Galley produced the album. Due to the work commitments of various band members it was impossible for the unit to play live, so Lee Payne was once again obliged to enlist new personnel.

Vocalist Russ North returned to England and rejoined the band, after a period of time spent living in Spain. Eventually the band's line-up was completed by Mick Powell and Ben Read on guitars, with Jon Brown on drums.

2008 onwards

A collection of re-recorded songs - *The Definitive Part One* - was released in early 2008,[2] with a new EP to be called *Throne of Damnation* scheduled for release in 2010.

In 2008, Cloven Hoof co-headlined the *Metal Brew* Festival in Mill Hill with Pagan Altar.[3] Both bands also performed at the *British Steel IV* Festival at the Camden Underworld in 2009.[4]

On 27 June 2009, Cloven Hoof appeared at the *Bang Your Head!!!* festival in Balingen, Germany. They featured on the bill alongside bands such as W.A.S.P., U.D.O., Blind Guardian and Journey, playing their set in torrential rain.

The track *Nightstalker*, from the band's debut album, was used in the soundtrack for the Brütal Legend computer game.

In early 2010, following the exit of Russ North, Matt Moreton was hired to record the vocals that appeared on the *Throne of Damnation* EP. Moreton left the band due to ill health soon afterwards.[5]

On 13 December 2010, Cloven Hoof released their first DVD, *A Sultan's Ransom - Video Archive*, comprising footage of a 1989 concert at Lichfield Art Centre and also featuring two music videos for the songs *Mad, Mad World* and *Highlander*, both from *A Sultan's Ransom*.

2011 saw Lee Payne rebuilding the band, bringing in guitarist Joe Whelan from the band Dementia and guitarist Chris Coss from UK/DC, along with drummer Mark Gould and Ash Cooper on vocals. This line-up released a music video called *I'm Your Nemesis* and an updated version of "Nightstalker".

Russ North parted company with Cloven Hoof for a final time in July 2012, following a controversial performance in Cyprus. Mark Gould left the band in August 2012, with Jake Oseland replacing him on drums in time for a series of live dates in 2013.

The 2013 line-up of Cloven Hoof scheduled a debut UK concert appearance with Jameson Raid and Hollow Ground at Wolverhampton Civic Hall on 30 March 2013.[6]

On 27 April 2013, Cloven Hoof played a concert at the Parkhotel Hall in Tirol, Austria. The show was recorded by producer Patrick Engel for a future live album release. A studio album, provisionally entitled *Resist or Serve*, was planned for release on High Roller Records.

On 23 June 2013, Cloven Hoof played at the *R-Mine* Festival in Belgium, on a bill which included Hell, Tygers of Pan Tang and Tank. This was followed by an appearance at the *Heavy Metal Night 6* Festival in Italy on 21 September 2013.

In 2014, Cloven Hoof were added to the bill for the Sweden Rock Festival, with Black Sabbath and Alice Cooper. An appearance at the *Power and Glory* Festival in Hatfield was scheduled for 23 August 2014, with further European tour dates due to take place throughout the year.

2.13.2 Discography

Studio albums

- *Cloven Hoof* (1984)
- *Dominator* (1988, re-released 2011 & 2012)
- *A Sultan's Ransom* (1989, re-released 2012)
- *Eye of the Sun* (2006)
- *Resist or Serve* (Due: 6 June 2014)

Live albums

- *Fighting Back* (1986)

Compilation albums

- *The Definitive Part One* (2008)

EPs

- *The Opening Ritual* (1982)
- *Throne of Damnation* (2010)

Demos

- *1982 Demo* (1982)
- *Second 1982 Demo* (1982)

Videos and DVDs

- *A Sultan's Ransom - Video Archive* (DVD) (2010)

2.13.3 Line-up

- Lee Payne - Bass (1979–1990, 2000-)
- Joe Whelan - Guitars/Vocals (2011-)
- Chris Coss - Guitars (2011-)
- Jake Oseland - Drums (2012-)

2.13.4 Former members (those featured on albums)

Vocals

- Russ North (1986-1990, 2006-2009, 2011–2012)
- Rob Kendrick (1985-1986)
- David Potter (1982–1984)
- Matt Moreton (2000-2006, 2009)

Guitar

- Steve Rounds (1982–1986)
- Andy Wood (1988–1990, 2004)
- Andy Shortland (2005–2006)
- Ben Read (2007–2010)
- Mick Powell (2007, 2008, 2009–2010)

Drums

- Kevin Pountney (1982–1986)
- Lynch Radinsky (2005–2006)
- Jon Brown (1987–1990, 2007–2010)

2.13.5 See also

- List of New Wave of British Heavy Metal bands

2.13.6 References

[1] "MusicMight :: Artists :: CLOVEN HOOF". Rockdetector.com. Retrieved 2014-07-28.

[2] "Cloven Hoof - The Definitive Part One - Reviews - Encyclopaedia Metallum". The Metal Archives. 2008-05-28. Retrieved 2014-07-28.

[3] "Blabbermouth.net". Legacy.roadrunnerrecords.com. 2013-04-17. Retrieved 2014-07-28.

[4]

[5] "CLOVEN HOOF (Lee Payne) - Interview 2012". Strikemet.com. Retrieved 2014-07-28.

[6]

2.13.7 External links

- Official website

2.14 Dedringer

Dedringer were a British hard rock band associated with the New Wave of British Heavy Metal. They were formed in 1977 in Leeds, United Kingdom, and released two albums (through Dindisc and Neat Records respectively) before finally quitting in 1985.

2.14.1 History

Originally titled **Deadringer**,[1] the band was formed in late 1977 as a covers band in Leeds by Johnny "JJ" Hoyle, Neil Hudson, Al Scott, Lee Flaxington and Kenny Jones.[2] They built up a core grassroots following throughout 1978,[3] and came to the attention of Virgin Records through their A&R man, who decided to manage the band when Virgin failed to sign them.[1] In 1980, they signed to the pop and new romantic label Dindisc and issued their debut single, "Sunday Drivers", in January; the band toured the UK with the likes of Praying Mantis, Gillan, Triumph and the Michael Schenker Group.[2][4]

February 1981 saw the release of Dedringer's debut album, *Direct Line*. Eduardo Rivadavia of Allmusic desccribed the album as a "fairly innocuous hard set",[2] and Martin Popoff, giving the album 6/10, summed it up as "a memorial to non-threatening pub rock, absorbing all the non-achieving affectations of those who slogged the wee stages before them."[5] The album however sold enough to gain the band a set on the Friday Rock Show, but following the release of the *Maxine* EP in April 1981, strife between the band and their record label, and serious car accident suffered by Hudson and Scott,[2] led the band to call it a day.

Hudson, Scott and Jones reformed the band in 1985, with new members Neil Garfitt (vocals) and Chris Graham (bass guitar). They signed to Neat Records and released their new single, "Hot Lady" (in November 1982) and second LP, *Second Arising* (in January 1983). The new style was compared to New Wave of British Heavy Metal bands Fist and Tygers of Pan Tang,[1][3] as well as older acts such as AC/DC, Quiet Riot, Dokken,[5] and Status Quo,[2] but after some final line-up shuffling, diminishing fan interest led Dedringer to disband in 1985.

2.14.2 Line-up

Last known line-up

- Neil Garfitt (vocals)
- Neil Hudson (guitar)
- Al Scott (rhythm guitar)
- Chris Graham (bass)
- Kenny Jones (drums)

Previous members

- John Hoyle (vocals)
- Lee Flaxington (bass)

Mike Kremastoules

2.14.3 Discography

- "Sunday Drivers" / "We Don't Mind" 7" (Dindisc, 1980)
- "Direct Line" / "She's Not Ready" 7" (Dindisc, 1981)
- *Direct Line* LP (Dindisc, 1981)
- *Maxine* 7" EP (Dindisc, 1981)
- "Hot Lady" 7" (Neat, 1982)
- *Second Arising* LP (Neat, 1983)

2.14.4 See also

- List of New Wave of British Heavy Metal bands

2.14.5 References

[1] Larkin, Colin (1995). *The Guinness Who's Who of Heavy Metal (2nd Edition)*, Guinness Publishing Ltd, ISBN 0-85112-656-1, page 97.

[2] Rivadavia, Eduardo. "Dedringer biography". Allmusic. Retrieved 2012-02-13.

[3] Strong, Martin (2001), *The Great Metal Discography (2nd Edition)*, MOJO Books, ISBN 978-1-84195-185-0, page 150.

[4] Sharpe-Young, Garry. "Dedringer biography". MusicMight. Retrieved 2012-02-13.

[5] Popoff, Martin (1997). *The Collector's Guide to Heavy Metal*, Collector's Guide Publishing, ISBN 1-896522-32-7, page 114.

2.14.6 External links

- Dedringer @ AllMusic
- Dedringer @ MusicMight

2.15 Def Leppard

Def Leppard are an English rock band formed in 1977 in Sheffield as part of the New Wave of British Heavy Metal movement. Since 1992, the band has consisted of Joe Elliott (lead vocals), Rick Savage (bassist, backing vocals), Rick Allen (drums, backing vocals), Phil Collen (guitar, backing vocals), and Vivian Campbell (guitar, backing vocals). This is the band's longest-standing line-up.

The band's strongest commercial success came between the early 1980s and the early 1990s. Their 1981 album *High 'n' Dry* was produced by Robert John "Mutt" Lange, who helped them begin to define their style, and the album's stand out track "Bringin' On the Heartbreak" became one of the first rock videos played on MTV in 1982. The band's next studio album *Pyromania* in January 1983, with "Photograph" as the lead single, turned Def Leppard into a household name. In the U.S, *Pyromania* was certified Diamond (10× Platinum). In 2003, the album ranked number 384 on Rolling Stone's 500 Greatest Albums of All Time.[6]

Def Leppard's fourth album *Hysteria*, released in August 1987, topped the UK and U.S. album charts. As of 2009, it has reached beyond the success of *Pyromania*, having been certified 12× Platinum for sales of over 12 million in the U.S. and has gone on to sell over 25 million copies worldwide.[7] The album spawned seven hit singles, including the U.S. *Billboard* Hot 100 number one "Love Bites", alongside "Pour Some Sugar on Me", "Hysteria", "Armageddon It", "Animal", "Rocket", and "Women". Their next studio album *Adrenalize* (the first following the death of guitarist Steve Clark) reached number one in the UK and U.S. charts in 1992, and contained several hits including, "Let's Get Rocked" and "Have You Ever Needed Someone So Bad". Their 1993 album *Retro Active* contained the acoustic hit song "Two Steps Behind", while their greatest hits album *Vault*, released in 1995, featured the UK hit "When Love & Hate Collide".

As one of the world's best-selling music artists, Def Leppard have sold more than 100 million records worldwide,[8] and have two albums with RIAA Diamond certification, *Pyromania* and *Hysteria*.[9] They are one of only five rock bands with two original studio albums selling over 10 million copies in the U.S.[10] The band were ranked No. 31 in VH1's "100 Greatest Artists of Hard Rock"[11] and ranked No. 70 in "100 Greatest Artists of All Time".[12]

2.15.1 History

Early years (1977–1979)

Rick Savage, Tony Kenning, and Pete Willis, all students at Tapton School in Sheffield, South Yorkshire, formed a band called Atomic Mass in 1977. The band originally consisted of Willis on guitar, Savage on bass (after originally playing guitar), and Kenning on drums. Only 18 at the time, Joe Elliott tried out for the band as a guitarist following a chance meeting with Willis after missing a bus, in November 1977. During his audition it was decided that he was better suited to be the lead singer. Their first ever gig was in the dining hall in A Block in Westfield School in Mosborough, Sheffield.[13]

Soon afterward they adopted a name proposed by Elliott, "Deaf Leopard", which was originally a band name he thought up while writing reviews for imaginary rock bands in his English class (and in at least partial reference to the band Led Zeppelin).[14] At Kenning's suggestion, the

Lead singer Joe Elliott

spelling was slightly modified in order to make the name seem less like that of a punk band. In January 1978, Steve Clark joined the band. According to Joe Elliott, he successfully auditioned for the band by playing Lynyrd Skynyrd's "Free Bird" in its entirety.[15]

In November, just prior to recording sessions for what would be a three-song release known as *The Def Leppard E.P.*, Kenning abruptly left the band; he would later form the band Cairo. He was replaced for those sessions by Frank Noon. By the end of the month, Rick Allen, then only 15 years old, had joined the band as its full-time drummer. Sales of the EP soared after the track "Getcha Rocks Off" was given extensive airtime by renowned BBC Radio DJ John Peel, considered at the time to be a champion of punk rock and new wave music.[16]

Throughout 1979, the band developed a loyal following among British hard rock and heavy metal fans and were considered among the leaders of the New Wave of British Heavy Metal movement. Their growing popularity led to a record deal with the major label Phonogram/Vertigo (Mercury Records in the US). Def Leppard's original management, MSB, a local duo consisting of Pete Martin and Frank Stuart-Brown, were fired after Martin and Joe Elliott got into a fist fight over an incident on the road. The band approached Peter Mensch of Leber-Krebs management, who had booked them on a tour of the UK supporting AC/DC. Mensch, who admitted that he had had his eye on the band, became their manager.[17]

Rise to fame (1980–1983)

Def Leppard's debut album, *On Through the Night*, was released on 14 March 1980. Although the album hit the Top 15 in the UK, many early fans were turned off by the perception that the band was trying too hard to appeal to American audiences by recording songs such as "Hello America" and touring more in the US (supporting Pat Travers, AC/DC, and Ted Nugent). A performance at the Reading Festival in August was marred when audience members expressed their displeasure by pelting the band with beer cans and bottles filled with urine. This incident was partially blamed on a cover story in *Sounds* music newspaper by the journalist Geoff Barton entitled "Has the Leppard changed its spots?" accusing the band of selling out to the American market. In a documentary on the band recorded for BBC 2, Barton recalls feelings of guilt over the story and having a "stand-up row" with the band's manager, Mensch, backstage at the show.[17][18][19] In the documentary series Metal Evolution, Joe Elliott says that the media had exaggerated the event and all bands on the day had experienced the 'abuse' from the crowd.[20]

Co-lead guitarist Phil Collen

The band had by then caught the attention of AC/DC producer Robert John "Mutt" Lange, who agreed to work on their second album, *High 'n' Dry*, released on 11 July 1981. Lange's meticulous approach in the studio helped them begin to define their sound. Despite the album's unimpressive sales figures, the band's video for "Bringin' On the Heartbreak" became one of the first metal videos played on MTV in 1982, bringing the band increased visibility in the U.S.[21] After the album's release, a European tour followed. The band opened for Ozzy Osbourne and Blackfoot.[22]

Phil Collen, former guitarist with the glam band Girl, on 12 July 1982 replaced Pete Willis, who had been fired the previous day because of excessive alcohol consumption on the job. (Willis would later resurface with the bands Gogmagog and Roadhouse.) This personnel change took place during the recording of their third album, *Pyromania*, which was released on 20 January 1983 and also produced by Lange. The cover artwork depicted an animated picture of a huge flame emerging from the top floor of a skyscraper, with a bullseye aimed at the flame. Though many stores would not carry the album due to the cover, the band did not change the artwork. The lead single, "Photograph", turned Def Leppard into a household name, supplanting Michael Jackson's "Beat It" as the most requested video clip on MTV and becoming a staple of rock radio (dominating the US Album Rock Charts for six weeks), and sparked a headline tour across the U.S.[23]

Fueled by "Photograph" and subsequent singles "Rock of Ages" and "Foolin'", *Pyromania* went on to sell six million copies in 1983 (more than 100,000 copies every week in that year) and was held off the top of the US album charts only by Michael Jackson's *Thriller*. With the album's massive success, *Pyromania* was the catalyst for the 1980s pop-metal movement.[24] In 2004, *Pyromania* was certified Diamond having sold over 10 million copies in the US.[25] Def Leppard's US tour in support of *Pyromania* began opening for Billy Squier in March and ended with a headlining performance before an audience of 55,000 at Jack Murphy Stadium in San Diego, California in September. As a testament to the band's popularity at the time, a US Gallup poll in 1984 saw Def Leppard voted as favourite rock band over peers such as The Rolling Stones, AC/DC, and Journey. However, in their native England, Duran Duran secured the number one spot.

Hysteria era (1984–1989)

Main articles: Hysteria (Def Leppard album) and Hysteria World Tour

Following their breakthrough, the band moved to Dublin in February 1984 for tax purposes to begin writing the follow-up to *Pyromania*. Mutt Lange initially joined in on the songwriting sessions but then suddenly declined to return as producer due to exhaustion. Instead, Jim Steinman (of Meat Loaf's *Bat Out of Hell* fame) was brought in.

Bassist Rick Savage

On 31 December 1984, drummer Rick Allen lost his left arm in a car crash on the A57 in the hills outside the band's home city of Sheffield. Allen was driving with his Dutch girl-friend, Miriam Barendsen, when his Corvette swerved off the road on a sharp bend and went through a drystone wall. Despite the severity of the accident, Allen was committed to continuing his role as Def Leppard's drummer, and realised that he could use his legs to do some of the drumming work previously done with his arms.[26] He then worked with Simmons to design a custom electronic drum kit.[27] The other members of the band supported Allen's recovery and never sought a replacement. Allen was placed in a separate studio to practice his new drums. After a few months, Allen gathered the band together and performed the intro to the Led Zeppelin version of "When the Levee Breaks" to showcase his progress to the band. Joe Elliott reports this as being a "very emotional moment." During this period, Mutt Lange returned as producer. Def Leppard brought in Jeff Rich in August 1986 to play alongside Allen during Def Leppard's warm-up mini tour of Ireland, but after Rich accidentally missed a gig, he and the band realised Allen could drum alone. Allen's comeback was sealed at the 1986 Monsters of Rock festival in England, with an emotionally charged ovation after his introduction by Joe Elliott.[28]

After losing his left arm in a car accident, drummer Rick Allen used his legs to do some of the drumming

After over three years of recording, Def Leppard's fourth album, *Hysteria*, was released on 3 August 1987. The first single from the album, "Animal", became the band's first Top 10 hit in the UK, reaching No. 6 on the UK Singles Chart.[29] "Animal" also started their run of ten consecutive U.S. *Billboard* Hot 100 Top 40 singles.[30] *Hysteria* immediately topped the UK Album Charts in its first week of release, and has since spent 105 weeks on the chart.[29] Initial US album sales were relatively slow (compared to *Pyromania*) until the release of the fourth single, "Pour Some Sugar on Me". The song hit Number 2, and *Hysteria* finally reached the top of the U.S. *Billboard* 200 in July 1988.[31] The "Pour Some Sugar on Me" video was No. 1 on Dial MTV for a record 73 days (from 26 May–5 September 1988). Often regarded as the band's signature song, "Pour Some Sugar on Me" was ranked No. 2 on VH1's "100 Greatest Songs of the 80s" in 2006.[32]

The band's UK success saw them nominated for the 1988 Brit Award for Best British Group.[33] In October 1988, the power ballad "Love Bites" reached number one on the *Billboard* Hot 100.[30] In January 1989, the band scored another US Top 5 hit with "Armageddon It", and by spring of 1989 the final single "Rocket" was in the Top 20.[30] Wanting to give fans something new after the massive radio and video airplay for not only the 7 singles but also the Album tracks that Radio DJs were playing off the album, the band performed "Tear It Down", a Hysteria B-side at the 1989 MTV Video Music Awards. Due to positive fan reaction the song was reworked for their following album *Adrenalize*.

Hysteria is one of only a handful of albums that has charted seven singles or more on the US Hot 100: "Women" (#80),

"Animal" (#19), "Hysteria" (#10), "Pour Some Sugar on Me" (#2), "Love Bites" (#1), "Armageddon It" (#3), and "Rocket" (#12).[30] It remained on the charts for three years and has sold over 25 million copies worldwide.[7] Equally successful was the accompanying 16-month tour, in which the band performed in the round. This concept proved wildly popular with fans (as seen in the videos for "Pour Some Sugar on Me" and "Armageddon It") and was used again for the *Adrenalize* tour.

At the 1989 Brit Awards held at the Royal Albert Hall in London, Def Leppard were again a nominee for Best British Group, and the band performed "Pour Some Sugar on Me" at the ceremony.[34][35] At the 1989 American Music Awards, Def Leppard won Favorite Heavy Metal/Hard Rock Artist, as well as Favorite Heavy Metal/Hard Rock Album (for *Hysteria*).[36]

Adrenalize, Clark's death, and change in musical direction (1990–1999)

Former co-lead guitarist Steve Clark died in London in 1991

Following *Hysteria*, the band quickly set out to work on their fifth album, hoping to avoid another lengthy gap. Steve Clark's alcoholism worsened to the point that he was constantly in and out of rehab. Recording sessions suffered from this distraction, and in mid-1990, Clark was granted a six-month leave of absence from the band. Clark died from an accidental mix of prescription drugs and alcohol on 8 January 1991, in his London home.[37]

The remaining band members decided to carry on and recorded the album as a four-piece, with Collen mimicking Clark's style on his intended guitar parts. Def Leppard's fifth album, *Adrenalize*, was finally released on 31 March 1992. The album simultaneously entered at number one on both the UK and US album charts, staying on the latter for 5 weeks.[31][38] The first single, "Let's Get Rocked", was an instant smash hit, and the band performed the song at the 1992 MTV Video Music Awards where it was nominated for Best Video of the Year.[39] In April 1992, Def Leppard appeared at the Freddie Mercury Tribute Concert at Wembley Stadium, London, performing a three-song set of "Animal", "Let's Get Rocked" and Queen's "Now I'm Here" with guitarist Brian May.[40] Joe Elliott later performed "Tie Your Mother Down" with the remaining members of Queen and Guns N' Roses guitarist Slash.[41]

Vivian Campbell replaced Steve Clark in 1992

In a period between late 1991 and early 1992, auditions to replace Clark commenced. Among the guitarists who auditioned included Adrian Smith, John Sykes, and Gary Hoey. Ultimately, the band chose Vivian Campbell in February 1992, formerly of Dio and Whitesnake. Another world tour followed but the band's fortunes began to be affected by the rise of alternative rock, including grunge.

A collection of b-sides and unreleased tracks recorded between 1984 and 1993, called *Retro Active*, was released in October 1993, preceded by the success of "Two Steps Behind" (from the Arnold Schwarzenegger film Last Action Hero). Another single, "Miss You in a Heartbeat", hit the Top 5 in Canada, becoming one of their biggest hits there. Retro Active has sold 3 million copies worldwide to date. Two years later, Def Leppard issued their first greatest hits collection, *Vault: Def Leppard Greatest Hits (1980–1995)*, which reached number 3 in the UK, and sold over 5 million copies in the US.[29][42] Alternate track listings of the album were issued for North America, the UK, and Japan. The compilation included a new track, the power ballad "When Love & Hate Collide", which became their biggest ever hit in the UK, hitting No. 2 on the UK Singles Chart.[43]

On 23 October 1995, the band entered the *Guinness Book of World Records* by performing three concerts on three continents in one day (Tangiers, Morocco; London, England; and Vancouver, Canada).[44]

Slang, released in May 1996, marked a drastic musical departure for the band by featuring darker lyrics and a stripped-down alternative rock edge. The band rehearsed and played the songs together in the studio instead of recording parts separately, resulting in a much more live-sounding album.[45] The US audience reception for *Slang* and its subsequent tour was a major dropoff from a decade earlier, but *Q Magazine* nonetheless listed *Slang* as one of their Top Ten Albums of 1996.[46] This album was the first recorded performance of Rick Allen playing a semi-acoustic drum kit since his accident, and not his electronic set as was first used with *Hysteria*.

VH1 revived the band's fortunes in the US in 1998 by featuring them on one of the first episodes of *Behind the Music*. Reruns of the episode yielded some of the series' highest ratings and brought the band's music back into the public consciousness (following years of burial by the alternative rock climate). The episode was even parodied on *Saturday Night Live*. In an effort to capitalise on this new momentum, Def Leppard returned to its classic sound with the 1999 album *Euphoria*. The first single, "Promises", reunited the band with Mutt Lange and hit the US Mainstream Rock charts at No. 1 for 3 weeks. The album was certified gold in the US and Canada.

2000–2007

On 5 September 2000, Def Leppard were inducted into the Rock Walk of Fame on Hollywood's Sunset Boulevard by their friend Brian May of Queen. In 2001, VH1 produced and aired *Hysteria - The Def Leppard Story*, a biopic that included Anthony Michael Hall as Mutt Lange and Amber Valletta as Lorelei Shellist (Steve Clark's girlfriend). The docudrama covered the band's history between 1977 through 1986, recounting the trials and triumphs of Rick Allen and Steve Clark. The 18 July broadcast still produced some of the channel's highest-ever ratings and is available on DVD.

Def Leppard's tenth album, *X*, saw the band's musical direction moving more towards pop and further away from the band's hard rock roots. *X* quickly disappeared from the charts, ultimately becoming the band's least successful release. However, the accompanying tour played to the band's strongest audiences since *Adrenalize*.

Def Leppard performing in Minot, North Dakota, US, on 26 July 2007

An expanded and updated best-of collection, *Best Of*, was released internationally in October 2004. The North America-only version, *Rock of Ages – The Definitive Collection*, was released the following May. Def Leppard participated at the Live 8 show in Philadelphia and toured in the summer with Bryan Adams. In 2005, the band left their longtime management team, Q-Prime, and signed with HK Management.

On 23 May 2006, Def Leppard released an all-covers album titled *Yeah!*. The disc pays homage to classic rock songs of their childhood, originally recorded by Blondie, The Kinks, Sweet, ELO, and Badfinger among others. It debuted at No. 16 in the US, their tenth consecutive Top 20 album.[31]

The band, along with Queen, Kiss, and Judas Priest, were the inaugural inductees of "VH1 Rock Honors" on 31 May 2006. During the show, The All-American Rejects paid homage to the band with a cover of "Photograph". Soon afterwards, they embarked on a US tour with Journey. That October, *Hysteria* was re-released in a two-disc deluxe edition format, which combined the original remastered album with b-sides, remixes, and bonus tracks from single releases. Def Leppard began their "Downstage Thrust Tour", on 27 June, which took them across the US and into Canada. Support bands were Foreigner and Styx.

Songs from the Sparkle Lounge (2008–2009)

Main articles: Songs from the Sparkle Lounge and Songs from the Sparkle Lounge Tour

On 28 April 2008, Def Leppard released their first album

Def Leppard at the 2008 Sweden Rock Festival

of new studio material in six years, *Songs from the Sparkle Lounge*. The album debuted at No. 5 on the *Billboard* 200 in the US. The first single was entitled "Nine Lives" and featured country singer Tim McGraw, who co-wrote the song with Joe Elliott, Phil Collen, and Rick Savage.

A tour in support of the album began on 27 March 2008 in Greensboro, North Carolina,[47] with Styx and REO Speedwagon joining the band on US dates. The band also played several European rock festivals. An arena tour of the UK took place in June in which the band co-headlined with Whitesnake and was supported by US southern rockers Black Stone Cherry. The band then returned to Europe before coming back for a second leg of the UK tour in June. The first of these dates was at the Glasgow SECC on 17 June. Again they were joined by Whitesnake; however, hard rock band Thunder supported at some of these shows. Black Stone Cherry continued to support most of the dates, including some of the Thunder ones. Six shows which were cancelled during the USA/Canada leg of their world tour due to illnesses affecting Joe Elliott and Phil Collen would be rescheduled and played in August of that year. On 11 June, Def Leppard announced further dates for their 2008 World Tour. The extension saw them visit Japan, Australia and New Zealand. Whitesnake continued to support Def Leppard for their Indian and Japanese dates. Def Leppard toured 41 US cities plus Toronto, Canada, during mid-2009 with Poison and Cheap Trick and also played the Download Festival with Whitesnake and ZZ Top.

In October 2008, Def Leppard played with country star Taylor Swift in a taped show in Nashville, Tennessee, in a show called CMT Crossroads: Taylor Swift and Def Leppard. This was released as a DVD on 16 June 2009 exclusively at Wal-Mart.[48] The release was the best-selling DVD of week, and the 10th best selling Wal-Mart music release.[49] A fan of the band since childhood, Taylor Swift chose Def Leppard to perform together for the show, and their crossover performance of "Photograph" was up for both Performance of the Year and Wide Open Country Video of the Year at the CMT Music Awards in 2009.[48] Taylor Swift said of the performance, "Performing with Def Leppard was awesome! They are the coolest guys on the planet! It was the coolest thing in the world to have my band on stage with them...It was the most amazing feeling in the world..."[50] Joe Elliott from Def Leppard said, "What an absolute pleasure it was to work with Taylor and her band who are a great set of musicians. Myself and Taylor blended really well together, I think, and everybody, both bands and the crowd, had a great time. I'm really glad we had the opportunity to do this."[51]

In October 2009 the band announced that they would be cancelling the last leg of the 2009 North American tour, a total of 23 shows. The band cited, "unforeseen personal matters," as the reason for the cancellations.[52] At the time, the band denied rumours about a breakup, saying, "We're not splitting. Not at all. We often joke, what else would we do? You just can't imagine doing anything else."[52][53]

Recent events and self-titled album (2010–present)

On 22 February 2011 *Mirror Ball – Live & More*, a two-disc live album, with three new studio tracks, was released in parts of Europe on 3 June, the rest of Europe on 6 June, and on 7 June in the US; it was announced at the same time that Def Leppard would perform at the Download Festival on 10 June 2011.[54] Three singles, all studio tracks, were released from the album, the first single being "Undefeated".

Def Leppard embarked on a two-month U.S. tour in the summer of 2011, with Heart.,[55] as well as another seven shows in Australia in October with The Choirboys and Heart,[56] two shows in Japan in November,[57] and six shows in the United Kingdom in December with Steel Panther and Mötley Crüe.[58] The following year, they then toured with Poison and Lita Ford in the US during the summer of 2012 from 20 June through 15 September, dubbed the "Rock Of Ages 2012 Tour".[59][60]

The year after, Def Leppard played an eleven show residency at the Hard Rock Hotel and Casino in Las Vegas, Nevada from 22 March through 13 April 2013. The residency, referred to as Viva! Hysteria, featured a two part show, with the first half featuring Def Leppard opening for themselves, under the alias "Ded Flatbird", (jokingly called the best Def Leppard cover band in the world), when they would then play songs they very rarely play live, going all the way back to "Good Morning Freedom", a b-side from the single "Hello America" released in February 1980, an era usually left untouched by the band. The opening set varied each night, from playing the best hits from albums like *On Through the Night*, *Slang*, and *Euphoria*, to being the entire first half of *High 'n' Dry*. The second half, and "main event" was Def Leppard, as themselves playing their best-selling album, *Hysteria*, from start to finish. A live album, also titled *Viva! Hysteria* was released on 22 October 2013. This was the first time the band has played an album live from start to finish.[61][62]

The band has re-recorded several hits and even the entire album *Hysteria* in an effort to circumvent their record label from future royalties, though of these re-recordings, only "Rock Of Ages", "Pour Some Sugar On Me", and "Hysteria" have actually been released.[63][64][65]

In June 2013, Vivian Campbell announced that he had developed Hodgkin's lymphoma, a malignant form of cancer that affects the Reed-Sternberg cells, located in the lymph nodes.[66] He continued performing with Def Leppard, and no shows were cancelled or rescheduled. The sole idea of cancelling any shows and not doing anything disgusted Vivian, believing performing would be the best way to remain optimistic.[67] In November 2013, he announced he was in remission. However, the cancer has since reemerged, and he is now receiving chemotherapy once again. Should the cancer once again enter remission, he will undergo a stem-cell transplant.

On 11 February 2014, the band released a remastered deluxe edition of their 1996 album *Slang* after much delay. The album, still coveted by many loyal fans of the band, now features 30 tracks including demos, B-sides, and unreleased material.[68] From 23 June 2014 to 31 August 2014, Def Leppard and Kiss toured 42 cities, with a dollar per ticket donated to such military charities as Wounded Warrior Project.[69] Def Leppard contributed one song Helen Wheels to the Paul McCartney tribute album The Art of McCartney released on November 18, 2014. Joe Elliott also contributed another track Hi Hi Hi.

At certain recent points in time, the band had projects, such as a cartoon and a documentary in development. However, these projects seem to be shelved indefinitely. The band had originally planned to do another residency in Las Vegas, this time in honour of *Pyromania* (called *Viva! Pyromania*), but due to the "Heroes 2014" tour with Kiss, and an upcoming, unnamed studio album, the project has been pushed back indefinitely.[70][71] The new album was originally planned to be an EP, but the set-list increased to 15 songs by June 2014.[72] The album is planned to be released in 2015 with a tour to follow.[73]

In December 2014, the band announced a 13-date Canadian tour in April and May 2015.[74] This was followed in February 2015 with the announcement of a 2015 US summer tour with Styx and Tesla from June to October 2015.[75] The tour has been extended to include dates in Japan and Australia throughout November, and a tour of the UK and Ireland with Whitesnake in December. Def Leppard will also return to North America with Styx and Tesla in early 2016.

An eleventh studio album, titled *Def Leppard*, was recorded in 2014 and 2015, and released on 30 October, 2015.[76] The band released the lead single from their self-titled album on September 15, 2015, titled "Let's Go", with a music video for the song being released on October 30.[77] The 14 track album debuted at number 10 on the *Billboard* 200 in the U.S.

2.15.2 Musical style and legacy

Def Leppard's music is a mixture of hard rock, AOR, pop and heavy metal elements, with its multi-layered, harmonic vocals and its melodic guitar riffs. However, even though they were often considered one of the top bands of the New Wave of British Heavy Metal movement of the late 1970s, in the mid-1980s the band were associated with the growing glam metal scene, mainly due to their mainstream success and glossy production. *Pyromania* has been cited as the catalyst for the 1980s pop-metal movement.[24] Def Leppard, however, expressed their dislike of the "glam metal" label, as they thought it did not accurately describe their look or musical style.[78] By the release of the *Hysteria* album, the band had developed a distinctive sound featuring electronic drums and effects-laden guitar sounds overlaid with a multi-layered wall of husky, harmonised vocals. Def Leppard has been cited as an influence by a wide range of musical acts, from heavy metal and thrash metal bands such as Slayer,[79] Pantera,[80] and Metallica[81] as part of the New Wave of British Heavy Metal movement as well as by popular contemporary artists Matt Nathanson[82] and Taylor Swift.[83]

With *Pyromania* and *Hysteria* both certified Diamond by the RIAA, Def Leppard is one of only five rock bands with two original studio albums selling over 10 million copies each in the US.[10] The others are The Beatles, Led Zeppelin, Pink Floyd and Van Halen.[10] Both *Pyromania* and *Hysteria* feature in *Rolling Stone*'s list of the 500 Greatest Albums of All Time.[6][26]

Def Leppard was among the most successful of the New Wave of British Heavy Metal bands in the early 1980s. They combined the raw power of metal with a pop emphasis on melody, catchy hooks and vocal harmonies that, particularly later on, contrasted sharply with harsher contemporary metal and punk bands.[84] Their early albums such as *On Through the Night* (1980) appealed to metal fans and influenced the likes of Dimebag Darrell of Pantera[85] and Jeff Hanneman of Slayer.[86] Their hugely popular later albums, such as *Hysteria* (1987), appeared irregular due to their perfectionism in the studio, but appealed to a broad range of music fans.[84]

2.15.3 Band members

Timeline

Lineups

2.15.4 Side projects

Phil Collen played guitar, uncredited, on Sam Kinison's "Wild Thing" from 1988. The video featured members of Poison, Bon Jovi, Mötley Crüe, Guns N' Roses, Ratt, and Aerosmith. Collen also produced and played on the 1991 album *On The Edge* from Australian band BB Steal.

Joe Elliott sang lead vocals on two tracks on Rolling Stones guitarist Ronnie Wood's 1992 solo album, *Slide on This*. His then-wife Karla appeared in the videos for "Always Wanted More" and "Somebody Else Might". Various members of Def Leppard have played on tribute records for Jeff Beck, AC/DC and Alice Cooper.

A fan of his local football club Sheffield United F.C., Elliott performed on two tracks to the soundtrack of the 1996 Sheffield-set motion picture, *When Saturday Comes* (featuring fellow Sheffield native Sean Bean as a star football player), the title track and an instrumental, "Jimmy's Theme".[90] Elliott sang and co-wrote the opening track, "Don't Look Down" on Mick Ronson's farewell album *Heaven and Hull*. A promotional video was issued for the song as well.

Cybernauts was a side project consisting of Elliott and Collen teamed with members of the Spiders From Mars (David Bowie's former band), minus the late Mick Ronson. The group played several shows, covering Bowie's Ziggy Stardust-era songs and released one internet only album (since deleted).

Vivian Campbell has played with two side bands in recent years, Clock and the Riverdogs, and recorded a solo album, *Two Sides of If*, released in 2005. Campbell toured with Thin Lizzy in early 2011 before joining Def Leppard on their latest tour.

Collen sings lead vocals and plays guitar in a side band called Man Raze with Sex Pistols drummer Paul Cook and former Girl bandmate Simon Laffy. They released their debut album *Surreal* in 2008 and a second album, *PunkFunkRootsRock*, in 2008.

Joe Elliott founded and fronts the band Down 'n' Outz with members of The Quireboys. The band plays covers of Mott the Hoople and related artists such as British Lions and Ian Hunter. They have released two studio albums of covers and one live album since their incarnation in 2009.

Following the death of Ronnie James Dio, Vivian Campbell reunited with the rest of the original Dio lineup with vocalist Andrew Freeman to form Last in Line. The band pays tribute to Dio by playing songs from their original tenure in the band and will also be releasing a studio album of original material in 2016.

Joe Elliott, along with various other musicians including Glenn Hughes, Duff McKagan, Sebastian Bach, Matt Sorum, Gilby Clarke and Steve Stevens formed a supergroup called Kings of Chaos, whose catalogue consists of songs by Deep Purple, Def Leppard, Guns N' Roses and others. In 2012, Kings of Chaos recorded their version of Deep Purple's classic, "Never Before" featuring Elliott singing lead vocals. Kings of Chaos played Stone Fest in Australia along with a few dates in South America in 2013.

Phil Collen formed a blues project by the name of Delta Deep with vocalist Debbi Blackwell Cook which released an eponymous debut in 2015.

2.15.5 Discography

Main article: Def Leppard discography

Studio albums

- *On Through the Night* (1980)
- *High 'n' Dry* (1981)
- *Pyromania* (1983)
- *Hysteria* (1987)
- *Adrenalize* (1992)
- *Slang* (1996)
- *Euphoria* (1999)
- *X* (2002)
- *Yeah!* (2006)
- *Songs from the Sparkle Lounge* (2008)
- *Def Leppard* (2015)

2.15.6 Awards and nominations

Main article: List of Def Leppard awards and nominations

2.15.7 See also

- List of best-selling albums
- List of best-selling music artists
- List of artists who reached number one on the Hot 100 (U.S.)
- List of artists who reached number one on the U.S. Mainstream Rock chart
- List of New Wave of British Heavy Metal bands

2.15.8 References

[1] Pierce, Olga (5 May 2008). "Hair metal grows back on the 'Net". *The Seattle Times*. Retrieved 15 April 2014.

[2] Rhodes, Paul. "Glam Metal 101". About.com. Retrieved 15 April 2014.

[3] Guitar World Staff. "Top 20 Hair Metal Albums of the Eighties". *Guitar World*. Retrieved 15 April 2014.

[4] "Def Leppard Biography". *Rolling Stone*. Simon & Schuster. Retrieved 15 April 2014.

[5] Thomas Erlewine, Stephen. "Def Leppard Biography". AllMusic. Retrieved 15 April 2014.

[6] 500 Greatest Albums of All Time: Pyromania – Def Leppard Rolling Stone. Retrieved 17 November 2011

[7] Kara, Scott (30 October 2008). "One giant Leppard". *The New Zealand Herald*. Retrieved 27 September 2011.

[8] Walker, Graham (10 September 2013). "VIDEO: Viva! Hysteria with Def Leppard's Joe Elliott". Sheffield Star. Retrieved 20 December 2013.

[9] (26 February 2009). Def Leppard Announces US Tour *Newsroom America*. Retrieved 1 March 2010.

[10] Cohen, Jane and Grossweiner, Bob. (9 January 2008). "Def Leppard Continues North American Tour" Ticket News. Retrieved 1 March 2010. "They are one of only five rock bands that can claim two separate, original 10 million-plus selling albums (certified "Diamond") in the U.S. The others are The Beatles, Led Zeppelin, Pink Floyd and Van Halen".

[11] "VH1: 100 Greatest Hard Rock Artists". Rock on the Net. Retrieved 22 July 2011.

[12] "VH1 100 Greatest Artists of All Time". Vh1.com. Retrieved 22 July 2011.

[13] Pete Frame (1999). "Pete Frame's Rockin' Around Britain: Rock'n'roll Landmarks of the UK and Ireland". p. 211. Music Sales Group

[14] According to the book "Bang Your Head: The Rise And Fall of Heavy Metal" by David Konow.

[15] Prato, Greg. Steve Clark Biography Allmusic. Retrieved 17 November 2011

[16] Bronson, Fred (1997). The Billboard book of number one hits. Billboard Books, 1 December 1997

[17] "Watch Videos Online | Rock Of Ages - The Def Leppard Story". Veoh.com. 2 May 2008. Retrieved 17 April 2014.

[18] Peter Buckley (2003) The rough guide to rock

[19] Colin Larkin (1995) *The Guinness encyclopedia of popular music*, Volumes 1–6. p.1118.

[20] Metal Evolution, Season 1 Director Sam Dunn

[21] Daniel Bukszpan, Ronnie James Dio (2003) The Encyclopedia of Heavy Metal

[22] Band Biography, DefLeppard.com. Archived 23 February 2006 at the Wayback Machine

[23] Bob Batchelor, Scott Stoddart The 1980s Greenwood Publishing Group, 2007

[24] Pyromania: Def Leppard Allmusic. Retrieved 17 November 2011

[25] Diamond Awards *RIAA* Retrieved 28 January 2011

[26] "500 Greatest Albums of All Time: Hysteria – Def Leppard". Rolling Stone. Retrieved 17 November 2011

[27] Legends of rock guitar: the essential reference of rock's greatest guitarists Hal Leonard Corporation, 1997

[28] Def Leppard Biography. Billboard. Retrieved 17 November 2011

[29] Neil Warwick, Jon Kutner, Tony Brown (2004) The complete book of the British charts: singles & albums Omnibus Press, 2004

[30] Def Leppard: Song Chart History Billboard. Retrieved 17 November 2011

[31] Def Leppard: Album Chart History Billboard. Retrieved 17 November 2011

[32] "VH1: 100 Greatest Songs of the 80s". Rock on the Net. Retrieved 22 July 2011.

[33] "1988 Brit Awards". *Awards & Winners*. Retrieved 5 August 2015.

[34] Def Leppard – Performance at Royal Albert Hall in 1989 Brits.co.uk. Retrieved 1 February 2012

[35] Best British Group – 1989 Brit Awards Brits.co.uk. Retrieved 1 February 2012

[36] 16th American Music Awards *Rock on the Net* Retrieved 28 January 2011

[37] Stanton, Scott The tombstone tourist: musicians

2.15. DEF LEPPARD

[38] Roberts, David (2006). British Hit Singles & Albums. London: Guinness World Records Limited

[39] 1992 MTV Video Music Awards Rock on the Net. Retrieved 17 November 2011

[40] 1992 The Freddie Mercury Tribute Concert Ultimate Queen. Retrieved 17 November 2011

[41] *The Rough Guide to Rock*. Books.google.com. 28 October 2003. Retrieved 22 July 2011.

[42] Week Ending 12 June 2011. Albums: The Tortoise & The Hare Yahoo. Retrieved 1 February 2012

[43] "UK Top 40 Hit Database". everyHit.com. Retrieved 22 July 2011.

[44] *The Guinness Book of Records, 1997* p.272

[45] Newman, Melinda (6 April 1996). "Def Leppard Shifts Gears With "Slang"". *Billboard- The International Newsweekly of Music, Video and Home Entertainment* (108.14): 12, 18.

[46] "Q lists". Rocklist.net. Retrieved 23 October 2010.

[47] Def Leppard.Com Archived 18 December 2007 at the Wayback Machine

[48] "PRESS RELEASE – CMT CROSSROADS: TAYLOR SWIFT and DEF LEPPARD on DVD 16 June". Defleppard.com. Retrieved 22 July 2011.

[49] "CROSSROADS is Wal-Mart's best-selling DVD this week". Defleppard.com. Retrieved 22 July 2011.

[50] "CMT Crossroads: Def Leppard and Taylor Swift sneak peek". Defleppard.com. Retrieved 22 July 2011.

[51] "CMT Crossroads: Def Leppard and Taylor Swift premieres Nov. 7". Defleppard.com. Retrieved 22 July 2011.

[52] "Def Leppard Cancels Third Leg of Tour" *The Associated Press*. Retrieved 3 February 2010.

[53] Def Leppard dismiss split rumours ahead of Sheffield gig *Sheffield Telegraph*. Retrieved 3 May 2010.

[54] "DEF LEPPARD: Live Album Title Revealed; DOWNLOAD Festival Appearance Announced". Blabbermouth.net. 22 February 2011. Archived from the original on 22 February 2011. Retrieved 23 February 2011.

[55] "DEF LEPPARD To Make 'Major' Announcement Soon". Roadrunnerrecords.com. Retrieved 22 July 2011.

[56] "Def Leppard Australian Tour Dates 2011". Triple M. 7 July 2011. Archived from the original on 25 January 2013. Retrieved 26 January 2013.

[57] "DEF LEPPARD: Japanese Dates Announced". Blabbermouth.net. 27 June 2011. Retrieved 26 January 2013.

[58] "DEF LEPPARD, MÖTLEY CRÜE, STEEL PANTHER To Join Forces For U.K. Tour". Blabbermouth.net. 30 August 2011. Retrieved 26 January 2013.

[59] "Def Leppard & Poison 2012 tour". 10 February 2012. Retrieved 10 February 2012.

[60] "U.S. Tour w/ Poison & Lita Ford – 1st Leg Dates Announced!". 9 March 2012. Retrieved 11 March 2012.

[61] Mansfield, Brian. (12 November 2012) Def Leppard setting off 'Hysteria' with Las Vegas run *USA Today*. Retrieved 12 November 2012.

[62] "Def Leppard to Record Las Vegas 'Hysteria' Shows for Live Album". Ultimateclassicrock.com. 12 March 2013. Retrieved 17 April 2014.

[63] "Def Leppard Release Re-Recorded "Hysteria"". .gibson.com. 21 March 2013. Retrieved 17 April 2014.

[64] "Def Leppard Re-Recording Hit Songs to 'Wrestle Back Career' From Record Label". Ultimateclassicrock.com. 10 January 2013. Retrieved 17 April 2014.

[65] Halperin, Shirley (8 January 2012). "Pour Some Sugar Again: Why Def Leppard is Rerecording Hits". The Hollywood Reporter. Retrieved 17 April 2014.

[66] "Def Leppard guitarist Vivian Campbell reveals all about life with lymphoma in this rocking film!". YouTube. Retrieved 17 April 2014.

[67] "A Message From Vivian". Def Leppard. Retrieved 17 April 2014.

[68] "Def Leppard Revisits Overlooked Album: 'It Went Against the Grain'". Billboard. Retrieved 17 April 2014.

[69] Elavsky, Cindy (22 March 2014). "Celebrity Extra". King Features. Retrieved 5 June 2014.

[70] "Def Leppard Plots 'Pyromania' Residency In Las Vegas; New Studio Album In View". Billboard. Retrieved 27 June 2014.

[71] "Vivian Says Pyromania Residency Will Not Happen In 2014". deflepparduk. Retrieved 27 June 2014.

[72] "Phil Collen Talks Delta Deep Side Project, Progress on New Def Leppard Album". Ultimate Classic Rock. 16 June 2014. Retrieved 15 November 2014.

[73] "Def Leppard plan new album and UK tour". Virgin media, 10 June 2014.

[74] "Def Leppard announce 2015 spring tour of Canada". AXS. 9 December 2014. Retrieved 3 September 2015.

[75] "DEF LEPPARD Set To Tour The U.S. This Summer with STYX & TESLA". *DefLeppard.com*. Retrieved 12 February 2015.

[76] "Q&A with Def Leppard's Joe Elliott". Grand Forks Herald. 27 August 2015. Archived from the original on 28 August 2015. Retrieved 28 August 2015.

[77] http://ultimateclassicrock.com/def-leppard-lets-go/

[78] McDevitt, Cody (5 July 2007). "Def Leppard craves respect in interview". heavymetalmusic.biz. Archived from the original on 9 March 2009. Retrieved 30 April 2014.

[79] http://www.guitarworld.com/tribute-complete-untold-story-slayers-jeff-hanneman

[80] http://www.guitarworld.com/dimebag_darrell_dime%E2%80%99s_dozen?page=0%252C1

[81] http://www.allmusic.com/artist/lars-ulrich-mn0000134416/biography

[82] "Alter Bridge & Matt Nathanson". *That Metal Show*. Season 3. 15 February 2014. VH1.

[83] "Taylor Swift Calls Rocking with Def Leppard 'A Dream'". People. 23 June 2015.

[84] Caulfield, Keith (2013). "Viva' Def Leppard!" **125** (43). p. 57. Retrieved 2 October 2014.

[85] http://www.guitarworld.com/dimebag_darrell_dime%E2%80%99s_dozen?page=0%252C1

[86] http://www.guitarworld.com/tribute-complete-untold-story-slayers-jeff-hanneman

[87] "wild heart management - Sinead Madden". Maggiereilly.de. Retrieved 17 April 2014.

[88] http://loudwire.com/trixter-guitarist-steve

[89] *Def Leppard Tour History* http://www.deflepparduk.com/2013newsnov159.html. Retrieved 3 February 2015. Missing or empty |title= (help)

[90] "When Saturday Comes". *The New York Times*.

2.15.9 External links

- Def Leppard's official website
- 2015 Phil Collen Interview on Guitar.com
- Def Leppard at DMOZ

2.16 Demon (band)

Demon is an English rock/metal group, formed in 1979 by vocalist Dave Hill and guitarist Mal Spooner, both hailing from Leek, Staffordshire. They are considered an important band in the New Wave of British Heavy Metal.

2.16.1 Early years

The original line-up was completed by Les Hunt (Lead guitar), Chris Ellis (bass guitar) and John Wright (drums). The band were signed by Mike Stone's Clay Records in 1980 and licensed to Carrere Records to join their stable of metal bands. Their debut album, *Night of the Demon*, was released in 1981.

After their 1982 follow-up album, *The Unexpected Guest*, the band experimented beyond the NWOBHM sound and moved the band in a more melodic direction whilst still retaining the more traditional heavy metal black magic lyrical style.[1]

In 1983 Demon took a change in direction.[1] *The Plague* marked a swing towards a more progressive sound, adding the keyboards of session musician Andy Richards to the album's sound. Lyrically the band also changed direction, switching to a more overtly political style that was to characterise their albums for the rest of their career.[1] The following album, the Pink Floyd influenced *British Standard Approved* (1984), released on the small independent Clay label, was not a huge commercial success, and with the death of Mal Spooner later that year, it appeared that the band would soon fold. At this point, the band had recruited a permanent keyboard player in Steven Watts.[1]

2.16.2 1985-1992

The following release *Heart of Our Time* (1985) showed that the remaining members of the band were determined to continue, and it was the start of a new songwriting partnership between Hill and Watts. Although the album is regarded as the weakest of the bands releases, it paved the way for the critically acclaimed *Breakout* (1987) and its follow-up *Taking the World by Storm* (1988).[1] The band would go onto release two more albums in the 1990s; 1991's *Hold onto the Dream* and 1992's *Blow Out* before splitting up in 1992 which, according to singer and founding member Dave Hill, was because of fatigue.[2]

2.16.3 Reunion 2001-present

Hill reunited the band with new members in 2001, and released a new album called *Spaced Out Monkey*. The band has since gone onto release a further two albums, *Better the Devil You Know* (2005) and their latest release *Unbroken*, which was released on 13 September 2012.[3] Both of the bands post reunion releases have received positive reviews from the press leading the band to go on and play many festivals across Europe Including Bang Your Head festival and Sweden Rock the band also toured with Magnum singer Bob Catley in 2005.[4]

The band released their twelfth studio album, *Unbroken*, in September 2012 and are planning a number of festival appearances in 2013 in support of it. The band are due to play at Sweden Rock Festival in June and Headbangers Open Air festival in July.[5]

2.16.4 Members

Current

- Dave Hill - Lead Vocals (1979-1992, 2001-present)
- Ray Walmsley - Bass (2012-present), Guitars (1997-2011)
- Karl Waye - Keyboards (2001, 2012-present)
- Neil Ogden - Drums, Percussion (2002-present)
- David Cotterill - Guitars (2007-present)
- Paul Hume - Guitars (2012-present)

Past

- Paul Riley - Bass (1979-1980)
- John Wright - Drums, Percussion (1979-1987)
- Clive Cook - Guitar (1979-1980)
- Mal Spooner - Guitar (1979-1984) †
- Les Hunt - Bass (1981) Guitar (1981-1983)
- Chris Ellis - Bass (1982-1983)
- Gavin Sutherland - Bass (1984-1985)
- Steve Watts - Keyboards (1984-1991)
- John Waterhouse - Guitar (1985-1992)
- Andy Dale - Bass 1987-1988, 1997-2011)
- Nick Bushell - Bass (1988-1991)
- Scott Crawford - Drums (1988-1991)
- Steve Brookes - Guitar (1988-1992, 1997-2001)
- Mike Thomas - Bass (1992)
- Paul Rosscrow - Drums, Percussion (1992)
- John Cotterill - Drums, Percussion (2001)
- Duncan Hansell - Keyboards (2001}
- Karl Finney - Guitar (2003-2005)
- Tim Read - Guitar (2005-2007)
- Paul Farrington - Keyboards (2002-2012)
- Paul Johnson - Bass (2011-2012)

2.16.5 Discography

Studio albums / EPs

- *Night of the Demon* (1981)
- *The Unexpected Guest* (1982) - UK Number 47
- *The Plague* (1983) - UK Number 73
- *Wonderland* (EP) (1984)
- *British Standard Approved* (1985)
- *Heart of Our Time* (1985)
- *Demon* (EP) (1986)
- *Breakout* (1987)
- *Taking the World by Storm* (1989)
- *Hold on to the Dream* (1991)
- *Blow-out* (1992)
- *Spaced out Monkey* (2001)
- *Better the Devil You Know* (2005)[6]
- *Unbroken* (2012)

Live albums / compilations

- *One Helluva Night* (live) (1990)
- *Anthology* (compilation) (1991)
- *The Best of Demon: Volume One* (compilation) (1999)
- *Time Has Come - The Best of Demon* (compilation) (2006)

DVDs

Hill/Stone Productions

- *The Unexpected Guest Tour - Live at Tiffany's 1982* (2009)
- *Up Close and Personal - Live in Germany at The Keep It True Festival warm up show 2006* (2009)

2.16.6 See also

- List of New Wave of British Heavy Metal bands

2.16.7 References

[1] Potts, Mark L. (2006-11-10). "Official DEMON biography 2001". Demon Official Website. Retrieved 2010-11-10.

[2] Ekdahl, Anders. "Demon_2001_Interview". Battlehelm. Retrieved 10 November 2012.

[3] "Demon_2012_Unbroken". Encyclopedia_Metallium. Retrieved 10 November 2012.

[4] Ritchie, Jason. "Demon_2005_Interview". Get_Ready_To_Rock. Retrieved 10 November 2012.

[5] "Demon_2013". *Site_Of_The_Demon*. Retrieved 10 November 2012.

[6] Roberts, David (2006). *British Hit Singles & Albums* (19th ed.). London: Guinness World Records Limited. p. 150. ISBN 1-904994-10-5.

2.16.8 External links

- Official website
- Demon discography at Discogs

2.17 Diamond Head (band)

Diamond Head are an English heavy metal band formed in 1976 in Stourbridge, England. The band is recognised as one of the leading members of the New Wave of British Heavy Metal and is acknowledged by thrash metal bands such as Metallica and Megadeth as an important early influence.[1]

2.17.1 Band history

Early history

Formed by school friends in 1976 Brian Tatler and Duncan Scott[2] with Tatler playing on a cheap fuzzy guitar and Scott on biscuit tins. The name "Diamond Head" came from a 1975 Phil Manzanera album that Tatler had a poster of in his room. Sean Harris later joined the band after they learned about his vocal abilities while on a school trip,[3] singing Gene Vincent's 1956 hit "Be-Bop-A-Lula", and auditioned him in Tatler's bedroom. The band played their first gig at High Park school hall (10th Feb 1977) and sold 151 tickets for a forty-minute set of their own original material which went down a storm. A very confident show but these songs were gradually replaced by better material as the band's writing skills developed. Bassist Colin Kimberley, a friend of Tatler's from primary school, joined the band in 1978 (and was in fact Diamond Head's fourth bassist).

In their early days, the band played very few cover songs and concentrated on their own material. Exceptions were Black Sabbath's "Paranoid", "Its All For The Love of Rock and Roll" by the Tuff Darts, "Motorhead" by Motörhead and Space Station #5 by Montrose. In one interview, Brian Tatler stated that they wrote some 100 songs before their first studio recorded release, and only one song (*It's Electric*) from their 1978 debut gig with Colin made it onto vinyl.

The band recorded self-financed demo tapes in 1979. Recorded within six hours on a four-track, their unique sound and quality of writing gained enough attention for the band to tour as support to AC/DC and Iron Maiden.[4] Although several record companies expressed interests in signing the band, no contracts were forthcoming. The band was at the time managed by Reg Fellows and Sean Harris' mother (Linda Harris),who reportedly turned down an offer from the influential Leiber/Krebs Management,.[5] Thus while other 'New Wave of British Heavy Metal' bands were signed to major labels and headlining their own tours Diamond Head remained independent. The management decided that they would release their material through a label owned by Muff Murfin called 'Happy Face Records'. Muff also owned a studio where Diamond Head did many of their early recordings.

The first release was the 1979 single "Shoot Out The Lights" (B-side *Helpless*), second single "Sweet and Innocent" (B-side "Streets of Gold") was released by Media Records in 1980.

In the same year the band also recorded their debut album on Happy Face. Most commonly known as *Lightning to the Nations*, (although it was officially untitled), the collection was recorded in seven days at The Old Smythy Studio in Worcester, a venue which the band described later as 'dead'.[6] The album was packaged in a plain sleeve with no title or track listings, simply bearing a signature of one of the band members. The management thought that it should be perceived as a 'demo' album so no fancy sleeve was required, making it very cheap to produce. the first 1000 copies were pressed and made available at concerts or via mail-order for £3.50. The only mail-order advertisement appeared in *Sounds* and ran for six weeks. The band did not pay for the advertisement and ended up being sued. The idea for recording this album came from Fellows and Linda Harris as an attempt to record tracks to entice attention from a record company, which would take care of the recording costs.[7]

This album has become one of the most sought after items among record collectors. Another 1000 copies were pressed along with the track listings once the first 1000 copies had sold out. Unfortunately, the original stereo master tapes were lost after they were sent to the German record company, Woolfe Records, and never returned. However, Woolfe Records released a vinyl version of the album with a new sleeve. The tapes were eventually tracked down around 1989.

Living on...Borrowed Time

The buzz surrounding the band's live shows eventually led to a record deal with MCA Records in 1982, and rush released the *Four Cuts EP*, which contained two early era songs *Shoot Out The Lights* and *Dead Reckoning*. Their new status afforded them a slot on the Reading festival bill in 1982, albeit as late and unadvertised replacements for Manowar. Their stunning set was recorded by the BBC and later released in 1992 through Raw Fruit Records as the *Friday Rock Show Sessions*.

The first MCA album, *Borrowed Time* featured a lavish Rodney Matthews-illustrated gatefold sleeve based on the album's Elric theme and was the most expensive sleeve commissioned by MCA at the time. The investment paid off as it was enthusiastically received and climbed to No. 24 in the UK album charts, enabling the band to perform a full scale UK tour at large venues such as London's Hammersmith Odeon.

To support the album Diamond Head's sixth single "In the Heat of the Night", backed with live versions of *Play it Loud* and *Sweet and Innocent* recorded at the Zig-Zag club, and an interview with DJ Tommy Vance (although the latter was not available on the 12").

Diamond Head tried a more experimental sounding followup to *Borrowed Time*, tentatively titled *Making Music* which later became *Canterbury* in 1983. The success of this album was stalled as the first 20,000 copies suffered vinyl pressing problems, causing the LP to jump.

Many fans disliked the progressive direction, expecting a reprise of *Borrowed Time*. During the recording of the album a split in the band occurred with Scott being fired and Kimberley quiting once all his bass parts had been recorded. Tatler explained that Kimberly found the band too much hard work and Scott did not seem to be improving quickly enough.[8] Mervyn Goldsworthy, formerly of Samson, and Robbie France, later a founding member of Skunk Anansie, came in on bass and drums respectively. Also introduced to the band was keyboard player Josh Phillips-Gorse. Live footage of this line up's live show at the University of Leicester on 12 February 1984 was officially released on VHS via the Diamond Head fan club.

Diamond Head opened the 1983 Monsters of Rock festival at Donington, and supported Black Sabbath on their 'Born Again' European tour. After getting dropped by MCA in January 1984 Diamond Head started work on their fourth studio album, entitled *Flight East*. Although never released, five tracks (*Be Good, A New Messiah, Someone Waiting, Today* and *Back In The Powerage*) emerged on bootleg and shows the band totally changing direction with the dropping of all the characteristic signature guitar solos and heavy dynamic riffs. The change in the band's musical direction was with the duo becoming bored of just playing Heavy Metal and felt that it was time to change. Another change the band made at the time was Brian switching from his Flying V to a Gibson Les Paul, saying that "I think the Les Paul's better, the V's more of a metal guitar. At one stage it was just me and Schenker with them, now the guy in Saxon's got one and all the European metal bands like Accept have them."[8] Harris' lyrics had also taken a religious route, as with one of the new songs *A New Messiah*. After little interest from any record label to pick up the project (and with no money coming in) Tatler and Harris decided to take a break from one another in 1985.

Reunion and National Bowl show

Metallica's increasing status and the often mentioned influence of Diamond Head on their sound kept the band's name relatively prominent and helped back-catalogue sales. Inevitably in 1990 Tatler and Harris began writing songs for a new album and in 1991 Diamond Head went back on the road with Karl Wilcox on drums and Eddie Moohan on bass.

The band also released a new 12" only single which contained *Wild on the Streets* and *I Can't Help Myself*, and was only available at concerts and specialised music stores. Sean Harris also wrote the lyrics to a song with Dave Mustaine for Megadeth called "Crown Of Worms" and both released as a B-side to Megadeth's 1994 single *Train of Consequences* and on the re-mastered version of *Countdown to Extinction*.

In 1993 the band released *Death and Progress* featuring guest contributions by Tony Iommi of Black Sabbath and Dave Mustaine. The band's reunion was short lived as they were on the verge of splitting up as soon as the record was released.

In November 1992 Diamond Head guested on stage with Metallica at Birmingham's NEC to jointly perform the Diamond Head classics *Helpless* and *Am I Evil?*. Footage of this show was released via the Metallica fan club on a video entitled *Metallican*.

Diamond Head opened for Metallica and Megadeth at the National Bowl in Milton Keynes on 5 June 1993. Sean Harris came out dressed as the Grim Reaper which Brian Tatler remarked (in the British rock magazine *Classic Rock*) was Harris' way of saying that the NWOBHM was over. Their performance was subdued, reportedly due to Tatler suffering from shingles at the time and the lack of rehearsal time prior to the gig.

In 1994 the band split again and did not reform until 2000.

2000s

In 2000 Harris and Tatler reformed with guitarist Floyd Brennan and performed a series of short acoustic gigs, including a support slot with Budgie, which ended in the release of the *First Cuts Acoustic EP*.

The band started touring again doing full electric shows with Moohan and Wilcox back in the band. This tour also saw Diamond Head play their first US show. The band went back into the studio to record a new album entitled *Host*, however the band ended in disagreement and turmoil as Harris wished the album to be put out under a new name as a fresh start.

After years of Tatler and the band tolerating Harris' creative desires Diamond Head and Sean Harris finally went their separate ways. Although Harris issued a press release on Blabbermouth.net[9] that said that as far as he was concerned he had as much right over the Diamond Head name as anyone else, and that as far he was concerned he was still in the band.

Nick Tart era

The rest of the band, determined to continue, soon announced his replacement as Nick Tart. Tart had previously worked with many midlands based bands. Robin George recruited Nick after seeing him perform live at JBs in Dudley with Alabama Bombshell, a new project was underway to re-record some of Robin's songs that artists such as, Glenn Hughes, Ruby Turner, Robert Plant and coincidentally Sean Harris had previously recorded. Between 1992 –1996 they toured the UK, performed a live TV appearance on The James Whale show and Radio 1 sessions with Tommy Vance under the name Life before releasing an album entitled Cocoon. Nick quit the music business in 1997 but joined a new band in 2003. After a few weeks Diamond Head drummer Karl Wilcox happened to drop in on a rehearsal (as he was a friend of their drummer) and after hearing Nick sing, Karl immediately got on the phone to Brian saying he had heard a great singer and passed on his phone number. After introductions Tart agreed to join.

The band's next album, *All Will Be Revealed* (the title apparently referring to Sean Harris), was released in 2005 and was very different from their early material. To pro-

Nick Tart & Brian Tatler at The Astoria, London, 2005

mote this album they toured with Megadeth. Brian Tatler commented that this was one of the best experiences of his life and regained his enjoyment playing live with the band again.[10]

Diamond Head headlined a celebration of the 25th anniversary of the NWOBHM at the London Astoria, supported by Witchfynde, Bronz, Praying Mantis and Jaguar. This concert was later released as a live CD entitled It's Electric and also the band's first DVD, To the Devil His Due in 2006. The band's rhythm guitarist Adrian Mills left the band and was replaced with Andy 'Abbz' Abberley,[11] previously in traditional heavy metal band Requiem with drummer Karl Wilcox.

The band released their sixth studio album, What's in Your Head?, through Cargo records with Dave 'Shirt' Nicholls, who has produced albums with bands such as Slipknot and The Wildhearts. The Japanese version included extra track *This is War*. The band have toured extensively over the last few years through the UK, Europe and Japan. In 2007 Diamond Head were special guests to Thin Lizzy in the UK.

In November 2009 Brian Tatler published his autobiography 'Am I Evil?' with forewords by Lars Ulrich and Dave Mustaine. A hardback book that documents the story of Diamond Head, featuring many rare and unseen photographs. All 500 copies have now sold out.

In 2010 Diamond Head were special guests to Europe on their nine date UK tour. They celebrated the 30th Anniversary of their first album 'Lightning To The Nations 'with a European tour beginning 7 November 2010, with all seven songs performed back to back for the first time at selected venues. Diamond Head were invited to open for the 'Big 4' at 2011's Sonisphere Festival at Knebworth, England on 8 July and Sonisphere France on 9 July. They also performed for the first time at the Heavy T.O. festival in Toronto on 23 July and Heavy MTL festival, Montreal, Canada, 24 July 2011. On 15 August 2011 Diamond Head embarked on their first ever U.S. tour, kicking off at El Corazon in Seattle and finishing up on 1 September at BB King's in New York City, 17 shows in all.

2012 saw a twelve date European tour in June and July including Bang Your Head festival in Germany. In 2013 Diamond Head completed a 17 date East coast US tour beginning 10 April, also a five date UK tour co-headlining with Uli Jon Roth. A West coast US tour is being planned for October 2013.

Due to the untimely death of his father Nick will be flying home to Brisbane to be with his family and unfortunately has had to withdraw from Diamond Head's upcoming US tour in October. In order to maintain their commitment to their fans and the tour, Diamond Head have called upon vocalist Chas West (The Jason Bonham Band, Lynch Mob, 3 Legged Dogg & Tribe Of Gypsies) who has been a long time friend of the band to help out for this tour. Diamond Head are delighted to have Chas be part of this upcoming tour which kicks off in Vancouver Canada 8 October 2013.

In 2014, due to the practical difficulties of touring and writing with Nick Tart being located in Brisbane, Australia, Danish born Rasmus Bom Andersen, from London, became Diamond Head's third singer. A successful tour of Europe and Britain followed in the Summer and Autumn of 2014.

2.17.2 Influences

Diamond Head have cited their early inspirations as classic British rock bands such as Free, Deep Purple, Led Zeppelin, UFO, Black Sabbath and Judas Priest.[12] Brian Tatler relating that some of the first albums he bought were Led Zeppelin's second album and Deep Purple's *Machine Head*, and said that although a lot of his guitar work was inspired by Ritchie Blackmore and Michael Schenker it was punk rock that showed him that anyone could form a band. Colin Kimberley commented Diamond Head got their complex sound from listening to bands like Black Sabbath and Rush and realising that a song with a single riff throughout was not interesting enough.[13]

In a recent interview Tatler stated that he now tries not to be influenced by modern bands and keep his sound, although he imagines that "little bits creep into the writing process."[14]

2.17.3 Lack of success

Many reasons have been cited why Diamond Head never achieved their full potential. That they changed musical direction with *Canterbury* and that they did not attain a record deal soon enough are two main reasons. Once they did sign to a major label, MCA proved to be the wrong label, forcing the band to sound more commercial.[15] Also, while bands like Iron Maiden and Def Leppard were managed by established music management, Diamond Head were managed by Reg Fellows, a cardboard factory owner from the Midlands and Harris' mother.

There are also many other smaller contributions to the decline of Diamond Head. One of these being that the band seemed to shy away from playing shows in London, where the main hub of activity was. Diamond Head did not play their first headline gig in the capital until April 1980 at the Marquee.[16] It also did not help that the band did not stick to a style and give it chance to succeed before trying something new.

Then later they had problems with a viable comeback, with problems associated with the National Bowl gig with Metallica and the lack of desire from Sean Harris to carry on performing heavy metal.

2.17.4 Influence on Metallica

Diamond Head are probably most famous among heavy metal fans for their influence on Metallica. Metallica openly acknowledge them as an important early influence and have covered Diamond Head songs at gigs such as "Sucking My Love", "Am I Evil" and "The Prince" . The earliest known recordings of these songs are a rehearsal demo recorded at then-bassist Ron McGovney's house in March 1982. The *Metal Up Your Ass* live demo, recorded in November of that year, featured a live rendition of "Am I Evil." "The Prince" was also played, but the tape ran out too soon to catch it. The song would see another demo release as part of the *Horsemen Of The Apocalypse* demo in 1983. "Sucking My Love" exists on various bootlegs that have been circulating since 1982 along with a recording on the early demo *No Life*

Til Leather.

The first official release of "Am I Evil" came in 1984 as part of the *Creeping Death* EP, paired with another NWOBHM classic "Blitzkrieg", by the band of the same name. The two songs were also included in the first pressing of the *Kill 'Em All* LP when it was re-released by Elektra Records.

"Helpless" would see a release with *The $5.98 EP: Garage Days Re-Revisited* in 1987 and "The Prince" was included as a B-side to the "One" single.

During the Wherever We May Roam Tour Metallica played "Am I Evil?" and "Helpless" with the original band members on 5 November 1992 at NEC Arena in Birmingham.[17]

The official recordings of "Helpless", "Am I Evil", and "The Prince" would also be featured on Metallica's 2-CD *Garage Inc.* compilation, a collection of numerous cover songs that the band had played over the years. The first CD in the set was newly recorded covers, one of which was Diamond Head's "It's Electric".

Metallica performed "Am I Evil" along with the other bands in the Big 4 (*Megadeth*, *Anthrax* and *Slayer*) at the 2011 Sonisphere festival, and with Diamond Head themselves at the Sonisphere festival in Knebworth on 8 July 2011. Lars Ulrich said that there was "a pretty good chance that none of us would be here" without Brian Tatler before playing the song. Brian performed "Helpless" with Metallica and Anthrax at the Sonisphere festival in *Amnéville* on 9 July 2011.[18]

On 5 December 2011 Brian Tatler and Sean Harris joined Metallica onstage at the legendary Fillmore Auditorium in San Francisco to celebrate Metallica's 30th Anniversary. Together they played "The Prince", "It's Electric", "Helpless" and "Am I Evil?". Brian and Sean also took part in a group encore of Seek and Destroy.

2.17.5 Band members

Current members

- Brian Tatler – lead guitar, rhythm guitar, backing vocals (1976–1985, 1991–1994, 2000–present)
- Eddie Moohan – bass (1991–1992, 2000–present)
- Karl Wilcox – drums (1991–1994, 2002–present)
- Andy "Abbz" Abberley – rhythm guitar (2006–present)
- Rasmus Bom Anderson – lead vocals (2014 – present)

Former members

- Duncan Scott – drums (1976–1983)
- Sean Harris – lead vocals (1976–1985, 1990–1994, 2000–2004)
- Colin Kimberley – bass, backing vocals (1978–1983)
- Mervyn Goldsworthy – bass (1983-1985)
- Robbie France – drums (1983–1985; died 2012)
- Josh Phillips – keyboard (1983–1984)
- Dave Williamson – bass (1976-1977)
- Pete Vuckovic – bass (1992–1994)
- Floyd Brennan – rhythm guitar (2000–2002)
- Adrian Mills – rhythm guitar (2003–2006)
- Nick Tart – lead vocals (2004–2014)

Timeline

2.17.6 Discography

Studio albums

- *Lightning to the Nations* (1980)
- *Borrowed Time* (1982)
- *Canterbury* (1983)
- *Death and Progress* (1993)
- *All Will Be Revealed* (2005)
- *What's in Your Head?* (2007)

Live albums

- *The Friday Rock Show Sessions / Live at Reading* (1992)
- *Evil Live* (1994)
- *It's Electric* (2006)
- *Live at the BBC* (2010)

Singles and EPs

- *Shoot out the Lights* (1980)
- *Sweet and Innocent* (1980)
- *Diamond Lights EP* (1981)
- *Call Me* (1982)
- *In The Heat Of The Night* (1982)
- *Four Cuts EP* (1982)
- *Makin' Music* (1983)
- *Out Of Phase* (1983)
- *Sucking My Love* (1983)
- *Wild On The Streets/I Can't Help Myself* (1991)
- *Acoustic: First Cuts EP* (2002)

Compilations

- *Behold the Beginning* (1986)
- *Am I Evil* (1987)
- *Sweet and Innocent* (1988)
- *Singles* (1992)
- *Helpless* (1996)
- *To Heaven from Hell* (1997)
- *The Best of Diamond Head* (1999)
- *Diamond Nights* (2000)
- *The Diamond Head Anthology: Am I Evil?* (2004)
- *The MCA Years* (2009)
- *Am I Evil?: The Best Of* (2013)

DVDs

- *To the Devil His Due* (21 November 2006)

2.17.7 See also

- List of New Wave of British Heavy Metal bands

2.17.8 References

[1] "Diamond Head Press Pack". Diamond-head.net. Retrieved 2014-07-28.

[2] Eduardo Rivadavia (2002-04-05). "Diamond Head | Biography". AllMusic. Retrieved 2014-07-28.

[3] "A Beginner's Guide To Diamond Head". Diamond-head.net. Retrieved 2014-07-28.

[4] "Supporting ACDC". Diamond-head.net. Retrieved 2014-07-28.

[5] "Am I Evil?". Diamond-head.net. Retrieved 2014-07-28.

[6] Kollektor's Klassik 3, pp16

[7] "News Article". Diamond-head.net. Retrieved 2014-07-28.

[8] 1983 interview with Steve Hammonds

[9] "Ex Diamond Head Singer Says He Was 'Shocked' By Announcement He Was Fired From Band - Blabbermouth.net". Roadrunnerrecords.com. 2004-08-27. Retrieved 2014-07-28.

[10] "Metal Invader - Diamond Head Interview". Diamond-head.net. 2005-10-19. Retrieved 2014-07-28.

[11] "Andy Abberley Interview". *Guitarhoo!*. Guitarhoo.com. 23 December 2013. Retrieved 21 February 2014.

[12] Tate Bengtson. "Interview". Diamond-head.net. Retrieved 2014-07-28.

[13] "News Article". Diamond-head.net. Retrieved 2014-07-28.

[14] "getreadytoroll.com". getreadytoroll.com. Retrieved 2014-07-28.

[15] *Survivors*, Classic Rock Vol.124, pg57

[16] "Diamond Head Tour Dates". Diamond-head.net. Retrieved 2014-07-28.

[17] "Metallica - Am I Evil / Helpless with Diamond Head - Birmingham 1992". YouTube. Retrieved 2014-07-28.

[18] "Diamond Head Homepage". Diamond-head.net. Retrieved 2014-07-28.

2.17.9 External links

- Official website

Dumpy at Coventry's General Wolfe 1985

2.18 Dumpy's Rusty Nuts

Dumpy's Rusty Nuts are a British rock band founded in 1981[1] by the lead singer Graham "Dumpy" Dunnell. Though unsuccessful as recording artists the band have been a successful and popular live act for decades. The band attracted a cult following for their live performances in small rock venues. Playing classic blues rock, their initial audiences were drawn from the New Wave Of British Heavy Metal[2] and 'Bikers' and they became particularly well-known at the London Marquee Club, where they were a regular and popular attraction. In the early to mid-1980s the band toured extensively around the UK playing at small rock/'Biker' pub and club venues including the Isle of Man TT, and music festivals, cementing their name and following.

The band were not successful recording artists, preferring to concentrate on live work. They released a debut single "Just For Kicks" in June 1982 but in order to get airplay the band had to change their name to "Dumpy's Rusty Bolts".[3] Sales of the single were poor, and the original band name was restored. A second single, "Box Hill Or Bust", was released. Subsequent sporadic releases have only found favour with their small core audience.

They released a double live album, *Somewhere In England*, in 1984, which was recorded at the Marquee Club.

Despite the group's longevity, they became for a time a favourite target for mockery from the British music press, especially *Melody Maker*,[4] where they were regularly portrayed as claiming to be jumping on the latest improbable bandwagon in the humorous section "Talk Talk Talk" written by David Stubbs.

As of 2010, the band is still performing in small venues, music festivals and bike rallies across Europe. The band has toured with and supported many bands including Hawkwind, Motörhead and Status Quo.

2.18.1 See also

- List of New Wave of British Heavy Metal bands

2.18.2 References

[1] "Top biker band at the Palladium". *North Devon Journal*. 16 March 2009. Retrieved 17 June 2014.

[2] New Wave of British Heavy Metal website

[3] Huey, Steve. "Dumpy's Rusty Nuts - Biography". Allmusic. Retrieved 17 June 2014.

[4] Carroll, Jim (21 April 2008). "The Monday morning randomiser". *The Irish Times*. Retrieved 17 June 2014.

2.18.3 External links

- Official website

2.19 E. F. Band

E.F. Band was a Swedish band that sometimes were mixed up with the New Wave Of British Heavy Metal movement, even though they were Swedish. The band formed in 1979 by Pär Ericsson and Bengt Fischer, two former members of the progressive rock band Epizootic. The "E.F." portion of the band's name was derived from the first letter of Ericsson and Fischer's last names. The band hired drummer Dave Dufort, who had played with Mike Oldfield and Screaming Lord Sutch and thus completed the trio. Dufort left the band before the release of their first full-length album and was replaced by drummer Dag Eliason, thereby making the band an entirely-Swedish trio. John Rich joined as lead vocalist in 1982 and featured on the second album

Deep Cut. London-based Roger Marsden (ex Deep Machine, Angel Witch) replaced Rich in 1983 and sang on the band's third album *One Night Stand*. E.F. Band broke up in 1986.

2.19.1 Discography

Singles

- Night Angel 7" (contains "Night Angel" and "Another Day Gone") (1979)
- Self Made Suicide 7" (contains "Self Made Suicide" and "Sister Syne") (1979)
- Devils Eye 7" (contains "Devils Eye" and "Comprende") (1980)

Albums

- *Metal for Muthas, Vol. 1* ("Fighting for Rock and Roll") (1980)
- *Last Laugh Is on You* (1981)
- *Deep Cut* (1982)
- *One Night Stand* (1985)

2.19.2 See also

- List of New Wave of British Heavy Metal bands

2.19.3 External links

- Official E.F. Band website

2.20 Elixir (band)

Elixir is a British heavy metal band, formed by Steve Bentley, Kevin Dobbs, Nigel Dobbs and Phil Denton in November 1983. They are notable for being associated with the New Wave of British Heavy Metal movement.

2.20.1 History

1983-1990

The band spent the first time after having formed writing material and rehearsing. After brief stints as "Purgatory" and "Hellfire" the members finally decided on naming the band "Elixir". According to the biography on the band's website the name was chosen through Steve Bentley closing his eyes and putting his finger on a word in a dictionary at random.[1] In need of a vocalist Elixir recruited singer Sally Pike, but after recording a four song demo tape and playing two gigs together, she left the band by the end of the year. In 1984 Pike was replaced by Paul Taylor, and later the same year guitarist Norman Gordon joined the band to fill the vacant spot left by Steve Bentley, who departured after Elixir had completed their second demo tape.

In 1985, Elixir released their debut single "Treachery (Ride like the Wind)" / "Winds of Time". This single was reviewed by Ronnie James Dio in *Kerrang!* (No 99), and was given the thumbs up.

In 1986, the band recorded their first album *The Son of Odin*. In issue 137 (November 2005) of Terrorizer magazine, the album was included in the top 20 power metal albums of all time, alongside Judas Priest's *Painkiller*, Helloween's *Keeper of the Seven Keys Part II* and Cirith Ungol's *King of the Dead*.

Elixir recorded their second album, initially called *Sovereign Remedy* in 1988 with Mark White on the bass and former Iron Maiden drummer Clive Burr. Stevie Hughes replaced Burr for the band's live commitments through 1989. At the end of the year, Phil Denton quit the band and was replaced by Leon Lawson for several live shows before the band came off the road. Their second album was released by the Sonic label as *Lethal Potion* in 1990. In 2004, the album was re-released as *Sovereign Remedy* on the TPL label, as it was originally intended, with all the tracks, the original mix and new artwork.[2]

2001-2012

In 2001 the band reverted to the Paul Taylor, Phil Denton, Norman Gordon, Kevin Dobbs and Nigel Dobbs line up and in 2003 recorded their third album *The Idol*, which was made up of material the band had written in the 1980s. With rising popularity, the band toured around various countries such as Greece, Germany and the USA.

Elixir recorded their fourth album *Mindcreeper* in 2006, which was released by Majestic Rock.[3]

Elixir released their latest album *All Hallows Eve* on 31 October 2010 on their own CTR label.[4]

Between 2006 and 2012, Elixir organised six editions of the "British Steel Festival", appearing on the bill at each event. From 2008 onwards, the festival was held at the Camden Underworld.[5]

Elixir disbanded in 2012, with members Paul Taylor and Phil Denton going on to form the metal/rock band Midnight

Messiah.

Clive Burr died a year later, due to complications related to MS.

2.20.2 Discography

Studio albums

- *The Son of Odin* (1986)
- *Lethal Potion* (1990)
- *The Idol* (2003)
- *Mindcreeper* (2006)
- *All Hallows Eve* (2010)

Live albums

- *Elixir Live* (2006)

Singles

- *Treachery* (1985)
- *Knocking on the Gates of Hell* (2006)

Alternative versions

- *Sovereign Remedy* (2004)

2.20.3 See also

- List of New Wave of British Heavy Metal bands

2.20.4 References

[1] "ELIXIR - THE HISTORY". cold town music. Retrieved 8 March 2007.

[2] "ELIXIR". Truemetalfan.org. Retrieved 2015-09-06.

[3] "Cult British Metallers Elixir Sign With Majestic Rock Records - Blabbermouth.net". Roadrunnerrecords.com. 2006-03-26. Retrieved 2015-09-06.

[4] "Elixir: 'All Hallows Eve' Album Out Now - Blabbermouth.net". Roadrunnerrecords.com. 2010-11-15. Retrieved 2015-09-06.

[5] British Steel VI Festival details at Planetmosh website, 31 March 2012

2.20.5 External links

- Official Web Elixir Page
- Elixir at MySpace
- Elixir on Facebook

2.21 Eric Bell

For other people named Eric Bell, see Eric Bell (disambiguation).

Eric Robin Bell (born 3 September 1947 in East Belfast, Northern Ireland)[1] is a Northern Irish rock musician and guitarist, best known as a founder member and the original guitarist of the rock group Thin Lizzy. After his time in the band, he had a brief period of fronting his own group.

2.21.1 Career

Early career

Bell began his career with local groups around the Belfast area, including the last incarnation of Them to feature Van Morrison, between September and October 1966.[2] He also played with a number of other bands including Shades of Blue, The Earth Dwellers and The Bluebeats, before joining an Irish showband named The Dreams.[2][3] He left in 1969 having tired of the showband format, and at the end of that year he formed a band with local musicians Phil Lynott, Eric Wrixon and Brian Downey. Bell named the group Thin Lizzy, after Tin Lizzie, a robot character in *The Dandy* comic.[4]

Thin Lizzy

Wrixon left Thin Lizzy after a few months, and the remaining trio later secured a contract with Decca Records.[5] As lead guitarist, Bell played on Thin Lizzy's first three albums *Thin Lizzy*, *Shades of a Blue Orphanage* and *Vagabonds of the Western World*, as well as their hit single "Whiskey in the Jar". He co-wrote a number of songs with Lynott and Downey, including "The Rocker" which became a live favourite throughout the band's career.[2] He also composed one song on his own, "Ray Gun", from their first album, *Thin Lizzy*.[6]

Although Thin Lizzy gained in popularity during the early 1970s, the pressures of recording, touring and the excesses of the rock star lifestyle began to take their toll. He left the band after a New Year's Eve concert in 1973, after throwing

Eric Bell with Thin Lizzy, 1972

Eric Bell and Bo Diddley performing with Mainsqueeze in Novi Sad, former Yugoslavia, 27 February 1984.

his guitar into the air in the middle of the concert, pushing the amplifiers into the audience and storming off stage. He stated later that he had no regrets about leaving: *"I really had to leave because of ill-health. It was exhaustion, and the majority of things that were available to me... I couldn't really handle it."*[2] He was temporarily replaced by Gary Moore.[5]

The Noel Redding Band

In 1974, after a brief period fronting his own Eric Bell Band,[7] Bell was recruited by ex-Jimi Hendrix sideman Noel Redding, along with keyboardist Dave Clarke and drummer Les Sampson, to form The Noel Redding Band. Bell was initially unsure of the musical direction Redding was taking,[8] but went on to record two albums with the group before they split in 1976. A third album of unused tracks was released in 1995. Bell composed the song "Love and War" for the second album, *Blowin'*.[9]

The 1980s and Mainsqueeze

In 1980, Bell reunited with Thin Lizzy to record a tribute song to Jimi Hendrix, "Song for Jimmy" [sic], which was released as an orange flexi disc and given away with *Flexipop* in August 1981.[10] It was later included on the Thin Lizzy *Vagabonds, Kings, Warriors, Angels* box set in 2002. Bell also appeared as a guest on Thin Lizzy's final tour in 1983, and the accompanying live album, *Life*.

Bell had also reactivated his own band in the late 1970s, and released an EP in 1981.[11]

Bell subsequently joined saxophonist Dick Heckstall-Smith's eight-piece blues rock ensemble Mainsqueeze.[11] They toured Europe,[12] recorded a live album in 1983, and later toured as Bo Diddley's backing group, recording the *Hey... Bo Diddley: In Concert* album in 1986.[11]

Later career

Bell has continued to perform and record with the Eric Bell Band throughout the 1990s and 2000s, releasing several albums.[11] He has also recorded with the Barrelhouse Brothers.[13]

In 2005, he joined Gary Moore onstage to perform "Whiskey in the Jar" at the Phil Lynott tribute concert "The Boy Is Back in Town" in the Point Theatre, Dublin. This was released on a DVD called *One Night in Dublin: A Tribute to Phil Lynott*.[14] In 2010, Bell moved from London where he had lived for many years to his new home in West Cork, Ireland.

2.21.2 Discography

Thin Lizzy

- *Thin Lizzy* (1971)
- *Shades of a Blue Orphanage* (1972)
- *Vagabonds of the Western World* (1973)
- "Song for Jimmy" – Flexipop single (1981)
- *Life* (1983)

The Noel Redding Band

- *Clonakilty Cowboys* (1975)
- *Blowin'* (1976)
- *The Missing Album* (1995)

Eric Bell Band

- "The Eric Bell Band E.P." (1981)
- "Lonely Man / Anyone Seen My Baby" – single version of the E.P. (1981)
- *Live Tonite* (Sweden, 1996)
- *Irish Boy* (Spain, 1998)
- *Live Tonite Plus* (Extra tracks, 2001)
- *A Blues Night in Dublin* (2002)
- *Lonely Nights in London* (2010)
- *Belfast Blues in a Jar* (2012)[15]

Mainsqueeze

- *Live at Ronnie Scott's Club* (France, 1983)
- *Hey... Bo Diddley: In Concert* – as backing group for Bo Diddley (1986)

Others

- The Dreams – *The Best of Dreams* (1969)
- Whistler – *Ho Hum* (1971)
- Brush Shiels – *Brush Shiels* (1977)
- Smiley Bolger – *Ode to a Black Man* (1991)
- Honeyboy Hickling – *Straight from the Harp* (2000)
- Barrelhouse Brothers – *Pick It Up, Pass It On* (2002)
- The Animals and Friends – *Instinct* (2004)

2.21.3 References

[1] IMDb.com

[2] Alan Byrne, "Thin Lizzy: Soldiers of Fortune", Firefly, 2004.

[3] "Irish Showband & Beat-Group Member's List". *List of members who performed in the Irish Showbands in the 1960s–1970s*. Ireland. 2001–2010. Retrieved 20 June 2011.

[4] "Thin Lizzy". Eric Bell Official Website. Retrieved 10 April 2011.

[5] Mark Putterford, "Philip Lynott: The Rocker", Castle, 1994

[6] "Thin Lizzy – Thin Lizzy". Allmusic.com. Retrieved 10 April 2011.

[7] "Eric Bell Band". Eric Bell Official Website. Retrieved 10 April 2011.

[8] "Noel Redding Band". Eric Bell Official Website. Retrieved 10 April 2011.

[9] "Noel Redding Band – Blowin'". Allmusic.com. Retrieved 10 April 2011.

[10] "Flexipop Label Discography". 45cat.com. Retrieved 10 April 2011.

[11] "IrishRock.org – Eric Bell". Irishrock.org. Retrieved 10 April 2011.

[12] "Mainsqueeze". Eric Bell Official Website. Retrieved 10 April 2011.

[13] "Barrelhouse Brothers". RockDetector. Retrieved 10 April 2011.

[14] "Thin Lizzy – One Night in Dublin – A Tribute to Phil Lynott". Encyclopedia Metallum. Retrieved 3 April 2011.

[15] "Belfast Blues in a Jar – Eric Bell | Songs, Reviews, Credits, Awards". AllMusic. Retrieved 2014-08-01.

2.21.4 External links

- Official Web Site
- Eric Bell in Concert

2.22 Ethel the Frog (band)

Ethel the Frog was a heavy metal band formed in 1976 in Hull, England. They are notable for being a part of the New Wave of British Heavy Metal movement. The band's unusual name was taken from a Monty Python sketch about the "Piranha Brothers".

2.22.1 Career

After building a local following, they released a heavy version of The Beatles song "Eleanor Rigby" in 1978. Ethel the Frog also contributed the song "Fight Back" to one of Neal Kay's *Metal for Muthas* compilations. In 1979, they signed a recording contract with EMI, which re-released the "Eleanor Rigby" single with "Whatever Happened to Love" as the B-side.[1]

Their self-titled debut album was released in 1980. A CD release on a small record label, British Steel, appeared in 1997.

2.22.2 Post Ethel

Hopkinson is now a lecturer at the University of Leicester School of Archaeology.[2]

Tognola and Conyers went on to join a band called Salem, releasing one single called "Reach for Eternity/Cold as Steel" in 1982. That band split in 1983, then reformed in 2009 and is currently achieving some success.

Doug Sheppard continued to play in cover bands, but then formed the band No Messiahs which lasted a couple of years, and he continues to play guitar in the Netherlands and has several original songs issued on Reverbnation.[3]

2.22.3 Line-up

The original line-up was:

- Paul "Doug" Sheppard (lead guitar)
- Terry Hopkinson (vocals, bass)
- Paul Tognola (vocals, lead guitar)
- Paul Conyers (drums).

2.22.4 Discography

- *Metal for Muthas* - Compilation (1980) EMI
- *Ethel the Frog* (1980) EMI

2.22.5 See also

- List of New Wave of British Heavy Metal bands

2.22.6 References

[1] "Ethel the Frog". Geocities. 2001-09-01. Archived from the original on 2005-08-30. Retrieved 2007-01-20.

[2] "Dr. Terry Hopkinson".

[3] Reverbnation.com

2.22.7 External links

- article and discography
- MusicMight bio

2.23 Fist (band)

Fist are an English heavy metal band hailing from South Shields, North East UK. Fist were one of the original bands that were considered to be part of the New Wave Of British Heavy Metal movement in the late 1970s and early 1980.[1] The band first formed in April 1978 as **Axe**, but only recorded one song ("S.S. Giro") under that name.[2] The group reformed in late 1979 under the new name of Fist, soon signing with Neat Records and releasing their first single, "Name, Rank and Serial Number" in April 1980. This single did good business with heavy radio rotation and good sales. The single was praised in the pages of *Sounds*, and bigger things were anticipated for the band as they signed with MCA, releasing a second single and preparing a full-length record for the end of the year. *Turn the Hell On* was released and the band toured with the likes of UFO, Judas Priest and Iron Maiden. Unfortunately, the LP suffered from a poor mix and MCA didn't have any real experience of dealing with metal bands and promoted the band poorly. *Turn the Hell On* inevitably failed to satisfy the label saleswise and Fist were dropped by MCA in early 1981.[2]

Apart from a couple of compilation appearances (including the old 1978 Axe recording of "S.S. Giro" showing up on the Neat compilation *Lead Weight*), Fist went unheard from for a short time, re-vamping the line-up in July 1981 and issuing their second LP, *Back with a Vengeance*, on Neat in early 1982. Ironically the album had a better mix but a truly awful album cover, almost the complete opposite of the previous effort *Turn the Hell On*. This new line-up included lead vocalist Glenn Coates from Hollow Ground, John Roach from Mythra, bassist Norman Appleby as well as Hill and Irwin. Reviews were favourable for this album, with a few minor quibbles about the band sounding "too American" due to Glenn Coates smoother vocals. However, due to limited distribution and scarce label funds the album never took off. The band seemed a little restrained also, mainly gigging locally in the North East UK. Fist went through a few more changes from that point until finally and officially disbanding in 1985.

Despite failing to sell in "significant numbers", Fist were singled out for praise by a number of critics for writing catchy choruses and resisting the clichéd heavy metal lyrics of many other NWOBHM bands, that primarily sang about the occult; "You'll Never Get Me Up (In One of Those)", for example, is about fear of flying, while "Throwing in the Towel" is about an ageing boxer unhappy to be back in the ring. "Name, Rank and Serial Number" in particular is considered an all-time classic by many rock and metal fans.[1]

In 2001, original frontman Keith Satchfield formed a new version of Fist which included members of Hollow Ground as well as guest musicians. This lineup released a new album, *Storm*, in 2005. The music on this album had a much heavier feel than anything Fist had previously released. The album received a mixed reception, with some camps preferring the older more classic sounding material and other camps criticising the "synthetic" sound of the recordings especially the drums. There was some initial activity with this line-up e.g., a one off show at Headbangers Open Air in Germany, however, due to ill health, the band remained inactive shortly afterwards and again the album failed to make any major impact.

In 2013, Fist reformed with original members Harry "Hiroshima" Hill, Davey Irwin and Norman Appleby from the *Back with Vengeance* period. Added to this line-up was new frontman Glenn S. Howes, a veteran of the NWOBHM scene after spending time in such luminaries as Blitzkrieg, Tygers of Pan Tang and Avenger. This line-up debuted at the Bro Fest festival in the UK in 2014, headlining the Friday night to much expectation and excitement. The resulting reviews pouring great admiration for the band and the new formation. Fist continue to play live across the world with this line up and as of 2015 have rumoured to be writing songs for a new album.

2.23.1 Discography

Albums

- *Turn the Hell On* (MCA November 1980)
- *Back with a Vengeance* (Neat 1982)
- *Storm* (Demolition April 2005)

Singles

- "Name, Rank and Serial Number" / "You'll Never Get Me Up (In One of Those)" (Neat April 1980 / MCA July 1980)

- "Forever Amber" / "Brain Damage" (MCA August 1980)
- "Collision Course" / "Law of the Jungle" (MCA January 1981)
- "The Wanderer" / "Too Hot" (Neat November 1982)

Compilation appearances

- "Brain Damage" (*Brute Force*, MCA September 1980)
- "S.S. Giro" / "Throwing in the Towel" (*Lead Weight*, Neat May 1981)
- "Lost & Found" (*60 Minute Plus Heavy Metal*, Neat November 1982)

Compilations

- *Back with a Vengeance: The Anthology* (Sanctuary 2002)

2.23.2 See also

- New Wave of British Heavy Metal
- List of New Wave of British Heavy Metal bands

2.23.3 References

[1] *Back With A Vengeance: The Anthology* (Inset). Fist. UK: Sanctuary Records. 2002. CMDDD585.

[2] Rivadavia, Eduardo. "Biography of Fist". *Allmusic*. Macrovision. Retrieved 25 August 2009.

2.23.4 External links

- Encyclopedia Metallum - Fist

2.24 Geoff Barton

Geoff Barton is a British journalist who founded the heavy metal magazine *Kerrang!* and was an editor of *Sounds* music magazine.[1]

He joined *Sounds* at the age of nineteen after completing a journalism course at the London College of Printing. He specialised in covering rock music and helped popularise the New Wave of British Heavy Metal after using the term for the first time (after editor Alan Lewis coined it) in the

May 1979 issue of *Sounds*.[2] In 1981 he edited the first issue of *Kerrang!*, which was published as a one off. This was successful so it became a fortnightly magazine. He left the magazine in 1995.

Barton's articles for *Sounds* which covered the NWOBHM helped to create the sense that an actual movement was taking place, and in a sense helped to create one in the process. Barton recalls: "The phrase New Wave of British Heavy Metal was this slightly tongue-in-cheek thing...I didn't really feel that any of these bands were particularly linked in a musical way, but it was interesting that so many of them should then be emerging at more or less the same time." [3] He currently works for *Classic Rock Magazine*.

2.24.1 References

[1] "Geoff Barton, behind the wheel". RockCritics.com.

[2] Steve Waksman, *This Ain't the Summer of Love: Conflict and Crossover in Heavy Metal and Punk* (Los Angeles, CA: University of California Press, 2009), 173-175.

[3] Mick Wall, Run to the Hills: Iron Maiden, the Authorised Biography (London: Sanctuary, 2000), 88. See also Steve Waksman, *This Ain't the Summer of Love: Conflict and Crossover in Heavy Metal and Punk* (Los Angeles, CA: University of California Press, 2009), 330, note 7.

2.25 Girl (band)

Girl were an English glam metal band formed in London, UK in 1979, which split up in 1982 with band members going on to join Def Leppard and L.A. Guns among others.

2.25.1 History

Girl were formed in 1979 by vocalist Phil Lewis, guitarists Gerry Laffy and Phil Collen, drummer Dave Gaynor, and bassist Mark Megary (replaced shortly thereafter by Simon Laffy. Collen had previously been in the bands Lucy, Tush, and Dumb Blondes. Girl were first discovered and managed by Jon Lindsay who was looking for bands for former manager of The Who, Kit Lambert for a proposed new record label. Lindsay and Girl separated over managerial decisions when the band wanted to sign a recording deal with Don Arden instead of a recording contract negotiated by Lindsay with music figure Simon Napier-Bell's Nomis Publishing.

The band were signed by Jet Records, releasing two singles prior to their debut album *Sheer Greed* (1980), which reached number 33 in the UK Albums Chart.[1] The band's profile was raised by tours with the Pat Travers Band and UFO, in the midst of the New Wave of British Heavy Metal explosion.[2] Girl recorded a pre-L.A. Guns version of the song "Hollywood Tease", which peaked at No. 50 in the UK Singles Chart in April 1980.[3]

Gaynor left in 1981, to be replaced by former Gillan/Broken Home drummer Pete Barnacle, who was replaced by Bryson Graham during the recording of the next album.[1] Their second album *Wasted Youth* was released in 1982 and reached number 92 in the UK.[1] Pete Bonas replaced Phil Collen, who left to join Def Leppard, though the band broke up soon after.

Girl still have six albums available through Sanctuary Records (previously released by Don Arden's Jet Records): *Sheer Greed*, *Wasted Youth*, *Killing Time*, *Live At The Marquee*, *Live At The Exposition Hall, Osaka, Japan*, the 37 track anthology *My Number: The Anthology*, *Bootleg - Live in Tokyo 1980* and *Girl-Sheer Greed-Gerry Laffy - The Rare DVD Collection*.

After the band's dissolution, Phil Lewis joined The London Cowboys, then Airrace, and in 1987 L.A. Guns.[1] Lewis also sang with New Torpedos, Torme, Filthy Lucre, and The Liberators.

Gerry Laffy, Simon Laffy, and Pete Barnacle went on to play in Sheer Greed, which also featured guest appearances from both Lewis and Collen. Sheer Greed also recorded two versions of "Hollywood Tease", one recorded in studio for the album *Sublime to the Ridiculous* and another live for *Live in London*.

Collen and Simon Laffy are currently in a band called Man Raze, along with former Sex Pistols drummer Paul Cook.[4]

2.25.2 Members

- Phil Lewis - vocals (1979-1982)
- Gerry Laffy - guitars (1979-1982)
- Phil Collen - guitars (1979-1982)
- Dave Gaynor - drums (1979-1981)
- Mark Megary - bass (1979)
- Simon Laffy - bass (1979-1982)
- Pete Barnacle - drums (1981-1982)
- Bryson Graham - drums (1982)
- Pete Bonas - guitars (1982)

2.25.3 Discography

Studio albums

- *Sheer Greed* (1980) - UK #33
- *Wasted Youth* (1982) - UK #92
- *Killing Time* (1997)[3]

Live albums

- *Live at the Marquee* (2001)
- *Live at the Exposition Hall, Osaka, Japan* (2001)
- *Live at the Greyhound* (2013)
- *Rainbow Tease* (2013)

Compilations

- *My Number: The Anthology*

Other

- *Live in Tokyo 1980* (Bootleg)

2.25.4 Videography

- *GIRL - The Rare DVD Collection* (2006)

2.25.5 See also

- List of New Wave of British Heavy Metal bands

2.25.6 References

[1] Strong, Martin C. (2001). *The Great Metal Discography*. Edinburgh, UK: MOJO Books. p. 224. ISBN 1-84195-185-4.

[2] Larkin, Colin (1999) *The Virgin Encyclopedia of Heavy Rock*, Virgin Books, ISBN 0-7535-0257-7, p. 183-4.

[3] Roberts, David (2006). *British Hit Singles & Albums* (19th ed.). London: Guinness World Records Limited. p. 228. ISBN 1-904994-10-5.

[4] "DEF LEPPARD Guitarist's MAN RAZE: New Single Cover Artwork Unveiled", Blabbermouth.net, 4 May 2011, retrieved 2011-05-07

2.25.7 External links

- Gerry Laffy's MySpace page
- Sheer Greed Facebook Group

2.25.8 Sources

- http://www.nwobhm.com/girl.htm

2.26 Girlschool

This article is about the band. For girls' schools, see single-sex education. For the song by Britny Fox, see Britny Fox (album).

Girlschool are a British heavy metal band originating out of the New Wave of British Heavy Metal scene in 1978 and frequently associated with contemporaries Motörhead. They are the longest running all-female rock band, still active after more than 35 years.[1][2] Formed from a school band called Painted Lady, Girlschool enjoyed strong media exposure and commercial success in the UK in the early 1980s with three albums of 'punk-tinged metal'[3] and a few singles, but rapidly lost their momentum in the following years.[4]

In the 1990s and 2000s, they concentrated their efforts on live shows and tours, reducing considerably the production of studio albums. During their long career, Girlschool travelled all over the world, playing in many rock and metal festivals and co-headlining with or supporting some of the most important hard rock and heavy metal bands. They maintain a worldwide cult following and are considered an inspiration for many succeeding female rock musicians.[5] Despite frequent changes of line-up, original members Kim McAuliffe, Enid Williams and Denise Dufort are still in the band to this day. The only original member no longer in the band, lead guitarist and singer Kelly Johnson, died of cancer in 2007.[6]

2.26.1 History

1975–1978: Painted Lady

In 1975, school friends and neighbours from Wandsworth, South London, Kim McAuliffe (rhythm guitar, vocals) and Dinah Enid Williams (bass, vocals) formed an all-girl rock cover band called Painted Lady, together with Tina Gayle on drums. Deirdre Cartwright joined the new band on lead guitar, Val Lloyd replaced Gayle on drums and they started playing the local pub scene.[7][8] "The reason we were all girls was we couldn't find any blokes who wanted to play with us! This was the natural thing to do", McAuliffe explained to Gary Graff in 1997 about the all-female composition of the band.[5]

Cartwright, who was older and more musically experienced than the other girls,[7] left in 1977 to form the band Tour De Force[8] and then followed different professional opportunities in the music business; she is now a renowned jazz guitarist.[9] Her place in the band was briefly taken by visiting American Kathy Valentine, who approached the band through an advertisement in the British music newspaper *Melody Maker*.[7] When Valentine returned to the United States in 1978 to form the Textones and later join The Go-Go's as bass player, Painted Lady broke up. However, McAuliffe and Williams were still willing to pursue a musical career to escape their day jobs in a bank and a bakery and reformed the band,[10] recruiting lead guitarist Kelly Johnson and drummer Denise Dufort in April 1978.[11] The new line-up changed their name to Girlschool, taking it from the B-side of the hit single "Mull of Kintyre" (1977) by Paul McCartney & Wings[12] and immediately hit the road, touring small venues in France, Ireland and Great Britain.[2]

1978–1982: N.W.O.B.H.M.

Girlschool original line-up: Kim McAuliffe, Enid Williams, Kelly Johnson, Denise Dufort (1981)

In December 1978, Girlschool released their first single, "Take It All Away", on the independent record label City Records, owned by Phil Scott, a friend of the band.[3][7] The single had some radio airplay[7] and circulated in the underground scene, coming to the ear of Ian Kilmister, commonly known as Lemmy, leader of the British rock band Motörhead, who wanted to meet the band. Lemmy, together with Motörhead and Hawkwind manager Doug Smith, went to see the band performing live and offered them a support slot on Motörhead's *Overkill* tour in the spring of 1979.[13][14] This was the start of an enduring relationship between the two bands that lasts to this day.[15] After the tour and a few other shows supporting Welsh band Budgie, Doug Smith became the manager of Girlschool and obtained an audition with the British label Bronze Records, at the time home of Uriah Heep, Motörhead and Juicy Lucy. Bronze's owner Gerry Bron himself attended the audition and was impressed by Girlschool's stage presence and musicianship, offering them a contract with his label in December 1979.[11]

I went to an early rehearsal and was surprised how well (Girlschool) played their instruments – how terribly chauvinistic of me. None of them were particularly good looking, although from a distance Kelly Johnson looked like that Charlie's Angels' actress, Farrah Fawcett, but there was something about them...

"

"

–Gerry Bron[16]

The British rock movement known as the New Wave of British Heavy Metal (frequently abbreviated in NWOBHM), which started in the late 1970s and broke in the mainstream in the early 1980s,[17] was just exploding in the United Kingdom and the band gained the support of a strong label at exactly the right time to exploit the moment and form a solid fan base.[18]

The band entered the recording studio with experienced producer Vic Maile in April 1980.[19] Vic Maile had been working as live sound engineer for many important acts, like The Who, Led Zeppelin, The Kinks and Jimi Hendrix,[20] producing also the first two seminal albums of Dr. Feelgood and a few punk bands in the late 70s.[21] He captured the raw but powerful sound of Girlschool in ten short songs, with lead vocals shared by Williams, McAuliffe and Johnson. Girlschool released their debut album, *Demolition*, in June 1980,[22] alongside the singles "Emergency", "Nothing to Lose" and "Race with the Devil". *Demolition* reached No.28 in the UK Album Chart in July 1980.[23]

In the same period, albums and singles from Judas Priest,[24] Saxon,[25] Def Leppard,[26] Iron Maiden,[27] Motörhead[28] and other bands of the NWOBHM reached high positions in the UK charts, while the same bands did tours and concerts all over Europe.[29][30][31][32] Girlschool participated in this frenzied touring activity, travelling in Great Britain and visiting Europe both as headliner act and as support to label mates Uriah Heep and Motörhead.[33] On 20 August, Girlschool and Motörhead were filmed performing live at the Nottingham Theatre Royal for the *Rockstage* programme, broadcast by the ATV station on 4 April 1981.[34] In this period, the band was subjected to intense media coverage by music magazines, radio and TV, interested in the novelty of a successful British all-female metal band.[35] The barrage of interviews and promotion did not stop the production of songs and the girls released the new single "Yeah Right" in November 1980.[22]

In December 1980, Girlschool officially started recording

the follow-up to *Demolition*, again with producer Vic Maile, who had meanwhile produced Motörhead's classic album *Ace of Spades*. During the sessions, Maile suggested a studio recording team-up with Motörhead, resulting in the release of the EP *St. Valentine's Day Massacre*.[36] The EP contains the cover of Johnny Kidd & The Pirates' song "Please Don't Touch" and two self-covers, with Motörhead performing Girlschool's "Emergency", and Girlschool playing Motörhead's "Bomber". Dufort played drums on all songs, because Motörhead's drummer Phil "Philthy Animal" Taylor was recovering from a neck injury. She also played the drums during the BBC One *Top of the Pops* TV show of 19 February 1981, where the two bands performed "Please Don't Touch" under the moniker Headgirl.[37] The EP reached No.5 in the UK Single Chart in February 1981[38] and was certified silver in December 1981,[39] the best sale performance for both bands at the time.

The album *Hit and Run* was released in April 1981,[22] soon followed by the eponymous single. Both releases were very successful in the UK, with the album reaching position No.5 and the single position No.33 in the respective charts.[23] The album charted also in New Zealand and in Canada,[40][41] where it went gold.[42] *Hit and Run* was not released in the USA until 1982, with a different track listing including songs from *Demolition*. The success of their second album made Girlschool a rising attraction in the boiling British hard rock and heavy metal scene, ensuring headliner slots in medium sized arenas in their sold-out UK tour[43] or guest slots in stadium size concerts of major attractions like Black Sabbath and Rush.[10] No dates in the USA were arranged, but Girlschool visited Canada in July. Their 1981 tour culminated on 28 August, headlining the Friday night of the three-day Reading Festival.[44] The Friday Rock Show on BBC Radio 1 would later broadcast the Reading set, but the recording has not received an official release.[10]

Headlining the Friday night of the 1981 Reading Festival was the highlight of Girlschool's career

At the beginning of 1982, Girlschool did a European tour and, at the last Danish date in Copenhagen with supporting act Mercyful Fate, McAuliffe received a potentially-fatal electric shock from her microphone.[45] She recovered fast enough to complete a Japanese tour, to do other European shows supporting Rainbow on their *Difficult to Cure* tour and to start working on new material for the next album. However, the gruelling schedule of recordings, promotional work and concerts had started to take its toll on the group, with bassist Enid Williams the first to give up, right after the release of *Wildlife* in March 1982, an EP designed to launch the upcoming album.[46][47] On the recommendation of Lemmy, Williams was replaced by Ghislaine 'Gil' Weston,[5] former bassist of the punk band The Killjoys.[48]

Girlschool's third album *Screaming Blue Murder* was recorded in February and March 1982 under the direction of Nigel Gray, the successful producer of The Police and The Professionals.[49] The album had a worldwide release in June 1982[22] but, despite the strong promotion, it reached only No.27 in the UK Album Chart.[23] Critics generally considered *Screaming Blue Murder* a weaker offering in comparison with the preceding two albums.[47][50]

Girlschool remained anyway a strong live attraction and their 1982 world tour led the band for the first time in the USA to play in stadiums, supporting Iron Maiden and Scorpions.[51] NWOBHM acts like Judas Priest and Def Leppard started to be very popular in America and the girls and their record label had no intention to fall back in the conquest of that large market.[46]

1983–1985: American sirens

Back in England, the continuous succession of recording sessions, gigs and promotional work started again, but the strain of this routine was wearing out Kelly Johnson,[52] who was also tired of the music the band had been playing for four years without a break.[5][53] The other members struggled to convince her to stay and the chance to record with British celebrities Noddy Holder and Jim Lea as producers persuaded the guitarist to carry on with Girlschool.[53] Holder and Lea, who had returned in those years to great success and popularity in Great Britain with the 70s rock band Slade,[54] were hired to produce only a single,[55] with the following album already scheduled to be recorded in Los Angeles with Quiet Riot producer Spencer Proffer.[8][10] However, the good chemistry found with the two Slade members led the band to decide to record not a single, but their whole fourth studio album in North London with Lea and Holder, giving up the trip to the USA.[7] This time the group changed sensibly both their appearance and their musical style in order to appeal to a large American audience, which Bronze considered more oriented toward AOR and glam rock than to the 'biker metal'[56] Girlschool had produced before.[53] *Play Dirty*, released in October 1983,[22] is an album with a very polished sound, filled with keyboards, choruses and melodies, but it lacks much of the aggression and power of the preceding works.[57] The album contains covers of the Slade songs "High & Dry" and "Burning in the Heat" and of T.Rex's "20th Century Boy", which was also released as a single. *Play Dirty* failed to enter the top 50 chart in the UK and had a lukewarm reception by fans and critics at home.[58] A struggle between Bronze and PolyGram for the worldwide contract of the band resulted also in poor promotion for the album in the USA.[53] Moreover, a disastrous performance at Wembley Arena supporting ZZ Top did not help Girlschool's already degraded image in Great Britain.[53]

Girlschool upgraded their look in 1983 to appeal to the US market

Girlschool embarked in a long US tour to promote the album, sometimes as support to Quiet Riot and Blue Öyster Cult, but more often as headliner in small venues after uncomfortable travels.[53] Johnson, unable to tolerate the unhealthy life on the road,[59] quit the band before completing the US tour, hurting the promotion of the album in America. She went to live in Los Angeles with Vicki Blue, former bassist of The Runaways.[59] With the departure of Kelly Johnson, who was often considered the visual[60] and musical focal point of the band, the almost bankrupt Bronze Records failed to extend the band's recording contract for a follow-up album.[3][53]

At the beginning of 1984, Girlschool were in need of a new lead guitar player and singer, of a new recording contract and chart success but, despite the difficult situation, the band did not give up.[53] The search for new members ended with the arrival of guitarist Cris Bonacci and singer and keyboard player Jackie Bodimead, both from the all-female hard rock band She.[61] She were playing in London clubs at the time, trying to get a record contract and attract the attention of the British music press.[62]

The new Girschool, now a five-piece group, signed with the PolyGram American subsidiary Mercury Records, once home of the American all-girls rock band The Runaways.[11] The label saw in the band an opportunity to produce a rival for chart-winning female-fronted bands like Heart and Lita Ford and pushed the music of the band even more towards FM friendly American hard rock.[63] The band was paired with producer Nick Tauber, who had produced the first albums of Thin Lizzy and the most successful albums of Toyah and Marillion, contributing also to the launch of the British glam metal act Girl.[64] The resulting album *Running Wild*, sported ten keyboard-laden tracks much different from Girlschool's most successful music. The record label decided to publish the album only in the USA in February 1985,[22] but actually gave little support to its marketing.[3] The review of the magazine *Kerrang!*[65] reflects the opinions of Dufort and McAuliffe, which described years later the album as rubbish or even worse.[14][63] *Running Wild* had insignificant sales on the US market, not representing the breakthrough the band and the label had hoped for.[46] A live performance of Girlschool as a quintet at Camden Palace in London was taped for the VHS *Play Dirty Live*,[66] which was released in 1985 and reissued on DVD with the title *Live from London* in 2005.[67]

The band did some shows supporting the glam rock band Hanoi Rocks in Great Britain,[68] before embarking in the Deep Purple comeback world tour, where Girschool played in a supporting role all over the USA.[69] A tour of India and the Far East completed their live activities for 1985.[70] Vocal duties were shared on stage between McAuliffe and Bodimead, who also played keyboards. At the end of the tour, Jackie Bodimead left the band to pursue a solo career.[63]

1986–1990: 'back to square one'

After the bad commercial results of *Running Wild*, Mercury broke the contract with Girlschool,[46] leaving the band without financial backup and with a career in dire straits.[63] "Back to square one again", McAuliffe said at the time.[63] The band decided to go back to their roots, remaining a quartet with only McAuliffe on vocals and going on a UK tour in November – December 1985 supporting Blue Öyster Cult; their immediate goal was to play as much as they could and regain some of their fan base.[63] In early 1986, thanks again to Lemmy's suggestion, they eventually signed for Doug Smith's new label GWR Records, which also included in their roster Motörhead.[11] The girls immediately started working on a new album with their old producer Vic Maile at Jackson's Studio in Rickmansworth.[63] The first output of their new work was a team-up with British glam rock singer Gary Glitter for the cover of his 1973 hit "I'm the Leader of the Gang (I Am)", which was released as a single in April 1986.[11][22] The album *Nightmare at Maple Cross*, released in July of the same year,[22] marked for the band the return to the sound of *Hit and Run* and to their trademark abrasive lyrics. The album received fairly good reviews,[71][72] but it did not enter the British charts and was released in North America only a year later.[73] The following European tour saw the girls supporting the Scottish hard rock band Nazareth.[74]

In January 1987, after five years with the group, bassist Gil Weston-Jones left Girlschool to spend more time with her American husband.[73] Her place was quickly taken by Tracey Lamb, who had been the bass player of the all-female NWOBHM band Rock Goddess and a band mate of Cris Bonacci in She.[73] Girlschool spent the rest of the year promoting the album with a US tour and appearances in various TV shows across Europe, followed by a long European tour supporting usual label mates Motörhead.[70]

At the beginning of 1988, the band started rehearsing material for a new album with producer André Jacquemin, who had worked on all the Monty Python's records.[70] The album *Take a Bite* was published by GWR in October 1988 and follows in the steps of *Nightmare at Maple Cross*, presenting powerful and melodic metal songs, tinged with the humour typical of the band.[75] To promote the album, Girlschool did a UK tour with Gary Glitter,[76] followed by a North American tour. In 1989, they travelled across Europe with Dio[11] and to the Soviet Union with Black Sabbath, till the end of the year.[77] After their return from Russia, GWR did not renew their contract and the band practically broke up.[3][46] Musical tastes were changing worldwide in favour of grunge and more extreme metal genres, compelling most acts originated from the New Wave of British Heavy Metal to disband or to reduce their activities, and the same thing happened to Girlschool.[12]

1990–1991: She-Devils and Strange Girls

Even if not officially disbanded, Girlschool had become "not a full-time thing anymore" for the members of the group.[5] In this period, Cris Bonacci joined British singer Toyah Willcox, for the promotion of the album *Ophelia's Shadow*.[78] A brief tour of Spain was Girlschool's only activity of 1990,[8] but in December, McAuliffe, Bonacci, Dufort and returning bass player Enid Williams, teamed up with Toyah Willcox under the name She-Devils for the first edition of the Women in Music festival at Shaw Theatre in London, performing both Girlschool and Toyah's songs.[46][79] A few months later, the same musicians reunited again under the new name Strange Girls, with Lydie Gallais replacing Dufort on drums.[8] Strange Girls toured clubs in Great Britain in 1991 and 1992[2] and supported The Beach Boys in their German dates in the summer of 1991.[80] The band wrote a few songs and produced a demo,[2] but the only published track from this period is the song "Lust for Love", which can be found on Toyah's album *Take the Leap!* (1993).[81]

1992–2002: living on tour

Lead guitarist Jackie 'Jax' Chambers playing live at Bloodstock Open Air 2009

Girlschool went back in action in 1992, recruiting Jackie Carrera on bass and recording *Girlschool*, their first self-produced album,[82] which was distributed worldwide by the British indie label Communiqué Records. The lower visibility of the album distributed by an indie label marked the definitive transition to cult status for the band, renouncing to many expectations of big sales. Girlschool were now the managers of themselves, relying on their solid live show[83] and on their reputation with promoters and other artists to get gigs and work.[76] As stated in an interview to the British TV show Raw Power, Girlschool would "play in every single toilet that we can find!"[82]

After a few European dates, returning bassist Tracey Lamb replaced Carrera before a new tour in the United States.[8] But more line-up changes were in store for the band because, at the end of 1992, Cris Bonacci left the band to become a touring musician and then a producer.[84] In 1993, her place as lead guitarist was taken back by Kelly Johnson,[85] who returned after nine years to England from LA, where she had played in a band with Kathy Valentine and written and produced her own music.[86][87] The plethora of compilations of old Girlschool material that had started to be published from 1989 kept the band alive on the CD market and guaranteed enough visibility to get a good number of gigs every year in every part of the world, often supporting other NWOBHM acts like Motörhead or Saxon.[87] In this period, the girls were also present at rock festivals all over Europe, both as Girlschool or separately in other outfits.[8] In 1995, Communiqué Records released *Girlschool Live*, a live album documenting the intense live shows of the band in that period and which included the new tracks "Knife" and "Little Green Men".[88] Girlschool continued their live activity in the 1990s, culminating with a participation to the Wacken Open Air festival on Friday, 6 August 1999.[89]

In all this time the band had been writing new songs[87] and, in September 1998, they began to record a new album,[3] but touring commitments and new line-up changes prevented Girlschool to complete it. In fact, Johnson quit amicably Girlschool in 1999, followed by Lamb in 2000.[90] They were replaced by new lead guitarist Jackie 'Jax' Chambers and by Enid Williams, who finally rejoined the group after eighteen years. Johnson, who had been diagnosed with cancer,[6] and Lamb remained anyway strictly associated with the other band members.[74][90]

21st Anniversary: Not That Innocent was finally released at the beginning of 2002 and co-produced by Girlschool and Tim Hamill. The album contains tracks recorded three years earlier by the previous line-up, with the addition of the songs "Coming Your Way" and "Innocent" recorded by the current one.[2] The influence of the American years spent by Johnson in Los Angeles is clearly audible in the music and in the vocal tracks of the album, which features Girlschool's first semi-acoustic ballad "A Love Too Far".[91]

2003– present: recent activities

In 2003, the band was again in a recording studio for *The Second Wave: 25 Years of NWOBHM*, a split album conceived by the label Communiqué, comprising five songs each for Oliver/Dawson Saxon, Tygers of Pan Tang and Girlschool. A tour of the three aforementioned bands could not be organized and, in October 2004, Girlschool toured supporting the album with Tygers of Pan Tang and Paul Di'Anno.[92]

Preceded by the publication of the re-mastered editions of their first four albums, Girlschool released the studio album *Believe* in July 2004.[93] The wish to explore new

Lead vocalist Kim McAuliffe at Bloodstock Open Air 2009

territories is obvious in some tracks of the album, which is the first one entirely composed by the new line-up at Chambers' home studio.[94] The changed line-up brought a new balance in the band, with Chambers involved in the composition of all songs.[95] Moreover, the chance to use again two lead singers led to improvements in the vocal and choral parts.[83] Unfortunately, the album was poorly distributed and remained unknown to large parts of its potential audience.[96] In 2005, the band re-released *Believe* in a new package with a DVD containing footage taken from concerts of the 2000s and sold it through their official website.[96][97] A US and European tour followed *Believe* first release, but the project for releasing in 2004 a live DVD tentatively titled *Girlschool Live at the Garage* never materialized.[98] In June 2005, Girlschool did a UK tour with Vixen[83] and another one in November–December with old pals Motörhead, celebrating Lemmy's band 30th anniversary.[99] During the same year, they were also on stage at summer festivals in the Netherlands and England and opened for Alice Cooper in Spain.[94]

Rock and metal festivals have become a constant for the band, that performed both in large open air meetings in Germany (Headbangers Open Air 2006,[100] Bang

Your Head!!! 2007,[101] Wacken Open Air 2008[102] and Wacken Rocks 2009[103]), France (Hellfest Summer Open Air 2009[104]), England (Hard Rock Hell 2007[105] and 2009,[106] Bloodstock Open Air 2009[107]) and the USA (Power Box Festival 2007[108]) and in smaller settings, like the Rock of Ages Fest in England in 2007[109] and the Metal Female Voices Fest in Belgium in 2008.[110] Girlschool were opening act for Heaven & Hell in 2007,[101] for Dio in 2008[111] and for Hawkwind and Motörhead in 2009.[7]

On 15 July 2007, Kelly Johnson died of spinal cancer, after six years of painful therapy and treatment of her illness.[6] At Kelly's memorial, Tracey Lamb read the eulogy she had written for her.[112] The band performed a tribute gig on 20 August 2007 at the Soho Revue Bar in London, with many of Johnson's friends and former Girlschool's members[113] and a concert for Cancer Research UK at Rock of Ages Fest in Tamworth on 8 September 2007.[109]

The new album *Legacy*, released in October 2008,[114] celebrates both the departed guitarist and the 30th anniversary of Girlschool, making them the so far longest running female rock band in the world.[1][2] The recording was auto-produced with the assistance of Tim Hamill and the compositions are more individual, revealing a large array of influences, going from NWOBHM, to punk, to West Coast alternative rock.[97] To emphasize the celebrative mood, the album features many guest musicians, with members of Heaven & Hell, Twisted Sister and Motörhead supplying vocals and guitars in many tracks.[106] Kelly Johnson's 'ghost' presence permeates the album[115] and the song "Legend" is especially dedicated to her.[116] The album received excellent reviews[117][118][119] and the German label SPV/Steamhammer guaranteed the worldwide distribution. Girlschool performed a special show celebrating their 30th anniversary on 16 December at the Astoria 2 in London.[120]

Girlschool are among the many female singers performing in veteran German hard rock singer Doro Pesch's single "Celebrate", published in 2008.[121] Jackie Chambers and Enid Williams were also present on stage at Doro's 25th anniversary celebrative concert on 13 December 2008 in Düsseldorf.[122]

At the beginning of 2010, Girlschool contributed to the release of the cover of their single "Emergency" by Cornish youth music charity Livewire, in order to raise funds for the victims of the 2010 Haiti earthquake.[123] The band went on tour in Europe with the Canadian metal band Anvil in 2010.[124] The band spent time in studio re-recording their classic 1981 album *Hit and Run*, during 2011.[125] The new version of the LP, titled *Hit and Run – Revisited*, was released on 26 September 2011 to celebrate the original album's 30th anniversary.[126]

Girlschool continued to tour Europe and South America in 2011-12 and returned in Japan in 2013.[127] In early 2015, they recorded a new album titled *Guilty as Sin* with producer Chris Tsangarides,[128] which was released on 13 November 2015.[129]

2.26.2 Music and style

Enid Williams and Lemmy singing "Please Don't Touch" live in 2009. The ties that bind Motörhead and Girlschool started in the 1980s and are still strong today

Revolver magazine editor Christopher Scapelliti aptly described Girlschool's music as a "punk-metal mix tough, but poppy enough for radio".[46] The influences of classic hard rock and heavy metal are present in the musical background of all the original band members[5][12] and they are particularly evident in the clean and sometimes bluesy solo guitar work of Kelly Johnson.[130] On the other end, punk rock had a direct influence in the birth of New Wave and New Wave of British Heavy Metal and that music was still very popular when the band was born.[131][132] Moreover, both Denise Dufort and Gil Weston had played in punk bands before joining Girlschool.[10][133][134] "We're both too heavy to be New Wave and too punk to be a heavy metal band", McAuliffe explained to Robbi Millar of *Sounds* in 1980.[33] The raw and almost live recording sound of their first two Vic Maile produced albums represents perfectly the core music of the band in the years from 1979 to 1982, which were the most successful for Girlschool. The combination of metal and punk was a large part of the sound which also propelled Motörhead to notoriety and chart success in the early 80s in the United Kingdom.[33] This sound, the tours and recordings made together with Lemmy's band, the girls' denim and leather look, as much as their rowdy and alcohol driven off-stage behaviour soon gained Girlschool the moniker of 'sisters of Motörhead', which they are often still identified with today.[87] Their close association with Motörhead at the beginning of Girlschool's career was anyway a useful springboard for their early success.[15]

The mounting pressure to appeal to a mainstream audience, the quick change of tastes in British rock fans with the decline of the NWOBHM phenomenon and the chance to have a breakthrough in the US market prompted Girlschool to change their music, starting with the album *Screaming Blue Murder* in 1982.[47] Their sound, following the success of Def Leppard's album *Pyromania*,[96] became more polished with the introduction of keyboards on *Play Dirty* and veered toward hard rock and glam metal, losing the raw edge of their early works.[135] "We were signed to an American label (...) there was a certain amount of pressure exerted on us to sound more American" was McAuliffe explanation, speaking about the tame sound of the album *Running Wild*.[63] The band appearance also changed to a more feminine and sophisticated style, imitating the successful American glam metal bands of the time and generally following the direction of the market. However, the failed attempt to create a niche for Girlschool in the USA and the rapidly changing record market behaviour made the band change their mind and go back to their original sound,[70] which they retain to this day. Girlschool's members themselves described their music in different ways, from "slapstick rock"[55] to "raucous (...) heavy metal rock 'n' roll",[82] and, even acknowledging the common origin of their music in the NWOBHM,[33][35] they sometimes found it difficult to associate their songs to a single genre or subgenre of rock music.[55][130]

Just like most punk songs, Girlschool's lyrics usually have short and direct texts, often reflecting the wild rock 'n' roll lifestyle and treating sex and romance as seen from a feminine point of view, with the use of reverse sexism and tongue-in-cheek sense of humour.[11][33] Some of their songs deal also with more serious matters, such as exploitation and abuse of women,[33] murder, addiction, the destruction of the environment,[15] social and political issues.[97]

2.26.3 Reception

The fact of being a band composed of girls, beside the obvious marketing gimmick based on sexuality,[18] has always been perceived as a handicap in the sexist and male-dominated heavy metal scene,[136] especially in the early 1980s, when metal was rapidly taking the place of punk music in the tastes of many young males in Great Britain.[35] However, Girlschool's good musicianship and their aggressive but fun-loving attitude quickly won the NWOBHM audience, which treated them with respect, forming a loyal fan base.[33] In Kelly Johnson's word, Girlschool were so well accepted because "most of the audience is headbangers and they spend most of the time banging their heads and hardly look at us".[130]

We're a bunch of fun-loving, ordinary people and that's the image we always like to present.

"

"

–Kim McAuliffe[63]

In 1980, Girlschool's fondest fans formed a club called 'The Barmy Army', which followed and supported the band during every tour in Great Britain and Europe. The fan club did not survive the decline of the band and almost ceased its activities by the end of 1982.[35][74]

British specialized press took notice of the band and especially weekly magazines like *Sounds* and later *Kerrang!* dedicated covers to Girlschool and had frequent articles for either their stage performances[33][137][138] or for their off-stage drinking bouts[13] and 'no-nonsense attitude',[139] during their period of maximum media exposition and chart success.[87] In 1980, *Sounds* voted the band second 'Best Newcomer' and Kelly Johnson third 'Best Female Vocalist'.[3] Two years later, *Kerrang!* still voted Kelly Johnson second 'Best Female Vocalist' and best 'Female Pin-up'.[60] In that period, British radio stations gladly broadcast Girlschool's singles and the band was also guest of music TV shows, culminating with a performance at *Top of the Pops* on April 1981 to promote the single "Hit and Run".[140]

On the contrary, Girlschool's change of musical style in 1984 and their sudden predilection for the US market were not well received by the British press and by their fans at home.[76][135] The change of attitude and image, exemplified by the music video for "Running Wild" on rotation on MTV, which showed the girls playing with heavy make-up, combed hair and fancy costumes, imitating a trendy American glam outfit,[141] alienated the love of British fans, whose perception of the band was still that of roughneck companions to Motörhead, instead of competitors of Mötley Crüe and Ratt.[53] In the time span of two years, Girlschool passed from headliner act to having serious difficulty to find a gig in the UK: "Nobody seems to want us in Britain anymore", confessed McAuliffe to journalist Malcolm Dome in 1984.[53] The return of Girlschool to the sound of their beginnings came too late to win back the large fan base of their heyday and the band fell to cult status already in the late 1980s.[18]

2.26.4 Legacy

Pete Makowski in an article of the August 1980 edition of *Sounds* defined Girlschool "the leading pioneers in the battle against sexism".[35] However, even if Enid Williams' showed interest in feminism,[97] the band never openly expressed opinions about female discrimination, happy of being appreciated simply as musicians instead of 'female musicians'.[12] Nonetheless, the simple fact of being a successful all-female group in the macho heavy metal scene was a statement of sexual equality, as many reviewers remarked,[33][35][142] arriving as far as to associate Girlschool with the American feminist Riot Grrrl movement.[5][143]

Reviewers and critics have also often associated the production of recent all-female metal acts to the sound and music of Girlschool,[144][145] identifying them as a band that, just like The Runaways before them, helped in paving the way to the presence of women in rock music.[3][5][146] However, Williams remembered in 2004 how, in her experience, Girlschool were more inspirational for young male musicians than for female ones in starting rock bands.[97] Moreover, important female metal bands of the 2000s, such as Crucified Barbara and Drain STH, denied even of knowing the music of Girlschool.[147][148] Only the American all-female rock band The Donnas publicly acknowledged the influence of Girlschool on their music.[149]

2.26.5 Band members

For more details on this topic, see List of Girlschool band members.

Current members

- Kim McAuliffe – rhythm guitar, lead and backing vocals (1978 - present)
- Enid Williams – bass guitar, lead and backing vocals (1978 - 1982, 1990 - 1991, 2000 - present)
- Jackie Chambers – lead guitar, backing vocals (2000 - present)
- Denise Dufort – drums (1978 - present)

2.26.6 Discography

For a more comprehensive list, see Girlschool discography.

- *Demolition* (1980)
- *Hit and Run* (1981)
- *Screaming Blue Murder* (1982)
- *Play Dirty* (1983)
- *Running Wild* (1985)
- *Nightmare at Maple Cross* (1986)

- *Take a Bite* (1988)
- *Girlschool* (1992)
- *21st Anniversary: Not That Innocent* (2002)
- *Believe* (2004)
- *Legacy* (2008)
- *Hit and Run – Revisited* (2011)
- *Guilty as Sin* (2015)

2.26.7 Videography

- *Play Dirty Live* (1985)
- *Girlschool - Live from London* (2005)
- *Around the World* (2008)

2.26.8 See also

- List of New Wave of British Heavy Metal bands
- List of female heavy metal musicians
- All-female band

2.26.9 References

[1] "Reviews". *Classic Rock (magazine)*. Girlschool official website. December 2004. Retrieved 3 September 2010. ...apparently listed in The Guinness Book Of Records for being the world's longest-surviving all-female rock band

[2] "Girlschool biography". Girlschool Official Website. Retrieved 27 January 2011.

[3] Corich, Robert M. (1998). *The Collection* (CD booklet). Girlschool. England: Sanctuary Records (CMDD014).

[4] Various (1992). "Appendix to Performers / Girlschool". In Lisa Dyer. *New Illustrated Rock Handbook*. London, UK: Salamander Books Limited. p. 201. ISBN 0-86101-595-9.

[5] Graff, Gary (1997). *King Biscuit Flower Hour Presents Girlschool* (CD booklet). Girlschool. New York, NY: King Biscuit Flower Hour Records. 70710-88032-2.

[6] Tunzi, Kristina (25 August 2007). "Mileposts". *Billboard* **119** (34): 68. ISSN 0006-2510. Retrieved 31 January 2014.

[7] "Girlschool guitarist Kim McAuliffe". Fullinbloom.com. 31 July 2009. Retrieved 23 June 2010.

[8] Sharpe-Young, Garry. "Girlschool". MusicMight. Retrieved 23 June 2010.

2.26. GIRLSCHOOL

[9] "Deirdre Cartrwright Official Website". Deirdrecartwright.com. Retrieved 23 June 2010.

[10] Bradley, Vicky (8 September 2007). "Girlschool video interview 2007". Angel of Metal.com. Retrieved 29 January 2011.

[11] Harp, John (15 August 2004). "Girlschool Band Page". Tartarean Desire Webzine. Retrieved 29 August 2010.

[12] "Girlschool interview". Ddays-revenge.com. 29 July 2004. Retrieved 23 June 2010.

[13] Kilmister, Ian and Garza, Janiss *White Line Fever* (2002) – Simon & Schuster pp. 126-128 ISBN 0-684-85868-1.

[14] Ricetti, Stefano (28 October 2008). "Girlschool (Denise Dufort)" (in Italian). Truemetal.it. Retrieved 23 June 2010.

[15] Shelton, Robert (1982). "Girlschool". In Liz Thomson. *New Women in Rock*. Omnibus Press. pp. 62–63. ISBN 0-7119-0055-8.

[16] Ling, Dave (18 Dec 1999). "Interview with Gerry Bron". *Classic Rock (magazine)* **9**. Bath, UK: Future Publishing.

[17] Bowar, Chad. "What Is New Wave Of British Heavy Metal?". About.com. Retrieved 31 December 2010.

[18] Vengadesan, Martin (20 July 2008). "Girlschool of rock". The Star (Malaysia). Retrieved 23 June 2010.

[19] "Girlschool". *Melody Maker*. 8 March 1980. Retrieved 27 January 2011.

[20] "The Isle of Wight Festivals 1968-70". UKRockfestivals.com. July 2010. Retrieved 27 January 2011.

[21] "Vic Maile Credits". *Allmusic*. Rovi Corporation. Retrieved 27 January 2011.

[22] Strong, Martin C. (1995). *The Great Rock Discography*. Edinburgh, Great Britain: Canongate Books. p. 326. ISBN 0-86241-541-1.

[23] "Girlschool - UK Singles & Albums Chart Archive". Chart Stats. Archived from the original on 21 October 2012. Retrieved 10 December 2010.

[24] "Judas Priest chart stats". Chart Stats. Archived from the original on 20 September 2012. Retrieved 2013-04-27.

[25] "Saxon - UK Singles & Albums Chart Archive". Chart Stats. Archived from the original on 21 October 2012. Retrieved 27 January 2011.

[26] "Def Leppard - UK Singles & Albums Chart Archive". Chart Stats. Archived from the original on 20 September 2012. Retrieved 27 January 2011.

[27] "Iron Maiden - UK Singles & Albums Chart Archive". Chart Stats. Archived from the original on 21 October 2012. Retrieved 27 January 2011.

[28] "Motorhead - UK Singles & Albums Chart Archive". Chart Stats. Archived from the original on 11 October 2012. Retrieved 27 January 2011.

[29] "Judas Priest - Tourdates Archive". Jugulator.net. Retrieved 2013-04-28.

[30] "Def Leppard On Through The Night Tour 1980 -- UK/Europe". Darren's UK Def Leppard Site. Retrieved 27 January 2011.

[31] "Iron Maiden tour April - December 1980". The Iron Maiden Commentary. Retrieved 27 January 2011.

[32] "Motörhead past tour dates 1980". Motörhead Official Website. Retrieved 27 January 2011.

[33] Millar, Robbi (1 March 1980). "The Dinosaur's Daughters". *Sounds*. Retrieved 30 December 2010.

[34] "BFI - Film & TV Database - ROCKSTAGE". British Film Institute. Retrieved 2 January 2011.

[35] Makowski, Pete (9 August 1980). "Back to Schooldays". *Sounds*. Retrieved 3 January 2011.

[36] Kilmister, Ian and Garza, Janiss *White Line Fever* (2002) – Simon & Schuster pp. 144 ISBN 0-684-85868-1.

[37] Burridge, Alan; Stevenson, Mick (1994). *Illustrated Collector's Guide to Motörhead*. Burlington, Ontario, Canada: Collector's Guide Publishing. ISBN 0-9695736-2-6.

[38] "Top 40 Official UK Singles Archive 28th February 1981". The Official Charts Company. Retrieved 21 June 2010.

[39] "BPI Certified Awards Searchable Database". BPI. Retrieved 14 August 2010. search keywords 'motorhead & girls school'

[40] "Girlschool - Hit and Run (Album)". Charts.org.nz. Retrieved 14 August 2010.

[41] "Top Albums/CDs - Volume 35, No. 4, July 04, 1981". Library and Archives Canada. 4 July 1981. Retrieved 14 August 2010.

[42] "Gold Platinum Database - Title:Hit and Run". Music Canada. Retrieved 22 November 2011.

[43] Tucker, John (2006). "Denise Dufort on Girlschool's Support Bands". *Suzie Smiles... The New Wave of British Heavy Metal*. Church Stretton, Shropshire, UK: Independent Music Press. p. 69. ISBN 978-0-9549704-7-5.

[44] "The 21st Reading Rock Festival". UKRockfestivals.com. January 2010. Retrieved 21 June 2010.

[45] Matera, Joe (February 2005). "It's Electric!". *Classic Rock* **76**. London, UK: Future Publishing. p. 54.

[46] Scapelliti, Christopher (March 2006). "Everything you ever wanted to know about Girlschool". *Revolver*. New York, NY: Future US. p. 114.

[47] Rivadavia, Eduardo. "Screaming Blue Murder review". Allmusic. Retrieved 21 June 2010.

[48] Ogg, Alex (5 October 2006). *No More Heroes: a Complete History of UK Punk from 1976 to 1980*. London, UK: Cherry Red Books. ISBN 978-1-901447-65-1.

[49] "Nigel Gray credits". *Allmusic*. Rovi Corporation. Retrieved 29 January 2011.

[50] Tuffnell, Scott (22 May 2010). "Girlschool Screaming Blue Murder". Metal Music Archives. Retrieved 4 January 2011.

[51] "Blackout Tour 1982 - 1983". Scorpions official website. Retrieved 23 June 2010.

[52] Rivadavia, Eduardo. "1-2-3-4 Rock'n'Roll EP review". *Allmusic*. Rovi Corporation. Retrieved 30 January 2011.

[53] Dome, Malcolm (3 May 1984). "Roots March". *Kerrang!* **67**. London, UK: Morgan Grampian. p. 9.

[54] Prato, Greg. "Slade biography". Allmusic. Retrieved 17 January 2011.

[55] James, Gary (1985). "Gil Weston Interview". FamousInterview.com. Retrieved 31 December 2010.

[56] Prato, Greg. "21st Anniversary: Not That Innocent review". Allmusic. Retrieved 15 August 2010.

[57] Rivadavia, Eduardo. "Play Dirty review". Allmusic. Retrieved 25 August 2010.

[58] "Chart History of "Girlschool - Play Dirty"". Chart Stats. Retrieved 30 January 2011.

[59] Dome, Malcolm (26 June 1986). "Kelly Johnson". *Kerrang!* **123**. London, UK: United Magazines ltd. p. 41.

[60] Various (30 December 1982). "Female pin-up". *Kerrang!*. Kerrang 1982 Poll Winners **32** (London, UK: Morgan Grampian). p. 5.

[61] van Poorten, Toine (7 April 2008). "Back To The Past (15): Rock Goddess". Metalmaidens.com. Retrieved 2 January 2011.

[62] Suter, Paul (5 April 1984). "She - Marquee, London". *Kerrang!* **65**. London, UK: Morgan Grampian. p. 39.

[63] Johnson, Howard (30 October 1986). "Hear No Evil". *Kerrang!* **132**. London, UK: United Magazines ltd. pp. 10–11.

[64] "Nick Tauber credits". *Allmusic*. Rovi Corporation. Retrieved 29 January 2011.

[65] Johnson, Howard (3 October 1985). "Girlschool 'Running Wild'". *Kerrang!* **104**. London, UK: Morgan Grampian. p. 14.

[66] "Girlschool - Play Dirty Live". Encyclopaedia Metallum. Retrieved 17 July 2010.

[67] "Girlschool - Live From London". EzyDVD. 2006. Retrieved 17 July 2010.

[68] Dome, Malcolm (1984). *Extra Kerrang!* **3**. Morgan Grampian. p. 56.

[69] "The Deep Purple Reunion, 1985...". Deep-purple.net. Retrieved 28 June 2010.

[70] "Girlschool Bio". *Roadrunner Records press release for* Take a Bite (Roadrunner Records). 3 October 1988.

[71] Dome, Malcolm (2 October 1986). "Girlschool - Nightmare At Maple Cross". *Kerrang!* **130**. London, UK: United Magazines ltd. p. 21.

[72] Christgau, Robert (1987). "Girlschool Nightmare at Maple Cross review". Robert Christgau. Retrieved 4 January 2011.

[73] Dome, Malcolm (28 May 1987). "Girlschool". *Kerrang!* **147**. London, UK: Spotlight Publications Ltd. p. 7.

[74] Sidiropoulos, Georgios (December 2004). "Girlschool interview". Tartarean Desire Webzine. Retrieved 4 July 2010.

[75] Hill, Gary. "Take a Bite review". *Allmusic*. Rovi Corporation. Retrieved 30 January 2011.

[76] Watts, Chris (19 November 1988). "Once Bitten... Twice Dry". *Kerrang!* **214**. London, UK: Spotlight Publications Ltd. pp. 28–29.

[77] Dwyer, Robert (2003). "Shows - Headless Cross". Sabbathlive.com. Archived from the original on 15 April 2008. Retrieved 4 July 2010.

[78] "Toyah & Cris Bonacci - Brilliant Day". YouTube. 23 October 2006. Retrieved 28 January 2011.

[79] "Women in Music history". Women in Music.org. Retrieved 29 June 2010.

[80] Knoll, Alex. "Out In The Green Festival". Retrieved 16 January 2011.

[81] Michinari, Yamada (1994). "1992". *Take the Leap!* (CD Booklet). Toyah Willcox. Japan: Discipline Records. p. 4.

[82] "Girlschool - Jackie and Kim interview". YouTube. 23 October 2006. Retrieved 4 July 2010.

[83] Sidiropoulos, Georgios (2005). "Girlschool & Vixen Live". Tartarean Desire Webzine. Retrieved 4 July 2010.

[84] "Chris Bonacci credits". *Allmusic*. Rovi Corporation. Retrieved 31 January 2011.

[85] "Kim and Kelly interview". *Raw Power*. YouTube. June 1993. Retrieved 29 January 2011.

[86] Drury, Anne. "World's Cutest Killers Page". *Anne's Guitar Tab Archive*. Angelfire. Retrieved 29 January 2011.

[87] van Poorten, Rita (1995). "The sisters of Motörhead on crusade". Metalmaidens.com. Retrieved 23 June 2010.

[88] "Girlschool - Girlschool Live". Encyclopaedia Metallum. Retrieved 25 May 2010.

[89] "Wacken 1999 Running order" (JPG). Wacken Open Air. 1999. Retrieved 12 September 2010.

[90] "Girlschool Interview with Jackie "Jax" Chambers". Morbidzine.com. 26 March 2010. Retrieved 31 January 2011.

[91] van Poorten, Toine (June 2002). "Girlschool 21st Anniversary - Not That Innocent". *Metal Maidens* **28**. Leerdam, The Netherlands.

[92] "Paul Di'Anno, Girlschool, Tygers of Pan Tang To Team Up For European Tour". *Blabbermouth.net*. Roadrunner Records. 24 June 2004. Retrieved 30 December 2010.

[93] "GIRLSCHOOL Name New Album: Audio Available". *Blabbermouth.net*. Roadrunner Records. 1 July 2004. Retrieved 27 January 2011.

[94] "Interview with Jackie Chambers". Jevitron.com. 2006. Retrieved 5 July 2010.

[95] "Reviews". *Classic Rock (magazine)*. Girlschool official website. December 2004. Retrieved 3 September 2010.

[96] Geesin, Joe (2005). "Interview: Girlschool". Get Ready to Rock! .com. Retrieved 5 July 2010.

[97] "L'intervista a Enid Williams" (in Italian). Long Live Rock n Roll.it. 3 October 2008. Retrieved 14 March 2010.

[98] "Girlschool Set Tentative Title For Live DVD". *Blabbermouth.net*. Roadrunner Records. 6 September 2004. Retrieved 30 December 2010.

[99] "Girlschool to support Motörhead in UK". *Blabbermouth.net*. Roadrunner Records. 15 April 2005. Retrieved 30 December 2010.

[100] "Headbanger's Open Air History". Headbangers Open Air. Retrieved 6 July 2010.

[101] "Bang Your Head!!! History". Bang Your Head!!! Festival. Retrieved 6 July 2010.

[102] "Billing/Bands 2008". Wacken Open Air. Retrieved 6 July 2010.

[103] "Wacken Rocks 2009 (Seaside) Lineup". Virtual Festivals.com. Retrieved 31 January 2011.

[104] "Hellfest 2009 (Photos de Murder-One)" (in French). Metalcroniques Photos. Retrieved 6 July 2010.

[105] "Hard Rock Hell 2007 Lineup". Virtual Festivals.com. Retrieved 31 January 2011.

[106] "Girlschool's Kim McAuliffe Interviewed On UK's Rock Radio - Dec. 9, 2009". *Blabbermouth.net*. Roadrunner Records. 9 December 2009. Retrieved 6 July 2010.

[107] "Bloodstock Open Air 2009 Lineup". Virtual Festivals.com. Retrieved 31 January 2011.

[108] "Kittie, Doro, Vixen, Girlschool Confirmed For Power Box Festival - July 14, 2007". *Blabbermouth.net*. Roadrunner Records. 14 July 2007. Retrieved 6 July 2010.

[109] Regards, Steve (30 August 2008). "Il metal festival Rock of Ages parte con i Tygers of Pan Tang". Musicalnews.com. Retrieved 31 January 2011.

[110] "MFVF 6 poster" (JPG). Metal Female Voice Fest. Retrieved 6 July 2010.

[111] "Dio past tour dates". Official Ronnie James Dio Website. Retrieved 31 January 2011.

[112] Lamb, Tracey (24 July 2007). "Kelly Johnson Eulogy". Girlschool official website. Retrieved 6 July 2010.

[113] Ling, Dave (26 September 2007). "Members of Girlschool perform at Tribute gig Aug 20th 2007". MySpace.com. Retrieved 6 July 2010.

[114] "GIRLSCHOOL: 'Legacy' Gydget Available". *Blabbermouth.net*. Roadrunner Records. 1 October 2008. Retrieved 27 January 2011.

[115] "GIRLSCHOOL: 'Legacy' Details Revealed". *Blabbermouth.net*. Roadrunner Records. 28 August 2008. Retrieved 1 February 2011.

[116] Chambers, Jackie (2008). ""Legend"". *Legacy* (CD Booklet). Girlschool. Dörpstedt, Germany: Wacken Records. p. 4.

[117] Henderson, Alex. "Legacy Review". Allmusic. Retrieved 15 August 2010.

[118] "Girlschool - Legacy review". Metal Storm. 9 December 2008. Retrieved 15 August 2010.

[119] Bowar, Chad. "Girlschool Legacy review". About.com. Retrieved 15 August 2010.

[120] "Blitzkrieg added to Girlschool anniversary show". *Blabbermouth.net*. Roadrunner Records. 8 December 2008. Retrieved 30 December 2010.

[121] "Doro: 'Celebrate (The Night Of The Warlock)'". *Blabbermouth.net*. Roadrunner Records. 10 October 2008. Retrieved 7 July 2010.

[122] "Doro 25th Anniversary". Metal-Experience.com. 2008. Retrieved 7 July 2010.

[123] "Girlschool's 'Emergency' Provides A Livewire To Haiti". *Blabbermouth.net*. Roadrunner Records. 17 February 2010. Retrieved 30 December 2010.

[124] Milligan, Glenn (7 July 2010). "Anvil/Girlschool – O2 Academy 2, Sheffield, Wednesday 7th July 2010". Metalliville webzine. Retrieved 1 January 2011.

[125] "Girlschool Re-Recording Classic 'Hit And Run' Album". *Blabbermouth.net*. Roadrunner Records. 10 December 2010. Retrieved 13 December 2010.

[126] "Girlschool Frontwoman Comments On 'Hit And Run Revisited' Album". *Blabbermouth.net*. Roadrunner Records. 14 September 2011. Retrieved 26 September 2011.

[127] "Japanese Assault Fest 13" (in Japanese). Spiritual Beast.com. Retrieved 2014-03-23.

[128] "Girlschool Putting Finishing Touches On 'Guilty As Sin' Album, Preparing For U.S. Tour". Blabbermouth.net. 4 March 2015. Retrieved 2015-03-08.

[129] "Girlschool To Release 'Guilty As Sin' Album In November". Blabbermouth.net. 9 September 2015. Retrieved 13 November 2015.

[130] "Kelly Johnson - Making Music in a Man's World". *Guitar World*: pp. 20. March 1984. Retrieved 27 December 2010.

[131] Gendron, Bernard (2002). *Between Montmartre and the Mudd Club: Popular Music and the Avant-Garde*. Chicago and London: University of Chicago Press. pp. 269–270. ISBN 0-226-28735-1.

[132] Erlewine, Stephen. "Motörhead Biography". Allmusic. Retrieved 19 December 2008. Motörhead wasn't punk rock... but they were the first metal band to harness that energy and, in the process, they created speed metal and thrash metal.

[133] Dufort, Denise (17 July 2009). "The School- 07-17-2009". Girlschool official forum. Retrieved 5 December 2010.

[134] Marko, Paul. "Interview - Gil Weston". Girlschool Unofficial site. Retrieved 28 January 2011.

[135] Huey, Steve. "King Biscuit Flower Hour Presents In Concert review". Allmusic. Retrieved 1 January 2011.

[136] Pinsonneault, Julie (19 March 2007). "Women in Metal". Stylus Magazine. Retrieved 1 February 2011.

[137] Ravendale, Ian (19 July 1980). "Demolition Derby". *Sounds*. Retrieved 5 January 2011.

[138] Jeffries, Neil (30 December 1983). "Girlschool Forest National, Brussel". *Kerrang!* 32. London, UK: Morgan Grampian. p. 37.

[139] Perrone, Pierre (17 July 2007). "Kelly Johnson obituary". *The Independent* (Independent Print ltd.). Retrieved 8 July 2010.

[140] "Hit & Run TOTP - Girlschool". YouTube. 30 December 2006. Retrieved 28 January 2011.

[141] ""Running Wild" video clip". YouTube. 4 November 2008. Retrieved 29 June 2010.

[142] Laing, Dave (23 July 2007). "Kelly Johnson obituary". *Guardian.co.uk*. Guardian Media Group. Retrieved 14 July 2010.

[143] Rivadavia, Eduardo. "Nightmare at Maple Cross review". Allmusic. Retrieved 5 January 2011.

[144] Chun, Kimberly (24 August 2010). "Girlschool 2010". *San Francisco Bay Guardian*. Retrieved 5 January 2011.

[145] "Crucified Barbara Bio". Retrieved 5 January 2011.

[146] Prato, Greg. "Girlschool biography". Allmusic. Retrieved 5 January 2011.

[147] Ansali, Paolo (3 July 2007). "Crucified Barbara: we love the italian audience!!" (in Italian). Musicalnews.com. Retrieved 5 January 2011.

[148] Kelter, Cristopher J. (14 August 1999). "Drain Sth - Don't call them Girlschool". Roughedge.com. Retrieved 5 January 2011.

[149] Robertson, Allison (18 July 2007). "The Donnas' Robertson Reacts To Kelly Johnson's Death". Rockdirt.com. Retrieved 5 January 2011.

2.26.10 External links

- Official website

2.27 Grim Reaper (band)

Grim Reaper are a British heavy metal band from the New Wave of British Heavy Metal era. The band was formed in 1979 in Droitwich, England, by guitarist Nick Bowcott.[1]

2.27.1 History

Early years (1979-1984)

They were discovered after winning a Battle of the Bands featuring over 100 bands. They were eventually signed to Darryl Johnston's Ebony Records, and their debut album was *See You in Hell*. The album was released in 1984 and was distributed worldwide through RCA Records.

Commercial success (1985-1986)

Grim Reaper soon became readily identifiable with Bowcott's guitar work and lead vocalist Steve Grimmett's head voice vocals. Their successful world tour included a support show at Texxas Jam playing to over 20,000 people. Their 1985 follow-up, *Fear No Evil*, showed improvement on the production front and also enjoyed moderate success in both the United States and Europe.

Legal battles and later years (1987-1988)

Legal battles with Ebony Records delayed the release of the band's third album *Rock You to Hell* by almost two years. The album was released directly through RCA Records in 1987. However, by this time Grim Reaper's melodic Heavy metal sound had fallen out of favor as much of the metal market moved toward heavier fare like thrash metal and speed metal. Even the major label distribution and popular video for the title track could not save the band. With the production of their fourth studio album (reportedly to be called *Nothing Whatsoever to Do with Hell*) about to start, another round of legal action from Ebony Records effectively dealt the death blow to Grim Reaper, subsequently disbanding in 1988.

Side projects (1988-2006)

Grimmett went on to front Onslaught and Lionsheart, as well as perform on several tribute albums. Bowcott became a freelance music writer, and later staff contributor, for publications like Circus and Guitar World. Bowcott also worked with Marshall Amplification's United States division. He also played in the band Barfly who recorded an album with Jack Ponti producing and Michael Wagener mixing for RCA records.

Current (2006-present)

In 2006, Eddie Trunk announced on Metal Mania that the band has reformed. The "original" lineup of Grim Reaper (without Nick Bowcott) played the Keep It True VI festival in Lauda-Königshoffen on 8 April 2006. The band played the annual MetalBrew festival in London's Mill Hill on Saturday 18 July 2009. Later they were scheduled to play at the Play it Loud IV in Bologna, Italy, in September 2009. The festival was then cancelled when the promoter forfeited, but the band (urged on by a crowd of fans who had already bought tickets) managed to play the date along with a number of originally billed acts (as a single-day event instead of a weekend-spanning one).[2]

The band made a successful appearance at the British Steel festival in Bolognia Italy in November 2010 at the Estragon venue on a bill that included other classic bands of the NWoBHM era - Diamond Head, Girlschool, Demon and Angelwitch. They also played at the Academy Birmingham with the band Jameson Raid.

The current line-up continues to tour the UK and Europe. They did a short tour of Greece and Cyprus in November 2011 and released the Limited Edition "Live in Europe 2011". Festival appearances in 2012 included Sweden's "Muskelrock" and headlining Germany's Sword Brothers.

In spring 2013, Steve Grimmett's Grim Reaper will be recording a new studio album, their first since 1987, for release later in the year. The band are confirmed as headliners of this year's British Steel festival in London in June and co-headliners of Belgium's Heavy Sound Festival in November with Tokyo Blade. More European Festivals and a US tour are planned for 2013.

In April 2014, Grim Reaper played their first show in the US since 1987, joined by original guitarist Nick Bowcott, and featured several tracks from the forthcoming album, *From Hell*.[3]

2.27.2 Band members

2.27.3 Discography

Studio albums

- *See You in Hell* (1983)
- *Fear No Evil* (1985)
- *Rock You to Hell* (1987)
- *From Hell* (2015)

Compilation albums

- *Heavy Metal Heroes* (1981) with the song "The Reaper" and in an earlier line-up including Paul DeMacardo - vocals, Nick Bowcott - guitar, Dave Wanklin - bass and Adrian Jacques - drums.
- *See You in Hell/Fear No Evil* (1999)
- *Best of Grim Reaper* (1999)

2.27.4 In popular culture

A slightly re-edited version of the video for Grim Reaper's 1985 hit "Fear No Evil" was initially used as the video for Weezer's song "We Are All on Drugs". That song (plus "Rock You to Hell" & "See You in Hell") all appeared in episodes of Beavis and Butt-head, with the duo mocking the songs and videos. Grim Reaper's song "Lust for Freedom" was used as the title track for a 1987 women's prison movie of the same name.

2.27.5 See also

- List of New Wave of British Heavy Metal bands

2.27.6 References

[1] "Grim Reaper". Angel Fire. Retrieved 12 May 2014.

[2] (registration required)

[3] "Original Grim Reaper Members Steve Grimmett and Nick Bowcott Interviewed at RAGNARÖKKR METAL APOCALYPSE (Video)". *Blabbermouth*. 22 April 2014. Retrieved 12 May 2014.

2.27.7 External links

- Grim Reaper "Official" Facebook page
- Grim Reaper at AllMusic
- Grim Reaper at Yahoo! Music

2.28 Haze (band)

Haze (1978–1988, 1998–present) are an English progressive rock band from Sheffield, England, mainly active in England in the 1980s.[1]

2.28.1 History

Formed in 1978 by the brothers Chris McMahon (bass, keyboards and vocals), and Paul McMahon (guitar and vocals), they played their first concert at Stephen Hill Youth Club, Sheffield on 10 November that year.[1] They had several drummers before the longest serving and most notable, Paul 'Chis' Chisnell, joined them at a concert at the White Lion, Huddersfield, on 19 June 1983.[1]

The band's first full album, *C'est La Vie*, was released on vinyl with a special concert at Sheffield's The Leadmill on 7 April 1984.[2]

Following a "final" sell-out gig at Sheffield University, the trio split up on the 10th anniversary of the band's founding, 29 May 1988,[1] but reunited for a "one-off" concert to mark the 20th anniversary, on 31 May 1998 at The Boardwalk, Sheffield.[1] They now play together on an occasional basis, and played two 30th anniversary gigs at The Peel, Kingston-upon-Thames, London on 31 May, and at The Boardwalk on 1 June 2008,[1] at which six new songs were performed.

Despite achieving no chart success, and never having a recording contract (they released their own albums, on their 'Gabadon' label), they attracted a considerable cult following, headlined at The Marquee,[1] and their original albums are highly sought after collectors' items.

In March 2013 the band released their first studio album in 26 years, called *The Last Battle*. The album features the band in its classic line-up (Paul and Chris McMahon and Paul Chisnell) with the addition of Ceri Ashton (on whistle, flute, cello, viola and clarinet) and Catrin Ashton (on fiddle and flute). The band have stated that this is the final recorded performance with their long time drummer Paul Chisnell. Following the release of the album Paul McMahon's son Danny McMahon will be playing drums with Haze.

2.28.2 Images

The band at a concert in the early 1980s

- Chris McMahon
- Paul McMahon
- Paul Chisnell

2.28.3 Discography

- *The Night*
- *The Cellar Tapes*
- *C'est La Vie* (1984)
- *Cellar Replay* (1985)
- *The Ember*
- *Warts'n'All* (live album) (1986)
- *Old New Burrowed & Blue*
- *Tunnel Vision/Shadows*
- *Stoat & Bottle* (1987)
- *The Peterborough Tapes*
- *Humphrey*
- *The 10th Anniversary Gig*
- *Last Orders*
- *In The End: 1978-88*
- *In Concert*
- *C'est La Vie/The Ember*
- *20th Anniversary Show* (1998)
- *30th Anniversary Show* (2008)
- *The Last Battle* (2013)

2.28.4 References

[1] "Haze/World Turtle/Von Daniken Gig List". Retrieved 26 November 2011.

[2] "Haze (UK) C'est la Vie". Retrieved 21 February 2013.

2.28.5 External links

- Official site
- Haze discography at MusicBrainz
- Haze at Allmusic.com

2.29 Hell (band)

Hell are an English heavy metal band from Derbyshire, formed in 1982 from the remaining members of bands Race Against Time and Paralex. Due to a series of unfortunate and tragic events, the band originally folded in 1987. They were amongst the first bands to wear proto-corpse paint as part of their stage show, which features hysterical ranting from a Gargoyle-adorned pulpit, along with the use of a pyrotechnic exploding Bible which caused outrage amongst the clergy when it originally appeared in 1983.

Although they were largely ignored by the media and record companies in the 1980s, their music became known through the underground tape trading phenomenon, and the band achieved a degree of cult status. In 2008 they reunited, and were signed by Nuclear Blast.[1] Their first full-length album, *Human Remains*, was released May 2011.[2] The album topped at No. 46 on the German album chart in its first week of release.[3]

2.29.1 Biography

Early years (1982-1987)

Hell was founded in 1982, in Derbyshire, England.

They signed to the Belgian label Mausoleum Records, but two weeks prior to the recording of their debut album, the label collapsed into bankruptcy. Guitarist Kev Bower subsequently quit the band. He was briefly replaced by Sean Kelley, though Hell split up soon afterwards, which led to the suicide of vocalist Dave Halliday by carbon monoxide poisoning.

Dave Halliday taught Andy Sneap (later to form heavy metal band Sabbat) to play guitar and Sneap mentions Hell as one of his main influences.[4] Sneap subsequently went onto become a world-renowned record producer, with over 100 albums and a Swedish Grammy Award to his credit.

Reformation (2008-2011)

The remaining original members of Hell reunited in 2008 to finally record their album which was entitled *Human Remains*. Sabbat members Martin Walkyier and Andy Sneap agreed to play on the album to replicate Dave Halliday's vocals and guitar tracks respectively, with Sneap also acting as the producer. Although Walkyier spent a few evenings (not the 'several months' he often claims in frequent social media rants) recording test vocals for various songs on the album, this process was halted once it became clear that his vocal style and somewhat ascerbic temperament were unsuitable for the task. Kev Bower's brother David (who is known as David Beckford in his career as a stage and television actor) was invited to do a voiceover for the song "Plague And Fyre" and subsequently joined the band as lead vocalist, re-recording all the lead vocal parts. Sneap subsequently also joined the band as their permanent second guitarist.

2011

The new lineup played their first gig at the MFN club in Nottingham on 20/05/2011, playing songs from Human Remains and also Race Against Time's "Bedtime" as a tribute to David Halliday.[5] This was rapidly followed up by a run of festival shows in Europe and the UK, including Metalfest Open Airs in Switzerland, Germany and Austria, Rockstad Falun in Sweden, UK's Download Festival, Tuska Open Air Metal Festival in Finland, Summer Breeze Open Air in Germany, and Bloodstock Open Air in the UK, for which they received the "2011 Best Mainstage Performance" vote. The band then went onto perform on the Sweden Rock Cruise, and closed out 2011 by having the *Human Remains* album being awarded Sweden Rock Magazine's "2011 Album Of The Year", as well as attaining position No. 6 in the Metal Hammer 'Best Of 2011' list. The album also attained "Best Of 2011" accolades on many internet webzines, as well as being nominated "2011 Album Of The Year" on the Bloodstock Open Air user forum.

2012

Hell opened their 2012 show run with a mainstage appearance at the Hammerfest in Prestatyn, North Wales. This was followed by the band gaining a prestigious support slot with Accept for the whole of their "Stalingrad" European tour, which started at Le Bataclan in Paris on 6 April.[6] The band were also nominated for a Metal Hammer Golden Gods Awards in the magazine's "Metal As F*ck" category. Numerous additional European shows were also played, including the Rock Hard Festival at the German Gelsenkirchen Amphitheatre, with this show being filmed and subsequently broadcast by WDR TV on the long-running Rockpalast mainstream TV show. Scandinavian shows included headlining appearances at the Muskelrock and Metal Magic festivals in Sweden and Denmark respectively, along with a Sweden Stage appearance at the Sweden Rock Festival. The band also featured in the July 2012 issue of the UK's *Metal Hammer* magazine, in which they appeared in a 3-page article. Hell's 2012 tour run also included their first shows in Eastern Europe at the Masters of Rock (festival) in the Czech Republic and Metalcamp in Slovenia, along with appearances at the Alcatraz (BE), Zwarte Cross (NL), and Into The Grave (NL) festivals. They closed out the year with headlining appearances in Dublin (IRE), a town festival at Molins de Rei near Barcelona (ES), and played their final show of 2012 at Rommelrock in Maasmechelen (BE), thus completing the 'Human Remains' tour run which had taken the band to no less than 16 different countries. Hell also entered the studio late in the year to commence work on the follow-up album to *Human Remains*.

2013

By the beginning of 2013, Kev Bower and Andy Sneap had completed demo recordings for the majority of songs which would appear on the band's sophomore album, with recording proper set to commence in the Spring. Since no early demo recordings were this time available to fill a bonus disc, the band elected to record a live DVD as a bonus complement to the album, and this was shot and recorded at the band's first 2013 show at Derby Assembly Rooms (UK) on 23 February. The sell out event also unveiled the band's full *Church Of Hell* stage set and pyrotechnic show, with fans travelling from 13 different countries to attend. The band played a headline show at the R-Mine Metalfest (BE) and also appeared at Turock Open Air (DE), Hammer Open Air (FIN), Bang Your Head Open Air (DE) and made a return mainstage appearance at Bloodstock Open Air as one of the most heavily requested bands on the BOA user forum, and once again won the 'Best Mainstage Performance' vote. It was subsequently discovered that technical problems with the DVD recording at Derby had made some material unsalvageable, so additional footage was added from the band's appearance at this festival.

It was announced in August that the second album would be entitled 'Curse and Chapter'. To coincide with the album release, Hell were subsequently announced as being principal support for Amon Amarth and Carcass on the whole of their extensive European tour, taking in 25 shows in 13 countries, opening in Oberhausen (DE) on 7 November.[7]

2014 and present

The first three months of 2014 saw the band on a temporary hiatus as Andy Sneap had production commitments in the USA with Accept and Exodus. The first large-scale show of 2014 was announced as being at Hyde Park in London, playing alongside Black Sabbath. The band played a warm-up show to this event at The Rescue Rooms in Nottingham. Following a main slot at the Leyendas Del Rock event in Alicante (ES) and a W.E.T.Stage appearance the 2014 Wacken Open Air festival, Andy Sneap and Kev Bower took to the saddle for charity on behalf of the band, participating in a 260 km cycle ride from London to Download Festival to raise money for the NSPCC, the Teenage Cancer Trust and Nordoff Robbins. The band played a run of shows in Europe supporting Kreator and Arch Enemy, immediately followed by a UK tour supporting Saxon throughout November and December. On the eve of the show at Newcastle 02 Academy, however, Saxon's drummer Nigel Glockler was rushed to hospital with a brain aneurysm, resulting in the last five shows being postponed until February 2015.

On August 5 2015, the band announced that after their last live show of 2015 in Finland, they will be starting work on their third studio album.[8]

2.29.2 Musical style

Hell are most often described as a NWOBHM band, although they strongly distance themselves from this movement, citing that the NWOBHM was already in rapid decline by the time the band actually formed. Their progressive musical style incorporates elements of thrash, power, symphonic, gothic, speed, doom and black metal, encompassing great variety, and with no two songs ever sounding exactly alike. Underlying lyrical themes in much Hell material focuses on the occult and the darker sides of human nature. Typical themes include a distaste for organised religion, alien abduction, political imprisonment, mental illness, and historical events such as the Black Death and the Bubonic Plague. Although primarily guitar-driven, the band's sound is fleshed out by the use of keyboards and digital sampling to add depth and texture to the material. Their approach to song writing is often unorthodox, with numerous complex tempo, time signature and key changes, along with a signature series of atmospheric, theatrical interludes and introductions to their songs.

2.29.3 Band members

Current

- David Bower - vocals (2010–present)
- Kev Bower - guitar, keyboard, vocals (1982–1987, 2008–present)
- Tim Bowler - drums (1982–1987, 2008–present)
- Andy Sneap - guitar (2008–present)
- Tony Speakman - bass (1982–1987, 2008–present)

Past

- Dave G. Halliday - vocals, guitar (1982–1987) (deceased)
- Sean Kelley - guitar (1987)

2.29.4 Discography

Studio albums

- *Human Remains* (2011, Nuclear Blast)
- *Curse and Chapter* (2013, Nuclear Blast)
- TBA

EPs

- *Save Us from Those Who Would Save Us* (1983, Self-financed by the band and released on their own 'Deadly Weapon' label, also included "Deathsquad")
- *Save Us* (2011, Nuclear Blast - also included "On Earth as It Is in Hell")
- *The Age Of Nefarious* (2013, Nuclear Blast)
- *End Ov Days* (2014, Nuclear Blast) - produced in support of the 2014 tour and given away free at shows

DVD's

- *The Greatest Show On Earth - As It Is In Hell* (2013, 'Curse And Chapter' bonus disc)

Videos

- *Deathsquad* (1983) - Shot in Derbyshire and at Wingfield Manor
- *On Earth as It Is in Hell* (2011) - Shot at Wingfield Manor

2.29.5 References

[1] "HELL - Nuclear Blast". Nuclearblast.de. Retrieved 2014-07-28.

[2] Phil Freeman (2011-05-17). "Human Remains - Hell | Songs, Reviews, Credits, Awards". AllMusic. Retrieved 2014-07-28.

[3] "charts.de". Officialcharts.de. 2011-05-13. Retrieved 2014-07-28.

[4] *METAL FORCES* No 25, 15 August 1987

[5] "Hell Live at the MFN Club, Nottingham | Gig Reviews". CackBlabbath. Retrieved 2014-07-28.

[6] "Hell live at the Bataclan in Paris, France, April 6 2012". Metal Traveller. 2012-04-06. Retrieved 2014-07-28.

[7] "AMON AMARTH: Deceiver of the Gods European headline tour announced". Metalblade.com. Retrieved 22 August 2013.

[8] "HELL: Start Working On Third Album". *Metal Shock Finland* (Metal Shock Finland). 5 August 2015. Retrieved 5 August 2015.

2.29.6 External links

- Hell at AllMusic
- Official Website
- Hell official myspace website

2.30 HellsBelles

Not to be confused with Hell's bells.

HellsBelles (formerly known as **Hell's Belles**) is a heavy metal band from England active from 1984 to 1987 and 1998 to present, considered part of the latter stages of the New Wave of British Heavy Metal (NWOBHM).

2.30.1 1980s - Hell's Belles

They gained a considerable following and achieved major airplay and media coverage, with radio plays on Tommy Vance's BBC Radio 1 Friday Rock Show, on lead singer Paul Quigley's Mancunian friend Terry Christian's award-winning radio show 'Barbed Wireless' on BBC Radio Derby during the band's 80s heydey, as well as on pirate rock station Alice's Restaurant Rock Radio.

In the press, the band received rave coverage for both their live performances and recordings in metal magazines *Kerrang!*[1] and *Metal Forces*.

They were unusual for their time for playing a distinct mix of punk rock and more traditional heavy metal, a genre subsequently emulated by many bands such as Metallica and others. The punk element came from the ex-Discharge and The Varukers drummer Garry Maloney, who had played on Discharge's 1982 seminal hardcore album *Hear Nothing See Nothing Say Nothing* and guitarist Pooch (born Peter Purtill), previously a guitarist for Discharge following the departure of Bones to join his brother in Broken Bones. Gareth Holder was a former member of Leamington Spa-based punk band The Shapes.

The heavy metal and classic rock influence was provided by vocalist/guitarist/lyricist Paul Quigley, formerly of seminal NWOBHM heavy rock band SwingFire with former The Hoax drummer Dave Raeburn and bassist Mick Paul. Quigley later formed London-based A.M. and later RAAM with former Metal Mirror guitarist Chris Haggerty (1960–2004). Quigley subsequently founded London scene glam rock band BellaDonna in 1987 who went on to perform with ex-drummer of Tokyo Blade, Andy 'A.D. Dynamite' Parsons (who later went on to play with former Iron Maiden vocalist Paul Di'Anno in Battlezone.

Drummer Anthony 'Spiv' Smith was previously a member of Brute Force, and replaced D-beat pioneer Discharge drummer Garry Maloney in April 1984 shortly after the band's inception. Maloney subsequently rejoined Cal (born Kelvin Morris) in Discharge for their 'Grave New World' and 'Massacre Divine' albums.

Paul Quigley also acted in the lead role in two promo videos for Bronze Records' heavy metal band Girlschool in their singles "20th Century Boy", a cover version of the Marc Bolan hit of the 1970s, and "Play Dirty", which both featured on Girlschool's 1983 album of the same name, produced by Slade's Noddy Holder and Jimmy Lea. Paul Quigley's acting also appeared on MTV favourite cartoon comedy show Beavis and Butthead which featured the "Play Dirty" Girlschool video.

Hell's Belles released one full-length album *Hell's Belles* (RAWLP015) in 1986, and one single "Barricades" on both 7" and 12" format in the same year (RAWSS001/RAWTS001), during their span on Castle Communications' Raw Power label. They also featured with two tracks on Castle's *Metal Killers Kollection Volume 1 & 2*, as well as other rock compilations 'Rock Legends' and 'Rock Classics' on other record labels.

Hell's Belles' guest keyboard player, classically trained Lyndsay Bridgwater had formerly been the touring keyboard player for former Black Sabbath lead vocalist Ozzy Osbourne the previous year on both the *Diary of a Madman* tour with Randy Rhoads, Bob Daisley and Lee Kerslake, and then on Ozzy's *Speak of the Devil* tour with Brad Gillis replacing Randy Rhoads on guitar after his untimely passing in a plane accident on the U.S. tour, and with Rudy Sarzo on bass. Bridgwater played the keyboard solo on the Hell's Belles single *Barricades* and the synth parts on album track *Strangelove* and *Looks Like Love*, which Metallica's James Hetfield used Quigley's lyrics from that song using them in a similar slow-paced section where both sing 'sleep with one eye open' in Metallica's multi-platinum-selling track 'Enter Sandman' on their Black album. Metallica's Hetfield, Ulrich and Burton and Megadeth's Dave Mustaine all had been long-time Discharge admirers in the early days, and used to go to Discharge gigs in the US in the early 1980s, and had subsequently recorded two of Discharge's songs for their Garage covers album work.

Discharge's Cal (Kelvin Morris) also later 'borrowed' Paul Quigley's 1986 'Overload' song title in no less than two other, subsequent album tracks: 'Fantasy Overload' from the Discharge album 'Shootin' Up The World' in 1993, and, 'Hype Overload' on the 'Discharge' 2002 album, such was the influence of Paul Quigley's lyrical symbolism.[2]

Soon after the release of the first album in 1986, Holder left the band and was replaced by bassist Jon Archer in late 1986. This line-up dissolved as a working band shortly thereafter.

2.30.2 2000s - HellsBelles

Paul Quigley reformed a new band called 'HellsBelles'[3] (one word, no apostrophes) in 1998.

HellsBelles released two new singles in 2011, "Abyssinian Demesne" and "(Why Did They Kill) Joe Hill", "Gone but Not Forgotten" in January 2013.

2.30.3 Current members

- Paul Quigley 'The Belle Lord' - vocals, guitars, keyboards
- Caddavirr - bass
- O'Jeopardoso - guitar
- St Eval Denies - drums

2.30.4 Original members

- Paul Quigley - vocals
- Peter "Pooch" Purtill - guitar

- Garry Maloney - drums
- Gareth Holder - bass

2.30.5 Other members

- Anthony "Spiv" Smith - drums
- Jon Archer - bass
- Lyndsay Bridgwater - keyboards (on LP *Hell's Belles* - ex-Ozzy Osbourne, Blizzard of Oz, Budgie)

2.30.6 See also

- List of New Wave of British Heavy Metal bands

2.30.7 References

[1] "Kerrang! Review of Hell's Belles live in London and 1986 album". Kerrang!.

[2] "Ginger Coyote Interviews Paul Quigley of HellsBelles". Punk Globe Magazine.

[3] "The 'original' British heavy metal band...". HellsBelles. Retrieved 2011-10-27.

2.30.8 External links

- HellsBelles official website
- HellsBelles on Reverbnation
- HellsBelles on Twitter
- - HellsBelles on facebook

2.31 Hollow Ground (band)

Hollow Ground were an English heavy metal band.

2.31.1 Biography

Formed in the North East of England in the late 1970s, Hollow Ground became one of the cutting edge groups of the NWOBHM period. Although they only released six tracks, these have come to be considered a classic example of the style of the era.[1] In 1980 they released the *Warlord* EP, containing the tracks "Flying high," "Warlord," "Rock on", and "Don't chase the dragon." This 7-inch record is difficult to find and now changes hands for £200 in mint condition.[2] Later in 1980, a further two tracks ("Fight with the devil" and "The holy one") were recorded and were used along with "Rock on" and "Flying high" on the *Roksnax* split album. Four more tracks were recorded, "Rock to love", "Promised land," "Easy action", and "Loser", but were never released. In 1990 the track "Fight with the devil" was included on the Lars Ulrich/Geoff Barton compilation album *NWOBHM '79 Revisited*. The original *Warlord* EP tracks can also be found on the compilation CD *Rare Metal: N.W.O.B.H.M. Metal Rarities, Volume 1*.

Singer Glenn Coates left Hollow Ground to join Fist in 1982 for their *Back With A Vengeance* album. This defection signalled the end for Hollow Ground.

Lead Guitarist Martin Metcalf later recorded the Classic Rock album 'POWERHOUSE' with former Geordie vocalist Dr.Rob Turnbull in 1986

In 2007 the band were asked to reform and play at the Headbangers Open Air Festival in Germany. They were received very favourably, particularly by fans of the NWOBHM, who were delighted to see one of the 'lost' bands of that era perform live.

Hollow Ground also appeared on the bill with Jameson Raid and Cloven Hoof for a gig at Wolverhampton Civic Hall on 30 March 2013.[3]

2.31.2 Members

- Glenn Coates - vocals
- Martin Metcalf - lead guitar
- Brian Rickman - bass guitar
- John Lockney - drums

2.31.3 Discography

EPs

- *Warlord* (1980; 7-inch; Guardian Records)

1. "Flying High" - 2:56
2. "Warlord" - 2:20
3. "Rock On" - 3:07
4. "Don't Chase the Dragon" - 3:49

Albums

- *Roksnax* (1980; split album; Guardian Records)

1. "Die or deliver" by Samurai - 4:39
2. "Rock on" by **Hollow Ground** - 3:04
3. "Speed of sound" by Saracen - 4:26
4. "Fight with the devil" by **Hollow Ground** - 3:14
5. "Temptress" by Samurai - 2:26
6. "Fast living" by Saracen - 3:46
7. "Flying high" by **Hollow Ground** - 2:52
8. "Feel just the same" by Saracen - 3:17
9. "Knights in painted castles" by Samurai - 2:36
10. "The holy one" by **Hollow Ground** - 3:34
11. "Spirits of the lost" by Samurai - 3:36
12. "Setting the world ablaze" by Saracen - 3:44

Other appearances

- "Fight with the Devil" appears on *NWOBHM '79 Revisited* (1990; CD; Caroline Records)
- The *Warlord* EP appears on *Rare Metal: N.W.O.B.H.M. Metal Rarities, Volume 1* (1996; CD; British Steel Records)

2.31.4 See also

- List of New Wave of British Heavy Metal bands

2.31.5 References

[1] Hollow Ground at AllMusic

[2] Hollow Ground at MusicMight

[3] Jameson Raid / Cloven Hoof / Hollow Ground concert at Wolverhampton Civic Hall on 30 March 2013 - details on official Cloven Hoof website

2.31.6 External links

- The band is listed at Encyclopaedia Metallum.
- The band is listed at New Wave Of British Heavy Metal.

2.32 Holocaust (band)

Holocaust is a heavy metal band which is based in Edinburgh, Scotland, founded in 1977 while still at high school.

Influenced by Black Sabbath, Judas Priest, Motörhead, UFO, Led Zeppelin, Rush and Budgie, the original lineup featured guitarists John Mortimer and Ed Dudley, vocalist Gary Lettice, bassist Robin Begg and drummer Nick Brockie. In 1983, guitar player Ed Dudley left the band, forming and releasing an album under the moniker Hologram.

Hologram's album "Steal the Stars" was a much more radio-friendly release, presented by Dudley as the official continuation of Holocaust, yet in 1984 John Mortimer revived the Holocaust name, releasing the first of many albums with himself as vocalist, guitarist and sole original member. The John Mortimer-led Holocaust incorporated many progressive metal, thrash metal and post-punk influences into its sound, releasing complex pieces such as the "Sound of Souls" EP and concept album "Covenant". The band's current 3-piece lineup has remained the same since 2003[1] and will soon release their tenth album, entitled "Sweet Liberty".[2]

2.32.1 Discography

Albums

- *The Nightcomers* (1981)
- *Live (Hot Curry & Wine)* (1983)
- *No Man's Land* (1984)
- *The Sound of Souls* (1989)
- *Hypnosis of Birds* (1992)
- *Spirits Fly* (1996)
- *Covenant* (1997)
- *The Courage to Be* (2000)
- *Primal* (2003)

EPs and Singles

- "Heavy Metal Mania" (1980, 7-inch)
- *Heavy Metal Mania* (1980, 12-inch)
- "Smokin' Valves" (1980, 7-inch)
- *Smokin' Valves* (1980, 12-inch)

- *Live from the Raw Loud 'n' Live Tour* (1981, 7-inch)
- *Comin' Through* (1982, 12-inch)
- *Heavy Metal Mania '93* (1993, CD)
- *Expander* (2013, CD)

Compilations

- *NWOBHM '79 Revisited* (1990)
- *Smokin' Valves: The Anthology* (2003)

Videos

- *Live from the Raw Loud 'n' Live Tour* (1981, VHS; 2004, DVD)

2.32.2 Cover versions

- Metallica covered the song "The Small Hours" on their 1987 EP *The $5.98 EP: Garage Days Re-Revisited* and their album *Garage Inc.*
- Gamma Ray covered the song "Heavy Metal Mania" on their 1996 live album *Alive '95*. There was also a studio version released as a bonus song with their 1995 album Land of the Free. Later on in 2013 Gamma Ray recorded the song "Death or Glory".
- Six Feet Under covered the song "Death or Glory" from *The Nightcomers* album on their 1997 *Warpath* record.

2.32.3 See also

- List of New Wave of British Heavy Metal bands

2.32.4 References

[1] https://www.facebook.com/Holometal/info

[2] http://www.rockpages.gr/detailspage.aspx?id=9929&type=1&lang=EN

2.32.5 External links

- http://www.metal-archives.com/bands/Holocaust/760

2.33 Iron Maiden

This article is about the band. For the supposed torture device, see iron maiden. For other uses, see Iron Maiden (disambiguation).

Iron Maiden are an English heavy metal band formed in Leyton, east London, in 1975 by bassist and primary songwriter Steve Harris. The band's discography has grown to thirty-eight albums, including sixteen studio albums, eleven live albums, four EPs, and seven compilations.

Pioneers of the New Wave of British Heavy Metal, Iron Maiden achieved initial success during the early 1980s. After several line-up changes, the band went on to release a series of UK and US platinum and gold albums, including 1982's *The Number of the Beast*, 1983's *Piece of Mind*, 1984's *Powerslave*, 1985's live release *Live After Death*, 1986's *Somewhere in Time* and 1988's *Seventh Son of a Seventh Son*. Since the return of lead vocalist Bruce Dickinson and guitarist Adrian Smith in 1999, the band have undergone a resurgence in popularity,[1] with their 2010 studio offering, *The Final Frontier*, peaking at No. 1 in 28 different countries and receiving widespread critical acclaim. Their sixteenth studio album, *The Book of Souls*, was released on 4 September 2015.

Despite little radio or television support,[2] Iron Maiden are considered one of the most successful heavy metal bands in history, with *The Observer* reporting in 2015 that the band have sold over 90 million albums worldwide.[3] The band won the Ivor Novello Award for international achievement in 2002. As of October 2013, the band have played over 2000 live shows throughout their career. For the past 35 years, the band have been supported by their famous mascot, "Eddie", who has appeared on almost all of their album and single covers, as well as in their live shows.

2.33.1 History

Early years (1975–1978)

Iron Maiden were formed on Christmas Day 1975 by bassist Steve Harris shortly after he left his previous group, Smiler. Harris attributes the band's name to a film adaptation of *The Man in the Iron Mask* from the novel by Alexandre Dumas, which he saw around that time and which had a verbal connection to the iron maiden torture device.[5] After months of rehearsal, Iron Maiden made their debut at St. Nicks Hall in Poplar on 1 May 1976,[6] before taking up a semi-residency at the Cart and Horses Pub in Maryland Point, Stratford.[7]

The original line-up did not last very long, however, with

The Cart and Horses Pub, located in Maryland Point, Stratford, was where Iron Maiden played some of their first shows in 1976.[4]

vocalist Paul Day being the first casualty as he lacked "energy or charisma onstage."[8] He was replaced by Dennis Wilcock, a Kiss fan who used make-up and fake blood during live performances.[8] Wilcock's friend Dave Murray was invited to join, to the dismay of the band's guitarists Dave Sullivan and Terry Rance.[9] Their frustration led Harris to temporarily disband Iron Maiden in 1976,[9] though the group reformed soon after with Murray as the sole guitarist. Steve Harris and Dave Murray remain the band's longest-standing members and have performed on all of their releases.

Dave Murray and Steve Harris in 2008. Harris and Murray are the only members to have performed on all of the band's albums.

Iron Maiden recruited yet another guitarist in 1977, Bob Sawyer, who was sacked for embarrassing the band onstage by pretending to play guitar with his teeth.[10] Tension ensued again, causing a rift between Murray and Wilcock, who convinced Harris to fire Murray,[11] as well as original drummer Ron Matthews.[6] A new line-up was put together, including future Cutting Crew member Tony Moore on keyboards, Terry Wapram on guitar, and drummer Barry Purkis. A bad performance at the Bridgehouse, a pub located in Canning Town,[12] in November 1977 was the line-up's first and only concert and led to Purkis being replaced by Doug Sampson.[13] At the same time, Moore was asked to leave as Harris decided that keyboards did not suit the band's sound.[13] A few months later, Dennis Wilcock decided that he had had enough with the group and left to form his own band, V1, and Dave Murray was immediately reinstated.[14] As he preferred to be the band's sole guitarist, Wapram disapproved of Murray's return and was also dismissed.[6]

Steve Harris, Dave Murray and Doug Sampson spent the summer and autumn of 1978 rehearsing while they searched for a singer to complete the band's new line-up.[15] A chance meeting at the Red Lion pub in Leytonstone in November 1978 evolved into a successful audition for vocalist Paul Di'Anno.[16] Steve Harris has stated, "There's sort of a quality in Paul's voice, a raspiness in his voice, or whatever you want to call it, that just gave it this great edge."[17] At this time, Murray would typically act as their sole guitarist, with Harris commenting, "Davey was so good he could do a lot of it on his own. The plan was always to get a second guitarist in, but finding one that could match Davey was really difficult."[18]

Record contract and early releases (1978–1981)

Main articles: The Soundhouse Tapes, Iron Maiden (album) and Killers (Iron Maiden album)

On New Year's Eve 1978, Iron Maiden recorded a demo, consisting of four songs, at Spaceward Studios in Cambridge.[19] Hoping the recording would help them secure more gigs,[19] the band presented a copy to Neal Kay, then managing a heavy metal club called "Bandwagon Heavy Metal Soundhouse", located in Kingsbury Circle, northwest London.[20] Upon hearing the tape, Kay began playing the demo regularly at the Bandwagon, and one of the songs, "Prowler", eventually went to No. 1 in the Soundhouse charts, which were published weekly in *Sounds* magazine.[21] A copy was also acquired by Rod Smallwood, who soon became the band's manager,[22] and, as Iron Maiden's popularity increased, they decided to release the demo on their own record label as *The Soundhouse Tapes*, named after the club.[23] Featuring only three tracks (one song, "Strange World", was excluded as the band were unsatisfied with its production)[24] all five thousand copies were sold out within weeks.[25]

In December 1979, the band secured a major record deal with EMI[26] and asked Dave Murray's childhood friend Adrian Smith to join the group as their second guitarist.[27] Smith declined as he was busy with his own band, Urchin, so Iron Maiden hired guitarist Dennis Stratton instead.[28] Shortly afterwards, Doug Sampson left due to health issues and was replaced by ex-Samson drummer Clive Burr at Stratton's suggestion on 26 December.[29] Iron Maiden's first appearance on an album was on the *Metal for Muthas* compilation (released on 15 February 1980) with two early versions of "Sanctuary" and "Wrathchild".[30] The release led to an ensuing tour which featured several other bands linked with the New Wave of British Heavy Metal.[31]

Paul Di'Anno and Steve Harris supporting Judas Priest on their British Steel Tour, 1980.

Iron Maiden's eponymous 1980 release, *Iron Maiden*, debuted at No. 4 in the UK Albums Chart.[32] In addition to the title track (a live version of which would be one of the first music videos aired on MTV),[33] the album includes other early favourites such as "Running Free", "Transylvania", "Phantom of the Opera", and "Sanctuary" – which was not on the original UK release but made the US version and subsequent remasters. The band set out on a headline tour of the UK, before opening for Kiss on their 1980 Unmasked Tour's European leg as well as supporting Judas Priest on select dates. After the Kiss tour, Dennis Stratton was dismissed from the band as a result of creative and personal differences,[34] and was replaced by Adrian Smith in October 1980.

In 1981, Iron Maiden released their second album, entitled *Killers*. Containing many tracks that had been written prior to their debut release, only two new songs were written for the record: "Prodigal Son" and "Murders in the Rue Morgue"[35] (the latter's title was taken from the short story by Edgar Allan Poe).[36] Unsatisfied with the production on their debut album,[37] the band hired veteran producer Martin Birch,[38] who would go on to work for Iron Maiden until his retirement in 1992.[39] The record was followed by the band's first world tour, which included their debut performance in the United States, opening for Judas Priest at The Aladdin Casino, Las Vegas.[40]

Success (1981–1985)

Main articles: The Number of the Beast (album), Piece of Mind, Powerslave and Live After Death

By 1981, Paul Di'Anno was demonstrating increasingly self-destructive behaviour, particularly through his drug usage,[6] about which Di'Anno comments, "it wasn't just that I was snorting a bit of coke, though; I was just going for it non-stop, 24 hours a day, every day... the band had commitments piling up that went on for months, years, and I just couldn't see my way to the end of it. I knew I'd never last the whole tour. It was too much."[41] With his performances suffering, Di'Anno was immediately dismissed following the Killer World Tour,[42] at which point the band had already selected his replacement.[43]

After a meeting with Rod Smallwood at the Reading Festival,[44] Bruce Dickinson, previously of Samson, auditioned for Iron Maiden in September 1981 and was immediately hired.[43] The following month, Dickinson went out on the road with the band on a small headlining tour in Italy, as well as a one-off show at the Rainbow Theatre in the UK.[42] For the last show, and in anticipation of their forthcoming album, the band played "Children of the Damned" and "22 Acacia Avenue", introducing fans to the sound towards which they were progressing.[45]

In 1982, Iron Maiden released *The Number of the Beast*, an album which gave the band their first ever UK Albums Chart No. 1 record[46] and additionally became a Top Ten hit in many other countries.[47] At the time, Dickinson was in the midst of legal difficulties with Samson's management and was not permitted to add his name to any of the songwriting credits, although he still made what he described as a "moral contribution" to "Children of the Damned", "The Prisoner" and "Run to the Hills".[48] For the second time the band embarked on a world tour, dubbed The Beast on the Road, during which they visited North America, Japan, Australia and Europe, including a headline appearance at the Reading Festival. A new and hugely successful chapter in Iron Maiden's future was cemented; in 2010 *The New York Times* reported that the album had sold over 14 million copies worldwide.[49]

The Beast on the Road's US leg proved controversial when

an American conservative political lobbying group claimed Iron Maiden were Satanic because of the new album's title track,[47] to the point where a group of Christian activists destroyed Iron Maiden records as a protest against the band.[50] In recent years, Dickinson has stated that the band treated this as "silliness",[51] and that the demonstrations in fact gave them "loads of publicity."[6]

Nicko McBrain has been Iron Maiden's drummer since 1982

In December 1982, drummer Clive Burr was fired from the band and replaced by Nicko McBrain, previously of French band Trust.[52] Although Harris states that his dismissal took place because his live performances were affected by offstage activities,[53] Burr objected to this and claimed that he was unfairly ousted from the band.[54] Soon afterwards, the band journeyed for the first time to The Bahamas to record the first of three consecutive albums at Compass Point Studios.[55] In 1983, they released *Piece of Mind*, which reached the No. 3 spot in the UK,[56] and was the band's debut in the North American charts, reaching No. 70 on the *Billboard* 200.[57] *Piece of Mind* includes the successful singles "The Trooper" and "Flight of Icarus", the latter of which being particularly notable as one of the band's few songs to gain substantial airplay in the US.[58]

Soon after the success of *Piece of Mind* and its supporting tour, the band released *Powerslave* on 9 September 1984. The album featured fan favourites "2 Minutes to Midnight", "Aces High", and "Rime of The Ancient Mariner",[59] the latter based on Samuel Taylor Coleridge's poem of the same name and running over 13 minutes long.

The tour following the album, dubbed the World Slavery Tour, was the band's largest to date and consisted of 193 shows in 28 countries over 13 months,[59] playing to an estimated 3,500,000 people.[60] Many shows were played back-to-back in the same city, such as in Long Beach, California, where the band played four consecutive concerts. It was here where the majority of their subsequent live release, *Live After Death*, was recorded, which became a critical and commercial success, peaking at No. 4 in the UK.[61] Iron Maiden also made their debut appearance in South America, where they co-headlined (with Queen) the Rock in Rio festival to an estimated crowd of 300,000.[62] The tour was physically gruelling for the band, who demanded six months off when it ended (although this was later reduced to four months).[63] This was the first substantial break in the group's history, including the cancellation of a proposed supporting tour for the new live album,[64] with Bruce Dickinson threatening to quit unless the tour ended.[65]

Experimentation (1986–1989)

Main articles: Somewhere in Time (Iron Maiden album) and Seventh Son of a Seventh Son

Returning from their time off, the band adopted a different style for their 1986 studio album, entitled *Somewhere in Time*, featuring, for the first time in the band's history, synthesised bass and guitars to add textures and layers to the sound.[66] The release charted well across the world, particularly with the single "Wasted Years", but notably included no writing credits from lead singer Bruce Dickinson, whose material was rejected by the rest of the band.[67] While Dickinson was focused on his own music, guitarist Adrian Smith, who typically collaborated with the vocalist, was "left to [his] own devices" and began writing songs on his own, coming up with "Wasted Years", "Sea of Madness", and "Stranger in a Strange Land",[68] the last of which would be the album's second single.[67]

The experimentation evident on *Somewhere in Time* continued on their next album, entitled *Seventh Son of a Seventh Son*, which was released in 1988. A concept album, based on the 1987 novel *Seventh Son* by Orson Scott Card,[69] this would be the band's first record to include keyboards, performed by Harris and Smith,[69] as opposed to guitar synthesisers on the previous release.[70] After his contributions were not used for *Somewhere in Time*, Dickinson's enthusiasm was renewed as his ideas were accepted for this album.[70] Another popular release, it became Iron Maiden's second album to hit No. 1 in the UK charts,[71] although it only achieved a Gold certification in the US, in contrast to its four predecessors.[72]

During the following tour, the band headlined the Monsters of Rock festival at Donington Park for the first time on 20 August 1988, playing to the largest crowd in the festival's history (107,000).[73] Also included on the bill were Kiss, David Lee Roth, Megadeth, Guns N' Roses and Helloween.[74] The festival was marred, however, by the deaths of two fans in a crowd-surge during the aforementioned Guns N' Roses performance; the following year's festival was cancelled as a result.[73] The tour concluded with several headline shows in the UK in November and December 1988, with the concerts at the NEC Arena, Birmingham recorded for a live video, entitled *Maiden England*.[75] Throughout the tour, Harris' bass technician, Michael Kenney, provided live keyboards.[76] Kenney has acted as the band's live keyboard player ever since, also performing on the band's four following albums before Harris took over as the group's sole studio keyboardist from 2000's *Brave New World*.[77]

Upheaval (1989–1994)

Main articles: No Prayer for the Dying and Fear of the Dark (Iron Maiden album)

During another break in 1989, guitarist Adrian Smith released a solo album with his band ASAP, entitled *Silver and Gold*,[78] and vocalist Bruce Dickinson began work on a solo album with former Gillan guitarist Janick Gers, releasing *Tattooed Millionaire* in 1990,[79] followed by a tour.[80] At the same time, to mark the band's ten-year recording anniversary, Iron Maiden released *The First Ten Years*, a series of ten CDs and double 12-inch singles. Between 24 February and 28 April 1990, the individual parts were released one-by-one, each containing two of Iron Maiden's singles, including the original B-sides.

Soon afterwards, Iron Maiden regrouped to work on a new studio record. During the pre-production stages, Adrian Smith left the band due to differences with Steve Harris regarding the direction the band should be taking, disagreeing with the "stripped down" style that they were leaning towards.[81] Janick Gers, having worked on Dickinson's solo project, was chosen to replace Smith and became the band's first new member in seven years.[80] The album, *No Prayer for the Dying*, was released in October 1990[82] and contained "Bring Your Daughter... to the Slaughter", the band's first (and to date, only) UK Singles Chart No. 1, originally recorded by Dickinson's solo outfit for the soundtrack to *A Nightmare on Elm Street 5: The Dream Child*.[83]

After another tour and some more time off, the band recorded their next studio release, *Fear of the Dark*, which was released in 1992 and included the stand-out title track, which is now a regular fixture in the band's concert setlists. Achieving their third No. 1 in the UK albums chart,[84] the disc also featured the No. 2 single "Be Quick or Be Dead" and the No. 21 single "From Here to Eternity". The album featured the first songwriting by Gers, and no collaboration at all between Harris and Dickinson on songs. The extensive worldwide tour that followed included their first ever Latin American leg (after a single concert during the World Slavery Tour), and headlining the Monsters of Rock festivals in seven European countries. Iron Maiden's second performance at Donington Park, to an audience of 68,500 (the attendance was capped after the incident in 1988),[85] was filmed for the audio and video release, *Live at Donington*, and featured a guest appearance by Adrian Smith, who joined the band to perform "Running Free".[85]

In 1993, Bruce Dickinson left the band to further pursue his solo career, but agreed to remain for a farewell tour and two live albums (later re-released in one package).[86] The first, *A Real Live One*, featured songs from 1986 to 1992, and was released in March 1993. The second, *A Real Dead One*, featured songs from 1980 to 1984, and was released after Dickinson had left the band. The tour did not go well, however, with Steve Harris claiming that Dickinson would only perform properly for high-profile shows and that at several concerts he would only mumble into the microphone.[87] Dickinson denies the charge that he was under-performing, stating that it was impossible to "make like Mr Happy Face if the vibe wasn't right," claiming that news of his exit from the band had prevented any chance of a good atmosphere during the tour.[88] He played his farewell show with Iron Maiden on 28 August 1993, which was filmed, broadcast by the BBC and released on video under the name *Raising Hell*.[89]

Blaze Bayley era, *The X Factor* and *Virtual XI* (1994–1999)

Main articles: The X Factor (album) and Virtual XI

In 1994, the band listened to hundreds of tapes sent in by vocalists before convincing Blaze Bayley, formerly of the band Wolfsbane who had supported Iron Maiden in 1990, to audition for them.[90] Harris' preferred choice from the outset,[91] Bayley had a different vocal style from his predecessor, which ultimately received a mixed reception among fans.[92]

After a two-year hiatus (as well as a three-year hiatus from studio releases – a record for the band at the time) Iron Maiden returned in 1995. Releasing *The X Factor*, the band had their lowest chart position since 1981 for an album in the UK (debuting at No. 8),[93] although it would go on to win *Album of the Year* awards in France and Germany.[94] The record included the 11-minute epic "Sign of the Cross", the band's longest song since "Rime of the Ancient Mariner", as well as the singles, "Man on the Edge", based on the film *Falling Down*,[95] and "Lord of the Flies", based on the novel of the same name.[96] The release is notable for its "dark" tone, inspired by Steve Harris' divorce.[94] The band toured for the rest of 1995 and 1996, playing for the first time in Israel and South Africa,[97] before stopping to release *Best of the Beast*. The band's first compilation, it included a new single, "Virus", whose lyrics attack the critics who had recently written off the band.[98]

Iron Maiden returned to the studio to record *Virtual XI*, released in 1998. The album's chart scores were the band's lowest to date,[99] including the UK where it peaked at No. 16[100] failing to score one million worldwide sales for the first time in Iron Maiden's history.[101] At the same time, Steve Harris assisted in remastering the band's entire discography, up to and including *Live at Donington* (which was given a mainstream release for the first time).[102]

Bayley's tenure in Iron Maiden ended in January 1999 when he was asked to leave during a band meeting.[103] The dismissal took place due to issues Bayley had experienced with his voice during the Virtual XI World Tour,[104] although Janick Gers has since stated that this was partly the band's fault for forcing him to perform songs which were beyond his natural register.[105]

Return of Dickinson and Smith, *Brave New World* (1999–2002)

Main articles: Ed Hunter and Brave New World (Iron Maiden album)
While the group were considering a replacement for Bayley, Rod Smallwood convinced Steve Harris to invite Bruce Dickinson back into the band.[106] Although Harris admits that he "wasn't really into it" at first, he then thought, "'Well, if the change happens, who should we get?' The thing is, we know Bruce and we know what he's capable of, and you think, 'Well, better the devil you know.' I mean, we got on well professionally for, like, eleven years, and so... after I thought about it, I didn't really have a problem with it."[106]

The band entered into talks with Dickinson, who agreed to rejoin during a meeting in Brighton in January 1999,[107] along with guitarist Adrian Smith, who was telephoned a few hours later.[108] With Gers, Smith's replacement, remaining, Iron Maiden now had a three-guitar line-up and embarked on a hugely successful reunion tour.[109] Dubbed The Ed Hunter Tour, it tied in with the band's newly released greatest hits collection, *Ed Hunter*, whose track listing was decided by a poll on the group's website, and also contained a computer game of the same name starring the band's mascot.[110]

One of Dickinson's primary concerns on rejoining the group "was whether we would in fact be making a real state-of-the-art record and not just a comeback album,"[106] which eventually took the form of 2000's *Brave New World*.[111] Having disliked the results from Harris' personal studio, Barnyard Studios located on his property in Essex,[112] which had been used for the last four Iron Maiden studio albums, the band recorded the new release at Guillaume Tell Studios, Paris in November 1999 with producer Kevin Shirley.[111] Thematic influences continued with "The Wicker Man" – based on the 1973 British cult film of the same name – and "Brave New World" – title taken from the Aldous Huxley novel of the same name.[113] The album furthered the more progressive and melodic sound present in some earlier recordings, with elaborate song structures and keyboard orchestration.[113]

The world tour that followed consisted of well over 100 dates and culminated on 19 January 2001 in a show at the Rock in Rio festival in Brazil, where Iron Maiden played to an audience of around 250,000.[114] While the performance was being produced for a CD and DVD release in March 2002, under the name *Rock in Rio*,[115] the band took a year out from touring, during which they played three consecutive shows at Brixton Academy in aid of former drummer Clive Burr, who had recently announced that he had been diagnosed with multiple sclerosis.[116] The band performed two further concerts for Burr's MS Trust Fund charity in 2005,[117] and 2007;[118] before his death in 2013.[119]

Adrian Smith re-joined Iron Maiden in 1999, resulting in a three guitar line-up.

Dance of Death and A Matter of Life and Death (2003–2007)

Main articles: Dance of Death (album) and A Matter of Life and Death (album)

Following their Give Me Ed... 'Til I'm Dead Tour in the summer of 2003, Iron Maiden released *Dance of Death*, their thirteenth studio album, which was met by worldwide critical and commercial success.[120] Produced by Kevin Shirley, now the band's regular producer, many critics also felt that this release matched up to their earlier efforts, such as *Killers, Piece of Mind* and *The Number of the Beast*.[121] As usual, historical and literary references were present, with "Montségur" in particular being about the Cathar stronghold conquered in 1244,[122] and "Paschendale" relating to the significant battle which took place during The First World War.[123] During the following tour, the band's performance at Westfalenhalle, in Dortmund, Germany, was recorded and released in August 2005 as a live album and DVD, entitled *Death on the Road*.[124]

In 2005, the band announced the Eddie Rips Up the World Tour which, tying in with their 2004 DVD entitled *The History of Iron Maiden – Part 1: The Early Days*, only featured material from their first four albums.[125] As part of this celebration of their earlier years, "The Number of the Beast" single was re-released[126] and went straight to No. 3 in the UK Chart.[127] The tour included many headlining stadium and festival dates, including a performance at Ullevi Stadium in Sweden to an audience of almost 60,000.[128] This concert was also broadcast live on satellite television all over Europe to approximately 60 million viewers.[129] Following this run of European shows, the band co-headlined the US festival tour, Ozzfest, with Black Sabbath, their final performance at which earned international press coverage after their show was sabotaged by singer Ozzy Osbourne's family,[130] who took offence to Dickinson's remarks against reality-TV.[131] The band completed the tour by headlining the Reading and Leeds Festivals on the 26–28 August,[132] and the RDS Stadium in Ireland on 31 August. For the second time, the band played a charity show for The Clive Burr MS Trust Fund, this time taking place at the Hammersmith Apollo.[117] The same year, the band were inducted into the Hollywood RockWalk in Sunset Boulevard, Los Angeles.

At the end of 2005, Iron Maiden began work on *A Matter of Life and Death*, their fourteenth studio effort, released in autumn 2006. While not a concept album,[133] war and religion are recurring themes in the lyrics, as well as in the cover artwork. The release was a critical and commercial success, earning the band their first top ten in the *Billboard* 200[134] and receiving the Album of the Year award at the 2006 *Classic Rock* Roll of Honour Awards.[135] A supporting tour

Vocalist Bruce Dickinson during A Matter of Life and Death World Tour. Throughout the tour's first leg, the band played the A Matter of Life and Death *album in its entirety.*

followed, during which they played the album in its entirety; response to this was mixed.[136]

The second part of the "A Matter of Life and Death" tour, which took place in 2007, was dubbed "A Matter of the Beast" to celebrate the 25th anniversary of *The Number of the Beast* album, and included appearances at several major festivals worldwide.[137] The tour opened in the Middle East with the band's first performance in Dubai at the Dubai Desert Rock Festival,[138] after which they played to over 30,000 people at the Bangalore Palace Grounds,[139] marking the first concert by any major heavy metal band in the Indian sub-continent.[138] The band went on to play a string of European dates, including an appearance at Download Festival, their fourth headline performance at Donington Park,[140] to approximately 80,000 people.[141] On 24 June they ended the tour with a performance at London's Brixton Academy in aid of The Clive Burr MS Trust fund.[118]

Somewhere Back in Time World Tour and *Flight 666* (2007–2009)

Main articles: Somewhere Back in Time World Tour and Iron Maiden: Flight 666

On 5 September 2007, the band announced their Somewhere Back in Time World Tour, which tied in with the DVD release of their *Live After Death* album.[142] The setlist for the tour consisted of successes from the 1980s, with a specific emphasis on the *Powerslave* era for set design.[142] The first part of the tour, commencing in Mumbai, India on 1 February 2008, consisted of 24 concerts in 21 cities, travelling nearly 50,000 miles in the band's own chartered aeroplane,[143] named "Ed Force One".[144] They played their first ever concerts in Costa Rica and Colombia and their first shows in Australia and Puerto Rico since 1992.

Iron Maiden performing in Toronto during the Somewhere Back in Time World Tour 2008. The stage set largely emulated that of the World Slavery Tour 1984–85.[142]

The tour led to the release of a new compilation album, entitled *Somewhere Back in Time*, which included a selection of tracks from their 1980 eponymous debut to 1988's *Seventh Son of a Seventh Son*, as well as several live versions from *Live After Death*.[145]

The Somewhere Back in Time World Tour continued with two further legs in the US and Europe in the summer of 2008, during which the band used a more expansive stage-set, including further elements of the original *Live After Death* show.[146] With the sole UK concert taking place at Twickenham Stadium, this would be the first time the band would headline a stadium in their own country.[147] The three 2008 legs of the tour were remarkably successful; it was the second highest grossing tour of the year for a British artist.[148]

The last part of the tour took place in February and March 2009, with the band, once again, using "Ed Force One".[149] The final leg included the band's first ever appearances in Peru and Ecuador, as well as their return to Venezuela and New Zealand after 17 years.[150] The band also played another show in India (their third in the country within a span of 2 years) at the Rock in India festival to a crowd of 20,000. At their concert in São Paulo on 15 March, Dickinson announced on stage that it was the largest non-festival show of their career, with an overall attendance of 63,000 people.[151] The final leg ended in Florida on 2 April after which the band took a break. Overall, the tour reportedly had an attendance of over two million people worldwide over both years.[152]

At the 2009 BRIT Awards, Iron Maiden won the award for best British live act.[153] Voted for by the public, the band reportedly won by a landslide.[154]

On 20 January 2009, the band announced that they were to release a full-length documentary film in select cinemas on 21 April 2009. Entitled *Iron Maiden: Flight 666*, it was filmed during the first part of the Somewhere Back in Time World Tour between February and March 2008.[155] *Flight 666* was co-produced by Banger Productions and was distributed in cinemas by Arts Alliance Media and EMI, with D&E Entertainment sub-distributing in the US.[156] The film went on to have a Blu-ray, DVD and CD release in May and June,[152] topping the music DVD charts in 22 countries.[157]

The Final Frontier and Maiden England World Tour (2010–2014)

Main articles: The Final Frontier, The Final Frontier World Tour, En Vivo! (Iron Maiden album) and Maiden England World Tour

Following announcements that the band had begun composition of new material and booked studio time in early 2010 with Kevin Shirley producing,[158] *The Final Frontier* was announced on 4 March.[159] The album, the band's fifteenth, was released on 16 August,[160] garnering critical acclaim[161] and the band's greatest commercial success in their history, reaching No. 1 in twenty-eight countries worldwide.[162] Although Steve Harris had been quoted in the past as claiming that the band would only produce fifteen studio releases,[163] band members have since confirmed that there will be at least one further record.[164]

The album's supporting tour saw the band perform 98 shows across the globe to an estimated audience of over 2 million,[165] including their first visits to Singapore, Indonesia and South Korea,[162] before concluding in London on 6 August 2011.[166] As the tour's 2010 leg preceded *The Final Frontier*'s release, the band made "El Dorado" available as a free download on 8 June,[160] which would go on to win the award for Best Metal Performance at the 2011 Grammy Awards on 13 February 2011.[167] It is the band's first win following two previous Grammy nominations ("Fear of the Dark" in 1994 and "The Wicker Man" in 2001).[168]

On 15 March, a new compilation to accompany 2009's *Somewhere Back in Time* was announced. Entitled *From Fear to Eternity*, the original release date was set at 23 May but was later pushed back to 6 June.[169] The double disc set covers the period 1990–2010 (the band's most recent eight studio albums),[169] and, as on *Somewhere Back in Time*, live versions with Bruce Dickinson were included in place of original recordings which featured other vocalists, in this case Blaze Bayley.

In a press release regarding *From Fear to Eternity*, band manager Rod Smallwood revealed that Iron Maiden will release a new concert video to DVD in 2011, filmed in Santiago, Chile and Buenos Aires, Argentina during The Final Frontier World Tour.[170] On 17 January 2012, the band announced that the new release, entitled *En Vivo!*, based on footage from the Chile concert, will be made available worldwide on CD, LP, DVD and Blu-ray on 26 March, except the United States and Canada (where it was released on 27 March).[171] In addition to the concert footage, the video release includes an 88-minute tour documentary, entitled Behind The Beast, containing interviews with the band and their crew.[172] In December 2012, one song from the release ("Blood Brothers") was nominated for a Grammy Award for Best Hard Rock/Metal Performance at the 2013 Grammy Awards.[173]

On 15 February 2012, the band announced the Maiden England World Tour 2012–14, which was based around the video of the same name.[174] The tour commenced in North America in the summer of 2012 and was followed by further dates in 2013 and 2014, which included the band's record-breaking fifth headline performance at Donington Park,[175] their first show at the newly built national stadium in Stockholm,[176] a return to the Rock in Rio festival in Brazil,[177] and their debut appearance in Paraguay.[178] In August 2012, Steve Harris stated that the *Maiden England* video would be re-issued in 2013,[179] with a release date later set for 25 March 2013 in DVD, CD and LP formats under the title *Maiden England '88*.[180]

The Book of Souls (2015–present)

Main articles: The Book of Souls and The Book of Souls World Tour

Following confirmation from the group that 2010's *The Final Frontier* would not be their last album,[164] Bruce Dickinson revealed plans for a sixteenth studio record in July 2013, with a potential release date in 2015.[181] In February 2015, drummer Nicko McBrain revealed that a new album had been completed, although the release has been put on hold while Dickinson recovers from treatment for a cancerous tumour found on his tongue.[182] On 15 May, after Dickinson had been given the all-clear, manager Rod Smallwood confirmed that the album would be released in 2015, although the band will not tour until 2016 to allow Dickinson to recuperate.[183] On 18 June 2015, the band's website announced its title, *The Book of Souls*, and confirmed a release date of 4 September 2015.[184] A critical and commercial success, it received positive reviews and became the band's fifth UK No. 1 album.[185]

The new record was recorded at Guillaume Tell Studios, Paris, which they had previously used for 2000's *Brave New World*, with regular producer Kevin Shirley in late summer 2014.[186] With a total time of 92 minutes, it is the group's first double studio album.[186] In addition, the release's closing song, "Empire of the Clouds", penned by Dickinson, replaces "Rime of the Ancient Mariner" (from 1984's *Powerslave*) as Iron Maiden's longest song, at 18 minutes in length.[184] A music video for the song "Speed of Light" was issued on 14 August.[187]

From February 2016, the band will embark on The Book of Souls World Tour, which will see them play concerts in 35 countries in North and South America, Asia, Australasia, Africa and Europe, including their first ever performances in China, El Salvador and Lithuania.[188] As with 2008-09's Somewhere Back in Time World Tour and 2010-11's The Final Frontier World Tour, the group will be travelling in a customised aeroplane, flown by Dickinson and nicknamed "Ed Force One", although this time they will be using a Boeing 747-400 jumbo jet.[189]

2.33.2 Image and legacy

Iron Maiden were ranked No. 24 in VH1's "100 Greatest Artists of Hard Rock",[190] No. 4 in MTV's "Top 10 Greatest Heavy Metal Bands of All Time"[191] and No. 3 in VH1 Classic's "Top 20 Metal Bands".[192] The band also won the Ivor Novello Award for international achievement in 2002[193] and were inducted into the Hollywood RockWalk whilst touring in the US in 2005.[194]

Iron Maiden frequently use the slogan "Up the Irons" in their disc liner notes, and the phrase can also be seen on several T-shirts officially licensed by the band. It is a paraphrase of "Up the Hammers," the phrase which refers to the London football club, West Ham United, of which founder Steve Harris is a fan.[195]

Iron Maiden's mascot, Eddie, is a perennial fixture in the band's science fiction and horror-influenced album cover art, as well as in live shows.[196] Originally a papier-mâché mask incorporated in their backdrop which would squirt fake blood during their live shows,[197] the name would be transferred to the character featured in the band's debut album cover, created by Derek Riggs.[198] Eddie was painted exclusively by Riggs until 1992, at which point the band began using artwork from numerous other artists as well, including Melvyn Grant.[84] Eddie is also featured in the band's first-person shooter video game, *Ed Hunter*,[199] as well as numerous T-shirts, posters and other band-related merchandise.[196] In 2008, he was awarded the "Icon Award" at the *Metal Hammer* Golden Gods,[200] while Gibson.com describes him as "the most recognisable metal icon in the world and one of the most versatile too."[201]

Iron Maiden's distinct logo has adorned all of the band's releases since their debut, 1979's *The Soundhouse Tapes* EP. The typeface originates with Vic Fair's poster design for the 1976 science fiction film, *The Man Who Fell to Earth*,[202] also used by Gordon Giltrap, although Steve Harris claims that he designed it himself, utilising his abilities as an architectural draughtsman.[203]

Influence on other artists

According to *Guitar World*, Iron Maiden's music has "influenced generations of newer metal acts, from legends like Metallica to current stars like Avenged Sevenfold,"[204] with Metallica drummer Lars Ulrich commenting that he has "always had an incredible amount of respect and admiration for them."[205] Kerry King of Slayer has stated that "they meant so much to me in their early days" and Scott Ian of Anthrax says that "they had a major impact on my life."[206]

M. Shadows of Avenged Sevenfold states that Iron Maiden "are by far the best live band in the world and their music is timeless," while Trivium singer Matt Heafy comments that "without Iron Maiden, Trivium surely wouldn't exist."[205] Slipknot frontman Corey Taylor says that "Steve Harris does more with four fingers than I've ever seen anybody do. And Bruce Dickinson? Dude! To me, he was the quintessential old-school heavy metal singer. He could hit notes that were just sick, and he was a great showman. Everything made me a fan. And there wasn't a dude that I hung out with that wasn't trying to draw Eddie on their schoolbooks,"[191] while their music also helped Jesper Strömblad of In Flames to pioneer the melodic death metal genre, stating that he had wanted to combine death metal with Iron Maiden's melodic guitar sounds.[207]

Other heavy metal artists who cite the band as an influence include Chris Jericho, lead singer of Fozzy,[208] Cam Pipes, lead vocalist of 3 Inches of Blood,[209] Vitaly Dubinin, bassist of Aria,[210] and Mikael Åkerfeldt, guitarist and lead vocalist of Opeth.[211] Both current and former Dream Theater members John Petrucci, John Myung and Mike Portnoy have stated that Iron Maiden were one of their biggest influences when their band first formed.[212]

Appearance in media

The band's name has been mentioned prominently in several songs, such as the singles "Teenage Dirtbag" by Wheatus,[213] "Back to the 80's" by Danish dance-pop band Aqua.[214] and "Fat Lip" by Sum 41.[215] Iron Maiden have also been referenced in Weezer's "Heart Songs" (from their 2008 self-titled "Red" album),[216] Blues Traveler's "Psycho Joe" (from 1997's *Straight on till Morning*),[217] and NOFX's "Eddie, Bruce and Paul" (from their 2009 album *Coaster*), which Sputnikmusic describes as "a humorous retelling of Paul DiAnno's departure."[218] Also, Swedish power metal band Sabaton have made references to the band in their songs "Metal Machine", "Metal Crue", and "Metal Ripper", with the former mentioning various Iron Maiden songs (namely "Fear of the Dark" and "Afraid to Shoot Strangers"),[219] and the latter including lyrics from "The Number of the Beast".[220]

In 2008, *Kerrang!* released an album, entitled *Maiden Heaven: A Tribute to Iron Maiden*, composed of Iron Maiden cover songs played by artists such as Metallica, Machine Head, Dream Theater, Trivium, Coheed and Cambria, Avenged Sevenfold, and others who were influenced by Iron Maiden throughout their careers.[205] In 2010, Maiden uniteD, an acoustic tribute band consisting of members of Ayreon, Threshold and Within Temptation, released *Mind the Acoustic Pieces*, a re-interpretation of the entire *Piece of Mind* album.[221] Many other Iron Maiden cover albums exist (each featuring various artists), including piano,[222] electro,[223] string quartet[224] and hip-hop tributes.[225]

Iron Maiden songs have been featured in the soundtracks of several video games, including *Carmageddon 2*,[226] *Grand Theft Auto: Vice City*,[227] *Grand Theft Auto: Episodes From Liberty City*,[228] *Grand Theft Auto IV: The Lost and Damned*,[229] *Tony Hawk's Pro Skater 4*,[230] *SSX on Tour*[231] and *Madden NFL 10*.[232] Their music also appears in the *Guitar Hero* and *Rock Band* series of rhythmic video games.[233] Iron Maiden songs have also appeared in films, such as *Phenomena* (entitled *Creepers* in the US),[234] and *Murder by Numbers*;[235] while MTV's animated duo Beavis and Butt-head have commented favourably on the band several times.[236]

Transformers author Bill Forster is an avowed Iron Maiden fan and made several Iron Maiden references, including song lyrics and the phrase "Up the Irons" in his books, including The Ark series and The AllSpark Almanac series.[237]

Claims of Satanic references

In 1982, the band released one of their most popular, controversial and acclaimed albums, *The Number of the Beast*. The artwork and title track led to Christian groups in the United States branding the band as Satanists, encouraging people to destroy copies of the release.[50] The band's manager, Rod Smallwood, later commented that Christians initially burnt the records, but later decided to destroy them with hammers through fear of breathing in the melting vinyl's fumes.[238] The claims were not restricted to the US, however, with Christian organisations managing to prevent Iron Maiden from performing in Chile in 1992.[170]

Contrary to the accusations, the band have always denied the notion that they are Satanists, with lead vocalist, Bruce Dickinson, doing so on-stage in the *Live After Death* concert video.[62] Steve Harris has since commented that, "It was mad. They completely got the wrong end of the stick. They obviously hadn't read the lyrics. They just wanted to believe all that rubbish about us being Satanists."[47] Harris has also stated that "The Number of the Beast" song was inspired by a nightmare he had after watching *Damien: Omen II*,[239] and also influenced by Robert Burns' *Tam o' Shanter*.[51] Furthermore, the band's drummer, Nicko McBrain, has been a born again Christian since 1999.[240]

Ed Force One

For their Somewhere Back in Time World Tour in 2008 and 2009, Iron Maiden commissioned an Astraeus Airlines Boeing 757 as transport.[241] The aeroplane was converted into a combi configuration, which enabled it to carry the band, their crew and stage production, thereby allowing the group to perform in countries which were previously deemed unreachable logistically.[143] It was also repainted with a special Iron Maiden livery,[143] which the airline decided to retain after receiving positive feedback from customers.[242]

The aircraft, named "Ed Force One" after a competition on the band's website,[144] was flown by Dickinson, as he was also a commercial airline pilot for Astraeus, and plays a major role in the award-winning documentary,[243] *Iron Maiden: Flight 666*, which was released in cinemas in 42 countries in April 2009.[155] A different aeroplane (G-STRX)[244] was used for The Final Frontier World Tour in 2011 with altered livery, adopting the artwork of *The Final Frontier* album,[245] and features heavily in the 2012 documentary "Behind the Beast". For the upcoming The Book of Souls World Tour (2016), the band have upgraded to a Boeing 747-400 jumbo jet, supplied by Air Atlanta Icelandic, which allows for more space without the aircraft having to undergo a significant conversion to carry their equipment.[189]

2.33.3 Musical style and influences

Steve Harris, Iron Maiden's bassist and primary songwriter,[246] has stated that his influences include Black Sabbath, Deep Purple, Led Zeppelin, Uriah Heep, Pink Floyd, Genesis, Yes, Jethro Tull, Thin Lizzy, UFO and Wishbone Ash.[247] In 2010 Harris stated, "I think if anyone wants to understand Maiden's early thing, in particular the harmony guitars, all they have to do is listen to Wishbone Ash's *Argus* album. Thin Lizzy too, but not as much. And then we wanted to have a bit of a prog thing thrown in as well, because I was really into bands like Genesis and Jethro Tull. So you combine all that with the heavy riffs and the speed, and you've got it."[204] In 2004, Harris explained that the band's "heaviness" was inspired by "Black Sabbath and Deep Purple with a bit of Zeppelin thrown in."[248] On top of this, Harris developed his own playing style, which guitarist Janick Gers describes as "more like a rhythm guitar,"[249] cited as responsible for the band's galloping style,[250] heard in such songs as "The Trooper"[251] and "Run to the Hills."[252]

The band's guitarists, Dave Murray, Adrian Smith and Janick Gers, each have their own individual influences and playing style. Dave Murray is known for his legato technique which, he claims, "evolved naturally. I'd heard Jimi Hendrix using legato when I was growing up, and I liked that style of playing."[253] Stating that he "was inspired by blues rock rather than metal," Adrian Smith was influenced by Johnny Winter and Pat Travers, leading to him becoming a "melodic player."[254] Janick Gers, on the other hand, prefers a more improvised style, largely inspired by Ritchie Blackmore,[255] which he claims is in contrast to Smith's "rhythmic" sound.[256]

Singer Bruce Dickinson, who typically works in collaboration with guitarist Adrian Smith,[257] has an operatic vocal style, inspired by Arthur Brown, Peter Hammill, Ian Anderson and Ian Gillan,[258] and is often considered to be one of the best heavy metal vocalists of all time.[259] Although Nicko McBrain has only received one writing credit, on the *Dance of Death* album,[260] Harris often relies on him while developing songs. Adrian Smith commented, "Steve loves playing with him. [They] used to work for hours going over these bass and drum patterns."[261]

Throughout their career, the band's style has remained largely unchanged, in spite of the addition of guitar synthesisers on 1986's *Somewhere in Time*,[82] keyboards on 1988's *Seventh Son of a Seventh Son*,[70] and an attempt to return to the "stripped down" production of their earlier material on 1990's *No Prayer for the Dying*.[81] In recent years, however, the band have begun using more progressive elements in their songs,[262] which Steve Harris describes as not progressive "in the modern sense, but like Dream Theater, more in a 70s way."[263] According to Harris, *Seventh Son of a Seventh Son* was the band's first album which was "more progressive,"[264] while they would only return to this style from 1995's *The X Factor*, which he states is "like an extension of *Seventh Son*..., in the sense of the progressive element to it."[94] The development contrasts with the band's raw sounding earlier material,[204] which AllMusic states was "clearly drawing from elements of punk rock,"[265] although Harris firmly denies this.[266]

2.33.4 Awards

Main article: List of awards and nominations received by Iron Maiden

2.33.5 Band members

For more details on this topic, see List of Iron Maiden band members.

2.33.6 Discography

Main article: Iron Maiden discography

Studio albums

- *Iron Maiden* (1980)
- *Killers* (1981)
- *The Number of the Beast* (1982)
- *Piece of Mind* (1983)
- *Powerslave* (1984)
- *Somewhere in Time* (1986)
- *Seventh Son of a Seventh Son* (1988)
- *No Prayer for the Dying* (1990)
- *Fear of the Dark* (1992)
- *The X Factor* (1995)
- *Virtual XI* (1998)
- *Brave New World* (2000)
- *Dance of Death* (2003)
- *A Matter of Life and Death* (2006)
- *The Final Frontier* (2010)
- *The Book of Souls* (2015)

2.33.7 Concert tours

Main article: List of Iron Maiden concert tours

* More dates to be announced

2.33.8 See also

- List of artists who reached number one on the UK Singles Chart
- List of New Wave of British Heavy Metal bands
- List of bands from England
- List of Iron Maiden songs
- Music in tribute of Iron Maiden
- The Iron Maidens

2.33.9 Notes

Citations

[1] Green 2010.

[2] Smith 2009.

[3] Munday 2015.

[4] Wall 2004, p. 29; Bushell & Halfin 1985, p. 9.

[5] Barton 1970.

[6] EMI 2004.

[7] Wall 2004, p. 29.

[8] Wall 2004, p. 32.

[9] Wall 2004, p. 33.

[10] Wall 2004, p. 44.

[11] Wall 2004, p. 46.

[12] Wall 2004, p. 23.

[13] Wall 2004, p. 48.

[14] Wall 2004, p. 50.

[15] Wall 2004, p. 52.

[16] Wall 2004, p. 54.

[17] Wall 2004, p. 53.

[18] Wall 2004, p. 64.

[19] Wall 2004, p. 66.

[20] Wall 2004, p. 67.

[21] Wall 2004, pp. 104–105.

[22] Wall 2004, p. 83.

[23] Wall 2004, p. 103.

[24] Wall 2004, p. 102.
[25] Wall 2004, p. 104-105.
[26] Wall 2004, p. 108.
[27] Wall 2004, pp. 163–164.
[28] Wall 2004, p. 121.
[29] Wall 2004, p. 123.
[30] Wall 2004, p. 137.
[31] Wall 2004, p. 139; Saulnier 2012.
[32] Wall 2004, p. 143.
[33] Roland 2013.
[34] Hinchcliffe 1999.
[35] Wall 2004, p. 183.
[36] Brannigan.
[37] Wall 2004, p. 145.
[38] Wall 2004, p. 181.
[39] Wall 2004, p. 300.
[40] Wall 2004, p. 251.
[41] Wall 2004, p. 194.
[42] Wall 2004, p. 219.
[43] Wall 2004, p. 218.
[44] Wall 2004, p. 217.
[45] Dome 2014.
[46] Wall 2004, p. 227.
[47] Wall 2004, p. 228.
[48] Shooman 2007, p. 82.
[49] Pfanner 2010.
[50] Young(1).
[51] Eagle Vision 2001.
[52] Wall 2004, p. 233.
[53] Wall 2004, pp. 232-233.
[54] Marlow 2011.
[55] Wall 2004, p. 246.
[56] Wall 2004, p. 247.
[57] Billboard.
[58] Wall 2004, p. 245.
[59] Wall 2004, p. 253.
[60] Stenning 2006, p. 102.
[61] Wall 2004, p. 257.
[62] EMI 2008.
[63] Wall 2004, p. 258.
[64] Stenning 2006, p. 104.
[65] Wall 2004, p. 255.
[66] Huey(3).
[67] Wall 2004, p. 260.
[68] Wall 2004, p. 261.
[69] Popoff 2005(d).
[70] Wall 2004, p. 265.
[71] Wall 2004, p. 263.
[72] RIAA.
[73] Wall 2004, p. 269.
[74] UK Rock Festivals.
[75] Wall 2004, p. 272.
[76] Wall 2004, p. 266; Johnson 1988.
[77] Gennet 2010.
[78] Wall 2004, p. 273.
[79] Wall 2004, p. 281.
[80] Wall 2004, p. 285.
[81] Wall 2004, p. 283.
[82] Prato.
[83] Wall 2004, p. 282.
[84] Wall 2004, p. 289.
[85] Wall 2004, p. 291.
[86] Wall 2004, p. 293.
[87] Wall 2004, p. 296.
[88] Wall 2004, p. 297.
[89] Wall 2004, p. 298.
[90] Wall 2004, p. 301.
[91] Wall 2004, p. 302.
[92] Stagno 2006(b).
[93] Wall 2004, p. 313.

[94] Wall 2004, p. 311.
[95] Paterson 2009, p. 44.
[96] Popoff 2005(b).
[97] Wall 2004, p. 314.
[98] Wall 2004, p. 316.
[99] Sverigetopplistan.
[100] Official Charts Company 1998.
[101] Stagno 2006(a).
[102] Saulnier 2010.
[103] Wall 2004, p. 324.
[104] Wall 2004, p. 321.
[105] Brave Words & Bloody Knuckles 2010.
[106] Wall 2004, p. 328.
[107] Wall 2004, p. 329.
[108] Wall 2004, p. 330.
[109] Wall 2004, p. 331.
[110] Adams.
[111] Wall 2004, p. 341.
[112] Berelian 2000.
[113] Wall 2004, p. 342.
[114] Wall 2004, p. 353; Shooman 2007, p. 176; Sanctuary 2002; Martins 2002.
[115] Wall 2004, p. 357.
[116] Wall 2004, p. 361.
[117] Blabbermouth.net 2005c.
[118] Blabbermouth.net 2007c.
[119] BBC News 2013.
[120] Wall 2004, p. 368.
[121] Wall 2004, p. 369.
[122] Wall 2004, p. 373.
[123] Wall 2004, p. 375.
[124] Blabbermouth.net 2005a.
[125] Blabbermouth.net 2005b.
[126] Blabbermouth.net 2004d.
[127] Official Charts Company 2005.
[128] Metal Underground 2004.
[129] Metal Underground 2005.
[130] KNAC 2004; Sullivan 2005.
[131] Wilde 2008.
[132] NME 2005; Williams 2005.
[133] Blabbermouth.net 2006.
[134] Billboard 2006.
[135] Blabbermouth.net 2006b.
[136] Vincentelli 2006; Evening Times 2006.
[137] Blabbermouth.net 2007b.
[138] Blabbermouth.net 2007a.
[139] Vulliamy 2007.
[140] Metal Underground 2007.
[141] Blabbermouth.net 2007d.
[142] Lane 2007.
[143] Metal Storm 2007.
[144] Cashmere 2008.
[145] Lane 2008.
[146] Sputnikmusic 2008.
[147] Thrash Hits 2007.
[148] Khan 2009.
[149] Bezer 2008.
[150] Soto 2008.
[151] Kaczuroski 2009.
[152] Bezer 2009d.
[153] Bezer 2009b.
[154] Blabbermouth.net 2009c.
[155] Bezer 2009a.
[156] Blabbermouth.net 2009d.
[157] Bezer 2009f.
[158] Masters 2009.
[159] Bezer 2010a.
[160] Blabbermouth.net 2010c.
[161] MetaCritic1.
[162] Coleman 2011.

[163] Daily Star 2009.

[164] Bezer 2010b; Dawson 2011.

[165] Blabbermouth.net 2011a.

[166] Blabbermouth.net 2010f.

[167] Blabbermouth.net 2010g.

[168] Rock on the Net.

[169] Blabbermouth.net 2011c.

[170] Brave Words & Bloody Knuckles 2011.

[171] Blabbermouth.net 2012.

[172] UpVenue.

[173] Alderslade 2012b.

[174] Alderslade 2012a.

[175] Kielty 2012.

[176] Nilsson 2012.

[177] Childers 2012; Rocha 2012.

[178] Crónica 2013.

[179] Jaedike 2012.

[180] Hartmann 2012.

[181] Tez 2013.

[182] Kielty 2015a; Kaufman 2015.

[183] Munro 2015.

[184] Grow 2015.

[185] MetaCritic2; Sexton 2015.

[186] Kielty 2015b.

[187] Lach 2015a.

[188] Lach 2015b; Alfa.lt 2015.

[189] Lach 2015b.

[190] VH1 2005.

[191] MTV 2006(a).

[192] VH1 2006.

[193] Sanctuary Group 2002.

[194] Guitar Center.

[195] Football Fancast.

[196] Wall 2004, p. 133.

[197] Wall 2004, p. 62.

[198] Wall 2004, p. 136.

[199] Popoff 2005(a).

[200] Thrash Hits 2008.

[201] Lefkove 2008.

[202] Meansheets 2010.

[203] EMI 1998.

[204] Bienstock 2011.

[205] Kerrang! 2008.

[206] Young(2).

[207] Metal Update 2010.

[208] MTV 2006(b).

[209] Charlesworth 2009.

[210] Lenta.ru 2010.

[211] Lawson 2013.

[212] Blabbermouth.net 2010e.

[213] Basham 2000.

[214] MetroLyrics(1).

[215] Sputnikmusic(1).

[216] MetroLyrics(2).

[217] MetroLyrics(3).

[218] Thomas 2009.

[219] MetroLyrics(4).

[220] MetroLyrics(5).

[221] Maiden United.

[222] AllMusic.

[223] Aquarius Records.

[224] Loftus.

[225] AllMusic(2).

[226] Giant Bomb.

[227] IGN.

[228] Allgame.

[229] Rockstar Games.

[230] Blabbermouth.net 2002.

[231] Cheat Code Central.

[232] Metal Insider 2009.

[233] East 2009; Rock Band.

[234] BillWyman.com 2014.

[235] JoBlo.com.

[236] Wardlaw; Ling 2005.

[237] Angelfire(1); Angelfire(2).

[238] Eagle Vision 2001; Young(1).

[239] Wall 2004, p. 224.

[240] Godscare.

[241] Bezer 2008; Metal Storm 2007.

[242] Blabbermouth.net 2008.

[243] Juno Awards 2010; Bezer 2009c.

[244] EMI 2012.

[245] Blabbermouth.net 2010d.

[246] MusicRadar 2010.

[247] Blabbermouth.net 2004c; EMI 2004; Wall 2004, p. 27; Wall 2004, p. 154.

[248] Blabbermouth.net 2004c.

[249] Popoff 2005(c).

[250] Fender.

[251] Huey(2).

[252] Lawson.

[253] McIver 2010(a).

[254] McIver 2010(c).

[255] Wall 2004, p. 277.

[256] McIver 2010(b).

[257] Wall 2004, p. 244.

[258] Dmme.net.

[259] Rosen 2011; HearYa.com 2006; Blabbermouth.net 2009a; Blabbermouth.net 2009b.

[260] Ling 2005b.

[261] Wall 2004, p. 241.

[262] Dome 2006a; Dome 2006b.

[263] Dome 2006b.

[264] Wall 2004, p. 264.

[265] Huey(1).

[266] VH1 2011.

[267] Blabbermouth.net 2011b.

[268] Bandit Rock 2015.

[269] Barton 2009.

[270] BBC News 2015.

[271] YLE.

[272] Gill 2011.

[273] Juno Awards 2010.

[274] Jones 2005.

[275] Anderson 2013.

[276] Blabbermouth.net 2004a.

[277] Bezer 2009e.

[278] Metal Storm 2011.

[279] Blabbermouth.net 2012b.

[280] Kielty 2014.

[281] Metal Storm (1).

[282] Metal Storm (2).

[283] Metal Storm (3).

[284] Blabbermouth.net 2004b.

[285] Cooper 2015.

[286] Wejbro 2011.

[287] Bezer 2009c.

2.33.10 References

- Adams, Bret. "Iron Maiden: *Ed Hunter*". *AllMusic*. Rovi Corporation. Retrieved 16 February 2014.

- Alderslade, Merlin (15 February 2012). "Maiden announce US tour". *Metal Hammer*. Archived from the original on 3 December 2013. Retrieved 15 February 2012.

- Alderslade, Merlin (6 December 2012). "Iron Maiden, Megadeth, Marilyn Manson, Lamb of God Among Grammy Nominees". *Metal Hammer*. Archived from the original on 9 June 2013. Retrieved 6 December 2012.

- "Metalo milžinai „Iron Maiden" pirmą kartą atvyksta į Lietuvą Skaitykite daugiau: Metalo milžinai „Iron Maiden" pirmą kartą atvyksta į Lietuvą". *Alfa.lt* (in Lithuanian). 2 November 2015. Retrieved 2 November 2015.

2.33. IRON MAIDEN

- "*Grand Theft Auto: Episodes from Liberty City* Credits". Allgame. Retrieved 25 February 2012.

- "Various Artists - *The Piano Tribute to Iron Maiden*". AllMusic. Retrieved 2 September 2014.

- "Various Artists - *Hip-Hop Tribute to Iron Maiden*". AllMusic. Retrieved 2 September 2014.

- Anderson, Steve (14 June 2013). "*Kerrang!* Awards 2013: Rock veterans Iron Maiden and Queen's Brian May and Roger Taylor honoured". *The Independent*. Retrieved 2 September 2014.

- "Annotated AllSpark Almanac I notes by Chris McFeely". Angelfire.com. Retrieved 27 August 2010.

- "Annotated AllSpark Almanac II notes by Chris McFeely". Angelfire.com. Retrieved 27 August 2010.

- "*Powerslaves: An Elektro Tribute to Iron Maiden*". Aquarius Records. Retrieved 2 September 2014.

- "Alla vinnare i Bandit Rock Awards 2015!". *Bandit Rock* (in Swedish). 27 February 2015. Retrieved 27 February 2015.

- Barton, Geoff (27 October 1970). "Blood and Iron: HM from the punky East End and nothing to do with Margaret Thatcher, sez Deaf Barton". *Sounds*. NWOBHM.com. Archived from the original on 29 June 2007. Retrieved 8 October 2006.

- Barton, Geoff (2 November 2009). "Iggy Pop 'Living Legend' At Classic Rock Awards". *Classic Rock*. Archived from the original on 19 December 2013. Retrieved 24 March 2013.

- Basham, David (23 August 2000). "Wheatus Digs Up "Dirtbag," Gives Props To Iron Maiden". MTV. Retrieved 7 October 2013.

- "Clive Burr, former Iron Maiden drummer, dies at 56". BBC News. 13 March 2013. Retrieved 15 March 2013.

- "Queen named 'living legends' at *Classic Rock* awards". BBC News. 11 November 2015. Retrieved 11 November 2015.

- Berelian, Essi (June 2000). "The Wicked Man". *Classic Rock* (15): 36–43.

- Bezer, Terry (12 November 2008). "Iron Maiden Announce Final 'Somewhere Back in Time' Dates". *Metal Hammer*. Archived from the original on 4 February 2014. Retrieved 19 April 2013.

- Bezer, Terry (20 January 2009). "Iron Maiden: The Movie! Catch The Trailer!". *Classic Rock*. Archived from the original on 6 May 2009. Retrieved 29 November 2012.

- Bezer, Terry (18 February 2009). "Iron Maiden wins Brit award". *Metal Hammer*. Archived from the original on 2 June 2013. Retrieved 1 September 2011.

- Bezer, Terry (23 March 2009). "SXSW award for Flight 666". *Metal Hammer*. Archived from the original on 14 May 2013. Retrieved 1 September 2011.

- Bezer, Terry (15 April 2009). "Iron Maiden Release *Flight 666* DVD Details". *Classic Rock*. Archived from the original on 15 January 2010. Retrieved 19 April 2013.

- Bezer, Terry (16 June 2009). "*Metal Hammer* awards 2009 winners". *Metal Hammer*. Archived from the original on 27 December 2013. Retrieved 1 September 2011.

- Bezer, Terry (18 June 2009). "Iron Maiden Hit Number One in Over 20 Countries". *Metal Hammer*. Archived from the original on 4 February 2014. Retrieved 19 April 2013.

- Bezer, Terry (4 March 2010). "Iron Maiden *The Final Frontier* Album Details Emerge". *Metal Hammer*. Archived from the original on 2 June 2013. Retrieved 26 November 2012.

- Bezer, Terry (10 August 2010). "Iron Maiden's Nicko McBrain: "It Ain't Gonna Be The Last Record. Not As Far As I'm Concerned"". *Metal Hammer*. Archived from the original on 29 October 2013. Retrieved 18 August 2010.

- Bienstock, Richard (3 July 2011). "Maiden Voyage". *Guitar World*. Retrieved 30 August 2011.

- "Piece of Mind". *Billboard*. Nielsen Business Media, Inc. Retrieved 1 August 2009.

- "Iron Maiden returns to the chart for the first time since 2003". *Billboard*. 13 September 2006. Retrieved 20 December 2011.

- "Bill Wyman's *Phenomena* 'Valley' soundtrack and videos". BillWyman.com. 24 March 2014. Retrieved 2 September 2014.

- "AC/DC Bassist To Tour Eastern Europe". Blabbermouth.net. 20 October 2002. Retrieved 24 February 2012.

- "*Metal Hammer* awards 2004 winners". Blabbermouth.net. 7 June 2004. Retrieved 1 September 2011.

- "Iron Maiden Receive Special Achievement Award". Blabbermouth.net. 18 June 2004. Retrieved 20 November 2011.

- "Iron Maiden Bassist Talks About His Technique And Influences". Blabbermouth.net. 24 September 2004. Retrieved 25 April 2008.

- "Iron Maiden To Release 'Number of the Beast' Single". Blabbermouth.net. 16 November 2004. Retrieved 20 November 2011.

- "Iron Maiden Announce Details Of *Death on the Road* DVD/CD". Blabbermouth.net. 11 May 2005. Retrieved 20 November 2011.

- "Iron Maiden: 'Eddie Rips Up the World' Tour Opener Setlist Revealed". Blabbermouth.net. 28 May 2005. Retrieved 1 January 2010.

- "Iron Maiden Announce eBay Auction and Hard Rock Café Event". Blabbermouth.net. 22 November 2005. Retrieved 20 November 2011.

- "Iron Maiden Drummer, Guitarist Talk About New Album". Blabbermouth.net. 5 July 2006. Retrieved 17 September 2006.

- "*Classic Rock* 2006 winners". Blabbermouth.net. 7 November 2006. Retrieved 1 September 2011.

- "Iron Maiden Announces First-Ever Appearance in India". Blabbermouth.net. 13 February 2007. Retrieved 20 November 2011.

- "Iron Maiden Announces 'A Matter of the Beast Summer Tour '07'". Blabbermouth.net. 8 May 2007. Retrieved 20 November 2011.

- "Iron Maiden Confirms Special Clive Burr Show". Blabbermouth.net. 25 May 2007. Retrieved 20 November 2011.

- "UK's Download named Top Festival". Blabbermouth.net. 15 November 2007. Retrieved 15 November 2007.

- "Iron Maiden Frontman Issues 'Bruce Air' Update". Blabbermouth.net. 7 July 2008. Retrieved 20 November 2011.

- "Robert Plant, Freddie Mercury, Axl Rose, Ian Gillan Among 'Greatest Voices in Rock'". Blabbermouth.net. 2 January 2009. Retrieved 1 August 2010.

- "Bruce Dickinson And Ronnie James Dio Are Heavy Metal's Top Singers". Blabbermouth.net. 1 June 2009. Retrieved 1 August 2010.

- "Iron Maiden wins Brit award". Blabbermouth.net. 18 February 2009. Retrieved 1 September 2011.

- "Iron Maiden's *Flight 666* Was Biggest-Ever Worldwide Simultaneous Release Of Documentary Film". Blabbermouth.net. 11 May 2009. Retrieved 27 October 2014.

- "Iron Maiden *Flight 666* To Be Screened As Part of BBC4's 'Heavy Metal Britannia' Weekend". Blabbermouth.net. 26 February 2010. Retrieved 20 November 2011.

- "Iron Maiden To Play Concert in Transylvania". Blabbermouth.net. 17 May 2010. Retrieved 20 November 2011.

- "Iron Maiden: New Album Details Revealed". Blabbermouth.net. 7 June 2010. Retrieved 20 November 2011.

- "Iron Maiden: Around The World In 66 Days". Blabbermouth.net. Roadrunner Records. 2 November 2010. Retrieved 8 June 2013.

- "Dream Theater and Iron Maiden Members Say 'Cheese' for Tour Photo". Blabbermouth.net. 22 July 2010. Retrieved 2 September 2014.

- "Iron Maiden To End 'The Final Frontier World Tour' In London". Blabbermouth.net. 20 November 2010. Retrieved 20 November 2011.

- "Iron Maiden, Slayer, Megadeth, Ozzy, Korn Among Grammy Awards Nominees". Blabbermouth.net. 1 December 2010. Retrieved 2 December 2010.

- "Iron Maiden Announces Support Acts For U.K. Tour". Blabbermouth.net. 18 February 2011. Retrieved 20 November 2011.

- "Bandit Rock Awards 2011". Blabbermouth.net. 4 April 2011. Retrieved 1 September 2011.

- "*From Fear To Eternity* New Release Date Announced; Promo-Only CD Single Detailed". Blabbermouth.net. 6 May 2011. Retrieved 20 November 2011.

- "Lady Gaga: Iron Maiden Changed My Life". Blabbermouth.net. 25 May 2011.

- "Iron Maiden To Release *En Vivo!* Concert Blu-Ray, Two-DVD Set And Double Soundtrack Album". Blabbermouth.net. 17 January 2012. Retrieved 17 January 2012.

- "Saxon, Anthrax, Fear Factory, Machine Head Honoured At 'Metal Hammer Golden Gods'". Blabbermouth.net. 12 June 2012. Retrieved 12 June 2012.

- Brannigan, Paul. "Hack Job?". *Kerrang! Legends* (2): 26–27.

- "Janick Gers interview- Talking Metal Pirate Radio No. 5". *Brave Words & Bloody Knuckles*. 26 August 2010. Retrieved 25 February 2012.

- "Iron Maiden To Release From Fear To Eternity – The Best of 1990 – 2010; Details Revealed, Manager Rod Smallwood Comments". *Brave Words & Bloody Knuckles*. 15 March 2011. Retrieved 20 November 2011.

- "Chilean Magazine Slams Iron Maiden Why Music Matters Animated Film As "Full of Lies"". *Brave Words & Bloody Knuckles*. 15 June 2011. Retrieved 20 September 2011.

- Bushell, Garry; Halfin, Ross (1985). *Running Free, The Official Story of Iron Maiden* (second ed.). Zomba Books. ISBN 0-946391-84-X.

- Cashmere, Tim (15 January 2008). "Iron Maiden Reveal Ed Force One". Undercover FM. Retrieved 20 November 2011.

- Charlesworth, Jenny (29 October 2009). "3 Inches of Blood's Cam Pipes Raised on Classical Music". Spinner.com. Archived from the original on 29 June 2013. Retrieved 26 January 2010.

- "*SSX on Tour* Review". Cheat Code Central. Retrieved 24 September 2011.

- Childers, Chad (16 October 2012). "Metallica + Iron Maiden Sign on to Headline Rock in Rio 2013". *Loudwire*. Archived from the original on 18 October 2012. Retrieved 17 October 2012.

- Coleman, Andrew (29 July 2011). "Music: Iron Maiden's final frontier". *Birmingham Mail*. Retrieved 24 September 2012. hitting the number one spot in 28 countries

- Cooper, Leonie (23 March 2015). "Iron Maiden win O2 Silver Clef 2015 Award for outstanding contribution to UK music". *NME*. Retrieved 23 March 2015.

- "Iron Maiden, Slayer y Ghost confirmaron su venida histórica al Paraguay". *Crónica* (in Spanish). 11 April 2013. Archived from the original on 11 April 2013. Retrieved 11 April 2013.

- "Iron Maiden cancel plans to quit". *Daily Star*. 17 March 2009. Retrieved 3 August 2011. We've always said we're only going to do 15 albums; we're coming up to it. There's going to be an ending point.

- Dawson, Kim (3 August 2011). "Iron Maiden play it cool". *Daily Star*. Retrieved 5 August 2011.

- "Interview with Bruce Dickinson October 2001". dmme.net. Retrieved 15 August 2011.

- Dome, Malcolm (September 2006). "The Good Life". *Classic Rock* (97): 76.

- Dome, Malcolm (September 2006). "Iron Maiden: War all the Time". *Metal Hammer* (157): 34–40.

- Dome, Malcolm (26 September 2014). "Remembering The Day Bruce Joined Maiden". *Metal Hammer*. TeamRock. Retrieved 26 September 2014.

- *Classic Albums: Iron Maiden – The Number of the Beast* (DVD). Eagle Vision. 4 December 2001.

- East, Tom (7 May 2009). "*Guitar Hero Greatest Hits* Tracklist Confirmed". *Official Nintendo Magazine*.

- "Part 2: Groundwork". *Iron Maiden: In Profile*. EMI. 1998.

- *The History of Iron Maiden – Part 1: The Early Days* (DVD). UK: EMI. 23 November 2004. ASIN B0006B29Z2

- "The History of Iron Maiden part 2". *Live After Death* (DVD). EMI. 4 February 2008.

- "Iron Maiden: Behind the Beast". *En Vivo!* (DVD). EMI. 26 March 2012.

- "Dickinson and his veteran boys can still rock..". *Evening Times*. vlex.co.uk. 14 December 2006. Retrieved 1 January 2009.

- "Steve Harris Precision Bass®". Fender.com. Retrieved 21 September 2011.

- "Steve Harris: West Ham's Top Ten Most Famous Fans". Footballfancast.com. Retrieved 30 August 2011.

- Fuentes Rodríguez, César (2005). *Iron Maiden: El Viaje De La Doncella*. ISBN 84-933891-2-9. (Spanish)

- Gamba, Marco; Visintini, Nicola (2000). *Iron Maiden Companion* (1st ed.). Moving Media & Arts.

- Gennet, Robbie (3 October 2010). "Michael Kenney - the Man Behind the Maiden". *Keyboard Magazine*. Retrieved 19 April 2012.

- "Carmageddon 2". Giant Bomb. Retrieved 24 September 2011.

- Gill, James (14 February 2011). "Iron Maiden Win at the Grammys". *Metal Hammer*. Archived from the original on 4 February 2014. Retrieved 7 October 2013.

- "The drummer with million". Godscare.net. Archived from the original on 23 July 2011. Retrieved 27 August 2010.

- Green, Thomas H (28 July 2010). "Iron Maiden: doing it their own way". *The Daily Telegraph* (London). Retrieved 24 December 2011. when Dickinson re-entered the fold in 1999 the band's ensuing career made them bigger than ever

- Grow, Kory (18 June 2015). "Iron Maiden Announce New Double Album *The Book of Souls*". *Rolling Stone*. Retrieved 18 June 2015.

- "Iron Maiden- Guitar Center Rockwalk". Guitar Center. Retrieved 1 September 2011.

- Hartmann, Graham (12 February 2013). "Iron Maiden to Release *Maiden England '88* Concert DVD With Never-Before-Seen Footage". *Loudwire*. Archived from the original on 12 February 2013. Retrieved 12 February 2013.

- "Hit Parader's Top 100 Metal Vocalists of All Time". HearYa.com. 4 December 2006. Retrieved 1 August 2010.

- Hinchcliffe, Jon (27 October 1999). "Dennis Stratton Interview: October 1999". Praying-Mantis.com. Retrieved 8 October 2006.

- Huey, Steve. "*Iron Maiden* – Review". *AllMusic*. Rovi Corporation. Retrieved 19 November 2011.

- Huey, Steve. "*Piece of Mind* – Review". *AllMusic*. Rovi Corporation. Retrieved 19 November 2011.

- Huey, Steve. "Iron Maiden – *Somewhere in Time* – Review". *AllMusic*. Rovi Corporation. Retrieved 12 October 2008.

- "*Grand Theft Auto: Vice City* Songs". IGN. Retrieved 2 September 2014.

- Iron Maiden (past and present band and management) (1996). *12 Wasted Years* (VHS). UK: Sanctuary Group. OCLC 23531749 ASIN 6301092643

- Jaedike, Jan (1 September 2012). "Steve Harris: Es Geht Voran". *Rock Hard* (in German) **304**: 16–21.

- "*Murder By Numbers* (2002)". JoBlo.com. Retrieved 2 September 2014.

- Johnson, Howard (20 August 1988). "Waiting for the (Seventh) Son". *Kerrang!* (201): 12.

- Jones, Sam (26 August 2005). "*Kerrang!* 2005 winners". *The Guardian* (London). Retrieved 3 December 2011.

- "Juno Winners – 2010 Gala Dinner & Awards". Juno Awards. 18 April 2010. Retrieved 1 September 2011.

- Kaczuroski, Thiago (16 March 2009). "Iron Maiden does biggest show of career in São Paulo" (in Portuguese). Terra Networks.

- Kaufman, Spencer (19 February 2015). "Iron Maiden's Bruce Dickinson Undergoes Treatment for Cancerous Tumor". *Loudwire*. Retrieved 19 February 2015.

- "The making of Maiden Heaven". *Kerrang!*. 16 July 2008. Archived from the original on 1 May 2013. Retrieved 13 January 2011.

- "Lady Gaga hearts Iron Maiden". *Kerrang!*. 1 July 2010. Archived from the original on 1 May 2013. Retrieved 16 October 2011.

- Khan, Urmee (6 April 2009). "The Police and Iron Maiden lead British music stars' foreign earnings to hit record levels". London: *The Daily Telegraph*. Retrieved 18 February 2011.

- Kielty, Martin (20 September 2012). "Iron Maiden confirmed for Download 2013". *Classic Rock*. Archived from the original on 20 September 2012. Retrieved 20 September 2012.

- Kielty, Martin (16 June 2014). "Maiden, A7X, others honoured at Metal Hammer Golden Gods". *Classic Rock*. Retrieved 19 June 2014.

- Kielty, Martin (27 February 2015). "Maiden album is ready but on hold". *Metal Hammer*. Retrieved 27 February 2015.

- Kielty, Martin (18 June 2015). "Iron Maiden name album No.16". *Metal Hammer*. Retrieved 18 June 2015.

- "Iron Maiden Manager's Official Statement Regarding Ozzfest Feud". KNAC. 23 August 2005. Retrieved 16 September 2012.

- Lach, Stef (14 August 2015). "Iron Maiden unveil "Speed of Light"". *Metal Hammer*. Retrieved 14 August 2015.

- Lach, Stef (25 August 2015). "Maiden to tour world in new Ed Force One". *Metal Hammer*. Retrieved 25 August 2015.

- Lane, Daniel (7 September 2007). "Iron Maiden Tour Plans". *Metal Hammer*. Archived from the original on 2 June 2013. Retrieved 29 November 2012.

- Lane, Daniel (27 March 2008). "Iron Maiden – New Album, Old Songs". *Metal Hammer*. Archived from the original on 2 June 2013. Retrieved 19 April 2013.

- Lawson, Dom. "666 of the Best". *Kerrang! Legends* (2): 36–37.

- Lawson, Dom (April 2013). "Infinite Dreams". *Metal Hammer* (242): 43.

- Lefkove, Aaron (5 June 2008). "Heavy Metal's Most Savage Mascots!". Gibson.com. Retrieved 23 September 2011.

- Группа "Ария" (in Russian). Lenta.ru. 5 November 2010. Retrieved 23 February 2013.

- Ling, Dave (November 2005). "Made in England". *Classic Rock* (86): 54.

- Ling, Dave (2005). "Nicko McBrain". *Metal Hammer presents: Iron Maiden 30 Years of Metal Mayhem*: 103.

- Loftus, Johnny. "Little Emo Quartet / Vitamin String Quartet - *Anatomy of Evil: The String Quartet Tribute to Iron Maiden*". AllMusic. Rovi Corporation. Retrieved 2 September 2014.

- "Maiden uniteD discography". MaidenuniteD.com. Retrieved 16 October 2011.

- Marlow, Lee (February 2011). "When drummer Clive Burr was ousted from Iron Maiden...". *Classic Rock* (154): 52–55.

- Martins, Thiago (5 April 2002). "Rock in Rio III Concert review". Metal Rules. Retrieved 4 September 2011. From the supposed attendance of 250,000 people...

- Masters, Tim (3 November 2009). "Rolling Stone Wood wins rock gong". BBC News. Retrieved 27 November 2009.

- McIver, Joel (December 2010). "Iron Maiden: Dave Murray". *Total Guitar* (208): 32–34.

- McIver, Joel (December 2010). "Iron Maiden: Janick Gers". *Total Guitar* (208): 36–38.

- McIver, Joel (December 2010). "Iron Maiden: Adrian Smith". *Total Guitar* (208): 40–42.

- "Fair Play " Meansheets – Vintage Movie Posters". Meansheets.com. 9 March 2010. Retrieved 9 July 2011.

- "*The Final Frontier* – Iron Maiden". *Metacritic*. CBS Interactive Inc. Retrieved 1 September 2011.

- "Reviews for *The Book of Souls* by Iron Maiden". *Metacritic*. CBS Interactive. Retrieved 1 September 2015.

- "Madden '10? More like Maiden '10! Game Soundtrack Revealed". Metal Insider. 27 July 2009. Retrieved 4 November 2009.

- "Metal Storm 2006 winners". Metal Storm. Retrieved 1 September 2011.

- "Metal Storm 2009 winners". Metal Storm. Retrieved 6 September 2011.

- "Metal Storm 2010 winners". Metal Storm. Retrieved 1 September 2011.

- "Iron Maiden – More Somewhere Back in Time World Tour Dates". Metal Storm. 1 November 2007. Retrieved 20 November 2011.

- "*Metal Hammer* awards 2011 winners". Metal Storm. 16 June 2011. Retrieved 1 September 2011.

- "Iron Maiden's Gothenburg Show Sold Out in 2.5 Hrs". Metal Underground. 30 October 2004. Retrieved 20 November 2011.

- "SVT To Broadcast Iron Maiden Live in Gothenburg". Metal Underground. 18 May 2005. Retrieved 20 November 2011.

- "Iron Maiden Headlining Download Festival". Metal Underground. 31 January 2007. Retrieved 20 November 2011.

- "Metal Update Interview with Jesper Strömblad". Metalupdate.com. 19 November 1999. Retrieved 27 August 2010.

- "Aqua- 'Back to the 80s' (lyrics)". MetroLyrics. Retrieved 16 October 2011.

- "Weezer- 'Heart songs' (lyrics)". MetroLyrics. Retrieved 16 October 2011.

- "Blues Traveler- 'Psycho Joe' lyrics". MetroLyrics. Retrieved 16 October 2011.

- "Sabaton- 'Metal Machine' (lyrics)". MetroLyrics. Retrieved 16 October 2011.

- "Sabaton- 'Metal Ripper' (lyrics)". MetroLyrics. Retrieved 16 October 2011.

- "The 60 greatest bassists of all time". MusicRadar. 24 September 2010. Retrieved 21 September 2011.

- "The Greatest Metal Bands of All Time, 4: Iron Maiden" (Official Website). MTV. 2006. Retrieved 7 October 2006.

- "Top 10s from Some Top 10 Metal Heads". MTV. 9 March 2006. Retrieved 13 January 2011.

- Munday, Matt (6 September 2015). "Bruce Dickinson: 'Hell would have to freeze over before you'd stop me getting on stage'". *The Observer*. London. Retrieved 13 September 2015.

- Munro, Scott (15 May 2015). "Dickinson given cancer all-clear". *Metal Hammer*. Retrieved 15 May 2015.

- Nilsson, Christoffer (25 September 2012). "Bruce Dickinson laddad inför konserten i Sverige". *Aftonbladet* (in Swedish). Archived from the original on 28 September 2012. Retrieved 25 September 2012.

- "Iron Maiden rise above Osbourne's drama at Leeds". *NME*. UK. 2005. Archived from the original (Official Website) on 20 July 2006. Retrieved 11 October 2006.

- "Official UK Albums Archive: 4 April 1998". Official Charts Company. Retrieved 17 October 2011.

- "UK Singles Chart- 15 January 2005". Official Charts Company. Retrieved 20 September 2011.

- Paterson, Lawrence (2009). *Blaze Bayley: At the End of the Day*. Blaze Bayley Recordings Ltd. p. 44.

- Pfanner, Eric (5 September 2010). "Die-Hard Fans Follow Iron Maiden into the Digital Age". *The New York Times*. Retrieved 10 October 2010.

- Popoff, Martin (2005). "Bullet in the Head". *Metal Hammer presents: Iron Maiden 30 Years of Metal Mayhem*: 43.

- Popoff, Martin (2005). "The X Offender". *Metal Hammer presents: Iron Maiden 30 Years of Metal Mayhem*: 63.

- Popoff, Martin (2005). "Maiden at the Movies". *Metal Hammer presents: Iron Maiden 30 Years of Metal Mayhem*: 104–105.

- Popoff, Martin (2005). "Commercial Break!". *Metal Hammer presents: Iron Maiden 30 Years of Metal Mayhem*: 108–109.

- Popoff, Martin (2013). *2 Minutes to Midnight: An Iron Maiden Day-by-Day*. Backbeat Books. ISBN 1-617-13565-8.

- Prato, Greg. "Iron Maiden – *No Prayer for the Dying*". *AllMusic*. Rovi Corporation. Retrieved 19 November 2011.

- "RIAA Searchable database – Gold and Platinum". Recording Industry Association of America. Retrieved 30 March 2008.

- Rocha, Pedro (16 October 2012). "Rock in Rio 2013 terá Springsteen, Metallica e Iron Maiden". *Jornal do Brasil* (in Portuguese) (Rio de Janeiro). Archived from the original on 18 October 2012. Retrieved 17 October 2012.

- "Iron Maiden: All Songs by Artist". *Rock Band*. Retrieved 24 September 2011.

- "Grammy Awards: Best Metal Performance". Rock on the Net. Retrieved 8 March 2009.

- "*The Lost and Damned* soundtrack". Rockstar Games. Retrieved 24 September 2011.

- Roland, Driadonna (13 March 2013). "Ex-Iron Maiden Drummer Clive Burr Dead at 56". MTV. Retrieved 13 May 2013.

- Rosen, Jeremy (7 December 2011). "The 50 Greatest Metal Front-men of All Time!". Roadrunner Records. Retrieved 1 August 2010.

- *Iron Maiden: Rock in Rio* (DVD). Sanctuary. 10 June 2002.

- "Iron Maiden honoured with Ivor Novello award". Sanctuary Group. 18 September 2002. Archived from the original (Official Website) on 10 March 2007. Retrieved 11 October 2006.

- Saulnier, Jason (30 April 2010). "Blaze Bayley Interview: Iron Maiden Singer talks Wolfsbane". Music Legends. Retrieved 24 May 2013.

- Saulnier, Jason (22 November 2012). "Paul Di'Anno Interview". Music Legends. Retrieved 6 May 2013.

- Sexton, Paul (11 September 2015). "Iron Maiden Earns Fifth No. 1 Album in U.K. With *The Book of Souls*". *Billboard. Retrieved 12 September 2015*.

- Shooman, Joe (2007). *Bruce Dickinson: Flashing Metal with Iron Maiden and Flying Solo*. Independent Music Press. ISBN 0-9552822-4-1

- Smith, Matt (21 April 2009). "Award Winning Iron Maiden Film Hits Cinemas". BSkyB. Retrieved 26 November 2011. ...largely without the help of radio airplay or the mainstream media.

- Soto, Jobana (1 December 2008). "Iron Maiden to perform in Lima March 2009". Living in Peru. Retrieved 6 December 2008.

- "Biography: Sum 41". Sputnikmusic. Retrieved 16 October 2011.

- "Iron Maiden: US Tour Dates". Sputnikmusic. 29 March 2008. Retrieved 20 November 2011.

- Stagno, Mike (11 June 2006). "Iron Maiden – *Virtual XI*". Sputnikmusic. Retrieved 28 January 2012.

- Stagno, Mike (2 August 2006). "Iron Maiden: *The X Factor* (Review)". Sputnikmusic. Retrieved 28 February 2012. ...the often criticised Blaze Bayley himself. With his lower vocal range, he may not have been able to sing the old Iron Maiden classics as well as Bruce...

- Stenning, Paul (2006). *Iron Maiden: 30 Years of the Beast – The Complete Unauthorised Biography*. Chrome Dreams. ISBN 1-84240-361-3.

- Sullivan, Caroline (24 August 2005). "The revenge of Sharon Osbourne". *The Guardian* (London).

- "Iron Maiden – *Virtual XI* Worldwide Charts". *Sverigetopplistan*. Swedishcharts.com. Retrieved 11 April 2012.

- Tez, Mehmet (26 July 2013). "Bir Bruce Dickinson röportajı: "Iron Maiden'ın farklı din ve kültürlerden İnsanları bİrleştİren yanını sevİyorum"". *Hafif Müzik* (in Turkish). Retrieved 27 February 2015.

- Thomas, Adam (29 April 2009). "NOFX- *Coaster*". Sputnikmusic. Retrieved 16 October 2011.

- "Iron Maiden live at Twickenham". *Thrash Hits*. 28 July 2007. Retrieved 12 October 2008.

- "*Metal Hammer* awards 2008 winners". Thrash Hits. 17 June 2008. Retrieved 1 September 2011.

- "Donington – Iron Maiden". UK Rock Festivals. Retrieved 12 October 2009.

- "Iron Maiden Releasing *En Vivo!* Blu-Ray, 2DVD and Soundtrack". *UpVenue*. 17 January 2012. Retrieved 17 January 2012.

- Carmen Electra (host) (11 August 2005). "VH1's 100 Greatest Hard Rock Artists". *The Greatest*. VH1.

- "VH1 Classic's Top 20 Metal Bands". 25 December 2006. VH1 Classic. Missing or empty |series= (help)

- Dunn, McFadyen (creators, directors) (10 December 2011). "New Wave of British Heavy Metal". *Metal Evolution*. VH1 Classic.

- Vincentelli, Elisabeth (31 December 2006). "Whole Albums in Concert". *The New York Times*. Retrieved 1 January 2009.

- Vulliamy, Ed (22 April 2007). "Maiden India". *The Guardian* (London). Retrieved 8 January 2012.

- Wall, Mick (2004). *Iron Maiden: Run to the Hills, the Authorised Biography* (third ed.). Sanctuary Publishing. ISBN 1-86074-542-3.

- Wardlaw, Matt. "Top 10 Beavis And Butthead Classic Rock Song Commentaries". Ultimate Classic Rock. Retrieved 20 December 2011.

- Wejbro, Sandra (31 August 2011). "Bästa liveakt hårdrock: Iron Maiden" (in Swedish). *Aftonbladet*. Retrieved 1 September 2011.

- Wilde, Jon (6 June 2008). "He ain't heavy he's your captain". *Daily Mail* (London). Retrieved 23 June 2011.

- Williams, Scott (31 August 2005). "Iron Maiden Reading 2005 Review". EFestivals.com. Retrieved 11 October 2006.

- "Emman historia" (in Finnish). YLE. Retrieved 4 September 2011.

- Young, Simon. "Raising Hell". *Kerrang! Legends* (2): 32.

- Young, Simon. "Iron Men". *Kerrang! Legends* (2): 90–93.

2.33.11 External links

- Official website
- Iron Maiden at Metal Archives

2.34 Jaguar (band)

This article is about the British heavy metal band Jaguar. For the Icelandic funk band Jagúar, see Jagúar (band).

Jaguar are an English heavy metal band, formed in Bristol, England, in December 1979. They had moderate success throughout Europe and Asia in the early 1980s, during the heyday of the New Wave of British Heavy Metal movement.

2.34.1 History

Early years

The band was formed in December 1979 in Bristol, England, trough an ad published in a local newspaper by Jeff Cox and Garry Pepperd looking for a drummer. The original line-up consisted of Garry Pepperd (guitar), Jeff Cox (bass, vocals) and Chris Lovell (drums). The same year they went straight into Sound Conception Studios to record their first demo, which was finished on 22 March 1980. The songs recorded on their first demo were "Feel the Heat", "Battle Cry" and "Piledriver". In April 1980, they put out another advertisement for a vocalist, to which Rob Reiss answered joining the band. In December 1980 the band went into another studio, Studio 34, and recorded another demo, which they later put together with the previous demo tracks. The band added now three new demo tracks to the previous ones. The new tracks were "Stormchild", "Ain't no Fantasy" and "War Machine".

Now the completed work consisted of six songs on a demo track tape. The songs were "Stormchild" (Cox); "Ain't No Fantasy" (Pepperd); "War Machine" (Pepperd); "Battlecry" (Cox/Pepperd) "Feel The Heat" (Pepperd); and "Piledriver" (Cox/Pepperd) . The demo was sold to the public through an ad in the music magazine *Sounds*, starting in February 1981. The band sold about 540 demos this way, a tremendous amount for a demo at that time.

The *Sounds* ad put Jaguar in contact with the Dutch fan and promoter Frits Gijsbertse, who arranged multiple gigs for the band in the Netherlands. The local metal magazine *Aardschok* often featured Jaguar in its pages and the magazine's owner, a man named 'Metal Mike', became later the band's promoter in that country.

Jaguar in 1980 sent their demo also to a Battle of the Bands competition and eventually a letter came through saying: "Congratulations, you've made it through to the Bristol heats!" Their first performance at that contest was on 2 May 1981 and they arrived to the final. Jaguar got a good reaction from the judges and they came fourth. This result and their demo earned Jaguar the chance to contribute with the song "Stormchild" to the compilation album *Heavy Metal Heroes*, released by Heavy Metal Records. The same label released in the second week of November 1981 the single "Back Street Woman", which went sold out within two months of its initial pressing of 4,000 copies.

Signed with Neat Records

At the beginning of 1982, after an appearance at a Dutch rock festival with Raven, Jaguar were noticed by Raven's manager and also owner of the indie label Neat Records Dave Wood, who proposed to release the band's next single through his label.

Jaguar signed the deal with Neat Records and replaced Reiss with Paul Merrell, former vocalist from the band Stormtrooper, just in time for the recording of the single "Axe Crazy", which was released later in 1982. The single sold really well and now Jaguar started to purr into a higher gear.

After intensive touring, the following year in June 1983 Jaguar released their first debut album, *Power Games*, which was a success with its no-nonsense high-speed approach. The band received great reviews from critics and fans and the album is regarded as the best ever made by Jaguar.

Signed with Roadrunner Records

Their follow-up album *This Time* was released in 1984 by Roadrunner Records and marked a change of musical direction for the band, towards a more melodic and AORish sound. At this time they were supported by Motörhead´s management, but by the end of the year Jaguar disbanded as Roadrunner did not fulfil the contract deal with the band.

Jaguar reformation

After a revival of interest in the New Wave of British Heavy Metal in Europe and Japan, and the successful re-release of their first album in those regions, Jaguar reformed in 1999, with the modified line-up of Pepperd, Jeff Cox, Nathan Cox on drums and the new vocalist Jamie Manton. An appearance at Wacken Open Air Festival the same year proved the new line-up was capable of recreating the energy of the early years.

The album *Wake Me* followed in 2000, after which Jeff Cox left the band to concentrate on solo material and family life. Jeff was replaced by Darren Furze.

The next album, *Run Ragged*, appeared in 2003. In 2007, the band released two live albums. The first release was a recording from a show the band performed in the Netherlands in 1982, which originally saw only a limited release. The second was the first of three planned releases covering early, unreleased recordings. Entitled *Archive Alive Vol.1*, it covered the period of the band's successful period, the birth of the band and their rise to NWOBHM prominence. Sleeve notes were written by the band's guitarist, Garry Pepperd, and the album cover included rare photographs.

Current activities

Jaguar released their latest album, "Metal X", in 2014. It was their first new material since 2003's *Run Ragged*. Jaguar did their first Sweden debut at Sweden Rock Festival in the summer of 2014.

In September 2014, Jaguar parted company with their previous vocalist Jamie Manton following their appearance at Sweden Rock Festival in June the same year. The band started to search for the perfect fitted vocalist for the band both in the U.K. and in Scandinavia and as the band founder Garry Pepperd planned to move to Sweden to settle down with his Swedish-born fiancée he started to search mostly in Sweden for a vocalist. In November the same year 2014 the band released its long-awaited album "Metal X" on Golden-Core Records/ZYX Music, mixed by Mike Exeter (JUDAS PRIEST, BLACK SABBATH).

In beginning of April 2015, Garry Pepperd moved to north Sweden with his fiancée, and in late August same year the band finally found the perfect fit in vocalist L-G Persson from the Swedish heavy metal/power metal band The Storyteller and ex Steel Attack from Gävle, Sweden after audition many different vocalists trough audition recordings. L-G Persson was then taken into a studio in Gävle after heard his audition recording of two of Jaguar's songs and it turned out after the band heard him live that he was right fitted for Jaguar. Lars G Persson also known as L-G are today regarded by many as one of the best heavy metal vocalists in Sweden today.

Jeff Cox has recently formed a new progressive metal band called This Raging Silence, which have an album entitled *Isotopes and Endoscopes* due for release in early 2015.

2.34.2 Music style

Jaguar played faster and more aggressively than any other band during the early days of the NWOBHM movement and, according to the band's history, they are considered among the inventors of the speed metal and thrash metal subgenres. They were influential for many other bands in later years, including US bands such as Metallica.

In an interview Garry Pepperd talked about Jaguar and their music style:

> I suppose you could say we were thrash metal and speed metal before there was such a thing, (...) we were part of the second generation of the New Wave of British Heavy Metal I suppose, ourselves and Raven were playing music a bit faster than bands like Saxon and Tygers of Pang Tang. We were really playing something that is gonna be influential, although we never knew it at that time.

2.34.3 Discography

Albums

- *Power Games* (1983) Neat Records
- *This Time* (1984) Roadrunner Records
- *Wake Me* (2000) Neat Metal Records
- *Run Ragged* (2003) Angel Air Records
- *This Time Remaster* (2009) Metal Mind Records
- *Metal X* (2014) GoldenCore Records/ZYX Music
- *Metal X* Limited Edition Vinyl LP (2015) GoldenCore Records/ZYX Music

Singles

- "Back Street Woman" (1981) Heavy Metal Records
- "Axe Crazy" (1982) Neat Records

Live Albums

- *Holland '82* (2006) Majestic Records

Compilations

- "Stormchild" on *Heavy Metal Heroes* (Heavy Metal Records, 1981)
- "Dirty Tricks" on *60 Min. Plus* (Neat Records, 1982)
- *The Anthology* (2001) Sanctuary Records
- *Power Games: The Anthology* (2002) Sanctuary Records
- *Archive Alive Volume I* (2007) Majestic Rock
- *Opening the Enclosure* (2010) High Roller Records
- "Stormchild" (2014 Edition) on *The Ultimate Oldschool Tracks*
- *Speed Metal* (2014) GoldenCore Records/ZYX Music

2.34.4 Present band members

- Garry Pepperd – guitar
- Simon Patel – bass
- Nathan Cox – drums
- Lars G Persson - Vocals (announces that he leaving the band 2015-11-14)

2.34.5 Past band members

- Jeff Cox – bass (1979–1985, 1998–2000), vocals (1979–1980)
- Chris Lovell – drums (1979–1984)
- Rob Reiss – vocals (1980–1982)
- Paul Merrell – vocals (1982–1985) See also: ex-Stormtrooper, ex-Hellrazer
- Gary Davies – drums (1984–1985)
- Les Foster – drums (1984) See also: ex-Tok-io Rose
- Darren Furze – bass (1998–2005)
- William Sealey – drums (2009–2011)
- Jamie Manton – vocals (1998–2014)

2.34.6 See also

- List of Bands from Bristol
- List of New Wave of British Heavy Metal bands

2.34.7 References

- NWOBHM Jaguar-Encyclopaedia Metallum The Metal Archives
- Jaguar at Discogs
- http://www.blabbermouth.net/news/nwobhm-legends-jaguar-recruit-the-storyteller-singer

2.34.8 External links

- NWOBHM Jaguar official website

2.35 Jameson Raid (band)

For The 1895 raid on Paul Kruger's Transvaal Republic, see Jameson Raid.

Jameson Raid are a British heavy metal band. They are usually considered to be part of the New Wave of British Heavy Metal, following their inclusion on EMI's album *Metal For Muthas II*, although they were established on the Birmingham circuit as a hard rock band several years before this.

2.35.1 Career

The band can originally be dated back to 1973, when bassist John Ace and guitarist Ian Smith, played together in Spectaté II at the school they attended in Sutton Coldfield. The band members went their separate ways to go to university – aside from Smith who went to sea – at which point Ace formed a covers outfit. When this split, Ace, together with rhythm guitarist Stewart Harrod, persuaded Smith to return and added the drummer Phil Kimberley. Their first gig took place on 26 August 1975, under the generally disliked name Notre Dame. The name Jameson Raid comes from an incident in the Transvaal at the turn of 1895/96. Their roadie Nick Freeman was credited with recalling the event from his school history books and proposing it to the band. With Hoi Polloi singer Terry Dark joining in December 1976, and Stewart leaving a few days later, Jameson Raid's most well-known line-up was complete.

Jameson Raid released their first single, the "Seven Days of Splendour" EP in February 1979. "The combination of influences which had given birth to the band's overall sound was quite difficult to pin down, as there were elements of 70's rock/pop (particularly David Bowie and Mott The Hoople), heavier acts such as Thin Lizzy and the occasional nod towards punk snottiness..." noted author Malc Macmillan,[1] and the three tracks on the EP ("Seven Days of Splendour", "It's a Crime" and "Catcher in the Rye") illustrated Macmillan's conundrum in terms of an inability to categorise the band's sound. Described in *The International Encyclopedia of Hard Rock & Heavy Metal* as "cult heroes for the Midland rock circuit... Their music is a poppy form of heavy metal...".[2] The EP was well received and, as Martin Popoff pointed out, showcased "a masterful bit of songwriting throughout these three tracks".[3] The first 1,000 copies came in a white sleeve, with a further pressing of 2,000 in a black sleeve; both featured what Popoff called "a spoofed band history" together with the lyrics to all three songs.

In March 1980 the band, along with Magnum, played support to Def Leppard at West Midland venues on the latter's

On Through the Night World Tour.

In May 1980, EMI released the second of its *Metal for Muthas* NWOBHM compilation albums. *Metal For Muthas II Cut Loud*, featured the Jameson Raid track "Hard Lines", although the band were unhappy that EMI had, unbeknownst to them, completely remixed the song (which the band had already mixed to their satisfaction) and in doing so pretty much destroyed it.[4] The band were credited as The Raid on this release.[5]

Fighting against a tide of apathy, Smith and Ace handed in their notice and played their final gig with the band in Birmingham in July 1980. A second 7" EP, widely referred to as *The Hypnotist* but actually entitled *End of Part One*, was released at this time. Featuring four tracks ("The Hypnotist", "The Raid", "Getting Hotter" and "Straight from the Butchers"), the EP proved to be the band's vinyl swansong.

Kimberley and Dark soldiered on, recruiting guitarist Mike Darby and bassist Peter Green. In 1981 Darby left and was replaced by The Handsome Beasts founder member James Barrett, who in turn gave way to Steve Makin in 1982. The four-track *Electric Sun* demo cassette (featuring "Electric Sun", "Run for Cover", "Poor Little Rich Girl" and "Getting Hotter") was made available, but later that year Kimberley and Dark quit and the band was effectively over. During an interview for *Classic Rock* magazine in 2010, Terry Dark said: "We just seemed to be either a year too early, or a year too late... But whatever the reason things never quite happened for us."[6] A green vinyl LP titled *Jameson Raid*, comprising the *End Of Part One* EP, the *Electric Sun* demo tracks, the *Metal for Muthas* take of "Hard Lines" and the unreleased track "Running Blind" from the final 1983 line-up was released as a bootleg and not an official release, although it has become an expensive collector's item. Both of the EPs featured in the 2010 edition of *Record Collector*.[7]

In 1983, Green and Makin drafted in drummer Roger Simms, and with Makin handling both guitar and vocal duties, they tried to resurrect the band as The Raid, but with no great success nor longevity. Makin went on to front several other bands before being invited to appear on the solo album by Cozy Powell, *The Drums Are Back* (1992). He joined Slade in 1993.

Malcolm Dome wrote: "Jameson Raid are one of the many bands who were definitely contenders for glory during the halcyon days of the New Wave of British Heavy Metal. Sadly, they never quite lived up to their obvious potential".[6]

The classic line-up of Terry Dark, Ian Smith, John Ace and Phil Kimberley re-united in 2008, and their back catalogue album, *Just as the Dust Had Settled*, was released by Shadow Kingdom Records in March 2010. The band played gigs both in Germany and the UK in July 2010.

In February 2011 John Ace left the band. They played the Download festival in June 2011 with a stand in bass player before Peter Green, the bass player from 1980 to 1983, rejoined in June 2011. By 2012 first Ian Smith and then Phil Kimberley had followed John Ace and returned to their day jobs. They were replaced by Kalli Kaldschmidt and Andreas 'Neudi' Neuderth from the band Roxxcaliber. In August 2013 drummer Lars Wickett was recruited due to Neudi's live gig commitments with Manilla Road.

Jameson Raid have remained active particularly in Europe with occasional gigs in the UK.

2.35.2 Members

Current lineup

- Terry Dark - vocals
- Kalli Kaldschmidt - guitar, vocals
- Pete Green - bass guitar, vocals
- Andreas "Neudi" Neuderth - drums, vocals

Past members

June 1975

- Ian Smith - guitar, vocals
- John Ace - bass guitar, vocals
- Phil Kimberley - drums, vocals
- Stewart Harrod - rhythm guitar, vocals

December 1976 to July 1980

- Terry Dark - vocals
- Ian Smith - guitar
- John Ace - bass guitar
- Phil Kimberley - drums, vocals

1980 to 1981

- Terry Dark - vocals
- Mike Darby - guitar
- Peter Green - bass guitar
- Phil Kimberley - drums, vocals

1981

- Terry Dark - vocals
- James Barrett - guitar
- Peter Green - bass guitar
- Phil Kimberley - drums, vocals

1982

- Terry Dark - vocals
- Steve Makin - guitar
- Peter Green - bass guitar
- Phil Kimberley - drums, vocals

1983

- Steve Makin - guitar, vocals
- Peter Green - bass guitar
- Roger Simms - drums

2008 to Feb 2011

- Terry Dark - vocals
- Ian Smith - guitar, vocals
- John Ace - bass guitar, vocals
- Phil Kimberley - drums, vocals

2.35.3 Discography

Albums

- *Seven Days of Splendour* EP (GBH Records, 1979)
- *End of Part One* EP (Blackbird Records, 1980)
- *Just as the Dust Had Settled* LP (Shadow Kingdom Records SKR030CD, March 2010)
- *Just as the Dust Had Settled* Limited Edition Vinyl LP (High Roller Records HR141, July 2010)
- *Jameson Raid Live at the O2 Academy* Limited Edition Vinyl LP (High Roller Records HR180, June 2011)
- *The Beginning of Part II* Limited Edition Vinyl LP (High Roller Records HRR220, September 2012)

Tracks on sampler albums

- *Metal for Muthas II* (EMI Records 1980) One Track, "Hard Lines".
- *NWoBHM Vol. 2* (1992) One track, "It's a Crime".

Compilation albums

- *Jameson Raid* (Phoenix Records)

2.35.4 See also

- List of New Wave of British Heavy Metal bands

2.35.5 References

[1] *The New Wave Of British Heavy Metal Encyclopedia* by Malc Macmillan, Iron Pages, 2001

[2] *The International Encyclopedia of Hard Rock And Heavy Metal* by Tony Jasper and Derek Oliver, Sidgwick & Jackson,, 1983

[3] *The New Wave Of British Heavy Metal Singles* by Martin Popoff, Scrap Metal Records, 2005

[4]

[5] 'Suzie Smiled: The New Wave Of British Heavy Metal' by John Tucker, 2006

[6]

[7] 'Record Collector 2010. Page 264. ISBN 978-0-9532601-9-5

2.35.6 External links

- Official website
- Fan website
- Jameson Raid on MySpace.com
- Rockdetector.com entry
- Metal-Archives.com entry
- New Wave Of British Heavy Metal entry

2.36 John McCoy (musician)

John Matthew McCoy (born c. 1950, Huddersfield, Yorkshire, England), is an English bass guitarist, who is best known for his work with Ian Gillan and *Mammoth* as well as numerous other bands and sessions since the late 1960s. He currently plays in British rock trio Guy McCoy Tormé with former Gillan/Ozzy guitarist Bernie Tormé and Bruce Dickinson/Sack Trick drummer Robin Guy. He is also an accomplished guitar, drum, trumpet, cello, and double bass player. Nearly as well known as his music is his appearance: he is always pictured wearing sunglasses, with the striking contrast of bald head and robust chin beard. Along with guitarist Vic Elmes and ZZebra colleague Liam Genockey on drums, McCoy can also be heard playing in the intro and end titles theme of the 1970s cult TV series *Space: 1999*.

2.36.1 Early career

In the 1960s, when he was 13, whilst still at school, McCoy began playing as lead guitarist with a working beat group, *The Drovers*. In 1966 he responded to an advertisement in the Yorkshire Post newspaper for a guitarist to join a band called *Mamas Little Children* who were about to begin touring Germany. McCoy went to audition only to find they had just given someone else the position, but still needed a bass player. He auditioned on a spare bass that was there and was given the job. In 1968 he was forced to resign from the band because he was working illegally under age. On his return to Britain he went to London where he found work as a session musician with former Drifters member Clyde McPhatter touring the UK.

In 1974, McCoy was playing with London-based band *Scrapyard* when they recruited Irish-born lead guitarist Bernie Tormé. Although Tormé eventually left to form his own punk rock band, the two were later reunited in former Deep Purple singer Ian Gillan's band.

On 18 July 2009, John McCoy performed at the Furnace in Swindon Wiltshire, England Performing in a group G.M.T with Bernie Tormé (guitar legend formerly with Gillan, and Ozzy Osbourne) Robin Guy (former Drummer with Iron Maiden's Bruce Dickinson and Faith No More)

2.36.2 Career with Gillan

Main article: Gillan (band)

In July 1978, the jazz-rock fusion Ian Gillan Band were altering direction, under the influence of keyboards player Colin Towns in a return to Ian Gillan's hard rock roots. Towns had begun writing new material, and Gillan gave him the task of recruiting the new line-up. Towns recruited session drummer Liam Genockey, McCoy and guitarist Richard Brampton, who was replaced by Steve Byrd - a former colleague of McCoy's from ZZebra - almost immediately. Within a month of their formation the band had recorded their first album, *Gillan*, and they made their live debut at the Reading Festival on 16 August 1978. They were originally listed there as the Ian Gillan Band but, in a move away from the jazz-rock connotations, they renamed the band, Gillan.

Gillan underwent a further three line-up changes, but McCoy remained as bass player until the band eventually split acrimoniously[1] in 1982.

2.36.3 Mammoth

Post-Gillan, McCoy recruited session drummer Vinnie "Tubby" Reed, guitarist "Big" Mac Baker and vocalist Nicky Moore to form a band initially called Dinosaur. The name was already in use by a Californian band, so McCoy renamed his new outfit Mammoth. The name was also a tongue-in-cheek reference to the large size of the band members: McCoy weighed 120 kg (19 st), Reed 140 kg (22 st), Baker 152 kg (23.9 st), and Moore 127 kg (20.0 st).

The band toured with Whitesnake and Marillion and were well received by fans. They released one single, "Fatman", and two albums, *Mammoth* and *Larger And Live*. In 1988, the entire band appeared in the film *Just Ask For Diamond*,[2] playing the henchmen. Musically, commercial success eluded them however and the band eventually split in 1989, with McCoy becoming an independent producer.

2.36.4 Equipment

McCoy usually uses a traditional four string fretted Fender Precision guitar and predominantly Marshall amplification in various configurations. Although he has used Trace Elliot, he has described it as "...a bit clean for my personal taste..." [3] Currently he uses a Marshall 200w integrated amp driving a 2x15 cab and a Marshall 100w lead amp driving 4x12 cabs.

His playing style utilises both pick and fingers, although he plays mostly with picks, preferring Fender extra heavy large triangles "...for greater precision and attack."[3][4]

2.36.5 List of bands and artists worked with

Tyla Gang

From The Fire Al Atkins

2.36.6 References

[1] "Get Ready to ROCK! Interview with John McCoy, bass guitarist with McCoy,Mammoth and Gillan". Getreadytorock.com. Retrieved 2013-06-18.

[2] "Just Ask For Diamond". IMDb.com. Retrieved 2013-06-17.

[3] "Planet Bass – The John McCoy Interview January 2006", URL accessed on 24 January 2007.

[4] McCoy. "McCoy - Music Biography, Credits and Discography". AllMusic. Retrieved 2013-06-18.

2.37 Judas Priest

Judas Priest is a British heavy metal band formed in Birmingham, England, in 1970.[1] The band has sold over 45 million albums to date.[2][3][4] MTV ranked them the second greatest metal band of all time.[5]

Despite an innovative and pioneering body of work in the latter half of the 1970s, the band struggled with indifferently-produced records, repeated changes of drummer and a lack of major commercial success or attention until 1980, when they adopted a more simplified sound on the album *British Steel*, which helped shoot them to rock superstar status. In 1989, they were named as defendants in an unsuccessful lawsuit alleging that subliminal messages on the song Better By You, Better Than Me had caused the suicide attempts of two young men.[6]

The band's membership has seen much turnover, including a revolving cast of drummers in the 1970s, and the temporary departure of singer Rob Halford in the early 1990s. The current line-up consists of lead vocalist Rob Halford, guitarists Glenn Tipton and Richie Faulkner, bassist Ian Hill, and drummer Scott Travis. The band's best-selling album is 1982's *Screaming for Vengeance* with their most commercially successful line-up, featuring Halford, Tipton, Hill, K. K. Downing (guitar), and Dave Holland (drums).

Their influence, while mainly Rob Halford's operatic vocal style and the twin guitar sound of K.K. Downing and Glenn Tipton, has been adopted by many bands. Their image of leather, spikes, and other taboo articles of clothing were widely influential during the glam metal era of the 1980s.[7] Their *British Steel* album has been referred to as the "record that, more than any other, codified what we mean by 'heavy metal'".[8] Despite a decline in exposure during the mid 1990s, the band has once again seen a resurgence, including worldwide tours, being inaugural inductees into the VH1 Rock Honors in 2005, receiving a Grammy Award for Best Metal Performance in 2010, and their songs featured in video games such as *Guitar Hero* and the *Rock Band* series.

2.37.1 History

Origins (1969–1974)

An earlier band with a different line-up had been formed in the West Midlands area in 1969 by Al Atkins (lead vocals), Bruno Stapenhill (bass, born Brian Stapenhill, in 1948, Stone Cross, W. Bromwich), John Partridge (drums, born c. 1948, W. Bromwich), and John Perry (guitar).[9][10] Stapenhill came up with the name *Judas Priest* from Bob Dylan's song "The Ballad of Frankie Lee and Judas Priest"[11] and they rehearsed at his house in Stone Cross. Perry died in a car accident shortly after the band's formation, and was subsequently replaced by Ernie Chataway.[12]). The band played their first gig on 25 November 1969 at The George Hotel in Walsall and then toured Scotland in December 1969 and January 1970. The group disbanded in April 1970 after their last gig on 20 April at The Youth Centre in Cannock.

The line-up that took over the name of Judas Priest included lead guitarist Kenny K. K. Downing, bassist Ian 'Skull' Hill and drummer John Ellis. The first two had known each other since early childhood, growing up on the Yew Tree estate in West Bromwich and became close friends in their early teens, when they shared similar musical interests (Black Sabbath, Led Zeppelin, Deep Purple, Jimi Hendrix, The Who, Cream, The Yardbirds) and learned to play instruments. The band was founded in October 1970 in Birmingham. They agreed to join with Atkins, who suggested using his old band's name, and rehearsed at Atkins' mother-in-law's house in Stone Cross. The reformed group played their first gig on 16 March 1971 at St John's Hall, Essington.

With Downing as acting leader, the band moved away from their original blues influences to play hard rock. The quartet played around Birmingham and the surrounding areas with various drummers until 1974, sometimes opening for bands such as Budgie, Thin Lizzy, and Trapeze. Eventually, financial difficulties and problems with their management, Tony Iommi's company, IMA, led to the departure of Alan Atkins and drummer Alan Moore in May 1973. At the time, Ian Hill was dating a Walsall woman who suggested her brother, Rob Halford,[13] as the band's singer. Halford joined them, bringing drummer John Hinch from his previous band, Hiroshima. This line-up toured the UK, often supporting Budgie, and even headlining some shows in Norway and Germany.

***Rocka Rolla* (1974–1975)**

Before the band entered the studio to record their first album, their record company suggested they add another musician to the line-up. As Downing was reluctant to incorporate a keyboard or horn player into the band, he chose another lead guitarist, Glenn Tipton, in April 1974, from the Stafford-based Flying Hat Band as their new member. The two guitarists worked together to adapt the existing material and Tipton also received credits as a songwriter. In August 1974, the band released their debut single "Rocka Rolla" and followed this a month later with an album of the same name.

Technical problems during the recording contributed to the poor sound quality of the record. Producer Rodger Bain, whose resume included Black Sabbath's first three albums as well as Budgie's first album, dominated the production of the album and made decisions with which the band did not agree.[14] Bain also chose to leave fan favourites from the band's live set, such as "Tyrant", "Genocide" and "The Ripper", off the album and he cut the song "Caviar and Meths" from a 10-minute song down to a 2-minute instrumental.

The tour for *Rocka Rolla* was Judas Priest's first international tour[15] with dates in Germany, Holland, Norway and Denmark including one show at Hotel Klubben[16] in Tønsberg, one hour from Oslo, Norway, which scored them a somewhat negative review in the local press.[17] The album flopped upon release, leaving Priest in dire financial straits. Priest attempted to secure a deal with Gull Records to get a monthly pay of 50 pounds, however, because Gull Records were struggling as well, they declined.[18] *Rocka Rolla* (1974) has been for the most part dismissed by the band and none of its songs were played live after 1976[19] except for "Never Satisfied", which was revived during the Epitaph Tour in 2011.

Sad Wings of Destiny (1975–1977)

The band participated more in the production of their next album, recorded during November and December 1975, and chose the producers themselves. The result, *Sad Wings of Destiny* (1976), included a variety of old material, including the aforementioned stage favourites and immediately shifted the band from a psychedelic sound to straight gritty metal with the opening track, the progressive epic "Victim of Changes". This song was a combination of "Whiskey Woman", a stage classic from the Al Atkins' era of Judas Priest, and "Red Light Lady", a song that Halford had written with his previous group, Hiroshima. This album and a strong performance at the 1975 Reading Festival[20] helped to raise wider interest in the band and expand their fanbase.

Major label debut (1977–1979)

Their next album, 1977's *Sin After Sin*, was the first Priest record under a major label, CBS and the first of eleven consecutive albums to be certified Gold or higher by the RIAA. With the termination of their contract with their previous label Gull, the band lost the rights to their first two albums. *Sin After Sin* was produced by ex-Deep Purple bass player Roger Glover. The band chose to use session drummer Simon Phillips for the recordings. He declined to become a permanent member of Judas Priest, so the band hired Les Binks on Glover's recommendation. Together, they recorded 1978's *Stained Class*, produced by Dennis MacKay, and *Killing Machine* (released in America as *Hell Bent for Leather*).[21] Binks, credited with writing the powerful "Beyond the Realms of Death", was an accomplished and technically skilled drummer and his addition added a dexterous edge to the band's sound. Binks also played on *Unleashed in the East* (1979), which was recorded live in Japan during the Killing Machine tour. While the first three Judas Priest albums had considerable traces of Black Sabbath, Led Zeppelin, and Deep Purple in them, as well as ballads, *Stained Class* did not contain any ballads aside from the very dark "Beyond the Realms of Death." *Killing Machine* was the first nod to a more commercial sound, with simpler songs that brought back some blues influences. At about the same time, the band members adopted their now-famous "leather-and-studs" image.[7]

Mainstream success (1979–1991)

Judas Priest performing in 1981, during their World Wide Blitz Tour.

Following the release of *Killing Machine* (1978) was the live release from the supporting tour, *Unleashed in the East* (1979). It was the first of many Judas Priest albums to go Platinum. There was some criticism of the band's use of studio enhancements and overdubbing in what was marketed as a live album.[22] By this point the playing style of the band had grown progressively heavier, with live versions of songs such as "Exciter" and "Diamonds and Rust" sounding much heavier and faster than their studio counterparts.

Les Binks quit in late 1979, as he was unhappy with the band's desire to move towards a simplified radio rock sound, so they replaced him with Dave Holland, formerly from the band Trapeze. With this line-up, Judas Priest recorded six studio and one live album, which garnered different degrees of critical and financial success.

In 1980, the band released *British Steel*. The songs were shorter and had more mainstream radio hooks, but retained the familiar heavy metal feel. Tracks such as "United", "Breaking the Law", and "Living After Midnight" were frequently played on the radio. The next release, 1981's *Point of Entry*, followed the same formula, and the tour in support of the album featured new songs such as "Solar Angels" and "Heading Out to the Highway".

The 1982 album *Screaming for Vengeance* featured "You've Got Another Thing Comin'", which became a major radio hit in the US. Songs such as "Electric Eye" and "Riding on the Wind" also appeared on this album, and proved to be popular live. "(Take These) Chains" (by Bob Halligan, Jr) was released as a single and received heavy airplay. This album went Double Platinum.[23]

Downing and Tipton performing in San Sebastián, Spain, during their World Conqueror Tour of 1984.

Priest continued their success through the mid-1980s. "Freewheel Burning", released in 1983, was a regular on rock radio. Its album *Defenders of the Faith* was released the following year. Some critics dubbed it "Screaming for Vengeance II", due to its musical similarity to the previous album.[24]

On 13 July 1985, Judas Priest, along with Black Sabbath and other performers, played at Live Aid. The band played at JFK Stadium in Philadelphia. Their setlist was "Living After Midnight", "The Green Manalishi (With The Two-Pronged Crown)" and "(You've Got) Another Thing Comin'".

Turbo was released in April 1986. The band adopted a more colourful stage look and gave their music a more mainstream feel by adding guitar synthesisers. The album also went Platinum and had a successful arena tour in support, with 100 concerts in North America, Europe and Japan in 1986. A live album recorded on the tour, titled *Priest...Live!*, was released the next year, offering live tracks from the era. The video documentary *Heavy Metal Parking Lot* was created by Jeff Krulik and John Heyn in 1986. It documents the heavy metal fans waiting on 31 May 1986 for a Judas Priest concert (with special guests Dokken) at the Capital Center (later renamed US Airways Arena) in Landover, Maryland.

Rob Halford in 1988. One of Priest's trademark stage stunts was to have Halford ride a motorbike on stage.

In May 1988, *Ram It Down* was released, featuring several reworked songs left over from *Turbo*, in addition to new songs. The band recorded three tracks with pop producers Stock-Aitken-Waterman: two originals, "Runaround"[25] and "I Will Return",[26] and a cover of The Stylistics' hit "You Are Everything"; however, they were ultimately not included on this album due to a management decision. A reviewer has called *Ram It Down* a "stylistic evolution" that resulted from the band's "..attempt to rid themselves of the tech synthesiser approach..and return to the traditional metal of their fading glory days." The reviewer argued the album showed "...how far behind they were lagging... the thrashers they helped influence" in earlier years.[27] As well, in the late 1980s, longtime drummer Dave Holland left the band.

In September 1990, the *Painkiller* album used a new drummer, Scott Travis (formerly from Racer X). This comeback album dropped the 1980s-style synthesisers for all songs except "A Touch of Evil". The tour used bands such as Megadeth, Pantera, Sepultura and Testament as opening bands, and culminated in the Rock in Rio performance in Brazil in front of 100,000+ fans.

Part of the Judas Priest stage show often featured Halford riding onstage on a Harley-Davidson motorbike, dressed in motorcycle leathers and sunglasses. In a Toronto show in August 1991, Halford was seriously injured as he rode on stage, when he collided with a drum riser hidden behind clouds of dry ice mist. Though the show was delayed, he performed the set before going to a hospital. Hill later noted "he must have been in agony". In a 2007 interview, Rob claimed the accident had nothing to do with his departure from the band.[28]

Subliminal message trial In the summer of 1990, the band was involved in a civil action that alleged they were responsible for the self-inflicted gunshot wounds in 1985 of 20-year-old James Vance and 18-year-old Raymond Belknap in Sparks, Nevada, USA.[29] On 23 December 1985, Vance and Belknap, after hours of drinking beer, smoking marijuana and allegedly listening to Judas Priest, went to a playground at a church in Sparks with a 12-gauge shotgun to end their lives. Belknap was the first to place the shotgun under his chin. He died instantly after pulling the trigger. Vance then shot himself but survived, suffering severe facial injuries. Following numerous complications, Vance too died in 1988, three years after the suicide pact.[6]

The men's parents and their legal team alleged that a subliminal message of "do it" had been included in the Judas Priest song "Better By You, Better Than Me" (a cover of the Spooky Tooth number) from *Stained Class* (1978). They alleged the command in the song triggered the suicide attempt.[29] The trial lasted from 16 July to 24 August 1990, when the suit was dismissed after the judge ruled that the so-called "do it" message was a result of an accidental mixup of background lyrics.[29] One of the defence witnesses, Dr. Timothy E. Moore, wrote an article for *Skeptical Inquirer* chronicling the trial.[29] The trial was covered in the 1991 documentary *Dream Deceivers: The Story Behind James Vance Vs. Judas Priest*.

Comedian Bill Hicks ridiculed the lawsuit as part of his act, pointing out the absurdity of the notion that a successful band would wish to kill off their purchasing fanbase.[30]

Halford leaves (1991–1992) After the *Painkiller* tour in 1991, Halford left Judas Priest. In September 1991, there were indications of internal tensions within the band.

Halford went on to form a street-style thrash metal group named Fight, with Scott Travis on drums for the recording sessions. He formed this band to explore new musical territory, but due to contractual obligations, he remained with Judas Priest until May 1992.[31]

Halford collaborated with Judas Priest in the release of a compilation album entitled *Metal Works '73-'93* to commemorate their 20th anniversary. He also appeared in a video by the same title, documenting their history, in which his departure from the band was officially announced later that year.

In a 1998 interview on MTV, Halford publicly came out as gay.[32]

Ripper Owens (1996–2003)

Tim "Ripper" Owens, who had previously sung in a Judas Priest tribute band called British Steel, was hired in 1996 as Judas Priest's new singer. This line-up released two albums, *Jugulator* (1997) and *Demolition* (2001), as well as two live double-albums – *'98 Live Meltdown* and *Live in London* (2003), the latter of which had a live DVD counterpart. Although *Jugulator* sold relatively well, it was given mixed reviews, though it contains the epic "Cathedral Spires", which became one of Ripper's most popular songs.

Reunion and Angel of Retribution (2003–2006)

The reunited Judas Priest performing in 2005

After eleven years apart, faced with an ever-growing demand for a reunion, Judas Priest and Rob Halford announced they would reunite in July 2003, to coincide with the release of the Metalogy box set (despite Halford's earlier insistence that he "would never do it"[33]). They did a concert tour in Europe in 2004, and co-headlined the 2004 Ozzfest, being named as the "premier act" by almost all

US media coverage of the event. Judas Priest and "Ripper" Owens parted amicably, with Owens joining American heavy metal band Iced Earth.

A new studio album, *Angel of Retribution*, was released on 1 March 2005 (US) on Sony Music/Epic Records to critical and commercial success. A global tour in support of the album ensued. As for the band Halford, writing for the fourth release was cut off. However, after the Retribution tour in June 2006, Halford announced he would create his own record company, Metal God Entertainment, where he would release all his solo material under his own control. In November 2006 he remastered his back catalogue and released it exclusively through Apple's iTunes Store. Two new songs allegedly set for the fourth release, "Forgotten Generation" and "Drop Out", were released through iTunes as well.

Judas Priest in typical heavy metal attire performing at the VH1 Rock Honors in Las Vegas on 25 May 2006.

VH1 Rock Honors Along with Queen, Kiss and Def Leppard, Judas Priest was an inaugural inductee into the "VH1 Rock Honors".[34] The ceremony took place 25 May 2006 in Las Vegas, Nevada, and first aired on 31 May.[34] Their presentation was preceded by Godsmack performing a medley of "Electric Eye"/"Victim of Changes"/"Hell Bent for Leather." Judas Priest then played "Breaking the Law", "The Green Manalishi (With The Two-Pronged Crown)" and "You've Got Another Thing Comin'", before which Halford rode a Harley onstage.

Nostradamus (2006–2010)

In a June 2006 interview with MTV.com, Halford said of the group's concept album about the 16th-century French writer Nostradamus, "Nostradamus is all about metal, isn't he? He was an alchemist as well as a seer – a person of extraordinary talent. He had an amazing life that was full of trial and tribulation and joy and sorrow. He's a very human character and a world-famous individual. You can take his name and translate it into any language and everybody knows about him, and that's important because we're dealing with a worldwide audience."[35] In addition to digging new lyrical ground for the band, the album would contain musical elements which might surprise fans. "It's going to have a lot of depth", Halford said. "There'll be a lot of symphonic elements. We might orchestrate it, without it being overblown. There may be a massive choir at parts and keyboards will be featured more prominently, whereas they've always been in the background before."[35] The album *Nostradamus* was released in June 2008; the band began a support tour in that same month.[36]

In early February 2009, the band joined the ranks of bands speaking out against ticket-touting ("scalping"), issuing a statement condemning the practice of selling tickets at well above face value, and urging fans to buy tickets only from official sources.[37] In the same month, Judas Priest continued their tour, bringing their "Priest Feast" (with guests Megadeth and Testament) to multiple arenas in England, Wales, Scotland, and Ireland in February and March 2009. From there the tour progressed to multiple venues in Sweden. Later in March, Judas Priest performed in Portugal (at Lisbon on the Atlantic Pavilion), which they had not visited since 2005. The tour then continued to Milan, Italy, and then Paris, France; Halford had last performed with Judas Priest in Paris in 1991.

Judas Priest headlined the Sweden Rock Festival in June 2008.

From June through August 2009, Judas Priest completed a North American tour to commemorate the 30th anniversary of the release of *British Steel* (1980); the album was performed in its entirety on each tour date, with some other songs thrown in. This tour was to be a joint effort with fellow Englishman David Coverdale and Whitesnake. Unfortunately, Whitesnake would have to leave the tour after the show in Denver, Colorado on 11 August 2009 due to Coverdale falling ill with a serious throat infection; he was advised to stop singing immediately to avoid permanently damaging his vocal cords.[38][39]

On 14 July 2009, Judas Priest released a new live album,

featuring 11 previously unreleased live tracks from the 2005 and 2008 world tours, *A Touch of Evil: Live*. The performance of "Dissident Aggressor" won the 2010 Grammy Award for Best Metal Performance.[40]

In May 2010, Halford said the band had been offered a star on the Hollywood Walk of Fame, but "we've just never been there when they wanted to do the ceremony." He also revealed that a *Nostradamus* tour was still being contemplated: "We were in Hollywood recently and met with some producers and agents, so there are a lot of things going on behind the scenes."[41] The Judas Priest song "Electric Eye" was used in the temp score for *Toy Story 3*[42] but was ultimately replaced by another piece of music.

Downing's retirement and Epitaph World Tour (2010–2011)

Judas Priest announced on 7 December 2010, that their Epitaph World Tour would be the band's farewell tour and would run up until 2012.[43] In a January 2011 interview, Rob Halford said about the band's impending retirement that:

> *"I think it's time, you know. We're not the first band to say farewell, it's just the way everyone comes to at some point and we're gonna say a few more things early next year, so I think the main thing that we just want to ask everybody to consider is don't be sad about this, start celebrating and rejoicing over all the great things we've done in Judas Priest."*[44]

Judas Priest on stage in 2011

On 27 January 2011, it was announced that Judas Priest was in the process of writing new material; the band also clarified their plans for the future, saying that "...this is by no means the end of the band. In fact, we are presently writing new material, but we do intend this to be the last major world tour."[45] Speaking at a press conference in Los Angeles on 26 May of the new material Glenn Tipton said: "It's quite a mixed bag. Really, there's more sentiment on this album. In a way, I suppose, it's also our farewell album, although it might not be our last one. There are some anthems on there, which pay tribute to our fans".[46]

On 20 April 2011, it was announced that K. K. Downing had retired from the band and would not complete the Epitaph World Tour. Downing cited differences with the band and management and a breakdown in their relationship. Richie Faulkner, guitarist for Lauren Harris's band, was announced as his replacement for the Epitaph World Tour.[47] Downing's retirement leaves bassist Ian Hill as the only remaining founder member of the band.

On 25 May 2011, Judas Priest played during the finale of *American Idol* season 10 with James Durbin, making it their first live performance without K.K. Downing.[48] The band played a mixture of two songs: "Living After Midnight" and "Breaking the Law".[48]

On 7 June 2011, the band announced that it planned to release the box set *Single Cuts*, a collection of singles, later that summer.[49]

***Redeemer of Souls* and future touring plans (2011-present)**

In an August 2011 interview with Billboard, Halford explained that he and Tipton "have about 12 or 14 tracks completely mapped out" for a new studio album. He went on to say that four of those were already recorded and mixed, and suggested a new album should be out in 2012.[50] However, the year ended without seeing a release. In another interview with Billboard in August 2012, Halford said that the band is taking its time with the album, and did not give a definite release date, saying "I'm of the attitude it'll be ready when it's ready [...] I don't think we're going to slack off. We're determined to do a lot of work and be just as dedicated as we've always been and take a lot of care and attention with all the songs. We're not going to just bang this one out, so to speak."[51]

On 13 September 2011, Priest announced its plans to release a new compilation album, *The Chosen Few*, a set of Priest songs chosen by other iconic heavy metal musicians.[52] On 5 June 2013, Rob Halford confirmed that the Epitaph World Tour would not be the band's final tour.[53] On 22 December 2013, Judas Priest released a short Christmas message on their official website, which confirmed that they would be releasing the new album sometime in 2014.[54]

On 5 January 2014, the band appeared in the episode "Steal This Episode" of comedy cartoon show *The Simpsons* playing the song "Breaking the Law". Their music was referred to as "death metal",[55] for which the producers subsequently apologised by having Bart Simpson write "Judas Priest is not 'Death Metal'" in the opening sequence chalkboard gag.[56]

On 17 March 2014 at the Ronnie James Dio Awards in Los Angeles, California, Rob Halford announced that the new album is finished:

> "The Priest album is finished. It's done. I just heard from the mastering sessions that [guitarist] Glenn [Tipton is] looking over in England, it's finished. It's done. It's coming out at some point. We've got some more information we're about to drop but in the process of the magic of building up expectation and tension to the climax."[57]

On 28 April 2014, the band released a brand new track for streaming on their official website entitled "Redeemer of Souls", which is the title track for their upcoming album of the same name.[58]

In an interview given by Eddie Trunk on 5 May 2014, Glenn Tipton says that the band is looking to go back on the road:

> "It's all a little bit 'play it by ear.' We're looking at starting some dates in the fall — exactly how many and what size, what capacity, we're not sure. But one thing that we have discussed is PRIEST have got such a wealth now of songs behind us, we probably won't go over the top on production like we've done before; the strength will be in the music. That's our feeling at the moment with this next tour."[59]

The band toured the album in 2014 and are due to play more shows in 2015.[60][61][62][63]

Redeemer of Souls sold around 32,000 copies in the United States in its first week of release to land at position No. 6 on The Billboard 200 chart, the band's highest charting position in the US after the double-disc concept album, "Nostradamus", debuted at No. 11. This was the band's first top 10 album in the US.[64]

2.37.2 Musical style and influence

Musical style

Judas Priest's style has always been rooted in heavy metal, and many of their albums reflect diverse aspects of the genre. For example, their first album, *Rocka Rolla* (1974), is primarily rooted in heavy blues rock. From *Sad Wings of Destiny* (1976) through *Stained Class* (1978), their style was somewhat progressive, with complex guitar passages and poetic lyrics. Songs would often shift in dynamics and tempo, and the music was some of the heaviest of its day. This would later have a major influence on progressive metal bands. 1977's *Sin After Sin* introduced the combination of the double bass drum and rapid 16th bass rhythms combined with rapid 16th guitar rhythms that came to define the genre.[65] While the double-bass rhythms of Judas Priest are generally measured and technical, the song "Dissident Aggressor" (1977) pushed an increase in "tempo and aggression" which was later adopted by bands like Motörhead with a much harder-edged approach.[65] Starting with their fifth album, *Killing Machine* (1978), the band began to incorporate a more commercial, radio-friendly style to their music. The lyrics and music were simplified, and this style prevailed up to their seventh album, *Point of Entry* (1981). With their eighth album, *Screaming for Vengeance* (1982), the band incorporated a balance of these two styles. This continued on *Defenders of the Faith* (1984). With the follow-up album, *Turbo* (1986), the band incorporated guitar synthesizers into its signature heavy metal sound. On 1988's *Ram It Down* the band retained some of the more commercial qualities of *Turbo* but also returned to some of the fast tempo heavy metal found on their earlier works. This fast-tempo style continued with 1990's *Painkiller*. *Jugulator* (1997) tried to incorporate some of the 1990s contemporary groove metal styles. *Demolition* (2001) has a more traditional heavy metal sound with nu metal elements. Following the return of Halford for Angel of Retribution and Nostradamus, the band returned to the style of its early albums.[1]

Media recognition

Judas Priest have influenced a great deal of metal music since the late-mid 70s. They were ranked by MTV as the second "Greatest Metal Band" of all time (after Black Sabbath), and VH1 named them the 78th greatest artist of all time in 2010.[5]

Fashion

In addition to the sound, Judas Priest is also known for being revolutionary in heavy metal fashion.[7] Rob Halford thus began incorporating a macho image of what today is known as hardcore metal/biker/S&M style into his look as early as 1978 (to coincide with the release of their album *Killing Machine*), and the rest of the band followed. It became a mainstay in heavy metal; soon, several other bands, particularly of the NWOBHM and early black metal movements, began incorporating Halford's fashion into their look as well.[66] This sparked a revival in metal in the early '80s, and catapulted them to fame, in both the mainstream and underground. Even in the present, it is not uncommon to find metal artists sporting such a look at concerts.

Their popularity and status as one of the exemplary and influential heavy metal bands has earned them the nickname "Metal Gods" from their song of the same name.[67]

2.37.3 Personnel

Main article: List of Judas Priest band members

Current members

- Ian Hill – bass, backing vocals (1970–present)
- Rob Halford – vocals (1973–1992, 2003–present)
- Glenn Tipton – guitars, keyboards, synthesiser, backing vocals (1974–present)
- Scott Travis – drums, percussion (1989–present)
- Richie Faulkner – guitars, backing vocals (2011–present)

Timeline

2.37.4 Discography

Main article: Judas Priest discography

Studio albums

- *Rocka Rolla* (1974)
- *Sad Wings of Destiny* (1976)
- *Sin After Sin* (1977)
- *Stained Class* (1978)
- *Killing Machine* (1979)
- *British Steel* (1980)
- *Point of Entry* (1981)
- *Screaming for Vengeance* (1982)
- *Defenders of the Faith* (1984)
- *Turbo* (1986)
- *Ram It Down* (1988)
- *Painkiller* (1990)
- *Jugulator* (1997)
- *Demolition* (2001)
- *Angel of Retribution* (2005)
- *Nostradamus* (2008)
- *Redeemer of Souls* (2014)

2.37.5 Tours

- Judas Priest Tour 1969
- The Return of the Priest Tour 1970–1971 (First gig of the tour with Black Sabbath)
- Whiskey Woman Tour 1972
- Never Turn Your Back on a Friend Tour 1973 (First Tour with Rob Halford, Judas Priest is the support act of Budgie)
- Gull Records Tour 1974 (First Tour with Glenn Tipton, Judas Priest is the support act of Budgie again)
- Rocka Rolla Tour 1974
- Sad Wings of Destiny Tour 1975–1976
- Sin After Sin Tour 1977
- Stained Class Tour 1978
- Hell Bent for Leather Tour 1978–1979
- British Steel Tour 1980
- World Wide Blitz Tour 1981
- World Vengeance Tour 1982–1983
- Metal Conqueror Tour 1984
- Live Aid 1985
- Fuel for Life Tour 1986
- Mercenaries of Metal Tour 1988
- Painkiller Tour 1990
- Operation Rock 'N' Roll Tour 1991
- Jugulator World Tour 1998
- Demolition World Tour 2001–2002
- Reunited Summer Tour 2004

- Ozzfest Tour 2004
- Retribution World Tour 2004–2005
- 2008/2009 World Tour 2008–2009
- Epitaph World Tour 2011–2012
- Redeemer of Souls Tour 2014-2015

2.37.6 References

[1] "Biography". Allmusic.com. Retrieved 13 February 2011.

[2] Riddle, Tree. "Original Singer: Judas Priest Would've Sounded 'More Like AC/DC' If I'd Stayed in Band". Loudwire. Retrieved 27 March 2012.

[3] "Judas Priest Confirm UK Dates As Part of Epitaph World Tour". CaughtOffside. 28 February 2011. Retrieved 10 July 2011.

[4] Glasgowvant (22 February 1999). "Glasgow SECC | Judas Priest Epitaph Tour 2011". Glasgowvant. Retrieved 10 July 2011.

[5] "MTVNews.com: The Greatest Metal Bands Of All Time". Mtv.com. 9 March 2006. Retrieved 10 July 2011.

[6] Cooper, Candy (1 July 2005). "The Judas Priest Trial: 15 Years Later". Blabbermouth.net. Retrieved 18 November 2006.

[7] Daniel Bukszpan (2003). "The Encyclopedia of Heavy Metal".

[8] Roy Wilkinson (20 May 2010). "How Judas Priest invented heavy metal". *The Guardian*. Retrieved 2014-08-10.

[9] "The Judas Priest History". Jugulator.net. Retrieved 2014-05-18.

[10] "Former Judas Priest Singer Completing Work On Autobiography". Blabbermouth.net. 2004-07-02. Retrieved 2014-05-18.

[11] "AL ATKINS EX-SINGER IN JUDAS PRIEST – JUDAS PRIEST 1969 – 1973". Allanatkins.pwp.blueyonder.co.uk. 19 January 1973. Retrieved 7 November 2010.

[12] "Early Judas Priest Guitarist Ernie Chataway Dies at 62". Loudwire.com. Retrieved 2014-05-18.

[13] Archived 15 September 2008 at the Wayback Machine

[14] "Judas Priest Info Pages - Rocka Rolla". Thexquorum.com. Retrieved 2014-08-10.

[15] "Judas Priest Info Pages - Forging The Metal". Thexquorum.com. Retrieved 2014-04-18.

[16] "Hotell Sentralt i Tønsberg - Quality Hotel Klubben". Nordicchoicehotels.no. Retrieved 2014-04-18.

[17] "Newspaper cutting : Lydsjokk pa Klubben". Kkdowning.net. Retrieved 2014-04-19.

[18] "Judas Priest Behind The Music Remastered: Judas Priest". MTV. Retrieved 2014-05-18.

[19] "Judas Priest Tour Statistics - setlist.fm". Setlist.fm. Retrieved 10 January 2015.

[20] https://vintagerock.wordpress.com/2013/06/13/judas-priest-newcastle-city-hall-october-1978/

[21] Daniels, Neil (2007). *The story of Judas priest: Defenders of the faith*. Omnibus Press. ISBN 9780857122391.

[22] "Unleashed in the East > Overview". AllMusic. Retrieved 23 April 2007.

[23] "Screaming for Vengeance Info Page". Judas Priest Info Pages.

[24] "Defenders of the Faith Info Page". Judas Priest Info Pages.

[25] http://www.mikestockmusic.com/songDisplay.php?id=49

[26] http://www.mikestockmusic.com/songDisplay.php?id=48

[27] "kickedintheface.com". kickedintheface.com. Retrieved 2014-08-10.

[28] "Q&A with Rob Halford > Overview". Montreal Gazette. Retrieved 22 August 2009.

[29] Moore, Timothy (November–December 1996). "Scientific Consensus and Expert Testimony: Lessons from the Judas Priest Trial". Skeptical Inquirer. Retrieved 18 November 2006.

[30] Hicks, Bill; Lahr, John (2004). *Love All the People: Letters, Lyrics, Routines*. Constable & Robinson. ISBN 1-84119-878-1. Retrieved April 20, 2015.

[31] "War of Words Info Page". Judas Priest Info Pages.

[32] "Rob Halford Discusses Sexuality Publicly For The First Time". MTV News. 5 February 1998. Retrieved 24 May 2010.

[33] "Interview with Rob Halford of Two". NY Rock. Retrieved 7 September 2012.

[34] Archived 3 July 2014 at the Wayback Machine

[35] "Work on New Album Is 'Going Incredibly Well'". Blabbermouth.net. 12 September 2006. Retrieved 18 November 2006.

[36] Saulnier, Jason (16 April 2011). "Rob Halford Interview, Judas Priest Singer talks Rare Recordings". Music Legends. Retrieved 3 May 2013.

[37] "Judas Priest Issues Warning About Ticket Prices". idiomag. 12 February 2009. Retrieved 13 February 2009.

[38] "Message from Judas Priest after US Tour". Judaspriest.com. 24 August 2009. Retrieved 7 November 2010.

[39] "Whitesnake tour announcement". Judaspriest.com. 13 August 2009. Retrieved 7 November 2010.

[40] "Judas Priest Grammy Nomination for Dissident Aggressor". Judaspriest.com. 4 December 2009. Retrieved 7 November 2010.

[41] Reesman, Bryan (4 June 2010). "Rob Halford: Back To The Future". Attention Deficit Delirium. Retrieved 29 June 2010.

[42] Reesman, Bryan (10 April 2010). "Judas Priest In "Toy Story 3"? Almost.". Attention Deficit Delirium. Retrieved 29 June 2010.

[43] "JUDAS PRIEST Announces Farewell 'Epitaph' Tour – Dec. 7, 2010". Blabbermouth.net. 7 December 2010. Retrieved 8 December 2010.

[44] "ROB HALFORD Doesn't Want Fans To Be Sad About JUDAS PRIEST's Upcoming Farewell Tour". Blabbermouth.net. 11 January 2011. Retrieved 13 January 2011.

[45] "JUDAS PRIEST Working on New Material – Jan. 27, 2011". Blabbermouth.net. 27 January 2011. Retrieved 28 January 2011.

[46] "JUDAS PRIEST: More Video Footage Of Los Angeles Press Conference – May 25, 2011". Roadrunnerrecords.com. Retrieved 3 October 2011.

[47] "News – K.K. DOWNING retirement Press Release". JudasPriest.com. 20 April 2011. Retrieved 10 July 2011.

[48] "JUDAS PRIEST Performs On 'American Idol' Finale; Video Available". Blabbermouth.net. 25 May 2011. Archived from the original on 29 May 2011. Retrieved 29 May 2011.

[49] "JUDAS PRIEST To Release 'Single Cuts' In August". Blabbermouth.net. 7 June 2011. Archived from the original on 10 June 2011. Retrieved 11 June 2011.

[50] "JUDAS PRIEST Singer Says '12 Or 14' Songs Have Been 'Completely Mapped Out' For Next Album". Blabbermouth.net. Retrieved 5 September 2011.

[51] "Judas Priest Hints at New Music for 2013". Billboard. 6 August 2012.

[52] "Judas Priest Announce New Compilation Album – Lars Ulrich, Ozzy Osbourne, Alice Cooper and more chose their favorite Priest songs for 'The Chosen Few'". Rolling Stone. 13 September 2011. Retrieved 13 September 2011.

[53] "JUDAS PRIEST's Rob Halford, Richie Faulkner Talk Epitaph, 40th Anniversary – "It's Not The End of Touring; We Are Still Going To Be Going Out There"". Bravewords.com. Retrieved 14 June 2013.

[54] "Official Judas Priest news: Christmas message". Judas-Priest.com. 22 December 2013.

[55] Beaumont-Thomas, Ben (14 January 2014). "The Simpsons apologise to Judas Priest for calling them 'death metal'". *The Guardian*. Retrieved 27 January 2014.

[56] "Bart Simpson Apologizes for Calling Judas Priest 'Death Metal'". *Rolling Stone*. 13 January 2014. Retrieved 27 January 2014.

[57] "Rob Halford: New Judas Priest Album Is 'Finished' and 'F—ing Heavy'". *Loudwire*. 19 March 2014. Retrieved 19 March 2014.

[58] "Judas Priest Unveil New Track from Upcoming Album". Tapp Out Music. Retrieved 2014-05-18.

[59] "Eddie Trunk Live (Trunk Nation) Judas Priest 5-5-14". YouTube. 5 May 2014. Retrieved 5 May 2014.

[60] "JUDAS PRIEST TO ANNOUNCE TOUR DATES IN SUPPORT OF 'REDEEMER OF SOULS'". judaspriest.com. 20 May 2014. Retrieved 20 May 2014.

[61] "Judas Priest announces 2014 Tour Dates, Barclays Center, Izod Center, Atlantic City, FFF Fest & more included". Brooklynvegan.com. 2014-06-27. Retrieved 2014-07-10.

[62] "Judas Priest 2015 Redeemer of Souls Tour Schedule With Saxon". January 11, 2015. Retrieved March 29, 2015.

[63] "Judas Priest Tour Schedule". Retrieved March 29, 2015.

[64] "Judas Priest Lands First Ever Top 10 Album In U.S. With 'Redeemer Of Souls'". Blabbermouth.net. 2014-07-16. Retrieved 2014-08-10.

[65] Cope, Andrew Laurence. *Black Sabbath and the Rise of Heavy Metal Music*. Ashgate Publishing. ISBN 9781409493983.

[66] "Hell Bent for Leather/Killing Machine Info Page". Judas Priest Info Pages.

[67] Berelian, Essi. *The Rough Guide to Heavy Metal*. Rough Guides. p. 172. ISBN 1-84353-415-0.

2.37.7 External links

- Official website

2.38 Lionheart (band)

Lionheart was a British hard rock band formed in late 1980, originally featuring singer Jess Cox (ex-Tygers of Pan Tang), guitarist Dennis Stratton (ex-Iron Maiden), guitarist Steve Mann (ex-Liar), bassist/vocalist Rocky Newton (ex-The Next Band, Wildfire), and drummer Frank Noon (ex-The Next Band, Def Leppard).

2.38.1 History

Lionheart made their debut one Saturday night at the Marquee Club in London but suffered from bad press thanks to criticism of Cox. This led to the cancellation of the next two appearances and saw Cox replaced by former Lautrec frontman, Reuben Archer. Former Judas Priest drummer Les Binks replaced the Wild Horses-bound Noon for the 1981 UK tour with Def Leppard with former Wild Horses drummer Clive Edwards eventually replacing Binks. Archer, too, would briefly spend time in Wild Horses before forming Stampede with his step son, guitarist Laurence Archer, Noon, and bassist Colin Bond.

The song "Lionheart", recorded by Reuben Archer, Dennis Stratton, Steve Mann, Rocky Newton, and Frank Noon would belatedly surface on the *Heavy Metal Heroes Vol. 2* (Heavy Metal Records) compilation in 1982. Said track remains the only representative recording of the band's early sound as they would change their style significantly later on.

A demo recorded by the core of Stratton, Mann, and Newton landed Lionheart a deal with the American branch of CBS Records in 1984. Enlisting new vocalist Chad Brown and securing the studio services of Leo Sayer band drummer Bob Jenkins, the band proceeded to record their debut album, *Hot Tonight*, with record producer Kevin Beamish (REO Speedwagon, Starship) in Los Angeles, California. This was a slick AOR-styled effort that failed to capture the old fans' interest or that of their target audience in the United States.

In 1985 the band continued with former Grand Prix members, drummer Andy Bierne and keyboardist Phil Lanzon, appearing on Channel 4's popular ECT program. Lanzon eventually left to join the reformed Sweet (and later Uriah Heep), while Brown gave way to new vocalist Keith Murrell (ex-Airrace).

Failing to make any headway, Lionheart split up in 1986, with Bierne going into management, Murrell fronting Irish rockers, Mama's Boys, and Newton and Mann joining the McAuley Schenker Group. Dennis Stratton later found fame in Japan as part of an all-star Praying Mantis touring line-up alongside former Iron Maiden band mate Paul Di'Anno.

Steve Mann would sign on with Sweet as the guitarist/keyboardist in late 1989, ironically replacing his former Lionheart band mate Lanzon. Mann stayed on into the mid 1990s when he was invited by Frank Bornemann, owner of Horus Sound Studio in Hannover, Germany to play guitar and some keyboards for his band Eloy, completing a line-up that consisted of Klaus-Peter Matziol on bass, Michael Gerlach on keyboards, and Bodo Schopf (ex-McAuley Schenker Group, Sweet) on drums. Mann guested on both *The Tides Return Forever* and *Ocean 2: The*

Answer and also took part in a tour of Germany.

Unearthed - Raiders of the Lost Archives, a 30-song collection of Lionheart demos, was issued in 1999 by Pony Canyon in Japan.

2.38.2 Discography

- *Hot Tonight* (1984)
- *Unearthed - Raiders of the Lost Archives* (1999)

2.38.3 See also

- List of New Wave of British Heavy Metal bands

2.38.4 External links

- Lionheart @ MusicMight.com
- Lionheart @ TartareanDesire.com
- SteveMann.net

2.39 List of New Wave of British Heavy Metal bands

This is a list of British bands which emerged during the New Wave of British Heavy Metal and released records in the period 1975-1985, as compiled by Malc McMillan in his *The New Wave of British Heavy Metal Encyclopedia*.

Contents :

- Top
- 0–9
- A
- B
- C
- D
- E
- F
- G
- H
- I

- J
- K
- L
- M
- N
- O
- P
- Q
- R
- S
- T
- U
- V
- W
- X
- Y
- Z

2.39.1 A

Angel Witch

- Ace Lane
- After Dark
- After Hours
- Alec Johnson Band
- Alkatrazz

- Amazon
- Angel Street
- Angel Witch[1][2]
- Anthem
- Apocalypse
- Aragorn[3][4]
- Arc
- A.R.C. Rock Band
- Argus
- Atlantis Rising
- Atomkraft[4][5][6]
- A II Z[7][8]
- Aurora
- Avalanche
- Avalon
- Avenger[4][9][10]
- Avenue
- Axis[11]

2.39.2 B

Blitzkrieg

- Baby Tuckoo[12][13]
- Backlash
- Badge
- Badger

- Baseline
- Bashful Alley
- Battleaxe[14][15]
- Battlezone[16][17]
- Beg to Differ
- Berlin Ritz
- Big Daisy
- Bill the Murderer
- Bitches Sin[4][18][19]
- Black Axe[20]
- Blackmayne[21]
- Blackout
- Black Rose[22][23]
- Blackwych
- Blade Runner
- Blazer Blazer
- Bleak House
- The Blitz
- Blitzkrieg[24][25]
- Blood Money[26][27]
- Bloodshot Eyes
- Blue Blud
- BollWeevil
- Bombay
- Boulevard
- Briar[28]
- Bronz[29][30]
- Brooklyn[30]
- Brunel
- Buffalo
- Buzzard

2.39.3 C

- Cagey Bee
- Camargue
- Canis Major
- Catch 22 (I)
- Catch 22 (II)
- Ceffyl Pren
- Centurion
- Chainsaw (I)
- Chainsaw (II)
- Challenger
- Charger
- Chariot[31]
- Charlie 'Ungry
- Chasar[31]
- Chase
- Chateaux[32][33]
- Cheeky
- Chemical Alice
- Chevy
- China Doll
- Chinatown[34]
- Chinawite[34]
- Chrome Molly[34][35]
- Clientelle[36]
- Cloven Hoof[36][37]
- Cobra (I)
- Cobra (II)[38]
- The Covenant
- Cracked Mirror
- Crazy Blaze
- Crucifixion[39]
- Cry
- Cryer
- Crys
- Cynic

2.39.4 D

Def Leppard

- Damascus
- Dark Earth
- Dark Star[40][41]
- Dawn Trader
- Dawnwatcher
- Deadly Atlantic Run
- Dealer[42]
- Dedringer[43][44]
- Deep Switch[45]
- Def Leppard[46][47]
- Demon[48][49]

Demon

- Demon Pact

- Denigh
- Desolation Angels[50]
- Destroyer
- Deuce (I)
- Deuce (II)
- Diamond Head[27][51][52]

Diamond Head

- Di'Anno[53]
- Diawled
- Dick Smith Band
- Die Laughing
- Distrainers
- Dorcas
- Dragonfly
- Dragonslayer
- Dragster
- Driveshaft
- Duchess
- Dumpy's Rusty Nuts[54][55]

2.39.5 E

- Earthbound
- Eazie Ryder
- Eazy Street
- EF Band[56][57]

Elixir

- Elixir[57][58]
- Emerson
- Energy
- Eric Bell Band
- E. S. P.
- Ethel the Frog[59][60]
- Everyone Else
- Excalibur[61]
- Exocet
- Explorer[62]
- Export[63]
- Expozer
- Ezy Meat[64]

2.39.6 F

- Factory
- Fair Warning
- False Idols
- Fast Kutz[65]
- Filthy Rich
- Firebird
- Firebrand
- Fireclown
- Fist[66][67]
- 5 A. M.

- Flash Harry
- Flashpoint[68]
- Flight 77
- Force
- Forger
- Founded
- Four Wheel Drive
- Framed
- Frenzy
- Friends
- Fugitive
- Full Moon
- Fury

2.39.7 G

Girlschool

- Garbo
- Gaskin[69][70]
- Geddes Axe[70][71]
- Gemage
- General Wolf
- Genghis Khan
- Girl[72][73]
- Girlschool[27][73][74]

- Glasgow
- Gogmagog[75]

Grim Reaper

- Goldsmith
- Golgotha
- Grand Prix[76][77]
- Grim Reaper[78][79]
- Ground Attack
- Gunslingers
- Gypp

2.39.8 H

- Hammer[80]
- Hammerhead[80]
- The Handsome Beasts[81][82]
- The Hard
- Harlequyn
- Harrier[83]
- Haze
- Hazzard
- Headbangers
- Heavy Pettin[84][85]
- Hell[86]
- Hellanbach[87][88][89]
- Hellrazer
- Hell's Belles[90]
- Heretic[91]
- Heritage[91]
- H. G. B.
- High Risk
- High Treason
- Hoggs
- Holland[92]
- Hollow Ground[93]
- Holocaust[89][94][95]
- Hologram[96][97]
- Horizon
- Horsepower

2.39.9 I

Iron Maiden

- Idle Flowers
- Idol Rich
- Incubus[98]
- Influence
- International Heroes
- Iona
- Ipanema Katz
- Iron Maiden[99][100]
- Isengard

2.39.10 J

- Jaguar[89][101][102]
- Jameson Raid[103]
- Janine
- Jeddah
- Jess Cox[104]
- JJ's Powerhouse
- Jodey
- Jody St.
- Joe Lethal
- Joker
- Jokers Wild
- Jonah
- Juno's Claw

2.39.11 K

- Karrier
- Kick
- Knightrider
- Knock Up
- Kooga
- Korea
- Kraken
- Kruza

2.39.12 L

- Lady Jane
- Last Flight
- Lautrec
- The Law
- Léargo
- Left Hand Drive
- Legend (I)
- Legend (II)[105][106]
- Le Griffe[107][108]
- Liaison
- Lighning Raiders
- Limelight
- Lionheart[109]
- Lonely Hearts
- Lone Wolf (I)
- Lone Wolf (II)
- Lorelei
- Lost Famous
- Lost Property
- Lotus Cruise
- Lyadrive
- Lynx

2.39.13 M

- Mad Dog
- Made in England
- Maineeaxe[110]
- Maison Rouge
- Malllet
- Mama's Boys[111][112]
- Mammath[113]
- Mammoth[112][114]
- Marionette
- Marquis De Sade
- Marseille[115][116]
- Marz
- Masai
- Mass
- Masterstroke
- Mayday

- McCoy
- Meanstreak
- Medusa
- Megaton
- Mendes Prey
- Metal Mirror
- Metal Virgins
- Midas
- Millennium[117]
- Mithrandir
- Moby Dick
- Money
- More[118][119]
- Moselle
- Mother's Ruin
- Mournblade[120]
- Movie Stars
- Mythra[121]

2.39.14 N

- National Gold
- Nato
- Neon Spirit
- Never Amber
- Next Band
- Nicky Moore Band
- Night Games
- Nighttime Flyer
- Nightwing[122][123]
- No Faith
- No Quarter[124]
- North Star
- No Sweat
- Nuthin Fancy

2.39.15 O

- Omega[125]
- Omen Searcher
- 100% Proof
- Onslaught
- Oral
- Ore
- Original Sin
- Orion
- Overdrive
- Overkill
- Oxym

2.39.16 P

Praying Mantis

- Pagan Altar[126][127]
- Pali Gap
- Panza Division
- Paradyne
- Paralex[128][129]
- Pariah[130]
- Paul Dale Band
- Penetrations

- Persian Risk[131][132]
- Pet Hate[132]
- Phasslayne[133]
- Pheetus
- Phoenix Rising[133]
- Phyne Thanquz
- Praying Mantis[134][135]
- Predator
- Predatür
- Presence
- Preyer
- Prowler (I)
- Prowler (II)
- Purple Haze
- Pyramid

2.39.17 Q

- Quartz[136][137]

2.39.18 R

Raven

- Radar

- Radium
- Rage[138]
- Rampent
- Rankelson
- Raven[139][140][141]
- Raw Deal (I)
- Raw Deal (II)
- Red
- Red Alert
- Red Rage
- Reincarnate
- Renegade (I)
- Renegade (II)
- Requiem
- Rhabstallion
- Ricochet
- Roadster
- Rock Goddess[142][143]
- Rogue Male[144][145]
- Rokka
- Rollin' Thunder
- Rough Justice (I)
- Rough Justice (II)
- Rox
- Runestaff

2.39.19 S

Satan

2.39. LIST OF NEW WAVE OF BRITISH HEAVY METAL BANDS

- Sabre[141][146]
- Sacred Alien
- Sacrilege
- Saigon
- Salem[147]
- Samson[148][149]
- Sam Thunder[150]
- Samurai[150]
- Sapphire
- Saracen[151][152]
- Satan[141][153][154]
- Satanic Rites (I)
- Satanic Rites (II)[155]
- Savage[156][157]

Saxon

- Saxon[141][158][159]
- Scarab (I)
- Scarab (II)
- Scorched Earth
- Scorpio
- Seducer[160]
- Seventh Son
- Severed Head
- Shader
- Shadowfax
- Shadowlands
- She[161]
- Sheer Khan
- Sherwood
- Shiva[161][162][163]
- Shock Treatment
- Shogun[161]
- Shy[164][165]
- Shywolf
- Sian
- Sidewinder
- Siege
- Silverwing[166]
- Singapore
- Sinner
- Skitzofrenic
- Sledgehammer[167]
- Slender Thread
- Slowtrain
- Smart
- Smokin' Roadie
- Snakebite
- Snatch-back
- Snowblind
- Soldier[163]
- So What
- Sparta
- Spartan Warrior[168][169]
- Speed
- Speed Limit
- Spider[170][171]

- Spitfire
- Spitzbrook
- Split Beaver[171][172]
- Splitcrow[171]
- Squashed Pyrannah
- Stagefright
- Stampede (I)[173][174]
- Stampede (II)
- Starfighters[174]
- Statetrooper[175]
- Static
- Steel
- Stolen Thunder
- Stormchild
- Stormtrooper
- Storyteller
- Strategy
- Stratus[176]
- Streetfighter
- Street Legal
- Strutz
- Stryder
- Surface[177]
- Suspect
- Sweet Savage[178]
- Syar
- S. Y. X.

2.39.20 T

- T34
- Tank[179][180]
- Target UK
- Tempest
- Terraplane[181]
- Thin Edge of the Wedge
- Thunderstick[182]
- Titan (I)
- Titan (II)
- TNT
- Toad the Wet Sprocket[183]
- Tobruk[184]
- Tok-io Rose
- Tokyo Blade[185][186]
- Tokyo Rose
- Too Much
- Tora Tora
- Torture
- Tosh
- Touched[187]
- Tracer
- Track 4
- Trader
- Traitors Gate
- Trans Am
- Traxx
- Tredegar[188]
- Trespass[163][189]
- Triarchy
- Trident
- Trobwll
- Trojan (I)[190][191]

- Trojan (II)[192]
- Troyen
- Truffle
- Trux
- Trydan
- Turbo
- Tutch
- Tuxedo
- 20/20 Vision
- Twisted Ace
- Tyga Myra[193]
- Tygers of Pan Tang[163][194][195]
- Tyrant
- Tysondog[196][197]
- Tytan[197][198]

2.39.21 U

- Urchin
- Us

2.39.22 V

Venom

- V8
- Vagabond

- Valhalla (I)
- Valhalla (II)
- Vardis[199][200]
- Venom[201][202]
- Vermillion
- Vhf
- Virginia Wolf
- Virgin Star
- Virtue
- Voltz[203]
- Voyager UK

2.39.23 W

- Warfare[204]
- War Machine
- Warrior (I)
- Warrior (II)[205]
- Warrior (III)
- Warrior (IV)[205]
- Weapon[206]
- Wendy House
- Whitefire
- White Heat
- White Lightning
- White Spirit[207][208]
- Widow
- Wikkyd Vikker
- Wildfire (I)
- Wildfire (II)[209]
- Wild Horses[210][211]
- Wildsmith St.
- Winter's Reign
- Witches Brew

- Witchfinder General[212][213]
- Witchfynde[214][215][216]
- Wolf (I)
- Wolf (II)[217]
- Wrathchild[218][219]

2.39.24 X

- Xero

2.39.25 Y

- Young Blood

2.39.26 Z

- Zenith
- Zorro

2.39.27 Notes

[1] Rivadavia, Eduardo. "Angel Witch biography". *AllMusic*. All Media Network. Retrieved 18 March 2015.

[2] Popoff: p.21

[3] Rivadavia, Eduardo. "Aragorn biography". *AllMusic*. All Media Network. Retrieved 25 March 2015.

[4] Tucker: p.203

[5] Rivadavia, Eduardo. "Atomkraft biography". *AllMusic*. Rovi Corporation. Retrieved 21 April 2013.

[6] Popoff: p.29

[7] Rivadavia, Eduardo. "A II Z biography". *AllMusic*. All Media Network. Retrieved 10 February 2012.

[8] Popoff: p.31

[9] Rivadavia, Eduardo. "Avenger biography". *AllMusic*. All Media Network. Retrieved 10 February 2012.

[10] Popoff: p.32

[11] Rivadavia, Eduardo. "Axis biography". *AllMusic*. All Media Network. Retrieved 25 March 2015.

[12] "Baby Tuckoo biography". *AllMusic*. All Media Network. Retrieved 10 March 2015.

[13] Popoff: p.35

[14] Ruhlmann, William. "Battleaxe biography". *AllMusic*. All Media Network. Retrieved 10 March 2015.

[15] Popoff: p.39

[16] "Battlezone biography". *AllMusic*. All Media Network. Retrieved 10 March 2015.

[17] Popoff: pp.39-40

[18] Rivadavia, Eduardo. "Bitches Sin biography". *AllMusic*. All Media Network. Retrieved 10 March 2015.

[19] Popoff: p.42

[20] Rivadavia, Eduardo. "Black Axe biography". *AllMusic*. All Media Network. Retrieved 25 March 2015.

[21] Popoff: p.46

[22] Ruhlmann, William. "Black Rose biography". *AllMusic*. All Media Network. Retrieved 10 March 2015.

[23] Popoff: p.47

[24] Rivadavia, Eduardo. "Blitzkrieg biography". *AllMusic*. All Media Network. Retrieved 10 February 2012.

[25] Popoff: p.52

[26] Popoff: p.53

[27] Tucker: p.204

[28] Popoff: p.60

[29] "Bronz biography". *AllMusic*. All Media Network. Retrieved 10 March 2015.

[30] Popoff: p.61

[31] Popoff: p.69

[32] Rivadavia, Eduardo. "Chateaux biography". *AllMusic*. All Media Network. Retrieved 10 February 2012.

[33] Popoff: p.70

[34] Popoff: p.72

[35] "Chrome Molly biography". *AllMusic*. All Media Network. Retrieved 10 March 2015.

[36] Popoff: p.74

[37] Rivadavia, Eduardo. "Cloven Hoof biography". *Allmusic*. All Media Network. Retrieved 10 February 2012.

[38] Popoff: pp. 74-75

[39] Popoff: p.80

[40] Rivadavia, Eduardo. "Dark Star biography". *AllMusic*. All Media Network. Retrieved 10 March 2015.

[41] Popoff: pp.85-86

[42] Popoff: p.88

[43] Rivadavia, Eduardo. "Dedringer biography". *AllMusic*. All Media Network. Retrieved 13 February 2012.

[44] Popoff: p.90

[45] Popoff: p.91

[46] Erlewine, Stephen Thomas. "Def Leppard biography". *AllMusic*. All Media Network. Retrieved 10 February 2012.

[47] Popoff: pp.92-93

[48] Rivadavia, Eduardo. "Demon biography". *AllMusic*. All Media Network. Retrieved 10 February 2012.

[49] Popoff: pp.93-94

[50] Popoff: p.94

[51] Rivadavia, Eduardo. "Diamond Head biography". *AllMusic*. All Media Network. Retrieved 10 February 2012.

[52] Popoff: pp.96-97

[53] Popoff: p.97

[54] Huey, Steve. "Dumpy's Rusty Nuts biography". *AllMusic*. All Media Network. Retrieved 10 March 2015.

[55] Popoff: p.104

[56] Rivadavia, Eduardo. "EF Band biography". *AllMusic*. All Media Network. Retrieved 10 February 2012.

[57] Popoff: p.106

[58] Rivadavia, Eduardo. "Elixir biography". *AllMusic*. All Media Network. Retrieved 10 February 2012.

[59] Rivadavia, Eduardo. "Ethel the Frog biography". *AllMusic*. All Media Network. Retrieved 10 February 2012.

[60] Popoff: p.108

[61] Popoff: p.110

[62] Popoff: p.112

[63] Popoff: pp.112-113

[64] Popoff: p.113

[65] Popoff: p.117

[66] Rivadavia, Eduardo. "Fist biography". *AllMusic*. All Media Network. Retrieved 10 February 2012.

[67] Popoff: p.121-122

[68] Popoff: p.122

[69] Rivadavia, Eduardo. "Gaskin biography". *AllMusic*. All Media Network. Retrieved 10 March 2015.

[70] Popoff: p.130

[71] "Geddes Axe biography". *AllMusic*. All Media Network. Retrieved 10 March 2015.

[72] Rivadavia, Eduardo. "Girl biography". *AllMusic*. All Media Network. Retrieved 10 March 2015.

[73] Popoff: p.133

[74] Prato, Greg. "Girlschool biography". *AllMusic*. All Media Network. Retrieved 10 February 2012.

[75] Popoff: p.135

[76] Leggett, Steve. "Grand Prix biography". *AllMusic*. All Media Network. Retrieved 10 March 2015.

[77] Popoff: p.136

[78] Rivadavia, Eduardo. "Grim Reaper biography". *AllMusic*. All Media Network. Retrieved 10 February 2012.

[79] Popoff: pp.139-140

[80] Popoff: p.145

[81] Rivadavia, Eduardo (20 August 2006). "Handsome Beasts biography". *AllMusic*. All Media Network. Retrieved 25 June 2012.

[82] Popoff: p.146

[83] Popoff: p.148

[84] Ankeny, Jason. "Heavy Pettin biography". *AllMusic*. All Media Network. Retrieved 10 March 2015.

[85] Popoff: p.153

[86] Freeman, Phil. "Hell - Human Remains review". *AllMusic*. All Media Network. Retrieved 10 February 2012.

[87] Rivadavia, Eduardo. "Hellanbach biography". *AllMusic*. All Media Network. Retrieved 10 March 2015.

[88] Popoff: p.155

[89] Tucker: p.205

[90] Popoff: p.158

[91] Popoff: p.159

[92] Popoff: p.161

[93] Rivadavia, Eduardo. "Hollow Ground biography". *AllMusic*. All Media Network. Retrieved 10 February 2012.

[94] Rivadavia, Eduardo. "Holocaust biography". *AllMusic*. All Media Network. Retrieved 10 February 2012.

[95] Popoff: pp.161-162

[96] Rivadavia, Eduardo. "Hologram biography". *AllMusic*. All Media Network. Retrieved 10 March 2015.

[97] Popoff: p.162

[98] Popoff: p.168

[99] Huey, Steve. "*Iron Maiden* review". *AllMusic*. All Media Network. Retrieved 10 February 2012.

[100] Popoff: p.169-172

[101] Rivadavia, Eduardo. "Jaguar biography". *AllMusic*. All Media Network. Retrieved 10 February 2012.

[102] Popoff: p.175

[103] Rivadavia, Eduardo. "Jameson Raid biography". *AllMusic*. All Media Network. Retrieved 10 February 2012.

[104] "Jess Cox biography". *AllMusic*. All Media Network. Retrieved 27 March 2015.

[105] Rivadavia, Eduardo. "Legend biography". *AllMusic*. All Media Network. Retrieved 10 February 2012.

[106] Popoff: pp.195-196

[107] "Le Griffe biography". *AllMusic*. All Media Network. Retrieved 10 March 2015.

[108] Popoff: p.196

[109] "Lionheart biography". *AllMusic*. All Media Network. Retrieved 24 March 2015.

[110] Popoff: p.207

[111] Prato, Greg. "Mama's Boys biography". *AllMusic*. All Media Network. Retrieved 10 February 2012.

[112] Popoff: p.210

[113] Rivadavia, Eduardo. "Mammath biography". *AllMusic*. All Media Network. Retrieved 10 March 2015.

[114] "Mammoth biography". *AllMusic*. All Media Network. Retrieved 10 March 2015.

[115] "Marseille biography". *AllMusic*. All Media Network. Retrieved 10 March 2015.

[116] Popoff: p.214

[117] Popoff: p.225

[118] Rivadavia, Eduardo. "More biography". *AllMusic*. All Media Network. Retrieved 10 February 2012.

[119] Popoff: p.231

[120] Popoff: p.235

[121] "Mythra biography". *AllMusic*. All Media Network. Retrieved 25 March 2015.

[122] "Nightwing biography". *AllMusic*. All Media Network. Retrieved 22 March 2015.

[123] Popoff: p.243

[124] Popoff: p.246

[125] Popoff: p.250

[126] Rivadavia, Eduardo. "Pagan Altar biography". *AllMusic*. All Media Network. Retrieved 22 March 2015.

[127] Marsicano, Dan. "Essential Doom Metal Albums". About.com. Retrieved 1 July 2012.

[128] Rivadavia, Eduardo. "Paralex biography". *AllMusic*. All Media Network. Retrieved 10 March 2015.

[129] Popoff: p.258

[130] Popoff: p.259

[131] Rivdavia, Eduardo. "Persian Risk biography". *AllMusic*. All Media Network. Retrieved 10 February 2012.

[132] Popoff: p.260

[133] Popoff: p.261

[134] Rivadavia, Eduardo. "Praying Mantis biography". *AllMusic*. All Media Network. Retrieved 10 February 2012.

[135] Popoff: p.268

[136] Torreano, Bradley. "Quartz biography". *AllMusic*. All Media Network. Retrieved 10 February 2012.

[137] Popoff: pp.271-272

[138] Popoff: p.277

[139] Rivadavia, Eduardo. "Raven biography". *AllMusic*. All Media Network. Retrieved 10 February 2012.

[140] Popoff: pp.283-286

[141] Tucker: p.206

[142] "Rock Goddess biography". *AllMusic*. All Media Network. Retrieved 10 March 2015.

[143] Popoff: p.290

[144] "Rogue Male biography". *AllMusic*. All Media Network. Retrieved 10 March 2015.

[145] Popoff: p.292

[146] Rivadavia, Eduardo. "Sabre biography". *AllMusic*. All Media Network. Retrieved 10 March 2015.

[147] Rivadavia, Eduardo. "Salem biography". *AllMusic*. All Media Network. Retrieved 10 March 2015.

[148] Huey, Steve. "Samson biography". *AllMusic*. All Media Network. Retrieved 10 February 2012.

[149] Popoff: pp.305-307

[150] Popoff: p.307

[151] Rivadavia, Eduardo. "Saracen biography". *AllMusic*. All Media Network. Retrieved 10 March 2015.

[152] Popoff: p.308

[153] Rivadavia, Eduardo. "Satan biography". *AllMusic*. All Media Network. Retrieved 10 February 2012.

[154] Popoff: p.309

[155] Popoff: p.310

[156] Rivadavia, Eduardo. "Savage biography". *AllMusic*. All Media Network. Retrieved 10 February 2012.

[157] Popoff: pp.310-311

[158] Rivadavia, Eduardo. "Saxon biography". *AllMusic*. All Media Network. Retrieved 10 February 2012.

[159] Popoff: pp.314-315

[160] Popoff: p.320

[161] Popoff: p.322

[162] "Shiva biography". *AllMusic*. All Media Network. Retrieved 10 March 2015.

[163] Tucker: p.207

[164] "Shy biography". *AllMusic*. All Media Network. Retrieved 10 March 2015.

[165] Popoff: p.323

[166] Popoff: p.324

[167] Popoff: p.328

[168] Monger, James Christopher. "Spartan Warrior Biography". *AllMusic*. All Media Network. Retrieved 19 July 2015.

[169] Popoff: p.333

[170] "Spider biography". *AllMusic*. All Media Network. Retrieved 10 March 2015.

[171] Popoff: p.334

[172] "Split Beaver biography". *AllMusic*. All Media Network. Retrieved 10 March 2015.

[173] "Stampede biography". *AllMusic*. All Media Network. Retrieved 24 March 2015.

[174] Popoff: p.336

[175] Popoff: p.337

[176] Popoff: p.343

[177] Popoff: p.345

[178] Prato, Greg. "Sweet Savage biography". *AllMusic*. All Media Network. Retrieved 10 February 2012.

[179] Rivadavia, Eduardo. "Tank biography". *AllMusic*. All Media Network. Retrieved 10 February 2012.

[180] Popoff: pp.350-351

[181] Popoff: p.352

[182] "Thunderstick biography". *AllMusic*. All Media Network. Retrieved 10 March 2015.

[183] Rivadavia, Eduardo. "Toad the Wet Sprocket biography". *AllMusic*. All Media Network. Retrieved 10 March 2015.

[184] Rivadavia, Eduardo. "Tobruk Biography". *AllMusic*. All Media Network. Retrieved 2 September 2015.

[185] Rivadavia, Eduardo. "*Tokyo Blade* review". *AllMusic*. All Media Network. Retrieved 10 February 2012.

[186] Popoff: p.358-359

[187] Popoff: p.361

[188] Popoff: p.364

[189] Stone, Doug. "Trespass biography". *AllMusic*. All Media Network. Retrieved 10 February 2012.

[190] "Trojan biography". *AllMusic*. All Media Network. Retrieved 10 March 2015.

[191] Popoff: p.366

[192] Popoff: p.365

[193] Popoff: p.370

[194] Rivadavia, Eduardo. "Tygers of Pan Tang biography". *AllMusic*. All Media Network. Retrieved 10 February 2012.

[195] Popoff: p.371-372

[196] Rivadavia, Eduardo. "Tysondog biography". *AllMusic*. All Media Network. Retrieved 10 March 2015.

[197] Popoff: p.373

[198] Rivadavia, Eduardo. "Tytan biography". *AllMusic*. All Media Network. Retrieved 10 February 2012.

[199] Rivadavia, Eduardo. "Vardis biography". *AllMusic*. All Media Network. Retrieved 10 February 2012.

[200] Popoff: p.386

[201] Ankeny, Jason. "Venom biography". *AllMusic*. All Media Network. Retrieved 25 March 2015.

[202] Popoff: pp.395-397

[203] Popoff: p.401

[204] Popoff: p.403

[205] Popoff: p.406

[206] Popoff: p.409

[207] Rivadavia, Eduardo. "White Spirit biography". *AllMusic*. All Media Network. Retrieved 10 February 2012.

[208] Popoff: p.412

[209] Popoff: p.414

[210] Rivadavia, Eduardo. "Wild Horses biography". *AllMusic*. All Media Network. Retrieved 25 March 2015.

[211] Popoff: pp.414-415

[212] Rivadavia, Eduardo. "Witchfinder General biography". *AllMusic*. All Media Network. Retrieved 10 February 2012.

[213] Popoff: pp.416-417

[214] Rivadavia, Eduardo. "Witchfynde biography". *AllMusic*. All Media Network. Retrieved 10 February 2012.

[215] Popoff: pp.417-418

[216] Tucker: p.208

[217] Popoff: p.418

[218] "Wrathchild biography". *AllMusic*. All Media Network. Retrieved 10 March 2015.

[219] Popoff: pp.419-420

2.39.28 References

- Macmillan, Malc (2012). *The New Wave of British Heavy Metal Encyclopedia*. Iron Pages Books (3 ed.) (Berlin, Germany: I.P. Verlag Jeske/Mader GbR). ISBN 978-3-931624-16-3.

- Popoff, Martin (1 November 2005). *The Collector's Guide to Heavy Metal: Volume 2: The Eighties*. Burlington, Ontario, Canada: Collector's Guide Publishing. ISBN 978-1-894959-31-5.

- Tucker, John (2006). *Suzie Smiled... The New Wave of British Heavy Metal*. Shropshire, UK: Independent Music Press. ISBN 978-0-9549704-7-5.

2.40 Magnum (band)

Magnum are an English rock band from Birmingham. Formed as a four piece by Tony Clarkin (guitar, songwriter), Bob Catley (vocals), Kex Gorin (drums) and Bob Doyle (bass) in order to appear as the resident band at The Rum Runner night club in Birmingham. Magnum have undergone several changes in personnel over the years; however, the core of Catley and Clarkin remain.

Magnum's most notable success during their early years was *Chase the Dragon* in 1982, which reached #17 in the UK Albums Chart,[1] and included several songs that would be mainstays of the band's live set, notably "Soldier of The Line," "Sacred Hour" and "The Spirit".

Their breakthrough came in 1985 with the album *On a Storyteller's Night*, which featured the single "Just Like an Arrow". This success continued in the following years with the Roger Taylor produced *Vigilante* in 1986, the Top 5 album *Wings of Heaven* in 1988, which featured three Top 40 singles, and the Keith Olsen produced *Goodnight L.A.* which reached #9 in the UK Album Chart in 1990.[1]

In 1995, Clarkin announced Magnum's split; he later formed another band, with Catley and Al Barrow called Hard Rain. Magnum reformed in 2001 and have released a further six studio albums since then. Their most recent album *Escape from the Shadow Garden* was released in March 2014.

2.40.1 History

Early years (1972—1978)

Magnum began as the house band at Birmingham's famous Rum Runner night club (later the home of Duran Duran). Joining Clarkin and Catley were drummer Kex Gorin and bassist Bob Doyle. The band line up remained the same until 1972, when Les Kitcheridge joined temporarily on guitar. Bob Doyle left Magnum in 1972 and joined Roy Wood's Wizzard, and was replaced by former Uglys and Balls bassist Dave Morgan (later a member of ELO). Morgan commented:

> I was absolutely broke, and the people who owned the Rum Runner club were building this new night club called Snobs, and they got all the musicians that worked at the Rum Runner helping out. I went to the Rum Runner one night, so Tony Clarkin said, "Come and earn some money building this new club." So I was down there every day helping them build this thing, and on the night I used to go down to the Rum Runner just to see the groups. I was in there one night, and to cut a long story short, Bob Doyle the original bass player with Magnum left the band, and Tony Clarkin said, "Can you play bass?", I said "Yeah", he said, "You got the job!" That was it, I just happened to be there when Doyle left, so I got his job![2]

They began to develop their own style by playing Clarkin's songs at a residency at The Railway Inn, in Birmingham's Curzon Street, in 1976. In 1975, Clarkin and Dave Morgan received an offer from Kim Holmes to help with the construction of a studio, rather than being paid with money,

Clarkin requested to be paid with studio time.[3] Much of Magnum's early demo material was recorded at Nest Studios in Birmingham, which would later lead to a recording contract with David Arden of Jet Records. During the "Nest" sessions, at least two songs written by Dave Morgan (and sung by Bob Catley) were recorded but never released. The titles were "Baby I Need" and "One More Round The Bend", which resurfaced on an acetate disc in 2005.[4][5]

A one off deal with CBS was arranged via producer Roger Greenaway, and the band released a cover of The Searchers' "Sweets for My Sweet" in February 1975; however, this failed to make the charts. The original recording included a medley of "God Rest Ye Merry, Gentlemen" but was edited out for the single release. Lead vocals on this song were by Morgan, who left the band soon after, and was replaced by Colin "Wally" Lowe. Success was still minimal; they were working as a backing band for artists, such as Del Shannon, on small tours.[4] The band was expanded to a five-piece with the addition of Richard Bailey on keyboards. In May 1977 the band supported Judas Priest on their *Sin After Sin* UK tour, still without the backing of a record label.

Jet Records (1978—1984)

Magnum's debut album *Kingdom of Madness* was released on Jet Records at the end of 1978 and reached #58 in the UK Chart;[1] it received a five star review from Geoff Barton of *Sounds magazine*. They toured the UK in October/November 1978, as support to David Coverdale's Whitesnake. Leo Lyons, formerly bassist with Ten Years After, produced the follow-up album *Magnum II* – which was released in 1979, but failed to chart. Another support tour was organised for November 1979, this time with Blue Öyster Cult. A live set, *Marauder*, was released as an album and reached #34 in the UK,[1] and a live double single ("Live at the Marquee", including "Invasion") reached #48 in the UK Singles Chart.[1] Bailey departed soon after and was replaced temporarily by Grenville Harding during Magnum's support of Def Leppard's *On Through the Night* UK tour in March. For the second leg in April, permanent replacement Mark Stanway took over keyboard duties. Magnum also appeared at the Reading Festival in 1980. April 1981 saw another support tour, this time with Tygers of Pan Tang on their *Spellbound* UK tour.

Their first successful album was the Jeff Glixman produced *Chase the Dragon* (1982), which reached #17 in the UK,[1] and included several songs that would be mainstays of the band's live set, including "Soldier of the Line", "Sacred Hour" and "The Spirit". Glixman was previously known for his work with Kansas, and this was the first Magnum release to feature the artwork of fantasy artist Rodney Matthews. The tour included a support slot in February with Krokus, on their *One Vice at a Time* UK tour. A few US dates were played during the summer of 1982, supporting labelmate Ozzy Osbourne – these would ultimately prove to be the only live gigs the band ever played outside Europe. The band returned to the UK in July for their own headlining tour.

Budgetary constraints at Jet denied Magnum the use of an outside producer for 1983's Clarkin-produced *The Eleventh Hour*, which peaked at UK #38.[1] A UK tour started in May 1983, featuring additional guitarist Robin George for live performances. Magnum also appeared at the 1983 Reading Festival, with George.

Magnum and Jet parted company shortly afterwards, Kex Gorin was replaced by Jim Simpson and Stanway took some time away from the band to work with Phil Lynott, being replaced by Eddie George. Local businessman Keith Baker(Time Music) engaged the band, an independent tour was organised for February 1984 without the backing of a record label. Lawrence Archer temporarily stood in for Tony Clarkin when he became ill.

***On a Storyteller's Night* and chart success (1985—1995)**

Stanway returned to the band in 1984, and they toured the UK in January 1985. Magnum signed a one-off deal with FM Records, and released *On a Storyteller's Night*, which had a cover by Rodney Matthews. It reached #24 in the UK,[1] and launched the band across Europe. For the May UK tour, Simpson was replaced by Mickey Barker. Keith and the band embarked on a journey that would change the lives of Magnum forever.

From the success of On a Storyteller's Night, Keith was able to negotiate the band a major label deal with Polydor Records, and they embarked on the most commercially successful period of their career – opening the famous Monsters of Rock festival at Castle Donington in August 1985, on a bill that also included Bon Jovi, Metallica, Marillion and headliners ZZ Top. A second leg for the *Storyteller's* tour was concluded in December 1985.

The first release for the label was co-produced by Queen drummer Roger Taylor in 1986, entitled *Vigilante*. The switch to Polydor saw an increase in the marketing budget, and promotional videos were made for the singles "Lonely Night" and "Midnight". A full UK and European tour was scheduled in March 1986, including appearances at The Garden Party Festival, Milton Keynes Bowl in June and the Out In The Green Festival. A second leg was organised in September 1986, which finished in Europe in November 1986. In March 1987, the band embarked on a third UK and European tour, including an appearance at 1987's Reading Festival.

Magnum enjoyed increased success with the album *Wings of Heaven* (#5 in the UK).[1] Three singles from *Wings of Heaven* reached the UK Top 40,[1] including a *Top of the Pops* appearance with "Start Talking Love". A successful tour followed in December and, by now, Magnum had been elevated to an 'arena' band in the UK, headlining the N.E.C. and several nights at London's Hammersmith Odeon, supported by the Norwegian band Stage Dolls.

The band went to Los Angeles for the Keith Olsen produced *Goodnight L.A.*, which peaked at #9 in the UK chart.[1] The band performed at Berlin's Arena Festival, followed by a full UK and European tour in September 1990. They toured the UK again in November. Following *Goodnight L.A.'s* lukewarm reception, Magnum parted company with Polydor. They released the live album *The Spirit* in 1991 and toured the UK and Europe again to support the album. During the concerts in Germany, the band played live with the Roger Taylor band The Cross. Magnum continued to release albums for various labels on one-off deals, the first being *Sleepwalking* in 1992 on Music for Nations with a full UK tour in October. This was followed by the acoustic album *Keeping the Nite Light Burning* in 1993 with a UK tour in April.

Rock Art was released in 1994 on EMI. A UK tour was scheduled for April, but dates in May and June were postponed or cancelled. A low key tour was arranged for August and Europe in September. In the summer of 1995, Tony Clarkin announced the band were to split and a farewell tour of the UK and Europe took place in March, documented on the live album *Stronghold* (titled *The Last Dance* in mainland Europe).

Split and Hard Rain years (1995—2001)

Main article: Hard Rain (band)

After Magnum split, a spin-off group featuring Catley and Clarkin was formed called Hard Rain, which released the albums *Hard Rain* and *When the Good Times Come*. It was around this time that Catley launched a solo career using various songwriters, including Gary Hughes of the band Ten. However, Hard Rain found bookings hard to come by, and there were discussions about renaming the band as Magnum. At the same time, Catley was becoming increasingly focused on his solo career, and he quit Hard Rain, marking the end of a working relationship with Clarkin that dated back to 1972. After a quiet period, Clarkin announced the end of Hard Rain.

Reformation and beyond (2001—present)

Eventually, Clarkin and Catley re-launched Magnum with the album *Breath of Life* in 2002 on SPV, with a UK tour in December. They were again joined by Stanway, as well as former Hard Rain bassist Al Barrow. They recorded the album without a drummer, before hiring Thunder drummer Harry James to complete the lineup. This was subsequently followed by *Brand New Morning* in 2004, and appearances at Germany's Bang Your Head Festival, the Lorca Rock Festival in Spain and a tour around the UK and Europe in December. Clarkin commented:

> The break since the middle of the Nineties was definitely necessary for me. Since the end of the Seventies, in fact since we embarked on the preparations for our debut recording *Kingdom of Madness*, not a single month had gone by in which I didn't work for Magnum, composed for the group, or at least thought of them permanently. For almost twenty years, all my thoughts had revolved around the band. I needed a break to clear my head and to be able to devote myself to the band again with renewed energy.[6]

When James returned to Thunder, Jimmy Copley became a full-time member of Magnum. The band toured in April 2005 to mark the 20th anniversary of *On a Storyteller's Night*; they released a live DVD of the Astoria concert entitled *Livin' the Dream*, which also included a short documentary and promotional videos from throughout the band's history.

Magnum completed work on a new studio album, *Princess Alice and the Broken Arrow*, which was released on 26 March 2007; this also marked the return to the cover artwork by Rodney Matthews. The album entered the UK Album Charts at No. 70, the first time Magnum had charted in the UK since 1994. It also reached No. 4 on the BBC Rock Album Charts and No. 60 in Germany.

Magnum toured the UK and Europe in May 2007. Harry James played drums temporarily for half the tour as Jimmy Copley was taken ill.

In 2005, former drummer Kex Gorin was diagnosed with kidney cancer. Gorin had a kidney removed and underwent radiotherapy and steroid treatment, but died of the disease on 21 December 2007.[7]

Magnum undertook a UK tour celebrating the 20th anniversary of *Wings of Heaven* in November 2007. These shows were recorded for *Wings of Heaven Live* album, which was released in March 2008.

In 2007, Magnum played a one off show at the Robin 2 in Bilston, Wolverhampton. This was a charity event in aid of former drummer Kex Gorin's family. An auction of memorabilia before the show raised over £10,000. Magnum then played a two-hour set of old and new material.[8]

On 15 June 2009, they released *Into the Valley of the Moonking* on SPV.

In 2010, the band released, *The Gathering*, on Universal/Sanctuary; their first ever cross-career collection spread over five discs featuring a 1988 live recording from Hammersmith Odeon.

The band released their next album, *The Visitation*, in 2011.[9] The band toured in support of the album, which charted at No. 55 in the UK and No. 19 in Germany, throughout March and April 2011.

On 30 August, Magnum announced a new compilation remix album *Evolution* celebrating the last 10 years on SPV GmbH since their reformation in 2001. The album was released on 11 November 2011 in Germany and 14 November in the rest of Europe and the UK. The album featured 10 songs from the band's previous five studio releases, eight were re-recorded, remixed and remastered, as well as two new songs.

The band released their 17th studio album *On the 13th Day* in September 2012. "So Let It Rain" was the first single, released in August 2012 via Steamhammer/SPV. The band toured in Europe to promote the album in late 2012 which charted in many countries across Europe including the UK at No. 43.

Soon after releasing and touring *On the 13th Day* Magnum revealed that Tony Clarkin was back in the studio writing and recording new songs via Facebook on 4 April 2013.[10] The new album, called *Escape from the Shadow Garden*, also was to feature Rodney Matthews's artwork, this time showing similarities to Magnum's early albums *Chase the Dragon* (the tree) and *On a Storyteller's Night* (the storyteller), along with elements from more recent albums such as *On the 13th Day*. *Escape From the Shadow Garden* was released in Scandinavia on 19 March 2014, and on 21 March for Germany, Austria and Switzerland, 24 March for the rest of Europe, and 1 April for the USA and Canada. As with *On the 13th Day* the band were hosts to their fans at a record launch party held at the Robin 2 in Bilston on 25 March 2014, the day after the UK release. Compared with Magnum's album releases since reformation it was a great commercial success reaching number 14 in the German Albums Chart, 19 in the Swedish Albums Chart, 22 in the Switzerland Albums Chart and 38 in the official UK Albums Chart, a position last achieved by Magnum with *The Eleventh Hour!* in 1983, and not bettered since 1992's *Sleepwalking*! It also reached number two in the UK Rock Albums Chart.

2.40.2 Band members

Timeline

2.40.3 Discography

Main article: Magnum discography

2.40.4 References

[1] Roberts, David (2006). *British Hit Singles & Albums* (19th ed.). London: Guinness World Records Limited. p. 344. ISBN 1-904994-10-5.

[2] Heath, Alan. "Dave Morgan Interview". Archived from the original on 21 August 1999. Retrieved 2015-09-18.

[3] Clarkin, Tony & Ling, David (2006). Sleeve Notes. In *Kingdom Of Madness: Expanded Edition* (pp. 2) [CD liner notes]. London: Sanctuary Records.

[4] "Prologue: Days of Wonder". Archived from the original on 10 March 2008. Retrieved 2015-09-18.

[5] "Scott Morgan Discography". Archived from the original on 26 June 2008. Retrieved 2015-09-18.

[6] "Magnum - New 'Breath Of Life' For Legendary Art Rock Band After 6 Year Hiatus". Workhardpr.com. 16 January 2002. Archived from the original on 14 May 2003. Retrieved 2015-09-18.

[7] "Drummer's fight to prolong life". *BBC News*. 2 August 2007. Retrieved 12 May 2010.

[8] Bennett, Debbie (11 December 2007). "Magnum raise roof - and funds". *Express & Star*. Archived from the original on 13 December 2007. Retrieved 2015-09-18.

[9] "Magnum". Magnumonline.co.uk. Retrieved 2014-08-14.

[10] "MAGNUM". Facebook. Retrieved 2014-08-14.

2.40.5 External links

- Official Magnum site

- Magnum at MySpace.com

- Express & Star interview with Tony Clarkin, June 2009

2.41 Mama's Boys

For the reality television series, see Momma's Boys.

Mama's Boys were a 1980s hard rock/heavy metal group from County Fermanagh, Northern Ireland featuring the three McManus brothers Pat, a.k.a. "The Professor", (guitar and occasionally fiddle), John (bass and vocals), Tommy (drums). Later in their career they became a four-piece adding Rick Chase on vocals in 1985 who was later replaced by Keith Murrell in 1987 due to Rick's ill-health. Keith was later replaced with Mike Wilson in 1989.

2.41.1 Biography

The McManus brothers, who grew up on a farm near the village of Derrylin, Co. Fermanagh, started off their musical career as award winning traditional Irish musicians, but were inspired by the Irish celtic rock band, Horslips, as well as younger brother Tommy's passion for the drums to form a rock band. In the late 70s the brothers had become big fans of Horslips and attended their gigs at every possible opportunity. They eventually got to know and became friends with the band members. It was around that time that they started their own band which was originally called Pulse before they changed it to Mama's Boys. Barry Devlin of Horslips heard about their band and went to see them rehearse at their home. He was suitably impressed and offered them a support slot for Horslips' 1979 tour.

Although their heroes Horslips mixed traditional music with hard rock and the McManus brothers were top notch traditional musicians, Mama's Boys didn't really go for the celtic fusion sound, apart from the occasional fiddle solo by Pat, but went for a harder edged more heavy metal sound.

By 1980 Mama's Boys had a bootleg circulating and were touring extensively in Ireland. In 1981 they were invited to support Hawkwind on their UK tour. They recorded and self-financed their first album, a raw blast of rock power entitled *Plug It In* in 1982 and achieved a hit single in Ireland with the most pop-oriented song on the album, "Needle in the Groove".

The second album *Turn It Up* was released in 1983. The same year they toured with Thin Lizzy on that band's farewell tour, played at the Reading Rock Festival and signed a worldwide record deal with Jive Records. The first album released on Jive was a self-titled compilation of *Plug It In* and *Turn It Up* with a few new songs added. One of the new songs, a cover of Slade's "Mama Weer All Crazee Now" was released as a single and reached number 54 in the American charts. The video for the song got a lot of airplay on MTV and helped the band to become known in the US which they toured in 1984. On Tuesday 24 January 1984 Mama's Boys played at The Odeon, Birmingham, UK when they were the warm up band to the German heavy metal/rock band Scorpions. They were booed and beer canned off the stage. Coincidentally, the American heavy metal band Quiet Riot also released their cover version of the song at the same time as Mama's Boys, but Quiet Riot's version gained more airplay.

1985's *Power and Passion* album broke into the Billboard top 100 in the US and the band toured in the US, Europe and Japan. During the European leg of the tour Tommy had a relapse of leukemia which he had been treated for as a child and a replacement drummer Jimmy DeGrasso was brought in to complete the tour. The recovering Tommy rejoined the tour in Ireland but had to be rushed back to hospital after another relapse.

In 1987, former Airrace vocalist Keith Murrell was brought in after Rick Chase started having trouble with his vocal cords and they recorded the album *Growing Up the Hard Way*. Jive Records chose Murrell with the idea of giving them a more polished commercial sound but it backfired as the unique raw sound of the band was replaced by a bland AOR type sound. This was also contributed by the Producer Phil Begley who produced the single "Pop music" by "M". The Jive contract, which ended that year, was not renewed and Murrell left shortly after to join Cliff Richard as a backing singer.

In 1989 with a new vocalist, Mike Wilson, and under new management they moved their base to the UK. The live album *Live Tonite* was released in 1991 and the band toured extensively in Europe. They released the album *Relativity* in 1992. While on tour in Italy in 1993, Tommy became ill again and the tour had to be cancelled. The following year Tommy underwent a bone marrow transplant but tragically he did not survive. His brothers were devastated and Mama's Boys did not continue after this blow. On the first anniversary of Tommy's death John composed a traditional lament on the low whistle for his brother and this led to himself and Pat revisiting their traditional Irish music roots and forming a celtic/new age group called Celtus.

In 2003, Pat McManus joined with Irish rock band 'Indian' for an album and live shows. Pat is on line with a searing lead on the song Burning it Up. He also shows with the annual Rory Gallagher festival at Ballyshannon. His playing is immense but sadly not well known in USA. Pat McManus has his own band with Marty McDermott on bass and Paul Faloon on drums. They have just released a new live CD and DVD called *Live and in time*. The live recording features songs from Pat's previous CD *In My Own Time* and Mama's Boys songs.

2.41.2 Band members

Former members

- Patrick Francis 'Pat' McManus – lead guitar, fiddle, backing vocals (1978–1993)
- John McManus – bass, lead vocals, backing vocals, low whistle, tin whistle, uilleann pipes (Irish bagpipes) (1978–1993)
- Thomas 'Tommy' McManus – drums, bodhran (Irish drum), backing vocals (1978–1993) (1966 - 16 November 1994)
- Rick Chase - lead vocals (1985-1986)
- Mickey Fenlon – lead vocals (1986–1987)
- Keith Murrell – lead vocals (1987–1989)
- Connor McKeon – lead vocals (1989-1990)
- Mike Wilson – lead vocals (1990–1992)
- Alan Williams – keyboards (1989–1993)
- Jimmy DeGrasso – drums (1985–1986)

2.41.3 Discography

Albums

- *Official Bootleg* (1980)
- *Plug It In* (1982)
- *Turn It Up* (1983)
- *Mama's Boys* (1984)
- *Power and Passion* (1985)
- *Growing Up the Hard Way* (1987)
- *Live Tonite* (1991)
- *Relativity* (1992)

Singles

- "Belfast City Blues" (1982)
- "In the Heat of the Night" (1982)
- "Needle in the Groove" (1982)
- "Too Little of You to Love" (1983)
- "Midnight Promises" (1984)
- "Mama Weer All Crazee Now" (1984)
- "Needle in the Groove" (1985)
- "Higher Ground" (1987)
- "Waiting for a Miracle" (1987)

2.41.4 See also

- List of New Wave of British Heavy Metal bands

2.41.5 References

2.41.6 External links

- History of Mama's Boys on Celtus website
- Mama's Boys on IrishRockers.com
- Mama's Boys Tribute page on myspace
- Pat McManus Official Homepage
- (http://www.johnmcmanus.biz John McManus Official Homepage)
- Mama's Boys at AllMusic

2.42 Marseille (band)

Marseille are a British heavy metal band from Liverpool, England.

2.42.1 History

Marseille formed in Liverpool in early 1976, and released their debut album, *Red, White and Slightly Blue* on the Mountain Records label in 1978. Original members were Paul Dale (vocals), Neil Buchanan (guitar), Andy Charters (guitar), Keith Knowles (drums) and Steve Dinwoodie (bass). Marseille were the first band to win "UK Battle of the Bands" with the finals judged by Brian May and Roger Taylor of Queen at Wembley Arena on 31 October 1977.[1]

Marseille gathered a small fan base while promoting their first album as support for other groups such as Judas Priest, Nazareth, Whitesnake and UFO.[2] Their debut album contained very raunchy lyrics but suffered somewhat from lack of promotion and limitation of release.[3] The single "Kiss Like Rock 'n' Roll" was produced by Nazareth guitarist Manny Charlton.

Their second album release, the eponymous *Marseille*, received radio airplay, extending their fanbase in the UK. Several tracks off this album featured in the "Alternative Top 20 Charts" published in *Sounds* magazine with other emerging New Wave of British Heavy Metal bands such as Saxon, Def Leppard and Iron Maiden.[4] Marseille were the first NWOBHM band to tour and have an album released in the U.S. on RCA Records. The band promoted their *Marseille* album on tour in the U.S. with Scottish rock band Nazareth and American south coast boogie band, Blackfoot during the summer of 1980.[5] Unfortunately, the band arrived back in the UK to witness the demise of Mountain, their record and management company.[6] With all their equipment still stranded in the U.S., the band were forced off the road and into a two year legal battle with liquidators, which precluded them pursuing another recording contract. During this time, Paul Dale, Andy Charters and Neil Buchanan left the band. Charters moved to the U.S. and Buchanan began a successful career in television. The two remaining members, Keith Knowles and Steve Dinwoodie later recruited vocalist Sav Pearse and guitarist Marc Railton from local Liverpool band Savage Lucy to complete a third album entitled *Touch the Night* on the Ultra Noise label in 1984.[7] However, industry disinterest in the band caused this iteration of Marseille to split up soon after. *Touch the Night* was labeled by *Kerrang!* magazine as a closet classic that should have taken the band to higher ground.

In 2003, a two-disc CD aptly titled *Rock You Tonight* became the *Marseille Anthology* and was released by Castle Communications, a subsidiary division of Sanctuary Records Group. The album, containing material from all three of Marseille's previous albums, garnered some critical acclaim being hailed "The best box set of 2003" by George Smith of *Village Voice* magazine.[3]

The original line-up reunited for a handful of gigs in 2008, however, Paul Dale soon left the band and was replaced in February 2009 by Nigel Roberts. The band recorded an EP, *FourPlay* which was released on the Gas Station Music label in 2009. In 2010, Keith Knowles and Steve Dinwoodie stepped down to be replaced by Gareth Webb (drums) and Lee Andrews (bass). The band recorded their first full album in 25 years, *Unfinished Business* in early 2010. The album was unveiled at the band's appearance at the Hard Rock Hell festival in December 2010. A full UK tour supported by Exit State followed.

In April 2011, Gareth Webb stepped down and was replaced by Ace Finchum (also a member of Tigertailz) on drums. The band continued a heavy gig schedule throughout 2011 and worked on new material for a release in 2012. Festival appearances were put on schedule for 2012 to promote this release in the UK and Europe.

2.42.2 Band members

Current members

- Nigel Roberts - Lead vocals
- Neil Buchanan - Lead guitar & backing vocals
- Andy Charters - Rhythm guitar & backing vocals
- Ace Finchum - Drums

Former members

- Paul Dale - Lead vocals
- Sav Pearce - Lead vocals
- Marc Railton - Rhythm & lead guitar & backing vocals
- Steve Dinwoodie - Bass guitar & backing vocals
- Lee Andrews - Bass guitar
- Keith Knowles - Drums & backing vocals
- Gareth Webb - Drums

2.42.3 Discography

Albums

- *Red White and Slightly Blue* (1978) - Mountain
- *Marseille* (1979) - Mountain
- *Touch the Night* (1984) - Ultranoise
- *Unfinished Business* (2010) - Gas Station Music

Compilations

- *Rock You Tonight: The Anthology* (2003) - Castle Communications

EPs

- *FourPlay* (2009) - Gas Station Music

7" singles

- "The French Way" (1978) - Mountain
- "Over and Over" (1979) - Mountain
- "Bring on the Dancing Girls" (1979) - Mountain
- "Kiss Like Rock 'n Roll" (1979) - Mountain
- "Kites" (1980) - Mountain
- "Walking on a Highwire" (1984) - Ultranoise (10,000 of which were pressed in limited edition silver vinyl)

12" singles

- "(Do It) The French Way" (1977) - Varesse

2.42.4 See also

- List of New Wave of British Heavy Metal bands

2.42.5 References

[1] "Marseille | artist management | music promotion | a&r | tour management services : A & R Incorporated". Aandrinc.co.uk. Retrieved 2012-10-04.

[2] en.academic.ru listing for Marseille

[3] village voice > music > Marseille's Rock You Tonight by George Smith

[4] NWOBHM#List of NWOBHM artists

[5] "Cleveland Rock And Roll". Cleveland Rock And Roll. 2012-09-24. Retrieved 2012-10-04.

[6] "Label: Mountain Records". Rate Your Music. Retrieved 2012-10-04.

[7] Amazon.co.uk: Profile For Paul J. Thomas: Reviews

2.42.6 External links

- Marseille discography at MusicBrainz
- Marseille official website

2.43 Mirage (metal band)

Not to be confused with Mirage (band).

Mirage was a heavy metal band which was formed in 1983 from the ashes of two Welsh Rock/ Metal bands: 'Rough Justice' and 'Exit'. The band were based in the valleys of South East Wales, UK. Its members were Richard Morgan (aka "Wretch") on vocals, Richard Price on guitar, Carl Skinner on bass and Gerry Turner on drums.[1] In 1984, they released one track 'Blind Fury' on a compilation album produced by local record company 'Notepad Productions'. This came to the attention of Malc Macmillan, author of the Encyclopaedia of New Wave of British Heavy Metal (NWoBHM) who described their track 'Blind Fury' as "truly one of the classic tracks of the entire NWoBHM genre".[2] The rare Notepad Productions VOLUME I album remains highly sought after by collectors - featured in Record Collector Magazine in January 2015.[3] The band has enjoyed some recent attention from High Roller Records who have re-released the band's tracks Blind Fury/ Twilight Zone on black and white vinyl. The cover features Richard Price's original 1979 Fender Stratocaster guitar alongside a Turner family artefact from WWII.

- Band Members: Gerry Turner, Richard Morgan, Carl Skinner, Richard Price

2.43.1 References

[1] "Mirage - Blind Fury 7". HR Records. Retrieved 21 February 2015.

[2] Macmillan, M. *New Wave of British Heavy Metal* (Third ed.). p. 789. ISBN 978-3-931624-16-3.

[3] "Notepad Productions Volume 1". *Record Collector* (436): 11. January 2015.

2.44 More (British band)

More is a UK heavy metal band who were part of the New Wave of British Heavy Metal scene in the early 1980s. They recorded two albums and two singles, and opened the 1981 Monsters of Rock festival at Donington Park.[1]

Initially the band was fronted by vocalist Paul Mario Day, who had sung in an early incarnation of Iron Maiden.

By the time of their second album, Frank Darch and Laurie Mansworth had left, the latter going on to form the band Airrace.[2] Andy John Burton was recruited as the new drummer and the band became a four-piece. Bassist Brian

Day also left during the recording of the second album, to be replaced by Barry 'Baz' Nicholls.

Following Paul Mario Day's subsequent departure from the band, the line-up of Cox, Nicholls, Burton and vocalist Mick Stratton released a 7" single called "Trickster" in 1982, before splitting up.

Kenny Cox revived More briefly in 1985, with vocalist Ron Jackson, guitarist Mel Jones, bassist Baz Nicholls, and Paul George on drums.

A further attempt to reform the band occurred in the spring of 1998, with Mike Freeland featuring on vocals. A track called "My Obsession" was recorded by this incarnation of the band, but they split up shortly afterwards in the year 2000.

In 2011, Andy John Burton recruited Baz Nicholls (bass; joined More in 1982), Mike Freeland (vocals; part of More's 1999 line-up), Paul Stickles (guitar; also with the band Dangerous Breed) and special guest Chris Tsangarides to form a More tribute band called **Exmore**. They performed live at the Headbangers Open Air Festival in July 2011,[3] with a warm-up show at the Scream Lounge in Croydon on 4 June, then in two shows at the Astor Theatre in Deal, Kent (in July and October 2011).[4]

Exmore played a co-headlining show with Marseille at the Sir Robert Peel venue in Kingston upon Thames, Surrey on 15 October 2011.

The following year, the band changed their name to **More 2012** and scheduled further shows, including: 26 May at the Railway venue in Bolton, a cancelled appearance on 25 August at the Borderline in London (where the band had been due to support Tokyo Blade), 23 November at the Red Lion pub in Gravesend, Kent, and 1 December at the Hard Rock Hell VI festival, with Steve Rix on drums.[5]

An appearance at the 'Metalwave UK' festival in Purfleet, Essex, alongside Praying Mantis, Dennis Stratton, Cloven Hoof, Chariot and Deep Machine, took place on 5 October 2013,[6] followed by a performance at the 'Heavy Metal Maniacs' festival in Amstelveen on 19 October 2013.[7]

In May 2014, Dave John Ross replaced Paul Stickles on guitar. Further concert appearances were then scheduled for the 'Bang Your Head!!!' festival in Balingen on 12 July 2014,[8] 'Rock and Metal Circus' festival at Sywell Aerodrome in Northamptonshire on 13 September 2014 (cancelled),[9] 'Rock Diabetes' festival in Trowbridge on 11 October 2014 (also cancelled),[10] and the Hard Rock Hell VII festival in Pwllheli on 15 November 2014.[11]

2.44.1 Line-ups

First line-up (1980–1981)

- Paul Mario Day - Vocals
- Kenny Cox - Guitar
- Paul Todd - Guitar
- Brian Day - Bass
- Frank Darch - Drums

Second line-up (1981–1982)

- Paul Mario Day - Vocals
- Kenny Cox - Guitar
- Laurie Mansworth - Guitar
- Brian Day - Bass
- Andy John Burton - Drums

Third line-up (1982)

- Mick Stratton - Vocals
- Kenny Cox - Guitar
- Brian Day - Bass
- Andy John Burton - Drums

Fourth line-up (1982)

- Mick Stratton - Vocals
- Kenny Cox - Guitar
- Baz Nicholls - Bass
- Andy John Burton - Drums

Fifth line-up (1985)

- Ron Jackson - Vocals
- Kenny Cox - Guitar
- Mel Jones - Guitar
- Baz Nicholls - Bass
- Paul George - Drums

Sixth line-up (1998–2000)

- Mike Freeland - Vocals
- Kenny Cox - Guitar

- Baz Nicholls - Bass
- Rick Dyat / Andy Robinson - Drums

Exmore / More 2012 line-up (2011–present)

- Mike Freeland - Vocals
- Paul Stickles / Dave Ross - Guitar
- Chris Tsangarides - Guitar
- Baz Nicholls - Bass
- Andy John Burton / Steve Rix - Drums

2.44.2 Discography

Albums

Warhead (Atlantic Records, 1981)

- "Warhead"
- "Fire"
- "Soldier"
- "Depression"
- "Road Rocket"
- "Lord of the Twilight"
- "Way of the World"
- "We are the Band"
- "I Have No Answers"

Blood & Thunder (Atlantic Records, 1982)

- "Killer on the Prowl"
- "Blood & Thunder"
- "I Just Can't Believe It"
- "I've Been Waiting"
- "Traitors Gate"
- "Rock and Roll"
- "I Wanna Take You"
- "Go Home"
- "The Eye"
- "Nightmare"

Singles

- "We Are the Band" / "Atomic Rock" (Atlantic Records, 1981) - UK No. 59[12]
- "Trickster" / "Hey Joe" (Atlantic Records, 1982)

2.44.3 See also

- List of New Wave of British Heavy Metal bands

2.44.4 References

[1] http://www.ukrockfestivals.com/donington-1981.html Monsters of Rock 1981 - Festival information

[2] http://www.rockdetector.com/artist/united+kingdom/airrace Airrace - Band information at MusicMight website

[3] http://www.last.fm/festival/1559521+Headbangers+Open+Air+2011 Headbangers Open Air 2011 - Festival information

[4] Steve Goldby. "Exmore Booked For Headbanger's Open Air". Metaltalk.net. Retrieved 2014-05-22.

[5] http://www.last.fm/festival/3137892+Hard+Rock+Hell+VI Hard Rock Hell VI - Festival information

[6] http://planetmosh.com/metalwave-uk-circus-tavern-purfleet-essex-05102013 Metalwave Festival 2013 - Review at Planetmosh.com

[7] http://www.heavymetalmaniacs.com/festival/bands-2013/more Heavy Metal Maniacs Festival 2013 - Official website

[8] http://www.bang-your-head.de/english/home.php Bang Your Head Festival 2014 - Official website

[9] http://rockmetalcircus.co.uk Rock & Metal Circus Festival 2014 - Official website

[10] http://www.rockdiabetes.co.uk Rock Diabetes Festival 2014 - Official website

[11] http://www.hardrockhell.com Hard Rock Hell Festival 2014 - Official website

[12] Roberts, David (2006). *British Hit Singles & Albums* (19th ed.). London: Guinness World Records Limited. p. 378. ISBN 1-904994-10-5.

2.44.5 External links

- Official website for More 2012
- Unofficial MySpace site for More
- Information about More
- An extended biography of More

2.45 Motörhead

For other uses, see Motorhead (disambiguation).

Motörhead (/ˈmoʊtərhɛd/) are an English rock band formed in June 1975 by bassist, singer, and songwriter Ian Fraser Kilmister, professionally known by his stage name Lemmy, who has remained the sole constant member. The band are often considered a precursor to, or one of the earliest members of, the New Wave of British Heavy Metal, which re-energised heavy metal in the late 1970s and early 1980s.[1] Despite this, Lemmy has always dubbed their music as simply "rock and roll".

To date, Motörhead have released twenty-three studio albums, ten live recordings, twelve compilation albums and five EPs. Usually a power trio, they had particular success in the early 1980s with several successful singles in the UK Top 40 chart. The albums *Overkill*, *Bomber*, *Ace of Spades*, and particularly *No Sleep 'til Hammersmith*, cemented Motörhead's reputation as a top-tier rock band.[2] As of 2012, Motörhead have sold more than 15 million albums worldwide.[3]

Motörhead are typically classified as heavy metal, and their fusion of punk rock into the genre helped to pioneer speed metal and thrash metal. Their lyrics typically cover such topics as war, good versus evil, abuse of power, promiscuous sex, substance abuse, and, most famously, gambling. The name "Motörhead" is a reference to users of the drug amphetamine.[4] The band's distinctive fanged-face logo, with its oversized boar's tusks, chains, and spikes, was created by artist Joe Petagno in 1977 for the cover of the *Motörhead* album and has appeared in many variations on covers of ensuing albums. The fanged face has been referred to variously as "War-Pig"[5] and "Snaggletooth".[6] The band is ranked number 26 on VH1's 100 Greatest Artists of Hard Rock.[7]

2.45.1 History

Formation and early years, 1975–77

Lemmy was fired from Hawkwind in May 1975 for, as he says, "doing the wrong drugs".[8] He was arrested on suspicion of possessing cocaine at the Canadian border and spent five days in prison, causing the band to cancel some of their North America tour dates.[9] Now on his own, Lemmy decided to form a new band called Motörhead, inspired by the final song he had written for Hawkwind.[10]

Lemmy wanted the music to be "fast and vicious, just like the MC5".[11] His stated aim was to "concentrate on very basic music: loud, fast, city, raucous, arrogant, paranoid, speedfreak rock n roll ... it will be so loud that if we move in next door to you, your lawn will die".[12] On the recommendation of Mick Farren, he recruited Larry Wallis (ex-Pink Fairies) on electric guitar and Lucas Fox on drums. According to Lemmy, the band's first practice was at the now defunct Sound Management rehearsal studios, located on Kings Road, Chelsea in 1975 (Sound Management leased the basement area of furniture store "The Furniture Cave", located in adjacent Lots Road). Kilmister has said they used to steal equipment, as the band was short on gear.[13] Their first engagement was supporting Greenslade at The Roundhouse, London on 20 July 1975.[14] On 19 October, having played 10 gigs, they became the supporting act to Blue Öyster Cult at the Hammersmith Odeon.[15]

The band were contracted to United Artists by Andrew Lauder, the A&R man for the band Lemmy was previously in, Hawkwind.[16] They recorded sessions at Rockfield Studios in Monmouth with producer Dave Edmunds, during which Fox proved to be unreliable and was replaced by drummer Phil "Philthy Animal" Taylor, a casual acquaintance of Lemmy's. Their record label was dissatisfied with the material and refused to release it, although it was subsequently issued as *On Parole* in 1979 after the band had established some success.[17]

In March 1976, deciding that two guitarists were required, the band auditioned "Fast" Eddie Clarke. Wallis, who was continuing to tour with a reformed Pink Fairies, quit immediately after the auditions and Clarke remained as the sole guitarist. This trio of Lemmy/Clarke/Taylor is today regarded as the "classic" Motörhead line-up.[18] In December, the band recorded the "Leaving Here" single for Stiff

A Motörhead Snaggletooth Belt Buckle

Records, but United Artists intervened to prevent its general release as the band were still under contract to them, despite their refusal to issue their debut album. Initial reactions to the band had been unfavourable; they won a poll for "the best worst band in the world" in the music magazine *NME*.[19]

By April 1977, living in squats and with little recognition, Taylor and Clarke decided to quit the band, and after some debate, they agreed to do a farewell show at the Marquee Club in London. Lemmy had become acquainted with Ted Carroll from Chiswick Records and asked him to bring a mobile studio to the show to record it for posterity. Carroll was unable to get the mobile unit to the Marquee Club, but showed up backstage after the engagement and offered them two days at Escape Studios with producer Speedy Keen to record a single. The band took the chance, and instead of recording a single they laid down 11 unfinished tracks. Carroll gave them a few more days at Olympic Studios to finish the vocals and the band completed 13 tracks for release as an album.[20] Chiswick issued the single "Motorhead" in June, followed by the album *Motörhead* in August, which spent one week in the UK Albums Chart at number 43.[14][21] The band toured the UK supporting Hawkwind in June, then from late July they commenced the "Beyond the Threshold of Pain" tour with The Count Bishops.[14]

In August, Tony Secunda took over the management of the band, and their cohesiveness became so unstable that by March 1978, Clarke and Taylor had formed and were performing as The Muggers with Speedy Keen and Billy Rath.[12]

Rise to success: *Overkill* and *Bomber*, 1978–79

The 1976–1982 Motörhead line-up: Lemmy Kilmister, Phil "Philthy Animal" Taylor and "Fast" Eddie Clarke

In July 1978, the band returned to the management of Douglas Smith, who secured a one-off singles deal with Bronze Records.[12] The resulting "Louie Louie" single was issued in September peaking at number 68 on the UK Singles Chart,[21] and the band toured the UK to promote it, recorded a BBC Radio 1 *John Peel in session* on 18 September (these tracks were later issued on the 2005 *BBC Live & In-Session* album), and appeared for the first time on BBC Television's *Top of the Pops* on 25 October.[14] Chiswick capitalised on this new level of success by re-issuing the debut album *Motörhead* on white vinyl through EMI Records.

The single's success led to Bronze extending their contract, and put the band back into the studio to record an album, this time with producer Jimmy Miller at Roundhouse Studios.[17] A hint of what the band had recorded for the album came on 9 March 1979 when the band played "Overkill" on *Top of the Pops* to support the release of the single ahead of the *Overkill* album, which was released on 24 March. It became Motörhead's first album to break into the top 40 of the UK Albums chart, reaching number 24, with the single reaching number 39 on the UK Singles Chart.[21] These releases were followed by the "Overkill" UK tour which began on 23 March.[14] A subsequent single was released in June, coupling the album track "No Class" as the A-side with the previously unreleased song "Like a Nightmare" on the B-side. It fared worse than both the album and previous single but reached number 61 on the UK singles chart.[21]

During July and August, except for a break to appear at the Reading Festival, the band were working on their next album, *Bomber*. Released on 27 October, it reached number 12 on the UK Albums Chart.[21] On 1 December, it was followed by the "Bomber" single, which reached number 34 on the UK Singles Chart.[21] The "Bomber" Europe and UK tour followed, with support from Saxon. The stage show featured a spectacular aircraft bomber-shaped lighting rig. During the "Bomber" tour, United Artists put together tapes recorded during the Rockfield Studios sessions in 1975–1976 and released them as the album *On Parole*, which peaked at number 65 on the UK Albums Chart in December.[21]

On 8 May 1980, while the band were on tour in Europe, Bronze released *The Golden Years*, which sold better than any of their previous releases, reaching number eight on the UK Singles Chart.[21] The band had, however, preferred the title *Flying Tonight*, in reference to the "Bomber" lighting rig. On 20 August, the band (40 minutes) and Girlschool (20 minutes) were filmed performing live at the Nottingham Theatre Royal for the *Rockstage* programme, broadcast on UK television by the ATV station on 4 April 1981.[22]

***Ace of Spades* and *Iron Fist*, 1980–82**

During August and September 1980, the band were at Jackson's Studios in Rickmansworth, recording with producer Vic Maile. The "Ace of Spades" single was re-

Cover of the "Ace Up Your Sleeve" tour booklet, using one of the shots taken during the photography session in Barnet for the Ace of Spades *album cover*

Motorhead playing at Port Talbot in 1982

leased on 27 October 1980 as a preview of the *Ace of Spades* album, which followed on 8 November.[17] The single reached No. 15 and the album reached No. 4 on the UK charts.[21] Bronze celebrated its gold record status by pressing a limited edition of the album in gold vinyl.

Motörhead made an appearance on *Top of the Pops* in November that year with "Ace of Spades", and between 22 October and 29 November the band were on their "Ace Up Your Sleeve" UK tour with support from Girlschool and Vardis, and also made an appearance as guests on the ITV children's show *Tiswas* on 8 November.[14] The "Arizona desert-style" pictures used on the album sleeve and tour booklet cover were taken during a photo session at a sandpit in Barnet.[23] "Ace of Spades", considered to be the definitive Motörhead anthem,[24] "put a choke on the English music charts and proved to all that a band could succeed without sacrificing its blunt power and speed".[25]

To coincide with the *Ace of Spades* release, Big Beat, who had inherited the Chiswick catalogue, put together four unused tracks from the Escape Studios sessions in 1977 and released them as *Beer Drinkers and Hell Raisers*, which reached No. 43 on the UK Singles Chart in November.[17][21]

The band had more chart hits in 1981 with the releases *St. Valentine's Day Massacre* EP, their collaboration with Girlschool which reached No. 5 on the UK Singles Chart in February; the live version of "Motorhead", which reached No. 6 on the UK Singles Chart in July; and the album it was taken from, *No Sleep 'til Hammersmith*, which reached No. 1 on the UK Albums Chart in June.[21] During March 1981, the band had been touring Europe, and in the final week of the month they conducted the "Short Sharp, Pain in the Neck" UK tour from which the recordings for *No Sleep 'til Hammersmith* were made.[14]

From April through to July, the band toured North America for the first time (*Ace of Spades* was their debut release in the region) as guests of Blizzard of Ozz, an early incarnation of Ozzy Osbourne's band, but were still able to make an appearance on *Top of the Pops* on 9 July to promote the live "Motorhead" single. In October the band recorded tracks at BBC's Maida Vale 4 studio for the David Jensen show broadcast on 6 October. The band commenced a European tour on 20 November, supported by Tank, followed by Clarke producing Tank's debut album *Filth Hounds of Hades* at Ramport Studios in December and January.

Between 26 and 28 January 1982, the band started recording their self-produced new album at Ramport Studios, before moving onto Morgan Studios to continue the sessions throughout February. On 3 April the single "Iron Fist" was released, reaching No. 29 on the UK Singles Chart, followed by the parent album *Iron Fist*, released on 17 April and peaking at No. 6 on the UK Albums Chart.[21] They were the last releases to feature the Lemmy, Clarke, Taylor line-up, though the line-up continued to perform in the *Iron Fist* UK tour between 17 March and 12 April, and the band's first headlining North America tour from 12 May until Clarke's last engagement at the New York Palladium on 14 May.[14]

Departures, *Another Perfect Day* and *No Remorse*, 1982–84

Clarke left as a consequence of the band recording *Stand By Your Man*, a cover version of the Tammy Wynette classic, in collaboration with Wendy O. Williams and the Plasmatics. Clarke felt that the song compromised the band's principles, refused to play on the recording and resigned, later forming his own band, Fastway. Lemmy and Taylor made numerous telephone calls to find a guitarist, including one to Brian Robertson, formerly with Thin Lizzy, who was recording a solo album in Canada. He agreed to help out and complete the tour with them. Robertson signed a one-album deal resulting in 1983's *Another Perfect Day* and the two singles from it, "Shine" and "I Got Mine".[17]

In June and July the band played five dates in Japan, and from mid-October until mid-November they toured Europe. From late May until early July, the band conducted the 'Another Perfect Tour', followed by an American tour between July and August, and another European tour in October and November.[14] Robertson began to cause friction in the band as a result of his on-stage attire, consisting of shorts and ballet shoes, and, furthermore, with his point blank refusal to play the old standards that every Motörhead audience expected to hear. This led to an amicable agreement that Robertson would leave,[17][26] playing his last engagement with the band at the Berlin Metropol on 11 November.[14]

After Robertson's departure in 1983, the band were sent tapes from all over the world from potential guitarists. The group returned to the concept of dual lead guitars by hiring unknowns Würzel and Phil Campbell (ex-Persian Risk).[17] In February 1984, the Lemmy, Campbell, Würzel, and Taylor line-up recorded "Ace of Spades" for the "Bambi" episode in the British television series, *The Young Ones*. Scenes of the band playing are interspersed with the characters' antics as they rush to the railway station, in a parody of The Beatles' comedy film *A Hard Day's Night*.[27] Taylor quit the band after that recording, causing Lemmy to quip: "Did I leave them or did they leave me?". Before joining Motörhead, Phil Campbell had met ex-Saxon drummer Pete Gill, and the trio decided to call him to see if he would like to visit London. The try-outs went well and Gill was hired.[17]

Bronze Records thought the new line-up would not make the grade and decided to "nail down the lid" on the group with a compilation album. When Lemmy found out, he took over the project, selecting tracks, providing sleeve notes and insisted that Motörhead record four brand new tracks to go at the end of each side of the album.[17] During the sessions between 19 and 25 May 1984 at Britannia Row Studios, London, the band recorded six tracks for the single's B-side and the album. The single "Killed by Death" was released on 1 September and reached No. 51 in the UK Singles Chart, the double album *No Remorse* was released on 15 September and reached silver disc status, attaining the position of No. 14 in the UK Album charts.[14][21]

The band were involved in a court case with Bronze over the next two years, believing that their releases were not being promoted properly, and the record company banned them from the recording studio.[17] The band looked to more touring for income; Australia and New Zealand in late July to late August, a brief tour of Hungary in September, and the *No Remorse* "Death on the Road" tour between 24 October and 7 November. On 26 October the band made a live appearance on the British Channel 4 music programme The Tube, performing "Killed By Death", "Steal Your Face" (over which the programme's end-credits were played) and the unbroadcast "Overkill", before going on to their next engagement that evening. From 19 November to 15 December the band toured America with Canadian speed metal band Exciter and Danish black metal band Mercyful Fate and from 26 to 30 December performed five shows in Germany.[14]

On 5 April 1985, ITV broadcast four songs that were recorded after the band went off air on their earlier appearance on *The Tube* programme. A week later the band, dressed in tuxedos, played four songs on the live Channel 4 music show *ECT* (Extra-Celestial Transmission). To celebrate the band's tenth anniversary, two shows were arranged at Hammersmith Odeon on 28 and 29 June, a video of the second show was taken and later released as *The Birthday Party*. From early June until early August the band were on their 'It Never Gets Dark' tour of Sweden and Norway, an American tour followed in mid-November until late December.[14]

Orgasmatron and *Rock 'n' Roll*, 1986–89

From 26 March to 3 April 1986, the band toured Germany, the Netherlands and Denmark on their "Easter Metal Blast" and in June, played two dates in Bologna and Milan in Italy. The court case with Bronze was finally settled in the band's favour. The band's management instigated their own label, GWR.[17] Recording took place in Master Rock Studios, London and the single "Deaf Forever" was released on 5 July as a taster for the *Orgasmatron* album, which was released on 9 August. On the same day as the release of the album, Lemmy and Würzel were interviewed by Andy Kershaw on the BBC Radio 1 *Saturday Live* show and "Orgasmatron" and "Deaf Forever" were played. The single reached No. 67 and the album reached No. 21 in the UK charts.[21]

On 16 August, the band played at the Monsters of Rock at Castle Donington and was recorded by BBC Radio 1 for a future *Friday Rock Show* broadcast. The performance closed with a flyover by a couple of Second World War German aircraft. Also that day Lemmy was filmed giving his views on spoof metal act "Bad News" for inclusion in a Peter Richardson Comic Strip film entitled "More Bad News" since the band featuring Rik Mayall, Peter Richardson, Nigel Planer and Adrian Edmondson were also performing at Donington. In September the band conducted their "Orgasmatron" tour in Great Britain, supported by fledgling act Zodiac Mindwarp and the Love Reaction. In October they toured America and in December were in Germany.[14]

In 1987, during the filming of *Eat the Rich* – in which Lemmy was taking a starring role alongside well-known comedy actors such as Robbie Coltrane, Kathy Burke, the regulars from The Comic Strip ensemble, and various other musician cameo appearances[28] – Gill left the band and Taylor returned to appear in the band's cameo as "In House Club Band" alongside Würzel and Campbell. The band wrote "Eat the Rich" especially for the film, its soundtrack featured tracks from *Orgasmatron* and Würzel's solo single "Bess". The band's second album for GWR was *Rock 'n' Roll*, released on 5 September, after a tight work schedule in the studio. While having some popular tracks and using "Eat the Rich" as its second track, the band commented that the album was virtually "nailed together".[17]

On 2 July 1988 Motörhead were one of the performers at the Giants of Rock Festival in Hämeenlinna, Finland. The tracks were released as *No Sleep at All* on 15 October. A single from the album was planned with the band wanting "Traitor" as the A-side, but "Ace of Spades" was chosen instead. When the band noticed the change, they refused to allow the single to be distributed to the shops, and it was withdrawn and became available only on the "No Sleep at All" tour and through the *Motörheadbangers* fan club. While they continued to play live shows during 1989 and 1990, Motörhead once again felt unhappy with their career, and a court case with GWR followed, which was not resolved until mid-1990.[17]

Epic/WTG years: *1916* and *March ör Die*, 1990–92

With the court case resolved, Motörhead signed to Epic/WTG and spent the last half of 1990 recording a new album and single in Los Angeles.[17] Just prior to the album sessions the band's former manager, Doug Smith, released the recording of the band's tenth anniversary show, much against the bands wishes, having previously told him that they did not want it released, in 1986. In the studio they recorded four songs with producer Ed Stasium, before deciding he had to go.

When Lemmy listened to one of the mixes of "Going to Brazil", he asked for him to turn up four tracks, and on doing so heard claves and tambourines that Stasium had added without their knowledge. Stasium was fired and Peter Solley was hired as producer. The story according to Stasium was that Lemmy's drug and alcohol intake had far exceeded the limitations of Stasium's patience so he quit.[29] The single "The One to Sing the Blues" issued on 24 December 1990 (7" and CD) and 5 January 1991 (12"), was followed by the album *1916* on 21 January. The single, which was issued in 7", cassette, shaped picture disc, 12" and CD single, reached No. 45 in the UK Singles Chart, the album reached No. 24 in the UK Album Charts.[14][21]

The band conducted their "It Serves You Right" tour of Britain in February, the "Lights Out Over Europe" tour followed, lasting until early April, when the band returned to Britain to play another six venues. In June the band played five dates in Japan and five dates in Australia and New Zealand. Between July and August, they played across the United States with Judas Priest, Alice Cooper, Metal Church and opener Dangerous Toys on the "Operation Rock 'n' Roll" tour. The band finished the year with six dates in Germany during December.[30]

On 28 March 1992, the band played what would turn out to be Taylor's last engagement at Irvine Meadows, Irvine, California.[30] The band had been wanting Lemmy to get rid of their manager, Doug Banker, for some time and after an unsolicited visit from Todd Singerman, who insisted he should manage them despite never having managed a band before, the band met with Singerman and decided to take him on board, firing Banker.[31] In the midst of this, the band were recording an album at Music Grinder Studios, in the city's east part of Hollywood during the 1992 Los Angeles riots. Three drummers participated in the making of the *March ör Die* album: Phil Taylor, who was fired because he did not learn the drum tracks on the song "I Ain't No Nice Guy"; Tommy Aldridge who recorded most of the material on the album; and Mikkey Dee, who recorded "Hellraiser", a song originally written by Lemmy for Ozzy Osbourne's *No More Tears* album. *March ör Die* features guest appearances by Ozzy Osbourne and Slash.[14]

Bastards, *Sacrifice* and *Overnight Sensation*, 1993–97

Lemmy had known Mikkey Dee from the time when King Diamond had toured with Motörhead. He had asked Dee to become Motörhead's drummer before, but Dee had declined due to his commitment to King Diamond. On this occasion, Dee was available and met the band to try out. Playing the song "Hellraiser" first, Lemmy thought "he was very good immediately. It was obvious that it was going to work." After recording "Hellraiser" and "Hell on Earth" in the studio,[32] Dee's first engagement with Motörhead was on 30 August at the Saratoga Performing Arts Center. The new line-up then went on tour, playing dates with Ozzy Osbourne, Skew Siskin and Exodus. On 27 September, the band played at the Los Angeles Coliseum with Metallica and Guns N' Roses. The band toured Argentina and Brazil during October and conducted the "Bombers and Eagles in '92" tour of Europe with Saxon throughout December.[30]

Motörhead played two dates at the Arena Obras Sanitarias in Buenos Aires in April 1993 and toured Europe from early June until early July, returning to the United States to play one show at the New York Ritz on 14 August.[30] A new producer was sought for the band's next album and eventually Howard Benson, who was to produce the band's next four albums, was chosen. The band recorded at A&M Studios and Prime Time Studios in Hollywood and the resultant album, titled *Bastards*, was released on 29 November 1993. The single "Don't Let Daddy Kiss Me" included the song "Born to Raise Hell", which also appeared on the album and would later be re-recorded with collaborative vocals from both Ice-T and Ugly Kid Joe frontman, Whitfield Crane and released as a single in its own right. Although *Bastards* received airtime, the record company ZYX Music would not pay for promotional copies, so the band sent out copies themselves.[33] A further tour of Europe was made throughout December that year.[30]

In February and March 1994, Motörhead toured the United States with Black Sabbath and Morbid Angel. In April the band resumed their tour of the States until early May, playing an engagement with the Ramones on 14 May at the Estadio Velez in Buenos Aires,[30] attracting a crowd of 50,000 people.[34] The band toured Japan in late May and Europe in June, August and December.[30]

The band's 1995 touring schedule began in Europe in late April. In June, they went on a second tour with Black Sabbath, this time supported by Tiamat, until the band succumbed to influenza and headed back to Los Angeles and Cherokee Studios in Hollywood where they were to record an album. During the sessions it became clear that Würzel was not extending himself and left the band after the recording.[35] The title track from the album, *Sacrifice*, was later used in the movie *Tromeo and Juliet*, a film in which Lemmy appears as the narrator. The band decided to continue as a three-man line-up and a tour of Europe was performed throughout October and the first two days of November. A three-day tour of South America followed the week after. Lemmy celebrated his 50th Birthday later that year with the band at the Whisky a Go Go in Los Angeles; Metallica played at the event under the name "The Lemmy's".[30]

In 1996, the band began touring the States in early January and played thirty venues up to 15 February; a seven-date tour of Europe in June and July was followed by two engagements in South America during August.

A tour of the United States with Belladonna and Speedball began with two shows (Los Angeles & Hollywood) in early October 1996 and concluded in Washington on 4 December.[30] During this time the band had recorded *Overnight Sensation*, at Ocean Studio and Track House Recording Studio. The album was released on 15 October, the first official album of the band as a three-piece since *Another Perfect Day* and the best distributed album the band had had for years.[36] The band concluded the year's touring with thirteen dates in Germany.[30]

During 1997, the band toured extensively, beginning with the first leg of the *Overnight Sensation* tour in Europe on 12 January at the London Astoria, where the guest musicians were Todd Campbell, Phil Campbell's son, on "Ace of Spades" and "Fast" Eddie Clarke for "Overkill". The European leg lasted until March and was followed by four dates in Japan, from late May to 1 June, and an American tour with W.A.S.P. throughout the rest of June. In August, three dates in Europe were followed by seven dates in Britain, which ended with a show at the Brixton Academy on 25 October, where the guest musician was Paul Inder, Lemmy's son, for "Ace of Spades". A further four dates in October in Russia concluded the year 1997.[30]

Snake Bite Love, *We Are Motörhead* and *Hammered*, 1998–2003

Lemmy recalled that the touring was going particularly well, with some countries like Argentina and Japan putting the band in larger venues, and the English promoters discovered that "they could turn a nice profit with Motörhead shows". In his opinion, the three-piece line-up was performing excellently and it was high time they made another live record.[37] The band did eventually, but made another studio album first, *Snake Bite Love*, recorded in various studios and released on 3 March 1998.

The band joined with Judas Priest at the Los Angeles Universal Amphitheatre on 3 April, to begin their "Snake Bite Love" tour. On 21 May, Motörhead were recorded at The Docks in Hamburg. The tracks from this performance were later released as *Everything Louder Than Everyone Else*. The band were invited to join the Ozzfest Tour and played dates across the States during early July until early August and were in Europe from early October until late November. The British leg of the tour was dubbed the "No Speak With Forked Tongue" tour and included support bands Groop Dogdrill, Radiator and Psycho Squad, which was fronted by Phil Campbell's son Todd.[30]

In 1999 Motörhead made a tour of the states between 20 April and 2 June, before going to Karo Studios in Brackel, Germany to record their next album, *We Are Motörhead*, which was released in May the following year. During the time the album sessions took place, the band played at venues around Europe, the first of which was at Fila Forum in Assago, near Milan, where Metallica's James Hetfield joined the band on-stage to play "Overkill". In October and early November, the band toured the states with Nashville Pussy. Throughout the rest of November, the band conducted their European "Monsters of the Millennium" tour with Manowar, Dio and Lion's Share, ending the Millennium with two shows at the London Astoria. The two shows were billed under the *Kerrang!* "X-Fest" banner and at the first show were supported by Backyard Babies and during the second show guest vocals were provided by Skin from Skunk Anansie and Nina C. Alice from Skew Siskin for "Born to Raise Hell", and Ace from Skunk Anansie played "Overkill" with the band.[30]

Entrance ticket for the 25th anniversary concert at the Brixton Academy on 22 October 2000

In May 2000, the release of *We Are Motörhead* and the single from it, a cover of the Sex Pistol's "God Save the Queen", coincided with the start of the band's "We Are Motörhead" tour across South and North America during May and June, with a further nine shows across in Europe in July. Shows in the United States and France were followed by the release of a double-disc compilation album, *The Best Of*, on 26 August.

Four dates in Japan preceded the band's 25th anniversary concert on 22 October at the Brixton Academy in London, where guest appearances were made by "Fast" Eddie Clarke, Brian May, Doro Pesch, Whitfield Crane, Ace, Paul Inder and Todd Campbell. The show also featured the return of the Bomber-lighting rig. The event was filmed and released the following year as the *25 & Alive Boneshaker* DVD, and the CD of the show, *Live at Brixton Academy*, was released two years after that.[30] Lemmy states the reason for the DVD as wanting "to record it for the posterity or whatever it is. I nodded off through the tenth anniversary, we never did anything on the twentieth, so the twenty-fifth made sense."[19]

A tour of West and East Europe followed the anniversary concert, taking the band through October, November and December.[30] The schedule for the Eastern European tour was quite brutal, involving two eighteen-hour drives back-to-back and little time off, at the Warsaw venue the band did not arrive until eleven o'clock and the crew were still loading into the venue at one in the morning, while the fans waited.[38]

After taking a month off, the band began working on a new album at Chuck Reid's house in the Hollywood Hills. This album, *Hammered*, was released the following year. On 1 April 2001, the band gave a one song performance for Triple H's entrance at WrestleMania X-Seven at the Reliant Astrodome in Houston. The second leg of the "We Are Motörhead" tour began in May in Ireland, moving across to the United Kingdom. In Manchester, the band were supported by Goldblade, and by Pure Rubbish at the two London shows. The second London show also included Backyard Babies and Paul Inder, who was guest musician for "Killed By Death". Between June and August, Motörhead played at a number of rock festivals in Europe; including as the Graspop Metal Meeting in Belgium, the Quart Festival in Norway, and the Wacken Open Air on 4 August, where four songs were recorded for the *25 & Alive Boneshaker* DVD. The band returned to the States for a seven show tour between late September and early October.[30]

In April 2002, a DVD of some of Motörhead's performances from the '70s and '80s along with some stock footage of the band was released as *The Best of Motörhead*. Two weeks earlier, the *Hammered* album was released and supported by the "Hammered" tour, which kicked off in the States at around the same time. The United States dates continued until late May, and a European leg followed between June and August. In October, the band played five dates in Great Britain with Anthrax, Skew Siskin and Psycho Squad. The final venue was the Wembley Arena in London, where instead of Psycho Squad, the band were supported by Hawkwind, with Lemmy performing "Silver Machine" on stage with them. Throughout the rest of October and better part of November, the band were on a European tour with Anthrax.[30]

In April and May 2003, the band continued to promote the *Hammered* album in the States, and on the three dates Phil Campbell had to miss, his mother having died, Todd Youth stood in for him. Between late May and mid-July the band played seven dates at Summer Festivals in Europe and from late-July until the end of August, they were touring the

United States with Iron Maiden and Dio. On 7 October a comprehensive five-disc collection of the band's recordings covering 1975–2002 was released as *Stone Deaf Forever!*. On 1 September 2003, the band returned to Hollywood's Whisky A Go-Go club for the Hollywood Rock Walk of Fame Induction. During October, the band performed a tour of Great Britain with The Wildhearts and Young Heart Attack. The band performed seven shows across Belgium, the Netherlands and Spain between 21 and 28 October and from late-November until early-December they were in Germany and Switzerland, touring with Skew Siskin and Mustasch. On 9 December, the previously recorded *Live at Brixton Academy* album was released.[30]

Inferno, *Kiss of Death* and *Motörizer*, 2004–09

On 22 February 2004 Motörhead performed an invitation-only concert at the Royal Opera House in Covent Garden, London; at Summer Festivals in South America during May; and also Europe during June, July and August. The band had already spent time in the recording studio, working on their next album, *Inferno*, which was released on 22 June and was followed by the "Inferno" tour of Ireland with Class of Zero for three dates, before being joined by Sepultura and taking it to Great Britain.[39]

Some of the London show at the Hammersmith Apollo was filmed for TV as Gene Simmons introduced the extra opening act, The Class – a band made up of school children appearing in his Channel 4 series, *Rock School* – and Würzel joined as guest musician for "Overkill". The band continued the tour with Sepultura across Europe through the rest of November and December. At the show in Magdeburg, Germany on 4 December Motörhead joined Sepultura on stage during their support slot playing the song "Orgasmatron", in celebration of Sepultura's 20th Anniversary. The show on 7 December at the Philipshalle in Düsseldorf was recorded and later released as the *Stage Fright* DVD.[30]

Motörhead on stage, 2005

Motörhead picked up their first Grammy in the awards of 2005 in the Best Metal Performance category for their cover of Metallica's "Whiplash" on *Metallic Attack: The Ultimate Tribute*.[40] From March until early May, the band toured the United States, and in June and August were on the "30th Anniversary" tour in Europe.[30] On 22 August, the band were the subject of an hour-long documentary, *Live Fast, Die Old*, which was aired on Channel 4 as part of *The Other Side* series of documentaries, filmed by new and established directors.[41][42]

On 20 September, a compilation album containing the band's appearances on BBC Radio 1 and a concert recording from Paris Theatre, London, was released as *BBC Live & In-Session*. In October, the band toured Europe with Mondo Generator before returning to Great Britain to tour with In Flames and Girlschool in October and November. During the show at the Brixton Academy on 19 November, Lemmy joined Girlschool on stage to play "Please Don't Touch". Motörhead finished the year's tours in December, with two engagements in New Zealand and five in Australia with Mötley Crüe.[30] Also in 2005, Motörhead played on the Vaya Con Tioz farewell festival Böhse Onkelz at Lausitzring.

In 2006, the band performed a four-date House of Blues tour in the States in March with Meldrum and from June until early August played at European open-air festivals with some indoor headlining shows. On 28 October, the band performed at The Rock Freakers Ball in Kansas City before heading off to tour Great Britain with Clutch and Crucified Barbara.

While that tour was still going, their next album, *Kiss of Death*, was released on 29 August 2006 via Sanctuary Records, with a video for "Be My Baby". The tour ended with an engagement on 25 November at the Brixton Academy, where Phil Campbell was guest guitarist for "Killed By Death" played during Crucified Barbara's support set. A further twelve shows in Europe with Meldrum took them through the end of November to early December, the first two shows also featuring Skew Siskin.[30]

In November, the band agreed to a sponsorship deal with the Greenbank B under-10s football team from North Hykeham, Lincoln, putting the band's name as well as War-Pig on the team's shirts; the under-10s run out to "Ace of Spades". Lemmy is old friends with Gary Weight, the team's manager; Weight "sent an email off to them and they came back and said it was a great idea" and hopes the deal will draw inspired performances from his team.[43] On 25 April 2007, the band played at the Poliedro de Caracas in Caracas, Venezuela, and on 29 April at the Fundiçao Progresso, Rio de Janeiro.[30] In June, Motörhead played an engagement at the Royal Festival Hall as part of Jarvis Cocker's Meltdown. On 26 February 2008, No Sleep 'Til

Motörhead at the Masters of Rock tour in 2007.

Hammersmith was reissued again as a two disc CD.

From March through to June 2008, the band convened in Los Angeles with producer Cameron Webb to begin work on their 19th album *Motörizer*. Mikkey Dee's drum tracks were recorded at Dave Grohl's studio. Motörizer was released on 26 August. It does not feature artwork from Joe Petagno, the artist who designed many of their classic album covers.

In June 2008 the band performed at the main stage of the Download festival. Between 6 and 31 August, Motörhead joined with Judas Priest, Heaven & Hell and Testament on the Metal Masters Tour. On 20 August the band played one date at the Roseland Ballroom, New York, as part of "The Volcom Tour 2008", which continued with bands The Misfits, Airbourne, Valient Thorr and Year Long Disaster at House of Blues, Anaheim, California on 2 September, playing a further thirteen dates. The band concluded the tour without the supporting bands, playing one more show at the Roseland Ballroom on 20 September, and the final engagement, at The Stone Pony, Asbury Park, New Jersey on 21 September.

On 30 September, Reuters reported that Neverdie Studios had signed a deal with Lemmy and Motörhead to develop and market Lemmy's Castle and Motorhead Stadium inside the virtual world of Entropia Universe, an online virtual universe.[44] The year's touring ended with a 34-date tour of Europe with a variety of support bands including Danko Jones, Saxon, Witchcraft, and Airbourne.[30] On 6 March 2009, the band played in the Middle East for the first time, at the annual Dubai Desert Rock Festival in Dubai. On 1 April Motörhead are reported to have entered into a two-year sponsorship deal with UK Roller Derby team the Lincolnshire Bombers Roller Girls.[45]

In November 2009, the band are being supported by NWOBHM veterans Sweet Savage on the Irish leg of the tour (30 years after first sharing the stage together) and punk and goth rock legends The Damned on the UK leg of their world tour. On The Damned's official website, Captain Sensible is quoted as saying:[46]

> "Ha ha ... we're working with Lemmy again are we? Excellent! He's the real deal, the absolute antithesis to all that the likes of Simon Cowell stand for. And for that we should all be grateful. This tour will be a celebration of all things rock 'n' roll ... pity the poor roadies is all I can say!"

The Wörld Is Yours, *Aftershock* and *Bad Magic*, 2010–present

Motörhead performing at the Norway Rock Festival 2010

In a November 2009 interview with ABORT Magazine's E.S. Day, Lemmy stated that Motörhead would enter the studio in February 2010 "to rehearse, write and record" their 20th studio album, to be released by the end of the year.[47][48] The album was recorded with Cameron Webb and Welsh producer Romesh Dodangoda in Longwave Studio, Cardiff.

In an interview with Hungarian television in July 2010, drummer Mikkey Dee announced that the album was finished, with 11 tracks. The album's name was said to be

The Wörld Is Yours. On 3 November 2010, Future PLC, a UK media company, announced that Motörhead were to release *The Wörld is Yours* via an exclusive publishing deal with *Classic Rock* magazine on 14 December 2010.[49][50] The standard CD release of *The Wörld is Yours* would go on sale on 17 January 2011, through Motörhead's own label, Motörhead Music.[50][51]

Phil Campbell of Motörhead – New York City 28 February 2011

To coincide with the release of their upcoming album, Motörhead embarked on a 35th Anniversary UK tour, from 8–28 November 2010,[52] and a European tour from 30 November 2010 – 19 December 2010. They also took their tour to the Americas in 2011.[53] In October, the band recorded a slow blues version of their longtime hit "Ace of Spades" for a TV spot for Kronenbourg beer.[54] On 5 December the single "Get Back in Line" was released,[55] followed by the release of a video for the single on 6 December.[56] In December, Mikkey Dee stated to French journalists that Motörhead are planning to release a boxset with several DVDs in 2011. He did not give any details but said that it will come in a "beautiful package including many surprises".[57]

On 17 January 2011, it was announced that Motörhead would be part of the Sonisphere Festival in Knebworth.[58] In August 2011, they headlined the Brutal Assault open-air festival in the Czech Republic. On 2 March 2011 Motörhead performed on *Late Night with Jimmy Fallon*.[59] On 9 July 2011, former guitarist Würzel died of a heart attack.[60] In celebration of 35 years' touring, in late 2011 the band released the live DVD *The Wörld Is Ours – Vol 1 – Everywhere Further Than Everyplace Else*, including performances at the O2 Apollo Manchester, Best Buy Theater, New York City and Teatro Caupolicán, Santiago de Chile.

On 19 December 2011, it was announced that Motörhead would play at the German festivals Rock am Ring and Rock im Park in Nürburgring and Nuremberg respectively in June 2012.[61][62] On 12 January 2012, it was announced that Motörhead were touring the US and Canada in early 2012, along with three other metal bands Megadeth, Volbeat and Lacuna Coil. The Gigantour took place from 26 January to 28 February 2012, but Motörhead missed the final four shows because Lemmy had a combination of an upper respiratory viral infection and voice strain, resulting in severe laryngitis. Lemmy wrote on Facebook, "I'm giving my voice a good rest", hoping he would recover soon to play at the Mayhem Festival, which was held from 30 June to 5 August 2012. Motörhead also took part on 23 June in the Rock-A-Field Luxembourg Open Air Festival in Roeser.

In an April 2012 interview with Classic Rock Revisited, Lemmy was asked if Motörhead were planning to make a follow-up to *The Wörld Is Yours*. He replied, "We have not started writing any songs yet but we will. We put out an album out every two years. I will continue to do that as long as I can afford an amp."[63] On 28 June 2012, Lemmy told Auburn Reporter that Motörhead will release their next album in 2013 and they had written "about 6 songs so far."[64] On 23 October 2012, Lemmy told Billboard.com that the band had planned to enter the studio in January to begin recording the album for a mid-2013 release.[65] On 28 February 2013, it was announced that Motörhead had begun recording their new album.[66] Motörhead released the live DVD *The Wörld Is Ours – Vol. 2 – Anyplace Crazy As Anywhere Else* in September 2012. On 18 June 2013, the new album's title was revealed to be *Aftershock*.

In mid November 2013, Motörhead were due to embark on a European tour alongside Saxon, followed by a tour in Germany and Scandinavia due to last until mid December 2013 but the dates were postponed and rescheduled for February and March 2014 due to Lemmy's health problems. However, in January 2014, Motörhead announced the cancellation of the new February and March dates of their European tour as Lemmy was still to reach full recovery from diabetes related health problems.[67] But the same month, the band was confirmed for Coachella Festival to take place across two weekends in spring 2014 (12–14 and 19–21 April) in Indio, California,[68] the exact dates to be revealed as 13 and 20 April 2014. In February 2014, Motörhead confirmed a Summer tour 2014 with eight European dates (from 24 June to 10 August) in France (2 dates), Switzerland, Italy, Germany (2 dates), Russia and Ukraine.[69] In March 2014, the band announced a Los Angeles date on 11 April 2014 at Club Nokia. Later on, two new dates on 17 and 18 April 2014 respectively in Las Vegas (Pearl) and San Francisco (Warfield) were added.[70] Still in March 2014, Motörhead announced that three heavy metal bands Megadeth, Anthrax and themselves would perform from 22 to 26 September 2014 at the first annual Motörhead's Motörboat cruise on board the Carnival Ecstasy (self-proclaimed "The Loudest Boat in the World"), due to sail from Miami and visit the ports of Key West and the Cozumel island just off Mexico's Yucatán Peninsula.[71]

In a September 2014 interview on Full Metal Jackie, Lemmy stated that Motörhead would "probably" enter the studio in January 2015 to start work on their 22nd studio album for a tentative late 2015 release.[72] On 25 February 2015, Motörhead officially confirmed that they were in the studio recording their new album in Los Angeles with longtime producer Cameron Webb.[73][74] On 27 May 2015, the band released teasers on their Facebook page with the roman number "XXXX" on it. On 4 June the new album *Bad Magic* was launched for pre-order on Amazon, revealing its title and cover art which also shows the "XXXX", coinciding with the 40th anniversary of the band. The album was released on 28 August 2015.[75][76]

While touring the album,[77] Motörhead had to cut short their Salt Lake City show on 27 August 2015 (in the Rocky Mountains) due to Lemmy's breathing problems (the result of an altitude sickness) and then they had to cancel completely day-off their Denver Riot Fest set on 28 August 2015. Their tour picked up again on 1 September 2015 at Emo's in Austin, Texas (moved from Cedar Park Center) but sadly the group were again forced to abandon their set after three songs[nb 1] and to cancel subsequent shows (from the show on 2 September 2015 in San Antonio, Texas to the show on 5 September 2015 in Houston, Texas included).[80]

Despite his ongoing health issues forcing Motörhead to cut short or cancel several US shows,[78][81][nb 2][nb 3] Lemmy Kilmister was able to bounce back in time for the trio's annual Motörboat heavy metal cruise from Miami to the Bahamas which ran from 28 September through 2 October 2015 including performances by heavy metal legends Slayer and underground heroes like Anthrax, Exodus, Suicidal Tendencies and Corrosion of Conformity. For this occasion, Motörhead performed live two entire (identical) sets on 30 September and 1 October 2015.[84][85][86]

2.45.2 Style

In a biography of the band, senior editor for AllMusic, Stephen Erlewine, wrote: "Motörhead's overwhelmingly loud and fast style of heavy metal was one of the most groundbreaking styles the genre had to offer in the late '70s"

Lemmy live in Edmonton, 2005

and though "Motörhead wasn't punk rock ... they were the first metal band to harness that energy and, in the process, they created speed metal and thrash metal."[87] Whether they created these genres might be subject to debate, but Motörhead were unquestionably influential.

Although Motörhead is often considered as a heavy metal band, Lemmy has always described Motörhead's music as simply rock and roll. In 2011 he said: "We were not heavy metal. We were a rock'n'roll band. Still are. Everyone always describes us as heavy metal even when I tell them otherwise. Why won't people listen?"[88] In 2014 he reiterated to *Der Spiegel* that he did not particularly like heavy metal.[89]

Lemmy has stated that he generally feels more kinship with punk rockers than with metal bands: Motörhead had engagements with fellow Brits The Damned, with whom he played bass on a handful of late 1970s engagements,[90] as well as having penned the song "R.A.M.O.N.E.S." as a tribute to the Ramones. Motörhead, Lemmy states, have more in common aesthetically with The Damned than Black Sabbath, and nothing whatsoever in common with Judas Priest. Lemmy says he feels little kinship with the speed metal bands Motörhead have inspired:

> "They've just got the wrong bit. They think that being fast and loud is the whole thing and it isn't. The guitar solos are not really difficult for a guitar player, it's just playing scales. To feel a solo and bend into it & I mean Hendrix is the best guitarist you've ever seen in your life. And he learned from people like Buddy Guy, Lightnin' Hopkins and people like that inspired Hendrix. To be influenced by something, you're gonna have to play it the same."[91]

The *NME* stated that their brief solos were just long enough "... to open another bottle of beer", while a 1977 *Stereo Review* commented that "they know they're like animals, and they don't want to appear any other way. In view of the many ugly frogs in heavy metal who think they are God's gift to womankind these Quasimodos even seem charming in their own way".[92] Motörhead's approach has not changed drastically over the band's career, though this is a deliberate choice: erstwhile Motörhead drummer Phil "Philthy Animal" Taylor said that rock icons like Chuck Berry and Little Richard never drastically altered their style, and, like them, Motörhead preferred to play what they enjoyed and did best.[93] This fondness for the first decade of rock and roll (mid-1950s to mid-1960s) is also reflected in some of Motörhead's occasional cover songs from that era.

Lemmy often plays powerchords in his basslines. When asked about whether he had begun as a rhythm guitarist, he stated:

> No, I play a lot of notes, but I also play a lot of chords. And I play a lot of open strings. I just don't play like a bass player. There are complaints about me from time to time. It's not like having a bass player; it's like having a deep guitarist.[94]

2.45.3 Cover art

The band's name is usually printed in a lowercase form of blackletter. The umlaut character ö is possibly derived from the similar "heavy metal umlaut" in the name of their 1975 acquaintances Blue Öyster Cult. However, this umlaut does not alter the pronunciation of the band's name. When asked if Germans pronounced the band "Motuuuurhead", Lemmy answered "No, they don't. I only put it in there to look mean".[95]

Snaggletooth is the fanged face that serves as the symbol of Motörhead. Artist Joe Petagno drew it in 1977 for the cover of the band's debut album (with designer Phil Smee who

War-Pig on Motörhead's first album

turned it into a negative and did the lettering to complete the logo),[96] having met Lemmy while doing some work with Hawkwind.[97] Petagno stated;

> The inspiration came from just being a naturally pissed-off bastard! And Lemmy's the same way! So it was bound to be an alchemal wedding of a more "primordial nature". I did a lot of research on skull types and found a cross-breed gorilla-wolf-dog combination would work nicely with some oversized boars horns. Lemmy added Helmet, chains, spit, spikes and grit.[97]

Eddie Clarke was less sure about the imagery to begin with:

> I shuddered when I saw it the first time. I thought, "Blimey, this ain't gonna go down that well", because it was just way over the top, then. But I grew to love it ... [At first] it was not scary or horrifying, it would've been, in those days, deemed bad taste.[98]

It has remained a symbol of Motörhead throughout the years, with Petagno creating many variations of War-Pig for the covers of ensuing albums. To date, only two of the original covers for Motörhead's 22 studio albums do not feature any variation of War-Pig on the cover: *On Parole* and *Overnight Sensation* (of which, *On Parole* was never sanctioned by the band), and was in any case reissued with a black War-Pig on a white background. Phil is wearing a War-Pig badge on the cover of *Ace of Spades*. The cover of "Iron Fist" depicts a metal gauntlet wearing four skull-shaped rings, one of which is War-Pig, while the rear of the album-sleeve shows a fully detailed 3-D metal sculpture of the symbol. Originally the War-Pig design included a swastika on one of the helmet's spikes. This was painted out on later re-releases of the albums on CD.

On 21 September 2007, Petagno announced that "there will be no more "HEADS" from my hand", citing irreconcilable differences between himself and the band's current management, Singerman Entertainment. Petagno stated:

> It has been a long, exciting and industrious journey, full of art and intuition, difference in repetition, and creative innovation. I feel I accomplished something unique in Metal history over the last 31 years by breathing life again and again into a figment of my own imagination, an image or better an entity which has taken on a life of its own, which I actually believe goes beyond the music it was created to represent. I'm damn proud of that!

In reply, Lemmy stated:

> As many of you know, we have been working with Joe Petagno for 31 years. We always treated Joe fairly, and I would like to stress that at no time did my manager demand what Joe thinks he demanded — it is all a colossal misunderstanding. We have always loved his artwork, obviously, and if he now decides to stop working with us, we have no choice but to use someone else. However ... if he will not discuss this personally and try to work things out, I think it's a great tragedy. If Joe continues with us, no one would be more delighted than me. If it's goodbye, Joe, I wish you well, but I hope, even at this stage, to be reconciled and continue our association.[99]

2.45.4 Members

For a more comprehensive list, see List of Motörhead band members.

Current members

- Ian "Lemmy" Kilmister – lead vocals, bass guitar (1975–present)
- Phil "Wizzö" Campbell – guitar, backing vocals (1984–present)
- Mikkey Dee – drums (1992–present)

2.45.5 Discography

For a more comprehensive list, see Motörhead discography.

- *On Parole* (1976/1979)
- *Motörhead* (1977)
- *Overkill* (1979)
- *Bomber* (1979)
- *Ace of Spades* (1980)
- *Iron Fist* (1982)
- *Another Perfect Day* (1983)
- *Orgasmatron* (1986)
- *Rock 'n' Roll* (1987)
- *1916* (1991)
- *March ör Die* (1992)
- *Bastards* (1993)
- *Sacrifice* (1995)
- *Overnight Sensation* (1996)
- *Snake Bite Love* (1998)
- *We Are Motörhead* (2000)
- *Hammered* (2002)
- *Inferno* (2004)
- *Kiss of Death* (2006)
- *Motörizer* (2008)
- *The Wörld Is Yours* (2010)
- *Aftershock* (2013)
- *Bad Magic* (2015)

2.45.6 Filmography

- 1987: *Eat the Rich*: soundtrack includes "Nothing up My Sleeve", "Built for Speed", "Orgasmatron", "Doctor Rock", "On the Road (live)", "Eat the Rich" and "Bess" – New Line Home Entertainment. Halfway through shooting, the idea of gradually replacing the members of the ballroom band with Motörhead was hit upon. At first there are no Motörhead personnel, then Phil Campbell appears, followed by Würzel and

Phil Taylor. The scene involving Lemmy riding a motorcycle is played by a female stunt double as Lemmy was on tour with Motörhead in America at the time the scene had to be shot.

- 2010: *Lemmy (49% Motherfucker. 51% Son of a Bitch.)* (rockumentary film profile of Ian "Lemmy" Kilmister)

- 2011: *The World Is Ours – Vol 1 – Everywhere Further Than Everyplace Else* (live DVD of Motörhead's last global tour to date including the entire performance on 9 April 2011 at Santiago de Chile's Teatro Caupolican and moments from the shows on 16 November 2010 at Manchester's O2 Apollo and on 28 February 2011 at New York City's Best Buy Theater)

2.45.7 Notes

[1] About the shortened show on 1 September 2015 at Emo's in Austin, Texas: after having played the two first songs ("Damage Case" and "Stay Clean"), Kilmister returned to the stage after he cut short the third one, "Metropolis." «You're one of the best gigs that I've ever played. And I would love to play for you. But I can't,» Kilmister said, adding that he feared collapse. «Please accept my apologies.»[78][79]

[2] Shortened shows: on 27 August 2015 at The Complex in Salt Lake City, Utah;[82] on 1 September 2015 at Emo's in Austin, Texas.[78]

[3] Cancelled shows: on 28 August 2015 at Riot Fest in Denver, Colorado (show drop off at the last minute due to Lemmy's breathing issues[83]);[82] on 2 September 2015 at the Aztec Theatre in San Antonio, Texas; on 4 September 2015 at The Bomb Factory in Dallas, Texas; on 5 September 2015 at the House of Blues in Houston, Texas.[78][81]

2.45.8 References

[1] "New Wave of British Heavy Metal". AllMusic. Retrieved 11 April 2009.

[2] "LosingToday reviews". LosingToday Magazine's review of BBC Live & In-Session. Retrieved 11 February 2007.

[3] "Motorhead". Motorheadphones. Retrieved 12 January 2015.

[4] Reynolds, Simon (1995). *The Sex Revolts: Gender, Rebellion, and Rock 'n' Roll*. Harvard University Press. p. 107. ISBN 0-674-80272-1.

[5] Carroll, Ted. "Motorhead". Ace Records. Retrieved 14 August 2009.

[6] "Devil in the Details: Orgasmatron". Shana Ting Lipton. Retrieved 14 August 2009.

[7] "VH1: 100 Greatest Hard Rock Artists: 1–50:". Rock on the Net:. 22 February 2009. Retrieved 10 May 2009.

[8] Lemmy, *White Line Fever*, p. 94. (2002). Simon & Schuster. ISBN 0-684-85868-1.

[9] Tyler, Tony (28 June 1975). "The Trials of Lemmy". *NME*.

[10] *White Line Fever*, p. 99.

[11] Motörhead (2013). "Aftershock". *Classic Rock*: 57.

[12] Frame, Pete (1983). *Rock Family Trees*. Omnibus Press. ISBN 978-0-7119-0465-1.

[13] Make 'em deaf forever Archived 26 May 2015 at the Wayback Machine

[14] Burridge, Alan *Illustrated Collector's Guide to Motorhead* Published: 1995, Collector's Guide Publishing ISBN 0-9695736-2-6. Used for the line up numbers as listed in albums in band members section as well as information on recordings and performances.

[15] *White Line Fever*, p. 101.

[16] Bell, Max (19 September 2004). "Paradise recalled". *The Independent*.

[17] Burridge, Alan (April 1991). "Motörhead". *Record Collector* (140): 16–22.

[18] Adams, Bret. "*Ace of Spades* DVD Review". AllMusic. Retrieved 14 April 2008.

[19] Dansby, Andrew. Motorhead Roll On. *Rolling Stone*. 23 August 2002. Retrieved 9 October 2006.

[20] *White Line Fever*, pp. 112–113.

[21] "Motorhead Official Charts". Official Charts Company. Retrieved 17 May 2015.

[22] "BFI – Film & TV Database – ROCKSTAGE". British Film Institute. Retrieved 5 July 2009.

[23] "Dr Rock VS Lemmy interview 19 July 2004". PlayLouder. Archived from the original on 5 December 2006. Retrieved 27 February 2007.

[24] Konow, David (2002). *Bang Your Head*. Three Rivers Press, c2002. p. 226 has "Motorhead's signature song, Ace of Spades". ISBN 0-609-80732-3.

[25] Christe, Ian (2004). *Sound of the Beast*. Allison & Busby. ISBN 0-7490-8351-4.

[26] Q & A Session with Lemmy. *Motörhead official website*. Retrieved 11 February 2007

[27] "The Young Ones – Bambi". *Transcription of the "Young Ones" episode "Bambi" as it aired on American MTV in the mid-'80s*. Retrieved 10 February 2007.

[28] "Eat the Rich (1987)". Internet Movie Database. Retrieved 2 March 2007.

[29] *White Line Fever*, p. 228.

[30] "Motörhead tour date compendium". 1991 1992 1993 1994 1995 1996 1997 1998 1999 2000 2001 2002 2003 2004 2005 2006 2007 2008 Motörhead official website. Retrieved 21 December 2008.

[31] *White Line Fever*, p. 247.

[32] *White Line Fever*, p. 258.

[33] *White Line Fever*, p. 265.

[34] *White Line Fever*, p. 267.

[35] *White Line Fever*, pp. 266–269.

[36] *White Line Fever*, pp. 276–277.

[37] *White Line Fever*, pp. 281–283.

[38] *White Line Fever*, pp. 284–285.

[39] "Motorhead & Sepultura @ The Octagon". BBC News South Yorkshire article. Retrieved 24 February 2007.

[40] "47th Grammy Awards – 2005". Rock on the Net archive. Retrieved 11 February 2007.

[41] "Motörhead Documentary To Air on British TV Tonight". Blabbermouth.net (Roadrunner Records). Retrieved 17 February 2007.

[42] "The Other Side". *BFI Film & TV Database*. Retrieved 17 February 2007.

[43] Rockers to sponsor under-10 team. *BBC News Lincolnshire article*. Retrieved 10 February 2007.

[44] "Neverdie Studios Presents The Queen of Sheba; International Siren Cheri London Crosses Virtual World Divide Into". Reuters. 30 September 2008. Retrieved 20 December 2008.

[45] "Now sponsored by Motörhead! – Lincolnshire Bombers:". Lincolnshire Bombers' News forum. 1 April 2009. Archived from the original on 14 May 2010. Retrieved 11 January 2010.

[46] "Tour dates added". The Damned. Retrieved 23 August 2009.

[47] "Motörhead To Enter Studio in February". Blabbermouth.net. 1 November 2009. Retrieved 1 November 2009.

[48] "Motorhead The World Is Yours UK CD ALBUM (522220)". Eil.com. Retrieved 8 July 2011.

[49] "Motorhead to Release New Album Through Magazine Publishing Deal". Spinner. 3 November 2010. Retrieved 15 July 2011.

[50] "Newswire / Future Reveals Classic Rock Presents – Motorhead – Music/Movie/Concert – Future Publishing Limited". NewswireToday. Retrieved 15 July 2011.

[51] Cardew, Ben (3 November 2010). "The Wörld is Classic Rock's, after Motörhead sign Future deal". *Music Week*. Retrieved 15 July 2011.

[52] "Motorhead Announce UK Tour". Ultimate-Guitar.com. 18 March 2010. Retrieved 23 March 2010.

[53] "Upcoming Tour Dates – Motorhead: The Official Website". Imotorhead.com. Retrieved 8 July 2011.

[54] "Blabbermouth.net – Motörhead's Slowed Down Version Of "Ace of Spades" In U.K. Beer Commercial; Video Available". Roadrunnerrecords.com. Retrieved 8 July 2011.

[55] "Lemmy – Rocking Onto DVD & Bluray". Lemmy-movie.co.uk. 24 January 2011. Retrieved 8 July 2011.

[56] "New Video | Motothead- Get Back in Line". Metal Call-Out. Retrieved 6 December 2010.

[57] "New Interview | Mikkey Dee, Motöthead – Interview". VerdamMnis Magazine. Retrieved December 2010.

[58] Bhamra, Satvir. "Motorhead, Mastodon, In Flames and Parkway Drive join Sonisphere line-up". Amplified.tv. Retrieved 8 July 2011.

[59] Sara Schaefer. "Motorhead Performs 'Ace of Spades' – Music". Late Night with Jimmy Fallon. Retrieved 8 July 2011.

[60] "BLABBERMOUTH.NET – Former Motörhead Guitarist Würzel Reportedly Dies at 61". Roadrunnerrecords.com. Retrieved 15 July 2011.

[61] Spielplan / Bands — Rock am Ring 2012 — Offizielle Festival Homepage. Rock-am-ring.com. Retrieved 17 April 2012.

[62] Spielplan / Bands – Rock im Park 2012 – Offizielle Festival Homepage. Rock-im-park.com. Retrieved 17 April 2012.

[63] "Interview: Lemmy". Classic Rock Revisited.

[64] "Fifth annual Mayhem Festival slams into White River Amphitheatre July 3". Auburn Reporter.

[65] "MOTÖRHEAD Preparing To Enter Studio". Blabbermouth.net.

[66] "MOTÖRHEAD Recording New Album". Blabbermouth.net.

[67] "MotÖrhead: Rescheduled European Tour Canceled". Blabbermouth.net. Retrieved 19 August 2015.

[68] "NME News Motorhead confirmed for Coachella Festival in California". *NME*. Retrieved 19 August 2015.

[69] "Motörhead". Retrieved 19 August 2015.

[70] Motörhead official website / Tour Dates

[71] "Motörhead". Retrieved 19 August 2015.

[72] "Lemmy: Motörhead Will 'Probably' Begin Work On New Album In January. New album release expected fall 2015.". Blabbermouth.net. 1 October 2014. Retrieved 1 October 2014.

[73] "In The Studio!". *imotorhead.com*. 25 February 2015. Retrieved 27 February 2015.

[74] "Motorhead in the Studio Working on New Album: Video Footage, Photos". *blabbermouth.net*. 27 February 2015. Retrieved 28 February 2015.

[75] "Motörhead – Bad Magic on Amazon". Amazon.com. 3 June 2015. Retrieved 11 June 2015.

[76] "Motörhead To Release 'Bad Magic' In August". *Blabbermouth.net*. 4 June 2015. Retrieved 11 June 2015.

[77] "Motorhead cut tonight's Austin show short due to illness (pics & video) (photos by Tim Griffin) / Motorhead – 2015 Tour Dates". *brooklynvegan.com*. 2 September 2015. Retrieved 9 October 2015.

[78] "Motorhead cancels Aztec Theatre concert (by Hector Saldana)". *mysanantonio.com*. 2 September 2015. Retrieved 9 October 2015.

[79] "Motörhead Setlist at Emo's, Austin, TX, USA on 1 September 2015". *setlist.fm*. 2 September 2015. Retrieved 9 October 2015.

[80] "Motorhead cancels US show amid health fears for frontman Lemmy". *The Guardian*. 3 September 2015. Retrieved 4 September 2015.

[81] "Motorhead Cancel Another Date as Lemmy Recovers From Altitude Sickness – "Lemmy will resume duties the moment he is properly rested and firing on all cylinders again," band writes (by Kory Grow)". *Rolling Stone*. 2 September 2015. Retrieved 9 October 2015.

[82] "Motorhead Cancel Gigs Over Lemmy's Altitude Sickness – "The Rocky Mountain High has affected Lemmy... It's been quite a while since Lemmy was this 'high' in the US," band says in statement (by Daniel Kreps)". *Rolling Stone*. 30 August 2015. Retrieved 9 October 2015.

[83] "Riot Fest Denver day 1: Iggy Pop, partial NWA reunion, more (by Andrew Sacher)". *brooklynvegan.com*. 29 August 2015. Retrieved 9 October 2015.

[84] "Motörhead Setlist at Motörboat 2015 30 September". *setlist.fm*. 2 October 2015. Retrieved 9 October 2015.

[85] "Motörhead Setlist at Motörboat 2015 1 October". *setlist.fm*. 2 October 2015. Retrieved 9 October 2015.

[86] "See Motorhead, Slayer, Anthrax Rock High Seas on Motorboat 2015 – Lemmy and friends set sail for a metalhead's dream cruise". *Rolling Stone*. 7 October 2015. Retrieved 9 October 2015.

[87] Erlewine, Stephen. "Motörhead Biography". AllMusic. Retrieved 11 February 2007.

[88] Duerden, Nick (28 November 2010). "Growing old disgracefully: Lemmy on heartbreak, ageing and his penchant for Nazi memorabilia". *The Independent*. Retrieved 4 May 2014.

[89] "Motörhead-Chef Lemmy Kilmister: "Ich kann Heavy Metal nicht leiden"". *Der Spiegel* (in German). 27 July 2014.

[90] See the notes for The Damned's *Smash It Up – The Anthology 1976–1987*

[91] "*Motorhead Interview with Lemmy 6-20-2000* Ear Candy interview.". Retrieved 6 May 2007.

[92] "MK Magazine Interviews: Motorhead". *MK Magazine*. Retrieved 26 June 2007.

[93] See the notes for the 1999 Castle Records reissue of *Ace of Spades*

[94] We Do Not Bend The Knee. Motorhead Interview. Motorhead.ru. Retrieved 2014-04-11.

[95] "Motorhead Madman". *The Wave Magazine*. Archived from the original on 16 December 2006. Retrieved 12 February 2007.

[96] Hepworth, David (21 January 2010). "Here's a bloke whose record collection may well be worth as much as your house". *The Word magazine*. Retrieved 14 February 2010.

[97] "Interview with Motörhead Artist Joe Petagno". *Motörhead official website*. Retrieved 11 February 2007. Inspiration for War-Pig is also covered in the "About Joe Petagno" interview section on *Inferno 30th Anniversary edition bonus DVD*, SPV69748.

[98] *About Joe Petagno*, interview section with Joe Petagno, bonus DVD with *Inferno 30th Anniversary edition* SPV69748.

[99] "Motorblog: September 2007". *Joe Petagno – Lemmy's Statement*. Alan Burridge blog archive. September 2009. Retrieved 9 April 2009.

2.45.9 Sources

- Lemmy, *White Line Fever*. Simon & Schuster (2002). ISBN 0-684-85868-1.

- Buckley, Peter (2003). *The Rough Guide to Rock*. London: Rough Guides. ISBN 1-85828-201-2.

2.45.10 Further reading

- Harry Shaw, *Lemmy ... In his own words*. Omnibus Press 2002. ISBN 0-7119-9109-X.
- Alan Burridge, *Motorhead Live To Win*. Cleopatra 2012. ISBN 0-9636193-8-1.
- Alistair Lavers, *Treasure Trove*. Matador 2015. ISBN 978-1784624-989.

2.45.11 External links

- Official website
- Motörhead at AllMusic
- Interview with Lemmy 12/8/2010 German/Swiss/Austrian culture channel 3sat "Kulturzeit"
- Article on Motorhead in Sabotage Times

2.46 Nicky Moore

Nicky Moore (born 1952, England) is an English heavy metal singer, who is best known as a former member of the British band Samson. He replaced Bruce Dickinson who left the band to join Iron Maiden in 1982. Moore left Samson in the late 1980s and rejoined in the late 1990s.

After his initial departure from Samson, Moore sang in the band Mammoth, which also featured former Gillan bassist John McCoy. Mammoth released two albums before splitting up in 1989.[1]

In 2006, Moore teamed up with former Nazareth guitarist Manny Charlton and three musicians from the Swedish band Locomotive Breath to record an album under the band name "From Behind".[2] The band performed at the Sweden Rock Festival on 9 June 2006.

Since 1994, Moore has been working with his own band, Nicky Moore and the Blues Corporation, who were voted 'Top Live Blues Band' by BBC Radio 2 listeners in the year 2000.[3]

2.46.1 Discography

Hackensack

- "Moving On" (Single with "River Boat" B-Side, 1972)
- *Up the Hard Way* (1974)
- *Live - The Hard Way* (Recorded in 1973, released in 1996)
- *Give It Some* (Recorded between 1969 & 1972, released in 1997)

Tiger

- "Crazy" / "Bloody Blue Monday" (Single, 1975)
- "I Am an Animal" (Single, 1975)
- *Tiger* (1976)
- *Goin' Down Laughing* (1976)

Samson

- "Life on the Run" (1982) (Single)
- "Losing My Grip" (1982) (Single)
- *Before the Storm* (1982)
- "Red Skies" (1982) (Single)
- "Are You Ready" (1984) (Single)
- *Don't Get Mad, Get Even* (1984)
- "The Fight Goes On" (1984) (Single)
- *Thank You & Goodnight...* (1985) (Live)
- "No Turning Back" / "Reach Out To Love" (1984) (Single)
- *Joint Forces* (1986)
- *Pillars of Rock* (1990) (Compilation)
- *The Masters* (1998) (Compilation)
- *Test of Time* (1999) (Compilation and unreleased material)
- *Past, Present & Future* (1999) (Compilation)
- *Wacken 2000 Special Report* (2001) (V.A. DVD, live)
- *Live in London 2000* (2001) (Live)
- *There & back* (2001) (Compilation of unreleased versions, mixes & outtakes)
- *Riding with the Angels - The Anthology* (2002) (Compilation)
- *P.S....* (2006)
- *Tomorrow & Yesterday* (2006) (Compilation)

Mammoth

- *Fatman* (EP, 1987)
- "Can't Take the Hurt" (Single, 1987)
- "All the Days" (Single, 1988)
- *Mammoth* (1989)
- *XXXL* (1997)
- *The Collection* (2001) (Compilation)
- *Larger & Live* (2003) (Compilation)
- *Leftovers, Relics & Rarities* (2007) (Compilation)

Mister Big Stuff

- ??? (1994)

From Behind

- *Game Over* (2006)

The Nicky Moore Band

- *1981 The Year of the Lie*
- ??? (Tape, ????)
- ??? (Tape, ????)

Nicky Moore's Blues Corporation

- *Just Got Back* (1994)
- *Holding On* (1995)
- *Take Me Home* (1997)
- *300 Pounds of Joy* (1999)
- *Old, New, Borrowed & Blue* (2000)
- *Live* (2001)
- *Hog on a Log* (2006)
- *The Whale & the Waah!* (TBA)

Collaborations

- Electric Sun - *Beyond the Astral Skies* (1985, background vocals on "The Night the Master Comes")
- Gerry Rafferty - *On a Wing and a Prayer* (1993, background vocals)
- Spearfish - *Back for the Future* (Guest vocals on "In the Ghetto")

Contributions

- "Ain't No Love in the Heart of the City" (Included on various compilations)
- "And That Ain't All" (Included on various compilations)
- "Gimme All Your Lovin'" (Included on *Gimme All Your Top - A Tribute to ZZ Top*)
- "Honky Tonk Women" (Included on "A Tribute to The Rolling Stones")
- "Is This Love" (Included on various compilations)
- "Let Me Be Your Dog" (Included on *Another Hair of the Dog - A Tribute to Nazareth*)
- "Only You Can Rock Me" (Included on *Only UFO Can Rock Me - A Tribute to UFO*)
- "Ruby Tuesday" (Included on *A Tribute to The Rolling Stones*)
- "Tonight's the Night" (Included on various compilations)
- "Whiskey in the Jar" (Included on *Top Musicians Play Thin Lizzy*)
- "You Wear It Well" (Included on various compilations)

2.46.2 See also

- List of New Wave of British Heavy Metal bands

2.46.3 References

[1] "MusicMight :: Artists :: MAMMOTH". Rockdetector.com. Retrieved 2014-08-02.

[2] "From Behind - Game Over CD Album". Cduniverse.com. Retrieved 2014-08-02.

[3] "Interview - Nicky Moore". Earlyblues.com. Retrieved 2014-08-02.

2.46.4 External links

- Nicky Moore's official website

- Nicky Moore at MySpace

2.47 Nightwing (band)

Nightwing is a British rock band, originally formed in 1978 as "Gordon and Friends" by bassist Gordon Rowley (formerly of Strife) and keyboardist Kenny Newton.[2]

The band's lineup changed fairly consistently since its inception and at one point included vocalist Max Bacon (pre-Bronz), who would go on to be in the supergroup GTR and Dave Evans (formerly of the band Days of Grace and not to be confused with the first AC/DC singer of the same name). Some of the band's longer-lasting members include founding members Rowley, Newton and guitarists Alec Johnson and Glynn Porrino and drummer Steve Bartley.

Nightwing disbanded in 1987, with Rowley and long-time drummer Steve Bartley, moving on to a short-lived band called "Razorback" (not to be confused with Razorback) before reforming in the 1990s.[3] Their most recent album, *8472*, was released in 2008 by Timeline Records and as of this writing the band continues to tour.

2.47.1 Formation, Something In The Air and Black Summer

Nightwing was formed when Gordon Rowley wanted to return to music, having left Strife due to heart attack. Gordon had done some session work between leaving Strife, also turning down a spot in Rainbow in favor of forming his own band.[4] This lead to the formation of Nightwing, with keyboard player Kenny Newton, guitarist Alec Johnson as the core early lineup. With a variety of session drummers, including Steve Bartley, joining Rowley, Newton and Johnson, *Something in the Air* was released in 1981, with "Barrel of Pain" by Graham Nash taken as a single release.[5] For the tour and the following album, *Black Summer*, Steve Bartley became the full-time drummer for the band, the group playing Redding Festival[6] and supporting Gillan.

In 1982, the lineup of Rowley, Newton, Johnson and Bartley recorded and released *Black Summer*[7] which did particularly well in Eastern Europe, where the band would do an extensive tour.[8]

2.47.2 Max Bacon, Stand Up and Be Counted and My Kingdom Come

For their third album, Nightwing incorporated a lead vocalist into their lineup, vocal duties previously being shared predominantly between Rowley and Newton. Max Bacon joined the band in 1983 and Nightwing released *Stand Up and Be Counted*,[9] from which "Treading Water" was released as a single.[10]

For 1984's *My Kingdom Come* the band had decided to do a cover of "Cell 151", written by Steve Hackett (of Genesis).[11] Hackett decided to join Nightwing in the studio to co-produced the single "Night of Mystery", playing additional guitar on that track as well.[12] The album cover was painted by Roger Dean[13] who had also painted album covers for Yes and Asia.

After the album was completed and before the resulting tour, Max Bacon left Nightwing with Steve Hackett to form the supergroup GTR with Steve Howe of Yes fame. Alec Johnson would leave too, causing Nightwing to be down a guitarist and singer before the tour was to begin.

2.47.3 Dave Evans, Glynn Porrino, Night of Mystery - Alive! Alive! and Nightwing VI

For the *My Kingdome Come* tour, Nightwing enlisted Dave Evans on vocals and Glynn Porrino on lead guitar. The band would also record their first and only live album, *Night of Mystery - Alive! Alive!* on this tour from concerts in Yugoslavia and West Germany.[14]

Nightwing returned to the studio in 1986 for their fifth studio album, sixth in total, named *Nightwing VI*, which also featured an album cover painted by Porrino and saxophone parts also by Porrino.[15] This would be Nightwing's last studio recording until 1996 (the last full album until 2008). Tensions in the group lead to Dave Evans and Kenny Newton leaving the band just after it's completion, Kerry Beswick having also played some keyboards on the album. The band would tour in 1986/1987 as a four-piece with Rowley, Bartley, Porrino and Beswick,[16] before disbanding completely later in the year.

2.47.4 1996 Reunion, Natural Survivors, 2006 reunion and 8472

After Nightwing split up in 1987, Gordon Rowley and Steve Bartley formed Razorback with Del Bonham of Stray.[17] The sessions for this band were never officially released, however in 1996, Gordon Rowley reunited Nightwing, bringing together Porrino, Newton and drummer Barry

Roberts to record another three tracks, one of which was *Mercenary Man* which had been first written by Bartley in a band called "The Skeleton Crew",[18] before being recorded by Razorback, before finally being recorded by Nightwing, along with two new compositions, one written by Porrino and an instrumental by Rowley, was put on a re-release of *Nightwing VI* named *Natural Survivors* which featured different artwork, the old cover being used for the back.[19]

Another song, *Out in the Cold* was recorded during these sessions, but didn't make the re-release, latter being put on the *79 to 86* compilation album[20] which was released when the band reformed again in 2006, with the lineup of Rowley, Bartley, Beswick and Porrino, with Roberts providing additional drums and Tony Reid (formerly of Strife) also playing additional guitar. This lineup would go on to record their most recent album *8472* in 2008.[21]

2.47.5 Personnel

Timeline

2.47.6 Discography

- *Something in the Air* (1981)
- *Black Summer* (1982)
- *Stand Up and Be Counted* (1983)
- *My Kingdom Come* (1984)
- *A Night of Mystery – Alive! Alive!* (live album) (1985)
- *Nightwing VI* (re-released in 1996 as *Natural Survivors* with some tracks from the Razorback sessions re-recorded by the band) (1986)
- *Nightwing* (compilation – Long Island Records) (1996)
- *79 to 86* (live) (compilation) (2006)
- *8472* (2008)

2.47.7 See also

- List of New Wave of British Heavy Metal bands

2.47.8 References

[1] "Nightwing - discography, line-up, biography, interviews, photos". Spirit-of-metal.com. Retrieved 2011-03-12.

[2] "Nightwing". Nightwing.uk.com. Retrieved 2011-03-12.

[3] "Nightwing". Dinosaurdays. Retrieved 2011-03-12.

[4] http://www.butterworth01.f2s.com/afterstrife.html

[5] http://www.discogs.com/Nightwing-Barrel-Of-Pain-Nightwing/release/6362564

[6] https://upload.wikimedia.org/wikipedia/en/4/42/Reading-81-poster.jpg

[7] http://www.discogs.com/Nightwing-Black-Summer/release/2971836

[8] http://www.butterworth01.f2s.com/afterstrife.html

[9] http://www.discogs.com/Nightwing-Stand-Up-And-Be-Counted/release/2260431

[10] http://www.discogs.com/Nightwing-Treading-Water/master/347829

[11] http://www.discogs.com/Nightwing-My-Kingdom-Come/release/2226384

[12] http://www.discogs.com/Nightwing-Night-Of-Mystery/release/5074343

[13] http://www.rogerdean.com/picture-database/#gallery/2635/789/cart

[14] http://www.discogs.com/Nightwing-A-Night-Of-Mystery-Alive-Alive/release/4765254

[15] http://www.discogs.com/Nightwing-Nightwing-VI/release/6666706

[16] https://www.youtube.com/watch?v=Fe5fdQoeaRs

[17] http://www.butterworth01.f2s.com/afterstrife.html

[18] https://www.youtube.com/watch?v=w3EDymaiRj0

[19] http://www.discogs.com/Nightwing-Natural-Survivors/release/6759207

[20] http://www.spirit-of-metal.com/album-groupe-Nightwing-nom_album-'79_to_'86_(Live)-l-en.html

[21] http://www.spirit-of-metal.com/album-groupe-Nightwing-nom_album-8472-l-en.html

2.47.9 External links

- http://www.nightwing.uk.com/
- http://www.tartareandesire.com/bands/Nightwing/5040/
- http://www.butterworth01.f2s.com/afterstrife.html

2.48 Pagan Altar

Pagan Altar is a doom metal band from England.

2.48.1 Biography

Pagan Altar was formed in 1978 by Alan and Terry Jones. Alongside Witchfinder General, they are one of the few NWOBHM bands to play doom metal.[1] The band's concerts are characterised by moody, epic and heavy music, blended with stage effects which accentuate their interest in occult themes.

Pagan Altar's only release from the NWOBHM era was an independent, self-released, self-titled cassette (which was bootlegged in later years). Their debut album was officially re-released on Oracle Records in 1998, retitled "Volume 1".

The group reformed in 2004 to re-record an album of previously unreleased material which had been written during their original tenure as a band. The resulting album, "Lords of Hypocrisy", met with a positive reception from fans, and a third full-length album duly followed in 2006, entitled "Mythical and Magical".

In 2008, Pagan Altar co-headlined the "Metal Brew" Festival in Mill Hill, alongside Cloven Hoof.[2] Both bands also performed at the "British Steel IV" Festival at the Camden Underworld in 2009.[3] Pagan Altar returned to headline the "British Steel V" Festival in April 2011[4] and the "Live Evil" Festival in October 2011.

In 2012, Pagan Altar began work on their next album "Never Quite Dead", in a purpose-built recording studio in the back garden of vocalist Terry Jones's home. The 2013 lineup included: Dean Alexander on drums and William Gallagher on bass guitar.

On May 15, 2015, Terry Jones died of cancer.[5] The band had finished recording their upcoming album and was in its final mastering stage.

2.48.2 Line-up

- Alan Jones - guitar
- Dean Alexander - drums
- William "WillyG" Gallagher - bass guitar

2.48.3 Discography

Albums

- *Volume 1* CD (1998)
- *Lords of Hypocrisy* CD (2004)
- *Mythical and Magical* CD (2006)

EP

- *The Time Lord* (2004, re-released as a special edition in 2012)

Singles

- Pagan Altar - *Walking in the Dark* / Jex Thoth - *Stone Evil* (Split single, 2007)
- Pagan Altar - *Portrait of Dorian Gray* / Mirror of Deception - *Beltaine's Joy* (*Imperial Anthems* split single, 2011)
- *Walking in the Dark / Narcissus* (2013)

Demo

- *Pagan Altar* (1982)

2.48.4 See also

- List of New Wave of British Heavy Metal bands

2.48.5 References

[1] Pagan Altar at BNR Metal

[2] http://legacy.roadrunnerrecords.com/blabbermouth.net/news.aspx?mode=Article&newsitemID=96237 Metal Brew Festival (2008) details on Blabbermouth website, 3 May 2008

[3] http://www.metalteamuk.net/review-britishsteeliv.htm British Steel IV Festival (2009) details at MTUK website, 4 April 2009

[4] http://www.rockersdigest.com/Article/362/British+Steel+Festival+V British Steel V Festival (2011) details at Rockers' Digest website, 2 April 2011

[5] http://noisey.vice.com/blog/rip-terry-jones-pagan-altar

2.48.6 External links

- Pagan Altar's official website
- Official Myspace site

2.49 Paul Di'Anno

Paul Andrews (born 17 May 1958, in Chingford, London),[1][2] better known as **Paul Di'Anno**, is an English singer best known as the first vocalist to record with heavy metal band Iron Maiden, from 1978 to 1981.

In his post-Maiden career, Di'Anno has issued numerous albums over the years, as both a solo artist and as a member of such bands as Gogmagog, Di'Anno's Battlezone, Praying Mantis, Killers and Rockfellas.

2.49.1 Career

Iron Maiden (1978–81)

Paul Di'Anno and Steve Harris of Iron Maiden supporting Judas Priest on their British Steel Tour, 1980.

Di'Anno grew up in Chingford, England – spending his teenage years singing in various rock bands and working as a butcher and chef. He became the band's singer after the departure of the very unpredictable Dennis Wilcock, who had pressured Iron Maiden founder and bassist Steve Harris into firing every member of the band (including Dave Murray), before becoming fed up himself. According to Iron Maiden's *The History of Iron Maiden – Part 1: The Early Days* DVD, he was introduced to the band by drummer Doug Sampson, an old friend of Harris' from his days in the band 'Smiler'. It was around this time that he first adopted the stage name Di'Anno, which he would later use to claim Italian descent.[3][4] Their first audition with Rod Smallwood reputedly failed when Paul was arrested for showing off his pocket-knife in public. 1980's self-titled release quickly became acknowledged as a classic of its genre, as the band merged punk's energy with metal's riffs and progressive rock complexity, serving as the blueprint for such future genres as thrash metal and speed metal. 1981 saw the release of their second album, *Killers*, as well as a stopgap live EP, *Maiden Japan*. After having cancelled gigs due to Di'Anno's inability and, at times, lack of desire to perform, which had resulted from cocaine abuse and heavy drinking, Iron Maiden decided that to progress they would have to find a singer capable of withstanding the rigours of being on tour. They found a replacement in former Samson frontman Bruce Dickinson.

In 1981, Di'Anno left Iron Maiden after a meeting with the band and their manager Rod Smallwood. In Di'Anno's words: "It's like having Mussolini and Adolf Hitler run your band. Because it is Rod Smallwood and Steve Harris and that's it. There can't be anyone else and my character is too strong for that so me an' Steve was always fighting".[5] Di'Anno was paid out by Smallwood at the time of his departure and does not receive royalties on Iron Maiden songs.

Di'Anno (1983–85)

Di'Anno was the first project by Paul Di'Anno after he was fired from Iron Maiden. This group was originally called Lonewolf but after disagreement with a group already called Lone Wolf, they changed their name and ended up recording only one album under the simple moniker of Di'Anno. On the tour Paul refused to play any Iron Maiden songs (much to the dismay of the crowd), playing only their own songs and a few other covers (most notably Van Halen's version of The Kinks' "You Really Got Me" and "Don't Let Me Be Misunderstood"). Having little success, the six-piece band disbanded shortly after they were done touring. The only other recordings available from this band are a single of "Heartuser", a Japanese single of "Flaming Heart" and a Sweden-only VHS release called *Live at the Palace* (also available on DVD as *Di'Anno Live from London*). During the latter performance, the band played an unreleased song entitled "Spiritual Guidance", which Paul told the audience would be on the band's forthcoming album. This album was never recorded.

Last known line-up:

- Paul Di'Anno – lead vocals
- Lee Slater – guitars, vocals

- P.J. Ward – guitars, vocals
- Kevin Browne – bass, vocals
- Mark Venables – keyboards, vocals

Gogmagog (1985)

In 1985, Di'Anno was to work on a project with a number of hired musicians. The group, called "Gogmagog" (see the Biblical book Ezekiel 38:1–2), was put together by DJ and record producer Jonathan King. Gogmagog was a rock opera project. King brought in Di'Anno, drummer Clive Burr, guitarists Janick Gers and Pete Willis along with Neil Murray on bass. Russ Ballard wrote the title song with King writing the other two songs and the 3 track EP called "I Will Be There" was recorded. However, although much praised by rock critics, the EP did not chart and the group disbanded.

Battlezone (1985–89, 1998)

After the breakup of his self-titled band, Di'Anno formed Strike with DeeRal (guitar) who recruited drummer Bob Falck (who had used the name Sid Falck while playing drums in Overkill) and the Hurley brothers John (2nd guitar) and Chaz (bass). The project was eventually named Battlezone, after a name straight from a comic book,[6] upon the vocalist's return to Britain in 1985.[7] Paul had previously known guitarists John Wiggins and John Hurley from bands such as Deep Machine and Iron Cross.[6]

The band's initial line-up comprised Di'Anno, guitarists John Wiggins & John Hurley, bassist Laurence Kessler and Adam Parsons on drums. The latter had gone under the stage name A.D. Dynamite whilst in Aunt May. However, Parsons left shortly after to replace Vince Hoare in the London-based glam band Belladonna (formed by former Hell's Belles vocalist Paul Quigley, with Paul Lewis, Jeff Fox and Neil Criss)[8] and Falck reappeared on the scene in time to record the band's first album *written by Di'Anno & DeeRal Fighting Back*. 1986 also saw the enrollment of former Lonewolf and Tokyo Blade guitarist John Wiggins.

Battlezone performed a club tour of America in 1987 to promote the début *Fighting Back*, but musical differences, arguments and physical fights within the band led to the departure of John Hurley and Bob Falck after the first tour. According to Di'Anno's book *The Beast*, Hurley had become an "egomaniac" and the drummer Falck a "liability", so they were thrown out the band. Their places were taken by ex-Persian Risk members Graham Bath and Steve Hopgood respectively, following the tour's completion.

The second album to be released was entitled *Children of Madness* and achieved considerable commercial success. It featured a track entitled "Metal Tears", which is about a guy who was unable to have a steady relationship and built a female robot who he subsequently fell in love with. The original idea came from a book titled "Clone".[9] However, the track received criticism from the media for being very similar to a track (entitled "London") on Queensrÿche's *Rage for Order* album.

Guitarist Graham Bath, who had been recruited to play second guitar, wasn't enthusiastic about touring, so he was fired from the band. Peter West, the bassist, recommended a replacement Alf Batz, who joined just in time to go to New York for the video shoot."[9] The video for "I Don't Wanna Know" was played in rotation on MTV in the US.

Drugs and infighting again put a strain on the band. Towards the end of the final tour, most members had quit leaving Di'Anno to complete the tour with a backing band in order to fulfil his contract.

Subsequently, American guitarist Randy Scott, along with Dave Harman on guitar and Eddie Davidson on bass, signed up with Battlezone. However, the band were without proper management and disbanded shortly after.

Following the breakup of Battlezone, Di'Anno and Hopgood formed the power metal band Killers releasing four albums. Hurley would later form glam rock band L.O. Girls and release the "Twelve Bore Honeymoon" single in 1990 and "Just Can't Say I Love You" in 1993. During 1990, Di'Anno fronted Praying Mantis for a tour of Japan, which was recorded for the subsequent *Live at Last* album release with ex-Iron Maiden guitarist Dennis Stratton. Wiggins joined a reformed Tokyo Blade in 1995.

By 1998, Di'Anno had resurrected the name Battlezone. Joining him were Wiggins and fellow ex-Tokyo Blade members bassist Colin Riggs and drummer Marc Angel. Second guitars were supplied by the Brazilian Paulo Turin. This line-up cut the album *Feel My Pain*, released by the fledgling "Zoom Club" label. Working titles for the album included "Spoon Face" and "Smack", both containing references to heroin use. The album had a heavier edge compared to the first two Battlezone albums. The band undertook a sold-out Brazilian tour in January 1998, with erstwhile Killers colleagues bassist Gavin Cooper and guitarist Nick Burr joining on this South American tour.

The band toured Brazil in the same year playing a three-week tour to sold-out audiences up to 6000 fans a night. Being brought back down to earth, Battlezone upon their return home put on a gig at the Walthamstow Royal Standard with an audience of only a hundred or so and a gig at JB's Dudley in the West Midlands attracting fewer than a dozen fans. A live track from the Walthamstow gig later appeared on a compilation of all three Battlezone albums, entitled *Cessation of Hostilities*. Ex-Battlezone bassist Gavin

Cooper joined Lionsheart in December 2004, then moved onto Statetrooper in May 2005. The bassist subsequently joined the ranks of Magnum singer Bob Catley's solo band for UK dates in April 2006.

In mid-2008, a Battlezone compilation entitled *The Fight Goes On* was released as on the Phantom Sound & Vision label as a 3-CD box set featuring all 3 Battlezone studio albums.

Last known line-up:

- Paul Di´Anno – Vocals
- Johnny "Bravo" Wiggins – Guitars
- Paulo Turin – Guitars
- Colin Riggs – Bass
- Mark Angel – Drums

Former/past member(s):

- DeeRal – Guitars
- John Hurley – Guitars
- Graham Bath – Guitars
- Alf Batz – Guitars
- Randy Scott – Guitars
- Dave Harman – Guitars
- Chaz Hurley – Bass
- Peter Vester – Bass
- Eddie Davidson – Bass
- Bob "Sid" Falck – Drums
- J. Michael D.- Drums
- Steve Hopgood – Drums

Praying Mantis (1990)

After being dropped by BMG, Praying Mantis disbanded. Then, in a Spinal Tap-ish twist of fate, Paul Di'Anno called Dennis Stratton in 1989, about the Japanese wanting to have a ten-year anniversary of the New Wave of British Heavy Metal. The band found themselves enjoying a renaissance in Tokyo, Japan, prompting a reformation and tour in April 1990, which yielded the *Live at Last* LP.[10]

Killers (1990–97, 2001–03 2013–)

Killers was formed back in the summer of 1991. Cliff Evans was living in New York with Arnie Goodman, the manager of Fastway. Steve Hopgood, who played in Battlezone with Di'Anno previously, called Evans and outlined his plans for a new band. Di'Anno and Hopgood flew over to New York from the U.K. where they formed a band.

Within a few days, Killers had hired John Gallagher (from Raven) to play bass on a short-term basis. Former member of [(Drive She Said)] and New York session player Ray Detone was brought in on second guitar.

Shortly afterward, a live album called *Assault on South America* was recorded, featuring a number of Iron Maiden and Battlezone tracks and covers of "We Will Rock You" and "Smoke on the Water". This was funded by Rock in Rio promoter Carlos Genesio and to be released primarily for the South American market.[11] "Recorded in Brazil, Argentina and Venezuela in Summer of 1993" is splashed on the back cover. However, according to John Gallagher, the South American tour fell thorough so the entire album was recorded on a mobile recording truck in New York.[12] Later, a Canada-based record company called Magnetic Air Productions issued a pirate (bootleg) release worldwide, under a different cover, with no royalties being paid to the band.

Killers then played 2 days of showcases at Arnie Goodman's New York City studio for several major record companies including Virgin, EMI, Sony and BMG. Representatives flew into New York from all over the world to see Killers play. They played only Iron Maiden songs because the band had not written any material. Maiden songs played included "Phantom of the Opera" and "Wrathchild" which evidently impressed a BMG representative enough to give the band a $250,000 contract. BMG were unaware that these songs had been recorded previously.

Once Killers had the record deal, they started to write the first album entitled *Murder One*. Rob Fraboni was recruited to produce the record. The band moved to Binghamton, where they stayed in a motel in which the owner had a set up rehearsal studio. The album was written in about in two weeks. Fraboni then took Killers to White Crow Audio (Burlington, Vermont) to record the drums which took about half a day. Finally, vocals and final mixing were performed at The Powerstation in New York.

Nick Burr left Killers after the completion of *Murder One* and was replaced by former Battlezone and Persian Risk guitarist Graham Bath. For the next 18 months the band toured around the world playing to fans all over Europe, Japan and coast to coast across the USA.

After the tour of *Murder One*, Killers returned to the

U.K. while Di'Anno stayed in the U.S. Around this time, Di'Anno married an English girl, whom he flew in to New York. Drugs and alcohol took their toll and the marriage quickly fell apart. Di'Anno left New York and moved in with his new American girlfriend in L.A. A fight between him and her involving a knife caught the attention of the police, who came into the apartment and arrested him for spousal abuse, cocaine possession and firearms offences. After a court appearance, he was sentenced to spend four months in an L.A. jail and Di'Anno was branded by the judge as a 'menace to society'. It was here that Di'Anno began writing songs for the next Killers album and posting tapes back and forth to the UK, where the band were now living.

Di'Anno returned to the UK after being deported. It was here that the band was already signed to Bleeding Hearts records located in Newcastle, where they recorded their second studio album. It was entitled *Menace to Society*. However, with a Pantera-like style it was poorly received by many critics with the exception of *Metal Hammer* magazine in Germany who voted it as the "Best New Album" for that year.

By 2003, Di'Anno and Cliff Evans went on tour as the only original members of Killers remaining. Di'Anno hired new musicians whom he remembered from touring in Germany and Austria. Marcus Thurston joined the band as second guitarist, Darayus Kaye took over bass duties and Pete Newdeck on drums. Steve Hopgood had to retire as he developed tinnitus in his ears. The guitarist Graham Bath damaged his hands from playing so much over the years and developed arthritis.[13] According to Di'Anno, he wanted Clive Burr (ex-Iron Maiden) on drums, but he couldn't get to rehearsals in time. Later on, Burr was to become severely ill from multiple sclerosis.

By 2004, Killers had disbanded. Cliff Evans, the former Killers guitarist and last original member of the band apart from Di'Anno, subsequently formed his own record company called Soundhouse Records and re-released the entire Killers back catalogue with the addition of another live album entitled *Killers Live at the Marquee* in 2008. *Murder One* album was reissued with 2 acoustic bonus tracks – "Wrathchild" and "Dreamkeeper". Following this, Paul Di'Anno made both Killers studio albums available for download free of charge through his own website. Following legal action, Evans was forced to cease selling any Killers material on his label.

In December 2013, Paul Di'Anno and Cliff Evans announced that the band would regroup and release a new album entitled *The Lazarus Syndrome*. Producer Phil Kinmanm who had worked on Tank's album *War Nation* was announced to be involved with the new project.

Last known line-up

- Paul Di'Anno – Vocals (Di'Anno, ex-Battlezone, ex-Gogmagog (UK), ex-Iron Maiden)
- Cliff Evans – Guitars (Chicken Shack, Headfirst, Tank)
- Graham Bath – Guitars (Persian Risk, Sphinx)
- Brad Wiseman – Bass
- Steve Hopgood – Drums (ex-Battlezone, ex-Chinatown, ex-Jagged Edge, Persian Risk, Shy, Tank, Wild)

Former/past member(s)

- John Gallagher – Bass (1991–1992) (Raven)
- Ray Ditone – Guitars (1991–1992)
- Nick Burr – Guitars (1992) (ex-Battlezone, ex-Idol Rich, ex-Tyrant, now Bad Back Band)
- Gavin Cooper – Bass (1992–1994) (ex-Battlezone)

Nomad /Di'Anno (1999–2001, 2003–08)

Following the demise of the new Battlezone unit put together in 1998, Di'Anno teamed up with expat Brazilian guitarist Paulo Turin and lived in São Paulo during 2000. A new band was created initially under the banner of "Nomad" and featured an all Brazilian line up. It was economically and logistically preferable for Di'Anno to live in Brazil during this period, in order to tour South America and release a self-produced album pleasing to that particular market. The album was distributed by Perris Records. However, complete worldwide distribution was not achieved.

The album was repackaged and released as *The Living Dead*. The package included a DVD video for the title track. This was recorded in the East London Docks and directed by Swedish director Mats Lundberg from Doom Films, who went to London to work on the concept with Di'Anno's manager Lea Hart. All of the special effects were added in Sweden and the story line was based on the lyrics and message of the song. Few previously released live Iron Maiden tracks were also added to the CD.[14]

RockFellas: 2008–10

Late 2008, Di'anno relocated to the southeast of Brazil and toured with a new band/project named RockFellas with three Brazilian musicians: Jean Dolabella (drummer) ex-Diesel/Udora/Sepultura, Marcão (guitarist) of Charlie Brown Jr. and Canisso of Raimundos/ex-Rodox, playing rock & roll and metal classics. There, he was nicknamed "Paulo Baiano" ("Paulo" = Paul in Portuguese, Baiano = Who was born in Bahia), (vfs), being the "Paulo Baiano" nickname a pun/joke, for his name, Paul Di'Anno, is pronounced in a very similar way to the nickname above.

Present

Di'Anno was, before being jailed in March 2011, recording a new solo album with Paulo Turin,[15] the guitarist who worked on *Feel My Pain* and *Nomad*. The album was being produced by Dieter Roth in his studio in Germany. However, work on the album ceased due to record company problems.

He maintained an extensive world tour schedule including two recent trips through America where traditional metal band, Icarus Witch served as both his opening and backing band. In June 2012, Paul Di'Anno was given the Freedom of The City of Bariloche in Argentina for charitable work carried out several years ago.

In 2013, Di'Anno is doing his last world tour before retiring due to a severe knee injury.

In 2014 Di'Anno sang on lead vocals on the bonus track "Fuck You All" on the album "Big Trouble" by hard rock band Hollywood Monsters. The album was released in 2014 on Mausoleum Records and features Steph Honde on vocals and guitars, Vinny Appice on drums, Tim Bogert on bass and Don Airey on keyboards.[16]

In August 2014 Di'Anno has scrapped his retirement plans and is in the process of recording a new album with his new band called Architects of Chaoz (also featuring members of Paul's longtime German touring backing group The Phantomz).[17]

2.49.2 The Beast

Di'Anno has released an autobiography titled *The Beast* (ISBN 1-904034-03-9) and has had interludes with various drugs. The book includes a chapter of stories and comments regarding Di'Anno from former bandmates including Dennis Stratton, John Wiggins and Steve Hopgood. The book features many accounts of Di'Anno's violence towards people, including women, and the explanation of his ban from America. It was controversial for these reasons.

2.49.3 Singing style

In comparison to the soaring, operatic vocals of his successor in Iron Maiden, Di'Anno is remembered for having a more guttural "punk" sound to his singing, in part because he began his singing career in punk band the Paedophiles. Though Di'Anno was able to hit high-notes, he does not typically sing in Dickinson's trademark high tenor range. He usually sang with a raspy and rougher sound, although he was capable of singing with a purer voice as demonstrated by slower numbers like "Remember Tomorrow", "Strange World" and "Prodigal Son".

Later in his career Di'Anno's style, along with his music, became darker and more aggressive as Iron Maiden evolved into a more progressive outfit.

2.49.4 Other interests

Di'Anno has had several businesses outside of the music industry, including an internet café and a hotel/restaurant in England, both of which he sold. He was last resident in Salisbury, Wiltshire.[5]

2.49.5 Personal life

In February 2011, Di'Anno was convicted on eight counts of benefit fraud for claiming more than £45,000 under false pretenses. On 11 March 2011, he was jailed for nine months at Salisbury Crown Court.[18] He has since been released early from prison, having only served two of the nine months to which he was sentenced.

Di'Anno's religious affiliation is made uncertain by his own words; he has given interviews that contradict each other on this subject, perhaps as a practical joke. He has a tattoo on the back of his head that says "666" and "GOD = SUCKER".[19] According to his autobiography, he converted to Islam in the 1990s after reading the Qur'an. However he has subsequently reversed that position: *I think religion kills everybody. I don't believe in it. ... No, my father was a Muslim, I must admit. But I don't give a fuck.*[20] In later interviews Di'Anno clarifies that he never was a true Muslim, that he never stopped drinking, but tried to become a better person by applying some of the Muslim philosophies to his life. His autobiography furthers the confusion, in various passages he claims to be Muslim, Catholic, Jewish and Aborigine.

Di'Anno has a grown up son, who lives in England.[21]

2.49.6 Band timeline

Note: List excludes Di'Anno's many guest appearances on tribute albums.

- Iron Maiden (1978–81)
- Di'Anno (1983–85)

- Gogmagog (1985)
- Paul Di'Anno's Battlezone (1986–89)
- Praying Mantis (1990)
- Killers a.k.a. Paul Di'Anno's Killers a.k.a. Paul Di' Anno & Killers (1990–97)
- The Original Iron Men (1995–96)
- Paul Di'Anno (1997)
- Paul Di'Anno's Battlezone (1997–98)
- The Almighty Inbredz (1999)
- Paul Di'Anno (1999–2000)
- Di' Anno (2000)
- Paul Di'Anno's Killers a.k.a. Paul Di' Anno & Killers (2001–03)
- Paul Di'Anno (2003–05)
- Paul Di'Anno & Maiden England (2005)
- Paul Di'Anno & Children of the Damned (2002–present)
- Paul Di' Anno & The Phantoms of the Opera (2005–2014)
- Architects of Chaoz (2014—present)

2.49.7 Discography

with Iron Maiden

- *The Soundhouse Tapes* (1979)
- *Live!! +one* (1980)
- *Iron Maiden* (1980)
- *Killers* (1981)
- *Maiden Japan* (also known as Heavy Metal Army) (1981)
- *Live at the Rainbow* (VHS, 1981)
- *The First Ten Years* (VHS, 1990)
- *From Here to Eternity* (VHS, 1992)
- *The Story So Far Part One* (Boxset, 1995)
- *Best of the Beast* (1996)
- *Eddie Head* (Boxset, 1998)
- *Eddie's Archive* (Boxset, 2002)
- *The Early Days* (DVD, 2004)

with Di'Anno

- *Live at the Palace* (VHS, 1984)
- *Di'Anno* (1984)
    - "Flaming Heart" (1984)
    - "Heartuser" (1984)
- *Nomad* (2000)
- *Live at the Palace* (DVD, 2005)

Solo

- *The World's First Iron Man* (1997)
- *As Hard as Iron* (1997)
- *Beyond the Maiden* (1999)
- *The Masters* (1999)
- *The Beast* (Live, 2001)
- *The Beast in the East* (DVD, 2003)
- *The Living Dead* (a re-release of *Nomad* with bonus tracks, 2006)
- *The Maiden Years - The Classics* (2006)
- *Iron Maiden Days and Evil Nights* (2007)
- *The Early Iron Maiden Songbook* (2010)
- *The Beast Arises* (Live, 2014)

with Battlezone

- *Fighting Back* (1986)
- *Children of Madness* (1987)
- *Warchild* (1988)
- *Feel My Pain* (1998)
- *Cessation of Hostilities* (Compilation with all three studio albums Battlezone released + Children of madness demo tracks and one new live track, 2001)
- *The Fight Goes On* (Boxset including all three Battlezone studio albums, 2008)

with Killers a.k.a. Paul Di' Anno & Killers

- *Murder One* (1992)
- *South American Assault Live* (1994)
- *Menace to Society* (1994)
- *Live* (1997)
- *New Live & Rare* (1998)
- *Killers Live at the Whiskey* (2001)
- *Screaming Blue Murder – The Very Best of Paul Di'Anno's Killers* (2002)

with Gogmagog

- *I Will Be There* EP (1985)

with Dennis Stratton

- *The Original Iron Men* (1995)
- *The Original Iron Men 2* (1996)
- *As Hard As Iron* (1996)

with Praying Mantis & Paul Di'Anno, Dennis Stratton

- *Live at Last* (1991)

with The Almighty Inbredz

- *The Almighty Inbredz* (1999)

on compilations

- *Metal for Muthas* (with Iron Maiden, 1980)
- *Kaizoku* (1989, Song: „Danger on the Street II")
- *All Stars Featuring The Best Of British Heavy Metal & Heavy Rock Musicians* (1991, Song „She is danger")
- *True Brits* (1993)
- *True Brits 2* (1994)
- *True Brits 3* (1995)
- *Rock Hard Hard Rock* (1994, Songs: „No Repair", „She goes down")
- *X-Mas: The Metal Way* (1994)
- *Killer Voices* (1995)
- *Metal Monsters* (1996)
- *Metal Christmas* a.k.a. *The 21st Century Rock Christmas Album* (1996)
- *Hard 'n' Heavy Rock* (2001, Song: „Lights Out")
- *Wacken Rocks* (2001, Song: „Wrathchild (live)")
- *Classic Rock, Classic Rockers* (2002)
- *Metal Masters – Killers* (2005, Song: „Killers")
- *Rock Hard – Das Festival* (2007, Song: „Prowler (live)")

on tribute albums

- *666 The Number One Beast* (Iron Maiden Tribute) (1999)
- *666 The Number One Beast Volume 2* (Iron Maiden Tribute) (1999)
- *The Maiden Years* (Iron Maiden Tribute) (2000)
- *Gimme all your Top* (ZZ Top Tribute) (2000)
- *The Boys are back* (Thin Lizzy Tribute) (2000)
- *Only UFO can rock me* (UFO Tribute) (2001)
- *Another Hair of the Dog* (Nazareth Tribute) (2001)
- *Numbers from the Beast – An All Stars Tribute to Iron Maiden* (2005)
- *World's Greatest Metal – Tribute to Led Zeppelin* (2006)
- *An '80s Metal Tribute to Van Halen* (2006)
- *Thriller – A Metal Tribute To Michael Jackson* (Song: "Bad") (2013)

Guest appearances

- *English Steel: Start 'em young* (1993, Song: „She goes down")
- *English Steel: Lucky Streak Vol. II* (1994, Songs: „Danger", „Dirty")
- *Aciarium: The Heavy Metal Superstars* (1996)
- *Re-Vision: Longevity* (2001)
- *Spearfish: Back, for the Future*

- *Destruction: Inventor of Evil* (2005)
- *Attick Demons: Atlantis* (2011, Song: "Atlantis")
- *Wolfpakk: Wolfpakk* (2011)[22]
- *Prassein Aloga: Midas Touch* (2011, "See the Bodies" und "Flesh of Life")[23]
- *Scelerata: The Sniper* (2012) (Guest vocals, co-writing, composing)
- *Rushmore: Kingdom Of Demons* (2013)
- *Red Dragon Cartell: Wasted* (2014)
- *Hollywood Monsters: Big Trouble* (2014, bonus track: „Fuck you all")
- *Maiden United: Prowler* (2015)

2.49.8 See also

- List of New Wave of British Heavy Metal bands
- Hollywood Monsters Official Facebook

2.49.9 References

[1] "Read more about Iron Maiden". Archived from the original on 2010-08-18.

[2] "El legendario vocalista británico Paul Di'Anno arribará hoy al Central". Uruguay: *La Republica*. 20 April 2008. Retrieved 8 June 2010.

[3] "PAUL DI'ANNO Interview". Archived from the original on 2011-07-27.

[4] "KAOS2000 Magazine interview with Paul DiAnno". Kaos2000.net. Retrieved 2014-08-01.

[5] "Interview with Paul Di'Anno in Stockholm, Sweden". Metal-Rules.com. Retrieved 2014-08-01.

[6] Di'Anno interview with Chris Welch

[7] "Artists :: BATTLEZONE". MusicMight. Retrieved 2014-08-01.

[8] "HELLSBELLES † | The 'original' British heavy metal band...". Hellsbelles.co.uk. Retrieved 2014-08-01.

[9] Di'Anno interview by Andre Verhuysen, Metal Hammer

[10] "Dennis Stratton". Praying Mantis. Retrieved 2014-08-01.

[11] "Interview: Garry Sharpe-Young". Archived from the original on 2008-02-13.

[12] "kickedintheface.com". kickedintheface.com. Retrieved 2014-08-01.

[13] "Interview with Paul Di'Anno in Stockholm, Sweden". Metal-Rules.com. Retrieved 2014-08-01.

[14] "themetalweb.com". themetalweb.com. Retrieved 2014-08-01.

[15] "Paulo Turin". Archived from the original on 2011-02-07.

[16] "Hollywood Monsters Signs With Mausoleum". Rock N Growl Records. May 5, 2014. Retrieved 18 December 2014.

[17] "Ex Iron Maiden Singer Paul Di'anno Scraps 'Retirement' Plans, Launches New Band Architects Of Chaoz". Blabbermouth.net. 2014-08-25. Retrieved 2015-07-23.

[18] "Ex-Iron Maiden singer Paul Di'Anno jailed for fraud". *BBC News*. 11 March 2007. Retrieved 11 March 2011.

[19] "maidennorway.com". maidennorway.com. Retrieved 2014-08-01.

[20] "maidennorway.com". maidennorway.com. Retrieved 2014-08-01.

[21] "Ex-Iron Maiden singer Paul Di'Anno, 52, jailed over £45k benefits swindle | Mail Online". Dailymail.co.uk. 2011-03-11. Retrieved 2014-08-01.

[22] "Wolfpakk". Wolfpakk. Retrieved 2014-08-01.

[23] "Paul Di'anno Featured On New Prassein Aloga Album". Blabbermouth.net. 2012-03-05. Retrieved 2014-08-01.

2.49.10 External links

- Paul Di'Anno at the Internet Movie Database
- Official website
- Interview at RockSomething
- Paul Di'Anno: 30 Years of the Beast

2.50 Persian Risk

Persian Risk are a heavy metal band from the New Wave of British Heavy Metal era formed in 1979 and hailing from Cardiff, Wales. The brainchild of ex-Stoned Soul Party guitarist Phil Campbell, he recruited vocalist Jon Deverill, second guitarist Dave Bell, bass player Nick Hughes, and drummer Razz. The group was active until 1986. In 2012, the band was re-activated by vocalist Carl Sentance albeit without the involvement of any other past members.

2.50.1 History

In late 1980, Deverill was headhunted by the Tygers of Pan Tang and replaced by Carl Sentance, a former band mate of Nick Hughes and Razz in Leading Star. New vocalist in place, Persian Risk issued the now highly collectible *Calling For You* b/w *Chase the Dragon* 7" in 1981 before sacking Dave Bell's replacement, Alex Lohfink, and soldiering on as a four-piece. The band made further headway by contributing the aforementioned *Calling For You* to the "Heavy Metal Heroes Vol.2" compilation (Heavy Metal Records, 1982) and a new cut, *50.000 Stallions*, to the "60 Minutes Plus" cassette compilation (Neat Records, 1982), also issued on vinyl as "All Hell Let Loose" by Neat in conjunction with Italy's Base Records label in 1983. Adding to their tally, the band followed it up with the *Ridin' High* b/w *Hurt You* 7" single through Neat, which earned Risk their strongest reviews yet.

It would turn out to be the final recording with drummer Razz who was sacked in late 1983. He was briefly superseded by Dixie Lee (ex-Lone Star, Wild Horses) before a more permanent replacement was a found in Steve Hopgood (ex-Chinatown, Shy). The band also added a new second guitarist, Graham Bath (ex-Sphinx). Persian Risk were dealt a significant blow when founding member Phil Campbell successfully auditioned for Motörhead, who would tap his old band for the support slot on their 1984 UK tour. Campbell's successor was Phil Vokins (ex-Tyrant, Wrathchild). Risk also signed a new record deal with London-based Zebra Records and issued the *Too Different* 12" EP in 1984 which saw the band temper their raw approach in favor of a somewhat more polished sound.

That same year, Persian Risk made their one and only national UK TV appearance when the band performed three songs - *Women In Rock*, *Rise Up*, and *Too Different* - on Channel 4's ECT program. All three songs would later feature on their "Rise Up" LP which finally saw the light of day in 1986 on Metal Masters. By that time, the band had already disintegrated, the result of mounting frustration after years of hard work and failing to get that elusive big break. Nick Hughes exited to join Idol Rich, drummer Steve Hopgood co-founded Wild! (and later joined Paul Di'Anno's Battlezone and Killers as well as an early version of Jagged Edge), while Carl Sentance stepped in with Tokyo Blade on their 1986 European tour; he was also brought in as a guest vocalist by fellow Welsh act Tredegar for their 1986 debut album. Graham Bath, too, would later serve a stint with the DiAnno fronted Battlezone and Killers.

In February 2012, vocalist Carl Sentance announced on his Facebook page that he had recorded seven new songs and re-cut four old Persian Risk tracks for inclusion on a new Persian Risk album, albeit without any of the original members involved. While a full list of players has not yet been revealed, the participation of Deep Purple keyboardist Don Airey and former Thunder bassist Chris Childs was confirmed by Sentance.

In a 29 July 2012 posting on the band's Facebook page, an August release was announced for the new album, entitled *Once A King*. On it, Sentance, Airey and Childs are joined by bassist Alex Meadows, drummer Tim Brown and the guitar duo of Danny Willson and Howie G. The above-mentioned album was released in October 2012; a limited edition vinyl version was issued by German label High Roller Records.

The new Persian Risk played the "Hard Rock Hell" festival in Wales on 29 November 2012, with a line-up consisting of Sentance, Brown, Howie G. and former Blaze bassist Wayne Banks. They are also scheduled to appear at the "Keep It True" festival in Germany in April 2014. their third album, named Who am I was released on 6 November 2014.

2.50.2 Post break-up activities

- **Carl Sentance** was recruited by Black Sabbath bassist Geezer Butler to front the Geezer Butler Band in 1986 but the group ultimately failed to score a record deal. In 1990, he was sought out by Welsh guitarist Paul Chapman of Lone Star, UFO, and Waysted fame to front a new band, Ghost, in Orlando, Florida. It too never got off the ground properly and was mostly ignored by the industry (although an archives release was put together posthumously by Chapman). Sentance also assembled an American version of Persian Risk with guitarist Mark Lanoue; the band gigged in the Southern US area until their demise in 1995. Back in the UK, the singer was involved in a project with members of Wraith before being asked to front legendary Swiss hard rockers Krokus in 1998; he appeared on their *Round 13* album and stayed on for the next three years. In 2005, Sentance emerged fronting Whole Lotta Metal alongside co-vocalist Tony Martin of Black Sabbath fame and other British metal session musicians, assembled for a touring cast of cover versions. The singer also served as the voice for the Power Project who issued the *Dinosaurs* album in 2006. It featured Sentance and veteran US musicians Carlos Cavazo (Quiet Riot, Ratt), Jeff Pilson (Dokken, Dio, Foreigner), and Vinny Appice (Black Sabbath, Dio). On the live front, the singer teamed up with Deep Purple's Don Airey & Friends and can also be heard on Airey's 2008 solo effort, *A Light in the Sky*. Sentance issued his debut solo album, *Mind Doctor*, in 2008; musical guests include Airey on keyboards and the Thunder rhythm section of Harry James and Chris

Childs. Now he is the sole original member in the band.

- **Steve Hopgood** was seen in a late 90's incarnation of Tank who released the *The Return of the Filth Hounds - Live* album in 1998 and toured Japan as part of a 20th Anniversary NWOBHM festival billing, documented on the *Metal Crusade '99* split CD, which also features Samson, Trespass, and Praying Mantis.

- **Phil Vokins** returned in 2006 with Psychowrath, a union with fellow ex-Wrathchild members, bassist Marc Angel and drummer Eddie Starr, and Beyond Recognition vocalist Gaz Harris. The band is still active and playing shows.

- **Nick Hughes** has re-emerged in recent years as a DJ and producer in Trance music circles under the pseudonym Toad. He is also involved in the promoting side of things with 'Toadstool', a psytrance party based in Gloucester, UK where he acts as resident DJ.

- **Jon Deverill** left the rock music world behind after a final pair of Tygers of Pan Tang albums, *The Wreck-Age* and *Burning in the Shade*, in the late 80's and now works as a successful stage actor. A graduate of the Royal Welsh College of Music and Drama in Cardiff, Deverill, stage name: Jon de Ville, most recently appeared in a national tour of *Blood Brothers* in 2007 and The Sound of Music in London in 2008. An album, recorded in the mid-90's under the name of Square World with fellow former Tyger, Fred Purser, remains unreleased.

- **Phil Campbell** has been a continuous member of Motörhead for almost 30 years and has recorded more than a dozen albums with the band. In 2004, Campbell made 'The 100 Welsh Heroes' list as a result of Wales' largest ever online poll, conducted by Culturenet Cymru. Campbell also won a prestigious Grammy Award with Motörhead in the *Best Metal Performance* category for their cover of Metallica's "Whiplash" in 2005.

2.50.3 Discography

Singles

- "Calling for You" b/w "Chase the Dragon" (SRT Records, 1981)
- "Ridin' High" b/w "Hurt You" (Neat Records, 1983)
- "Too Different" 12" EP (Zebra Records, 1984)

Albums

- *Rise Up* (Metal Masters, 1986 / High Vaultage, 1997 / Powerage, 2002)

01. "Hold the Line"
02. "Jane"
03. "Rise Up"
04. "Brave New World"
05. "Don't Turn Around"
06. "Sky's Falling Down"
07. "Break Free"
08. "Dark Tower"
09. "Rip It Up"
10. "Women in Rock"

Note: The High Vaultage re-issue added the 3 songs from the *Too Different* 12" EP as bonus tracks.

- *Once a King* (2012)

01. "Asylum"
02. "Riding High"
03. "Killer"
04. "Once a King"
05. "Soul Deceiver"
06. "Battle Cry"
07. "Spirit in My Dreams"
08. "Ride the Storm"
09. "Fist of Fury"
10. "Women and Rock"
11. "Wasteland"

Note: "Riding High" and "Women and Rock" are re-recordings of earlier Persian Risk songs.

Compilations

- *Heavy Metal Heroes Vol.2* (Heavy Metal Records, 1982)
- *60 Minutes Plus* (Neat Records, 1982)
- *All Hell Let Loose* (Base Records/Neat, 1983)

2.50.4 See also

- List of New Wave of British Heavy Metal bands

2.50.5 References

2.50.6 External links

- Persian Risk official website

- Persian Risk Facebook page
- Carl Sentance website
- Music Might on Persian Risk
- Persian Risk on Encyclopaedia Metallum: The Metal Archives
- BNR Metal Pages on Persian Risk
- Leather Warriors pages on Persian Risk

2.51 Pet Hate

Pet Hate is a British heavy metal band who released two albums in the 1980s, titled *Bad Publicity* and *The Bride Wore Red*. Pet Hate took their name from the idea of a pet peeve.

The band was previously known as **Silverwing** and they had an album out in 1983 called *Alive and Kicking*. Several of the band members later formed a group called Wild Ones and in this guise they released an album in 1991 called *Writing on the Wall*.

The band hailed from Macclesfield and featured three ex Silverwing members Dave Roberts, Steve Roberts and Alistair Terry. After debuting *The Bride Wore Red* in 1984, renowned producer Eddie Leonetti was persuaded to produce the follow up *Bad Publicity*. Leonetti had produced albums from the American band Angel in the late 1970s, including one titled *Bad Publicity* whose artwork was rejected as being too controversial by the record company and the title was changed to *Sinful*. Pet Hate borrowed the cover idea for their own *Bad Publicity*.

The band supported Hanoi Rocks on a British tour and disbanded in 1985. Alistair Terry released a solo album entitled *Young at Heart* in 1986. Dave and Steve Roberts later played in Belinda Carlisle's backing band for lip-synced TV appearances throughout Europe, circa her first solo hit "Heaven Is a Place on Earth" in late 1987 / early 1988.

2.51.1 See also

- List of New Wave of British Heavy Metal bands

2.52 Praying Mantis (band)

Praying Mantis are an English rock band. Although a part of the New Wave of British Heavy Metal scene, they pursued a musical direction more melodic and AOR-sounding than their contemporaries.

2.52.1 Career

Their formation considerably pre-dated the NWOBHM movement. They were formed in 1974 by the Troy brothers, Tino and Chris, both college students. Like several NWOBHM bands they made their first available recording at Neal Kay's Soundhouse recording studio, which was released as the *Soundhouse Tapes* EP in 1979.

1980 saw their profile considerably raised with support slots for Iron Maiden and Ronnie Montrose's Gamma and "Captured City" was included on the Metal for Muthas compilation. The attention won them a recording contract with Arista Records and they released their best-known work *Time Tells No Lies* in 1981. Management and line-up instability undermined their success and Arista dropped them. The following year they signed for Jet Records, but two subsequent singles flopped and the band folded. They had recorded a version of the Russ Ballard penned track "I Surrender", but ran into conflict with Rainbow, who went on to release their version, and had a Top 10 worldwide hit. Instead, Praying Mantis recorded another single, "Cheated". It reached No. 69 in the UK Singles Chart in January 1981.[1]

The band maintained a strong fan base in Japan, and when the Troys temporarily reformed Praying Mantis for a NWOBHM nostalgia tour in 1990, they were encouraged by the response to resurrect the band full-time. Their live work was released as *Live at Last*, and a follow-up studio album *Predator in Disguise* was released the following year, and the band soldiered on into the new century. A compilation album, *The Best of Praying Mantis*, was released in 2004. Following further line-up changes, a new album, *Sanctuary*, was released in the spring of 2009 and has gained worldwide media acclaim.

In 2013 the band announced they are to release a new single in October 2013. The single is to officially introduce new members, John Cuijpers (vocals) and Hans in't Zandt (drums) to the band's fanbase after playing Colchester, Ipswich (with support from MGR Records band Kaine) and Cambridge Rock Festival with the brand new line up.[2][3][4] A new album called Legacy is due for release on 21 August 2015.[5]

2.52.2 Discography

Studio albums

- *Time Tells No Lies* (Arista 1981) - UK No. 60[1]
- *Throwing Shapes* (billed as *Stratus*) (Steel Trax 1984)
- *Predator in Disguise* (Pony Canyon 1991)

- *A Cry for the New World* (Pony Canyon 1993)
- *To the Power of Ten* (Pony Canyon 1995)
- *Forever in Time* (Pony Canyon 1998)
- *Nowhere to Hide* (Pony Canyon 2000)
- *The Journey Goes On* (Pony Canyon 2003)
- *Sanctuary* (Frontiers 2009)
- *Legacy* (Frontiers 2015)

Singles

- "Praying Mantis" / "High Roller" 7" (GEM, 1980)
- *The Soundhouse Tapes Part 2* ("Captured City" / "The Ripper" / "Johnny Cool") 12" (Ripper Records, 1981)
- "Cheated" / "Thirty Pieces of Silver" / "Flirting With Suicide" / "Panic in the Streets" 2x7" (Arista, 1981)
- "All Day and All of the Night" / "Beads of Ebony" 7" (Arista, 1981)
- "Turn the Tables" / "Tell Me the Nightmare's Wrong" / "A Question of Time" 7" EP (Jet, 1982)
- "Only the Children Cry" / "Who's Life is it Anyway?" / "A Moment in Life" / "Turn the Tables" CD EP (Canyon International, 1993)
- *Metalmorphosis* CD EP (self-released, 2011)

2.52.3 Compilations

- *The Best of Praying Mantis* (Pony Canyon 2004)

2.52.4 Lineups

2.52.5 See also

- List of New Wave of British Heavy Metal bands

2.52.6 References

[1] Roberts, David (2006). *British Hit Singles & Albums* (19th ed.). London: Guinness World Records Limited. p. 433. ISBN 1-904994-10-5.

[2] "New album "Legacy". August 2015". Praying Mantis. 2014-06-20. Retrieved 2015-09-06.

[3] "Praying Mantis UK Rock - Metal". Facebook. Retrieved 2015-09-06.

[4] "Kaine SUPPORTING PRAYING MANTIS @ The Railway, Ipswich ! Saturday, August 3rd 2013 | Ipswich". Allevents.in. 2013-08-03. Retrieved 2015-09-06.

[5] "Praying Mantis Legacy". Frontiers. Retrieved 2015-08-17.

2.52.7 External links

- Official website
- Praying Mantis discography at Discogs
- MusicMight bio
- Interview with Chris Troy (2009)
- Audio Interview with Praying Mantis from Hard Rock Hell Festival 2011

2.53 Quartz (metal band)

Quartz are a British heavy metal band.

2.53.1 History

Quartz dates back to as early as 1974 when they were known as Bandy Legs.[1] They signed to Jet Records in 1976 and supported Black Sabbath and AC/DC. The band changed their name to Quartz for their 1977 debut album, *Quartz*. The album was produced by Tony Iommi and Quartz toured with Black Sabbath to support this release. Queen guitarist Brian May handled guitar on "Circles," which also features Ozzy Osbourne on backing vocals. This track did not appear on the album but would turn up as the B-side to the "Stoking the Fires of Hell" single.

Quartz toured heavily during this time, playing the Reading Festival three times (1976, 1977 and 1980) and touring in support of some of the larger hard rock bands of the time (Iron Maiden, Saxon, UFO and Rush).[1]

Quartz released their second studio album, *Stand Up and Fight*, in 1980 and their third, *Against All Odds*, in 1983 before calling it quits. In 1979 Geoff Nicholls left to join Black Sabbath. He contributed keyboards and songwriting from 1980s *Heaven and Hell* to 2004.[1]

In 2004, doom metal band, Orodruin covered "Stand Up and Fight" on their album *Claw Tower*.

Prior to the founding of Quartz, Hopkins had played in Wages of Sin, a short-lived Birmingham band which toured as a backing band for Cat Stevens in 1970.[2] After that band's dissolution, two of his bandmates, expatriate Canadians Ed and Brian Pilling, returned to Canada and formed the band Fludd; Hopkins briefly joined that band in 1972 as a replacement for founding guitarist Mick Walsh, but left by the end of the year after they were dropped from their original record label.[2]

Quartz reformed in 2011 playing a reunion gig on 16 December 2011 at The Asylum in Birmingham, England. The line up consisted of Geoff Nicholls, Mike Hopkins, Derek Arnold, Malcolm Cope and vocalist David Garner.

2.53.2 Members

- Mike Taylor - vocals (1974–1982)
- Geoff Bate - vocals (1983)[3]
- David Garner - vocals (2011 – present)
- Mike Hopkins - guitar
- Geoff Nicholls - guitar/keyboards
- Derek Arnold - bass
- Malcolm Cope - drums

2.53.3 Discography

Studio albums

- *Quartz* (Jet Records 1977, rereleased in 1980 and renamed *Deleted*)
- *Stand Up and Fight* (MCA Records 1980)
- *Against All Odds* (Heavy Metal Records 1983)
- *Too Hot to Handle* (Skol Records 2015)

Singles

- "Street Fighting Lady" / "Mainline Riders" (Jet Records 1977)
- "Stoking Up the Fires of Hell" / "Circles" (MCA Records 1980)
- "Satan's Serenade" / "Bloody Fool" / "Roll Over Beethoven" (live) (Logo Records 1980)
- "Nantucket Sleighride" / "Wildfire" (Reddingtons Rare Records 1980)
- "Stand Up and Fight" / "Charlie Snow" (MCA Records 1981)
- "Tell Me Why" / "Streetwalker" (Heavy Metal Records 1983)

Live and compilation albums

- *Live Quartz* (Reddingtons Rare Records 1980) - Recorded at Digbeth Civic Hall, Birmingham, England on 1 December 1979
- *Resurrection* (Neat Records 1996)
- *Satan's Serenade* (Castle Records 2004)
- *Live and Revisited* (Private Release 2013)

2.53.4 See also

- List of New Wave of British Heavy Metal bands

2.53.5 References

[1] MusicMight

[2] Fludd at canoe.ca's Pop Music Encyclopedia.

[3] Popoff, Martin (1993). *Riff Kills Man! 25 Years of Recorded Hard Rock & Heavy Metal*. Power Chord Press. ISBN 0-9697707-0-7.

2.53.6 External links

Official Facebook Page. www.facebook.com/QuartzBackintheBand

2.54 Rainbow (rock band)

Rainbow (also known as **Ritchie Blackmore's Rainbow** or **Blackmore's Rainbow**) are a British rock band led by guitarist Ritchie Blackmore from 1975 to 1984 and 1993 to 1997. A limited number of European appearances have been announced by Blackmore for the summer of 2016. They were originally established with Ronnie James Dio's American rock band Elf, but after the first album, Blackmore fired the backing members and continued with Dio until 1979. Three British musicians joined in 1979, singer Graham Bonnet, keyboardist Don Airey, former Deep Purple bassist Roger Glover, and this line-up gave the band their commercial breakthrough with the single "Since You Been Gone". Over the years Rainbow went through many line-up changes with no two studio albums featuring the same line-up. Other lead singers Joe Lynn Turner and Doogie White would follow, and the project consisted of numerous backing musicians. The band's early work primarily featured mystical lyrics with a neoclassical metal style, but went in a more streamlined, commercial direction following Dio's departure from the group.[1]

Rainbow were ranked No. 90 on VH1's *100 Greatest Artists of Hard Rock*.[2] The band has sold over 28 million albums worldwide.

2.54.1 History

Formation (1975)

Ronnie James Dio in 2006.

By 1973, Blackmore had steered Deep Purple through a significant personnel change, with Ian Gillan and Roger Glover being replaced by David Coverdale and Glenn Hughes. However, the new members were keen to add new musical styles and Blackmore found his request to record the Steve Hammond-penned "Black Sheep of the Family" with "Sixteenth Century Greensleeves" turned down by the band.[3] He decided to record the song with Dio instead, using Dio's band Elf as additional musicians.[4] He enjoyed the results, and a full album, billed as *Ritchie Blackmore's Rainbow* was recorded between February and March 1975 at Musicland Studios in Munich, Germany.[5] The band name was inspired by the Rainbow Bar and Grill in Hollywood.[6]

Rainbow's music was partly inspired by classical music since Blackmore started playing cello to help him construct interesting chord progressions,[7][8] and Dio wrote lyrics about medieval themes. Dio possessed a versatile vocal range capable of singing both hard rock and lighter ballads, and, according to Blackmore, "I felt shivers down my spine."[9] Although Dio never played a musical instrument on any Rainbow album, he is credited with writing and arranging the music with Blackmore, in addition to writing all the lyrics himself.[5][10][11] Blackmore and Dio also found a common ground in their sense of humour.[12]

Following the positive experience of recording with Dio, Blackmore decided to leave Deep Purple, playing his last show in Paris in April.[3][13] The album had a positive critical reception and was a top 20 UK and top 30 US hit. Blackmore's departure from Deep Purple was publicly announced on 21 June.[14]

First world tour and initial success (1975–78)

Rainbow performing in Munich in 1977. The electric rainbow that spanned the stage used so much power, it frequently interfered with the guitars and amplifiers.[15]

Blackmore was unhappy about carrying the Elf line-up along for live performances, and so he fired everybody except Dio shortly after the album was recorded, due to Driscoll's style of drumming and the funky bass playing of Gruber.[16] Blackmore would continue to dictate personnel for the remainder of the band's lifetime, with drummer and former bandmate Ricky Munro remarking "he was very difficult to get on with because you never knew when he would turn around and say 'You're sacked'."[17] Blackmore recruited bassist Jimmy Bain, American keyboard player Tony Carey and drummer Cozy Powell, who had previously worked with Jeff Beck and had some solo success.[16] Powell also greatly appealed to Blackmore in their mutual fondness for practical jokes.[18]

This line-up also commenced the first world tour for the band, with the first date in Montreal on 10 November 1975. The centrepiece of the band's live performance was a computer-controlled rainbow including 3000 lightbulbs, which stretched 40 feet across the stage.[19] [18] A second album, *Rising*, was recorded in February at Musicland. By the time of the European dates in the summer of 1976, Rainbow's reputation as a blistering live act had been established. The band added Deep Purple's Mistreated to their setlist, and song lengths were stretched to include improvisation.[20] Carey recalls rehearsing the material was fairly straightforward, saying "We didn't work anything out, except the structure, the ending ... very free-form, really progressive rock."[21] The album art was designed by famed fantasy artist Ken Kelly, who had drawn Tarzan and Conan the Barbarian.[22][23]

In August 1976, following a gig at Newcastle City Hall, Blackmore decided to fire Carey, believing his playing style to be too complicated for the band. Unable to find a suitable replacement quickly, Carey was quickly reinstated,[24] but as the world tour progressed onto Japan, he found himself regularly being the recipient of Blackmore's pranks and humour.[25] Blackmore subsequently decided that Bain was substandard and fired him in January 1977. The same fate befell Carey shortly after. Blackmore, however, had difficulty finding replacements he liked. On keyboards, after auditioning several high profile artists, including Vanilla Fudge's Mark Stein, Procol Harum's Matthew Fisher and ex-Curved Air and Roxy Music man Eddie Jobson, Blackmore finally selected Canadian David Stone, from the little-known band Symphonic Slam. For a bass player, Blackmore originally chose Mark Clarke, formerly of Jon Hiseman's Colosseum, Uriah Heep and Tempest, but once in the studio for the next album, *Long Live Rock 'n' Roll*, Blackmore disliked Clarke's fingerstyle method of playing so much that he fired Clarke on the spot and played bass himself on all but four songs: the album's title track, "Gates of Babylon", "Kill the King", and "Sensitive to Light". Former Widowmaker bassist, Australian Bob Daisley was hired to record these tracks, completing the band's next line-up.

After the release and extensive world tour in 1977–78, Blackmore decided that he wanted to take the band in a new commercial direction away from the "sword and sorcery" theme.[26] Dio did not agree with this change and left Rainbow.

Commercial success (1978-84)

Graham Bonnet in 2008.

Blackmore asked Ian Gillan, also formerly of Deep Purple, to replace Dio, but Gillan turned him down. After a series of auditions, former singer/guitarist of The Marbles, Graham Bonnet was recruited. Powell stayed, but Daisley and Stone were both fired, the latter replaced by keyboardist Don Airey. At first the band auditioned bass players, but at Cozy Powell's suggestion Blackmore hired another former Deep Purple member, Roger Glover, as a producer, bassist and lyricist.[27] The first album from the new line-up, *Down to Earth*, featured the band's first major singles chart successes, "All Night Long" and the Russ Ballard-penned "Since You Been Gone". In 1980, the band headlined the inaugural Monsters of Rock festival at Castle Donington in England. However, this was Powell's last Rainbow gig: he had already given his notice to quit, disliking Blackmore's increasingly pop rock direction. Then Bonnet resigned to pursue a solo project.

For the next album, Bonnet and Powell were replaced by Americans Joe Lynn Turner and Bobby Rondinelli, respectively. The title track from *Difficult to Cure* was a version of Beethoven's Ninth Symphony. The album spawned their most successful UK single, "I Surrender" (another Ballard song), which reached No.3. After the supporting tour, Don Airey quit over musical differences and was replaced by David Rosenthal.

The band attained significant airplay on Album-oriented rock radio stations in the US with the track "Jealous Lover", reaching No. 13 on Billboard Magazine's Rock Tracks chart. Originally issued as the B-side to "Can't Happen Here", "Jealous Lover" subsequently became the title track

Joe Lynn Turner in 2008.

to an EP issued in the US that featured very similar cover art to *Difficult to Cure*.

Rainbow's next full-length studio album was *Straight Between the Eyes*. The album was more cohesive than *Difficult to Cure*, and had more success in the United States. The band, however, was alienating some of its earlier fans with its more AOR sound.[1] The single "Stone Cold" was a ballad that had some chart success (#1 on Billboard's Rock Tracks chart) and its video received heavy airplay on MTV. The successful supporting tour skipped the UK completely and focused on the American market. A date in San Antonio, Texas, on this tour was filmed, and the resulting "Live Between the Eyes" also received repeated showings on MTV.

Bent Out of Shape saw drummer Rondinelli fired in favour of former Balance drummer Chuck Burgi. The album featured the single "Street of Dreams". Blackmore claims on his website that the song's video was banned by MTV for its supposedly controversial hypnotic video clip,[28] but Dr. Thomas Radecki of the National Coalition on Television Violence criticised MTV for airing the video, contradicting Blackmore's claim.[29] The resulting tour saw Rainbow return to the UK, and also to Japan in March 1984 where the band performed "Difficult to Cure" with a full orchestra. The concert was also filmed.

Dissolution and temporary revival (1993-97)

Doogie White in 2009.

Rainbow's management Thames Talent co-ordinated attempts to successfully reform Deep Purple MK. II. By April 1984, Rainbow was disbanded. A then-final Rainbow album, *Finyl Vinyl*, was pieced together from live tracks and B-sides of singles, including the instrumental "Weiss Heim" (All Night Long B-side), "Bad Girl" (Since You Been Gone B-side), and "Jealous Lover" (Can't Happen Here B-side).

In 1988, after joining the band Impelliteri, Graham Bonnet covered "Since You Been Gone" on the group's debut album, *Stand In Line*.

In 1993 Blackmore left Deep Purple permanently due to "creative differences" with other members, and reformed Rainbow with all-new members featuring Scottish singer Doogie White. The band released *Stranger in Us All* in 1995, and embarked on a lengthy world tour.

The tour proved very successful, and a show in Germany was professionally filmed for the *Rockpalast* TV show. This show, initially heavily bootlegged (and considered by many collectors to be the best Rainbow bootleg of the era), was officially released by Eagle Records on CD and DVD as

Black Masquerade in 2013.[30] The live shows featured frequent changes in set lists, and musical improvisations that proved popular with bootleggers and many shows are still traded over a decade later.

However, Blackmore turned his attention to his long-time musical passion, Renaissance and medieval music. Rainbow was put on hold once again after playing its final concert in Esbjerg, Denmark in 1997. Blackmore, together with his partner Candice Night as vocalist then formed the Renaissance-influenced Blackmore's Night. Around the same time as production of *Stranger in Us All* (1995), they were already gearing up their debut album *Shadow of the Moon* (1997).[31]

Rainbow after 1997

Many Rainbow songs have been performed live by former members of the band since the group's split in 1984 and then in 1997, particularly former frontmen Ronnie James Dio, Graham Bonnet and Joe Lynn Turner in recent years. Also, Don Airey often plays 1979-1981 era songs during his solo shows. Blackmore's Night occasionally performs one or two Rainbow songs live, namely "Ariel", "Rainbow Eyes" and "Street of Dreams". The latter two were also re-recorded by Blackmore's Night in studio.

In 2002–2004 the Hughes Turner Project played a number of Rainbow songs at their concerts. On 9 August 2007 Joe Lynn Turner and Graham Bonnet played a tribute to Rainbow show in Helsinki, Finland. The concert consisted of songs from the 1979-1983 era.

In 2009, Joe Lynn Turner, Bobby Rondinelli, Greg Smith and Tony Carey created the touring tribute band Over The Rainbow with Jürgen Blackmore (Ritchie's son) as the guitarist. Over The Rainbow performed songs from every era of the band's history. After the first tour Tony Carey had to leave the band due to health concerns; he was replaced by another former Rainbow member, Paul Morris.

In 2015, Blackmore announced that he would play four "all rock" concerts in the summer of 2016. Two shows have currently been confirmed in Germany under the banner of 'Ritchie Blackmore's Rainbow and Friends', with a further show at the Birmingham Genting Arena in England.[32] Later on November 6, the line up was revealed as Lords Of Black singer Ronnie Romero, Stratovarius keyboardist Jens Johansson, Blackmore's Night drummer David Keith and bassist Bob Nouveau.[33][34]

2.54.2 Band members

2016 touring line up

- Ritchie Blackmore - guitar (1975–1984, 1993–1997, 2015-present)
- Jens Johansson - keyboards (2015-present)
- David Keith - drums (2015-present)
- Bob Nouveau - bass (2015-present)
- Ronnie Romero - lead vocals (2015-present)

Past members

2.54.3 Lineups

2.54.4 Discography

Main article: Rainbow discography

- *Ritchie Blackmore's Rainbow* (1975)
- *Rising* (1976)
- *Long Live Rock 'n' Roll* (1978)
- *Down to Earth* (1979)
- *Difficult to Cure* (1981)
- *Straight Between the Eyes* (1982)
- *Bent Out of Shape* (1983)
- *Stranger in Us All* (1995)

2.54.5 References

[1] Rivadavia, Eduardo. "Rainbow". Allmusic. Retrieved 10 July 2010.

[2] "VH1's 100 Greatest Artists of Hard Rock". Rate Your Music. Retrieved 13 November 2010.

[3] Robinson, Simon (1996). *Mk III: The Final Concerts* (Media notes). Deep Purple. Connoisseur Collection. DPVSOPCD-230.

[4] "Rainbow - 1975-1978". *Ronnie James Dio (Official Site)*. Retrieved 24 June 2009.

[5] *Ritchie Blackmore's Rainbow* (Media notes). Rainbow. Polydor Records. 1990. 825-089-2.

[6] Bloom 2007, p. 193.

[7] MORDECHAI KLEIDERMACHER (February 1991). "When There's Smoke.. THERE'S FIRE!". *Guitar World*.

[8] Warnock, Matt (28 January 2011). "Ritchie Blackmore: The Autumn Sky Interview". *Guitar International Magazine*.

[9] Bloom 2007, p. 186.

[10] *Rainbow Rising*. CD liner notes: Polydor Records.

[11] *Long Live Rock 'N' Roll*. CD liner notes: Polydor Records.

[12] Bloom 2007, p. 187.

[13] Bloom 2007, p. 184.

[14] Thompson 2004, p. 176.

[15] Robinson, Simon (1977). *Rainbow Live in Munich 1977 (liner notes)*. Eagle Rock Entertainment Ltd.

[16] "Tony Carey Interview". Music Legends. Retrieved 28 May 2013.

[17] Bloom 2007, p. 189.

[18] Bloom 2007, p. 190.

[19] Thompson 2004, pp. 195-196.

[20] Thompson 2004, p. 196.

[21] Bloom 2007, p. 194.

[22] Mark Voger (22 October 2006). "Criss eager to meet television idol Zacherley". *Asbury Park Press*. p. 6E.

[23] "Manowar truck to make its debut in Austria this weekend". *Austria Today*. 8 September 2006.

[24] Bloom 2007, p. 201-202.

[25] Bloom 2007, p. 203.

[26] Davies, Roy (2002). *Rainbow Rising: The Story of Ritchie Blackmore's Rainbow*. Helter Skelter Publishing.

[27] "Roger Glover. 1973-2006 History". Retrieved 23 September 2009.

[28] "Ritchie Blackmore Bio". Blackmores Night. 8 May 1998. Retrieved 13 November 2010.

[29] Denisoff, R. Serge (1988). "MTV: Some People Just Don't Get It". *Inside MTV*. Transaction. p. 284. ISBN 978-0-88738-864-4. Retrieved 13 October 2009. 'Street of Dreams' by Rainbow has a psychiatrist dominating a man through hypnosis intermixed with male-female violent fantasies including a bound and gagged woman.

[30] http://www.amazon.co.uk/dp/B00DBNWAZ6/

[31] Adams, Bret (26 February 2011). "Stranger in Us All". allmusic.

[32] "Ritchie Blackmore's Rainbow: Revealed UK Show Date". *Metal Shock Finland*. Retrieved 6 November 2015.

[33] "Blackmore's touring lineup revealed". *ClassicRock*. TeamRock. Retrieved 6 November 2015.

[34] "RITCHIE BLACKMORE'S RAINBOW: Touring Line-Up Announced". *Metal Shock Finland*. Retrieved 6 November 2015.

Books

- Bloom, Jerry (2007). *Black Knight*. Music Sales Group. ISBN 9780857120533.
- Thompson, Dave (2004). *Smoke on the Water: The Deep Purple Story*. ECW Press. ISBN 9781550226188.

2.54.6 Bibliography

- Roy Davies, *Rainbow Rising - The Story of Ritchie Blackmore's Rainbow* (Helter Skelter, 2002)
- Martin Popoff, *Rainbow - English Castle Magic* (Metal Blade, 2005)
- Jerry Bloom, *Black Knight - Ritchie Blackmore* (Omnibus Press, 2006)
- Jerry Bloom, *Long Live Rock 'n' Roll Story* (Wymer Publishing, 2009)

2.54.7 External links

- The Rainbow Fanclan Legacy
- Rainbow (rock band) at AllMusic

2.55 Raven (British band)

For the American blues band, see Raven (American band).

Raven are an English heavy metal band associated with the New Wave of British Heavy Metal movement. They had a hit with the single "On and On", and refer to their music as "athletic rock".

2.55.1 History

Formation

Raven was formed in 1974 in Newcastle, England, by brothers John and Mark Gallagher, and Paul Bowden.

Raven began creating a sound which was rooted in British hard rock, with progressive rock tendencies, and a willingness to take musical chances. The band's highly energized live show and interaction between band members developed a unique image and style of play, described as "athletic". They began wearing guards, helmets, and plates from various sports (hockey, baseball, etc...), and incorporating them into the playing of their instruments (for instance, elbow pads and hockey masks were used to strike cymbals). Their music began to develop into a unique amalgam of speed and power - heavily influencing the genres of speed/thrash metal and power metal. The band have a reputation as an extremely energetic live band - and for regularly destroying their equipment.

They started by playing local pubs and working men's clubs in the North East of England - occasionally opening shows for punk bands such as The Stranglers and The Motors.

Early years

Eventually, the band signed with Neat Records, the legendary, low-budget metal label of the North. They released their 1st single "Don't Need Your Money" in 1980 and embarked on a number of UK shows opening for bands such as Ozzy Osbourne's Blizzard of Ozz, Motörhead, Whitesnake and Iron Maiden. Their first album *Rock until You Drop* was released to wide acclaim in 1981, leading the band to tour Italy and the Netherlands. Their second album, *Wiped Out* was released in 1982 and was influential on creating the burgeoning thrash and speed metal genres, making an impressive showing on the UK charts at the time.

Sufficient noise was made for the American market to take notice and New Jersey's Megaforce Records signed them, issuing their next recording in the States as *All for One* in 1983. The band came stateside in 1983, and toured extensively on the "Kill 'em All For One" tour with young thrashers Metallica (on their first tour) as their opening act.

Commercial success

The manager and founder of Megaforce Jon Zazula believed that Raven was major-label material and kept them touring constantly until the big labels noticed. The infamous *Live at the Inferno* recording, released in 1984, was a product of one of those tours. Atlantic Records signed Raven to a worldwide contract after a minor bidding war (major label contracts would follow for Metallica and Anthrax in the following year). The band moved its permanent base from Newcastle to New York City.

Stay Hard was released in 1985, and proved a minor hit on the strength of single and video "On and On". The Atlantic years proved to be less than stellar for the band. A drastic shift in a more commercial direction came at the label's behest, with many die-hard fans being alienated by the slick, lightweight production of *The Pack Is Back*. However, the band redeemed themselves with a return to form on the *Mad* EP in 1986 and the *Life's a Bitch* album in 1987, before arranging their departure from Atlantic.

After the tour for *Life's a Bitch*, drummer Rob "Wacko" Hunter left the band in late 1987 to spend more time with his new wife and family. He would later pursue a career in audio production and engineering, eventually working with jazz musicians Branford Marsalis and Harry Connick, Jr..

Post Atlantic era

Virginian Joe Hasselvander (ex-Pentagram) joined as drummer in late 1987 and the band dropped the outlandish image for a more conventional denim-and-leather look for their 1988 release *Nothing Exceeds Like Excess*, which was self-produced and continued the band's return to form with fast, involved compositions. A concert at the Trocadero Theatre in Philadelphia was released by Combat Records as *Ultimate Revenge 2* and featured the band on 4 cuts, alongside a number of thrash bands such as Death, Forbidden and Dark Angel. Next was a US tour opening for Testament, and then a European tour with German band Kreator. The advent of grunge and the dissolution of their record label Combat Records led the band to concentrate on continental Europe and Japan, where they retained more of a following.

In 1990 the band recorded the album *Architect of Fear* in Germany (again self-produced) showcasing the band's heavier side. They toured Europe in 1991 as special guests of German band Running Wild. 1992 had the band releasing an EP called *Heads Up*, featuring 4 new studio songs and 3 live tracks from the 1991 tour. They again toured Europe with German band Risk as openers.

The band spent the first half of 1993 writing and demoing new material, delays ensued due to John Gallagher having a house fire and thieves stealing guitars from the remains. In 1994 the band regrouped and inked a deal with Japanese label Zero - an album entitled *Glow* was recorded at Showplace Studios, Dover NJ (notable for having a strip club connected to the tape closet!) The album was self-produced and varied in feel, even sporting a few ballads alongside heavier material such as "Altar" and "Enemy". A cover of Thin Lizzy's "The Rocker" also made the album.

In 1994 the band attended and played live at the Foundations Forum metal convention in Burbank, California, and stole the show alongside acts as disparate as Korn, Yngwie Malmsteen and Machine Head.

The band toured Japan for the first time in May 1995, a live album called *Destroy All Monsters/Live in Japan* was recorded featuring songst from *Glow*, as well as older cuts such as "For the Future".

1996 was spent writing and recording a new studio album

Everything Louder - sessions took place in Manassas VA at future Brett Michaels guitarist Pete Evick's studio and the recording was a frantic affair done over 4 weekends with almost no reheasal - the better to get a "live" feel onto tape. The album came out in 1997 in Japan, Europe and the US, and the band went on the road in Europe with support acts Tank and HammerFall.

1999 promised a Raven box set with the NY label Spitfire Records. However, after a "lack of communication" John took the extra live/studio/bootleg tracks and working with engineer S.A. Adams compiled a collection entitled *Raw Tracks*, featuring unreleased material from 1984 to the present. The band also reunited with producer Michael Wagener and worked on an album titled *One for All* recorded at Wagener's Wireworld Studio in Nashville TN. Following its release, the band toured opening for old friend Udo Dirkschneider's band U.D.O. in Europe and also with them in the US in 2000.[1]

Mark's accident - 2000's

The band recorded and toured until 2001, when a wall collapsed on guitarist Mark Gallagher, crushing his legs. Raven went on hiatus for nearly 4 years, from 2001 to 2004, while the guitarist rehabilitated. A number of shows were played in 2004 with Mark in the North East of the US with him in a wheelchair.[2] Following a number of US shows and European festival appearances (Bloodstock Open Air in the UK in 2005, Keep it True in Germany in 2005, Bang Your Head!!! in Germany in 2006) the band started work on the new album *Walk Through Fire*, initially released in Japan on King Records in 2009, then securing releases in 2010 for Europe on SPV and in North America on Metal Blade. The album was well received both critically and by the fans, and the band have been steadily playing live, playing the European festival circuit, making a triumphant return to Japan, and playing their first shows in South America, returning there in 2012. [3]

2013 brought a retrospective DVD entitled *Rock Until You Drop - A Long Day's Journey*, edited by Mark Gallagher and featuring a voluminous amount of never before seen footage of the band from 1982 onwards, interviews with Lars Ulrich, Dee Snider, Dave Ellefson, Chuck Billy, Jon Zazula, Chris Jericho, etc.[4] The band played the first full-scale tour of the US since 1989 headlining on the East Coast and joining forces for a double headlining jaunt through the West Coast with fellow UK NWOBHM stalwarts Diamond Head.[5] November/December had the band playing Europe with old mates Girlschool as support, garnering favorable reviews for the energetic performances.

In January 2014 the band were featured on the 70000 Tons Of Metal cruise from Miami to Mexico and played South America in March.[6] Metallica invited the band to open for them at a soccer stadium in São Paulo Brazil in March 2014 in front of almost 70,000 fans. The band started work on a new album "ExtermiNation" in September 2014 and were special guests on 3 USA showcase gigs with Accept. They then played a 43 date USA tour in October/November [7]

ExtermiNation (2015)

In order to cover total recording costs for a new album the band initiated a Kickstarter crowdfunding project; in the process they recorded an 11 song cover album "party killers" for the contributors. In 2015 the band played their first shows in Colombia - in Pereira & Bogota, where they were present for a 6.2 earthquake. *ExtermiNation* was released in late April 2015 and consists of 14 songs plus a bonus track. It was released worldwide via SPV, except in Japan via Spiritual Beast and in South America via Die Hard.

2.55.2 Members

Lineups

2.55.3 Discography

Main article: Raven discography

Studio albums

- *Rock Until You Drop* (1981)
- *Wiped Out* (1982)
- *All for One* (1983)
- *Stay Hard* (1985)
- *The Pack Is Back* (1986)
- *Life's a Bitch* (1987)
- *Nothing Exceeds Like Excess* (1988)
- *Architect of Fear* (1991)
- *Glow* (1994)
- *Everything Louder* (1997)
- *One for All* (2000)
- *Walk Through Fire* (2009)
- *ExtermiNation* (2015)

2.55.4 See also

- List of New Wave of British Heavy Metal bands

2.55.5 References

[1] john gallagher

[2] john gallagher

[3] john gallagher

[4] No Life 'til Metal - CD Gallery - Raven

[5] john gallagher

[6] John Gallagher

[7] john gallagher

2.55.6 External links

- Official website
- Magazine clippings of Raven
- Raven at AllMusic

2.56 Rock Goddess

Rock Goddess are an all-female heavy metal band from the New Wave of British Heavy Metal era who enjoyed cult status in the 1980s in Great Britain and who have recently reformed.

2.56.1 History

The band was formed in Wandsworth, South London in 1977, by sisters Jody Turner (guitar and vocals) and Julie Turner (drums) when they were thirteen and nine years old respectively.[1] They recruited school friend Tracey Lamb on bass guitar and that completed their first line-up. Later Donnica Colman joined, adding a second guitar, and after her departure, Jackie Apperley replaced her, also on a second guitar. After Jackie left the girls rehearsed intensively as a trio, and placed a track on a sampler album, which circulated in the London music underground.[1] Meanwhile, manager John Turner, Jody and Julie's father, who had a music shop and rehearsal rooms, used his musical connections to get the band their first gigs. Finally, after an appearance at the Reading Festival in 1982, the band obtained a recording contract with A&M.[1]

They released their eponymous debut album with producer Vic Maile in 1983, and at that time there were temporary legal problems - Julie Turner was still a minor attending school and she was restricted in the number of live shows she could play.[1] Also in this period, Kat Burbella briefly joined the band as a second guitarist, and Tracey Lamb became disgruntled and quit Rock Goddess, initially forming the band She with Burbella, but then joining Girlschool in 1987. She was replaced by Dee O'Malley, who played bass and keyboards on the band's second album, *Hell Hath No Fury*, produced by Chris Tsangarides that was released in 1984. The band co-headlined with Y&T, supported Iron Maiden and Def Leppard on UK and European tours and embarked on their own headlining tours. O'Malley announced her pregnancy just before Rock Goddess' first US tour and left the band, and Rock Goddess left A & M records with their third album unfinished and unreleased.[2] She was replaced by Julia Longman on bass and Becky Axten on keyboards.[1]

A fourth album was released only in France, with the title *Young and Free*, however, due to insurmountable problems Rock Goddess disbanded shortly thereafter. In 1988, the Turner sisters reappeared as The Jody Turner Band with two male musicians, but they did not go beyond the local club circuit.[2] Jody Turner fronted a new line-up of Rock Goddess in 1994, but after a name change to Braindance,[1] the group disbanded again in 1995, after playing their last gig at the Thomas O'Becket public house.

The band reformed in 2009 to play the Hard Rock Hell music festival in Prestatyn, Wales, but were forced to split before they had a chance to perform.[3]

In March 2013 it was announced that the original line up of Jody Turner, Julie Turner and Tracey Lamb had reformed and would start recording a new album. The three of them are now in the process of recording a new album tentatively titled *Unfinished Business*.[4]

2.56.2 Discography

Albums

- *Rock Goddess* (1983) - UK No. 65[5]
- *Hell Hath No Fury* (1983) - UK No. 84
- *Young and Free* (1987)

Singles

- "Heavy Metal Rock'n'Roll" (1982)
- "My Angel" (1983) - UK No. 64[5]
- "I Didn't Know I Loved You (Till I Saw You Rock 'n' Roll)" (1984) - UK No. 57

- "Love Has Passed Me By" (1986)

2.56.3 See also

- List of New Wave of British Heavy Metal bands
- List of all-female bands

2.56.4 References

[1] van Poorten, Toine (7 April 2008). "Back To The Past (15): Rock Goddess". Metalmaidens.com. Retrieved 2 January 2011.

[2] Watts, Chris (11 June 1988). "Band of Jo(d)y". *Kerrang!* **191**. London, UK: Spotlight Publications Ltd. p. 10.

[3] Barton, Geoff (4 September 2009). "News in brief". Classic Rock Magazine. Retrieved 15 January 2011. Rock Goddess split

[4] "ROCK GODDESS Is Back For 'Unfinished Business'". Blabbermouth.net. 29 April 2014. Retrieved 2014-07-12.

[5] Roberts, David (2006). *British Hit Singles & Albums* (19th ed.). London: Guinness World Records Limited. p. 456. ISBN 1-904994-10-5.

2.56.5 External links

- Musicmight Rock Goddess biography
- Rock Goddess at Encyclopaedia Metallum
- Rock Goddess MySpace page
- Rock Goddess at Metaladies.com

2.57 Rogue Male (band)

Rogue Male are a British heavy metal band, formed in 1983.

Rogue Male was the brainchild of Northern Ireland born singer/guitarist Jim Lyttle, who had previously been in the Northern Irish punk band Pretty Boy Floyd and The Gems. Moving to London in the late 70s, he decided to put together a band that would mix punk styles and aggression with the more metal sounds of the NWOBHM bands of the time. The band signed to the UK metal label Music for Nations and subsequently Elektra in the USA. Shortly afterwards, the band were invited to appear on the *E.C.T. (Extra Celestial Transmission)* Heavy Metal music programme on England's Channel 4 where they performed 2 songs live on 19 April 1985.

The first Rogue Male album, *First Visit*, was recorded by Lyttle on guitar and vocals, John Fraser-Binnie on lead guitar, Kevin Collier on bass, and Steve Kingsley on drums. Kinglsey was later replaced by Danny Fury. The album was produced by Steve James. Rogue Male toured the UK/Europe and the USA in support of it. *Kerrang* magazine in the UK gave the band several features, and a front cover article. "All Over You" was released as a 12-inch single. The second album *Animal Man*, was released a year later. Rogue Male subsequently dropped their record companies and started legal proceedings. The 1980s incarnation of the band played their final show in late 1987.

Both the original albums were re-released on on the Polish label Metal Mind records in 2007. In an interview in the March 2009 edition of *Classic Rock Magazine*, Lyttle stated that he had recently written, arranged, recorded and produced a new Rogue Male album. This featured Bernie Tormé on guitar on some tracks with John McCoy on bass and Robin Guy on drums and was called *Nail It*. A new track, "Cold Blooded Man" appeared on the CD which accompanied the magazine. Original lead guitarist John Fraser Binnie subsequently rejoined the band and a new DVD entitled *Liar* was recorded and released. Bass player Tony Forsythe joined the band on a permanent basis.

2.57.1 Discography

Studio albums

- *First Visit* (1985) Music for Nations MFN40 /Elektra Records 96 04231
- *Animal Man* (1986) Music for Nations MFN68 / Elektra Records
- *First Visit* (2007) Re-release on Metal Mind Productions
- *Animal Man* (2007) Re-release on Metal Mind Productions
- *Nail It* (2009) RM2K Music RMCD01

Singles

- "All Over You" (1985) - 12" Music for Nations 12KUT114 / Elektra Records
  - "All Over You (full version)", "All Over You (edit)", *The Real Me*
- "Belfast *(1986) - 12" Music for Nations 12KUT122*
  - "Belfast, Rough Tough (Pretty Too), Take No Shit

Compilation albums

- "Crazy Motorcycle" on *Welcome to the Metal Zone* (1985) Music for Nations MFN49

- "Belfast" on *MFN: The Singles Album* (1986) Music for Nations MFN71

- "The Passing" on *Nightmare on Carnaby St* (1988) Music for Nations MFN83

2.57.2 See also

- List of New Wave of British Heavy Metal bands

2.57.3 External links

- Official Website
- Official Facebook page
- Official YouTube page

2.58 Ronnie James Dio

Ronnie James Dio (born **Ronald James Padavona**, July 10, 1942 – May 16, 2010) was an American heavy metal vocalist and songwriter. He fronted and/or founded numerous groups including Elf, Rainbow, Black Sabbath, Dio and Heaven & Hell. He is credited with popularizing the "metal horns" hand gesture in metal culture and is known for his medieval themed lyrics. Dio possessed a powerful versatile vocal range capable of singing both hard rock and lighter ballads; according to Rainbow/Deep Purple guitarist Ritchie Blackmore upon hearing him sing, "I felt shivers down my spine."[3][4] Dio sold over 47 million albums throughout his career.

2.58.1 Early years, education and musical training

Ronnie James Dio was born in Portsmouth, New Hampshire, to Italian American parents who had moved to Portsmouth from Cortland, New York, where they had grown up.[5] The family resided in Portsmouth for only a short time before Dio's parents returned to Cortland. Dio listened to a great deal of opera while growing up, and was influenced vocally by American tenor Mario Lanza.[6] His first and only formal musical training began at age 5 learning to play the trumpet.[6] During high school, Dio played in the school band and was one of the youngest members selected to play in the school's official Dance Band. It was also during high school that Dio formed his first rock-n-roll group, the Vegas Kings (the name would soon change to Ronnie and the Rumblers, and then Ronnie and the Red Caps). Though Dio began his rock-n-roll career on trumpet, he quickly added bass guitar to his skillset once he assumed singing duties for the group.

Dio graduated from Cortland High School in 1960. Though he claimed in a later interview to have been offered a scholarship to the prestigious Juilliard School of Music, he did not pursue it due to his continuing interest in rock-n-roll music.[7] Instead, after graduation, he attended the University at Buffalo, majoring in Pharmacology.[8] He only attended from 1960 to 1961, and played trumpet in the university's concert band, and did not graduate.[5]

Despite being known for his powerful singing voice, Dio claimed never to have taken any vocal training.[4] Rather, he attributed his singing ability to the use of correct breathing techniques learned while playing trumpet.

2.58.2 Career

Early career

Dio's musical career began in 1957 when several Cortland, New York musicians formed the band, The Vegas Kings. The group's lineup consisted of Dio on bass guitar, Billy DeWolfe on lead vocals, Nick Pantas on guitar, Tom Rogers on drums, and Jack Musci on saxophone.

In 1958, the band again changed their name from Ronnie & The Rumblers to Ronnie and the Redcaps. Musci left the band in 1960, and a new guitarist, Dick Botoff, joined the lineup. The Redcaps released two singles: The first single was "Conquest"/"Lover" with the A-side being an instrumental reminiscent of The Ventures and the B-side featuring DeWolfe on lead vocals. The second single was "An Angel Is Missing"/"What'd I Say" which featured Dio on lead vocals for both tracks.

Explanations vary for how Padavona adopted the stage name "Dio". One story is that Dio was a reference to mafia member Johnny Dio.[9] Another has it that Padavona's grandmother said he had a gift from God and should be called "Dio". ("God" in Italian.) Whatever the inspiration, Padavona first used it on a recording in 1960, when he added it to the band's second release on Seneca. Soon after that the band modified their name to Ronnie Dio and the Prophets. The Prophets lineup lasted for several years, touring throughout the New York region and playing college fraternity parties. They produced one single for Atlantic[10] and one album. Some of the singles (such as "Mr. Misery", released on Swan) were labeled as being by Ronnie Dio as a solo artist even if the rest of the Prophets contributed to the recording. The group released several singles during the following years, until early 1967. Dio continued to use his birth name on any songwriting credits on those releases.

In late 1967 Ronnie Dio and the Prophets transformed into a new band called The Electric Elves and added a keyboard player. Following recovery from a deadly car accident in February 1968 (which killed guitarist Nick Pantas and put Dio and other band members in the hospital briefly), the group shortened its name to The Elves and used that name until mid 1972 when it released its first proper album under the name Elf. Over the next few years, the group went on to become a regular opening act for Deep Purple. Elf recorded three albums until the members' involvement recording the first Rainbow album in early 1975 resulted in Elf disbanding.

Rainbow

Dio and Ritchie Blackmore performing with Rainbow

Dio's vocals caught the ear of Deep Purple guitarist Ritchie Blackmore in the mid-1970s, who was planning on leaving then due to creative differences over the band's new direction. Blackmore invited Dio along with Gary Driscoll to record two songs in Tampa, Florida on December 12, 1974. Blackmore stated in 1983, "I left Deep Purple because I'd met up with Ronnie Dio, and he was so easy to work with. He was originally just going to do one track of a solo LP, but we ended up doing the whole LP in three weeks, which I was very excited about."[11] Being satisfied with the results, Blackmore decided to recruit more of Elf's musicians and form his own band, initially known as Ritchie Blackmore's Rainbow. They released the self-titled debut album *Ritchie Blackmore's Rainbow* in early 1975. After that, Dio recorded two more studio albums (*Rising* and *Long Live Rock 'n' Roll*) and two live albums ("Live in Germany 1976") and (*On Stage*) with Blackmore. During his tenure with Rainbow, Dio and Blackmore were the only constant members. Dio is credited on those albums for all lyrical authorship as well as collaboration with Blackmore on musical arrangement. Dio and Blackmore split, with Blackmore taking the band in a more commercial direction, with Graham Bonnet on vocals and the album "Down to Earth".

Black Sabbath

Dio left Rainbow in 1979 and soon joined Black Sabbath, replacing the fired Ozzy Osbourne. Dio met Sabbath guitarist Tony Iommi by chance at The Rainbow on Sunset Strip in Los Angeles in 1979.[11] Both men were in similar situations, as Dio was seeking a new project and Iommi required a vocalist. Dio said of the encounter, "It must have been fate, because we connected so instantly."[11] The pair kept in touch via telephone until Dio arrived at Iommi's Los Angeles house for a relaxed, getting-to-know-you jam session. On that first day the duo wrote the song, "Children of the Sea", which would appear on the *Heaven and Hell* album, the first the band recorded with Dio as vocalist in 1980.

The follow-up album, *Mob Rules*, featured new drummer Vinny Appice. Personality conflicts began emerging within the band. "Ronnie came into the band and he was doing whatever we told him, basically because he wanted the gig. The next album was a little different," Iommi recalled.[11] In 1982, conflict arose over the mixing of the *Live Evil* album. Iommi asserted that the album's engineer began complaining to him that he would work all day long on a mix, only to have Dio return to the studio at night to "do his own mix" in which his vocals were more prominent.[11] This was denied by Dio. The conflict led to Dio and Appice ultimately quitting the band later that year.

In 1992, Dio briefly returned to Black Sabbath to record the *Dehumanizer* album. The album was a minor hit, reaching the Top 40 in the United Kingdom and #44 on the *Billboard 200*. The single "Time Machine" was featured in the movie *Wayne's World*, the tenth highest-grossing film of 1992. Soon Dio and Appice again left the band, citing an inability to work with Iommi and Butler.

Dio

Main article: Dio (band)

Wanting to continue together as a band, Ronnie James Dio and Vinnie Appice formed Dio, the band, in 1982. Vivian Campbell played guitar and Jimmy Bain was on bass; the latter of whom Dio had known since the old Rainbow days. Their debut album, *Holy Diver*, included the hit singles "Rainbow in the Dark" and "Holy Diver", the album's title track.

The band added keyboardist Claude Schnell and recorded

two more full-length studio albums, *The Last in Line* and *Sacred Heart*. A notable live recording, *A Special From The Spectrum*, was filmed during the band's second world tour and released in VHS format only. The band changed members over the years, eventually leaving Dio as the only original member in 1990. Except for a few breaks, Dio, the band, were always touring or recording. They released ten albums, with *Master of the Moon* being the last one, recorded in 2004.

Heaven and Hell

Main article: Heaven & Hell (band)
In October 2006, it was confirmed that Dio would be joining Black Sabbath members Tony Iommi, Geezer Butler, and former Black Sabbath drummer Vinny Appice to tour under the moniker Heaven & Hell, the title of the first Dio era Black Sabbath album. They chose the name Heaven & Hell as Tony Iommi and Geezer Butler were still in Black Sabbath with Ozzy Osbourne and felt it was best to use a different moniker for the Dio version of the band. Original Black Sabbath drummer Bill Ward was to be involved in this project, but he later withdrew.

In 2007, the band recorded three new songs under the Black Sabbath name for the compilation album *Black Sabbath: The Dio Years*.

In 2008, the band completed a 98-date world tour. The band released one album under the Heaven & Hell name, *The Devil You Know*, to critical and commercial acclaim. They also had planned to release a follow-up in 2010.

Dio "throwing horns", a gesture commonly used by both artists and fans of heavy metal music

Other projects

In 1974, Dio sang on the Roger Glover conducted and produced concept album *The Butterfly Ball and the Grasshopper's Feast*. Along with other guest-singers, the album featured Deep Purple alumni Glenn Hughes and David Coverdale. Dio provided vocals for the songs "Homeward", "Sitting in a Dream", and the UK single "Love is All".

In 1980, Dio sang the tracks "To Live for the King" and "Mask of the Great Deceiver" on Kerry Livgren's solo album, *Seeds of Change*. Dio, who was between stints as singer for Ritchie Blackmore's Rainbow and Black Sabbath, later proved somewhat controversial among Livgren's Christian fans, as Black Sabbath and Dio were then perceived as "satanic" by many Christians. Dio said in an interview that he did not consider the album to be a "Christian" album and had performed on it as a favor to Livgren.

In 1985, Dio contributed to the metal world's answer to Band Aid and USA for Africa with the Hear 'n Aid project. With a heavy metal all-star ensemble which was the brainchild of his fellow Dio band mates Vivian Campbell and Jimmy Bain, he sang some of the vocals on the single "Stars" and an album full of songs from other artists given to charity.

The project raised $1 million within a year.

In 1997, Dio made a cameo on Pat Boone's *In a Metal Mood: No More Mr. Nice Guy*, an album of famous heavy metal songs played in big band style. Dio can be heard singing backup on Boone's take of "Holy Diver". In 1999, he was parodied in the TV show South Park, in the episode Hooked on Monkey Fonics, which he later went on to describe as "wonderful".[12]

In 1999, Dio participated in a significant Deep Purple project, Concerto for Group and Orchestra, where he recorded cover versions of Deep Purple songs, and reprised his songs from the earlier The Butterfly Ball and the Grasshopper's Feast album.

Tenacious D included a tribute song entitled "Dio" that appeared on their self-titled album. The song explains how he has to "pass the torch" for a new generation. Reportedly, Dio approved of it, and had Tenacious D appear in his video "Push" from *Killing the Dragon* in 2002. He also appeared in the film *Tenacious D in The Pick of Destiny*, playing himself.

In 2005, Dio was revealed to be the voice behind Dr. X in *Operation: Mindcrime II*, the sequel to Queensrÿche's seminal concept album *Operation: Mindcrime*. His part was shown in a prerecorded video on the subsequent tour, and Ronnie appeared onstage to sing the part live on at least one occasion (both shown on the *Mindcrime at the Moore* DVD).

On January 17, 2007, he was inducted into the Rock Walk of Fame at Guitar Center on Hollywood's Sunset Boulevard.

Dio is thanked in the end credits of the 2011 film *Atlas Shrugged: Part I*, due to his being "one of the people who kept the project alive."[13]

2.58.3 Personal life

Dio and drummer Vinny Appice performing with Heaven & Hell in Katowice, Poland, on June 20, 2007

Dio and his first wife, Loretta Berardi (born 1941), adopted a son, novelist Dan Padavona.[5]

After divorcing Berardi, he married Wendy Gaxiola (born 1945) who also served as his manager. In the 1980s, she managed the Los Angeles rock bands Rough Cutt, and Hellion. Dio remained married to Gaxiola until his death.

Illness and death

On November 25, 2009, Wendy announced that Dio had been diagnosed with stomach cancer[14] and was being treated at the M.D. Anderson Cancer Center in Houston, Texas, but that he would be back on stage when recovered.

On May 4, 2010, Heaven & Hell announced they were canceling all summer dates as a result of Dio's ill health.[15] His last live performance was with Heaven & Hell on August 29, 2009, in Atlantic City, New Jersey.

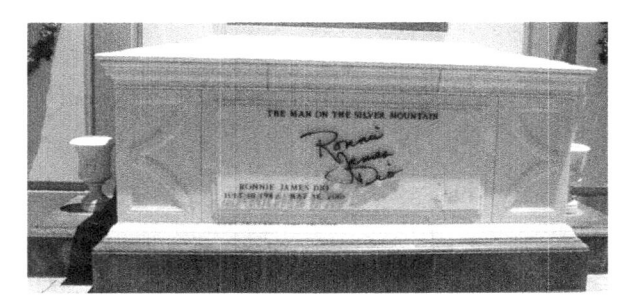

The tomb of Ronnie James Dio (note the "throwing horns" sign on the flanking urns)

Dio died at 7:45 am (CDT) on May 16, 2010, of metastasized stomach cancer, according to official sources.[16][17][18]

A public memorial service was held on May 30, 2010 at The Hall of Liberty, Forest Lawn Hollywood Hills, Los Angeles.[19] The hall was filled to capacity, with more fans sitting outside the hall watching from a screen. Friends, family, and former and current band mates of Dio gave speeches and performed including Rudy Sarzo, Geoff Tate, John Payne, Glenn Hughes, Joey Belladonna, and Heaven & Hell keyboard player, Scott Warren. On the screen was an accompanying documentary covering Dio's career from his early days with Elf to his final project with Heaven & Hell.

2.58.4 Legacy

A tribute monument of Ronnie James Dio in Kavarna, Bulgaria

Dio's career spanned over fifty years. During this period,

and particularly in the 21st century, he received a number of distinctions and awards. He was inducted into the Cortland City Hall of Fame in 2004, and has a street named after him there called Dio Way. *Classic Rock Magazine* awarded Dio with the "Metal Guru Award" at their yearly "Roll of Honour" awards ceremony in 2006. On January 17, 2007, Dio was inducted into Guitar Center's Rock Walk of Fame in Hollywood. Dio was named "Best Metal Singer" at the *Revolver* Golden Gods Awards in April 2010 for his work on *The Devil You Know*, making him the oldest recipient of this award at age 67. He accepted the award in person at what was to be his final public appearance, less than one month before his death.[20] The main stage of Bloodstock Open Air is also named after him in tribute after Heaven & Hell pulled out upon his death. Also the main stage on Masters of Rock festival carries his name since summer 2010. A Dio monument has been unveiled in Kavarna, Bulgaria.[21] In Mexico the biggest metal fest was named "Hell and Heaven" in honor of Dio; the organization says that the festival was named that way since they had worked with Dio, referring to him as "the greatest singer and person we ever had worked with, a really humble person"

Rolling Stone magazine eulogized Dio with these words: "It wasn't just his mighty pipes that made him Ronnie James Dio — it was his moral fervor...what always stood out was Dio's raging compassion for the lost rock & roll children in his audience. Dio never pretended to be one of the kids — he sang as an adult assuring us that we weren't alone in our suffering, and some day we might even be proud of conquering it".[22]

On July 10, 2011, in parallel to Dio's birthday, his home town of Cortland, New York, held a day-long event featuring many central New York local bands and talent for a benefit to the Stand Up and Shout Cancer foundation for cancer research and Dio Memorial concert. Part of the proceeds from the event went to fund a memorial music scholarship for the local city high-school in his name.[23]

On March 31, 2014, the tribute album *Ronnie James Dio This Is Your Life* was released. It was organized and produced by Wendy Gaxiola, with album proceeds benefiting the Ronnie James Dio Stand Up and Shout Cancer Fund.[24]

The character Dio Brando from JoJo's Bizarre Adventure is a reference/homage to the singer.

2.58.5 Band timeline

- The Vegas Kings (1957–1958)
- Ronnie & The Rumblers (1958)
- Ronnie & The Red Caps (1958–1961)
- Ronnie Dio & The Prophets (1961–1967)
- The Electric Elves (1967–1969)
- The Elves (1969–1970)
- Elf (1970–1975)
- Rainbow (1975–1979)
- Black Sabbath (1979–1982, 1991–1992, 2007)
- Dio (1982–1991, 1993–2010)
- Hear 'n Aid (1985)
- Heaven & Hell (2006–2010)

Timeline

2.58.6 Discography

Main article: Ronnie James Dio discography

2.58.7 References

[1] "Ronnie James Dio, Rock Vocalist, Dies at 67".

[2] "Ronny Dio's Early Years". Pavadona.com. Retrieved 2011-12-08.

[3] Bloom 2007, p. 186.

[4] Van Pelt, Doug (May–June 1997). "What Dio Sez". *HM Magazine* (65). ISSN 1066-6923. Archived from the original on December 12, 2000. Retrieved 2007-04-30.

[5] Sweeting, Adam (May 17, 2010). "Ronnie James Dio obituary". *The Guardian* (London).

[6] "Talk Today – Ronnie James Dio". USA Today. June 17, 2002. Retrieved June 26, 2013.

[7] "fortunecity.com". Rivendell.fortunecity.com. Retrieved 2010-11-13.

[8] "Ronnie James Dio interview". Ronniejamesdiosite.com. Retrieved 2010-11-13.

[9] Wilson, Dave. *Rock Formations: Categorical Answers to How Band Names Were Formed*. San Jose, Calif.: Cidermill Books, 2004. ISBN 0-9748483-5-2

[10] "Tapio's Ronnie James Dio Pages: Ronnie Dio & The Prophets 7" Discography". Dio.net. Retrieved 2013-02-06.

[11] Hotten, Jon. "The Dio Years" (PDF). Archived (PDF) from the original on January 24, 2009. Retrieved June 13, 2013.

[12] "Ronnie James Dio on Reality Check TV (2002)". YouTube. June 25, 2009. Retrieved 2014-05-18.

[13] Weigel, David (March 3, 2011) Libertarians Shrugged, *Slate.com*

[14] "Ronnie James Dio Diagnosed With Stomach Cancer". Blabbermouth.net. November 25, 2009. Retrieved November 26, 2009.

[15] "HEAVEN & HELL: All Summer Shows Canceled". Roadrunnerrecords.com. Retrieved 2010-11-13.

[16] "CNN.com: Metal rocker Ronnie James Dio has died, wife says". News.blogs.cnn.com. May 16, 2010. Retrieved 2010-11-13.

[17] "Legendary Heavy Metal Vocalist RONNIE JAMES DIO Dies". Roadrunnerrecords.com. Retrieved 2010-11-13.

[18] "Officially communicated of Dio's death". Ronniejamesdio.com. Retrieved 2010-11-13.

[19] The Associated Press (May 31, 2010). "Ronnie James Dio remembered in L.A". Cbc.ca. Retrieved 2010-11-13.

[20] "The Second Annual Revolver Golden Gods Winners Are Revealed! – Revolver Golden Gods Awards". Revolvermag.com. April 9, 2010. Retrieved 2010-11-13.

[21] "Паметник на Рони Джеймс Дио откриха в Каварна". Vesti.bg. October 13, 2010. Retrieved 2010-11-13.

[22] "Farewell, Dio: You Got to Bleed for the Dancer".

[23] Dick Bottoff (July 10, 2011). "DIO Tribute Web Site". Standupandshoutcortland.org. Retrieved 2011-08-21.

[24] Archived March 29, 2014 at the Wayback Machine

2.58.8 Sources

Pillsbury, Glenn (2013). "Dio's Lost Decade: Recovering the 1960s Career of Ronnie James Dio". Retrieved from http://www.peteofthestreet.net/dioslostdecade

2.58.9 External links

- Official website
- Ronnie James Dio at Billboard.com
- Memorial benefit event
- MTV
- Early career

2.59 Salem (UK band)

Not to be confused with Salem (Israel band) or Salem (Michigan band).

Salem is a hard rock/metal band from Hull, England. The band was formed following the split of the New Wave of British Heavy Metal band Ethel The Frog who featured on the *Metal for Muthas* compilations alongside the likes of Iron Maiden, Toad the Wet Sprocket, Praying Mantis and Samson. Salem recorded three demos and a single in the early 1980s; a compilation album of these recordings was released in 2010.

The band re-formed (aka Salem UK) in 2009 and has since released two new EPs "New Tricks" and "X Rated" EP, and the album "Forgotten Dreams". The band has also filmed two videos and has played numerous festivals and gigs in UK, across Europe and beyond. A re-mastered and rearranged edition of the 2010 "In The Beginning ..." album was released in July 2015 and the next new album is due for release in early 2016.

2.59.1 Career

1979 – 1983

Salem (I) was founded in late 1979 by two members of Ethel The Frog, Paul Tognola (singer/guitar) and Paul Conyers (drums), with Adrian Jenkinson (bass) and Paul Macnamara (lead guitar). The first band met up on 2 January 1980 in The Red Lion pub in Anlaby, East Riding of Yorkshire. After a period of song writing and rehearsal, Salem gigged regularly and built a solid following in the Hull area. They recorded their first demo at Fairview Studios, Willerby in January 1981.

Salem (III) - Hull, 1983

Soon after this first demo,Tognola left the band to be replaced by Simon Saxby as the new singer and later in the year by Mark Allison as the second guitarist. With this new line-up, **Salem (II)** released its double A-side single, "Cold As Steel"/"Reach To Eternity", recorded again at Fairview on 4 April 1982; this considered to be one of the notable recordings from Fairview. Following the interview with Macnamara in the May 1982 *Kerrang!* (No. 15), the single appeared in the 'local chart' section of the magazine and singles were sold globally. According to the *NWOBHM Encyclopaedia*,[1] the single is now, "a highly collectable and valuable rarity", and is also listed in Record Collector's "Rare Record Price Guide".[2]

Salem (III) continued with a new drummer Paul Mendham to perform in the North and North East of England and recorded another demo in September 1982, at Adda Studios in East Hull. Then as a result of their winning a Battle of bands competition at Huddersfield Polytechnic, Salem recorded the final demo at September Sound, Huddersfield, in March 1983.

Salem played their final gig on 31 May 1983, when the members left to follow different projects.

2009 – present

A double album compilation of the band's 1980s recordings, entitled *In The Beginning ...*, was released in June 2010 on High Roller Records (LP) and Pure Steel Records (CD).

Salem (III) reformed and played their first performance in 27 years in hometown Hull at The Adelphi on 20 November 2010, the story attracting interest in the press.[3][4]

In 2011, the band produced the limited edition, 'pre-release' "New Tricks" EP featuring three new tracks, "Retribution", "This Heart Is Mine" and "High Stakes." and a played another gig in Hull.[5]

In July 2012, Ricky Squires, formerly of the dEAd End KIdS[6] and the Heavy Metal Kids joined on drums to play festivals and gigs with Salem in Europe, including the Heavy Metal Night V[7] in Martinsicuro, Italy, Negosonic in Aalst and Ages of Metal IV[8] in Oostrozebeke, Belgium, and the Metieval Winterfest[9] back in Hull.

The band, as with Mendham again, continued to record further music and released their limited edition "X Rated" EP for the BROFEST#1 in Newcastle on 2 March 2013, including a bonus new recording of "Reach To Eternity". Further gigs in 2013 included shows in Netherlands, Germany, and back home in the UK at The Fleece in Bristol with Jaguar and at Fruit in Hull.

Salem signed with Pure Steel Records again[10] to release a new album "Forgotten Dreams" on 6 December 2013.[11] The album, recorded at Hairy Monster Studios,[12] has received critical acclaim as an "expertly crafted"[13] "masterpiece".[14]

In 2014, the band shot a short film at Fort Paull and in the crypt of Holy Trinity in Hull for "Forgotten Dreams" on YouTube. Salem also played numerous festivals and gigs in UK, Europe and beyond, including Play It Loud[15] in Italy, Very 'Eavy Festival[16] in Netherlands, Headbangers Open Air in Germany, and Rock You To Hell[17] in Greece. The final 2014 gig was in Dubai,[18] United Arab Emirates with deputy drummer, Oli Davis.

Salem has played gigs in Belgium and England in 2015, and at festivals including Wildfire, Scotland,[19] BÄÄÄM in Germany, Power & Glory II and headlining RockWich in UK. Also earlier in the year, the band filmed a second videos of the song "The Answer" on YouTube at sites in Barton-upon-Humber and Beverley.

In July 2015, a new re-mastered version of the *In The Beginning ...*[20] album was released by High Roller Records. The songs have been re-arranged into the original chronological order. Salem also contributed the track "Forgotten Dreams" to the RockWich 2015 commemorative CD,[21] with all the other bands from the festival; all profits from the sale of the CD go to the Sophie Lancaster Foundation.[22]

The band is completing the recording of a new album at Hairy Monster Studios again. Macnamara revealed in an interview[23] with PlanetMosh that Salem is working on a collaboration with Manny Charlton. The album is expected to be ready for release in early 2016.

In October 2015, Salem was invited to play at British Steel festival in Fismes, France in place of Oliver/Dawson Saxon who had to cancel. Salem is already booked at gigs and festivals for 2016 including a return to Headbangers Open Air and gigs with Diamond Head, Witchfynde and Spartan Warrior.

Salem has been cited, along with Iron Maiden, Saxon and Tygers of Pan Tang, as one of the "top 10 NWOBHM bands that are better than ever!",.[24]

2.59.2 Line-up

Salem (I)

- Paul Tognola (vocals, guitar) – formerly of Ethel the Frog

- Paul Macnamara (lead guitar)

- Adrian Jenkinson (bass)

- Paul Conyers (drums) – formerly of Ethel the Frog

Salem (II)

- Simon Saxby (vocals)
- Paul Macnamara (guitar)
- Mark Allison (guitar)
- Adrian Jenkinson (bass)
- Paul Conyers (drums)

Salem (III)

- Simon Saxby (vocals)
- Paul Macnamara (guitar)
- Mark Allison (guitar)
- Adrian Jenkinson (bass)
- Paul Mendham (drums)

2.59.3 Discography

- "Cold as Steel" / "Reach to Eternity" (1982) Hilton Records
- "Reach to Eternity" appears on the *NWOBHM Vol. 6* (1992) bootleg CD
- "Reach to Eternity" is also on the *NWOBHM – Vinyl revenge I (2005) bootleg*
- *In the Beginning ...* (double album) (2010), High Roller Records (vinyl), Pure Steel Records (CD)
- *New Tricks* (2011) EP
- *X Rated* (2013) EP
- *Forgotten Dreams* (2013) Pure Rock Records (vinyl and CD)
- *In the Beginning ...* version 2, (2015), High Roller Records CD
- "Forgotten Dreams" appears on the *RockWich 2015* commemorative CD

2.59.4 See also

- List of New Wave of British Heavy Metal bands

2.59.5 References

[1] "The New Wave of British Heavy Metal Encyclopaedia", Malc MacMillan, IP Verlag (16 November 2001), (ISBN 978-3931624163) pp. 500–501

[2] "Rare Record Price Guide 2010", Ian Shirley, Andy McDuff, Jeff Ball, and Val Cutts, Diamond Publishing Group Ltd; 9th Revised edition (1 October 2008), (ISBN 0953260194), p. 1046

[3] Hull Daily Mail 22 July 2010

[4] Hull Daily Mail 18 November 2010

[5] Hull Daily Mail 24 November 2011

[6] dEAd End KIdS

[7] Heavy Metal Night V festival 2012

[8] Ages of Metal

[9] Hull Daily Mail 13 December 2012

[10] Pure Steel Records 23 October 2013

[11] Bravewords 29 October 2013

[12] Hairy Monster Studios

[13] Metal Forces Magazine November 2013

[14] Metal Temple 21 November 2013

[15] Play It Loud Festival Facebook Official Page

[16] www.AllMetalFest.com 2014

[17] Rock You To Hell Festival 2014

[18] Salem UK to perform in Dubai - Gulf News 9 September 2014

[19] Review of Wildfire Festival, Scotland - All About The Rock 28 June 2015

[20] In The Beginning ... re-released, High Roller Records 21 July 2015

[21] RockWich 2015

[22] WorshipMetal - 1 October 2015

[23] Salem interview at Rockwich Festival - PlanetMosh 30 August 2015

[24] 10 New Wave Of British Heavy Metal Bands That Are Better Than Ever - What Culture, 19 September 2014

2.59.6 External links

- Official Salem website
- High Roller Records
- Pure Steel Records
- The NWOBHM Online Encyclopedia
- Encyclopaedia Metallum
- Fairview Studios
- Hairy Monster Studios, Hull

2.60 Samson (band)

Samson were a British hard rock band formed in 1977 by guitarist and vocalist Paul Samson. They are best known for their first three albums with future Iron Maiden singer Bruce Dickinson, then known as "Bruce Bruce", and drummer Thunderstick (real name Barry Graham Purkis), who wore a leather mask and performed on stage in a metal cage. Drummer Clive Burr was also a member of the band, both before and after his tenure with Iron Maiden. Drummer Mel Gaynor had a successful music career being a member of Simple Minds for over 20 years. Dickinson's replacement on vocals, Nicky Moore, performed with Samson throughout the mid-1980s and again from the late 1990s onwards; he has also been a member of the bands Mammoth and Nicky Moore and the Blues Corporation.

2.60.1 Career

In 1976 Paul Samson replaced Bernie Tormé in London-based band Scrapyard, joining bassist John McCoy and drummer Roger Hunt. The band name was changed to McCoy, and they built up a busy gigging schedule, whilst also independently playing various sessions. Eventually, McCoy left to join Atomic Rooster. His replacement was the band's sound engineer and a close friend of Paul Samson's, Chris Aylmer. Aylmer suggested a name change to Samson, and recommended a young drummer, Clive Burr, whom he had previously played with in the band Maya. Burr joined, and Samson was born, although for a time Paul Samson used bassist Bill Pickard and drummer Paul Gunn on odd gigs when Aylmer and Burr were honouring previous commitments. Various other people were tried out to expand the line up: Paul Samson got in touch with an old bandmate, bass player Stewart Cochrane, and asked him to try out with the group as a four-piece, with the current bass player Chris Aylmer on second guitar alongside Paul. Only one gig was played in this incarnation, at The Nag's Head pub in Rochester, Kent on 11 March 1978, where it was decided that Paul Samson and Aylmer's playing styles were not compatible, so they went back to being a three-piece. Cochrane joined the avant-garde jazz-rock band Spanish Fly; he later continued his career as an orchestra-leader for Holland America Line, Windstar Cruises and performed and recorded with members of bands The Animals, Nashville Teens and Steve Hackett Band. In October 1978, lead vocalist Mark Newman joined, but after about six shows, Paul Samson resumed lead vocals and they reverted to a three-piece line-up.

At the end of 1978, Burr left. They auditioned over 60 drummers, and eventually decided on Barry Purkis. The band were offered a recording contract, but Aylmer would not commit, so Paul Samson and Purkis decided that, as John McCoy was producing and had co-written much of the material, they would ask him to play bass on the album. The album was recorded for release on Lazer records, and given the title *Survivors*. In late 1979 Bruce Dickinson joined as lead vocalist under the name 'Bruce Bruce'.

The band's second album, *Head On*, was released in July 1980 and peaked at No. 34 in the UK Albums Chart[1] The supporting tour was full of controversy and legal issues, due to problems with their management.[2] They kept writing and rehearsing for a new record. Ten songs had already been composed, by October 1980, and were ready to be recorded.[2] At the same time, the band re-issued their debut album, *Survivors*, now with Dickinson handling vocal duties. The tour continued until the end of the year, when Samson entered the studio to record their third album, *Shock Tactics*. This was the last album Dickinson recorded with the band. Samson faced an innumerable amount of problems with their management.[3] They were always being booked on ill-matched support tours. After leaving their management in 1981 they discovered that their record company was going bankrupt. Dickinson said they "made every mistake in the business".[3] His last performance with Samson was at the Reading Festival in 1981. This was recorded by the BBC and released in 1990, as the live album *Live at Reading 1981*.

The group posted three entries in the UK Singles Chart. These were "Riding With The Angels (1981, No. 54), "Losing My Grip" (1982, No. 63) and "Red Skies (1983, No. 65).[4]

Following Dickinson's departure, former Hackensack and Tiger vocalist Nicky Moore was recruited to front the band who had also signed a new recording contract with Polydor. Samson's first release with Moore was the "Losing My Grip" EP in 1982. The title track as well as "Pyramid to the Stars" had originally been cut with Dickinson. Those versions would remain unreleased until they surfaced on the *Shock Tactics* CD re-release in 2001. Samson issued two albums with Moore, 1982's *Before the Storm* and 1984 *Don't Get Even, Get Mad* before the group disbanded with Paul Samson carrying on solo.

In 1990, Paul Samson asked New York singer/songwriter Rek Anthony to write lyrics and vocal melodies for Samson's studio reformation project. As a collaboration, Anthony wrote and recorded the lyrics and vocal melodies for eight songs while in New York, and in London re-recorded five demos at Picnic Studios. With limited time and budget, the band could only record five demo songs and the project was never completed. The Picnic demos were never picked up by Samson's record company, and sat idle for almost nine years. Anthony, Paul Samson, Gerry Sherwin and Tony Tuohy played some shows in Germany and the Netherlands under the name English Rogues, and as Samson whilst opening for Girlschool. After the dates in Europe, Anthony returned to New York. In 1999, Paul Samson released a CD containing five of the compositions from the Picnic Demos, entitled *Past, Present and Future*.

In 1999, the Samson-Aylmer-Thunderstick line-up reformed for a live show in Tokyo, and in 2000, with Nicky Moore back on board, a series of live dates, including a "25th Anniversary of the NWoBHM" concert at the London Astoria on 26 May 2000, which also featured Angel Witch on the bill. Samson's performance was recorded and released as a live album. The same line-up later appeared at the Wacken Open Air rock festival on 4 August 2000.

The group effectively disbanded with Paul Samson's death from cancer on 9 August 2002. Moore paid tribute to his late bandmate at the Sweden Rock Festival on 12 June 2004, with a set entitled "Nicky Moore plays Samson".[5]

Bass player Chris Aylmer born Christopher Robin Aylmer, 7 February 1948 died on 9 January 2007 following a battle with throat cancer.

The band appeared in a short-movie *Biceps of Steel* in 1980, directed by Julien Temple,[2] which was intended as the B-film to a major feature produced and promoted by the record company. The film featured two music-video type sequences which form the 15 minute film. Though it has been largely forgotten, clips from it were seen in the movie *The Incubus* (1981). However, in 2006 *Biceps of Steel* resurfaced on Bruce Dickinson's *Anthology* DVD.

Drummer Clive Burr died on 12 March 2013 after many years suffering from multiple sclerosis.

2.60.2 Discography

2.60.3 Members

2.60.4 Lineups

2.60.5 See also

- List of New Wave of British Heavy Metal bands

2.60.6 References

[1] "UK Top 40 Chart Archive, British Singles & Album Charts". everyHit.com. Retrieved 2008-12-16.

[2] "Samson Biography-sing365". Retrieved 28 May 2009.

[3] "The Bruce Dickinson biography". Book of Hours. Retrieved 12 November 2008.

[4] Roberts, David (2006). *British Hit Singles & Albums* (19th ed.). London: Guinness World Records Limited. p. 480. ISBN 1-904994-10-5.

[5]

2.60.7 External links

- The Official Samson/Paul Samson Website
- *Allmusic*: Samson

2.61 Satan (band)

Satan are a heavy metal band originating from Newcastle, England in 1979, known as part of the New Wave of British Heavy Metal movement. The band is considered influential for playing a form of proto-thrash/speed metal that was fairly advanced by the standards of the early 1980s.[1]

Their line-up has undergone a number of personnel changes and even name changes; for a time the band was called **Blind Fury**, putting out one album, 1985's *Out of Reach*, under that moniker before reverting to Satan. In 1988, the group changed its name to **Pariah**, releasing two albums under that name before folding in the early 90s. In 1998, Pariah released another album. The band's shifting line-up has included members of many other heavy metal bands such as Blitzkrieg, Atomkraft, Avenger, Persian Risk, Cronos and Battleaxe. In 1990, Steve Ramsey (guitar) and Graeme English (bass) together with singer Martin Walkyier of UK thrash metal band Sabbat founded folk metal band Skyclad.

Satan performed a one-off gig at Germany's Wacken Open Air in 2004[2] and finally reunited in 2011. Since their reunion, the band has performed at several European festivals and released a new album, *Life Sentence*, in April, 2013 via Listenable Records.[3] In 2014 the band increased their global reach by touring in North and South America.

On 2 October 2015 the band released their fourth studio album, *Atom by Atom*, while two days earlier the entire album was made available for streaming via *Invisible Oranges*.[4]

2.61.1 Members

2.61.2 Discography

Studio Albums

Singles and EPs

- *Kiss of Death* (1982)
- *Into the Future* (1986)

Demos

- *The First Demo* (1981)
- *Into the Fire* (1982)
- *Dirt Demo '86* (1986)

Compilations and live albums

- *Blitzkrieg in Holland* (2000)
- *Live in the Act* (2004)
- *Into the Fire / Kiss of Death* (2011)
- *The Early Demos* (2011)

2.61.3 See also

- List of New Wave of British Heavy Metal bands

2.61.4 References

[1] Popoff, Martin (2005). *The Collector's Guide to Heavy Metal Volume 2: The Eighties*. Toronto: Collector's Guide Publishing. p. 309. ISBN 1-894959-31-0.

[2] "SATAN Perform Live for First Time in 20 Years: Photos Available". Blabbermouth.net. Retrieved 2012-09-17.

[3] "'Life Sentence' Cover Art & Release Date". Satanmusic.com. Retrieved 2013-02-16.

[4] "'Atom by Atom' Available For Streaming In Its Entirety!". 30 September 2015.

2.61.5 External links

- Official website
- Official Facebook
- Official Twitter

2.62 Savage (band)

This article is about the English heavy metal band. For the Italian musician, see Roberto Zanetti.

Savage is a heavy metal band from Mansfield, England.

Savage's first album Loose 'N Lethal

The band is most remembered for the song titled 'Let it Loose', a track which made significant impact on the early 1980s metal scene (indeed, it was later covered by Metallica on Ron McGovney's Garage demo, and would later give rise to the name of their first album, *Loose 'N Lethal*, released in 1983 and nowadays considered a classic.

The group was formed in 1976 by 16-year-old bass player Chris Bradley, vocalist Chris Gent, guitarist Lee Statham and drummer Mick Percival, but after only one official gig the band disbanded and was re-formed in 1978 by Bradley, joined by Andy Bradbury on guitar, Simon Dawson on drums and his 15-year-old brother Andy Dawson on guitar. Line-up issues continued as Andy Bradbury was replaced by Wayne Renshaw, and Simon Dawson left to be replaced after a long period of searching by Dave Lindley. This was the line up that appeared on the compilation albums *Scene of the Crime* (the album picked up by a young Lars Ulrich, featuring 'Let it Loose'), *Metal Fatigue* and the double A-side single 'Aint No Fit Place'/'The China Run'. Lindley left shortly after this as was replaced by Mark Brown of Tyrant (another Mansfield based band that had appeared on *Scene of the Crime*).

In 1980, they released their first demo tape. In 1981, they managed to release *Scene of the Crime* and, what would be their most renowned song, 'Let it Loose'. The song incorporated a sound bordering on speed and thrash metal, and influenced many bands to follow similar styles.

In 1982, Ebony Records picked up the band. Their first release under the Ebony label was a track for a compilation titled *Metal Fatigue*. The release was met with good reviews, so Savage decided to release a self-financed double A-side single through the Ebony label, which also sold well. Their debut album, *Loose 'N Lethal* was released the following year.

Although being an impressive unit receiving compliments from magazines, fans, and bands, Savage lacked support, since small label Ebony did not know how to promote them beyond semi-pro levels.

In 1984 the band decided to leave Ebony Records and signed to a new label, Zebra Records, part of Cherry Red Records. At the end of the year they issed their first release for Zebra, the 12" EP *We Got the Edge*. This was followed by what was considered a radically different sounding second album, *Hyperactive*, which although gaining great reviews, the band were unable to capitalise on due to a lack of support from management or record company. Finally the band disbanded in 1986, resurfacing in 1995 at the request of fans during the height of Grunge releasing their third album *Holy Wars*, once again to critical acclaim. Albums followed in 1998, *Babylon*, and 2001, *Xtreme Machine*. A protracted hiatus then followed, fuelled by significant personal and family issues that were impacting all members of the band. The band resurfaced in 2011 with a new album *Sons of Malice*, again receiving significant critical acclaim with founding and driving members Chris Bradley and Andy Dawson, joined by Kris Bradley (Chris's son and Andys nephew) on guitar and Mark Nelson on drums. The band have returned to the festival circuit and are currently writing the follow-up album to *Sons of Malice* for a planned release in 2014 as part of a double album that will feature the entire *Loose 'n' Lethal* album recorded live.

2.62.1 Discography

Albums

- *Scene of the Crime* (Compilation album, Suspect Records, 1981)
- *Metal Fatigue* (Compilation album, Ebony Records, 1982)
- *Loose 'N Lethal* (Ebony Records, 1983)
- *Hyperactive* (Zebra Records, 1985)
- *Holy Wars* (Neat Records, 1995)
- *Babylon* (Neat Records, 1996)
- *Xtreme Machine* (Neat Records, 2001)
- *This Ain't No Fit Place* (Best of Compilation, Sanctaury Records, 2002)
- *Sons of Malice* (Minus2Zebra & Infestdead Records,[1][2] 2012)

Singles/EPs

- "Ain't No Fit Place" (Ebony Records, 1982)
- "We Got the Edge" (Zebra Records, 1984)
- "Cardiac" (Black Dragon, 1986)

2.62.2 See also

- List of New Wave of British Heavy Metal bands

2.62.3 References

[1] http://tntmagazine.in/tnt-y-news/northeast-gets-its-first-metal-label-signs-savage-uk/

[2] http://www.metallife.com/news/display_news.php?id=4666

2.63 Saxon (band)

Saxon are an English heavy metal band formed in 1976, in South Yorkshire. As one of the leaders of the New Wave of British Heavy Metal, they had eight UK Top 40 albums in the 1980s including four UK Top 10 albums and two Top 5 albums. The band also had numerous singles in the UK Singles Chart and chart success all over Europe and Japan, as well as success in the US. During the 1980s Saxon established themselves as one of Europe's biggest metal acts. The band tours regularly and have sold more than 15 million albums worldwide. They are considered one of the classic metal acts and have influenced many bands such as Metallica, Mötley Crüe, Pantera, Sodom, Skid Row, and Megadeth.[1]

2.63.1 History

Formation and early years (1976-1979)

Saxon began as with a lineup formed by Peter "Biff" Byford on vocals, Paul Quinn and Graham Oliver on guitars, Steve "Dobby" Dawson on bass and drummer David Ward and were originally named "Son of a Bitch". The band changed their name to Saxon shortly afterwards, replacing Walker with Peter Gill, and gained support slots on tour with more established bands such as Motörhead. In 1979, the band signed to the UK record label Carrere run by Freddy Cannon and the first group signed to the UK label and released their eponymous debut album.

Success in the UK (1980-1982)

In 1980, the band's follow-up album *Wheels of Steel*, was released and charted at #5 in the UK. It spawned two hit singles: the title track, and the crowd favourite "747 (Strangers in the Night)". The album quickly provided the band with success and they began a series of long-lasting tours across the UK. On 16 August 1980 Saxon appeared at the first Monsters of Rock Festival where they received a very positive reception from the crowd. The band's set was recorded but was not officially released until 2000. On April 1980, Saxon made the first of many appearances on *Top of the Pops*, where they performed the hit single "Wheels of Steel".

Strong Arm of the Law was released later in the year, charting at #11 in the UK. It is considered by many fans to be their best album, and it helped to keep the band's popularity increasing. Two singles were released from this album: the title track and Dallas 1PM, the latter written about the assassination of U.S. President John F. Kennedy. Sold out tours of Europe and the UK followed as the album charted in several European countries. The band had also gained great success in Japan where the single Motorcycle Man had stayed in the charts for almost 6 months.

By 1981, the band had toured most of the world and found themselves with less time to record new material. But recording finally started at several European locations, and at the end of 1981 the band released their fourth album *Denim And Leather* which the band dedicated to their fan base. The album is still popular today and the title track "Denim And Leather" is regarded as a metal anthem. The album also featured many other fan favourites such as "Princess of the Night", "Never Surrender" and "The Bands Played On" which were all UK Top 20 hits. *Denim And Leather* followed its predecessor's success and charted in several European countries and was certified gold in the UK. By this time the band was seen as the leaders of the NWOBHM movement with future greats Iron Maiden and Def Leppard following close behind.

Just as the band was about to embark on a long tour to follow the success of *Denim And Leather*, drummer Pete Gill left the band after injuring his hand. The band had to quickly replace him with Nigel Glockler formerly of Toyah, who had to learn the entire set within a day and a half just before the tour was about to begin. Glockler is still with the band today.

A series of headlining tours around the UK and a sold out tour in Europe with Ozzy Osbourne supporting, highlighted Saxon's immense touring ability and was set in stone with the classic live release *The Eagle Has Landed* (1982 UK no 5). Originally planned as a double live album, the record company decided to release it as a single live album despite protests from the band. The Eagle Has Landed is still a highly regarded live metal album. Saxon also played the 1982 Monsters Of Rock Festival again and became the first band to appear twice.

***Power & the Glory* and EMI years (1983-1987)**

As the NWOBHM movement began to fade, 1983's *Power & the Glory*, their highest selling album to date, saw Saxon cement themselves as the leading metal act in Europe along with Iron Maiden and Judas Priest. The "Power and Glory Tour" of 1983 was an arena tour that began in Europe, and was a huge success. The US leg of the tour with support act Accept proved to be successful and Saxon found themselves becoming a major act in the US as the album, in its first week of release, sold more than 15,000 copies in Los Angeles alone. The emerging glam metal scene in America would however prevent the band's conquest of the American market, as the genre was increasing in mainstream popularity. The cover art of the album was produced by Hollywood film director Ridley Scott. In late 1983 Saxon left Carrere.

Saxon signed with EMI Records in 1984, with their first release on the label being *Crusader*. Though still heavy, critics felt the album had a more commercial sound, and fans began to wonder what direction the band was taking. Despite its commercial sound, the title track became a fan favourite. The album sold over 2 million copies and the 1984 world tour "The World Crusade" was a success both in Europe and America. In the US they had Mötley Crüe and Krokus as support for many shows of the tour as the band spent one year on the road. By this time the band was considered as headliners for 1984's Monsters of Rock at Donington, but scheduling issues and record label disputes kept the band from participating.

The band continued to take a more commercial direction. *Innocence Is No Excuse* released in 1985, created a division amongst fans as the band's once raw, heavy sound had been watered down to gain more attraction to the large US market. The album has, however, gained more appreciation both from fans and critics as time has passed since its initial release. A huge sold out world tour in support of the album followed, but tensions began to appear within the band and by early 1986, bassist Steve Dawson was fired from the band,[2] and Saxon was forced to record their eighth studio album *Rock the Nations* without a replacement bassist. With Elton John making guest appearances as pianist on 2 tracks, and Byford recording the bass parts, the album charted higher than its predecessor and was considered a success. They hired bassist Paul Johnson to play for the band's European arena tour that followed. In the summer of 1986, Saxon headlined the Reading Festival and toured the United States.

In 1987 the band took time off from constant touring and recording that had begun in the mid 1970s, and only a minor tour of the U.S. and Canada was scheduled. In early 1987, Nigel Glockler left the band and was replaced by Nigel Durham.

Decline of fanbase and continued European success (1988-1993)

The band found it hard to attain chart success in America; the release of *Destiny* (1988) did not change this, and Saxon were later dropped by EMI. In 1988 Paul Johnson was replaced by Nibbs Carter. At the time, Carter was only 22 and would later be credited for revitalising the band. Nigel Glockler also decided to return to the band. 1989 saw the release of *Rock n Roll Gypsies* a live album recorded on an arena tour of eastern Europe in 1988, but by 1989 the gigs at the big stadiums and arenas of Europe and the US were few and far between and with no record deal, Saxon´s future was uncertain.

The band eventually decided to embark on a European tour titled '10 Years Of Denim And Leather' which proved to be a successful move as the band was re-established as a popular act. In 1990, they signed to Virgin Records and started work on their new album *Solid Ball of Rock*, which was released in 1991 and proved to be a successful album for Saxon. New bass Player Nibbs Carter co-wrote three songs. In 1992, Saxon carried on this success with the release of *Forever Free*. The album was produced by Biff Byford and Herwig Ursin. A UK version of the album featured an alternate cover with a "Space Marine" from the Warhammer 40,000 tabletop wargame. "Iron Wheels" was released as a single. The song was written about and dedicated to Byford's father who worked in the coal mines of Yorkshire.

Departure of Graham Oliver and return to heavier sound (1994-2002)

Doug Scarratt joined the band in 1996.

During 1994 Saxon recorded the album *Dogs of War*. Just after recording was completed, Graham Oliver was fired by the band for attempting to sell copies of their 1980 performance at Donington without the band's consent, and later joined forces with former member Steve Dawson, forming what would become their incarnation of Saxon.[3] The band replaced Oliver with Doug Scarratt, a long time friend of drummer Nigel Glockler. Saxon recorded a new music video for *Dogs of War*. 1996 saw the release of another live album, *The Eagle Has Landed Pt II*. They also recorded a cover of the Judas Priest song "You've Got Another Thing Comin'", for a tribute album entitled *A Tribute to Judas Priest: Legends of Metal*.

Saxon released *Unleash the Beast*, which was produced by Kalle Trapp and Saxon, in 1997. Saxon began their Unleash The Beast tour in May, where they played in Europe. *Unleash the Beast* reached the top 100 in the charts in Sweden, Germany and Switzerland. In November they played two gigs in Brazil (São Paulo and Santos) and ended the year with a Christmas show in Belgium. In 1998, the band toured the US, as well as also playing the Brazilian Monsters Of Rock. After relentless touring drummer Nigel Glockler took time off to recover from a neck and shoulder injury. He was temporally replaced by Fritz Randow.

September 1999 saw the release of *Metalhead*. The al-

2.63. SAXON (BAND)

bum received praise in Germany where Saxon had begun to play the Wacken Open Air Festival, where they later became a regular fixture. Saxon also headlined the first Bloodstock Festival in the UK. In 2001 they again headlined the Wacken Open Air Festival and recorded the live DVD "Saxon Chronicles". Saxon also released the album *Killing Ground* during the same year. In 2002 Saxon released *Heavy Metal Thunder*, a compilation album featuring re-recorded versions of songs from the band's biggest selling albums.

Battle for band name and *Lionheart* (2003-2006)

In 1999, former members Graham Oliver and Steven Dawson registered 'Saxon' as a trade mark. They then maintained that they had exclusive rights to the name and tried to prevent Biff Byford and Saxon's promoters and merchandisers from using the name. Byford applied to the Trade Mark Registry to have the trade mark declared invalid. He applied on the basis that the registration had been obtained in bad faith and that he was entitled to prevent use of the trade mark by bringing an action for 'passing off', that is an action to stop others misrepresenting themselves as Saxon. In 2003, the High Court declared that it was Byford and the current members of the band who owned the name, and were therefore in a position to prevent Oliver and Dawson passing themselves off as Saxon.[4] After this Oliver and Dawson renamed their band Oliver/Dawson Saxon.

Fritz Randow left the band in 2004. His replacement was former Stratovarius member Jörg Michael. 2004 also saw the release of *Lionheart* their 16th studio album. The album title was inspired from Richard Lionheart, King of England. "Beyond the Grave" was released as a single and a music video. The album received positive reviews and the title track remains a fan favorite.[5] Glockler rejoined the band in 2005. In 2006 the band released the live album, *The Eagle Has Landed – part 3*. The band were due to play that year's Dubai Desert Rock Festival and perform alongside Megadeth. Just before the band were due to play Dubai's Department of Tourism and Commerce Marketing had withdrawn the band's permission to play the festival. It was rumored that the historical lyrics in *Crusader* were the reason for this.[6]

Re-establishment in the UK (2007-2010)

In 2007, Saxon were the subject of an episode of *Harvey Goldsmith's Get Your Act Together*. As part of his programme, Goldsmith wanted to try and restore their popularity and cement their reputation once again. He drafted in two new producers to oversee the production of a new single "If I Was You" (a song about gun culture), which went to number one in the Rock Charts in over 10 countries (becoming their most successful single for over 12 years).[7] At the end of the programme, Saxon played at the sold out Sheffield City Hall. Saxon also performed at the 2008 Download Festival.

Saxon's *The Inner Sanctum* album, released in Europe on 5 March 2007, and North America on 3 April, was seen by critics as their best work in years.[8] The band then started a world tour in support of the album.

Saxon performing at Sweden Rock Festival, 2008.

Saxon released a new studio album, *Into the Labyrinth*, on 12 January 2009. The album received positive reviews and continued the success that *The Inner Sanctum* had created.[9] The band also headlined the Wacken Open Air Festival in Germany. In February, it was announced that the band were cancelling the Spanish leg of their European tour with Iced Earth, due to scheduling issues.[10] At the start of 2009 they toured the UK with Doro, and again at the end of the year they did a UK tour. In August of that year, they played at Sonisphere. In September Saxon announced the release of *Heavy Metal Thunder - The Movie*, a documentary on the band's history from the beginning.

Continuing their success in the UK, Saxon performed at the 2010 Download Festival, which took place at Donington Park between 11 and 13 June. The band played the *Wheels of Steel* album in its entirety to mark the 31st anniversary of its release.[11]

Call to Arms and *Sacrifice* (2011-2014)

Saxon released their nineteenth studio album, *Call to Arms*, on 3 June 2011. It debuted at number 6 on the UK Rock Albums chart.[12] The band embarked on a world tour which saw them visit the US; Saxon also revisited the UK for a second leg of the tour. The band announced on their Call To Arms tour that a number of fans at each venue each paying £10 would be able to watch them soundcheck. This was do-

Nibbs Carter performing at Download Festival 2012

nated to the Nordoff Robbins Music Therapy and Childline charities.[13]

In December, Byford joined Metallica on stage to perform "Motorcycle Man" for the band's 30th anniversary show. Saxon were billed as special guests supporting Judas Priest at Hammersmith Apollo on 26 May 2012. Saxon also played Download Festival 2012, and were recorded playing "Wheels Of Steel" for the festival's Highlights show shown on Sky Arts. On 13 February 2012, the band announced that they were releasing a new live DVD and CD package entitled *Heavy Metal Thunder - Live: Eagles Over Wacken*, which compiled their 2004, 2007 and 2009 performances at the Wacken Open Air across various formats. In March, Saxon won the Metal Hammer 2012 Golden God award for 'Best UK band'.

In October 2012, the band announced that their next studio album would be titled *Sacrifice* and it was released on 25 February 2013.[14] On 11 December 2012 *Heavy Metal Thunder - The Movie* saw an international release and was the first Blu-ray release for the band. 2013 also saw the release of a new compilation album *Unplugged and Strung Up*. 2014 saw the release of a new live album named *St. George's Day Sacrifice - Live in Manchester*. The band also embarked on a tour in October of that year named Warriors of the Road.

***Battering Ram* (2015-present)**

During an interview in November 2014, Biff Byford revealed plans for the band's next studio album, saying: "We're making the new album in January, February and March".[15] During a more recent interview, Byford described the album as a mixture of Rock and roll and Heavy metal. When asked about a possible release date, Byford said: "We're looking at maybe at a summer release. It just depends on whether it's ready or not. We're looking at finishing the album by the end of April. We're keeping our fingers crossed."[16]

On August 1, the band announced October 16th as the release date of *Battering Ram* and also premiered the official video of the title track worldwide.[17]

2.63.2 Personnel

Temporary members

- Sven Dirkschneider - drums (2015) sat in for Nigel Glocker on 'Warriors of the Road' tour - 4 shows only

Timeline

2.63.3 Discography

Main article: Saxon discography

- *Saxon* (1979)
- *Wheels of Steel* (1980)
- *Strong Arm of the Law* (1980)
- *Denim and Leather* (1981)
- *Power & the Glory* (1983)
- *Crusader* (1984)
- *Innocence Is No Excuse* (1985)
- *Rock the Nations* (1986)
- *Destiny* (1988)
- *Solid Ball of Rock* (1991)
- *Forever Free* (1992)
- *Dogs of War* (1995)
- *Unleash the Beast* (1997)
- *Metalhead* (1999)
- *Killing Ground* (2001)
- *Lionheart* (2004)
- *The Inner Sanctum* (2007)
- *Into the Labyrinth* (2009)
- *Call to Arms* (2011)
- *Sacrifice* (2013)
- *Battering Ram* (2015)

2.63.4 See also

- List of New Wave of British Heavy Metal bands

2.63.5 References

[1] "SAXON: Heavy Metal Thunder - Live: Eagles Over Wacken' Third Video Podcast". Blabbermouth.Net. Retrieved 2013-03-22.

[2] http://www.blabbermouth.net/news/oliver-dawson-saxon-s-steve-dawson-we-have-never

[3] "BLABBERMOUTH.NET - OLIVER/DAWSON SAXON's STEVE DAWSON: 'We Have Never Ever Tried To Be The Original Band'". Legacy.roadrunnerrecords.com. Retrieved 2013-03-22.

[4] "BLABBERMOUTH.NET - SAXON Name Dispute Settled". Legacy.roadrunnerrecords.com. Retrieved 2013-03-22.

[5] "Saxon - Lionheart (album review)". Sputnikmusic. 2005-07-30. Retrieved 2013-03-22.

[6] "BLABBERMOUTH.NET - SAXON Barred From Dubai Because Of 'Crusader' Song Lyrics". Legacy.roadrunnerrecords.com. Retrieved 2012-04-24.

[7] "Sunday Old School: Saxon - in Metal News". Metal Underground.com. Retrieved 2013-03-22.

[8] "Lords of Metal ezine". Lordsofmetal.nl. Retrieved 2013-03-22.

[9] Archived 3 June 2011 at the Wayback Machine

[10] "Saxon and Iced Earth Forced To Cancel Spanish Leg Of Metal Crusade". idiomag. 2009-02-17. Retrieved 2009-02-19.

[11] "Saxon, HIM, Coheed & Cambria added to Download 2010 line-up". NME. 23 March 2010. Archived from the original on 20 February 2012. Retrieved 21 February 2012.

[12] "SAXON Announce Official Call To Arms Release Dates". Bravewords.com. Retrieved 2011-05-21.

[13] "Classic Rock » Blog Archive » See Saxon Soundcheck For Charity". Classicrockmagazine.com. 2011-03-30. Retrieved 2012-04-24.

[14] "Announce 'Sacrifice Tour' in Spring". Saxon747.com (Official band website). Retrieved 30 October 2012.

[15] "SAXON To Begin Recording New Album In January". Blabbermouth.Net. 17 November 2014.

[16] "SAXON's BIFF BYFORD On Upcoming Album: 'It's A Mixture Of Rock And Roll And Heavy Metal'". Blabbermouth.Net. 21 March 2015.

[17] "SAXON To Release 21st Studio Album 'Battering Ram' On October 16th, Official Video For Title Track Released". *Metal Shock Finland*. 14 August 2015. Retrieved 14 August 2015.

2.63.6 External links

- Official website
- Saxon Record Label website
- Czech website

2.64 Shy (band)

For the fictional band that appears in the 'Buffy the Vampire Slayer' TV series, see Music in Buffy the Vampire Slayer and Angel.

Shy are a British metal band formed in 1980 under the name "Trojan", hailing from Birmingham, England.

2.64.1 Biography

Formerly known as Trojan, Shy featured vocalist Tony Mills, Steve Harris (guitars) (not to be confused with Iron Maiden's bass player, Steve Harris), Paddy McKenna (keyboards), Mark Badrick (bass) and drummer Alan Kelly. Their first album, called *Once Bitten...Twice...*, was released in 1983. Initial reports from *Kerrang!* were positive, however, a reporter was sarcastic to the band in the interview that would follow. After the release, Mills dropped his David Bowie-esque make up, and Mark Badrick was replaced by former Trouble bassist Roy Davies.

Shy made their major label debut on RCA Records with 1985's *Brave the Storm*. This release gained success despite the single "Hold On (To Your love)" being disqualified from the charts, as early copies included a shrink-wrapped T-shirt. Reviews from *Kerrang!* were more positive, comparing Mill's soaring vocals with those of Geoff Tate, vocalist of Queensrÿche. In the eighteen months that preceded the band's third album, Shy toured with Bon Jovi, Meat Loaf, Twisted Sister, Gary Moore and UFO.

The band's 1987 album, *Excess All Areas*, was recorded in the Netherlands with producer Neil Kernon. The album featured Shy's biggest hit, "Break Down the Walls", co-written with Don Dokken. The album reached Britain's top 75, with *Metal Hammer* magazine being appreciative. 1989 saw the release of *Misspent Youth* on MCA. The album, produced by Roy Thomas Baker, was promoted with American and European tours.

By 1994, Mills had been replaced by vocalist Jon Francis. The band's 1994 album, *Welcome to the Madhouse* was released in Japan by Phonogram but failed to get distribution elsewhere. The band released a live album in 1999, recorded in Europe, and two albums containing previously unreleased songs, *Let the Hammer Fall* and *Regeneration*.

Mills returned to the band in 2000. In 2002, Shy recorded and released an album featuring Mills, *Unfinished Business* which saw Man drummer Bob Richards replacing Kelly.

In 2005, Shy released *Sunset and Vine* on the MTM Music label. In addition to Mills, Harris and Davis, this album featured Mills' ex Siam colleague Ian Richardson on rhythm guitar, and keyboard player Joe Basketts who had previously worked with Mills on his solo album.

In 2006, Mills met with Norwegian rock act TNT, and announced he was leaving Shy to take up the vocalist slot, empty since the announced departure of Tony Harnell. Shy supported TNT on their final tour.

Shy originally had planned for Tony O'Hora to replace Mills. However, Lee Small, formerly of Surveillance and Phenomena, took the helm for a handful of gigs before parting company with Shy in January 2009, he is now once again Shy's vocalist. The band's latest album, entitled simply *Shy* was released in Japan in September 2011 on the Marquee Avalon label, and in Europe in October on Escape Music. Ian Richardson (previously in Siam) has since left Shy but provided some additional rhythm guitar on the latest release. Steve Harris died of a brain tumour in October 2011.[1] A posting on the band's own website dated 29 October 2011, also announced his death. Steve is irreplaceable and the present line-up is the final one.

2.64.2 Discography

- *Once Bitten...Twice...* (1983)
- *Brave the Storm* (1985)
- *Excess All Areas* (1987)
- *Misspent Youth* (1989)
- *Welcome to the Madhouse* (1994)
- *Regeneration* (1999)
- *Let the Hammer Fall* (1999)
- *Live in Europe* (1999)
- *Breakaway* (2001) (EP)
- *Unfinished Business* (2002)
- *Sunset and Vine* (2005)
- *Reflections: The Anthology 1983-2005* (2006)
- *Shy* (2011)[2]

2.64.3 Current members

- Lee Small - Vocals
- Roy Davis - Bass
- Joe Basketts - Keyboards
- Bob Richards - Drums

2.64.4 Previous members

- Tony Mills - Vocals
- Ian Richardson - Guitars
- Steve Harris (Deceased) - Guitar
- Alan Kelly - Drums
- Paddy McKenna - Keyboards
- John Ward (Wardi) - Vocals
- Mark Badrick - Bass

2.64.5 See also

- List of New Wave of British Heavy Metal bands

2.64.6 References

[1] Thedeadrockstarsclub.com - accessed October 30, 2011

[2] Shy Official Website, August 2011.

2.64.7 External links

- Band official website: www.shyonline.co.uk
- In Memory of Steve Harris Fundraising for The Brain Tumour Charity:
- Aorock fan site: www.aorock.com
- Lee's Official Site: www.leesmall.co.uk
- Shy 1980-2000 website (run by Alan Kelly, ex drummer): (http://www.shy-england.4t.com)
- Madhouse Rehearsals (owned by Roy): www.madhouserehearsals.com

- Once Bitten Music (Roy's publishing company): www.oncebittenmusic.com
- Interview with vocalist Lee Small

2.65 Spider (British band)

For British band Spiders, see Spiders (British band). For other similarly named bands, see Spider (disambiguation)

Spider were a British NWOBHM (New Wave of British Heavy Metal) band from Liverpool that formed in 1976.

The band, who were often compared to Status Quo, offered an upbeat sound, which was described as boogie rock. Spider released three albums in the 10 years they were together, titled *Rock 'n' Roll Gypsies* (1982)[1] *Rough Justice* (1984)[2] and *Raise the Banner (For Rock 'n' Roll)* (1986)[3]

The band split in 1986.

2.65.1 Career

Spider formed in 1976, consisted of four young men from Wallasey, including 2 brothers, none of whom had played in bands before.

After releasing "Children of the Street" on the Alien Record Label, Spider were playing, on average 20 dates a month, which included a support slot on the Uriah Heep 1980 Winter Tour.[4]

1982 proved to be the band's most lucrative year. It began in late 1981 when the band were contracted to record for BBC Radio 1 Friday Rock Show.[5] The producer, Tony Wilson, introduced them to Maggi Farren, who set up a recording deal with Creole Records as well as getting the band a support slot on the 1981 Slade Winter Tour.

Spider released the single "Talkin' 'bout Rock 'n' Roll" with Creole, which featured as part of Radio 1's play list.[5] They then went into the studio to begin recording their first album *Rock 'n' Roll Gypsies*,[1] to be released on the Creole label also. However RCA, who had made a late bid for the band, and after negotiations, Spider signed a 6-year recording contract with the record label.

1982 continued with Spider packing out the Marquee Club once a month. They played at the Reading Festival on Sunday 29 August 1982,[6] as well as securing a support slot on the mammoth Gillan Tour in coincidence with the release of their first album.

Dave Bryce, guitarist, currently plays with London rock band AWOL.

2.65.2 Band members

- Colin Harkness - lead vocals, guitar
- Dave "Sniffa" Bryce - guitar, backing vocals
- Brian Burrows - bass, backing vocals
- Rob E. Burrows - drums

2.65.3 Discography

Albums

Singles

- 1977: "Back to the Wall"
- 1980: "Children of the Street"
- 1980: "College Luv"
- 1981: "All the Time"
- 1982: "Talkin' 'Bout Rock 'n' Roll"
- 1982: "Rock 'n' Roll Forever Will Last"
- 1982: "Amazing Grace Medley" (Free with Rock 'n' Roll Forever Will Last)
- 1983: "Why D'Ya Lie to Me"
- 1984: "Here we go Rock 'n' Roll"
- 1984: "Breakaway"
- 1986: "Gimme Gimme It All"

2.65.4 See also

- List of New Wave of British Heavy Metal bands

2.65.5 References

[1] "IronMaid's NWOBHM space: Spider - Rock 'n' Roll Gypsies (160kbps) - 1982". Nwobhmstuff.blogspot.com. 2009-10-24. Retrieved 2014-07-25.

[2] "IronMaid's NWOBHM space: Spider - Rough Justice (192kbps) - 1984". Nwobhmstuff.blogspot.com. 2009-10-24. Retrieved 2014-07-25.

[3] "IronMaid's NWOBHM space: Spider - Raise the Banner (320kbps) - 1986". Nwobhmstuff.blogspot.com. 2009-10-22. Retrieved 2014-07-25.

[4] "Official Uriah Heep Homepage". Uriah Heep. Retrieved 2014-07-25.

[6] "Reading Rock Festival 1982". Ukrockfestivals.com. Retrieved 2014-07-25.

2.65.6 External links

- SPIDER BOOGIE FANWAGON
- Spider Fan Site
- Classic Rock Magazine - Cult Heroes no. 32

2.66 Stampede (band)

Stampede are a British hard rock band formed in 1981 by songwriting partnership Reuben Archer and Laurence Archer. The band signed to Polydor Records, emerging as part of the New Wave of British Heavy Metal scene. Stampede disbanded in 1983, and guitarist Laurence Archer went on to play with UFO, Phil Lynott's Grand Slam amongst other projects.[1] The band reformed 26 years later in 2009, and a new studio album titled 'A Sudden Impulse' was released on 9 May 2011 on the Grind That Axe label,[2] a subsidiary of Rock Candy Records.

2.66.1 History

Pre-Stampede (Lautrec, Lionheart & Wild Horses)

Stampede emerged from the partnership of Reuben Archer (vocalist, songwriter) and stepson Laurence Archer (guitarist, songwriter). Their first major project being the 1977 hard rock band Lautrec, for which they recruited Steve Holbrook of Frome on keyboards, and Simon Riddler of Shepton Mallet on bass. The drummer was Clive Deamer of Frome, who later played in Portishead and Robert Plant's Strange Sensation, as well as session work for many other important projects.[3]

Prior to a Saxon support tour, Deamer left to finish an apprenticeship and was replaced by Steve Jones. The band completed two support tours with Saxon and released a single on the Street Tunes Label: "Shoot Out the Lights" / "Mean Gasoline", now reputed to be one of the rarest 45s of the NWOBHM era.[4] auctioning on eBay for £1800.

In 1980, with no major deal in place, Reuben joined Lionheart, a new supergroup headed by ex-Iron Maiden guitarist Dennis Stratton.[5] Within 4 months with no record deal in the offing, Reuben took the offer to join Wild Horses with Jimmy Bain, late of Rainbow. The band required a guitarist to partner John Lockton and a new drummer, so Reuben suggested Laurence Archer on guitar and Frank Noon of Lionheart on drums. This completed the final line-up of Wild Horses. However, the project never took off and a disillusioned Reuben, Laurence and Frank left to form Stampede.[6] They recruited Alan Nelson (ex-Wildfire) on keyboards and Bristol-based bass player Colin Bond (formerly of Stormtrooper) to complete the original Stampede line-up.

Stampede (1981 - 1983)

***Days of Wine & Roses* EP and *The Official Bootleg* (1981-1982)** Under management from Roulette Music and with an advance from Polydor Records, Stampede went into Cave Studios in Bristol to record 6 tracks. The tracks were taken up by Polydor Records who consequently signed the band in 1981 for a major deal, immediately releasing four of the new tracks on an EP called *Days of Wine and Roses*.

The band continued to play residencies at the London Marquee Club and various other venues in and around London, and were booked for the Mildenhall and Reading Festivals of 1982. Before these festival dates, drummer Frank Noon left Stampede to join Bernie Tormé, and was replaced by Bristol-based Eddie Parsons who stayed with the band until the end. Prior to the Festivals, Reuben broke his hip and left thigh running to catch a bus with Iron Maiden's Bruce Dickinson, and only just made it out of hospital to appear onstage at the festivals on crutches. Prior to the Mildenhall Festival, Stampede decided to remain a four piece when keyboardist Alan Nelson left to pursue other things. It was felt that Bond's bass style and Taurus pedals more than filled out the sound, and that's how the band remained until their demise.

Polydor recorded the Mildenhall and Reading Festival sets of 1982 putting the live album out as *Stampede: The Official Bootleg*.

Between 1982 and 1983 Stampede also recorded a BBC show for Tommy Vance, a Capital Radio show with 4 tracks for Fluff Freeman's Rock Show, and a BBC In Concert show at the Paris Theatre with contemporaries Girlschool.

***Hurricane Town* and "The Other Side" (1983)** In 1983, Stampede followed up the *Official Bootleg* with a studio album, entitled *Hurricane Town*, recruiting Magnum's Mark Stanway for keyboard duties. At this time Polydor also released a 7" single called "The Other Side".

Hurricane Town was promoted by a support tour with Gary Moore, before which the band went off to Portugal to play a week's residency as warm up for the tour, which was extended after the Christmas of 1983.

2.66.2 Disbandment

After *Hurricane Town* a second studio album was scheduled and Stampede commenced writing material, however, when singer Reuben returned to hospital to have all the metalwork removed from his hip and thigh, he caught a virus during the op and became seriously ill. Due to this and the fact that rock and metal were having a hard time due to the onslaught of Punk and New Wave, plus with little support from Polydor, Stampede decided to split.

Reuben formed his own design company and Colin Bond went off to work with Meat Loaf, while Laurence joined Phil Lynott and Mark Stanway in Grand Slam. When Lynott died Laurence joined Brit rockers UFO, before retiring from music to work in the film industry.[7]

2.66.3 Reunion

In 2006 Rock Candy Records re-released Stampede's last studio offering *Hurricane Town* (originally released by Polydor Records in 1983). The album consisted of all the original tracks re-mastered, and four bonus tracks from the Lautec catalogue, and featured a 16-page colour booklet with sleevenotes by journalists Malcolm Dome, Dante Bonutto and Derek Oliver, along with a foreword by Reuben Archer.

On 2 January 2009, Reuben called Colin Bond and Laurence Archer with a view to reunite Stampede, and the first gig was staged at London's Embassy Club in Mayfair on 25 May 2009. After several gigs they made the unanimous decision to commence recording a new album.[7]

This was easier said than done as it soon transpired that the availability of each band member was impossible to schedule, and when Laurence became unavailable during a period in the recording schedule due to work commitments, Reuben brought in guitarists Rob Wolverson and Chris Clowsley to finish the job. Laurence and Reuben had written and recorded 5 tracks and Reuben with Rob and Chris along with original bassist Colin Bond and new drummer Steve Graystone completed the album.[8] The album, entitled *A Sudden Impulse* was recorded at Track 21 Studios in Weston-super-Mare, Dartington Hall Studios in Devon, and Mad Hat Studios in Wolverhampton.[9]

With the new album nearly completed Stampede's first live appearance was in 2010 at Birmingham's Meltdown Festival where they were main support to headliner Blaze Bayley.

The new album was released on Rock Candy Records on 9 May 2011 to much critical acclaim,[10][11] the single "Having Fun" being released a month prior to the album.

Stampede have since been announced for more live dates throughout 2011, including Festival appearances at Devon Rox in Exeter and Hard Rock Hell V in Prestatyn, and are currently scheduled to record the second comeback album for release in 2012.[12] On 29 September in Wolverhampton, Stampede will be playing at the Denim and Leather NWOBHM festival at the Slade Rooms alongside Praying Mantis, Weapon, Gaskin and Agincourt.[13]

2.66.4 Current members

- **Reuben Archer** (vocals)
- **Laurence Archer** (lead guitar)
- **Chris Clowsley** (guitar)
- **Rob Wolverson** (guitar)
- **Colin Bond** (bass)
- **Steve Graystone** (Drums)

Stampede today consists of original founding members Reuben and Laurence Archer and Colin Bond, along with new additions Chris Clowsley (guitar) and drummer Stevie G (Steve Graystone). In 2010, during the recording of new studio album *A Sudden Impulse*, Laurence became unavailable for recording for a period of time due to work commitments. As a result the band brought in guitarist Rob Wolverson for outstanding writing and recording duties.[14]

2.66.5 Discography

- *Days of Wine and Roses* EP - (Polydor Records 1982)

1. "Days of Wine and Roses"
2. "Moving On"
3. "Photographs"
4. "Missing You"

- *The Official Bootleg* Live album - (Polydor Records, 1982)

1. "Missing You"
2. "Moving On"
3. "Days of Wine and Roses"
4. "Hurricane Town"
5. "Shadows of the Night"
6. "Baby Driver"

7. "The Runner"

8. "There and Back"

- *Hurricane Town* Studio album - (Polydor Records, 1983)

1. "I've Been Told"
2. "Love Letters"
3. "Casino Junkie"
4. "The Other Side"
5. "Turning in Circles"
6. "Hurricane Town"
7. "Girl"
8. "The Runner"
9. "Mexico"

- "The Other Side" 7" Single - (Polydor Records, 1983)

1. "The Other Side"
2. "The Runner"

- *Hurricane Town* - Re-mastered & Re-released studio album - (Rock Candy Records, 2006)

1. "I've Been Told"
2. "Love Letters"
3. "Casino Junkie"
4. "The Other Side"
5. "Turning in Circles"
6. "Hurricane Town"
7. "Girl"
8. "The Runner"
9. "Mexico"
10. "Midnight at the Moulin Rouge" (Lautrec - bonus track)
11. "Red Light Ruby" (Lautrec - bonus track)
12. "Mean Gasoline" (Lautrec - bonus track)
13. "Shoot Out the Lights" (Lautrec - bonus track)

- *A Sudden Impulse* Studio album - (Grind That Axe/Rock Candy Records, 2011)

1. "Send Me Down an Angel"
2. "Jessie"
3. "Having Fun"
4. "Make a Change"
5. "Hard Rock Hell"
6. "This Road"
7. "Homeward Bound"
8. "Shame on You"
9. "Natural Disaster"
10. "Humble Pie"
11. "Flaming Gold"
12. "Recharged" (bonus track)
13. "Flaming Gold" - Acoustic version (bonus track)

2.66.6 See also

- List of New Wave of British Heavy Metal bands

2.66.7 References

[1] "MusicMight :: Artists :: LAURENCE ARCHER". Rock-detector.com. Retrieved 2014-07-16.

[2] "Stampede". Stampederock.com. Retrieved 2014-07-16.

[3] Michael G. Nastos. "Get the Blessing | Biography". AllMusic. Retrieved 2014-07-16.

[4] MacMillan, Malc. *The New Wave of British Heavy Metal Encyclopedia*. P Verlag, 16 Nov 2001

[5]

[6]

[7] "Stampede Biography". Stampede Official Website. Retrieved 2015-08-16.

[8] Stampede Official Press Pack, May 2011

[9] sleevenotes, A Sudden Impulse. Rock Candy Records 2011

[10] Dome, Malcolm. Review in Classic Rock Magazine, June 2011.

[11] Russell, Xavier. Review in Classic Rock Presents AOR Magazine, June 2011.

[12] Steve Goldby. "Stampede Announce More Live UK dates And Release Promo Video For 'Send Me Down An Angel'". Metaltalk.net. Retrieved 2014-07-16.

[13] "Denim and Leather NWOBHM Festival". Nwobhmgigs.co.uk. 2012. Archived from the original on 20 September 2012. Retrieved 2015-08-16.

[14] "Reformed Stampede To Release New Studio Album In April - Blabbermouth.net". Roadrunnerrecords.com. 2011-01-21. Retrieved 2014-07-16.

2.66.8 External links

- Stampede Official Website
- Rock Candy Records Stampede Catalogue Page

2.67 Starfighters (band)

Starfighters are an English heavy metal band from the New Wave of British Heavy Metal movement founded in Birmingham, England, in 1979. They attracted a strong British cult following but were not able to translate this into any lasting success, producing just two full studio albums in the early 1980s. Ex-member Stevie Young brought in some attention to the group after he joined the iconic hard rock band AC/DC in 2014.

2.67.1 Career

Initially called Savage (named after the original lead vocalist, Phil Savage), the founding members, Stevie Young and Barry Spencer Scrannage changed the band's name to Starfighters and released the single, "Heaven and Hell" (A Side) and "I'm Falling" (B Side), on the independent record label, Motor City Rhythm Records. A further two single were recorded and produced in 1980, prior to the band winning their support slot, but were never released. This line-up consisted of Steve Burton (vocals), Pat Hambly (guitar) Stevie Young (guitar), Doug Dennis (bass) and Barry Spencer Scrannage (drums). They were then signed up by Jive Records (a part of Zomba).

They then won a support slot with AC/DC on their 1980 'Back in Black' tour, during which, Barry Spencer Scrannage left for personal reasons (the death of close personal friend, John Bonham), his position was later filled by Steve Bailey. (Stevie Young is the nephew of AC/DC leaders Malcolm and Angus Young). Signing up with Krokus manager Butch Stone, in 1983 they released the follow-up album, *In-Flight Movie*, again produced by Tony Platt. Jive however were not prepared to pay for further tour promotions, and the band resorted to appearing in small British clubs. Despite receiving good reviews and publicity, particularly in *Kerrang!* magazine, this album did no better and Jive dropped them. The band consequently folded.

In 1987, the band reformed with the line-up of Burton (vocals), Young (guitars), Rik Sandford (guitars), Redvers (bass) and Jamie Hawkins (drums). Redvers had been known as Steve Hill up to this point, but was rechristened with his middle name, to avoid the confusion of having three 'Steves' in the band. Despite attracting a strong local following in Birmingham, they could not secure another recording contract, and the band folded after little more than a year. Sandford and Hawkins had very brief stints with UFO and Hawkwind respectively. Redvers became Steve Redvers and joined The Grip, before linking up with Young and Ian Charles (Chaz) in Little Big Horn.

Starfighters reformed again for a one off show on 10 November 2006 at 'The Roadhouse' in South Birmingham to raise money for charity, with the line-up of Burton (vocals), Young (guitars and vocals), Hambly (guitars), Dennis (bass and vocals) and Tony Bayliss (drums).

As of January 2015, Burton is fronting Birmingham blues band Vincent Flatts Final Drive

When bassist Doug Dennis died in 2011, the remaining Starfighters reformed to play at his wake with Stevie Young's son Angus on bass.

In May 2014, Stevie Young replaced his uncle Malcolm Young for the recording of a new AC/DC album and tour.

2.67.2 Discography

- *Starfighters* (1981) - Jive Records
- *In-Flight Movie* (1983) - Jive Records

2.67.3 See also

- List of New Wave of British Heavy Metal bands
- Heavy metal music
- Stevie Young

2.67.4 References

2.67.5 External links

- MusicMight bio
- detailed discography

2.68 Stratus (English band)

Stratus (originally "Clive Burr's Escape", then briefly known as "Tygon" and "Stratas"), was a short-lived English melodic hard rock supergroup. It was formed by ex-Iron Maiden drummer Clive Burr, the Troy brothers from then-inactive Praying Mantis plus ex-Gran Prix vocalist Bernie Shaw.

The track "Run for Your Life" was featured on the soundtrack to the movie *Class of Nuke 'Em High*.

2.68.1 Discography

- *Throwing Shapes* - 1985
    1. "Back Street Lovers" (3:51)
    2. "Gimme Something" (4:14)
    3. "Even if It Takes" (4:22)
    4. "Give Me One More Chance" (4:47)
    5. "Never Say No" (4:01)
    6. "Romancer" (3:22)
    7. "Enough Is Enough" (3:40)
    8. "Run for Your Life" (4:33)
    9. "So Tired" (4:46)

2.68.2 Line-up

- Bernie Shaw - lead vocals
- Tino Troy — lead guitar, vocals
- Alan Nelson — keyboard
- Chris Troy — bass, vocals
- Clive Burr - drums, vocals

2.68.3 See also

- List of New Wave of British Heavy Metal bands

2.68.4 References

- Praying Mantis: Side projects
- Praying Mantis: Stratus

2.69 Sweet Savage

Sweet Savage are a metal band from Belfast, Northern Ireland, formed in 1979. The band once included former Dio and Def Leppard guitarist Vivian Campbell.[1] Since forming in 1979, Sweet Savage have released three studio albums, three singles and one demo.

Considered one of the pioneers of the New Wave of British Heavy Metal movement alongside acts such as Iron Maiden, Saxon, Motörhead and Def Leppard. However, even though they were often considered among the forerunners of the NWOBHM movement, success eluded them and they disbanded shortly after 1982.

The band reformed in 1984 with a different line-up, but did not last long. Sweet Savage was once again reformed in the 90s, due to Metallica covering their song "Killing Time" as a B-side for their "The Unforgiven" single.

Sweet Savage released a new studio album, entitled *Regeneration*, in May 2011.

2.69.1 History

Early days (1979-1983)

Sweet Savage began with a line-up of Trev Fleming and Vivian Campbell on guitars, David Bates on drums and Ray Haller on bass and vocals. The band gained a support slot for Thin Lizzy on their Renegade tour[2] and supported acts such as Ozzy Osbourne, Wishbone Ash and Motörhead.

In 1981 the band signed to Park Records and released their first single "Take No Prisoners" which was limited to 1000 copies[3] - this single included the song "Killing Time". A self-released demo known as *Demo 81* was released at this time, which contained a BBC session of 4 songs.

In early 1983, guitarist Campbell accepted an offer to join Dio and subsequently left the band.

Reform (1984-1985)

After a year long break, Sweet Savage decided to reform, but without Campbell and Fleming. Ian "Speedo" Wilson joined Sweet Savage on guitar and the band recorded a single with vocalist Robert Casserly, "Straight Through the Heart" and was released on Crashed Records. In 1985, the band recorded their third single "The Raid". After this, Sweet Savage disbanded for a second time.

The albums (1996-1998)

Much later in the late 90's after Metallica covered "Killing Time" in 1991 as a B-side for "The Unforgiven", there was renewed interest for Sweet Savage. Fueled by this interest, the band reformed and signed to Neat Records in 1996, releasing their first studio album entitled *Killing Time*. The band at this stage were joined by Simon McBride on lead guitar and the return of Trev Fleming on additional guitar. Ian Wilson was concentrating on other projects and was not present on the *Killing Time* record, with Simon McBride taking over from him. *Killing Time* contained re-worked and re-recorded versions of songs that were originally released early on in their career.

Two years later in 1998, the band recorded and released an album of completely new material entitled *Rune*. Following the two albums, the band went on hiatus as each member wanted to follow different musical routes.

Present day revival (2008 onward)

In 2008, Maniacal Records from the USA was to release the band's early studio material on vinyl, but the band abruptly cancelled the project, citing lawsuit concerns from a former member. 23 April 2008 saw the long awaited return to the stage by Sweet Savage, as they supported Saxon on the St. Georges Day concert in London's Shepherds Bush Empire.[4] Bates decided to leave the band and was replaced by Jules Watson. A trip to Germany ensued in early August where they played the Headbangers Festival[5] and the Wacken Festival[6] to great acclaim. Later that month they supported Metallica & Tenacious D in Dublin, Marlay Park, 20 August 2008.[7] On 1 August 2009, again in Marlay Park, Ray Haller joined Metallica on stage for "Killing Time".[8]

The current line-up of Haller, Wilson, Fleming and Watson has been cited as being "the strongest version of the band" by the industry professionals and as frontman Ray Haller explains "All this interest lately, has come out of the blue and it's phenomenal how well the band is being received by everyone. We played Germany for the first time recently and were surprised to hear the kids singing our tunes back to us, we really had no idea how popular the band are."

In 2009 Sweet Savage were confirmed as the support along with Doro for Saxon's Battalions Of Steel World Tour II.

2009 also saw the release of their newest studio effort entitled *Warbird*, on SPV Records. The album features Vivian Campbell making a guest appearance on a cover of Thin Lizzy's "Whiskey in the Jar".[9]

At the band's support show with Motörhead, lead singer Ray Haller confirmed that the new record *Warbird* would have been released in Spring 2010 and not 2009 as planned.[10]

On 7 July 2010 Sweet Savage were announced as replacement support for the first date of Iron Maiden's Final Frontier European Tour at the O2 in Dublin on 30 July 2010. Heaven & Hell were originally announced as support, but were forced to cancel all of their summer dates due to Ronnie James Dio's death. At the show, Sweet Savage introduced a packed Dublin crowd to new drummer Marty McCloskey who would be taking over from Jules Watson. Jules went on to drum for Conjuring Fate. The band revealed that the new record *Warbird*, which had been postponed due to the current economic climatic in the music business, would be seeing a full release in Oct/Nov 2010.

On 2 October 2010, guitarist and songwriter Trev Fleming died after treatment for a recent illness, he had been missing from the band's line-up since February 2010 and was not present for support slots with Deep Purple and Iron Maiden or for Sweet Savage's performance at Sonisphere Festival.

Ray Haller joined Metallica onstage on 7 December 2011 at The Fillmore in San Francisco, CA for Metallica's 30th Anniversary show. Ray sang "Killing Time" with Metallica and also backing vocals on their track "Seek & Destroy". This was the second of 4 shows that Metallica played.

2.69.2 Band members

Current

- Ray Haller - lead vocals, bass guitar (1979–present)
- Marty McCloskey - drums (2010–present)
- Phil Edgar - guitar (2011–present)

Former

- Trev Fleming - guitar (1979–1983, 1996, 2008–2010) †
- Vivian Campbell - guitar (1979–1983)
- Simon McBride - guitar (1996–1998)
- David Bates - drums (1979–2008)
- Jules Watson - drums (2008–2010)
- Robert Casserly (1983–1985)
- Ian Wilson - guitar (1984–2012)

2.69.3 Discography

Studio Albums

- *Killing Time* (Metal Blade; 1996)

1. "Killing Time"
2. "Vengeance"
3. "Welcome to the Real World"
4. "Thunder"
5. "Eye of the Storm"
6. "Parody of Wisdom"
7. "DUD"
8. "Prospector of Greed"
9. "Why?"
10. "The Raid"
11. "Reach Out"
12. "Ground Zero"

- *Rune* (Neat Metal Nation; 1998)

1. "Ditch"
2. "Life's a Game"
3. "Trust"
4. "I Am Nothing (You Are Less)"
5. "Who Am I?"
6. "Shangri-La"
7. "Survive"
8. "Communication"
9. "Why Me?"
10. "Walk On By"

- *Regeneration* (Candyman; 2011)

1. "Warbird"
2. "Powder Monkey"
3. "Regenerator"
4. "No Guts, No Glory"
5. "Saviour (I Am Not)"
6. "Do or Die"
7. "Money"
8. "Razor's Edge"
9. "Whiskey in the Jar"
10. "Eye of the Storm"
11. "Queen's Vengeance"
12. "Achilles"
13. "The Raid"

Singles

- *Take No Prisoners* (Park Records- PKR 1001; 1981)

1. "Take No Prisoners"
2. "Killing Time"

- *Straight Through the Heart* (Crashed Music - CAR 48; 1984)

1. "Straight Through the Heart"
2. "Teaser"

- *The Raid* (Park Records– PKR 1003; 1985)

1. "The Raid"
2. "The Ripper"
3. "The Raid (1980 demo)"

Live Sessions

- *Friday Rock Show* (BBC; 1981)

1. "Eye of the Storm"
2. "Into the Night"
3. "Queen's Vengeance"
4. "Killing Time"

Compilations

- *The Friday Rock Show* (BBC Records; 1981)
  Featured track: "Eye of the Storm"
- *Now in Session* (Downtown Radio; 1982)
  Featured track: "Lady of the Night"
- *NWOBHM '79 Revisited* (Caroline Records; 1990)
  Featured track: "Eye of the Storm"
- *Lightnin' to the Nations: 25th Anniversary of NWOBHM* (2005)
  Featured track: "Killing Time"
- *Full Metal Garage: The Songs That Drove Metallica* (2006)
  Featured track: "Killing Time"

Canceled Releases

- *Eye of the Storm - The Early Years* (Maniacal Records/High Roller Records; 2008)[11][12]

    - Side A:

1. "Eye of the storm" (studio)
2. "Into the Night"
3. "Prospector of Greed (studio)"
4. "The Raid (studio)"
5. "Queen's Vengeance"

    - Side B:

1. "Killing Time (studio)"
2. "Ground Zero (studio)"
3. "The Ripper"
4. "Lady Marion"
5. "Take no Prisoners"

    - Side C:

1. "Teaser"
2. "DUD"
3. "The Raid (remix)"
4. "Prospector of Greed (remix)"
5. "Sweet Surrender"
6. "Crucify"

    - Side D:

1. "Sweet Surrender (live)"
2. "Prospector of Greed (live)"
3. "Eye of the Storm (live)"
4. "Take no Prisoners (live)"
5. "Killing Time (remix)"
6. "Eye of the Storm (remix)"

2.69.4 See also

- List of New Wave of British Heavy Metal bands

2.69.5 References

[1] Vivian Campbell's biography

[2] Tour posters from the era

[3] Encyclopaedia Metallum entry for Take No Prisoners

[4] News Article retrieved 28 March 2008

[5] Festival line-up for 2008

[6] News Article Sweet Savage Confirmed For Germany's WACKEN OPEN AIR Festival - retrieved 21 June 2008

[7] Video of Sweet Savage joined on stage by James Hetfield 20 August 2008 Marlay Park in Dublin, Ireland

[8] Video of Metallica joined on stage by Ray Haller 1 August 2009 Marlay Park in Dublin, Ireland

[9] retrieved May 2009 from the band's website

[10] was present at the show where these details were announced

[11] SWEET SAVAGE: 'Eye Of The Storm - The Early Years' Two-LP Collection Due This Summer - 5 June 2008

[12] Sweet Savage Added To Wacken Line Up

2.69.6 External links

- Official Myspace page
- Sweet Savage at AllMusic
- In The Irish Punk & New Wave Discography

2.70 Tank (band)

Tank is a British heavy metal band, formed in 1980 by Algy Ward, a former member of The Damned. The band is known as part of the New Wave of British Heavy Metal movement. Tank was often compared to Motörhead as both bands, trios fronted by singing bassists, played a loose, almost punk-styled metal music with often colourful lyrics.[1][2]

2.70.1 History

Their 1982 debut album, *Filth Hounds of Hades*, was positively received by both punk and metal fans as well as most critics, regarded now as one of the best albums of the NWOBHM movement.[3] Allmusic critic, Eduardo Rivadavia; described it as "Tank's best album ever, and qualifying it as an essential item in the record collection of any serious '80s metal fan."[4]

As was the case with many other bands of the era, Tank was never able to build on the promise shown by their first album. The band continued on for years through lineup changes and waning commercial fortunes before finally disbanding in 1989. Ward resurrected the band in 1997 playing tour dates around Europe and Japan for a couple of years. A new album, *Still At War*, emerged in 2002. In August 2006 Ward reported that he was putting the finishing touches on the demos for the next Tank album, *Sturmpanzer*.[5] The band's website has listed the release date for this album as "TBA" for years.

On 20 December 2008 a new lineup was announced. Guitarists Mick Tucker and Cliff Evans were joined by original drummer Mark Brabbs and former Bruce Dickinson bassist Chris Dale. Algy Ward was replaced by former Rainbow singer Doogie White. For 2010 the band replaced Brabbs with Voodoo Six drummer, Dave Cavill and released the new Tank album *War Machine*, with this lineup in released in October 2010. For 2011 the band replaced Cavill with heavy metal drummer, Mark Cross.

In February 2012 the band announced their first live DVD recorded the previous summer in Poland with additional footage to be recorded in March 2012. The band also released details of the return of former drummer, Steve Hopgood, along with details of the forthcoming album, *War Nation*. The album was released on 4 June on Metal Mind Productions, produced by Phil Kinman at his west London studios.[6]

In 2013 it emerged that Algy Ward has resurrected his own version of the band, with all tracks on a new album called *Breath of the Pit* being "written, played and shouted" by Ward himself.[7] According to Algy Ward, *Sturmpanzer* will finally be released sometime in 2015.[8] Tank led by Tucker/Evans will also release an album in 2015. The album called *Valley of Tears* was scheduled to be released on 9 June, but was pushed back to 18 September.[9][10]

2.70.2 Discography

2.70.3 Members

Timeline

2.70.4 See also

- New Wave of British Heavy Metal
- List of New Wave of British Heavy Metal bands

2.70.5 References

[1] "NWOBHM Encyclopedia". Retrieved 20 July 2009.

[2] Popoff, Martin (2005). *The Collector's Guide To Heavy Metal Volume 2: The Eighties*. Toronto: Collector's Guide Publishing. p. 350. ISBN 1-894959-31-0.

[3] "Tank - Filth Hounds of Hades - Reviews - Encyclopaedia Metallum". The Metal Archives. Retrieved 2014-07-26.

[4] Eduardo Rivadavia. "Filth Hounds of Hades - Tank | Songs, Reviews, Credits, Awards". AllMusic. Retrieved 2014-07-26.

[5] "TANK Mainman Putting Finishing Touches On 'Sturmpanzer'".

[6] "Metalmind". Metalmind.pl. 2012-03-09. Retrieved 2014-07-26.

[7] "Algy Ward's Tank: 'Breath Of The Pit' Cover Artwork Unveiled". Blabbermouth.net. 2013-04-29. Retrieved 2014-07-26.

[8] "ALGY WARD TO RELEASE NEW TANK ALBUM 'STURMPANZER' IN 2015". *Zero Tolerance*. 10 October 2014. Retrieved 28 March 2015.

[9] "TANK: 'Valley Of Tears' Artwork, Track Listing Unveiled". *Blabbermouth.net*. 9 March 2015. Retrieved 3 April 2015.

[10] "TANK's 'Valley Of Tears' Pushed Back To September". *Blabbermouth.net*. 29 April 2015. Retrieved 12 June 2015.

2.70.6 External links

- Algy Ward's Tank
- Tucker/Evans Tank

2.71 Terraplane (band)

Terraplane were a 1980s pop rock band from London, England. Composed of five musicians, they released two albums before disbanding in 1988. The band featured three musicians who would go on to form the hard rock act, Thunder.

2.71.1 Biography

Singer Danny Bowes, guitarist Luke Morley and drummer Harry James and bassist Nick Linden were the original recording line-up. After releasing a single on the independent 'City' label, they soon signed with Epic Records. With the much-delayed debut album almost completely recorded, they recruited second guitarist Rudi Rivière in time for him to appear on just one track on that release. That first studio album, *Black and White* (originally titled *Talking to God on the Great White Telephone*) was released by Epic Records in January 1986 and was critically well received. However, by 1987 their record label was exerting pressure on the band to follow up with another album of a soulful direction, with the resulting album *Moving Target* alienating the band's fan base.

Morley, Bowes and James regrouped in 1989 to form Thunder; all three remain in that band as of July 2015. Thunder supported Journey and Whitesnake in an arena tour of the UK in May 2013[1]

2.71.2 Discography

Albums

- *Black and White* (Epic, 1985) – UK Albums Chart No. 74[2]
- *Moving Target* (Epic, 1987)
- *We Survive* (compilation album) (Castle, 2005)

Singles

- "I Survive" (City Records, 1983) [b/w "Gimme The Money", "Turn Me Loose", "I Want Your Body"]
- "I Can't Live Without Your Love" (Epic, 1985)
- "When You're Hot" (Epic, 1985)
- "Talking to Myself" (Epic, 1985)
- "If That's What It Takes" (Epic, 1986)
- "Good Thing Going" (Epic, 1987)
- "Moving Target" (Epic, 1987)

2.71.3 See also

- List of New Wave of British Heavy Metal bands

2.71.4 References

[1] MEN Arena

[2] Roberts, David (2006). *British Hit Singles & Albums* (19th ed.). London: Guinness World Records Limited. p. 553. ISBN 1-904994-10-5.

2.72 The Handsome Beasts

The Handsome Beasts are a British heavy metal band who surfaced during the New Wave of British Heavy Metal.[1] Currently enjoying a resurgence in popularity,[2] their album *Beastiality* is infamous for being featured on several "Worst album cover of all time" lists.[3]

2.72.1 Career

Original line up

- Garry Dallaway (Vocals)
- Pete Malbasa (Drums)
- Steven Hough (Bass)
- James Stephen Barrett (Lead/Rhythm Guitar, Backing Vocals)

2.72.2 Discography

Albums

- *Beastiality* (Heavy Metal Records, 1981)
- *The Beast Within* (Heavy Metal Records, 1990)
- *04* (Heavy Rock Records, 2004)
- *Rock and a Hard Place* (Q Records, 2007)

Singles

- *All Riot Now* EP (Heavy Metal Records, 1980)
- *Breaker* EP (Heavy Metal Records, 1981)
- *Sweeties* EP (Heavy Metal Records, 1981)

2.72.3 See also

- List of New Wave of British Heavy Metal bands

2.72.4 References

[1] Rivadavia, Eduardo (2006-08-20). "Handsome Beasts - Music Biography, Credits and Discography". AllMusic. Retrieved 2012-06-25.

[2] "JAMESON RAID, THE HANDSOME BEASTS, AGINCOURT â€" Robin 2, Bilston, 18th July 2010 â€" John Tucker Online". Johntuckeronline.com. 2010-07-18. Retrieved 2012-06-25.

[3] "Museum of bad album covers: the worst album covers ever! No. 3". Zonicweb.net. Retrieved 2012-06-25.

2.72.5 External links

Official website

2.73 Thin Lizzy

Thin Lizzy are an Irish rock band formed in Dublin in 1969. Two of the founding members, drummer Brian Downey and bass guitarist and vocalist Phil Lynott, met while still in school. Lynott assumed the role of frontman and led them throughout their recording career of twelve studio albums. Thin Lizzy's most successful songs, "Whiskey in the Jar", "Jailbreak" and "The Boys Are Back in Town", were all major international hits which are still played regularly on hard rock and classic rock radio stations. After Lynott's death in 1986, various incarnations of the band have emerged over the years based initially around guitarists Scott Gorham and John Sykes, though Sykes left the band in 2009. Gorham later continued with a new line-up including Downey.

Lynott, Thin Lizzy's *de facto* leader, was composer or co-composer of almost all of the band's songs, and the first black Irishman to achieve commercial success in the field of rock music. Thin Lizzy boasted some of the most critically acclaimed guitarists throughout their history, with Downey and Lynott as the rhythm section, on the drums and bass guitar. As well as being multiracial, the band drew their members not only from both sides of the Irish border but also from both the Catholic and Protestant communities during The Troubles. Their music reflects a wide range of influences, including blues, soul music, psychedelic rock, and traditional Irish folk music, but is generally classified as hard rock or sometimes heavy metal. *Rolling Stone* magazine describes the band as distinctly hard rock, "far apart from the braying mid-70s metal pack".[1]

AllMusic critic John Dougan has written that "As the band's creative force, Lynott was a more insightful and intelligent writer than many of his ilk, preferring slice-of-life working-class dramas of love and hate influenced by Bob Dylan, Van Morrison, Bruce Springsteen, and virtually all of the Irish literary tradition."[2] Van Morrison, Jeff Beck and Jimi Hendrix were major influences during the early days of the band, and later influences included the pioneering twin lead guitars found in Wishbone Ash and American artists Little Feat and Bob Seger.

In 2012, Gorham and Downey decided against recording new material as Thin Lizzy so a new band, Black Star Riders, was formed to tour and produce new releases such as the *All Hell Breaks Loose* album. Thin Lizzy plan to reunite for occasional concerts.[3]

2.73.1 History

Early years (1969–74)

Thin Lizzy were founded one night in late December 1969 in Dublin, Ireland, when Belfast guitarist Eric Bell met up with organist Eric Wrixon in a pub and found that they shared an ambition to form a group. Both musicians had previously played with Them, fronted by Van Morrison.[4] The same night, they went to see the band Orphanage, which featured vocalist Phil Lynott and drummer Brian Downey. Bell and Wrixon introduced themselves after the gig and suggested the four of them form a band together. Lynott and Downey were aware of Bell's good musical reputation,[5] and agreed with the condition that Lynott play bass guitar as well as sing, and that they perform some of his own compositions.[4]

In July 1970, Thin Lizzy released a single, "The Farmer"/"I Need You", on EMI with the B-side written by John D'ardis, who owned Trend Studios where the single was recorded. The single sold just 283 copies and is now a collectors' item.[4] Wrixon left the band before the single's release, meaning there was a greater share of income for the three remaining members.[5] He moved to mainland Europe before returning to Belfast, rejoining his old band, Them.[6] Wrixon died on 13 July 2015.[7]

By the end of the year, Thin Lizzy were signed to Decca Records and they travelled to London in January 1971 to record their debut album, *Thin Lizzy*. The album sold moderately well but did not chart in the UK despite airplay and support from influential DJs John Peel and Kid Jensen.[4]

Around March 1971, the band permanently relocated to London, before the release of the unsuccessful "New Day" EP in August.[6] Despite poor sales, Decca agreed to finance the band's second album *Shades of a Blue Orphanage*, released in March 1972. Like the previous LP, the songs were filled with Lynott's personal anecdotes and references to his life in Dublin and the people he knew there. Musically the style was Celtic, with little warning of the hard rock direction that the band were to take in the future.[4] Again, the album did not chart in the UK.

In mid-1972, Thin Lizzy were asked to record an album of Deep Purple covers, which was released under the title *Funky Junction Play a Tribute to Deep Purple*. No mention was made of Thin Lizzy on the record. Vocals and keyboards were handled by members of another band, Elmer Fudd, and a few instrumental tracks composed by the band were also included on the album.[5] The album was released in January 1973.

Thin Lizzy in early 1974. Left to right: Brian Downey, Phil Lynott, Gary Moore.

"Whiskey in the Jar" In late 1972, the band embarked upon a high-profile tour of the UK with Slade, who were enjoying a string of hit singles at the time, and Suzi Quatro. Around the same time, Decca decided to release Thin Lizzy's version of a traditional Irish ballad, "Whiskey in the Jar", as a single. The band was angry at the release, feeling that the song did not represent their sound or their image,[6] but the single topped the Irish chart, and reached no. 6 in the UK in February 1973, resulting in an appearance on *Top of the Pops*. It also charted in many countries across Europe. However, the follow-up single, "Randolph's Tango", was a return to Lynott's more obscure work, and it did not chart outside Ireland.[8]

The band's next album, *Vagabonds of the Western World*, was released in September 1973 to positive reviews, but again failed to chart.[8] The accompanying single "The Rocker" also found little success outside Ireland, and the momentum gained from their hit single was lost.[5]

Eric Bell suddenly left the band on New Year's Eve 1973 after a gig at Queen's University Belfast, due to increasing ill-health and disillusionment with the music industry,[5] and young ex-Skid Row guitarist Gary Moore was recruited to help finish the tour. Moore stayed until April 1974, but the band recorded three songs with him in that time, including the version of "Still in Love with You" that was included on the fourth album *Nightlife*.

With the departure of Moore, Lynott decided to expand the line-up with two guitarists, and recruited two temporary members to complete a tour of Germany in May 1974. These were ex-Atomic Rooster and Hard Stuff guitarist John Cann, and Berliner Andy Gee, who had played with Peter Bardens and Ellis. Neither were considered as permanent members, as Lynott and Cann did not get on well personally,[5] and Gee was under contract to another record label. The tour was ended early, and with Thin Lizzy's contract with Decca coming to an end, a disillusioned Downey quit the band and had to be begged to return.[6]

Auditions were held for new members, and Lynott and Downey eventually settled on Glaswegian guitarist Brian Robertson who was only 18 years old at the time, and Californian Scott Gorham. The new line-up gelled quickly, dropped most of the old songs when they played live,[6] and secured a new record deal with Phonogram, but the resulting album *Nightlife* was a disappointment for the band due to its soft production and underdeveloped style.[4] Robertson described Ron Nevison's production as "pretty naff" and Gorham said the record was "ridiculously tame".[5] Like the previous three albums, it failed to chart.

"The Boys Are Back in Town" (1975–77)

In early 1975, Thin Lizzy toured the United States for the first time, in support of Bob Seger and Bachman–Turner Overdrive. When BTO toured Europe later in the year to support their hit single "You Ain't Seen Nothing Yet", Thin Lizzy again accompanied them on what was a very high-profile tour.[5] They then recorded the *Fighting* album, which became the first Thin Lizzy album to chart in the UK, reaching no. 60, although the singles still did not chart. Opening with Seger's "Rosalie", the album showed the first real evidence of the twin guitar sound that would lead the band towards their greatest successes, particularly with the dual harmonies of "Wild One" and both guitarists' soloing on "Suicide".[4]

After a successful multi-band tour in support of Status Quo, the band recorded the album *Jailbreak*, which proved to be their breakthrough record. Released on 26 March 1976, it featured the worldwide hit "The Boys Are Back in Town"

L to R: Brian Robertson, Phil Lynott, Scott Gorham performing during the Bad Reputation Tour, 24 November 1977

which reached no. 8 in the UK, and no. 12 in the US,[9] their first charting record in that country. The twin guitar sound had been fully developed by this time and was in evidence throughout the album, particularly on the hit single, and other tracks such as "Emerald" and "Warriors". The album also charted well on both sides of the Atlantic, and the follow-up single, "Jailbreak", also performed well. Thin Lizzy toured the US in support of various bands such as Aerosmith, Rush and REO Speedwagon, and they planned to tour there again in June 1976, this time with Rainbow. However, Lynott fell ill with hepatitis and the tour was cancelled, which set them back a few months.[4]

While Lynott was ill, he wrote most of the following album, *Johnny the Fox*. The album was recorded in August 1976 and the sessions began to reveal tensions between Lynott and Robertson; for example, there was disagreement over the composition credits of the hit single "Don't Believe a Word".[5] Lynott was still drawing on Celtic mythology and his own personal experiences for lyric ideas, which dominated *Johnny the Fox* and the other albums of Thin Lizzy's successful mid-1970s period.[4] The tour to support the album was very successful and there were further high-profile TV appearances, such as the *Rod Stewart BBC TV Special*.[6]

A further tour of the US was planned for December 1976, but it had to be cancelled when, on 23 November, Brian Robertson suffered a hand injury when trying to protect fellow Glaswegian, singer and friend Frankie Miller in a fracas at the Speakeasy Club in London. Miller had been jamming onstage with the reggae band Gonzalez, but had been drunk, offending Gonzalez guitarist Gordon Hunte. Hunte attacked Miller with a bottle in the dressing room, and Robertson intervened, suffering artery and nerve damage to his hand.[5][6] Robertson subsequently broke Hunte's leg, broke the collarbone of another man, and headbutted another, before being hit on the head with a bottle, rendering him unconscious.[5]

Robertson maintains that, contrary to reports at the time, he was not drunk and had only gone to the venue for a meal.[4][5] Lynott was angry and replaced Robertson with Gary Moore for another tour of the States in January–March 1977, this time supporting Queen. The tour was a success and Lynott asked Moore to stay on, but he returned to his previous band, Colosseum II. Robertson had not been sacked but was unsure of his position and made plans to start another band with Jimmy Bain of Rainbow.[5] Before the American tour, Lynott had also invited Irish guitarist Jimi Slevin to "try out a few things" with Thin Lizzy, prompting speculation that the ex-Skid Row member could replace Robertson.[10]

Thin Lizzy flew to Canada in May 1977 as a trio to record *Bad Reputation*, with Gorham handling all the guitar parts. A month into the sessions Robertson joined them, in his own words, "as a session player"[4] and in Lynott's words, "as a guest".[6] Robertson added lead guitar tracks to three songs as well as rhythm guitar and keyboards, and was officially reinstated in July. The album was released in September and sold well, reaching no. 4 in the UK, after a successful single, "Dancing in the Moonlight (It's Caught Me in Its Spotlight)". Also in 1977, Thin Lizzy headlined the Reading Festival.

The return of Gary Moore (1978–79)

In 1978, Lizzy released their first live album *Live and Dangerous*. There is some disagreement over just how much of the album is actually recorded live – producer Tony Visconti claimed that the only parts that were not overdubbed were the drums and the audience. However Brian Robertson has disputed this, saying that he had refused Lynott's request to re-record a guitar solo, and that the only overdubs were backing vocals and some guitar parts by Gorham. He added, "It's just not true. The only reason we said that it was recorded all over was obviously for tax reasons... so everything that Visconti claims is bollocks."[4] Gorham concurs,

Thin Lizzy 8 August 1977; Robertson, Lynott, Gorham, Downey

stating that he attempted to re-record a solo but could not recreate the live sound, adding, "I re-did *one* rhythm track and a few backing vocals. But that's it."[11] The album was a huge success, reaching no. 2 in the UK, and was ranked as the best live album of all time by Classic Rock Magazine in 2004.[12] But this success was overshadowed by the permanent departure of Robertson some time after a gig in Ibiza on 6 July 1978, the disagreements with Lynott having developed to an impossible level.[6] Robertson soon teamed up with Jimmy Bain to front their new band, Wild Horses.

Lynott replaced Robertson with Gary Moore again, and around this time the band loosely joined forces with Steve Jones and Paul Cook of the Sex Pistols, and also Chris Spedding and Jimmy Bain, to form The Greedy Bastards, who played a small number of gigs playing a varied selection of songs. In this way Lynott was able to align his band with the punk movement and avoid being tagged as a 'dinosaur' as many other 1970s rock bands had been.[5]

In August the band began another tour of the US, followed by a trip to Australia and New Zealand. Brian Downey did not accompany them, having contracted pneumonia and preferring to spend some time in Ireland. He was replaced for the tour by American drummer Mark Nauseef.[6] On their return, Downey rejoined the band and at the beginning of 1979 they recorded *Black Rose: A Rock Legend* in Paris. The sessions were marked by the increasing drug habits of Lynott and Gorham, and the general presence of drugs around the band.[5] This also showed in the subject matter on the album, in songs such as "Got to Give It Up". Celtic influences remained, however, particularly in the album closer "Róisín Dubh", a seven-minute medley of traditional Irish songs given a twin guitar rock veneer. Two singles, "Waiting for an Alibi" and "Do Anything You Want To", were successful, and the album reached no. 2 in the UK.[13] A third, moderately successful single, "Sarah" was Lynott's ode to his new-born daughter.[8]

However, on 4 July 1979, Gary Moore abruptly left Thin Lizzy in the middle of another tour of the US. Years later, Moore said he had no regrets about walking out, "but maybe it was wrong the way I did it. I could've done it differently, I suppose. But I just had to leave."[5] He subsequently pursued his solo career, releasing several successful albums. He had collaborated with Lynott and Downey on his 1978 album *Back on the Streets* and the hit single "Parisienne Walkways" before leaving Thin Lizzy, and in 1985 he and Lynott teamed up again on the UK no. 5 hit single "Out in the Fields". Gary Moore died of a heart attack in Estepona, Spain on 6 February 2011, aged 58.[14][15]

After Moore's departure, Thin Lizzy continued the tour for a few nights as a trio before Lynott brought in Midge Ure to replace him on a temporary basis. Ure had prior plans to join Ultravox, but had co-written a song, "Get Out of Here", with Lynott on *Black Rose: A Rock Legend*, and agreed to help Thin Lizzy complete their touring commitments.[4] He also contributed guitar parts for *The Continuing Saga of the Ageing Orphans*, a compilation album of remixed and overdubbed versions of Eric Bell-era tracks. On their return to the UK, the band were to headline the Reading Festival for the second time on 25 August 1979, but had to cancel due to the disruption within the line-up.[4]

Before a tour of Japan beginning in September, Lynott decided to bring in another guitarist, Dave Flett, who had played with Manfred Mann's Earth Band, to enable Ure to switch to playing keyboards where necessary. The tour was completed successfully, but the line-up now contained two temporary members, and Lynott was spending a lot of time on projects outside Thin Lizzy, including composing and producing material for other bands, as well as putting together his first solo album, *Solo in Soho*.[5] Lynott also reactivated The Greedy Bastards, who released a one-off Christmas single, "A Merry Jingle", in December 1979 as simply The Greedies. With the group now composed of Lynott, Gorham and Downey with Sex Pistols Jones and Cook, the single reached no. 28 in the UK.[8]

Later years and break-up (1980–83)

While Lynott searched for a permanent guitarist, he and the other members of Thin Lizzy, past and present, worked on *Solo in Soho* which was released in April 1980, and the next Thin Lizzy album, *Chinatown*. Lynott got married on 14 February, and his wife gave birth to a second daughter in July.[16] Dave Flett had hoped to be made a permanent member of Thin Lizzy but Lynott chose Snowy White, who had played with Pink Floyd and Peter Green.[4] Midge Ure was still acting as a temporary keyboard player at gigs during early 1980, but was replaced by Darren Wharton in April, shortly after White joined the band. Wharton

Thin Lizzy in concert, 1981

was only 17 at the time and was initially hired on a temporary basis.[4] This new line-up completed the *Chinatown* album between short tours, and two singles were released from it. The first, "Chinatown", reached no. 21 in the UK, but the second, "Killer on the Loose", reached the top 10 amid much adverse publicity due to the ongoing activities of serial killer Peter Sutcliffe, known as "The Yorkshire Ripper".[6]

Chinatown was finally released in October 1980, and reached no. 7 in the UK, but by this time Thin Lizzy albums were not even reaching the top 100 in the US. After a successful tour of Japan and Australia, the band undertook what was to be their final tour of the US in late 1980.[4] At the beginning of 1981, Lynott began work on his second solo album, using Thin Lizzy members among a large group of backing musicians. Around the same time, the band were recording material for the next Thin Lizzy album, and as before, the sessions seemed to merge to the extent that musicians were not always sure which album they were working on. Producer for the Thin Lizzy sessions, Chris Tsangarides, stated, "The feeling of confusion was in the air in that sometimes nobody knew if they were working on a Phil solo record or a Lizzy album."[4] Snowy White had previously felt that, as a member of Thin Lizzy, he should have been paid as a session player to appear on Lynott's solo recordings.[5]

In April 1981, the band's first 'greatest hits' album was released, and *The Adventures of Thin Lizzy* reached no. 6 in the UK, although a stand-alone single, "Trouble Boys", only reached no. 53, the band's worst chart placing since 1975.[6] According to White[4] and Wharton,[5] Lynott was the only person who wanted to release it, and nobody else liked the song. "Trouble Boys" had even been pencilled in as the title for the new album, but the single's chart failure resulted in the song being dropped from the album and the title changed to *Renegade*.[4] One highlight for the band at this time was headlining the first-ever Slane Castle concert on 16 August, with support from Kirsty McColl, Hazel O'Connor and U2.[4]

Lynott's second solo album, *The Philip Lynott Album*, was delayed until 1982 while *Renegade* was completed and released in November 1981. *Renegade* was not successful, only reaching no. 38 in the UK and no. 157 in the US.[4] A single, "Hollywood (Down on Your Luck)", also flopped,[8] although it did reach no. 24 on the US Mainstream Rock chart.[17] Despite only two songs from the album being written solely by Lynott, and other members of the band contributing more to the compositions, both Gorham and Wharton have since stated their dissatisfaction with some of the songs, such as "Angel of Death", "Fats" and "Mexican Blood".[5] Wharton was omitted from the band photos on the back of the record sleeve, despite the fact that he was by this time a permanent member of the band. "It hurt me a great deal", he said.[5]

Thin Lizzy performing at the Manchester Apollo, showing their famous dual guitars on each side

Thunder and Lightning The beginning of 1982 was marred by both Downey and Gorham having to take breaks from the European tour to recover from personal problems. Downey was involved in a fight in a nightclub in Denmark in February,[4] and Gorham was suffering from drug-induced exhaustion.[6] Downey missed five concerts, and was replaced by Mark Nauseef again for three of them, and by Mike Mesbur of support band The Lookalikes for the other two.[18] In March, Gorham collapsed and returned home; eight concerts were performed as a quartet and six others were postponed.[18]

Later in the year, Lynott went on a solo tour and released his second solo album, which did not sell particularly well. Snowy White left the band in August 1982, having tired of the disorganised schedules and Lynott's drug problems, although by his own admission he was too restrained and quiet to fit in well with his more raucous bandmates.[19] White went on to achieve top ten chart success in the UK with his single "Bird of Paradise" in 1983. Long-time co-manager Chris O'Donnell also left at this time, later stating, "A once-brilliant band was turning to crap before my very eyes."[5]

Lynott wanted to find a replacement for White before starting to record the next album, which would turn out to be the band's last. By September 1982, he had settled on John Sykes who had been a member of Tygers of Pan Tang, and he co-wrote the first single from the album, "Cold Sweat", although the rest of the album had already been written. *Thunder and Lightning* was released in March 1983, and was much more successful than its predecessor, reaching no. 4 in the UK.[8] Sykes' presence had rejuvenated the band musically, the composing credits were evenly shared, and the style had grown much heavier, veering towards heavy metal.[4]

The tour to support the album was to be a farewell tour, although Lynott was not convinced that this would be the end of the band. Sykes wanted to continue, although Gorham had had enough.[5] The tour was successful, and some concerts were recorded to compile a live album. Partway into the tour, many of Thin Lizzy's past guitarists were invited onstage to contribute to some of the songs they had originally recorded, the only exception being Snowy White. The album was released in October 1983 as *Life*, which included an older performance of "Renegade" featuring White, and reached no. 29 in the UK.[8] The tour continued while two more singles were released, the last of them, "The Sun Goes Down", only reaching no. 52 in August. Lynott also undertook another solo tour, accompanied by Downey and Sykes, under the name of The Three Musketeers.[4]

After a difficult leg of the tour in Japan, where some members of the band had difficulty obtaining heroin,[5] Thin Lizzy played their final UK concert before their break-up at the Reading Festival on 28 August 1983, which was eventually released in 1992 as their *BBC Radio One Live in Concert* album. The last concert came in Nuremberg on 4 September, at the Monsters of Rock festival, after which the band members went their separate ways.[8]

Post-Thin Lizzy projects and tributes (1985–96)

Before the end of 1983, Phil Lynott formed a new band called Grand Slam, but they were never able to secure a contract with a record company and split by the beginning of 1985.[6] Sykes and Downey initially agreed to be a part of the band, but Sykes joined Whitesnake and Downey also changed his mind. Lynott began to focus more on his solo career and enjoyed a no. 5 hit single "Out in the Fields" with Gary Moore in May 1985.[6] The song, composed by Moore, was taken from his solo album *Run for Cover* featuring various contributions from Lynott. Lynott's solo efforts did not fare so well, and his last single, "Nineteen", only reached no. 76 in the UK.[20]

Before his death, Lynott was planning a third solo album, and had spoken to Downey about a possible reformation of Thin Lizzy around March 1986, with Gorham and Sykes, and had booked studio time for January of that year.[21] However, he died in hospital in Salisbury, Wiltshire, on 4 January 1986, aged 36, having suffered from internal abscesses, pneumonia and septicaemia, brought on by his drug dependency, which led to multiple organ failure.[4][5][8]

On 17 May, Thin Lizzy reformed for the Self Aid concert, with a line-up of Gary Moore, Downey, Gorham, Wharton and Bob Daisley on bass. Bob Geldof and Moore handled most lead vocals, though various singers got onstage for "Whiskey in the Jar". A compilation album, *Soldier of Fortune*, was released in 1987, and also that year, the "Vibe for Philo" tribute concert in Lynott's memory was organised by Dublin DJ and promoter Smiley Bolger, which continues on an annual basis on the anniversary of Lynott's death.[22]

Brian Robertson performing at the 25th annual "Vibe for Philo" on 4 January 2011

The remaining members of Thin Lizzy did not work together until the recording of the single "Dedication" in October 1990, when a rough demo of Lynott's was worked into a finished song to commemorate the fifth anniversary of his death. The song dated from the Grand Slam days and had been originally written with guitarist Laurence Archer.[4][5] Modern recording techniques were used to replace the guitar and drum tracks with new work by Downey and Gorham. Gary Moore had agreed to participate as well, but ultimately did not do so.[5] The song charted in the UK at no. 35 during early 1991, and no. 2 in Ireland,[23] and featured on another greatest hits compilation album, *Dedication: The Very Best of Thin Lizzy*, released in February of that year, which reached no. 8 in the UK album chart.[6] However, a follow-up reissue of "The Boys Are Back in Town" only reached no. 63 in the UK,[13] although it peaked at no. 16

in Ireland.[23]

Following this, numerous small reunion projects began to appear. In 1991, a line-up featuring Robertson and Downey performed with Bobby Tench on lead vocals, ex-Grand Slam member Doish Nagle on guitar and Doug Brockie on bass. They toured Ireland briefly with a series of "An Evening of Thin Lizzy" concerts.[5] In August 1994, Downey, Bell, Robertson and Wharton held a tribute concert in Wolverhampton, together with tribute bands Limehouse Lizzy, Ain't Lizzy and Bad Habitz.[6] Another version of Thin Lizzy was formed later that year by John Sykes (now also performing lead vocals) with Downey, Gorham and Wharton, and with bass parts played by Marco Mendoza, who had played with Sykes in Blue Murder from 1991–93. The tour was advertised as a tribute to Phil Lynott.[4] This line-up also played at the Vibe for Philo gig on 4 January 1996, with a number of other notable musicians including Eric Bell, Midge Ure, Henry Rollins, Therapy? and Joe Elliott and Rick Savage from Def Leppard.[6]

In 1994, a collection of Thin Lizzy tracks from the BBC Radio 1 Peel Sessions was released, and yet another compilation album was brought out in 1996, called *Wild One: The Very Best Of Thin Lizzy*. This was successful, although strangely it did not feature the title track, "Wild One".

On 20 August 1996, Rude Awakening bassist Robert Ryder held "A Celebration of the Life of Philip Lynott" at the Palace in Hollywood, California at the request of Lynott's mother, Philomena, to commemorate both Phil Lynott's birthday and the tenth year of his passing. Philomena Lynott, her partner Dennis Keeley, and Smiley Bolger (Ireland's Vibe for Philo promoter) were flown to Los Angeles by Ryder to make a personal appearance at the show. It featured concert performances by Rude Awakening, Billy Sheehan, Rudy Sarzo, John Norum, Carmine Appice, Phantom Blue, Soma, producer Roy Z and his band the Tribe of Gypsies, Mark Ferrari, Oslo, Bang Tango, Stash, Iron Cross and Irish singer-songwriter Mark Dignam.

Thin Lizzy without Lynott (1996–present)

In 1996 John Sykes decided to reactivate Thin Lizzy, presenting the band as a tribute to Phil Lynott's life and work.[24] He decided to take on the role of lead vocals himself in the absence of Lynott, and persuaded Scott Gorham, Brian Downey and Darren Wharton to return to the fold. To complete the line-up, Marco Mendoza continued in Lynott's role as bass player. They received criticism for using the Thin Lizzy name without Lynott being present,[4] but the band only played hits from Thin Lizzy's back catalogue, and did not compose any new material.[24]

In 1997, Tommy Aldridge filled in on drums when Brian Downey was unable to, and became a full member when

The reformed version of Thin Lizzy at Gods of Metal, 2007

Downey left shortly thereafter. This line-up remained stable through to 2000, when the group recorded a live album, *One Night Only*. The band went on to tour the US playing clubs in early 2001, but Wharton had already left the band by the time of the tour. From 2000 to 2003, Mendoza toured with Ted Nugent, and with Whitesnake in 2004. Sykes released two solo albums in the gap in between 2002–03, while Gorham worked with his band 21 Guns.

Wharton later stated that Thin Lizzy would have been better suited to playing fewer concerts, in bigger venues. He also felt that after the experience of fronting his own band Dare, it was not satisfying enough to play keyboards behind Gorham and Sykes.[25] Sykes said that all the previous Thin Lizzy members were welcome to play with Thin Lizzy at any time.[26]

In 2004, Thin Lizzy worked together again, with Sykes and Gorham bringing in ex-Angel bassist Randy Gregg, and drummer Michael Lee, who had played with Robert Plant and The Cult among others. They toured in North America in both the winter and then the summer as special guests of Deep Purple. This line-up proved temporary however, with Mendoza returning in 2005, and Aldridge returning in 2007. There were no plans for a new album though Thin Lizzy continued to tour. At the London Hammersmith Apollo concert of 13 December 2007, the line-up was Sykes, Gorham, Aldridge and Francesco DiCosmo on bass.[27]

Sykes stated that Thin Lizzy was now "more of a tribute thing"[24] and that it would be wrong to record new material under that name. He added that while the existing band members might record together, it would not be as Thin Lizzy.[24] In 2007, Gorham said that Lynott still received the biggest cheer of the night at concerts, and that the current Thin Lizzy was not active simply for money.[28] "We'd stop if we thought we were just going through the motions...

I think that has a lot to do with the songs – if they were inferior, then maybe we would have got tired of it all. But they're not and we haven't," he said.[28] In January 2011, Gorham maintained that Lynott would have approved of the continuation of the band: "He worked long hours and travelled thousands of miles to get it to a certain level. There's no way he would have said 'No-one should play those songs again.'"[29]

Vivian Campbell and Brian Downey with Thin Lizzy on 6 January 2011

It had been announced that Thin Lizzy, along with The Answer, were to support AC/DC at stadium shows in England, Ireland and Scotland at the end of June 2009, but these appearances were cancelled after drummer Aldridge broke his collarbone in an accident. On 30 June, the band's website announced that Sykes had left Thin Lizzy and all shows for the rest of 2009 were cancelled or postponed. Gorham stated that he would announce Thin Lizzy's future plans shortly. In a statement, he said, "It's been a very tough time of late for myself and the band, firstly with drummer Tommy Aldridge's injury and now the subsequent decision for John and the rest of the group to go their separate ways. I can only apologise to everyone who has supported us over the years, but we will be back up to full speed soon."[27]

In September 2009, Gorham began to assemble a new version of Thin Lizzy, and in May 2010 a new line-up was announced. Joining Gorham was original drummer Brian Downey, long-standing keyboardist Darren Wharton, Def Leppard guitarist Vivian Campbell, and singer Ricky Warwick from The Almighty, while Marco Mendoza returned to fill the bass guitar role. Ex-Lizzy guitarist Brian Robertson was asked if he wanted to participate but had previous commitments to his own solo career.[30]

In addition to a full UK and European tour beginning in January 2011, the band initially announced a concert for 4 January at the O2 Arena in Dublin, which was in conflict with the 2011 "Vibe for Philo". The tour itself started on 6 January at the Music Hall Aberdeen in the UK, with the band finishing the tour in The Olympia, Dublin on 17 February 2011, having cancelled the O2 show.[31]

It was announced in April 2011 that Vivian Campbell would have to leave Thin Lizzy to rejoin Def Leppard after one final gig on 28 May. He was replaced by Guns N' Roses guitarist Richard Fortus.[32] On 28 August, it was announced that Damon Johnson of Alice Cooper's band would be replacing Fortus for Thin Lizzy's tour of the US with Judas Priest. Fortus returned to tour with Guns N' Roses for the rest of the year, and Johnson has since replaced Fortus permanently.[33]

Ricky Warwick (foreground) *and Brian Downey in June 2011 at the Download Festival*

In March 2011, Gorham told Billboard.com that Thin Lizzy may record a new album in the future, saying, "That's the No. 1 question we're getting from people – are we gonna record some new material? The fans seem to trust this line-up, and I don't blame them. We've kind of jumped this emotional hurdle together. Ricky's writing some fucking killer lyrics, and with the kind of talent that's in Thin Lizzy now I think we can pull off a really cool set of tunes. At least it's something that we can think about now, where before it wasn't on the table."[34] On 25 June 2012, Thin Lizzy were in the studio recording new material, although it was not clear how many songs would be recorded or released.[35]

On 10 October 2012, Thin Lizzy announced that the new material would not be released under the Thin Lizzy name, but would be released under a different name in due course. According to Gorham, this was "out of respect to Phil Lynott and the legacy he created", though he confirmed that the new material would feature the classic Thin Lizzy sound.[36] Ricky Warwick announced that the group would cease regular touring as Thin Lizzy at the end of 2012, but that this did not necessarily mean they would never play as Thin Lizzy again.[36]

On 20 December 2012, Gorham announced that the new material would be recorded under the name of Black Star Riders, and that Downey and Wharton had chosen not to participate in the new band project. Downey has decided to take a break from touring, and Wharton will be working on his own band Dare, and a film project. It was also announced that in March 2013, the band would tour Australia under the Thin Lizzy name, with Downey and Wharton, as the opening act on a triple bill with Mötley Crüe and Kiss. Gorham stressed that Thin Lizzy would still perform together occasionally: "We'll still go out as Thin Lizzy. There are still certain big festivals that we will do. Thin Lizzy is still on the horizon, we will still go out and do that but in the meantime we have Black Star Riders that we are going to concentrate on also."[3]

2.73.2 Other Thin Lizzy releases and tributes

A boxed set of four CDs of Thin Lizzy material was released in December 2001 as *Vagabonds, Kings, Warriors, Angels*. It contained all of the band's major hits, and included some rare songs, such as the first single "The Farmer", and single B-sides.[37] In 2004 and 2006, two further greatest hits compilations were released, with 2004's double CD *Greatest Hits* climbing all the way to No. 3 in the UK album chart.[38]

On 19 August 2005, Gary Moore staged a concert at the Point Theatre, Dublin, promoted as "The Boy Is Back in Town". The concert was staged to mark the unveiling of a bronze statue of Lynott on Dublin's Harry Street in the city centre. The performance also featured Brian Downey, Eric Bell, Brian Robertson and Scott Gorham, and included many classic Lizzy songs, such as "Whiskey in the Jar", "Still in Love With You", "Cowboy Song", "Emerald" and "The Boys Are Back in Town." A DVD of the concert was released as *One Night in Dublin: A Tribute to Phil Lynott*.[39]

On 8 September 2008, a 15-track album *UK Tour '75* was released featuring the band performing at Derby College on 21 November 1975. The album includes a 20-page booklet of previously-unseen photos, liner notes written by Brian Downey and extra material of the band jamming during their soundcheck.[40]

In March 2009, VH1 Classic Records issued the band-authorised *Still Dangerous: Live At The Tower Theatre Philadelphia, 1977*, a live CD recorded on the Bad Reputation tour. It was produced by Gorham and Glyn Johns, and Johns also mixed the record. It reached No. 98 in the UK chart.[41] Gorham has suggested there will be further archival releases in the future.[42]

On 24 January 2011, Universal Music issued remastered and expanded editions of *Jailbreak*, *Johnny the Fox* and *Live and Dangerous*. *Jailbreak* and *Johnny the Fox* are double CD editions with the second disc containing outtakes, BBC session recordings and newly remixed versions of two of that particular album's tracks. *Live and Dangerous* also comes as a double CD set, with two bonus tracks which are both unused live recordings. Previous CD editions of *Live and Dangerous* were single discs.[43]

Universal followed this with remasters of *Bad Reputation*, *Black Rose* and *Chinatown*, and in early 2012, *Nightlife* and *Fighting*. Finally, *Renegade* and *Thunder and Lightning* were remastered and re-released in 2013.

2.73.3 Origin of the band name

The band's original guitarist Eric Bell, who was a fan of John Mayall & the Bluesbreakers, bought a copy of *The Dandy* comic[4][44] after seeing Eric Clapton depicted reading a copy of its sister publication *The Beano* on the cover of the 1966 album *Bluesbreakers with Eric Clapton*. He suggested Tin Lizzie, the name of a robot character from the comic, itself named after a popular nickname for the Ford Model T car. Bell also suggested they change 'Tin' to 'Thin' to play on the Irish accent's propensity to drop the 'h'. After a while, Lynott and Downey agreed to the idea and the name stuck, as they thought the confusion was amusing and would create a talking point.[5][6] For some of their early gigs, the band were mistakenly promoted as "Tin Lizzy" or "Tin Lizzie".[8]

2.73.4 Style and legacy

From 1974, Thin Lizzy switched from using one lead guitarist to two. Though others had earlier used similar techniques, Thin Lizzy are widely recognised as one of the first hard rock bands to employ double lead guitar harmony sound – a technique pioneered by Peter Green's Fleetwood Mac and Wishbone Ash in the UK, whilst independently in the US by Lynyrd Skynyrd and The Allman Brothers Band. This style was later refined and popularised in the mid-1970s by bands like Thin Lizzy and Judas Priest, and later by the emerging New Wave of British Heavy Metal groups such as Iron Maiden and Def Leppard. Iron Maiden covered the song "Massacre" from Thin Lizzy's *Johnny the*

The classic line-up showing the band's famous "twin guitar" sound. L to R: Brian Robertson (guitar), Phil Lynott (bass guitar), and Scott Gorham (guitar)

Fox album, and released it on their 1988 single "Can I Play with Madness". A cover of "Cowboy Song" appears on *Sound of White Noise* by Anthrax as the bonus track for the album's Japanese release.

Thin Lizzy are also a major inspiration for modern heavy metal bands such as Metallica,[45] Alice in Chains,[46] Mastodon[47] and Testament.[48][49] Mastodon covered Thin Lizzy's classic "Emerald", which was included as a bonus track for the Japanese release of their album *Remission*. They have played the song live several times, including an acoustic version with Scott Gorham on guitar.[47] Henry Rollins has expressed a fondness for Thin Lizzy,[50] and the Rollins Band covered their song "Are You Ready?" on their album *Get Some Go Again* (2000). The 2005 release from The Great Divide included a cover of "Cowboy Song" in two parts. Megadeth covered Thin Lizzy's "Cold Sweat" on their 2013 release, *Super Collider*.

2.73.5 Band members

Main article: Thin Lizzy band members

2.73.6 Discography

Main article: Thin Lizzy discography

- *Thin Lizzy* (1971)
- *Shades of a Blue Orphanage* (1972)
- *Vagabonds of the Western World* (1973)
- *Nightlife* (1974)
- *Fighting* (1975)
- *Jailbreak* (1976)
- *Johnny the Fox* (1976)
- *Bad Reputation* (1977)
- *Black Rose: A Rock Legend* (1979)
- *Chinatown* (1980)
- *Renegade* (1981)
- *Thunder and Lightning* (1983)

2.73.7 References

[1] Thin Lizzy. *Rolling Stone*.

[2] Thin Lizzy: Biography. *AllMusic*

[3] "Thin Lizzy to End, Black Star Riders to Begin". noise11.com. 20 December 2012.

[4] Alan Byrne, "Thin Lizzy: Soldiers of Fortune", Firefly, 2004

[5] Mark Putterford, "Philip Lynott: The Rocker", Castle, 1994

[6] Stuart Bailie, "The Ballad of the Thin Man", Boxtree, 1996.

[7] "R.I.P. Eric Wrixon". Hot Press. 13 July 2015.

[8] Ken Brooks, "Phil Lynott & Thin Lizzy: Rockin' Vagabond", Agenda, 2000

[9] "The Boys Are Back in Town". *Rolling Stone*. 20 June 2008. Archived from the original on 20 June 2008. Retrieved 2011-07-17.

[10] *Starlight* Magazine, 16 December 1976

[11] "Thin Lizzy's Scott Gorham talks Les Pauls, tour and memoir". Gibson official website. 13 December 2012. Retrieved 13 March 2014.

[12] "Thin Lizzy top live album poll". BBC. 1 August 2004. Retrieved 17 April 2011.

[13] "Chart Stats – Thin Lizzy". Chart Stats. Archived from the original on 25 May 2012. Retrieved 25 June 2008.

[14] "Former Thin Lizzy guitarist Moore dies". *The Irish Times*. 6 February 2011.

[15] "Guitarist Gary Moore 'died of heart attack'". BBC. 8 February 2011.

[16] Philomena Lynott, "My Boy: The Philip Lynott Story", Virgin, 1995.

[17] "Thin Lizzy Billboard statistics". *AllMusic*. Retrieved 4 December 2011.

[18] "Thin Lizzy Tour 1982". Thin Lizzy Guide. Retrieved 4 June 2012.

[19] Interview with Snowy White, BBC Radio 1, "The Friday Rock Show", 8 January 1986.

[20] Adam C. Winstanley, "Black Rose" magazine, Issue 4, 1990.

[21] Interview with Brian Downey, BBC Radio 1, "The Friday Rock Show", 8 January 1986.

[22] "The Vibe for Philo". The Vibe for Philo. Retrieved 3 April 2011.

[23] "Irish Charts – Thin Lizzy". irishcharts.ie. Retrieved 21 June 2011.

[24] "Interview with John Sykes, July 1999". Melodicrock.com. Retrieved 3 April 2011.

[25] "Interview with Darren Wharton". Lords of Metal. Retrieved 17 April 2011.

[26] "Interview with John Sykes c.2004". *Komodo Rock, hosted at johnsykes.com*. Archived from the original on 10 April 2008. Retrieved 18 April 2011.

[27] "Thin Lizzy official website". Thinlizzyonline.com. Retrieved 3 April 2011.

[28] "Interview with Scott Gorham, December 2007". Liverpool F.C. Retrieved 3 April 2011.

[29] "The show must go on: when bands replace their dead stars". *The Guardian*. 27 January 2011. Retrieved 11 December 2011.

[30] "Rock Pages interview with Brian Robertson".

[31] "Thin Lizzy move Dublin date to the Olympia". *Hot Press*. 18 August 2010. Retrieved 25 February 2012.

[32] "Thin Lizzy Tour Dates". ents24.com. Retrieved 17 April 2011.

[33] "Thin Lizzy recruit guitarist Damon Johnson for US tour". blabbermouth.net. 28 August 2011.

[34] "Thin Lizzy Considering Return to the Studio". *Billboard*. 14 September 2009. Retrieved 3 April 2011.

[35] "Thin Lizzy Enter Recording Studio". *Ultimate-Guitar.com*. 25 June 2012. Retrieved 25 June 2012.

[36] "Thin Lizzy announce 'farewell' to touring and new album". Thin Lizzy Official Website. 10 October 2012.

[37] "Thin Lizzy – Vagabonds Kings Warriors Angels". *AllMusic*. Retrieved 17 April 2011.

[38] "Thin Lizzy Greatest Hits at Chartstats". Chartstats.com. Archived from the original on 29 July 2012. Retrieved 3 April 2011.

[39] "Gary Moore & Friends – One Night in Dublin – A Tribute to Phil Lynott". *AllMusic*. Retrieved 17 April 2011.

[40] "Thin Lizzy – UK Tour '75". Uncut, IPC Media. Retrieved 3 April 2011.

[41] "Still Dangerous at Chartstats". Chartstats.com. Archived from the original on 28 July 2012. Retrieved 3 April 2011.

[42] "Interview with Scott Gorham". Metal Express Radio. 9 April 2009.

[43] "Thin Lizzy Re-Release Classic Albums". Classic Rock Magazine, Future Publishing. 9 November 2010.

[44] "Dandy". Comics UK. Archived from the original on 12 June 2009. Retrieved 3 April 2011.

[45] *Classic Albums: Metallica: Metallica*, Eagle Eye/Pioneer, 2001.

[46] "GuitarPlayer: Jerry Cantrell talks 'Devils & Dinosaurs'". *Guitar Player*. Retrieved 6 March 2014.

[47] Kies, Chris (May 2009). "Interview: Mastodon's Brent Hinds & Bill Kelliher". *Premier Guitar, Gearhead Communications, LLC*. Retrieved 21 May 2010.

[48] "Testament's Chuck Billy Discusses New Album 'Dark Roots of Earth' + Randy Blythe Situation". Loudwire. 30 July 2012. Retrieved 18 October 2015.

[49] "Testament Frontman Talks Songwriting, Influences". Blabbermouth.net. 20 August 2013. Retrieved 18 October 2015.

[50] See Rollins's spoken word album *The Boxed Life*

2.73.8 External links

- Official website tour news
- The Official Thin Lizzy website
- Thin Lizzy at DMOZ
- 2015 Scott Gorham Interview on Guitar.com
- The Roisín Dubh Trust
- 2005 Rolling Stone.com article on Lizzy/Lynott
- Lizzy Days – Album artwork, photos and remembrances by Lizzy/Lynott friend, Irish artist Jim Fitzpatrick
- Andy Gee Interview (1974 Lizzy guitarist)

2.74 Thunderstick

This article is about the Samson drummer. For the noisemaker, see Thundersticks.

Thunderstick, real name **Barry Graham Purkis** (7 December 1954), is an English drummer who wore various masks and used to perform on-stage closed in a cage. He was in the popular cult-band Samson which his name is most associated with.

In 1979 he developed his persona modelled on horror icons such as The Rocky Horror Show, Dr. Phibes and the old Hammer horror films, alternatively wearing black and white make-up, an old man/schoolteacher mask, a black cotton mask and his trademarked rhinestone covered mirrorball mask.. He played inside a cage, including during a brief Samson reunion in 2000. With Samson he enjoyed a certain degree of success, especially when their album *Head On* was released in 1980 and reached No. 34 in the UK charts. The following single *Riding With The Angels*, from the album *Shock Tactics*, charted in the UK at No. 54.

In a rare occurrence his face was seen when he performed the main-role in the b-movie *Biceps of Steel*, featuring his band at the time Samson. In the film his then brother-in-law Ben K. Reeves performed as Thunderstick in his stead, only for the shots where Purkis and Thunderstick were set to appear at the same time.

In the June 2005 issue of Classic Rock Magazine, Thunderstick was listed as no. 36 in the "50 Greatest Drummers in Rock" feature.

2.74.1 Early days and Iron Maiden

Purkis started playing drums on a semi-professional level when joining the highly successful English-born band The Primitives (also known as "Mal Ryder & The Primitives" - not to be confused with the eighties UK band) in 1974. They extensively toured south-Italy.

Then he became a drummer for the English band Iron Maiden briefly in 1977, long time before he would create his masked persona. A lot of fantastic stories about the behaviour of Purkis during his tenure in Iron Maiden exist, one of which was that during a gig he fell asleep whilst on stage. During his early Samson tenure, Purkis was also asked to rejoin Iron Maiden in 1980 after the band had been touring with Samson but declined in favour of staying with Samson. This was mainly because his bizarre theatrical image had gained recognition, and he was then seen to be "the face of the New Wave Of British Heavy Metal". His Samson predecessor Clive Burr eventually took the Maiden position.[1]

2.74.2 Self-named band and beyond

After he left Samson for artistic divergences, Thunderstick then went on to form his own eponymous band called *Thunderstick* consisting of two guitarists, bass and female vocalist. They recorded two hard rock albums, the EP *Feel like Rock 'n' Roll?* (1983) and a full feature LP *Beauty and the Beasts* (1984) via Magnum/Thunderbolt Records. These have been restored and remastered for a 2011 CD release, an anthology called *Echoes from the Analogue Asylum* which also features previously-unreleased material.

The band disbanded in 1986, after having recorded their yet-to-be-released final album *Don't Touch, I'll Scream*. Both Thunderstick and vocalist Jodee Valentine went to the United States to try to secure a new deal. A new American line-up was considered, but was soon abandoned in favour of maintaining their identity within the NWOBHM scene. Both returned to the UK. A fifth incarnation emerged in 1988, secured by a high profile management contract, but Thunderstick disbanded again after failing to sign a major deal with a label.

As Barry Purkis, in the late eighties he worked with Bernie Tormé and the Electric Gypsies, and other artists.

He performed as Thunderstick again in a series of Paul Samson solo gigs in America along with bassist Eric Mauriello, in 1989. Ace Frehley jammed with them during an encore at the New York Roxy. Thunderstick rejoined Samson twice, once in 1990 to write and record new material (later issued on 1999's *Past Present & Future*) and then again in 1999-2000, for reunion gigs either in Japan and on the *Wacken Festival* set in Germany. His songwriting input is present on Paul Samson's posthumous solo album *P.S... 1953-2002* originally scheduled to be Samson's new album with the title of "Brand New Day".

Purkis still writes music, and is involved in production for other artists. On 25 April 2009 he played at the Keep It True Festival in Germany with a reunion of various New Wave Of British Heavy Metal artists, marking the return of his Thunderstick persona.

2.74.3 Thunderstick band line-ups

1981-82: Vinnie Munro (vocals), Neil Hay (guitar), Colin Heart (guitar), Ben K. Reeve (bass), Thunderstick (drums).

1982-83: Ana Marie Carmella Borg (vocals), Wango Wiggins (Neil Hay's new stage name, guitar), Cris Martin (guitar), Ben K. Reeve (bass), Thunderstick (drums).

1983-84: Jodee Valentine (vocals), Wango Wiggins (guitar), Christopher Martin (guitar), Ben K. Reeve (bass), Thunderstick (drums), Ana Marie Carmella Borg (vocals for the 1983 EP were provided by Ana but the cover featured a photo of Jodee Valentine who had by then replaced her and was touring with the band).

1984-86: Jodee Valentine (vocals), Wango Wiggins (guitar), Bengt Sorenssen (guitar), Ben K. Reeve (bass), Thunderstick (drums).

1987-88: Jodee Valentine (vocals), Dave Kilford (guitar), John Slight (bass), Thunderstick (drums).

2.74.4 Discography

2.75 Tobruk (band)

Tobruk was an English rock band, Its second incarnation formed in 1981 when vocalist Stuart "Snake" Neale (born 26 April 1963 - died 20 December 2006), guitarist Nigel Evans, and keyboard player Jem Davies from the Bedford-based band, Stranger, joined forces with guitarists Mick Newman, lead Martin Gregory, bassist Steve (Woody) Woodward and drummer Alan Vallance. Prior to this, the band had already had one single released in Ireland. Original members were Newman, Woodward, Vallance (previously Chris Thomas on drums), Nick Petty on guitar and Terry on vocals. Although the band came to the fore during the tail-end of the New Wave of British Heavy Metal movement, their sound was more melodic and polished.[1]

The band relocated to Birmingham and commenced touring. A demo brought them exposure on the Friday Rock Show in 1982. They gigged to promote their debut single "Wild on the Run" with "The Show Must Go On" which was released on Neat Records around 1983. Steve Woodward, who was a founding member and main songwriter, left the band in 1983 after a tour with Diamond Head just as EMI was showing interest in the band. A new rhythm section was recruited, when drummer Eddie Fincher and bassist Mike Brown joined. Vallance went on to stints in Sons of Eden and Proteus. Woodward currently plays guitar and sings in the band Three Chord Trick.[2]

The band's management at the time, Light And Sound Design, hired out the Birmingham Odeon, rigged it with expensive lights and sound and invited various talent scouts. This led the band to sign a deal. After signing to EMI (Parlophone) in 1984 Tobruk went on a club tour before playing some dates with Diamond Head. They also toured the UK supporting UFO (band).[3]

They then ventured to Philadelphia to start recording their debut album, also titled *Wild on the Run* at Warehouse Studios. Lance Quinn from Lita Ford and Bon Jovi-fame co-produced the album with the band.[4] The album was released in May 1985 and tours followed supporting UFO, Tokyo Blade and Manowar.

The band's 1985 single "Falling" gained some airplay. The 7" single release contained a prize draw competition in which the prize was a parachute jump (i.e. free-'falling') with the band at Bovingdon Green Airfield in Buckinghamshire. The winner (23-year-old John Michael Dunn (later known as John Michael Richards), of Thatto Heath, St.Helens, Merseyside (Lancashire)) had to sign a disclaimer/waiver relinquishing Parlophone Records of any responsibility for death, injury or loss. John Richards was a prominent Rock DJ on radio in Northwest England.

Unfortunately, the band could not break in the UK, as they sounded too American. The album's sales disappointed and the band left Parlophone around 1987. A second album was released through FM Revolver, called *Pleasure + Pain*.

By this stage, the band started falling apart with Snake and Fincher leaving the band to join the band Idol Rich. Tobruk tried to soldier on and recorded some demos with ex-The Alliance vocalist, Tony Martin, but nothing came of it and the band split for good. Martin went on to join Black Sabbath. Nigel spent some time touring with Shy.

Snake also had a stint in an early incarnation of The Wildhearts, but never recorded officially with them, although some demos were produced. Mike Brown played bass in a short-lived band with Alan Kelly (drummer, ex-Shy) called Why The Rabbit shortly after Tobruk broke up. Jem Davis and Fincher started the band Midnight Blue with one-time Yngwie Malmsteen and Rainbow singer Doogie White and recorded *Take The Money and Run* circa 1994. Davis also toured with UFO and had stints in Praying Mantis and FM.

Phoenix Music re-issued a Tobruk retrospective in 2001 with rare tracks and video footage, called *Recaptured*. Rip Tide Records also re-released *Wild on the Run* on CD in that year.

2.75.1 Discography

- *The Girl with the Flyaway Hair* (WEA - Ireland) 1981
- "Wild on the Run" 7" (Neat) 1983
- *Wild on the Run* (Parlophone / EMI) 1985
- *Wild on the Run* [Re-released with Bonus Live Disc] (Majestic Rock Records) 2007
- *Pleasure + Pain* (FM Revolver) 1987
- *Recaptured* (Phoenix) 2001

2.75.2 See also

- List of New Wave of British Heavy Metal bands

- The Wildhearts

2.75.3 References

[1] "Tobruk on MySpace Music". Retrieved 2009-03-26.

[2] Ling, Dave (2004). *Wild On The Run* (CD Booklet). Tobruk. Majestic Rock Records. pp. 1–5. 842051 003902.

[3] Dave Ling (3 July 2004). "Tobruk". *Classic Rock* (London).

[4] "Album Review - Tobruk - Wild On The Run - RevelationZ Magazine". 4 July 2007. Retrieved 2009-03-26.

2.75.4 External links

- Unofficial Tobruk Myspace Page

2.76 Tokyo Blade

Tokyo Blade is an English heavy metal band, active since 1982.[1] Tokyo Blade is one of the many acts considered part of the New Wave of British Heavy Metal (**NWOBHM**) movement from the late 1970s / early 1980s. Tokyo Blade went through many changes of formation and disbanded twice, often changing their musical style during the years of activity. However, the band is still active today, with three of the original members in the line-up.

2.76.1 History

NWOBHM (1978-1985)

The band was formed in Salisbury in the late 1970s under the moniker White Diamond later changed to Killer in 1981 and then changed again to Genghis Khan.[2] The original line-up consisted of Alan Marsh (vocals), Andy Boulton (guitar), Ray Dismore (guitar), Andy Robbins (bass), and Steve Pierce (drums). Later in the year, the band changed their name again, signed with the British independent record label Powerstation Records and recorded their first album. This album was self-titled in all regions, except in the United States, where it came out as *Midnight Rendezvous* on the Combat Records label. Also in 1981, the band shared the stages of clubs and festivals with notable acts such as Metallica and Venom.

Like many other acts of the period, Tokyo Blade was plagued by frequent changes of band members. By the time the follow-up album was released, vocalist Alan Marsh was replaced with Vic Wright. The album *Night of the Blade* was issued in 1984 with Wright on vocals. However, in 1998, an edition of the album featuring Marsh's original vocals was eventually released as *Night of the Blade... The Night Before*. In that period, Tokyo Blade took part in tours and festival packages with Blue Öyster Cult and others with Dio, Ozzy Osbourne and Scorpions. The band's third record *Black Hearts & Jaded Spades* was released in 1985 by the band's own label in Europe and available in the USA as an import only. The band filmed a concert at London's Camden Palace, which was aired on Channel 4 in 1985, and has since made its way on to multiple bootleg DVD releases. By the end of the year, Tokyo Blade disbanded, with all members dedicating their time and efforts to other projects.

Andy Boulton's Tokyo Blade (1985-1989)

Original vocalist Alan Marsh formed another Far East-influenced band called Shogun, alongside former Chinatown guitarist Danny Gwilym. They released two albums, and worked with noted producer Bob Ezrin. Shogun eventually worked with Tokyo Blade bandmates Steve Pierce, Andy Wrighton and Andy Robbins. Guitarist John Wiggins (Deep Machine, Slam) would go on to play in the first edition of Battlezone with ex-Iron Maiden vocalist Paul Di'Anno. Original bassist Andy Robbins would be a part of the bands Jagged Edge and Taste, which recorded a single with Iron Maiden's Bruce Dickinson and later became the hard rock band Skin. Vic Wright formed the band Johnny Crash, being the first project related to Tokyo Blade to have a major label home in the USA, releasing the album "Neighbourhood Threat." A new line-up of the band, including future Guns N' Roses members Dizzy Reed and Matt Sorum, recorded a second album, originally called "Damnation Alley," which saw release in 2008 on Sun City Records, re-titled "Unfinished Business."

Original guitarist Andy Boulton continued recording under the name "Andy Boulton's Tokyo Blade", with an entirely new line-up. This new incarnation of Tokyo Blade released the album "Ain't Misbehavin'" in 1987 and toured on the festival circuit, playing also on the same stage of Black Sabbath. In 1988, Boulton recruited members of the German band The Dead Ballerinas (featuring former Kin Ping Meh vocalist Michael Pozz) to record "No Remorse," issued under the GAMA International sub-label Hot Blood Records. Like the debut, the album has since been reissued with multiple covers. Tokyo Blade again disbanded, with Boulton returning to work with Alan Marsh.

Mr. Ice and reformation (1989-1998)

As record company problems plagued Shogun, Marsh formed a group called Mr. Ice, which eventually included guitarist Andy Boulton. As the group featured two key members from Tokyo Blade, a move from the band's management to resurrect the old name for a European tour with Uriah Heep led to additional issues. Boulton exited the group and was replaced by guitarist Steve Kerr. At the conclusion of the tour, both Kerr and the management exited. Some of the tracks from Mr. Ice were released as a Tokyo Blade record in the mid-1990s.

By 1994, Marsh and Boulton were again playing together and creating new music, releasing "Burning Down Paradise"'on SPV in 1996. Key tracks were also released as a Tokyo Blade record in the mid-to-late 1990s.

The early records by the band were reissued in 1997 by High Vaultage, and the later period recordings were gathered by Zoom Club, and a live album, "Live in Germany" was released in 2009.

Solo projects and new activities (2008-present)

Andy Boulton went on to be in the band XFX, later concentrating his efforts on a solo album and on teaching electric and bass guitar. Alan Marsh joined for a while the cast of a musical based on Jack the Ripper. Second vocalist Vic Wright has written a book, has a comedy show in production and is currently seeking a publishing deal. However, after over 12 years of inactivity, a new version of Tokyo Blade was rebuilt by guitarist Bryan Holland and included Boulton, new members, singer Chris Gillen, drummer Lorenzo Gonzalez and bassist Frank Sapardi, the band successfully toured through Europe through 2008-2009.

Andy Boulton quit the band just prior to the bands 2009 fall European tour, citing health reasons and gave Bryan Holland the nod to continue on without him, the band carried on with the remaining members to fulfill the touring contracts and commitments. Following the conclusion of the 2009 tour and release of the "Live in Germany" album, the US line-up dissolved and Andy Boulton re-enlisted four parts of the classic line up, John Wiggins, Andy Wrighton and Steve Pierce, reformed Tokyo Blade with vocalist Chris Gillen staying on board. Gillen did not perform or record with the band again and was soon replaced by Domain singer Nicolaj Ruhnow, the band recorded the new album "Thousand Men Strong" with producer Chris Tsangarides, released in March 2011.[3] Tokyo Blade was a live attraction at metal festivals in 2010, 2011, 2012 and 2013.

Nicolaj Ruhnow left the band abruptly in 2014, citing a fallout with Andy Boulton, and Chris Gillen has since returned to the band as lead vocalist.

Bassist Andy Wrighton (Deep Machine, Shogun) and guitarist John Wiggins (Deep Machine, Slam) are currently in the reformed Deep Machine with guitarist Bob Hooker, singer Lenny Baxter (Ex-Gangland) and drummer Chas Towler (Slam). Formed in East London in the 1980s, Deep Machine's roots go back to the early NWOBHM movement.

2.76.2 Members

Current members

- Andy Boulton - lead guitar (1982-1986; 1987; 1995-1996; 2007-2009; 2010-present)
- John Wiggins - rhythm guitar (1983-1986; 2010–present)
- Andy Wrighton - bass guitar (1984-1986; 2010–present)
- Steve Pierce - drums (1982-1986; 1987; 2010–present)
- Chris Gillen - Vocals (2008-2010, 2014-present)

Former members

- Alan Marsh - lead vocals (1982-1984; 1990-1991; 1995-1996)
- Vic Wright - lead vocals (1984-1986)
- Bryan Holland - lead guitar (2007-2010)
- Michael Pozz - lead vocals (1989)
- Pete Zito - lead vocals (1986-1988)
- Brian George - lead vocals (1987)
- Carl Sentance - lead vocals (1986)
- Danny Gwilym - rhythm guitar (1990-1991)
- Sean Cooper - rhythm guitar (1987)
- Ray Dismore - rhythm guitar (1982-1983)
- Steve Kerr - lead guitar
- Andy Robbins - bass guitar (1982-1984)
- Dave Donaldson - bass guitar (1987)
- Dave Sale - bass guitar (1989)
- Colin Riggs - bass guitar (1990-1991;1995-1996)
- Frank 'Sapardi' Kruckle- bass guitar (2008-2010)
- Ace Finchum - drums
- Alex Lee - drums (1987)
- Marc Angel - drums (1990-1991; 1995-1996)

- Lorenzo Gonzalez - drums (2008-2010)
- Martin Machwitz - keyboards (1989)
- Nicolaj Ruhnow - lead vocals (2010–2014)
- Atilla - keyboards (1990)

2.76.3 Discography

Studio albums

- *Tokyo Blade* (1983)
- *Midnight Rendezvous* (1984, US release)
- *Night of the Blade* (1984)
- *Black Hearts & Jaded Spades* (1985)
- *Ain't Misbehavin'* (1987)
- *No Remorse* (1989)
- *Burning Down Paradise* (1995)
- *Pumphouse* (1998)
- *Mr. Ice* (1998)
- *Eye of The Storm* (2008, re-release of *No Remorse*)
- *Thousand Men Strong* (2011)

EPs

- *Lightning Strikes* (1984)
- *Midnight Rendezvous* (1984)
- *Madame Guillotine* (1985)
- *Camp 334* (2012)
- *Stick it ...* (2012)

Live albums

- *Live in Germany* (2009) CD and DVD

2.76.4 Related releases

- Shogun - *Shogun* (Alan Marsh)
- Shogun - *31 Days* (Alan Marsh/Andy Wrighton/Steve Pierce)
- Johnny Crash - *Neighbourhood Threat* (Vic Wright)
- Battlezone - *Fighting Back* (John Wiggins)
- Battlezone - *Children of Madness* (John Wiggins)
- Battlezone - *Feel My Pain* (John Wiggins/Colin Riggs/Marc Angel)
- 12 Apostel - *12 Apostel* (Martin Machwitz)
- Dead Ballerinas - *Dead Ballerinas* (Michael Pozz)
- Kin Ping Meh - *Kin Ping Meh* (Michael Pozz)
- Skin - Multiple records/CD's (Andy Robbins)
- Reverence - *When Darkness Calls* (2012) (Bryan Holland)
- Reverence - *Gods of War* (2015) (Bryan Holland, Lorenzo Gonzalez)
- Reverence - *Live* (2016) (Bryan Holland, Lorenzo Gonzalez)
- Nick Hellfort - *The Mask Within* (2013) (Nicolaj Ruhnow)

2.76.5 See also

- List of New Wave of British Heavy Metal bands

2.76.6 References

[1] "Tokyo Blade - Encyclopaedia Metallum". The Metal Archives. Retrieved 2012-12-03.

[2] "Killer - Encyclopaedia Metallum". The Metal Archives. Retrieved 2012-12-03.

[3] Tokyo Blade Completes Recording New Album, "1000 Men Strong"

Nicolaj Ruhnow parts away with TOKYO BLADE

2.76.7 External links

- Official Homepage
- US Label
- Reverence Official website
- Reverence Official Facebook
- Vicki James Wright Interview
- Official MySpace Page
- Official Lost and Found Records website Retrieved 27 August 2009.
- Nick Hellfort Official Facebook
- Nick Hellfort Official Homepage

2.77 Tredegar (band)

Tredegar were a Welsh heavy metal band formed in 1982. It was named after the town in Wales.

2.77.1 History

Tredegar were formed by former Budgie members Tony Bourge and Ray Phillips. Their debut album was recorded in 1986 with the help of Persian Risk's Carl Sentance as a guest vocalist as the band did not have a permanent singer at the time. Russ North joined the band in time to record vocals for one song, and stayed with the band for around one year before leaving with guitarist Andy Wood to join Cloven Hoof.

The band went through many line-up changes, eventually leading to Ray Phillips being the only original member left. Phillips took over vocal duties for an album that was recorded in 1991, but not released after the record company that agreed to distribute it had a change of heart at the last minute.

After the break-up of Tredegar, Phillips, his guitarist son Justin and Tom Prince went on to form Six Ton Budgie. A remixed version of the debut album that had previously only been released in Germany was re-issued along with the entire unreleased second album on a single disc by Axel Records in 1994 under the title *Remix & Rebirth*.

2.77.2 Discography

Singles

- "Duma" (1986)

Studio albums

- *Tredegar* (1986)

Compilations

- *Remix & Rebirth* (1994)

2.77.3 Former members

Drums

- Ray Phillips (1982-92; also vocals in 1991–92)

Vocals

- Ian Hornsby (1982–86)
- Carl Sentance (1986)
- Russ North (1986–87)
- Paul Parry (1987–89)
- Trixie Thorne (1989-91)

Guitars

- Tony Bourge (1982-90)
- Andy Wood (1986–87)
- Lee Jones (1987-91)
- Sam Lees (1990-92)

Bass guitar

- Alan Fish (1982–85)
- Tom Prince (1985–86)
- Mike Taylor (1986-88)
- Jason Marsh (1988-92)

2.77.4 See also

- List of New Wave of British Heavy Metal bands

2.77.5 External links

- Tredegar band profile on Metal-Archives.com.

2.78 Trespass (band)

Trespass are a heavy metal band from Suffolk, England. They were part of the New Wave of British Heavy Metal at the beginning of the 1980s. The band reformed in 2015.[1]

2.78.1 Lineup

Initially the band consisted of brothers Mark Sutcliffe (voice and guitar) and Paul Sutcliffe (drums), Dave Crawte (guitar), and Richard Penny (bass). Later they replaced Richard Penny with Cris Linscott and added vocalist Steve "Sleeve" Mills, all under 21 at the time. They all had day jobs, as the band never became financially viable: "Sleeve" was employed by the Social Security Department, Mark and Paul worked at a factory, Dave worked at a record shop, and Cris was an income tax collector. The band's manager was Steve Kendall.[2]

Mark Sutcliffe cites as a musical influence Ritchie Blackmore of Deep Purple fame, Cris Linscott admired Lynyrd Skynyrd and Rush, while "Sleeve" liked David Coverdale and Paul Rodgers.

Trial Records

The band came to sign with Trial Records and their first single, "One of These Days", had a pressing of only 2000 copies, which were sold out in a short time. After that they enlisted vocalist Rob Eckland to record their "Jealousy/Live It Up" single, which was a double a-side.[3] The final release for the label was the *Bright Lights* EP which also had a pressing of 2000 copies. Interestingly, the a-side ran at 45 RPM but the b-side ran at 33⅓ RPM.

The Enid and Lodge Studios

In 1982 the band were represented for a brief period by Lester Mortimer, the manager for British pomp rock band The Enid. Lead vocalist Adrian Grimes (aka Adrian Lynden) joined them for the recording of a 6-track demo, produced by Steven Stewart at The Enid's Lodge Studios. Some of these tracks were included on *One Of These Days: The Anthology*. The band played a few gigs with this line-up (the biggest being the Quay Theatre in Sudbury, Suffolk), but disbanded after a family tragedy.

Other Releases

The band recorded a session for Tommy Vance's Friday Rock Show, which secured them an inclusion in *Metal Explosion*, a BBC compilation record.

They also managed to have two of their songs included in the second volume of the *Metal For Muthas* compilation series.

In 1990 Lars Ulrich, the drummer and co-founder of the band Metallica, released a compilation entitled *NWOBHM '79 Revisited* celebrating the tenth anniversary of the New Wave Of British Heavy Metal. The double-CD includes some of the top acts of the time, with Trespass being represented with their biggest hit "One of These Days" from the BBC session.

Trespass Hiatus

After Trespass's break-up, the long-term members of the band (Mark, Paul, and Dave) formed a glam metal band by the name of Blue Blud (later Blue Blood), releasing two albums: *The Big Noise* (1989) and *Universal Language* (1991). After Blue Blood's break-up in 1992, the brothers revived the Trespass name and released an album of original material in 1993 by the name of *Head*.

Various compilations of released and unreleased material have been issued during the years, both officially by the band and in unofficial bootlegs. Some of these include: *Through the Ages*, *The Works*, *The Works 2*, and *One Of These Days: The Trespass Anthology*.

Trespass Reform

Trespass started to reform in 2013 into 2014 when they entered the studio once more to rerecord their classic material so it had a consistent sound and feel.

The band launched an official Trespass Facebook page in December 2013.[4]

In 2014 Paul Sutcliffe decided he wanted to pursue other musical avenues so the remaining members of the band Mark Sutcliffe and Dave Crawte recruited James Last on Drums, Paul Martin on Guitars and Danny B (who engineered the new album) on Bass.

The band's new line up debuted at the Brofest #3 festival in Newcastle upon tyne, UK on 28 February 2015. The new eponymously titled album and accompanying website were launched in March 2015.

2.78.2 Recording Sessions[5]

1979, October - Hillside Studios

1. "One of these days" (*released as the a-side of the single "One of these days"*)

2. "Bloody moon" (*released as the b-side of the single "One of these days"*)

3. "Frogeye"

4. "Bombay mix"

5. "Ace of spades"

1980, February - Spaceward Studios

1. "8 'til 5"

2. "Stormchild" (*released on the compilation album Metal For Muthas, Volume 2: Cut Loud*)

3. "Lightsmith"

4. "One of these days" (*released on the compilation album Metal For Muthas, Volume 2: Cut Loud*)

1980, April - EMI Studios

1. "Live it up"

2. "Change your mind"

3. "Visionary"

4. "Assassin"

1980, 2 May - BBC Studios
(the Friday Rock Show session)

1. "One of these days"

2. "Stormchild"

3. "Live it up"

4. "Visionary" (*released on the compilation album Metal Explosion*)

1980, August - Spaceward Studios

1. "Live it up" (*released as the aa-side of the single "Jealousy"*)

2. "Jealousy" (*released as the a-side of the single "Jealousy"*)

1981, March - Hillside Studios

1. "Bounty hunter"

2. "Point of no return"

3. "Vendetta"

1981, July - RG Jones Studios

1. "Bright lights" (*released as the a-side of the EP "Bright lights"*)

2. "Duel" (*released as the first b-side of the EP "Bright lights"*)

3. "Man and machine" (*released as the second b-side of the EP "Bright lights"*)

4. "Life beat"

5. "It's all over"

1982, May - The Lodge Studios

1. "Make it metal"

2. "Rockin' on the radio"

3. "Midnight hour"

1982, November - The Lodge Studios

1. "Long way to Hollywood"

2. "Rockin' the hard way"

3. "Hot on your heels"

2014 various - recorded at Long Track studios mixed at HVR Studios

1. "Stormchild"

2. "Assassin"

3. "Ace of Spades"

4. "Eight til Five"

5. "Bloody Moon"

6. "One of these Days"

7. "Live it Up"

8. "Jealousy"

9. "The Duel"

10. "Lightsmith"

2.78.3 See also

- List of New Wave of British Heavy Metal bands

2.78.4 References

[1] http://www.trespassband.com

[2] Chris Collingwood, Sounds, 1980-08-03

[3] Sounds, 1980-08-16

[4] https://www.facebook.com/pages/Trespass

[5] Trespass. "One Of These Days: The Anthology". Sanctuary Records, 2004

2.79 Tygers of Pan Tang

Tygers of Pan Tang are a heavy metal band, part of the New Wave of British Heavy Metal movement. They formed in 1978 in Whitley Bay, England, and were active until 1987. The band reformed in 1999 and continue to record and perform. The name is derived from Pan Tang, a fictional archipelago in Michael Moorcock's Elric of Melniboné fantasy series whose wizards keep tigers as pets.

2.79.1 Biography

Early days, 1978–1983

The Tygers of Pan Tang was originally formed by Robb Weir (guitar), Richard "Rocky" Laws (bass), Jess Cox (vocals) and Brian Dick (drums). They played in working men's clubs[1] and were first signed by local independent label Neat Records before MCA gave them a major record deal. After several singles, they released their first album, *Wild Cat*, in 1980. The album reached No. 18 in the UK Album Chart in the first week of its release.

Subsequently John Sykes (formerly of Streetfighter, later in Badlands, Thin Lizzy, Whitesnake, and Blue Murder) was added as second guitarist. Jess Cox had a falling out with the others and quit, to be replaced by Persian Risk vocalist Jon Deverill. This lineup released *Spellbound* in 1981.

Sykes quit after the release of the third album, *Crazy Nights*, to audition for Ozzy Osbourne's band. He was replaced by ex-Penetration guitarist Fred Purser who had to learn the set in two days before touring.

Tygers of Pan Tang's fourth album, *The Cage*, was released in 1982. The band then had a disagreement with MCA, who were not prepared to promote them unless they agreed to play more cover recordings (following the band's hit with "Love Potion No. 9"). They subsequently tried to break free from their contract, but MCA's demands exceeded the willingness of any other record company to pay to free the band, and the band broke up in frustration.

John Sykes later achieved success with Thin Lizzy and then Whitesnake, and as a guitarist in Japan.

Reformation, 1985–1987

In 1985, Jon Deverill and Brian Dick reformed the band with Steve Lamb (formerly of Sergeant) on guitar, Neil Sheppard on guitar, and ex-Warrior, ex-Satan member Clin Irwin on bass. Dave Donaldson later replaced Clin Irwin. Meanwhile, Robb Weir and Jess Cox formed the spin-off band Tyger-Tyger.

The reformed Tygers of Pan Tang released *The Wreck-Age* in summer 1985 through Music for Nations, and *Burning in the Shade* in 1987, through Zebra Records. *Burning in the Shade* received poor reviews and they disbanded again.

Various compilations and live albums were produced by the band's two first labels, Neat Records and MCA.

Latter days, 1999–present

During the 1998 Wacken Open Air festival, Jess Cox joined on stage with Blitzkrieg, playing three old Tygers songs. The audience's response was very positive, and a year later, to celebrate the 20th anniversary of Tygers of Pan Tang and the 10th Wacken Open Air, the band was invited to play on the main stage. Brian Dick and Rocky were unable to join the band, but the Tygers (now Jess Cox and Robb Weir, backed up by Blitzkrieg guitarist Glenn S Howes, bassist Gavin Gray, and drummer Chris Percy) did perform. Recordings of their performance resulted in the *Live at Wacken* album.

In 2000, Robb Weir reformed the band as the only original member. The other musicians were Tony Liddell (vocals), Dean Robertson (lead guitar), Brian West (bass), and Craig Ellis (drums). They released *Mystical* through Z-Records. They toured in several festivals, but eventually were dropped by Z-Records in 2002, due to poor record sales.

The band went on to produce the split album *The Second Wave: 25 Years of NWOBHM* with Girlschool and Oliver/Dawson Saxon on Communique Records, and in 2004 released *Noises in the Cathouse* with new singer Richie Wicks who although a singer by trade was at the time still playing bass in Angel Witch.

Later that year, Richie Wicks left and was replaced by Italian vocalist Jacopo Meille. Wicks later joined Shadowkeep, appearing on their 2008 album *The Hourglass Effect*, before leaving in 2009. As of 2010, he was the vocalist in Heavenly Hell, a Dio-era Black Sabbath tribute band, and in 2013 he commenced fronting the band Black, White & Purple with fellow ex-Angel Witch guitarist Keith Herzberg and current Praying Mantis drummer Gary MacKenzie, along with Shadowkeep's ex-bassist Mark Fielden.[2]

Jon Deverill went on to work as an actor under the name of Jon De Ville, and as of October 2007 was performing in 'The Sound of Music' at the London Palladium with television star Connie Fisher.[3]

In October 2007, the band issued a limited edition five track EP titled *Back and Beyond*, which featured reworkings of three Tygers songs from the early 1980s, along with two new tracks taken from their forthcoming album. *Animal Instinct* was released on 19 May 2008, the first with vocalist Jacopo Meille. On 2011 bassist Gavin Gray retur in the band to replace Brian West. On 15 July 2011 it was announced that Tygers Of Pan Tang have signed an agreement with Rocksector Records for the worldwide release of their next studio album, with a current working title of "Ambush", provisionally planned for February/March 2012. The album came out on 24 September.

In January 2013 the band announced via their official website that guitarist Dean Robertson had left the band and that they had begun the search for a replacement.[4] The following month, the band announced Micky Crystal as their new guitarist.[5]

2.79.2 Members

Current members

- Robb Weir – Guitar (1978–1983, 1999, 2000–present)
- Craig Ellis – Drums (2000–present)
- Jacopo Meille – Vocals (2004–present)
- Gavin Gray – Bass (1999, 2011–present)
- Micky Crystal – Guitar (2013–present)

Past members

Vocals

- Richie Wicks (2004)
- Tony Liddell (2000–2004)
- John Deverill (1981–1987)
- Jess Cox (1978–1981, 1999)

Guitar

- Glenn S. Howes (1999)
- John Sykes (1980–1982)
- Fred Purser (1982–1983)
- Aynsley Merritt (1985–1985)
- Steve Lamb (1984, 1985–1987)
- Neil Shepherd (1984, 1985–1987)
- Dean Robertson (2000–2013)

Bass

- Brian West (2000–2011)
- Dave Donaldson (1985–1987)
- Clin Irwin (1983–1985)
- Richard "Rocky" Laws (1978–1983)

Drums

- Steven Plant (1999–2001)
- Chris Percy (1999)
- Brian Dick (1978–1983, 1985–1987)

Timeline

2.79.3 Discography

Studio albums

- *Wild Cat* – 1980 – No. 18 UK
- *Spellbound* – 1981 – No. 33 UK
- *Crazy Nights* – 1981 – No. 51 UK
- *The Cage* – 1982 – No. 13 UK
- *The Wreck-Age* – 1985
- *Burning in the Shade* – 1987
- *Mystical* – 2001
- *Noises From the Cathouse* – 2004
- *Animal Instinct* – 2008[6]
- *Animal Instinct x2* – 2009
- *Ambush* – 2012

Compilation albums

- *Tygers of Pan Tang* – 1982
- *The Best of Tygers of Pan Tang* – 1984
- *First Kill* – 1986
- *Hellbound* – 1989
- *Singles* – 1992
- *On the Prowl: The Best of* – 1999
- *Detonated* – 2005
- *Big Game Hunting (The Rarities)* – 2005
- *Bad Bad Kitty* – 2005

Live albums

- *BBC in Concert* – 1981
- *Live at Wacken* – 2001
- *Live at Nottingham Rock City* – 2001
- *Live in the Roar* – 2003
- *Leg of the Boot: Live in Holland* – 2005

EPs

- *Back And Beyond* (limited edition of 3,000) – 2007[7]
- *The Wildcat Sessions* – 2010[7]
- *The Spellbound Sessions* (limited edition of 1,000) – 2011[8]

Singles

- "Don't Touch Me There" / "Burning Up" / "Bad Times" – 1979
- "Rock 'N' Roll Man" / "All Right on the Night" / "Wild Cats" – 1980
- "Suzie Smiled" / "Tush" – 1980
- "Euthanasia" / "Straight as a Die" – 1980
- "Don't Stop By" / "Slave to Freedom" (live) / "Raised on Rock" (live) – 1981
- "Hellbound" / "Don't Give a Damn" / "Don't Take Nothing" / "Bad Times" – 1981 – No. 48 UK
- "The Story So Far" / "Silver and Gold" / "All or Nothing" – 1981
- "Love Don't Stay" / "Paradise Drive" – 1981
- "Do It Good" / "Slip Away" – 1982
- "Making Tracks" / "What You Sayin'" – 1982
- "Paris By Air" / "Love's a Lie" – 1982 – No. 63 UK
- "Rendezvous" / "Life of Crime" – 1982 – No. 49 UK
- "Love Potion No. 9" / "The Stormlands" – 1982 – No. 45 UK
- "Lonely at the Top" / "You Always See What You Want" – 1983

[6]

2.79.4 See also

- List of New Wave of British Heavy Metal bands

2.79.5 References

[1] Christe, Ian (2004). *Sound of the beast: the complete headbanging history of heavy metal*. HarperCollins. p. 49. ISBN 978-0-380-81127-4.

[2] Richie Wicks at Myspace

[3] "Jon De Ville – Franz". *The Official Sound of Music London Web Site*. The Really Useful Group Ltd.

[4] "Dean_Robertson_Leaves". Encyclopedia_Metallium. Retrieved 16 January 2013.

[5] "New Guitarist 2013". Tygers Of Pan Tang Official. Retrieved 3 March 2013.

[6] Roberts, David (2006). *British Hit Singles & Albums* (19th ed.). London: Guinness World Records Limited. p. 572. ISBN 1-904994-10-5.

[7] "Encyclopaedia Metallum: The Metal Archives – Tygers of Pan Tang". The Metal Archives. 2002-07-23. Retrieved 2012-04-27.

[8] Tygers Of Pan Tang Reveals New EP Details

2.79.6 External links

- Absolutely full discography and Band Photos
- Allmusic
- Biography at MusicMight
- Audio Interview with the Tygers Of Pan Tang from Hard Rock Hell Festival 2011
- Audio Interview with Robb Weir and Jack from Hard Rock Hell Festival 2008

2.80 Tytan

Tytan was a British rock band which lasted about two years during the early 1980s, and which reformed in 2012. They formed out of the New Wave Of British Heavy Metal movement and are best known for their strong melodies.

2.80.1 History

Tytan was a British heavy metal band formed at the height of the New Wave Of British Heavy Metal in the autumn of 1981 by the former Angel Witch rhythm section, bassist Kevin Riddles and drummer Dave Dufort (ex-E. F. Band), Scottish vocalist Norman 'Kal' Swan, and guitarists Steve Gibbs and Stuart Adams. The latter left within months and was superseded by Gary Owens (ex-A II Z, Aurora) before Steve Mann (ex-Liar, Lionheart) settled in more permanently.

Signed to Kamaflage Records, a subsidiary of DJM, Tytan recorded their lone album at Ramport Studios in Battersea with Will Reid-Dick manning the boards. Former Judas Priest and Lionheart drummer Les Binks joined the band just in time for the recording in place of Dave Dufort. Jody Turner of Rock Goddess made a guest vocal appearance on the song 'Women On The Frontline.' Binks would be replaced by Tony Boden on the band's October 1982 UK tour with the Tygers Of Pan Tang who was gone shortly thereafter, replaced by Simon Wright (ex-Tora Tora, A II Z, Aurora).

Unfortunately, Kamaflage folded before the album had chance to be released but managed to release the single 'Blind Men and Fools' in both 7" and 12" formats in September 1982 before the band split up the following summer. Wright would join AC/DC and subsequently work with Dio, Rhino Bucket, and UFO. Vocalist Kal Swan moved to Los Angeles, CA where he formed the band Lion with former Lone Star guitarist Tony Smith whose replacement was future Dio and Whitesnake axeman Doug Aldrich. Swan and Aldrich went on to record a further 3 albums in the 1990s under the name Bad Moon Rising. Steve Mann returned to Lionheart and recorded the 1984 *Hot Tonight* album with the band before joining the McAuley Schenker Group, The Sweet, and German prog rock institution Eloy.

In 1985, London-based label Metal Masters released the shelved Tytan tapes as the *Rough Justice* LP. A Japanese CD bootleg followed in the early 1990s, before Majestic Rock Records gave the album an official CD re-issue in 2004 and again in 2006, with 4 BBC 'Friday Rock Show' session live tracks ('Cold Bitch', 'The Watcher', 'Far Side of Destiny' & 'Blind Men and Fools') and a live DVD added as bonus on the second edition.

In 2012, following an invitation to perform at the Keep It True XV Festival in Germany, Tytan reformed, albeit with a revised line-up. Joining original bandmembers Kevin Riddles, Steve Gibbs and Steve Mann were vocalist Tom Barna (from the band Diamond Faith), Andrew Thompson on keyboards, and Angel Witch drummer Andrew Prestidge. Steve Gibbs left the band in early 2014. Drummer's Chris Benton and then Mikey Ciancio joined during 2012 and 2013 and in 2015 James Wise joined as the current drummer. Meanwhile Dave Strange (Midnight Messiah) joined the band in Nov 2014 when Steve Mann moved to the role of consultant/producer to the band. The band are currently writing a second follow up album to "Rough Justice" and touring UK and confirmed to appear at several European festivals in 2016.

2.80.2 Discography

- *Blind Men and Fools* 7"& 12" (Kamaflage, 1982)
- *Rough Justice* (Metal Masters, 1985 / Majestic Rock, 2004 & 2006)

2.80.3 See also

- List of New Wave of British Heavy Metal bands

2.80.4 References

- Tytan @ MusicMight.

2.80.5 External links

- Tytan - official website
- Japanese Tytan Site of Destiny
- Tytan @ MetalArchives.com

- Tytan Last.fm page
- www.facebook.com/TytanOfficial

2.81 UFO (band)

UFO are an English heavy metal and hard rock band that was formed in 1969.[2] UFO became a transitional group between early hard rock and heavy metal and the New Wave of British Heavy Metal. UFO were ranked No. 84 on VH1's "100 Greatest Artists of Hard Rock".[3]

2.81.1 History

Beginning (1969–72)

Singer Phil Mogg, guitarist Mick Bolton, bassist Pete Way, and drummer Andy Parker formed the band in August 1969. Originally taking the name Hocus Pocus, the group changed their name in October 1969 to UFO in honour of the London club where they were spotted by Noel Moore, who signed them to Beacon Records label, which was headed by Antiguan-born Milton Samuel. Their eponymously titled first album debuted in 1970 and was a typical example of early hard rock including a heavy version of the Eddie Cochran's classic "C'mon Everybody". Both *UFO 1* and its follow-up *UFO 2: Flying*, were successful in Japan (especially the single "C'mon Everybody" which became a huge hit there) and Germany (the song "Boogie For George," also from the first album, reached No. 30 in German singles charts as well as "Prince Kajuku" from *Flying* reached No. 26), but generated poor interest in Britain and America. Consequently, their third effort, *Live* (later re-issued as *UFO Lands In Tokyo*), was originally only released in Japan in 1971.

Part of UFO's early work was strongly influenced by space rock (their second album, including a 26-minute title track and a 19-minute-long opus "Star Storm", was subtitled *One Hour Space Rock*) that was modestly popular at the time, but the band soon realised the style was somewhat limited. In January 1972, Mick Bolton left the group, and UFO set out to find a guitarist who could provide the band with a more standard rock sound.

International success (1973–78)

After brief trial runs with Larry Wallis (February - October 1972) and Bernie Marsden (he toured with UFO in Europe and recorded a pair of demos, "Oh My" and "Sixteen") the band recruited Michael Schenker from Scorpions in June 1973. Schenker was only 18 at the time but was already a well-respected guitarist. On a new label, Chrysalis Records, the revamped UFO recorded a non-LP single in 1973, "Give Her The Gun" and "Sweet Little Thing" with producer Derek Lawrence. In 1974 and with a new producer, Leo Lyons (formerly of Ten Years After), UFO recorded *Phenomenon*, which highlighted the band's harder-edged guitar sound. *Phenomenon* contains many fan favorites such as "Doctor Doctor" (later a minor hit single as a live track) and "Rock Bottom" (which was extended live to provide a showcase for Schenker). By the time of the *Phenomenon* tour, ex-Skid Row guitarist Paul Chapman joined the group, but he left in January 1975 to form Lone Star.

Two later albums, *Force It* (July 1975) and *No Heavy Petting* (May 1976) (the last was recorded with a regular keyboardist, Danny Peyronel as well as harmony vocalist and also songwriter), and extensive touring brought UFO increased visibility with American audiences and increased their following in the UK. Song *Belladonna* from *No Heavy Petting* was very popular in USSR (and then became popular in Russia) after the cover version of Alexander Barykin.

In July 1976, the band recruited keyboardist and rhythm guitarist Paul Raymond from Savoy Brown to make 1977's *Lights Out*. This album was the pinnacle of UFO's studio career containing songs such as "Too Hot To Handle," "Lights Out," and the 7-minute opus "Love To Love." With *Lights Out*, the band received substantial critical acclaim. With their new-found success, the band went back into the studio to record *Obsession* in 1978. Later that year, the band went on tour in the USA and recorded a live album, *Strangers In The Night*, which was released in January 1979. *Strangers* was a critical and commercial success, reaching Number 8 in the UK Albums Chart in February 1979.

Schenker's departure (1978)

Along with Michael Schenker's increasing alcohol abuse, tensions had begun to grow between Mogg and Schenker in the late 1970s. Soon after UFO's final US show in Palo Alto, California in October 1978 Schenker left the band. He made a brief return to the Scorpions before going on to form his own Michael Schenker Group.[4]

Post-Schenker years (1979–90)

After Schenker's exit, UFO rehired Paul "Tonka" Chapman on guitar who brought over unused track ideas from Lone Star's drummer Dixie Lee. Shortly after they released their next LP, *No Place To Run* in January, 1980. Produced by the former Beatles producer, George Martin *No Place To Run* failed to match up to the success of its predecessors, though it fractionally missed the UK Top 10. Paul Raymond left the band at the end of the *No Place To Run* tour and was replaced by John Sloman from Uriah Heep for a couple of months and then by former Wild Horses guitarist and keyboardist Neil Carter, who helped fill the void in the songwriting left by Schenker's departure. Carter debuted with UFO on stage at the three-day Reading Festival on 23 August 1980, when the band played as the Saturday night headline act.[5] At the beginning of the following year, UFO released the self-produced *The Wild, the Willing and the Innocent*, which had a lighter pop rock sound, which was popular at the time. The album achieved mild success in the UK, reaching the UK Top 20, and the single "Lonely Heart" was released.

In February 1982 the band released *Mechanix*. It was very successful in the UK, where it reached No.8, the band's highest ever placing. Later that year, founding member Pete Way left the band to form Fastway with Motörhead guitarist "Fast" Eddie Clarke and then his own band, Waysted. He was replaced by Talas bassist, Billy Sheehan. UFO released *Making Contact* in 1983, but the album was a critical and commercial failure. Thus, that March, UFO decided to disband.[6] The band played a UK farewell tour with Paul Gray (ex Eddie and the Hot Rods and The Damned bassist). However, there was a hint that this might not be permanent, when UFO released a compilation album featuring songs by UFO (as well as other groups featuring ex-members of UFO) entitled *Headstone*, the sleeve of which showed a headstone, denoting UFO with their formation date but an incomplete end date.

This proved to be a short hiatus as, just short of two years later, in late 1984, Mogg assembled a new UFO line-up, featuring Paul Gray on bass again, ex- Diamond Head drummer Robbie France (replaced in 1985 by former Magnum drummer Jim Simpson), and Atomic Tommy M (Tommy Mc Clendon), a former roadie who also wrote lyrics for Loudness, on guitar, with Paul Raymond rejoining shortly after[7] and released *Misdemeanor*. This was followed by the 1988 EP *Ain't Misbehavin*. Despite the renewed activity of the band, neither release was financially successful and they officially disbanded again in 1989 after a string of guitarists replacing McClendon: Myke Gray of Jagged Edge in late 1987,[8] in 1988 former Legs Diamond guitarist Rik Sanford and Tony Glidewell, while Pete Way rejoined on bass, and finally in 1989 future Cold Sweat guitarist Erik Gamans.[9]

The reunion(s) (1991–2003)

In 1991, Mogg and Way decided to put a new UFO line-up together with Clive Edwards and Laurence Archer in the band and released *High Stakes & Dangerous Men*. While only released on a small independent label, *High Stakes* was enough to generate serious interest in a full-blown reunion.

The following year, the classic late-1970s UFO line-up – Mogg, Schenker, Way, Raymond and Parker – reunited, and the resulting album was *Walk on Water* (1995). This line-up (barring Parker's replacement by AC/DC's Simon Wright on drums) went on a world tour. However, tensions arose again, and Schenker left the band only 4 shows into the tour, walking off stage mid-set at (ironically) the very same Palo Alto venue where their October '78 tour died. Thereafter, the other members again went their separate ways. However, Schenker returned to the fold in 1998 and the band embarked on another tour, with Parker again replaced by a new drummer. They played at the Astoria, Charing Cross Road, London in 1998.

Phil Mogg and Pete Way continued working together throughout this fluctuating band membership, releasing two albums under the Mogg/Way name in the late 1990s, *Edge of the World* and *Chocolate Box*.

In 2000, Schenker rejoined UFO again and the band released the double CD *Covenant* (with Aynsley Dunbar on drums), which contained a disc of new material and a disc of live classics. In 2002, the band recorded *Sharks*; shortly after *Sharks* was released, Schenker left the band yet again and was replaced with Vinnie Moore.[10] and the official announcement was made in July 2003[11] In 2003, Michael Schenker and Pete Way released *The Plot* with drummer Jeff Martin.

Vinnie Moore and a return to chart success (2004–present)

In 2004 UFO released their 17th studio album *You Are Here* with their new permanent guitarist Vinnie Moore and Jason Bonham on drums (intermittently). UFO recorded their live set and released a double-DVD recording titled *Showtime* (2005) along with a double live CD on SPV in November 2005, mixing a number of re-recorded studio songs. In November 2005, Andy Parker returned to the band to play in the *Piorno Rock Festival* in Granada, Spain. UFO's eighteenth studio album, titled *The Monkey Puzzle*, was released in 2006.

Andy Parker returned in early 2007 after recovering from leg surgery. On the 2008 tour, Pete Way was unable to get a work visa to enter the United States, Rob De Luca (Sebastian Bach's band, Of Earth, Spread Eagle) filling in.[12]

UFO released their 19th studio album, *The Visitor*, in June 2009,[13] and followed with a tour of the UK, but without Pete Way, who was suffering from a medical condition.[14] Bass tracks on *The Visitor* were also played by Peter Pichl, and Pete Way was not credited as a band member on *The Visitor* cover, nor was any other bassist. However, the album saw UFO's return to the UK Top 100 album charts for the first time in almost 15 years.

In July 2009, UFO released a six-CD live concert box set, containing recordings of six concerts between 1975 to 1982, as well as previously unreleased live songs.

On their 2011 tour, they were accompanied by Barry Sparks playing bass.

Since December 2010, UFO had been working on a twentieth studio album, which was supposed to be released in June 2011.[15] Titled *Seven Deadly*,[16] was released on 27 February 2012 to almost universally good reviews and a higher chart position than The Visitor also charting in Germany, Sweden, and the Billboard indie charts.[17]

In 2011, former band members Danny Peyronel, Laurence Archer, and Clive Edwards teamed up with bassist Rocky Newton (ex-McAuley Schenker Group) to form a band entitled X-UFO. In live performances, X-UFO played sets of vintage UFO songs.

As of September 2013, according to Paul Raymond, a new UFO album is in the works, but there is "no detailed talk of that yet."[18]

The new album, *A Conspiracy of Stars*, was released on 23 February 2015.

2.81.2 Band members

Current members

- Phil Mogg – vocals (1969–83, 1984–89, 1992–present)
- Andy Parker – drums (1969–83, 1988–89, 1993–95, 2005–present)
- Paul Raymond – keyboards, rhythm guitar (1976–80, 1984–86, 1993–99, 2003–present)
- Vinnie Moore – guitar (2003–present)

Current touring members

- Rob De Luca – bass (2008–present)[19]

Former members

- Pete Way – bass (1969–82, 1988–89, 1992–2004, 2005–11)
- Mick Bolton – guitar (1969–72)
- Colin Turner – drums (1969)
- Larry Wallis – guitar (1972)
- Bernie Marsden – guitar (1973)
- Michael Schenker – guitar (1973–78, 1993–95, 1997–98, 2000, 2001–03)
- Paul Chapman – guitar (1974–75, 1977, 1978–83)
- Danny Peyronel – keyboards, piano (1975–76)
- John Sloman – keyboards (1980)
- Neil Carter – keyboards, guitar (1980–83)
- Billy Sheehan – bass (1982–83)
- Paul Gray – bass (1983–87)
- Tommy McClendon (aka Atomik Tommy M) – guitar (1984–86)
- Robbie France† – drums (1984–85)
- Jim Simpson – drums (1985–87)
- David Jacobson – keyboards (1986)
- Myke Gray – guitar (1987)
- Rik Sandford – guitar (1988)
- Tony Glidewell – guitar (1988)
- Fabio Del Rio – drums (1988)
- Erik Gamans – guitar (1988–89)
- Laurence Archer – guitar (1991–95)
- Jem Davis – keyboards (1991–93)
- Clive Edwards – drums (1991–93)
- Simon Wright – drums (1995–96, 1997–99)
- Leon Lawson – guitar (1995–96)
- John Norum – guitar (1996)
- George Bellas – guitar (1996)
- Aynsley Dunbar – drums (1997, 2000, 2001–04)
- Matt Guillory – guitar (1997)
- Jeff Kollmann – guitar (1998–99), bass (2005)
- Jason Bonham – drums (2004–05)
- Barry Sparks – bass (2004, touring: 2011)

Timeline

2.81.3 Discography

Main article: UFO discography

- *UFO 1* (1970)
- *UFO 2: Flying* (1971)
- *Phenomenon* (1974)
- *Force It* (1975)
- *No Heavy Petting* (1976)
- *Lights Out* (1977)
- *Obsession* (1978)
- *Strangers in the Night* (live album) (1979)
- *No Place to Run* (1980)
- *The Wild, the Willing and the Innocent* (1981)
- *Mechanix* (1982)
- *Making Contact* (1983)
- *Misdemeanor* (1985)
- *High Stakes & Dangerous Men* (1992)
- *Walk on Water* (1995)
- *Covenant* (2000)
- *Sharks* (2002)
- *You Are Here* (2004)
- *The Monkey Puzzle* (2006)
- *The Visitor* (2009)
- *Seven Deadly* (2012)
- *A Conspiracy of Stars* (2015)

2.81.4 Videography

- *Too Hot To Handle* (1994)
- *Showtime* (2005)

Tristan Greatrex – album artwork

2.81.5 References

[1] "Legends of Rock Guitar: The Essential Reference of Rock's Greatest Guitarists" by Pete Prown, H. P. Newquist

[2] Strong, Martin C. (2000). *The Great Rock Discography* (5th ed.). Edinburgh: Mojo Books. pp. 1014–1016. ISBN 1-84195-017-3.

[3] "The Greatest I Show Cast, Episodes, Guides, Trailers, Web Exclusives, Previews". VH1.com. Retrieved 2014-06-28.

[4] Saulnier, Jason (23 January 2009). "Michael Schenker Interview". Music Legends. Retrieved 6 May 2013.

[5] Tobler, John (1992). *NME Rock 'N' Roll Years* (1st ed.). London: Reed International Books Ltd. p. 345. CN 5585.

[6] Tobler (1992). *NME Rock 'N' Roll Years*. p. 378. CN 5585.

[7] "UFO - Family Tree - 1980 to 1990". Beatsworking.tv. Retrieved 2014-06-28.

[8] "UFO - Press Articles - 1987". Beatsworking.tv. Retrieved 2014-06-28.

[9]

[10] UFO on Allmusic

[11] "It's Official: Vinnie Moore, Jason Bonham Join Ufo". Blabbermouth.net. 2003-07-29. Retrieved 2014-06-28.

[12] Archived 3 November 2013 at the Wayback Machine

[13] "UFO To Release 'The Visitor' In The Spring".

[14] "UFO". Ufo-music.info. Retrieved 2014-06-28.

[15] "Ufo Announces Initial Batch Of 2011 North American Tour Dates - Blabbermouth.net". Roadrunnerrecords.com. 2010-12-01. Retrieved 2014-06-28.

[16] "Ufo: New Album Title Announced - Blabbermouth.net". Roadrunnerrecords.com. 2011-11-11. Retrieved 2014-06-28.

[17] "Ufo: New Album Release Date Announced - Blabbermouth.net". Roadrunnerrecords.com. 2011-11-07. Retrieved 2014-06-28.

[18] "Music News & Reviews". Music Street Journal. Retrieved 2014-06-28.

[19] "Rob De Luca Interview". Music Legends. Retrieved 3 July 2013.

2.81.6 External links

- Official UFO website
- UFO fansite
- UFO from A to Z
- Pete Way's Official website
- Interview with vocalist Phil Mogg
- UFO Feature and Interview with Andy Parker 2007

2.82 Urchin (band)

Urchin (originally **Evil Ways**)[1] were an English hard rock band.

2.82.1 Early years

The band was formed in 1972 by childhood friends Dave Murray and Adrian Smith. Along with bassist John Hoye and various drummers, they entered a few local talent competitions and played their first gigs in Hoye's school.

Early in 1974 Murray decided to leave and join a 'proper' band and Smith and Hoye met up with guitarist Maurice Coyne who was a friend of a friend. After a jam session in Hoye's school hall, they decided to form a band and Evil Ways was reborn. A drummer Barry Tyler then joined the band. After gigging around local pubs they decided that they needed a singer/frontman, and recruited Dubliner David Hall.

By this time Evil Ways were playing regularly at most of the well known London venues. In August 1976 they were signed by Nomis/Morgan (owned by Simon Napier-Bell) who changed the band's name to Urchin, and got them a recording contract with DJM Records. Their first single was going to be 'Without Love', written by Dave Hall, with "Rocka Rolla" (the Judas Priest song) as the B-side. They were recorded in a studio in Denmark Street, London but were never released. Soon after, Hoye left the band and was replaced by Alan Levett (an old school friend of Tyler's).

2.82.2 Line-up changes

"Black Leather Fantasy", was released on 13 May 1977 and is now a very rare collectors item. Hall left the band in July 1977, followed by Coyne in January 1978. Coyne was replaced, briefly, by Dave Murray who had left Iron Maiden after an argument. Murray decided not to stay and after playing on the recording of the band's second single - "She's a Roller" (originally called "I'm a Roller")/ "Long Time No Woman" - he returned to Iron Maiden.[2] Urchin carried on and recruited guitarist Andy Barnett and later keyboard player Richard (Dick) Young. However, the advent of punk rock led to the loss of their recording contract and meant that live work was drying up as their brand of hard rock was no longer fashionable. Eventually the band broke up and in early 1980 Smith and Barnett formed The Broadway Brats with ex members of Blazer Blazer. Later that year Smith was invited to replace guitarist Dennis Stratton in Iron Maiden.[3]

2.82.3 Reunions

On 19 December 1985 Smith organised a reunion of his mates and performed the live recording *The Entire Population of Hackney* at the Marquee Club in London along with Nicko McBrain. Later in this recording, the rest of his bandmates from Iron Maiden appeared on stage. In 1989, Smith got some of his Urchin bandmates and some friends together to form his separate project, ASAP (Adrian Smith and Project). They recorded two singles, "Silver and Gold" and "Down the Wire" and one album, *Silver and Gold*. They did not tour and split after Smith left Iron Maiden in 1990.

In 1992, Smith once again got together some of the ASAP bandmates to form the band The Untouchables, which lasted until 1994 when he decided to rename the band and hire a lead singer. This was called Psycho Motel.

In 2004, High Roller Records released a limited and hand-numbered 330 copies on silver vinyl album, *Urchin*, including four single tracks, one live recording and five unreleased songs. In 2010, High Roller Records released a full length album called High Roller, first released on a limited number of 1500 copies, 300 black vinyl with white border, 400 white vinyl and 800 black vinyl with a 20 pages booklet, and later in 2011, was released a CD version with a 24 pages booklet and a limited number of 1000 copies.

There are unofficial live albums, recorded on K7 tapes and currently distributed on the internet.

2.82.4 Discography

Singles

- "Black Leather Fantasy" (1977)

1. "Black Leather Fantasy"
2. "Rock 'n' Roll Woman"

- "She's a Roller" (1978)

1. "Long Time No Woman"

Albums

- *Urchin* (2004)

1. "She's a Roller"
2. "Long Time No Woman"
3. "Black Leather Fantasy"
4. "Rock & Roll Woman"
5. "See Me Through" (Live '85 by The Entire Population)
6. "See Me Through"
7. "Walking Out on You"
8. "Somedays"
9. "Watch Me Walk Away"
10. "The Latest Show"
11. "Lifetime"

- *Urchin - High Roller* (2010)

1. "Keeping It Mellow"
2. "Life in the City"
3. "Watch Me Walk Away"
4. "Countdown"
5. "Lifetime"
6. "The Late Show"
7. "My Lady"
8. "Animals"

- *Urchin - Get Up and Get Out* (2012)

1. "Madman"
2. "Need Somebody"
3. "Get Up and Get Out"
4. "Little Girl"
5. "Countdown" (Alternate Version)
6. "Lifetime"
7. "Don't Ask Me"
8. "Suicide"

Unofficial Live Albums

- *Urchin - Live in Oxford* 1980 (This is NOT the last Urchin show as some like to think!)

1. "Life in the City"
2. "Countdown"
3. "Walking Out on You"
4. "Little Girl"
5. "Steal My Heart"
6. "The User"
7. "Ain't Got No Money"
8. "30 Days in the Hole"
9. "Music"
10. "Somebody Like You"
11. "Rocky Mountain way"
12. "Lifetime"
13. "Animals"
14. "Statesboro Blues"
15. "Watch Me Walk Away"
16. "See Me Through"

- *Urchin Radio 1 BBC Session 1979* - (wrongly titled: *BBC Friday Rock Show* (1977))

1. "See Me Through"
2. "Walking Out on You"
3. "Some Days (I Only Want to Rock'n Roll)"
4. "Watch Me Walk Away"
5. "The Latest Show"
6. "Lifetime"

2.82.5 Members

Last known line-up

- Adrian Smith - guitar (1974–1980), vocals (1977–1980)
- Andy Barnett - guitar (1978–1980)
- Richard Young - keyboards (1979–1980)
- Alan Levett - bass guitar (1976–1980)
- Barry Tyler - drums (1974–1980)

Former members

- Maurice Coyne - guitar (1974–1978)
- David Hall - vocals (1975–1977)
- John Hoye - bass (1974–1976)
- Dave Murray - guitar (1977–1978)

2.82.6 See also

- List of New Wave of British Heavy Metal bands

2.82.7 References

[1] Wall, Mick (2004). *Iron Maiden: Run to the Hills, the Authorized Biography* (3rd ed.). Sanctuary Publishing. p. 167. ISBN 1-86074-542-3.

[2] Wall, Mick (2004). *Iron Maiden: Run to the Hills, the Authorised Biography* (3rd ed.). Sanctuary Publishing. p. 168. ISBN 1-86074-542-3.

[3] Wall, Mick (2004). *Iron Maiden: Run to the Hills, the Authorized Biography* (3rd ed.). Sanctuary Publishing. p. 169. ISBN 1-86074-542-3.

2.82.8 External links

2.83 Vardis

Vardis are an influential three-piece hard rock, boogie rock and heavy metal band from Wakefield, West Yorkshire, who enjoyed hits between 1978 and 1986.

They formed a prominent part of the New Wave of British Heavy Metal scene, then prevalent in the United Kingdom. They consisted of frontman Steve Zodiac on guitar and lead vocals, Alan Selway on bass guitar and Gary Pearson on drums. Alan Selway was later replaced by Terry Horbury (previously of Dirty Tricks) on bass guitar.

The band were originally formed under the name 'Quo Vardis' (Latin for 'whither goest thou?') because they did not know which direction they were going. This was later abbreviated to Vardis. Their first recordings were made at Holyground Studios in Cass Yard, Kirgate, Wakefied. The first ever track laid down on vinyl was titled "Jiving All Night Long" with the B-side titled "Stay with Me", both penned by Zodiac. This was followed up with a second record, both cover versions, those being "Roll Over Beethoven" (Chuck Berry) and "Don't Waste My Time" (Status Quo).

Vardis quickly gained notoriety for their high energy live performances, the unique approach of incorporating elements of 70's glam rock and heavy metal music and frontman Steve Zodiac's searing Fender Telecaster sound. Zodiac was reputable for playing Vardis concerts barefoot and bare chested, his look completed by long, naturally ice-blonde hair.

They took the unorthodox approach of comprising their debut album, *100MPH* (1980), of entirely live recordings. This is largely considered to be their finest hour and gained the band a large following early on in their career. They were invited to play the Heavy Metal Holocaust music festival in August 1981 alongside Motörhead, Ozzy Osbourne and Triumph. Around 30,000 heavy metal fans were estimated to have attended with the PA reportedly reaching new heights of amplification at over 100,000 watts.

Their second album, released in April 1981 and called *The World's Insane*, featured a cover version of Hawkwind's "Silver Machine", and featured bagpipes played by Judd Lander, making it one of the few heavy metal albums of that time to ever feature bagpipes. The album also featured a guest appearances from Status Quo's Andy Bown on keyboards. In 1982, Steve Zodiac was voted in the top 15 rock guitarists by *Sounds* magazine readers.

Vardis dissolved in the mid 1980s amid lengthy legal disputes with former management.

Two compilation albums, *The Best of Vardis* (1997) and *The World's Gone Mad: Best of Vardis* (2002) have been released since their premature split, but no new material. Original Vardis records are rare and are valued in most record collector's books and guides. An original copy of *100 M.P.H.* including the enclosed tour guide and poster has an estimated value of approximately £500 ($940).

Vardis reformed with the Zodiac/Horbury/Pearson lineup in March 2014,[1] and performed at festivals in the U.K. and Germany until Gary Pearson's resignation at the end of the year. New drummer Joe Clancy was unveiled in January 2015, as Vardis announced plans to write and record new material.[2]

2.83.1 Discography

Studio albums

- *100 M.P.H.* (Logo, 1980) - UK No. 52[3]
- *The World's Insane* (Logo, 1981)
- *Quo Vardis* (Logo, 1982)
- *Vigilante* (Raw Power, LP022, 1986) - featuring Terry Horbury

Compilation albums

- *New Electric Warriors* (Logo, 1980)
- *Metal Power* (Logo, 1981)
- *The Lion's Share* (Razor, 1983)
- *NWOBHM* (Phonogram, 1990)
- *New Electric Warriors* (British Steel, 1997)
- *The World's Gone Mad* (Essential, 2000)
- *NWOBHM Rarities* (British Steel, 2000)
- *Metal* (Sanctuary, 2001)
- *Rock of Ages* (Sanctuary, 2002)

Singles and EPs

- "Jiving All Night Long" (Holyground Enterprises, 1973)
- "Roll Over Beethoven" (Holyground Enterprises, 1973)
- "100 M.P.H. EP" (Redball, 1979)
- "If I Were King" (Castle, 1980)
- "Let's Go" (Logo, 1980) - UK No. 59[3]
- "Too Many People" (Logo, 1980)
- "Silver Machine" (Logo, 1981)
- "All You'll Ever Need" (Logo, 1981)
- "Gary Glitter Part One" / "To Be With You" (Logo, 1982) - (double A-side single)
- "Standing in the Road" (Big Beat, 1984)
- "200 M.P.H. - EP" (Hoplite Records, 2015)

2.83.2 See also

- List of New Wave of British Heavy Metal bands

2.83.3 References

[1] http://newwaveofbritishheavymetal.com/vardis-reform-to-appear-at-brofest-2014

[2] http://classicrock.teamrock.com/news/2015-01-28/vardis-name-new-drummer

[3] Roberts, David (2006). *British Hit Singles & Albums* (19th ed.). London: Guinness World Records Limited. p. 582. ISBN 1-904994-10-5.

2.83.4 External links

- Official website: www.VardisRocks.com
- Follow Vardis on Twitter
- Like Vardis on Facebook
- See Vardis on youtube
- Hear Vardis on soundcloud
- Vardis on Last.fm
- http://published.massivelinks.com/articles/_/entertainment/music/vardis-the-greatest-rock-band-ever-r22579
- Musicmight
- Photos and links
- NWOBHM archive
- CDs on Amazon.com
- European Tour Book 1981
- Heavy metal charts archive and links

2.84 Venom (band)

For other uses, see Venom (disambiguation).

Venom are an English extreme metal band that formed in 1979 in Newcastle upon Tyne.[1] Coming to prominence towards the end of the New Wave of British Heavy Metal, Venom's first two albums—*Welcome to Hell* (1981) and *Black Metal* (1982)—are considered a major influence on thrash metal and extreme metal in general.[1] Venom's second album proved influential enough that its title was used as the name of an extreme metal subgenre: black metal.

2.84.1 Band history

Early years (1978–1981)

Venom's original personnel came from three different bands: Guillotine, Oberon and Dwarf Star. The original Guillotine featured Jeffrey Dunn and Dave Rutherford on guitars, Dean Hewitt on bass guitar, Dave Blackman on vocals and Chris Mercater on drums who replaced Paul Burke, the original drummer when the band was founded. Blackman and Mercater were later also replaced by drummer Anthony Bray (b. 17 September 1957 in Jarrow, Tyne and Wear) and vocalist Clive Archer of Oberon after due to not living up to the expectations of Paul Burke on drums, and later on Dean Hewitt was replaced by Alan Winston on bass. Around that time a number of personnel changes occurred. Clive Archer, Eric Cooke, Tony Bray and Ian Kell formed a band called Venom while working at Reyrolles. Ian Kell was replaced in summer of 1978 and went on to play in folk band "Kropotkin Lied" In the late autumn of 1979 Conrad Lant, from the bands Dwarf Star and Album Graecum, replaced Dave Rutherford. Lant later switched to bass after the departure of Winston. The band members took on new stage names. Archer became "Jesus Christ", Lant "Mr. Cronos", Tony Bray "Abaddon", and Jeff Dunn "Mantas".

Prime influences of the formative band were Black Sabbath, Judas Priest, Motörhead[2] and KISS.[3] Other bands cited by Venom as an inspiration are Queen, The Who, Deep Purple, Sex Pistols, Van Halen, The Tubes and The Rolling Stones.[3][4]

Since the beginning of their career, Venom have often used 'Satanic' lyrics and imagery. However, the band were not Satanists, and such references were mostly for shock value.[5][6]

In April 1980, the band recorded a three-song disc, featuring "Angel Dust", "Raise the Dead", and "Red Light Fever". Soon afterward, six more tracks were recorded for just £50, with Lant taking vocal duties on the song "Live Like an Angel". Archer soon left the band, and Venom's line-up became a trio.

Classic lineup (1981–1986)

Venom's recording debut was the 1981 single "In League with Satan"/"Live Like an Angel" which was released by Neat Records. Later that year they released their full-length debut, *Welcome to Hell*.

Though crudely recorded with sometimes dubious musicianship, *Welcome to Hell* was still a big influence on future thrash bands. Venom's music was faster and harsher than most heavy metal contemporaries and while Satanism and other dark topics had been featured in metal before, the subject had rarely been more prominent. Lant was quoted as saying that this celebration of evil subjects was inspired by the perceived need to out-do musicians like Ozzy Osbourne of Black Sabbath, who would "sing about evil things and dark figures, and then spoil it all by going: 'Oh, no, no, please, God, help me!'"[7]

Their second album, 1982's *Black Metal* is cited as perhaps the most important influence in the development of black metal, thrash metal, death metal, and other related styles that are often grouped under the extreme metal umbrella.[1] Many defining elements of these genres are first found in the lyrics and song titles created by Lant and his unique singing style as well as the guitar work and solos performed by Dunn. Though they would later be cited as important, neither of Venom's first two albums sold well upon their original release. And while many of their British metal peers had found measures of popular success or critical acclaim (or, like Def Leppard, were moving away from metal towards hard rock), Venom were still regarded by critics as "a trio of buffoons".[8]

In an attempt to prove their status as serious musicians, Venom recorded *At War with Satan* in 1984. The epic 20-minute title track, with substantial progressive rock influences, took up the first side of the LP. The B-side was focused on the rapid-fire, three-minute "scorchers" Venom were known for. In 1985, Venom released their fourth album, *Possessed*, which was not as successful as previous albums. Dunn then left the band to pursue a solo career. Cronos however cites the Possessed album as underestimated. *"I don't think there's any songs that are kind of overlooked, I just think some songs maybe weren't recorded as well as we could have recorded them. Like say for example on the 'Possessed' album, I still think there are great songs[9]"*.

Lineup changes and departure of Lant (1987–1996)

Two guitarists, Mike Hickey and Jim Clare, were hired to replace Dunn. Their fifth album, 1987's *Calm Before the Storm*, moved away from Satanic themes in favor of "sword and sorcery" material.[10] This was even less successful than *Possessed*, and Lant, Clare and Hickey all left Venom after subsequent touring to form Lant's eponymous solo band Cronos.

Bray was left as the only group member, but he was able to convince Music for Nations for a deal to release a new Venom album on the Under One Flag label, using *Deadline* demo tracks which were recorded with previous line-ups but never released. In 1988, Bray offered a vocals/bass role to Tony Dolan from Atomkraft. Bray and Dolan wrote new material prior to Dunn's rejoining the band along with rhythm guitarist Al Barnes. Together they recorded *Prime Evil* (1989), *Tear Your Soul Apart* (1990) and *Temples of Ice* (1991). Barnes then left the band, and Steve White from Atomkraft was hired as his replacement. They released *The Waste Lands* in 1992, also without success. Music for Nations refused to release any more Venom albums, so Dolan and Dunn quit, effectively disbanding Venom. Bray continued to release compilation and live albums up to 1995.

Reunion of classic lineup (1995–1999)

In 1995, Lant, Dunn and Bray reunited the "classic" lineup, beginning by headlining the Waldrock Festival on 24

June 1995. They recorded and self-released the *Venom '96* EP with four re-recorded and one new song, resulting in a record deal with the SPV label. An album, *Cast in Stone*, was next released in 1997, split between new material and re-recordings of popular early-'80s songs.

Recent work (1999–present)

Bray left Venom in 1999 and was replaced by Lant's brother Antony "Antton" Lant. This lineup released *Resurrection* in 2000 on SPV. However, in 2002 Dunn again left the group and was replaced by a returning Hickey. In late 2005, Venom released a career-spanning 4-disc box set *MMV*, which includes an exclusive mini-poster of the band's seven-date tour of Europe with Metallica and a 60-page picture book, with interviews and pictures. The set includes all their best-known songs, along with rarities like live tracks, demos and outtakes. This lineup of the band released the *Metal Black* album.

Hickey was replaced by guitarist La Rage in 2007. This lineup released the record *Hell* the following year. Antton Lant left the group thereafter concentrate on his band DEF-CON-ONE and was replaced by drummer Danny "Dante" Needham. They released the *Fallen Angels* album on 28 November 2011.

Venom released their fourteenth studio album *From the Very Depths* on January 27, 2015.[11] The band also played one song, "Rise", they were working on in the studio, live for the audience at Rockfest 2014.[12]

2.84.2 Genre

As Venom were one of the first incarnations of extreme metal, influencing many thrash metal, black metal, death metal and other extreme metal bands,[13] their exact genre has been a topic of debate. Venom have been labeled various genres by members of the press. Most prominent genres are black metal, thrash metal, and speed metal.[14]

Cronos insists on calling it black metal, without passing judgment on the genre that later on flourished in Norway:

> ...It's one of the things when I first saw when I saw the Norwegian scene beginning in the early nineties. I thought: ok, I know they said Venom are an influence, etcetera, etcetera; let's see where these guys are coming from. And then when I started to read the lyrics, read the interviews and see they were kind of saying the same thing, but about their country, they had their religion, with all the Norse gods like Wodan and Thor. And then all of the sudden the Christians came in and they tried to destroy their religion. It's great that they stayed within in their country's beliefs for their lyrics as well. So, they're not the exactly the same things as Venom, they invented something of their own, which I think is fucking great...[9]

2.84.3 Legacy and influence

Welcome to Hell influenced several later bands.[13] Venom's music helped shape the development of many thrash metal bands, specifically the "Big Four of Thrash" (who in turn were highly influential): Metallica, Slayer, Anthrax and Megadeth (Metallica opened for Venom on an early 1980s tour[7] and Slayer played with them and Exodus on the *Combat Tour* in 1985). Venom would also be of extreme importance to the black metal and even the early death metal scene, with numerous bands copying styles, themes and imagery from the band, such as the Swiss band Hellhammer which also helped pioneer the genres. Music critic Bradley Torreano wrote that Venom "[caught] the attention of both metalheads and punks, the band was emulated by the former and turned into camp icons by the latter."[6]

Although they did not make it to MTV's top 10 heavy metal bands list, they were given an "honorable mention".[15]

2.84.4 Criticism

While many fans and musicians see Venom as an important band, their music has nonetheless been the subject of debate and criticism. Critic Eduardo Rivadavia of AllMusic writes that though *Welcome to Hell* influenced "literally thousands" of bands, Venom were "critically reviled".[13] However, critic James Christopher Monger declares that the members of Venom 'grew as musicians' as their careers progressed.[16] Ethnographer Keith Kahn-Harris argues that Venom's limited technical skill, particularly early in their career, was a profound, though inadvertent factor in Venom's influence: being unable to mimic more technically proficient metal of their predecessors or peers, Venom instead opted to focus on sheer speed, creating music that was inspired by earlier metal, yet simultaneously blazed new trails.

2.84.5 Members

Main article: List of Venom band members

2.84.6 Discography

2.84.7 See also

- List of New Wave of British Heavy Metal bands

2.84.8 References

[1] Kahn-Harris, Keith. *Extreme Metal: Music and Culture on the Edge*. Oxford: Berg, 2007. ISBN 1-84520-399-2.

[2] "Interview with Mantas". www.fortunecity.com. Retrieved 10 August 2009.

[3] "Interview with Abaddon and Cronos". www.fortunecity.com. Retrieved 10 August 2009.

[4] Ankeny, Jason. "Venom". AllMusic. Retrieved 21 May 2012.

[5] Moynihan, Michael; Søderlind, Didrik (2003) [1998]. *Lords of Chaos: The Bloody Rise of the Satanic Metal Underground* (revised and expanded ed.). Feral House. p. 13.

[6] Bradley Torreano: "In League with Satan - Venom". AllMusic. Retrieved 24 January 2013.

[7] "MMV: Review by James Christopher Monger". AllMusic. Retrieved 24 January 2013.

[8] "At War with Satan: Review by Eduardo Rivadavia". AllMusic. Retrieved 26 May 2010.

[9] "Lords of Metal interview with Cronos of Venom by Ramon van H". Lordsofmetal.nl. Retrieved 11 October 2013.

[10] "Calm Before the Storm: Review by Steve Huey". AllMusic. Retrieved 24 January 2013.

[11] "Venom To Release 'From The Very Depths' Album In January". Blabbermouth.net. Retrieved 26 November 2013.

[12] "Venom Putting Finishing Touches On New Album". Blabbermouth.net. Retrieved 6 November 2013.

[13] "Welcome to Hell: Review by Eduardo Rivadavia". AllMusic. Retrieved 26 May 2010.

[14] Black metal according to:
- MusicMight Venom page
- AllMusic Venom page
- Eduardo Rivadavia *Black Metal* review

Thrash metal according to:
- Keith Kahn-Harris *Extreme Metal* book
- Popmatters.com Celtic Frost article

Speed metal according to:
- *Revolver* Venom update

[15] "Metal's Honorable Mentions". *MTV.com*. Retrieved 15 March 2011.

[16] "Darkest Hour: Review by James Christopher Monger". AllMusic. Retrieved 26 May 2010.

2.84.9 External links

- Venom Legions official website

2.85 White Spirit (band)

This article is about the band. For the solvent, see White spirit.

White Spirit was a heavy metal[1] band from Hartlepool, England, best remembered for guitarist Janick Gers who went on to play with Ian Gillan, Bruce Dickinson, and ultimately, Iron Maiden. Other members of the band were Bruce Ruff (vocals), Malcolm Pearson (keyboards), Phil Brady (bass), and Graeme Crallan (drums).

2.85.1 History

White Spirit, co-founded by Gers and Crallan in 1975, are considered part of the New Wave of British Heavy Metal although their sound was closer to that of 1970s hard rock acts such as Deep Purple or Uriah Heep. The band issued their debut single, "Backs to the Grind", on the fledgling heavy metal independent label Neat Records in 1980.[2] It was backed with "Cheetah", which would also appear on Neat's *Lead Weight* compilation (and again on the retrospective *New Wave of British Heavy Metal '79 Revisited* double LP/CD in 1990, compiled by noted NWOBHM enthusiast Lars Ulrich of Metallica and former *Kerrang!* editor Geoff Barton). White Spirit featured on various other notable NWOBHM compilations such as Volume 2 of *Metal for Muthas*, the *Muthas Pride* EP, *Brute Force*, and *60 Minutes Plus*.

With the upsurge of the NWOBHM, White Spirit moved to the MCA label on which they released their first and only album in 1980. The album was simply titled *White Spirit* and featured cover artwork by Michael Spaldin who later worked on stage set design for Gillan. That same year White Spirit made an appearance at the prestigious Reading Festival. The group suffered a serious blow in 1981 when guitarist Janick Gers accepted an offer from former Deep Purple frontman Ian Gillan to join his solo outfit Gillan in place of Bernie Torme. Gers would go on to record the albums *Double Trouble* and *Magic*, before Ian Gillan decided to dissolve the band and join Black Sabbath for their

1983 album *Born Again*. Gers was part of the short lived UK supergroup Gogmagog, also featuring former members of Def Leppard, Iron Maiden and Whitesnake, who folded after releasing a sole EP, *I Will Be There*, in 1985.

White Spirit bassist Phil Brady later played with the Teesside metal band Therapy from 1990–1991, helping them reach the semi-finals of the Battle Of The Bands competition at Rio's in Bradford in 1990. He left White Spirit after their first studio album and was replaced by Ian Shuttleworth. Drummer Graeme Crallan, also known as 'Crash', joined Tank in 1984 and played on their *Honour & Blood* album. He quit the following year. Crallan died at Royal Free Hospital, Hampstead on 27 July 2008 after a fall in York Way, London.[3]

The band's eponymous album was re-issued in 2005 on the Castle label with an entire second disc's worth of bonus material, including rarities, demos, alternate versions and takes, and B-sides. Most notable amongst these additional tracks is one entitled "Watch Out", originally found on the *60 Minutes Plus* compilation in 1982, recorded after vocalist Bruce Ruff had left the band. Instead, future Ted Nugent and Bad Company singer Brian Howe contributed lead vocals.[4]

The re-issue is currently in print in Japan only, where Universal Music Japan issued the album as a re-mastered Limited Edition SHM (Super High Material technology) Mini-LP Sleeve CD in 2008. However this latest re-issue does not include various bonus tracks found on the original Castle edition.

2.85.2 Members

Former

- Bruce Ruff - lead vocals (1975-1981)
- Brian Howe - lead vocals (1981)
- Janick Gers - guitar (1975-1981)
- Phil Brady - bass guitar (1975-1981)
- Graeme Crallan - drums (1975-1981)
- Malcolm Pearson - keyboards (1975-1981)

2.85.3 Discography

Studio albums

- *White Spirit* (1980)

Compilation appearances

- *Metal for Muthas Volume II* (1980, EMI Records) ("High Upon High")
- *Muthas Pride* 12" EP (1980, EMI Records) ("Red Skies")
- *Brute Force* (1980, MCA Records) ("Back to the Grind")
- *Lead Weight* LP (1981, Neat/Base Records) ("Cheetah")
- *60 Minutes Plus* cassette (1982, Neat Records) ("Watch Out")
- *All Hell Let Loose* LP (1983, Base Records) ("Watch Out")
- *Metal Minded* CD (1987, Prism Entertainment) ("Watch Out")
- *New Wave of British Heavy Metal '79 Revisited* CD (1990, Metal Blade) ("Cheetah")

Singles & EPs

- "Backs to the Grind" b/w "Cheetah" (1980, Neat Records) (UK Indie No. 3)[5]
- "Midnight Chaser" b/w "Suffragettes" (1980, MCA Records)
- "High Upon High" b/w "No Reprieve", "Arthur Guitar" (1980, MCA Records)

2.85.4 See also

- List of New Wave of British Heavy Metal bands

2.85.5 References

[1] , additional text.

[2] "White Spirit". nwobhm.info. 2007-05-07. Retrieved 2010-08-13.

[3] "TANK News". Tankfilthhounds.net. Retrieved 2010-08-13.

[4] Source: CD liner notes

[5] Lazell, Barry (1997) *Indie Hits 1980-1989*, Cherry Red Books, ISBN 0-9517206-9-4

2.85.6 External links

- White Spirit page at allmusic at AllMusic
- NWOBHM.info - White Spirit page
- Encyclopedia Metallum - White Spirit

2.86 Whitesnake

For other uses, see White snake.

Whitesnake are a rock band, formed in England in 1978 by David Coverdale after his departure from his previous band, Deep Purple. Their early material has been compared by critics to the blues rock of Deep Purple, but they slowly began moving toward a more commercially accessible rock style.[2] By the turn of the decade, the band's commercial fortunes changed and they released a string of UK top 10 albums, *Ready an' Willing* (1980), *Come an' Get It* (1981), *Saints & Sinners* (1982) and *Slide It In* (1984), the last of which was their first to chart in the US and is certified 2x platinum.

The band's 1987 self-titled album was their most commercially successful worldwide, and contained two major US hits, "Here I Go Again" and "Is This Love", reaching number one and two on the Hot 100. The album went 8 times platinum in the US,[3] and the band's success saw them nominated for the 1988 Brit Award for Best British Group.[4] *Slip of the Tongue* (1989), was also a success, reaching the top 10 in the UK and the US, and received a platinum US certification.[5] The band split up shortly after this release, but had a reunion in 1994, and released a one-off studio album, *Restless Heart* (1997).

Whitesnake officially reformed in 2002 and have been touring together since, releasing three studio albums, *Good to Be Bad* (2008), *Forevermore* (2011) and *The Purple Album* (2015). In 2005, Whitesnake was named the 85th greatest hard rock band of all time by VH1.[1]

2.86.1 History

Formation (1978)

David Coverdale founded Whitesnake in 1978[6][7] in Middlesbrough, Cleveland, north-east England. The core line-up had been working as his backing band **The White Snake Band** on the *White Snake* (1977) album tour and they retained the title before officially being known as Whitesnake. They toured with Coverdale as his support band and for both of the solo albums he released, *White Snake* (1977) and *Northwinds* (1978), between exiting Deep Purple and founding Whitesnake. At this time, the band was made up of David Coverdale, Bernie Marsden, Micky Moody, Neil Murray and drummer David "Duck" Dowle with keyboardist Brian Johnston. Johnston would soon be replaced by Procol Harum organ player and keyboardist Pete Solley. Because of Solley's producing commitments he was replaced by the former Deep Purple keyboard player Jon Lord, during sessions for the first LP.

Early years and commercial success (1978–1983)

Whitesnake at the Reading Festival in Reading, Berkshire, England, 1980

Whitesnake recorded the EP *Snakebite*, which was released in 1978 and included a cover of a Bobby "Blue" Bland song "Ain't No Love in the Heart of the City", their first hit song proving the New Wave of British Heavy Metal could have a chart hit.[8] The EP had some success in the UK and subsequent reissues of this EP included four bonus tracks from Coverdale's second solo album *Northwinds* (1978) produced by Roger Glover.

A blues rock debut album *Trouble*, was released in the autumn of 1978 and peaked at No. 50 in the UK album charts. Whitesnake toured Europe to promote the album and their first live album *Live at Hammersmith* was recorded on this tour and released in Japan in 1979. Tracks from the EP Snakebite were included in a reissue of the album *Trouble* in 2006.

Whitesnake released *Lovehunter* in 1979, which courted controversy due to its risqué album cover by artist Chris Achilleos, which featured an illustration of a naked woman straddling a coiled snake. The album made the UK Top 30 and contained the minor hit "Long Way from Home", which reached No. 55 in the single charts. Shortly after that drummer Ian Paice replaced David Dowle giving Whitesnake three ex-Deep Purple members. The new line-up recorded the 1980 release *Ready an' Willing* (1980), which was a breakthrough hit for the band reaching the UK Top 10 and becoming their first entry into the U.S. Top 100. The single "Fool for Your Loving", which the band originally wrote for

B.B. King, made No. 13 in the UK single charts and No. 53 in the US, and the title track also hit No. 43 in the UK charts.

Whitesnake on stage at the Hammersmith Odeon, London, 1981

Whitesnake performing live in 1983

The Ready an' Willing tour included the Saturday night headline appearance at the 1980 Reading Festival, the highlights of which were broadcast by BBC Radio 1 in the UK. While still mostly unknown in the US, the modest success of *Ready an' Willing* (1980) helped Whitesnake increase awareness there as an opening act for established bands such as Jethro Tull and AC/DC.[9] The band also released *Live...In the Heart of the City*, which contained recordings made in 1978 and 1980 at the Hammersmith Odeon in London, and achieved a No. 5 ranking in the UK album charts.[10]

In 1981 the band recorded the album *Come an' Get It*, which climbed to No. 2 in the UK album charts and produced the Top 20 hit "Don't Break My Heart Again" and the Top 40 hit "Would I Lie to You". During 1982 Coverdale took time off to look after his sick daughter and decided to put Whitesnake on hold.

When David Coverdale returned to music he reformed the band and after the recording of the album *Saints & Sinners* (1982) replaced Bernie Marsden, Ian Paice and bass player Neil Murray with Mel Galley from Trapeze, bassist Colin Hodgkinson, and Cozy Powell as the new drummer. *Saints & Sinners* was another Top 10 UK album and contained the hit "Here I Go Again", which featured guest keyboard player Malcolm Birch from Chesterfield-based band Pegasus. The new lineup toured in 1982–83, headlined the Monsters of Rock Festival at Castle Donington UK in August 1983 and the single "Guilty of Love" reached No. 31 in the UK singles chart.[11]

Breakthrough and a change in musical style (1983–1985)

In late 1983, the band recorded *Slide It In*, which was released in Europe in early 1984. It was the band's fourth top 10 album in their native UK, peaking at number 9.[10] At this same time, the band secured a major US record deal with the Geffen label. The *Slide It In* (1984) album had drawn mixed reviews, the negatives particularly focusing on its "flat" mix.[12] While a personnel change saw the touring band replace Moody with former Thin Lizzy guitarist John Sykes, plus the return of bassist Neil Murray in place of Hodgkinson,[13] producer David Geffen insisted that the album be remixed for the US release. In addition to the remix, Sykes and Murray re-recorded the lead guitar and bass parts. This revised version of the album had its US release in April 1984. Despite Coverdale's misgivings regarding the lack of edge in these new tracks, *Slide It In* (1984) just barely missed the US Top 40, and went double platinum there three years later after the release of the band's eighth album.[3] The *Slide It In* (1984) album led to the album-oriented rock hits in the US: "Slow an' Easy" and "Love Ain't No Stranger", as well as the album's title track. It was at this point that Geffen suggested to Coverdale that he "start taking America seriously."[14]

While touring in spring 1984, Mel Galley suffered a broken arm in an accident, leaving John Sykes as the sole guitarist for the remaining dates. A few weeks later, Jon Lord left to reform Deep Purple Mk. II, and keyboard player Richard Bailey was brought in. The band was booked in the US to open for acts such as Dio and Quiet Riot. The tour ended with a performance in front of a crowd of over 100,000 people, at the Rock in Rio festival held in Rio de Janeiro, Brazil. Galley remained a member — "he's still getting paid," said Coverdale — until Galley rashly discussed plans to reform Trapeze in an interview, and Coverdale then fired him.

The self-titled album and success in the US (1985–1988)

John Sykes co-wrote their 1987 album with Coverdale

Starting in 1985, Coverdale and Sykes began writing the material for a follow-up studio album.[15] The approach was more modern, adding a slick Eighties studio polish to a band that up until *Slide It In* (1984) had a bluesier sound rooted in the Seventies. Sykes would play the rhythm and lead guitars for almost the entire album. Cozy Powell had left to join Emerson, Lake & Powell. Two musicians from the north of England were brought in for the recording of the album: drummer Aynsley Dunbar, and keyboardist Don Airey from the Ozzy Osbourne band and Rainbow. The album was put on hold for much of 1986, when Coverdale contracted a serious sinus infection that put his singing career in jeopardy. He eventually recovered, and the *Whitesnake* album was finished in 1987. But shortly before the album's release, Coverdale had dismissed Sykes. Adrian Vandenberg and Vivian Campbell mimed Sykes' guitar parts in the videos and played in subsequent live shows.

The album was entitled *1987* in Europe and *Serpens Albus* in Japan and marked the band's biggest mainstream success in the US. With the guidance of A&R guru John Kalodner, it has sold 8x platinum in the US.[3] The success of *Whitesnake* (1987) also pushed sales of *Slide It In* (1984) from its RIAA certified gold status to platinum status, and made the band a bona fide arena headliner for the first time in North America. The album continued to sell throughout 1987 and 1988, peaking at No. 2 in the US, and No. 8 in the UK.[11][16] The album was their most commercially successful, and in 1988, they were nominated for the Brit Award for Best British Group.[4] The album's biggest hits were "Here I Go Again" (#1 US *Billboard* Hot 100 and No. 9 UK Singles Chart) and power ballad "Is This Love" (#2 US and No. 9 UK).[11][17] "Here I Go Again" was a re-recording of a song originally on 1982's *Saints & Sinners*, and another track on *Saints & Sinners*, "Crying in the Rain", was also a redone song. Other hit singles from the album were "Still of the Night" (#16 UK and No. 79 US) and "Give Me All Your Love" (#18 UK and No. 48 US in 1988).[11][17] The album's exposure was boosted by heavy airplay of its videos on MTV, which featured actress Tawny Kitaen, whom Coverdale later married. None of the band members who played on the album appeared in these videos with the exception of Adrian Vandenberg, who had been hired after the others had been fired by Coverdale. Vandenberg's only work on the album was the solo on "Here I Go Again" though he became a full-time member of the band shortly afterwards. The resulting music videos from *Whitesnake* (1987) also featured new band members Rudy Sarzo, Tommy Aldridge and Vivian Campbell (who also re-recorded the solo for the "Give Me All Your Love" remix).

While some long-time fans viewed the *1987* album as a sell-out and attempt to pander to mainstream tastes at the time, Coverdale was still reaching back to his musical roots, including most prominently Led Zeppelin, but even older artists like Elvis. "I remember the *Jailhouse Rock* EP," Coverdale said. "It's interesting because you don't know what it is, but it gets you fluffed up. And 'Jailhouse Rock', contrary to what a lot of people imagine, was the inspiration for the verses of 'Still of the Night'."[18]

Slip of the Tongue and more success (1988–1990)

Guitarist Vivian Campbell left Whitesnake in late 1988 due to creative differences, and so the band's line-up changed yet again for the 1989 album *Slip of the Tongue*. Although he co-wrote all of the songs, while preparing for the recording of the album, guitarist Adrian Vandenberg sustained a serious wrist injury, making it impossible for him to play without experiencing great discomfort. Coverdale had no choice but to find a new guitar player to record the parts. He eventually found former Frank Zappa and David Lee Roth guitar player Steve Vai, whom Coverdale had seen in the 1986 film *Crossroads*. Upon its release, *Slip of the Tongue* (1989) sold three million copies and hit No. 10 in both the US and UK album charts.[11][16] The album also spawned three successful singles: a reworking of the band's 1980 classic "Fool for Your Loving" (#37 US and

David Coverdale backstage at the Donington Festival in 1990

Greatest Hits, *Restless Heart* and *Starkers in Tokyo* (1994–1998)

A new line-up of the band was assembled for 1994's *Whitesnake's Greatest Hits* album. They embarked on a short tour in Europe, with former Ratt guitarist Warren DeMartini playing lead guitar, drummer Denny Carmassi, the return of bassist Rudy Sarzo and guitarist Adrian Vandenberg, and the addition of keyboard player Paul Mirkovich before their recording contract with Geffen expired.

In 1997 Coverdale and Vandenberg re-grouped to work together on a new Whitesnake album *Restless Heart*. This was originally to be a solo album for Coverdale, but the record company pressured them to release it under the Whitesnake name. However, despite a release in both Japan and Europe, it was never available officially in the US. The album marked a return to the band's earlier R&B music. The album reached the UK Top 40 album chart and produced the blues ballad "Too Many Tears", which reached No. 46 on the UK singles chart.[11] The album featured Coverdale, Carmassi, Vandenberg, Pink Floyd touring bassist Guy Pratt with keyboardist Brett Tuggle who had played with Coverdale and Page. The touring lineup featured Coverdale, Vandenberg, Carmassi, Mr. Mister guitarist Steve Farris, keyboardist Derek Hilland and The Firm bassist Tony Franklin. During the tour, Coverdale and Vandenberg recorded unplugged show in Japan entitled *Starkers in Tokyo* (released in 1998). The two also played another unplugged show, this time for VH1. In the end of '97, Coverdale folded the band at the end of the tour, and took another break from the music business.

25th anniversary reformation (2002–2007)

In December 2002 Coverdale reformed Whitesnake for Whitesnake's 25th anniversary the upcoming year. Joining Coverdale for a 2003 tour were guitarists Doug Aldrich of Dio and Reb Beach of Winger, bass player Marco Mendoza, drummer Tommy Aldridge and keyboard player Timothy Drury. During 2003 they headlined the Rock Never Stops Tour with other popular rock bands.

The anniversary tour line up remained stable until early 2005, when Mendoza left to pursue the Soul SirkUS project and was replaced by Uriah Duffy. In February 2006, Whitesnake released a live DVD titled, *Live... In the Still of the Night* and announced a Spring and Summer tour of Japan and Europe. In June 2006 it was announced Coverdale had signed Whitesnake to a new record deal with Steamhammer/SPV Records who released a double live album entitled, *Live: In the Shadow of the Blues* during November 2006 in UK, Germany, Switzerland and Austria. The album had tracks recorded since 2003, and also included four new studio tracks: "Ready to Rock", "If You

No. 43 UK), the melodic "The Deeper the Love" (#28 US and No. 35 UK) and "Now You're Gone" (#31 UK and No. 96 US).[11][17] Steve Vai became an official member of the band and appeared in all of the band's new music videos.

With Vai and Vandenberg both as a full-time members, the band hit the road to support the album. During the Liquor and Poker tour for *Slip of the Tongue*, the band co-headlined the 1990 Monsters of Rock festival (their third time appearing and second headlining). After the last show of the Liquor and Poker tour in 1990, Coverdale decided he would fold the band. Coverdale announced that he would be taking a break from the music business, but the next year he started to work with former-Led Zeppelin guitarist, Jimmy Page, which resulted in the album *Coverdale•Page* (1993). Vandenberg, Sarzo, and Aldridge remained together, forming the new band Manic Eden.

Want Me", "All I Want Is You" and "Dog". These songs have been described by Coverdale as "three balls-to-the-walls rockers and a ballad".

In June 2007 the band released a dual CD/DVD titled *1987 20th Anniversary Collector's Edition* to mark the 20th anniversary of the mega-selling album *1987*. This was the re-mastered album along with a host of bonus material of four live tracks from the *Shadow of the Blues Live* set. It also includes the four promo videos for the album on the DVD.[19] In December 2007 Aldridge left the band, and was replaced by Chris Frazier, who had previously worked with Eddie Money, Edgar Winter and The Tak Matsumoto Group.[20]

Good to Be Bad and back on the road (2008–2010)

In March 2008 Whitesnake played at the Rock2Wgtn two-day festival, which also featured Ozzy Osbourne, Kiss, Poison, Alice Cooper and Lordi, with special effects by the Academy Award winning WETA Workshop. In April 2008 the band released their tenth studio album, *Good to Be Bad*, which reached No. 5 in the UK Album Chart.[19] During the summer of 2008 Whitesnake co-headlined a UK tour along with Def Leppard,[21] with Black Stone Cherry opening the UK arena shows in June and Thunder opening the July shows. In early November 2008, Whitesnake received the Classic Rock *Best Album* award for *Good to Be Bad*.

On 11 February 2009, Whitesnake announced they would be playing a festival slot at Download Festival, UK on 14 June via their official website. They also announced Def Leppard would be playing on the same day as the headliners. It was also announced that Whitesnake, and Journey would play The O2 in Dublin as support for headliners Def Leppard on 12 June 2009.

On 17 March 2009, it was announced that Whitesnake would be supporting Judas Priest on the 2009 North American Summer tour. On 11 August 2009 Whitesnake was playing a show at Red Rocks in Morrison, Colorado, when front man David Coverdale suffered a vocal injury. After seeing a specialist, it was announced on 12 August 2009 that Coverdale was suffering from severe vocal fold edema and a left vocal fold vascular lesion, and the band had to withdraw from the remainder of Judas Priest tour.

In early February 2010, David Coverdale announced that his voice seemed to have fully recovered from the trauma that sidelined him and the band on the Priest tour. He stated that he had been recording new demos, aiming for a new Whitesnake album.

In June 2010, Whitesnake announced they would be releasing their own wine, a 2008 Zinfandel, described by David Coverdale as "filled to the brim with the spicy essence of sexy, slippery Snakeyness ... I recommend it to complement any & all grown up friskiness & hot tub jollies ..." [22]

On 18 June 2010, it was announced that Whitesnake had parted ways with bassist Uriah Duffy and drummer Chris Frazier and that their new drummer is former Billy Idol drummer Brian Tichy.[23] On 20 August 2010, Whitesnake announced that their new bassist was to be Michael Devin.[24] On 13 September 2010, keyboardist Timothy Drury announced his departure from Whitesnake to pursue a solo career.[24] Drury has returned as a guest musician to record keyboards for the band's 2011 album *Forevermore*.[25]

Forevermore (2011–2015)

Coverdale at the O2 Apollo Manchester, England on 17 June 2011

Whitesnake released *Forevermore*, on 25 March 2011 in Europe, and on 29 June in North America.[26]

They have released a number of scheduled 2011 tour dates on their website, with six scheduled UK tour dates and other European dates. In February 2011, Whitesnake was announced as one of the headliners to play the annual Rocklahoma festival in Pryor, Oklahoma, on Memorial Day weekend. A digital single for the song "Love Will Set You Free" was released, along with a video for the song, on 21 February.[26]

The album *Forevermore* was released as a special edition 'Snakepack' through *Classic Rock* magazine on 25 March 2011, a full 3 weeks before its commercial release. The fan pack includes the full, official new album *Forevermore*, a 132-page magazine, poster and pin badge. On 20 March 2011, Whitesnake announced that Brian Ruedy would play keyboards on the Forevermore World Tour.[27]

In July 2012, David Coverdale said that a live album and DVD from the Forevermore tour were in production, as well as expanded editions of 'Into the Light' and 'Restless

Heart'.[28]

The album did not chart highly upon its official release in the UK (number 33, possibly due to the copies released as part of the aforementioned *Classic Rock* Snakepack, which are not eligible for the charts). It did, however, show signs of Whitesnake's slow rebuild of support in the US with the album charting at number 49 – the band's highest charting album since the 80s.

A live album, *Live at Donington 1990*, was released on 20 May 2011 in Japan, on 3 June in Europe and 7 June in the US.[29]

In November 2012, Whitesnake and Journey (along with special guests Thunder) announced an eight date UK Tour in 2013, where the two bands will appear onstage together for the first time ever.[30]

Drummer Brian Tichy announced on 4 January 2013 that he had left Whitesnake in order to focus on his other band, S.U.N.[31] According to Whitesnake, the band planned to continue its 2013 touring as scheduled and had already begun to look for a new drummer. On 25 January 2013, it was announced that former drummer Tommy Aldridge would be rejoining the band.[31]

On 13 February 2013, Whitesnake announced a new live DVD/album, *Made in Japan*, which had been recorded at the band's performance at the Loud Park Festival in Saitama, Japan on 15 October 2011, with release scheduled for 23 April on Frontiers Records.[32]

On 9 May 2014, it was announced that guitarist Doug Aldrich would leave Whitesnake.[33] The band is currently in the studio to work on an upcoming album.

On 21 August 2014, Joel Hoekstra (former Night Ranger) was announced as their new guitarist.

The Purple Album (2015–present)

On 25 February, it was announced *The Purple Album* would contain re-recorded Coverdale era songs of Deep Purple. The new cover album was released May 15, 2015 via Frontiers Records.

On 17 April, the Italian vocalist and instrumentalist Michele Luppi (Secret Sphere, former Vision Divine) was announced as their new keyboardist and backing vocalist, replacing Brian Ruedy.[34] The album debuted at #84 on the Billboard 200 album chart in the US selling over 6,900 units in its first week of release.[35]

2.86.2 Discography

Main article: Whitesnake discography

- *Trouble* (1978)
- *Lovehunter* (1979)
- *Ready an' Willing* (1980)
- *Come an' Get It* (1981)
- *Saints & Sinners* (1982)
- *Slide It In* (1984)
- *Whitesnake* (1987)
- *Slip of the Tongue* (1989)
- *Restless Heart* (1997)
- *Good to Be Bad* (2008)
- *Forevermore* (2011)
- *The Purple Album* (2015)

2.86.3 Members

Main article: List of band members in David Coverdale's bands

- David Coverdale – lead vocals (1978–1991, 1994, 1997, 2002–present)
- Tommy Aldridge – drums, percussion (1987–1991, 2002–2007, 2013–present)
- Reb Beach – guitar, backing vocals (2002–present)
- Michael Devin – bass, harmonica, backing vocals (2010–present)
- Joel Hoekstra – guitar, backing vocals (2014–present)

Current touring members

- Michele Luppi – keyboards, backing vocals (2015–present)

Timeline

2.86.4 In other media

In films

- *JoJo's Bizarre Adventure*
- *Talladega Nights: The Ballad of Ricky Bobby*
- *Old School*
- *Just My Luck*
- *The Rocker*
- *The Fighter*
- *Bad Teacher*
- *Rock of Ages*

On TV

- *CSI New York* - in the episode "Blacklist" (season 6, episode 2), Lindsay Monroe comes into work wearing a Whitesnake T-shirt because it was the only clean shirt she had (thanks to her newborn baby spitting up all the time) and her coworker Sheldon Hawkes commented on it.
- *The Venture Bros.* "Fallen Arches" episode includes the "Here I Go Again" video
- *The Simpsons* in the "Treehouse of Horror X" episode
- In *Smallville*, Lois Lane's favorite band is Whitesnake, and has a throw pillow she made from a concert T-shirt. Also in the episode "Crimson" she gave Clark a mix CD of their power-ballads.
- *Joey* – Season One episode 11 "Joey and the Road Trip" & 16 "Joey and the Tonight Show" Season Two episode 1&2 "Joey and the Big Break, Part 2"
- *Will & Grace* – In the fifth season finale, Karen Walker remarks that Danny Mordy (Nicollette Sheridan) was hot enough to be in a Whitesnake video.
- *Frasier* – Roz tells Frasier her boyfriend thinks she was in a Whitesnake video.
- "And the Wiener Is..." episode of *Family Guy* – Lois tells Meg about the music "mommies and daddies listen to."
- *How I Met Your Mother* – Season 2 Episode 19 "Bachelor Party": Barney Stinson says to Marshall that "every bachelor deserves to watch a stripper dance to Whitesnake's "Here I Go Again" before getting married".
- In the first season episode of *Psych* "Game, Set...Muuurder?", Henry donates some of Shawn's stuff to charity, including an old Whiteshake T-shirt. Shawn tells Henry off for giving the shirt away because they're no longer available in stores.

In musical theatre

The Whitesnake song "Here I Go Again" appears in both the Off-Broadway production Power Balladz and the award-winning Broadway hit Rock of Ages.

In songs

- The band Bowling for Soup in the song "1985"

"Here I Go Again" (as soundtrack)

- On the computer game *World in Conflict*
- BBC Three TV series *Nighty Night*
- In the *American Dad!* episode "Dungeons and Wagons"
- In the 2003 comedy film *Old School*[36]
- In the 2009 film "Adventureland".
- During the credits of the 2009 film *Fired Up* after Nicholas D'Agosto sang the chorus as a joke
- On the *Axe Men* TV show advert on Channel 5
- In the episode of *It's Always Sunny in Philadelphia* titled "Mac's banging the Waitress"
- In the *Life* season 2 episode 14 "Mirror Ball"
- In the 2010 film *The Fighter*, the chorus was briefly sung along to by Mark Wahlberg and Christian Bale. It was depicted as fighter Micky Ward's entrance music before his fight against Shea Neary.
- In the *Californication* episode "Here I Go Again"
- In the 2012 musical Rock of Ages.

2.86.5 Tours

- Trouble Tour (1978-1979)
- Love Hunter Tour (1979)
- Ready an' Willing Tour (1980)
- Come an' Get It Tour (1981)

- Saints & Sinners Tour (1982-1983)
- Slide It In Tour (1984-1985)
- Whitesnake 1987-88 World Tour (1987-1988)
- Slip of the Tongue Tour (1990)
- Greatest Hits Tour (1994)
- Restless Heart: Farewell Tour (1997)
- VH1 Classic Presents "mmm...Nice Package Tour" (2003)
- Monsters of Rock (Europe) Tour (2003)
- Rock Never Stops (USA) Tour (2003)
- 25th Anniversary Greatest Hits Tour Japan 03 (2003)
- Live...In the Still of the Night - European Tour (2004)
- The Rock & Roll, Rhythm & Blues Show Tour (2005)
- Live... In the Shadow of the Blues Tour (2006)
- Good to Be Bad World Tour (2008-2009)
- Forevermore World Tour (2011)
- UK Tour with Journey (2013)
- Year Of The Snake Tour (2013)
- Globar Warming Tour with Aerosmith (2013)
- The Purple Tour (2015-2016)

2.86.6 Notes

[1] "Ep. 036 | 100 Greatest Artists of Hard Rock - Hour 1 | The Greatest | Episode Summary, Highlights, and Recaps". VH1.com. Retrieved 24 April 2014.

[2] Pete Prown & Harvey P Newquist (1 February 1997). *Legends of Rock Guitar: The Essential Reference of Rock's Greatest Guitarists*. Hal Leonard Corporation. pp. 210–212. ISBN 978-0793540426.

[3] "RIAA Searchable Database: search for Whitesnake". Recording Industry Association of America. Retrieved 8 May 2015.

[4] "Whitesnake". Brits.co.uk. 19 February 2014. Retrieved 24 April 2014.

[5] "Gold & Platinum Searchable Database - April 24, 2014". RIAA. Retrieved 24 April 2014.

[6] "Whitesnake timeline 1978–1981". Deep-purple.net. Retrieved 18 July 2011.

[7] Classic Rock presents Whitesnake The Official Magazine pg.127

[8] Dave Thompson (2004). "Smoke on the Water: The Deep Purple Story". p. 216. ECW Press, 2004

[9] "David Coverdale bio at". Musicianguide.com. Retrieved 18 July 2011.

[10] "ChartArchive - Whitesnake". Archive.is. Retrieved 24 April 2014.

[11] Roberts, David (2006). British Hit Singles & Albums. London: Guinness World Records Limited

[12] *Deep Purple Appreciation Society – Whitesnake History'*, The Deep Purple Appreciation Society, 1984

[13] *Deep Purple Appreciation Society Magazine, Issue 29'*, The Deep Purple Appreciation Society, July 1984

[14] "David Coverdale bio at musicianguide.com, paragraph 9". Musicianguide.com. Retrieved 18 July 2011.

[15] Wall, Mick (2010). "Appetite for Destruction: The Mick Wall Interviews". Hachette UK, Retrieved 15 June 2012

[16] "Whitesnake | Music Biography, Credits and Discography". AllMusic. Retrieved 24 April 2014.

[17] Whitburn, Joel (2006). The Billboard Book of Top 40 Hits. Billboard Books

[18] Bryan Reesman (17 March 2011). "Digital Playlist: David Coverdale". Attention Deficit Delirium. Retrieved 18 March 2011.

[19] "David Coverdale news". Deep-purple.net. Retrieved 24 April 2014.

[20] Archived 15 August 2009 at the Wayback Machine

[21] Archived 3 April 2015 at the Wayback Machine

[22] Archived 29 October 2013 at the Wayback Machine

[23] "WHITESNAKE Parts Ways With DUFFY, FRAZIER; New Drummer Announced". BlabberMouth.

[24] "Whitesnake.com". Whitesnake.com. Retrieved 7 July 2011.

[25] "WHITESNAKE Keyboardist Quits To Pursue 'Solo' Career". BlabberMouth.

[26] "WHITESNAKE – Forevermore Tracklisting, Release Dates Revealed; New Song Streaming". *Bravewords.com*. Retrieved 18 January 2011.

[27] "Whitesnake – Introducing Brian Ruedy". Retrieved 20 March 2011.

[28] Henne, Bruce (9 July 2012). "Whitesnake update from David Coverdale". hennemusic. Retrieved 17 October 2012.

[29] ""Live at Donington 1990" CD and DVD". *Whitesnake.com*. Retrieved 21 May 2011.

[30] "Journey And Whitesnake Announce 2013 UK Tour With Special Guests Thunder". New York Music News. 6 November 2012. Retrieved 6 November 2012.

[31] "Drummer BRIAN TICHY Quits WHITESNAKE". Blabbermouth.net. 4 January 2013. Retrieved 10 January 2013.

[32] "WHITESNAKE To Release 'Made In Japan' In April". Blabbermouth.net. 13 February 2013. Archived from the original on 15 February 2013. Retrieved 16 February 2013.

[33] http://www.blabbermouth.net/news/guitarist-doug-aldrich-quits-whitesnake/

[34] "Whitesnake announce new keyboardist and singer". *Metalrocknews.com*.

[35] "Whitesnake's 'The Purple Album: First Week Sales Revealed". *Blabbermouth.net*.

[36] "Old School (2003) : Soundtracks". IMDb.com. Retrieved 24 April 2014.

2.86.7 References and further reading

- *Whitesnake*. Simon Robinson. Omnibus Press (1989) ISBN 0-7119-1550-4
- Record Collector magazine No 56. Peter Doggett. Diamond Publishing Group (1984) ASIN: B0018KXRB0
- *Purple Rainbows*: A Definitive Rock History Featuring the Best of Deep Purple, Rainbow, Whitesnake. Graham Bonnett. Stave House (1994) ISBN 1-85909-148-2
- *Whitesnake*. Tom Hibbert. Omnibus Press (1981) ISBN 0-86001-964-0
- *The Best of Whitesnake.*Aaron Stang. Warner Bros Publications Inc (1989) ISBN 0-7692-1352-9
- *Sail Away Whitesnake's Fantastic Voyage- Martin Popoff, soundcheck books (2015) ISBN 9780957570085*

2.86.8 External links

- Official website

2.87 Wild Horses (British band)

Wild Horses were a British rock band, active during the late 1970s and early 1980s.

2.87.1 History

Wild Horses was formed in the summer of 1978 by ex-Thin Lizzy guitarist Brian Robertson and ex-Rainbow bassist Jimmy Bain. At an early stage, the line-up featured former Stone the Crows and Wings guitarist Jimmy McCulloch and former Small Faces drummer Kenney Jones, but eventually stabilized with the addition of drummer Clive Edwards (ex-Pat Travers, Uli Roth) and guitarist/keyboardist Neil Carter (ex-Wilder, Gilbert O'Sullivan). This line-up recorded the Trevor Rabin-produced eponymous album in 1980, released by EMI who signed the band after their 1979 Reading Festival appearance.

Carter left the band in August 1980 after the band's UK tour with Ted Nugent in order to join UFO and later Gary Moore. His replacement was guitarist John Lockton (ex-Next Band, Red Alert) whose first appearance was on the band's Japanese tour in the autumn of 1980 followed by the release of the *Stand Your Ground* album in the spring of 1981.

In June 1981, Robertson and Edwards both left Wild Horses in the wake of the band's Paris Theatre show in London. Robertson teamed up with Motörhead a year later and recorded *Another Perfect Day* in 1983, before moving on to join fellow Scotsman Frankie Miller on the *Dancing in the Rain* album in 1986. Edwards continued with a number of different acts, including Bernie Marsden's S.O.S., Grand Prix, and Lionheart.

Bain assembled a new Wild Horses line-up featuring Lockton, former Lautrec stepfather and son team, Reuben (vocals) and Laurence Archer (guitar), and *The Def Leppard E.P.* credited drummer Frank Noon. The Archers and Noon left only months later and went on to form their own band, Stampede, and Wild Horses ceased to exist, with Bain joining his former Rainbow bandmate Ronnie James Dio in Dio, while Lockton became a member of German hard rockers Victory.

Wild Horses members Laurence Archer and Clive Edwards were part of the UFO line-up that recorded the *High Stakes & Dangerous Men* and *Lights Out in Tokyo* albums in the early 1990s, before spending time in Medicine Head. After being involved with the reformed Stampede, Archer and Edwards launched X-UFO in the summer of 2011 along with Rocky Newton and Danny Peyronel.

Both *Wild Horses* and *Stand Your Ground* have seen repeated re-issues over the years, the first coming in 1993 via EMI-Toshiba Japan as part of the 'Legendary Masters' series. European re-issues, including various bonus tracks, followed in 1999 (Zoom Club), 2009 (Krescendo), and 2013 (Rock Candy).

On 25 February 2014, a bootleg quality Wild Horses live

album, titled *Live In Japan 1980*, recorded at the band's Nakano Sun Plaza, Tokyo gig on 29 October 1980, was issued via Krescendo. The same recording had first surfaced in 2012 as a Japanese bootleg titled *Heavy Ride*.

2.87.2 Members

Wild Horses Mk I

- Jimmy Bain - bass/vocals
- Brian Robertson - guitar
- Jimmy McCulloch - guitar
- Kenney Jones - drums

Wild Horses Mk II - UK tour 1978 line-up:

- Jimmy Bain - bass/vocals
- Brian Robertson - guitar
- Neil Carter - guitar/keyboards
- Dixie Lee - drums

Wild Horses Mk III - 'The First Album' line-up (1979/80):

- Jimmy Bain - bass/vocals
- Brian Robertson - guitar/vocals
- Neil Carter -guitar/keyboards
- Clive Edwards - drums

Wild Horses Mk IV - 'Stand Your Ground' line-up (1980/81):

- Jimmy Bain - bass/vocals
- Brian Robertson - guitar
- John Lockton - guitar
- Clive Edwards - drums

Wild Horses Mk V - final live line-up (1981):

- Reuben Archer - vocals
- Jimmy Bain - bass/vocals
- John Lockton - guitar
- Laurence Archer - guitar
- Frank Noon - drums

2.87.3 Discography

Studio albums

- *Wild Horses* (EMI, 1980 / Toshiba-EMI/Insideout, 1993 / Zoom Club 1999 / Krescendo 2009 / Rock Candy, 2013)[1]

- *Stand Your Ground* (EMI, 1981 / Toshiba-EMI/Insideout, 1993 / Zoom Club 1999 / Krescendo, 2009 / Rock Candy, 2013)

Live albums

- *Live In Japan 1980* (Krescendo, 2014)

UK singles

- "Criminal Tendencies" / "The Rapist" (EMI, 1979)
- "Face Down" / "Dealer" (EMI, 1980)
- "Flyaway" / "Blackmail" (EMI, 1980)
- "I'll Give You Love" / "Rocky Mountain Way" (live) (EMI, 1981)
- "I'll Give You Love" / "Rocky Mountain Way" (live) / "The Kid" / "Saturday Night" (live) (EMI, 1981 - double single pack)
- "Everlasting Love" / "The Axe" (EMI, 1981)

Japan singles

- "Face Down" / "Dealer" (EMI, 1980)
- "Fly Away" / "The Rapist" (EMI, 1980)

2.87.4 See also

- List of New Wave of British Heavy Metal bands

2.87.5 References

[1] Roberts, David (2006). *British Hit Singles & Albums* (19th ed.). London: Guinness World Records Limited. p. 602. ISBN 1-904994-10-5.

2.87.6 External links

- Wild Horses Facebook
- Wild Horses MySpace
- Wild Horses @ MusicMight.com
- Wild Horses bio @ Allmusic.com

2.88 Witchfinder General (band)

Witchfinder General were a doom metal band from Stourbridge, England. They were part of the New Wave of British Heavy Metal scene and have been cited as a major influence on the doom metal genre. They were named after the 1968 British horror film *Witchfinder General*.

2.88.1 Biography

Witchfinder General formed in 1979 by Zeeb Parkes & Phil Cope in Stourbridge, England, as part of the New Wave of British Heavy Metal movement during the early 1980s. They are strongly influenced by Black Sabbath, and are widely recognised today as one of the pioneers of the doom metal style. The band's importance became acknowledged mostly after they disbanded.

The band (minus vocalist & writer Zeeb Parkes) reformed in November 2006, with new vocalist Gary Martin. In 2007 the band released *Buried Amongst the Ruins*, a compilation CD featuring the "Burning a Sinner" single, the *Soviet Invasion* EP, and four live tracks including a live version of the unreleased track "Phantasmagorical". Whilst stating they would not perform live again, the band released their third full-length album, entitled *Resurrected*, in 2008.

2.88.2 Members

- **Phil Cope** - Guitar (1979-1984, 2006-2008), Bass (1982)
- **Johnny Fisher** - Bass (1979-1980)
- **Steve Kinsell** - Drums (1979-1982)
- **Zeeb Parkes** - Vocals (1979-1984)
- **Kevin McCready** - Bass (1981-1982)
- **Graham Ditchfield** - Drums (1982-1983)
- **Rod Hawkes** - Bass (1982-1984, 2006-2008)
- **Dermot Redmond** - Drums (1983-1984, 2006-2008)
- **Gary Martin** - Vocals (2007-2008)

2.88.3 Discography

Studio albums

- *Death Penalty* - (1982)
- *Friends of Hell* - (1983)
- *Resurrected* - (2008)

Live albums

- *Live '83* CD - (2006)

Singles/EPs

- "Burning a Sinner" - (1981)
- *Soviet Invasion* - (1982)
- "Music" - (1983)

Other releases

- *Buried Amongst the Ruins* - (2007)

2.88.4 See also

- List of New Wave of British Heavy Metal bands

2.88.5 References

2.88.6 External links

- Official website

2.89 Witchfynde

Witchfynde are a British heavy metal band, which was one of the forerunners of the New Wave of British Heavy Metal in the late 1970s.

2.89.1 Early days

Witchfynde were formed in Derbyshire, England in 1974 by bass guitarist Richard Blower and vocalist Neil Harvey. Richard Blower discovered Montalo (Trevor Taylor) in a band called Atiofel. When Richard left the band in 1975, they reformed Witchfynde with lead guitarist Montalo, bassist Andro Coulton and drummer Gra Scoresby, and soon recruiting vocalist Steve Bridges. The band released their first single, "Give 'em Hell" in 1979 and released its first full-length album, also entitled *Give 'em Hell*, on Rondelet Records in 1980. A major attribute to success may have originated by the frequent airplay on the Friday Night Rock Show, hosted by Tommy Vance on BBC Radio 1. The band gained some exposure by touring the United Kingdom with Def Leppard in the summer of 1980. The band's sound incorporated a mix of influences, such as progressive and hard rock, with various aspects of the heavy metal sound as well as prominent use of satanic imagery.

2.89.2 Second album and change of musical direction

In 1980 the band released their second album *Stagefright*. Like their debut, it was recorded at Fairview Studios in Hull and is considered their most experimental work to date. During the period the album was released, bassist Andro Coulton was replaced by Pete Surgey, who was an obvious choice for the band as he had a good reputation on the local scene.

2.89.3 Departure with Rondelet Records

Around the time of the band's second release the relationship with their label Rondelet Records became increasingly strained to the point the label withdrew the band's funding. This made things very difficult for Witchfynde and eventually led to the departure of vocalist Steve Bridges. The band then recruited the new singer Luther Beltz and began working on the third album *Cloak and Dagger*; it was released on the small label Expulsion Records but due to bad production and the fact the label went bankrupt shortly after the album's release, it did not receive good promotion.

2.89.4 Mausoleum Records, fourth album and split

In 1984 the band signed a deal with Mausoleum Records to release their 4th album *Lords of Sin*. During the recording of the album, bassist Pete Surgey left the band and was replaced by Edd Wolfe, who had played in one of Luther Beltz's former bands but by the time the album was released he was replaced by Al Short, who played in the band Race Against Time. Although the band considered the album their strongest to date, it received very bad reviews from critics, with the final blow delivered when Mausoleum Records went bankrupt; as the result of the album's bad promotion the band became totally disillusioned with the music business and split up.

2.89.5 Reunion, 1999-present

In October 1999 Montalo, Gra and Luther began to discuss the possibility of a reunion due to a resurgence of interest in the band after the release of the *Best of Witchfynde* CD in 1996, which sold well. Pete Surgey rejoined the band on bass, but during rehearsals Luther Beltz announced that he no longer wanted to participate to the reunion and the band replaced him with vocalist Harry Harrison, a longtime fan of the band that was introduced by Pete Surgey. The band then began to work to their 5th album *The Witching Hour* which they released on Edgy Records in 2001. Their first three albums were re-released by Cherry Red and Lemon Recordings. A new *Best Of* album was released in 2007 by Lemon Recordings.

The band then began work on their 6th studio album called *Play It to Death* which they recorded at Bandwagon Studios and released in July 2008. Towards the end of 2008 due to Harry Harrison's ill health and other commitments, Luther Beltz returned to front the band for the Play It to Death UK Tour.

2.89.6 Line-up

Current line-up

- Luther Beltz - Lead Vocals (1980–1984, 1999, 2008–present)
- Montalo (Trevor Taylor) - Guitar (1973–1984, 1999–present)
- Pete Surgey - Bass Guitar (1980–1983, 1999–present)
- Gra Scoresby - Drums & Percussion (1973–1984, 1999–present)
- Tracey Abbott - 2nd Guitar (2014–present)

Former members

- Steve Bridges (vocals)
- Andro Coulton (bass)
- Alan Edwards ("Edd Wolfe") (bass)
- Dave Lindley (drums)
- Ron Reynolds (guitars)
- Dave Hewitt (bass/vocals)
- Neil Harvey (vocals)
- Luther Beltz (vocals)

- Richard Blower (bass guitar)
- Tez Brown (drums)
- Harry Harrison (vocals)

2.89.7 Discography

Albums

- *Give 'Em Hell* (Rondelet, 1980; reissued by Lemon, 2004)
- *Stagefright* (Rondelet, 1980; reissued by Lemon, 2005)
- *Cloak and Dagger* (Expulsion, 1983; reissued by Witchfynde Music, 2000)
- *Lords of Sin* (Mausoleum, 1984; first 10,000 copies came with *Anthems* live EP)
- *The Best of Witchfynde* (British Steel, 1996)
- *The Witching Hour* (Neat, 2001)
- *Play It to Death* (Neat, 2008)
- *Royal William Live Sacrifice* (live album) (Neat, 2011)
- *The Lost Tapes of 1975* (Vyper Records, 2013)

Singles

- "Give 'Em Hell" / "Gettin' Heavy" 7" (Rondelet, 1979)
- "In the Stars" / "Wake Up Screaming" 7" (Rondelet, 1980)
- "I'd Rather Go Wild" / "Cry Wolf" 7" (Expulsion, 1983)
- *Anthems* 12" (Mausoleum, 1984)
- "Conspiracy" / "Scarlet Lady" 7" (Mausoleum, 1984)

Wytchfynde

- Demo 2000
- *The Awakening* LP (Demolition, 2001)

2.89.8 See also

- List of New Wave of British Heavy Metal bands

2.89.9 References

[1] Witchfynde biography @ Rockdetector

[2] Popoff, Martin (1997). *The Collector's Guide to Heavy Metal*, pp. 515-516, Collector's Guide Publishing, ISBN 1-896522-32-7.

[3] Strong, M. C. (2001). *The Great Metal Discography*, p. 608, Canongate, ISBN 1-84195-185-4.

2.89.10 External links

- Official Witchfynde website
- Official Witchfynde Myspace page
- Witchfynde @ Lemon Recordings
- Allmusic Witchfynde biography
- The Official website of Andro Coulton ex-Witchfyde bass player

2.90 Wrathchild

For the song of the same name by Iron Maiden, see Killers (Iron Maiden album).

Wrathchild (sometimes known as **Wrathchild UK** in the United States due to a naming conflict with Wrathchild America) are an English heavy metal band. Formed in 1980, the group was an early band of the glam metal genre, starting off about the same time as bands of the genre such as Mötley Crüe. They are indeed the "Godfathers" of the glam/sleaze metal movement back in the early 80s.

In their home country, the band's speciality was in its D.I.Y. aesthetic (common for many NWOBHM bands), over the top stage shows, and striking image. During their early days, they would often play in pubs but still used confetti, pyrotechnics, and dressed in full glam metal gear, including their trademark platform boots and huge, teased hair.

2.90.1 History

Wrathchild was formed in 1980 in Evesham, England by Marc Angel and Philip Vokins. They recruited Rocky Shades for lead vocals, and Brian Parry on drums. Phil Vokins left in 1981 to join Bill Ward (Black Sabbath) in America with the new band Max Havoc, and Brian Parry left, too.

The band added two members from the band Medusa; guitarist Lance Rocket and drummer Eddie Star, who became mainstays in the band and completed the much recognised over the top line-up for a decade of touring and recording.

After releasing a string of demos, such as *Mascara Massacre* in 1982, the band was offered a record deal by Bullet Records. On this label the group put out their first official release in 1983, an EP called *Stackheel Strutt*.

In 1984, the band recorded and released their debut studio album, *Stakk Attakk*. It would spawn two singles; a cover version of the Gary Glitter classic "Doing Alright with the Boys" and "Trash Queen".

Unfortunately, just as Wrathchild became successful, they came embroiled in contractual problems with their label, Heavy Metal Records. RCA Records, a major label, unsuccessfully attempted to sign the band from Heavy Metal Records in an effort to free them from their contract. Meanwhile, the group released a video compilation called *War Machine* in 1984.

After settling the dispute with Heavy Metal Records, nearly four years later, the band released their second album, *The Biz Suxx*, in 1988. The album spawned a single, *Nukklear Rokket*, which had a promotional video that was produced by Bruce Dickinson of Iron Maiden. Bruce plays the protester in the video whilst the performance was filmed in the car park at his home in Chiswick. Ron Kennedy directed and edited the video as well as appearing as the mad professor. Steve Prior was the cameraman.

The band's third and final studio album, *Delirium*, was released shortly after in 1989. It featured Grim Reaper's Steve Grimmet on backing vocals. Soon after the release Rocky Shades left to join the punk band Discharge and with the onset of grunge, Wrathchild broke up.

In 2005 Marc Angel and Eddie Star got back together along with original guitarist Phil 'Wrathchild' Vokins and recruited vocalist Gaz 'Psychowrath' Harris, formerly of the band Beyond Recognition. This new line-up went under the name Psychowrath until 2009, then acquired the trademarks for Wrathchild & Wrathchild UK and reverted to using their original name Wrathchild. They have played several gigs between 2005 and 2009.

Wrathchild & Psychowrath

Marc Angel, Eddie Star, and Phil Vokins, with new singer Gaz Harris started a band in 2005 called Psychowrath. In 2009 they acquired the trademarks for Wrathchild & Wrathchild UK and reverted the name Wrathchild and released *Stakkattakktwo* in 23 August 2011 from Perris Records.

Marc Angel explained in an interview[1] how important the name "Wrathchild" is for them: "I spent my entire youth putting together and propagating the band known the world over as the mighty 'Wrathchild'. Wrathchild as a collective is unique, we forged an entire new glam-metal scene borne of mine and Eddie (Star's) punk roots".

Stakkattakktwo was voted the Best Album of 2011 by both Grande-Rock.com and the site's Readers' Poll.[2][3]

In August 2013 Gaz Harris and Wrathchild parted ways, Gaz joined Gypsy Pistoleros. As of present Wrathchild do not have a lead singer.

Rocky Shades Wrathchild

Rocky Shades Wrathchild, also known as R.S.W., was founded by former lead vocalist Rocky Shades in 2006. They recorded the demo *Dead Good* which was featured on their Myspace website for a short time. The line-up included Rocky Shades, Jon Sudbury and James Crofts. They were set to play the Hard Rock Hell III festival in December 2009, but were removed from the bill in October; reason as quoted by Hard Rock Hell promotors "All involved in Hard Rock Hell felt that without being able to use the name to advertise, and without more than one member of the original line-up in the band, what we were left with was simply not what we booked. It's as if we had booked Genesis and got Phil Collins. Hence it was not a proper booking, to which the agent who booked it agreed too." [4]

Wildside Riot

In December 2010, Rocky Shades decided to start afresh by creating a new band with no relation to the Wrathchild name, Wildside Riot. The initial line-up was Rocky Shades on vocals, Gaz Wilde (Gary Hunt) on drums, Iggie Pistolero and Rob D'Var on guitars. Natt Kid took on bass duties initially, eventually replaced by James Crofts (previously of Rocky Shades Wrathchild). The present line-up is Shades and Wilde, with Joss Riot and Jimmy Gunn on guitars, and Marty Mayhem on bass.[5][6][7]

Wildside Riot was launched in July 2011, and have played a handful of U.K dates from May 2012-July 2012 promoting the new outfit. Debut album "No Second Take" was released 28 January 2013 on CD and as a digital download. The band released a video to their self-titled track "Wildside Riot" ahead of the album which can be seen on the website.[8] Among several other promotional gigs in late 2012 and early 2013, they also secured a Saturday slot at Hard Rock Hell VI in December 2012.

2.90.2 Line-ups

2.90.3 Discography

Albums

- *Stakk Attakk* (1984)
- *Trash Queens* (1985)
- *The Biz Suxx* (1988)
- *Delirium* (1989)
- *Stakkattakktwo* (2011)

EPs

- *Stackheel Strutt* (1983)

Singles

- "Do You Want My Love?" (1982)
- "Alrite with the Boyz" (1984)
- "Trash Queen" (1984)
- "(Na Na) Nukklear Rokket" (1988)

Demos

- *Mascara Massacre* (1982)

Video albums

- *Live in London/War Machine* (1984)

2.90.4 Members

- **Gaz Psychowrath** - Vocals (former)2009-2013
- **Phil Wrathchild** - Lead guitar, backing vocals 1980-1981, 2009-2013
- **Marc Angel** - Bass guitar, backing vocals 1980-1990, 2009-2013
- **Eddie Star** - Drums 1981-1990, 2009-2013
- **Rocky Shades** - Vocals (former)1980-1990
- **Lance Rocket** - Lead guitar, backing vocals (former)1981-1990
- **Brian Parry** - Drums (former)1980-1981

2.90.5 See also

- List of New Wave of British Heavy Metal bands

2.90.6 References

[1] "Wrathchild - Interview with Marc Angel". Grande-Rock.Com. 28 January 2012.

[2] Best Album of 2011, Reader's Poll.

[3] Best Album of 2011, Grande-Rock.com - Best of 2011.

[4] "Classic Rock Magazine". Classic Rock Magazine. Retrieved 2012-11-09.

[5] "Former Wrathchild Vocalist Posts Video Of New Band Wildside Riot". Sleaze Roxx. 2012-06-25. Retrieved 2012-11-09.

[6] "Original Wrathchild Vocalist Rocky Shades Resurfaces In Wildside Riot". Sleaze Roxx. 2011-06-12. Retrieved 2012-11-09.

[7] "Wildside RIOT". Facebook. Retrieved 2012-11-09.

[8] "Rocky Shades Ex Wrathchild - Wildside Riot Official Website". Wildside Riot. Retrieved 2012-11-09.

2.90.7 External links

- Official website
- Wrathchild at NWOBHM.com

Chapter 3

Related Topics & Heavy Metal Magazines

3.1 Heavy metal fashion

Judas Priest, in typical heavy metal attire, performing at the VH1 Rock Honors on May 25, 2006.

Heavy metal fashion is the style of dress, body modification, make-up, hairstyle, and so on, taken on by fans of heavy metal, or, as they are often called, metalheads or headbangers.

3.1.1 Origins

The clothing associated with heavy metal has its roots in the biker,[1] rocker, and leather subcultures. Heavy metal fashion includes elements such as leather jackets; hi-top basketball shoes (more common with old school thrash metalheads); blue or black jeans, camouflage pants, shirts, jackets or shorts, and denim jackets or kutte vests, often adorned with badges, pins and patches. As with the bikers, there is a fascination with Germanic imagery, such as the Iron Cross.[2][3]

Distinct aspects of heavy metal fashion can be credited to various bands, but the band that takes the most credit for revolutionizing the look was Judas Priest, primarily with its singer, Rob Halford.[1] Halford wore a leather costume on stage as early as 1978 to coincide with the promotion for the *Killing Machine* (*Hell Bent for Leather* in the USA) album. In a 1998 interview, Halford described the leather subculture as the inspiration for this look.[4] Shortly after appropriating the leather look, Halford started appearing onstage on a roaring motor bike. Soon, the rest of the band followed.

It was not long before other bands appropriated the leather look; Iron Maiden's original singer Paul Di'Anno began wearing leather jackets and studded bracelets,[5][6] Motörhead innovated with bullet belts, and Saxon introduced spandex. This fashion was particularly popular with followers of the NWOBHM (New Wave of British Heavy Metal) movement in the early 1980s, and sparked a revival for metal in this era.

The studded leather look was extended in subsequent variations, to the wearing of combat boots, studded belts and bracelets, bullet belts, spiked gauntlets, etc. The codpiece, however, appears to have been less popular among the general public.

3.1.2 Other influences

The style and clothing of metal has absorbed elements from influences as diverse as the musical influences from which the genre has borrowed. It is from this linking of different sub-styles of clothing and music influences that one can sometimes determine a person's specific taste in music simply from overall appearance. However, such signs are not hard and fast rulings in the majority of cases. This uncertainty is what makes the first key aspect of the metalheads' identity below so important.

Some of the influences of modern military clothing and the Vietnam War can be seen by the fans and bands of thrash metal, with the members of thrash metal bands of the 1980s like Metallica, Destruction, and Megadeth wearing bullet belts around their waists on stage[7][8] (it is likely that the thrash metal bands got the idea of wearing bullet

Spike "bands" or gauntlets are a common element among fans.

belts from NWOBHM bands such as Motörhead, who have incorporated the bullet belt as part of their aesthetic since their inception, since many thrash metal bands in the 1980s were influenced by Motörhead). This style is often connected to punk-metal and anti-fashion, as akin to the hardcore punk scene, as the formentioned style reflects similar attitudes. German Heavy Metal band Accept ex lead singer Udo Dirkschneider also contributed to the military clothing by wearing military pants from 1982, being considered as the first Heavy Metal musician to wear them.

Fans of glam metal often have long or very long, teased hair, and are dressed in spandex pants and/or leather jackets. They also may use (but it's not necessary) some makeup (lipsticks, eye-shadows, tonal creams, etc.). Bands who play in glam metal genre may have instruments with an extravagant colour and attributes, like guitars with pink, violet, dalmatian or pink rose colour; microphone stands with (usually) a leopard or silk scarf (there may be some different attributes attached to the microphone stand, but mostly only leopard-colour scarfs have been seen); drumkits with some artwork (this kind of drumkit is seen in other metal genres as well, not only in glam metal).

The imagery and values of historic Celtic, Saxon, Viking and Chivalric culture is reflected heavily in metal music, by bands such as Blind Guardian, and has its impact upon the everyday fashion and especially the stagegear of metal artists. The independence, masculinity and honor of the warrior ethos is extremely popular amongst metalheads, as is the rejection of modern day consumerist and metrosexual culture. Folk metal, viking metal, black metal and power metal fans often grow long thick hair and beards reminiscent of a stereotypical Viking, Saxon and Celt, and wear Thor's Hammer pendants and other pagan symbols. On stage, in photoshoots, and in music videos, it is very common for bands of these genres such as Turisas and Moonsorrow to wear chain mail, animals skins, warpaint (such as woad) and other Dark Ages themed battle gear.

Corpse paint is another style of black-and-white makeup, used mainly by black metal bands. It is often composed of a white layer covering a person's face with black details on top, often in the shape of crosses or around the eyes. Bands such as Cradle of Filth have stated that this has been born as a homage to early silent black-and-white horror movies. Black metal fans also sport goatees, all black outfits, leather jackets (sometimes with black and white band patches sewed on), spikes, jewelry, facial piercings and boots.

Power metal fans and musicians such as Rhapsody of Fire often wear attire reminiscent of the Renaissance and the Middle Ages including tight black or brown leather trousers and wide sleeved, buttonless shirts of various colors. The imagery of bards and minstrels as well as knights is a popular part of power metal fashion.

Some stoner metal bands and fans have incorporated "retro" looks- boot-cut or bell-bottom jeans, headbands, and tie-dye or other colorful shirts inspired by 60's and 70's psychedelic rock as well as cannabis culture.

Nu metal fashion includes baggy pants or cargo shorts (borrowing from hip hop culture), spiked hair or dreadlocks, and an abundance of accessories.

Also notable is that the dark business suit now relates to some metalbands, most often Doom, Gothic or Stoner acts. Bands such as Akercocke, The Vision Bleak, Lacrimosa and Queens of the Stone Age are known for use of formal clothing in music videos and stage performances, sometimes followed by fans.

3.1.3 References

[1] *Heavy Metal: The Music and Its Culture*

[2] *Design Culture*

[3] *Popular Music: The Key Concepts*

[4] Interview with Rob Halford

[5] *Hell Bent for Leather*

[6] *Sound of the Beast*

[7] *Sound of the Beast*

[8] *Extreme Metal*

3.1.4 External links

- Community gallery of heavy/black/thrash metal T-Shirts from collectors

- *Is Image Important For Metal?*

- Women's Heavy Metal Fashion

3.2 Heavy metal subculture

A man wearing clothing typically associated with heavy metal and displaying the "metal horns" gesture

Fans of **heavy metal** music have created their own **subculture** which encompasses more than just appreciation of the style of music. Fans affirm their membership in the subculture or scene by attending metal concerts, buying albums, in some cases growing their hair, and most recently, by contributing to metal websites.[1] Some critics and musicians have suggested that the subculture is largely intolerant to other musical genres.

3.2.1 Nomenclature

Heavy metal fans go by a number of different names, including metalhead,[2] headbanger,[3] and thrasher.[4] These vary with time and regional divisions. But just "headbanger" and "metalhead" are universally accepted to refer to fans or the subculture itself.

3.2.2 Subculture

Heavy metal fans have created a "subculture of alienation" with its own standards for achieving authenticity within the group.[5] Deena Weinstein's book *Heavy Metal: The Music And Its Culture* argues that heavy metal "...has persisted far longer than most genres of rock music" due to the growth of an intense "subculture which identified with the music". Metal fans formed an "exclusionary youth community" which was "distinctive and marginalized from the mainstream" society.[6] The heavy metal scene developed a strongly masculine "community with shared values, norms, and behaviors". A "code of authenticity" is central to the heavy metal subculture ; this code requires bands to have a "disinterest in commercial appeal" and radio hits as well as a refusal to "sell out".[6] The metal code also includes "opposition to established authority, and separateness from the rest of society". Fans expect that the metal "...vocation [for performers] includes total devotion to the music and deep loyalty to the youth subculture that grew up around it..." ; a metal performer must be an "idealized representative of the subculture".[6]

While the audience for metal is mainly "white, male, lower/middle class youth," this group is "...tolerant of those outside its core demographic base who follow its codes of dress, appearance, and behavior".[6] The activities in the metal subculture include the ritual of attending concerts, buying albums, and most recently, contributing to metal websites. Attending concerts affirms the solidarity of the subculture, as it is one of the ritual activities by which fans celebrate their music.[7] Metal magazines help the members of the subculture to connect, find information and evaluations of bands and albums, and "express their solidarity".[7] The long hair, leather jackets, and band patches of heavy metal fashion help to encourage a sense of identification within the subculture. However, Weinstein notes that not all metal fans are "visible members" of the heavy metal subculture.

Authenticity

In the musical subcultures of heavy metal and punk, the word *poseur* (or *poser*) is "a person who habitually pretends to be something he/she is not."[8] In a 1993 profile of heavy metal fans' "subculture of alienation", the author noted that the scene classified some members as "poseurs," that is, heavy metal performers or fans who pretended to be part of the subculture, but who were deemed to lack authenticity and sincerity.[9] Jeffrey Arnett's 1996 book *Metalheads: Heavy Metal Music and Adolescent Alienation* argues that the heavy metal subculture classifies members into two categories by giving "...acceptance as an authentic metalhead or rejection as a fake, a poseur."[10]

Since decades ago, heavy metal fans began using the term "sell out" to refer to bands who turned their heavy metal sound into radio-friendly rock music. In metal, a sell out is "...someone dishonest who adopted the most rigorous pose, or identity-affirming lifestyle and opinions". The metal bands that earned this epithet are those "... who adopt the visible aspects of the orthodoxy (sound, images) without contributing to the underlying belief system."[11]

Ron Quintana's article on "Metallica['s] Early History" argues that when Metallica was trying to find a place in the L.A. metal scene in the early 1980s, "American hard-rock scene was dominated by highly coiffed, smoothly-polished bands such as Styx, Journey, and REO Speedwagon." He claims that this made it hard for Metallica to "...play their [heavy] music and win over a crowd in a land where poseurs ruled and anything fast and heavy was ignored."[12] In David Rocher's 1999 interview with Damian Montgomery, the frontman of Ritual Carnage, he praised Montgomery as "...an authentic, no-frills, poseur-bashing, nun-devouring kind of gentleman, an enthusiastic metalhead truly in love with the lifestyle he preaches... and unquestionably practises.[13]

In 2002, "[m]etal guru Josh Wood" claimed that the "credibility of heavy metal" in North America is being destroyed by the genre's demotion to "...horror movie soundtracks, wrestling events and, worst of all, the so-called 'Mall Core' groups like Limp Bizkit." Wood claims that the "...true [metal] devotee's path to metaldom is perilous and fraught with poseurs."[14] In an article on metal/hard rock frontman Axl Rose, entitled "Ex–'White-Boy Poseur'", Rose admitted that he has had "...time to reflect on heavy-metal posturing" of the last few decades. He notes that "We thought we were so badass...[until] N.W.A came out rapping about this world where you walk out of your house and you get shot." At this point, Rose argues that "It was just so clear what stupid little white-boy poseurs we were."[15]

Christian metal bands are sometimes criticized within metal circles in a similar light; their faith and adherence to the Church an indicator to some extreme metal adherents as membership to an established authority, and therefore rendering Christian bands as "posers" and a contradiction to heavy metal's purpose.[16] Some proponents argue personal faith in right hand path beliefs should not be tolerated within metal.[17] A small number of Norwegian black metal bands have threatened violence (and, in extremely rare instances, exhibited it) towards Christian artists or believers, as demonstrated in the early 1990s through occasional church burnings throughout Scandinavia.[16][18]

3.2.3 Social aspects

In place of typical dancing, metal fans are more likely to mosh[19] or headbang, a movement in which the head is shaken up and down in time with the music.[20]

Fans from the heavy metal culture often make the "Corna" hand-signal formed by a fist with the "pinkie" and index fingers extended, known variously as the "devil's horns", the "metal fist" and other similar descriptors.[21] This gesture was popularised by Dio and Black Sabbath vocalist Ronnie James Dio, who died in 2010.

3.2.4 Intolerance to other music

On a 1985 edition of Australian music television show *Countdown*, renowned music critic Molly Meldrum spoke about intolerance to other music within the subculture, observing "sections who just *love* heavy metal, and they actually don't like anything else."[22] Queen frontman Freddie Mercury, a guest on the program, readily concurred with Meldrum's view, and opined that his comments were "very true". Directly addressing the resistance to alternate genres seen among certain heavy metal fans, Mercury asserted: "that's *their* problem".[22]

Interviewed in 2011, Sepultura frontman Derrick Green said: "I find that a lot of people can be very closed minded – they want to listen to metal and nothing else, but I'm not like that. I like doing metal music and having a heavy style, but I don't like to put myself in such a box and be trapped in it."[23] Also that year, Anthrax drummer Charlie Benante admitted that hardened members of the heavy metal subculture "are not the most open-minded people when it comes to music."[24]

Ultimate Guitar reported in 2013 that thrash metal fans had directed "hate" towards Megadeth for venturing into more rock-oriented musical territory on that year's *Super Collider* album. Singer Dave Mustaine stated that their hostility was informed by an unwillingness to accept other genres and had "nothing to do with Megadeth or the greatness of the band and its music"; he also argued that the labelling of music fans contributed to their inability to appreciate other types of music.[25] That same year Opeth frontman Mikael Åkerfeldt also alleged that most members of the subculture are resistant to the musical evolution of artists within the metal genre, stating that it "doesn't seem to be that important" to those listeners. He added: "I think most metal fans just want their Happy Meals served to them. They don't really want to know about what they're getting. For a while, I thought metal was a more open-minded thing but I was wrong."[26]

Journalists have written about the dismissive attitude of many metal fans. MetalReviews.com published a 2004 article entitled "The *True*, *Real* Metalhead: A Selective Intellect Or A Narrow-Minded Bastard?", wherein the writer confessed to being "truly bothered by the narrow-mindedness of a lot of [his] metal brothers and sisters".[27] Critic Ryan Howe, in a 2013 piece for *Sound and Motion* magazine, penned an open letter to British metal fans, many of whom had expressed disgust about Avenged Sevenfold – whose music they deemed too light to qualify as metal – being booked to headline the 2014 instalment of popular metal event the Download Festival. Howe described the detractors as "narrow minded" and challenged them to attend the Avenged Sevenfold set and "be prepared to have [their] opinions changed."[28]

Despite widespread lack of appreciation of other music genres, some fans and musicians can profess a deep devotion to genres that often have nothing to do with metal music. For instance, Fenriz of Darkthrone is also known to be a techno DJ,[29] and Metallica's Kirk Hammett is seen wearing a t-shirt of post-punk band The Sisters of Mercy in the music video for "Wherever I May Roam".[30] Ted Kirkpatrick, Tourniquet band leader is a "great admirer of the classical masters".[31]

3.2.5 Attire

Main article: Heavy metal fashion

Another aspect of heavy metal culture is its fashion. Like the metal music, these fashions have changed over the decades, while keeping some core elements. Typically, the heavy metal fashions of the late 1970s – 1980s comprised tight blue jeans or drill pants, motorcycle boots or hi-top sneakers and black t-shirts, worn with a sleeveless kutte of denim or leather emblazoned with woven patches and button pins from heavy metal bands. Sometimes, a denim vest, emblazoned with album art "knits" (cloth patches) would be worn over a long-sleeved leather jacket. As with other musical subcultures of the era, such as punks, this jacket and its emblems and logos helped the wearer to announce their interests. Metal fans often wear t-shirts with the emblem of bands.

Around the mid-2000s, a renaissance of younger audiences became interested in 1980s metal, and the rise of newer bands embracing older fashion ideals led to a more 1980s-esque style of dress. Some of the new audience are young, urban hipsters who had "previously fetishized metal from a

Rob Halford of Judas Priest wearing studded leather jacket

A man wearing a denim jacket with band patches and artwork of heavy metal bands including Metallica, Guns N' Roses, Iron Maiden, Slipknot and Led Zeppelin

distance".[32]

3.2.6 International variations

Heavy metal fans can be found in virtually every country in the world. Even in some of the more orthodox Muslim countries of the Arab World a tiny metal culture exists, though judicial and religious authorities do not always tolerate it. In 2003, more than a dozen members and fans of Moroccan heavy metal bands were imprisoned for "undermining the Muslim faith." Heavy metal fans in many Arab countries have formed metal cultures, with movements such as Taqwacore.

3.2.7 References

[1] Heavy Metal: The Music And Its Culture, Revised Edition by Deena Weinstein Da Capo Press; Revised edition (April 4, 2000) ISBN 0-306-80970-2 ISBN 978-0-306-80970-5. Page 294

[2] "Metalhead - Definition and More from the Free Merriam-Webster Dictionary". Merriam-webster.com. 2012-08-31. Retrieved 2014-05-19.

[3] "Headbanger - Definition and More from the Free Merriam-Webster Dictionary". Merriam-webster.com. 2012-08-31. Retrieved 2014-05-19.

[4] "Cleveland - Music - Talkin' Thrash". Web.archive.org. 2007-08-10. Retrieved 2014-05-19.

[5] "Three profiles of heavy metal fans: A taste for sensation and a subculture of alienation." In *Journal Qualitative Sociology*. Publisher Springer Netherlands. ISSN 0162-0436 (Print) 1573-7837 (Online). Issue Volume 16, Number 4 / December, 1993. Pages 423-443

[6] Heavy Metal: The Music And Its Culture, Revised Edition by Deena Weinstein Da Capo Press; Revised edition (April 4, 2000) ISBN 0-306-80970-2 ISBN 978-0-306-80970-5

[7] Heavy Metal: The Music And Its Culture, Revised Edition by Deena Weinstein Da Capo Press; Revised edition (April 4, 2000) ISBN 0-306-80970-2 ISBN 978-0-306-80970-5

[8] "Definition of scotch, forgo, temporize, simulate". English-test.net. Retrieved 2014-05-19.

[9] "Three profiles of heavy metal fans: A taste for sensation and a subculture of alienation." In *Journal Qualitative Sociology*. Publisher Springer Netherlands. ISSN 0162-0436 (Print) 1573-7837 (Online). Issue Volume 16, Number 4 / December, 1993. Pages 423-443.

[10] *Metalheads: Heavy Metal Music and Adolescent Alienation* - by Jeffrey Jensen Arnett - 1996 - Music - 196 pages.

[11]

[12] "JoyZine - Interview with Metallica by Ron Quintana". Artistwd.com. 1982-03-14. Retrieved 2014-05-19.

[13] "CoC : Ritual Carnage : Interview : 2/13/1999". Chronicles-ofchaos.com. Retrieved 2014-05-19.

[14]

[15] Yuan, Jada (2006-09-18). "Axl Rose: Ex-'White-Boy Poseur' - New York Magazine". Nymag.com. Retrieved 2014-05-19.

[16] Khan-Harris, Keith. *Extreme Metal: Music and Culture on the Edge*. Oxford: Berg, 2006. ISBN 978-1-84520-399-3

[17] Norsk Black Metal (2003). Norwegian Broadcasting Corporation.

[18] Grude, Torstein (1998). Satan Rides The Media.

[19] Robin Pogrebin. "Hard-Core Threat to Health: Moshing at Rock Concerts". New York Times. Retrieved 2014-05-19.

[20]

[21] "The Devil's Horns: A Rock And Roll Symbol | Guitar Columns @". Ultimate-guitar.com. Retrieved 2014-05-19.

[22] Meldrum, Molly (5 May 1985). *Countdown*. Australian Broadcasting Corporation.

[23] "Exclusive – Sepultura Interview". Rushonrock.Com. 2011-07-18. Retrieved 2014-05-19.

[24] Coe, Matt (21 September 2011). "Anthrax - Worshipping Metal Legacy". *Eternal Terror*. Retrieved 25 September 2013.

[25] "Dave Mustaine: 'Thrash Metal Fans Don't Want to Accept Rock'". *Ultimate Guitar Archive*. 3 July 2013. Retrieved 25 September 2013.

[26] "OPETH Frontman Thinks Metal Fans Are Close-Minded". Metal Injection. Retrieved 2014-05-19.

[27] "Editorial - The *True*, *Real* Metalhead: A Selective Intellect Or A Narrow - Minded Bastard?". Metalreviews.com. 2004-01-24. Retrieved 2014-05-19.

[28] "An Open Letter to UK Metal Fans Regarding Avenged Sevenfold | Sound And Motion". Soundandmotionmag.com. 2013-11-04. Retrieved 2014-05-19.

[29] Hughes, Dylan (2012-03-13). "A Fist in the Face of God Presents... DJ Fenriz' Dance Mix | VICE Canada". Vice.com. Retrieved 2014-05-19.

[30] "Metallica - Wherever I May Roam [Official Music Video]". YouTube. 1992-05-21. Retrieved 2014-05-19.

[31] "Ted Kirkpatrick Bio". Tourniquet.net. Retrieved 2014-05-19.

[32] Stosuy, Brandon (2005-08-19). "Heavy metal for hipsters". Slate.com. Retrieved 2014-05-19.

3.3 Kerrang!

Kerrang! is a UK-based magazine devoted to rock music, currently published by Hamburg based Bauer Media Group. It was first published on 6 June 1981 as a one-off supplement in the *Sounds* newspaper. Named after the onomatopoeic word that derives from the sound made when playing a power chord on a distorted electric guitar, *Kerrang!* was initially devoted to the New Wave of British Heavy Metal and the rise of hard rock acts.[2] In the early 2000s it became the best-selling British music newspaper.[3]

3.3.1 History

Kerrang! was founded in 1981.[4] The magazine commenced publication on 6 June 1981 and was edited by Geoff Barton, initially as a one-time supplement in the *Sounds* newspaper, which focused on the New Wave of British Heavy Metal phenomenon and on the rise of other hard rock acts.[5] Angus Young of AC/DC appeared on *Kerrang!*'s first cover. Launched as a monthly magazine, *Kerrang!* began to appear on a fortnightly basis later, and in 1987 it went weekly. The original owner was United Newspapers who then sold it to EMAP in 1991.

During the 1980s and early 1990s the magazine placed many thrash and glam metal acts on the cover (like Mötley Crüe, Slayer, Bon Jovi, Metallica, Poison, and Venom) but later discarded them when grunge acts such as Nirvana rose to fame. Readers often criticise the magazine for repeating this process every time a new musical trend becomes popular.

Kerrang!'s popularity rose again with the hiring of editor Paul Rees circa 2000 when the nu metal genre, featuring bands like Limp Bizkit and Slipknot were becoming more popular.[6] Rees went on to edit *Q* magazine and Ashley Bird took over as editor from 2003 to 2005. However the magazine's sales went quickly into decline in 2003 and Paul Brannigan took over as editor in May 2005.[7]

The term "Thrash Metal" was first referred to in the music press by *Kerrang* journalist Malcolm Dome while making a reference to the Anthrax song "Metal Thrashing Mad" in issue number 62, page 8 published on 23 February 1984. Prior to this Metallica's James Hetfield referred to their sound as Power Metal.[8]

With the emergence of emo and metalcore, *Kerrang!* began to heavily feature this musical trend. However, the revamp was not welcomed by all readers and many complaints were received about *Kerrang!*'s sudden emphasis on emo and metalcore music. Brannigan took the magazine into its most commercially successful period with a record ever ABC for the title of 80,186 copies.[9]

In 2008, EMAP sold its consumer magazine to current owner Bauer Media Group. Brannigan left *Kerrang!* in 2009 and Nichola Browne was appointed editor.[10] She later stepped down in April 2011. Former *NME* features editor and *GamesMaster* deputy editor James McMahon was appointed as editor on 6 June 2011.[11]

3.3.2 Website

'Kerrang!''s website, www.kerrang.com was launched summer 2001 by Dan Silver. Kerrang!'s parent company Emap acquired the domain name from a Norwegian cybersquatter by the name of Steingram Stegane for a token sum of £666.[12]

Kerrang!'s website is dedicated to finding out more information to do with the magazine and also the latest information on the current bands and upcoming events. The website hosts *Kerrang!*'s online shop, podcasts, message board, TV and radio segments ensuring even more opportunities to sell associated merchandise and products.[13] In 2001, *Kerrang!* launched its own online forum with the "rants and raves" section taking up most of the traffic. Though initially extremely popular, the number of users began to peter out around 2005 with the number of people online dropping to as low as 10 when previously it had been closer to the 100 figure.

According to Alexa www.kerrang.com generates 60,000 pageviews per month and is ranked 66,798th globally.[14]

3.3.3 Kerrang! Awards

Main article: Kerrang! Awards

Since 1993, the magazine has held an annual awards ceremony to mark the most successful bands in the interests of their readers. The awards became one of Britain's most recognised events by the now defunct *Guinness Book of British Hit Singles & Albums*, often listing some of the winners in their annual round-up of the previous year. The event is presented by major music celebrities, with many others outside the industry who attend the event.[15]

3.3.4 Kerrang! Radio

Main article: Kerrang! 105.2

In 2000, EMAP launched *Kerrang!* as a digital radio station, across the United Kingdom. This was principally a 'jukebox' station, playing a back-to-back sequence of rock and alternative music. On 10 June 2004, Kerrang! 105.2

was launched as a regional radio station in Birmingham with an advertising campaign by London-based creative agency ODD.[16] The radio had a number of specialist programmes dedicated to the many subgenres of rock music. The radio output included interviews with those affecting popular culture and society as well as those involved with music. It stopped broadcasting on FM as of 14 June 2013 and once again became a digital station, with listeners able to tune in on DAB or the Kerrang! Radio app. With this broadcasting change came a move in Kerrang! Radio's offices from Birmingham to London. Planet Rock is now broadcasting on its FM frequency.

3.3.5 Kerrang! TV

Main article: Kerrang! TV

In 2001 EMAP launched Kerrang! TV. As with the radio station, the television channel covers the more mainstream side of the rock music as well as classic rock bands like Aerosmith and AC/DC, and classic heavy metal bands such as Guns N' Roses and Metallica. Kerrang TV is now a joint venture between Bauer Media Group and Channel 4.[17]

3.3.6 Kerrang! Tour

Main article: Kerrang! Tour

Kerrang! held throughout January a tour of rock music concerts around the United Kingdom.[18] The tour has featured bands such as Bullet for My Valentine, Good Charlotte, Sum 41, and Coheed and Cambria among others.

Although the 2012 Kerrang! Relentless Energy Tour had billed Sum 41, New Found Glory, letlive. and While She Sleeps to play, unfortunately Sum 41 had to pull out due to a back injury of their frontman. They were promptly replaced by The Blackout.[19]

3.3.7 The Official Kerrang! Rock Chart

In March 2012, Kerrang announced a new rock chart for the UK which is based upon airplay across Kerrang Radio, Kerrang TV and sales figures from the Official Charts Company. Charts are announced on Saturday mornings and feature twenty tracks. The latest chart can be viewed on Kerrang! every Saturday at midday.

3.3.8 International editions

Emap launched *Kerrang! Australia* in the late 1990s. Unlike its weekly counterpart in the UK, the Australian edition was published monthly due to stiff competition from free local music publications. *Kerrang!* is also published in Spanish and German.

3.3.9 References

[1] "ABC". Audit Bureau of Circulations. Retrieved April 17, 2015.

[2] Brannigan, Paul (6 June 2006). "25 Most Important Bands Of Our Lifetime". *Kerrang!* (Bauer Media Group) (1110).

[3] Baran, Pete (15 February 2002). "Kerrang topples NME as best selling music weekly". Freaky Trigger. Retrieved 23 November 2011.

[4] Andy R. Brown (2007). ""Everything Louder than Everything Else"". *Journalism Studies* **8** (4). Retrieved 10 November 2015.

[5] Ward, Steven. "Geoff Barton, behind the wheel". Rock Critics. Retrieved 22 November 2011.

[6] "Kerrang! overtakes NME". BBC News. 15 February 2002. Retrieved 7 May 2010.

[7] "ABC report: film and music". *Campaign* (Haymarket Group). 20 February 2004. Retrieved 22 November 2011.

[8] Dome, Malcolm (23 February 1984). "Anthrax 'Fistful Of Metal'". *Kerrang!* **62**. London, UK: Spotlight Publications Ltd. p. 8.

[9] Tryhorn, Chris (17 August 2006). "Kerrang! rocks NME's world". *The Guardian* (Guardian Media Group). Retrieved 22 November 2011.

[10] Brook, Stephen (17 August 2009). "Nichola Browne to edit Kerrang!". *The Guardian* (Guardian Media Group). Retrieved 28 October 2010.

[11] Cardew, Ben (6 June 2011). "Kerrang! names new editor". *Music Week* (Intent Media). Retrieved 9 June 2011.

[12] http://www.theguardian.com/media/2001/aug/27/mondaymediasection12

[13] "Kerrang! Stuff". *Kerrang!*. Bauer Media Group. Retrieved 22 November 2011.

[14] "Site Overview". Alexa. Retrieved April 17, 2015.

[15] Ng, Justin (4 May 2011). "Kerrang! Awards Fuelled By Relentless Energy Drink Nominations Announced". Entertainment Focus. Retrieved 22 November 2011.

[16] "About Kerrang! Radio". *Kerrang! Radio*. Bauer Media Group. 14 March 2002. Retrieved 22 November 2011.

[17] Plunkett, Joe (21 November 2008). "Bauer Radio mulls rebrand of Kerrang! station in West Midlands". *The Guardian* (Guardian Media Group). Retrieved 7 September 2010.

[18] Gregory, Jason (28 September 2011). "New Found Glory, Sum 41, letlive For 2012 UK And Ireland Tour – Tickets". Gigwise.com (Giant Digital). Retrieved 23 November 2011.

[19] "The Kerrang! Tour 2012 sponsored by Relentless Energy Drink featuring New Found Glory and The Blackout". Relentless Energy. 20 January 2012. Retrieved 11 May 2012.

3.3.10 External links

- Official website

3.4 Metal Forces

Metal Forces is a British publication founded in 1983 which promotes the music genres heavy metal and hard rock. *Metal Forces* was well known for its coverage of unsigned bands through its *Demolition* feature and championed the likes of Metallica,[1] Slayer, Megadeth, HellsBelles, Overkill, Death and Poison long before they had secured record deals. They are credited as contributing in this fashion to the success of the band Anacrusis.[2][3] Dave Reynolds, a former writer for *Metal Forces*, has claimed that the magazine was the first to coin the terms thrash metal and death metal.[4] A *Metal Forces* compiled vinyl album, *Demolition - Scream Your Brains Out!*, based on the magazine's popular *Demolition* column, was released in 1988 through Chain Reaction Records featuring Anacrusis, Atrophy, Hobbs' Angel of Death, Aftermath and the Chris Barnes fronted Leviathan. In addition to metal acts, the magazine also featured interviews with alternative rock acts such as Nirvana.[5]

In August 1991 *Metal Forces* created the offshoot publication *Thrash 'n Burn*, a monthly title dedicated to extreme metal.

3.4.1 Background

Metal Forces was created in 1983 by Bernard Doe, with the first issue released in August 1983. Articles covered and promoted mainly bands that were relatively unknown at the time. *Metal Forces* aided greatly in promoting unknown bands and heavy metal and hard rock during the 1980s and early 1990s, becoming one of UK's top music magazines during that period.

During the early 1990s, *Metal Forces* changed from their policy of balancing their articles between established and unknown bands, to a style which covered more mainstream and famed rock and heavy metal bands. The changes implemented were not profitable and the magazine lost readers and advertisers. In this period and for a brief time, *Metal Forces* launched the appreciated spin-off *Thrash 'n Burn* (later renamed *Xtreme Noize*). *Metal Forces* released seventy-two issues before rebranding under the abbreviated title of *MF*. The latter ceased publication in February 1993. As of 2012, *Metal Forces* launched its official website online, which has information from its magazine issues and new information and coverage of bands.

In an interview, rock columnist Dave Reynolds indicated that the magazine was created in response to difficulties working with rival publication *Kerrang!*[6] According to Reynolds, the magazine gained national distribution in the late 1980s and, with its success, inspired *Kerrang!* to produce a spin-off publication of its own, *Mega Metal Kerrang!*[6] The magazine disseminated information about the metal music scene; in 2007, the senior VP of Roadrunner Records indicated that *Metal Forces*, along with similar publication *Kick Ass*, "was my Bible... the way I discovered new bands and fed my insatiable appetite for all things emerging in the underground".[7]

Controversy

In 1984, *Metal Forces* printed a review of black metal band Hellhammer so negative that the band's guitarist, Tom Warrior, indicated the band would never play in England because of it; after forming a new band, Celtic Frost, the guitarist continued to refuse requests for an interview with the magazine for some time, notwithstanding that *Metal Forces* was, in the guitarist's own words, "the second biggest magazine in heavy metal".[8] In 2007, the *Metal Forces* editor and reviewer wrote the band history for Century Media Records remastered CD editions of Hellhammer albums.[9]

In 1986, Dave Mustaine, early guitarist of Metallica and founder of Megadeth, complained that replacement guitarist Kirk Hammett was unfairly named "number 1" in the reader poll of *Metal Forces* on the basis of Mustaine's guitar playing; Hammett indicated that the guitar playing was his own, re-rerecorded from the demo release.[10]

3.4.2 *Metal Forces* Official Website

As of 2012 *Metal Forces* launched their official website. The website was officially opened March 2012.

3.4.3 Metal Forces presents: Demolition - Scream Your Brains Out!

Track listing

1. "Violent Slaughter" - Leviathan
2. "Chainsaw Massacre" - Hobbs' Angel of Death
3. "War for Freedom" - Aftermath
4. "Imprisoned" - Anacrusis
5. "Chemical Dependency" - Atrophy
6. "Leviathan" - Leviathan
7. "Satan's Crusade" - Hobbs' Angel of Death
8. "When Will You Die" - Aftermath
9. "Disembowled/Annihilation Complete" - Anacrusis
10. "Preacher, Preacher" - Atrophy

3.4.4 Notes

[1] Lew, Brian. (May 9, 2000) Metallica, how could you? Salon.com. Accessed April 10, 2008.

[2] King, Louise. (March 8, 1990) "Anacrusis: Crashing into heavy metal". *St. Louis Post-Dispatch."* Page 8G.

[3] Durchholz, Daniel. (June 18, 1993). "Proving their metal". *St. Louis Post-Dispatch*, Everyday Magazine. Page 4D.

[4] Ritchie, Jason. (2003) Backstage heroes: interview with Dave Reynolds "Contrary to what anyone may have told you, 'Metal Forces' coined the terms 'death metal' and 'thrash metal'. The former almost as a lighthearted piss-take to anything that sounded as bad as Hellhammer!". getreadytorock.com. Accessed April 10, 2008.

[5] (a) 46, January 1990, page 24.

[6] Ritchie, Jason. (2003) Backstage heroes: interview with Dave Reynolds. getreadytorock.com. Accessed April 10, 2008.

[7] Metal Hammer. Bob Muldowney dies. metalhammer.co.uk. Accessed April 10, 2008.

[8] Doe, Bernard. (1985) "Celtic Frost". *Metal Forces Magazine* #14.

[9] Doe, Bernard. (2007). Hellhammer. Century Media Records. Accessed April 10, 2008.

[10] Putterford, Mark. *Metallica Talking: Metallica in Their Own Words*. 2004. Omnibus Press. ISBN 1-84449-099-8 p. 12.

3.4.5 External links

- Official website
- Official Facebook page
- Official Twitter page

3.5 Metal Hammer

Metal Hammer (sometimes *MetalHammer*) is a monthly heavy metal music magazine published in the United Kingdom by TeamRock, and in several other countries by different publishers. *Metal Hammer* articles feature both mainstream bands and more unusual acts from the whole spectrum of heavy metal music.

3.5.1 History

London-based Wilfried F. Rimensberger instigated the concept of *MetalHammer* magazine in 1983.[2] At the time, he suggested to the infant *Kerrang!* magazine in London that they should publish a German version, but the editors of the time were not interested. Rimensberger took the idea to Jürgen Wigginghaus, publisher of German *MusikSzene* magazine where Rimensberger was Chief-Editor, and proposed the idea of a multi-lingual rock music publication. He also approached some of Europe's largest publishers such as Springer, Ringier and Bauer, but none were interested.

Eventually, Wigginghaus used the *Dortmunder Rocknacht* as a test ground for the publication in Germany and Rimensberger started the international English version *Metalhammer* UK from London. He developed the multilingual concept that propelled the magazine to a monthly circulation of over 1 million and, during its peak, published in 11 different languages across the globe - at the time largely outselling *Kerrang!*. *Metalhammer* had local language editions in countries such as Israel, Japan, Serbia, Spain, The Netherlands, Italy, Poland, Hungary, France. *Metalhammer* was also the first Western youth publication in the Soviet Union. Rimensberger made up the original and, at the time, unique concept of a heavy metal lifestyle magazine which was embedded in a network of *Metalhammer* branded multi-national radio shows, awards, tours, festivals, recordings, etc. This organization made the publication into the leading genre platform of the 80's - and the global leader in his segment of the publishing market.

Rimensberger, who started and owned Metalhammer UK Ltd and the registered rights of the name, later sold them to Wigginghaus whilst remaining in the background until the early Nineties as an adviser to Wigginghaus. Rimensberger was the promoter of the first Metalhammer Lorelei Festival, with leading metal acts such as Metallica, Motörhead and Venom. It was him who recommended Metallica to Peter Mensch (AC/DC) for management. Rimensberger also linked the name *Metal Hammer* with other successful brands such as the BBC (*Friday Rock Show* with Tommy Vance), MTV Metal Show with Bailey Brothers and Castle Donington Monsters of Rock Festival.

Harry Doherty, formerly of *Melody Maker*, became the launch editor of the English-language *Metal Hammer*, also producing the Metal Hammer TV Show on satellite television. He left to found the video magazine, *Hard'n'Heavy*, before being asked back by Wigginghaus to take over all the European issues of *Metal Hammer* and other associated magazines, such as *Rock World*. In association with Picture Music International, the video arm of EMI Records, Doherty also launched the *Metal Hammer Video Magazine*, in direct competition with his earlier creation, *Hard'n'Heavy*. Doherty left after a management dispute with Wigginghaus. Harry Doherty's original personal assistant **Sue Powell** went on to manage the London-based offices under Wilfried F. Rimensberger.

Rimensberger joined the start-up crew of MTV Europe as a consultant to the director of Network Development. He also became a co-producer of Tom Galley's Phenomena project, organising its worldwide record deal and linking it with some of the best rock musicians and singers. He co-produced with Tom Galley *Dream Runner*, Phenomena's best selling album which has become somewhat of a rock classic, uniting the best rock voices of the time on one studio album. Rimensberger also represented Stiletto Entertainment Los Angeles in Europe, produced Nina Corti at the Royal Albert Hall and various TV productions for Swiss, German and UK TV. He is the sourcing producer of Barry Manilow's movie project and Broadway-bound musical *Harmony*, the founder of The Children's Arts Academy and the producer of further cross-culture based projects such as 'Europa - The Woman'[3] and EuropeanIcons.[4] In the 1990s, Wigginghaus lost control over the publication and, advised by Rimensberger, sold the German edition to Jürg Marquart, the publisher of *Penthouse* and *Cosmopolitan* magazines in Germany. Later, Wigginghaus had to sell the remaining UK publication to cover personal financial liabilities.

With their November 2011 issue, the magazine celebrated "25 years of keeping it heavy".[5]

3.5.2 Metal Hammer Golden Gods Awards

Main article: Metal Hammer Golden Gods Awards

The Golden Gods Awards were established in 2003 by Chris Ingham from TeamRock.com. The annual ceremony takes place in United Kingdom.[6][7][8]

3.5.3 MetalHammer.co.uk

Metal Hammer in the UK also includes its website and iPhone application which both feature original and exclusive content from news, reviews and interviews to multimedia and Metal Hammer TV.[9]

Metal Hammer Podcast

The Metal Hammer Podcast was originally presented by James Gill and Terry Bezer and contained "All of the news, headlines, general rantings and reviews" of the week. Gill and Beez coined the phrase "You Clahn" when describing a silly person.

As of June 2011, Terry left Metal Hammer to work elsewhere and Comedian Stephen Hill replaced him on the Podcast. James left Metal Hammer on 3 February 2012 and this was also the date of his last podcast.[10] He was replaced on the Podcast by Metal Hammer Deputy Editor Merlin Alderslade.

The Podcast has developed a cult following among listeners, with a Facebook page containing over 5000 fans who, at their peak, have been influential in increasing exposure for bands such as britrockers Max Raptor and progressive metal band Bleeding Oath. The Podcast was taken off the air in September 2013.

3.5.4 Publishers

Metal Hammer UK changed hands several times, being bought first by Dennis Publishing and then by Future plc. is now owned by Axel Springer. There remain Greek and Italian *Metalhammer* publications, both published independently. Today, Rimensberger is Founding Chairman of The Children's Art Academy CAA in London, is further involved in international magazine publications and is co-producer of Tom Galley's superstar rock music concept Phenomena and remains producer and director of the related multi-media project Phenomena. Wigginghaus is now publishing a local event publication in Germany. Serbia's edition is published by Color Media Group. It has over 20000 sold copies each month, and magazine covers Croatia, Serbia, Montenegro as well as all other former Yugoslavia republics.

3.5.5 See also

- *Classic Rock*
- Malcolm Dome
- Joel McIver

3.5.6 References

[1] "ABC Consumer Magazines Circulation Certificate Metal Hammer January to December 2011" (PDF). Retrieved 2012-08-20.

[2] Story in Metalhammer Germany special edition 2009, celebrating the publication's 25 years anniversary

[3] "░░░░░░░░░░░░░░░░░ ░░░". Europathewoman.org. Retrieved 2015-08-11.

[4]

[5] "Metal Hammer website". Metal Hammer. 2011-10-19. Retrieved 2011-11-16.

[6] "Orange Amplification presents The Metal Hammer Golden Gods 2015 in association with World Of Warships". develop-online. 15 June 2015. Retrieved 22 July 2015.

[7] "MARILYN MANSON, LEMMY, MURDERDOLLS Attend METAL HAMMER Awards: Photos Available". BLABBERMOUTH.NET. 5 June 2003. Retrieved 22 July 2015.

[8] "ESP Bands Dominate Golden Gods Nominations". ESP Guitars. 25 March 2015. Retrieved 22 July 2015.

[9] "Metal Hammer website". Metal Hammer. 2009-08-07. Retrieved 2009-08-07.

[10]

3.5.7 External links

- Metal Hammer UK Official website
- Metal Hammer Germany Official website

3.6 Raw Power (TV series)

Raw Power is a weekly Heavy Metal/Rock Music television programme, with connections to Raw magazine, and produced by Music Box Ltd, which aired in Britain on ITV from 1990 until 1993. The name was eventually changed to **Noisy Mothers** which aired Nationwide in 1994 and 1995 and the format of the show changed. The show was axed in late 1995, to make way for an overhaul of scheduling.

3.6.1 Origins

Before the advent of rock-focussed satellite television stations such as MTV2 and Kerrang, heavy metal & rock music in general got very little airplay on British National Network television. Featuring live performances (from UK acts such as Steevi Jaimz's band St. Jaimz), music videos, interviews and competitions (all with a heavy metal theme) the show aired in the early hours of Saturday mornings (sometime between Midnight and 3:00am), and sought to redress the balance.

Before Raw magazine got involved, the show was known as The Power Hour, originally presented by Dante Bonutto and Amanda Redington, and later by Alison Craig, Jacky Lynn and Nikki Groocock. It used to be shown from 1985 to 1990 on cable and satellite music channel Music Box, which stopped being a channel on its own to become producer of music shows for major British broadcasters including ITV.

The theme tune of Raw Power was an edited version of the guitar solo from "Love in an Elevator" by Aerosmith. The show was filmed at The Marquee in London and on various locations across the country, in Europe and the USA. Megadeth and Pantera were also used as theme tunes on Raw Power and Noisy Mothers.

3.6.2 Presenters

Originally presented by Phil Alexander (then editor of *Raw* magazine) and Nikki Groocock, the show was later to feature Ann Kirk replacing Nikki Groocock in mid-1991. Ann Kirk was the producer of later episodes of The Power Hour and created and produced "Raw Power" and "Noisy Mothers". Phil Alexander was replaced by Krusher as presenter and also appeared in a segment entitled *Krusher's Kouch* (later in Noisy Mothers *Krusher's Kosmos*). The show was Directed by Andrew Nicholson and Jerry Duller. The segment would always start with Krusher's greeting of *"Droogies, boozers, strumpets and losers"* and featured CD reviews, competitions and irreverent comment. Krusher would usually be accompanied by a Jack Russell Terrier named *Bullseye* (who died in 1995).

Later editions also featured various bands presenting the show, including The Almighty, Thunder, Alice Cooper, Megadeth, Iron Maiden and Motörhead and later on Noisy Mothers, Sepultura, Pride & Glory, Extreme, and Paradise Lost. Raw Power/Noisy Mothers would film band performances and cover the major rock festivals such as Donington Monsters of Rock and Reading. Bands performances filmed include The Black Crowes, Blind Melon, and Megadeth. Raw Power and Noisy Mothers won "Best TV Show" category in all the Rock Music Magazines in Britain during its run on ITV.

3.6.3 References

3.6.4 External links

Raw Power / Noisy Mothers at the Internet Movie Database

3.7 Terrorizer (magazine)

Terrorizer is an extreme music magazine published by Dark Arts Ltd. in the United Kingdom. It is released every four weeks with thirteen issues a year and features a "Fear Candy" covermount CD, a twice yearly "Fear Candy Unsigned" CD, and a double-sided poster.

3.7.1 History

1993

Terrorizer published its first issue in October 1993[2] with Sepultura on the cover and a price of £1.95. "Sure, the layout was a bit ropey, with several 'cut out'-style pictures in the live section and some horribly lo-fi video stills in the Pestilence feature, but what a line-up of bands! Sepultura, Morgoth, Entombed, Morbid Angel, At the Gates, Coroner, Dismember, Sinister, Death...it was a veritable smorgasbord of brutality."[3]

The magazine's name derives from seminal grindcore band Terrorizer (which got the name from the death metal band Master's first demo in 1985)[4] and as such the magazine was an early champion of the emerging death metal scene, a tradition that it carried on and expanded to include all sub-generes of heavy metal adopting the slogan "extreme music - no boundaries" in 2003 with issue 108, also the first part of the Thrash Special.

After a second issue with cover stars Carcass, the then editor, Rob Clymo, took a risk by putting Metallica on the cover which, although it caused controversy with elitists, symbolised a move towards broader musical coverage. Despite this, *Terrorizer*'s pulse remained firmly on the extreme metal underground with Cradle of Filth winning best demo and Fear Factory best newcomer in the 1993 Readers' Poll.

1994–1995

Issue 11 saw *Terrorizer* celebrate its first birthday, covering hardcore punk in force with features on Suicidal Tendencies, Madball, Chaos UK and Pro-Pain. "There was a sense that the team were finally properly honouring the magazine's original pledge to cover all forms of extreme music."[3]

In 1994, death metal began to get wider acceptance in the mainstream metal press, but black metal continued to be vilified or ridiculed, or both, creating a gap that *Terrorizer* filled by giving pages to bands like Enslaved, Emperor and Dissection, whilst the demo reviews continued to beat the trend, getting first listens of Behemoth and Amon Amarth.

The first covermount CD, entitled *Noize Pollution 3* (the first two having been cassettes), appeared on issue 23 in 1995 and featured At the Gates, Six Feet Under, In Flames, Moonspell and Dissection. That year, *Terrorizer* also launched two phone services, "Deathline" and "Metal Mates", that were swiftly discontinued. "The former was a number you could call to actually listen to the whole of the interviews you'd read snippets of in the magazine, and the latter where you could register your personal details with a metal matchmaking agency."[3]

1996–1998

With issue 28 in 1996, Nick Terry replaced Rob Clymo as editor and the issue saw a Burzum artwork poster. With issue 29, the new editor overhauled and expanded the album reviews, live reviews and introduced a black metal news column. The next two years were dominated by black metal vs hardcore punk debates, as the two forces then dominant in extreme music came head-to-head in the magazine. Issue 33 also featured a demo review of Public Disturbance, a Cardiff-based hardcore band whose members would go on to form Lostprophets. In 1997, the first incarnation of the *Terrorizer* website was launched; Emperor, Deicide, Vader and the return of Mayhem made the covers, and hardcore continued to get heavy coverage with Integrity, Shelter, the reformed Agnostic Front and a UK HC scene report that introduced Knuckledust.

In 1998, coverage embraced both nu metal (albeit in a critical fashion), which the magazine tried to christen 'woolly hat' music, as well as more traditional fare; the former, however, saw them receive a great deal of criticism from the underground. *Terrorizer* also featured the last ever interview with Death frontman Chuck Schuldiner in issue 59. Although the next year saw the emergence of noisecore with Neurosis, Today Is the Day and The Dillinger Escape Plan, Slipknot, who would receive a cover by issue 73, got their first interview. Joey Jordison would later reveal how he had been reading the magazine since its first issue.

Terrorizer released its first cover mounted CD on its December 1998 issue and did so every four months until 2001, which it was released every two months. From 2002, every issue came with a CD.

1999–present

Terrorizer ended 1999 with a Christmas show that saw Hecate Enthroned and Akercocke support Morbid Angel at The Astoria 2 in London. In late 2000, Jonathan Selzer replaced Nick Terry as editor and 2001 saw a doom metal revival with coverage of Cathedral and Spirit Caravan so intensive that British doom metallers Warning split up following an argument inspired by quotes in their *Terrorizer* interview that year.[3]

Issue 91 saw cover placement for London-based Satanic metallers Akercocke and later coverage of emerging British black metallers Anaal Nathrakh which would culminate in the previously studio-only band headlining *Terrorizer*'s 2005 Christmas event, "A Cold Night in Hell", as their first ever live appearance. With news of Chuck Schuldiner's death, issue 97 saw him appear on the cover in tribute along with six pages inside.

For issue 116, the covermount CD changed its name from "Terrorized" (then on its 26th volume) to "Fear Candy" and is currently on its 70th volume, with some volumes given over to the yearly "Fear Candy Unsigned" (previously called "The Abominable Showcase") CD in which unsigned bands compete for an interview in the magazine. For 2006, the "Fear Candy Unsigned" was mounted on the CD along with a regular "Fear Candy". Previous entrants for the "Fear Candy Unsigned" who have since had a level of success include Season's End, a symphonic metal band now on I Records, zombie-themed thrash band Send More Paramedics on In at the Deep End Records, post-hardcore band Million Dead (now split-up) and avant-garde grindcore band Tangaroa on Anticulture Records.

In September 2007, Jonathan Selzer left *Terrorizer* for *Metal Hammer*, and was replaced as editor by Joseph Stannard, the magazine's news editor until that time. Currently the role of editor is occupied by former *Rock Sound* and *Kerrang!* staffer Darren Sadler, after previous editor Louise Brown left *Terrorizer* to create specialist heavy metal magazine *Iron Fist*. Other roles are filled by Tom Dare (web editor), Darrell Mayhew (designer) and notable contributors include Morat, Ronnie Kerswell-O'Hara, Olivier "Zoltar" Badin, Jose Carlos Santos, Kim Kelly, John Mincemoyer, J. Bennett, Lee Macbride, Mike Kemp, Ian Glasper and Kevin Stewart-Panko.

3.7.2 Genre Specials

To date *Terrorizer* has produced nine genre specials and one "issue" special, the Art Special, part one of the Black Metal Special being the magazine's second best selling single issue on the UK newsstands and part one of the second Prog Special.

Punk Special (#96, 2002)

Initiated to celebrate the 25th anniversary of punk hitting the mainstream with the Sex Pistols' appearance on *Today* with Bill Grundy, the cover featured a striking image of a spikey haired female punk and led with a feature on Alan Parker's newly released punk history, *England's Dreaming*, all the punk retrospectives across CD, DVD and book were compiled into one reviews spread, appropriately followed by a feature on punk reissues, a feature on anarcho-punk, the UK's DIY punk underground, the validity of US claims to 'inventing' punk versus UK claims, Oi!, hardcore punk, the punk/metal crossover, and the legacy of punk in post-punk, industrial and goth, interviews with Deadline, Sick on the Bus, Bad Religion, Alec Empire and author Stewart Home. The special ended on a list of the top 50 punk albums, which was topped by Discharge's *Hear Nothing See Nothing Say Nothing*.

Gore Special (#98, 2002)

With a Necrophagia cover designed to mimic the EC Comics horror titles of the 1950s, the Gore Special opened with a four page Necrophagia interview, a Desecration interview, a Goregrind Round-Up that included Autopsy and Visceral Bleeding, a feature on cover art, censorship, horror movies and Gorerotted's own top ten.

Prog Special (#101, 2002)

Cover stars Arcturus and Opeth were photoshopped to hold the glowing covermount CD, a design that failed with the last minute change from a clear CD sleeve to a card one. The special opened with "A Brief History of Prog", an interview with Arcturus, Opeth, Ihsahn, Rush, Dream Theater and Cave In. A feature on the prog/metal crossover and a top ten.

Thrash Special (#108 & #109, 2003)

The first special to be done in multiple parts, issue 108 feature Anthrax's Scott Ian on the cover and 109 featured Nuclear Assault. The *Terrorizer* logo was coloured to resemble a classic thrash metal logo and the Thrash Special logo done as a patch on a denim background.

Part one started with a history of thrash, an interview with Anthrax, Overkill, Warhammer and Voivod, an overview of the global thrash metal scene, personal recollections from members of Testament, Kreator and Destruction as well as former *Metal Forces* editor Bernard Doe and producer Andy Sneap. Reviews of classic gigs and overview of the main labels involved.

Part two opened with cover-stars Nuclear Assault, the second part of the global thrash report, classic gigs and the personal recollections, an overview of forgotten bands, politics, thrash fashion, crossover thrash, the legacy of thrash, the art of Ed Repka and a top twenty trumped by Slayer's *Reign in Blood*.

Black Metal Special (#128, #129 & #130, 2005)

Opening with a striking Pete Beste image of Satyricon/1349's Frost breathing fire, the first part of the Black Metal Special opened with a brief history of black metal entitled "The Boys from the Black Stuff", a look at the black metal scene in Europe, the philosophy of black metal, the top twenty of the first wave, and a look at the black metal underground.

Part two of the black metal special began with a look at Supernatural Records, black metal labels, the scene in South America, the top twenty of the second wave, the black metal mainstream and the scene in North America. The third part contained a look at the scene in the UK and Ireland, Scandinavia, Australasia and a look at post-black metal.

Power Metal Special (#135, #136 & #137, 2005)

Part one of the Power Metal Special featured a DragonForce cover, a brief history of the genre, a look at the scene in Germany and in the UK as well as interviews with DragonForce and Dream Theater. The poster had Manowar on one side and the fantasy art of Paul Raymond Gregory on the other. Another fantasy artist, Chris Achilléos, gave a harsh blow-by-blow critique of power metal album covers.

The second part contained an interview with Stratovarius, a scene report from the USA, a look at power metal labels and selection of prominent power metal artists. The issue also contained a Judas Priest poster. Part three contained an interview with Gamma Ray and Helloween, a scene report for Europe, a top twenty and an A-to-Z of power metal themes.

Doom Special (#142, #143 & #144, 2006)

Although only the first part dominated the cover, a Black Sabbath-era image of Ozzy Osbourne, the Doom Special featured a specially compiled *Bleak and Destroyed* compilation CD that included classic tracks by The Obsessed, Pentagram, Candlemass, My Dying Bride, Reverend Bizarre, Witchcraft and more. Part one began with a look at Black Sabbath, a review of the entire Black Sabbath discography, a double-sided Cathedral and Wino poster, a look at 'true doom', death/doom and oral histories from Scott "Wino" Weinrich and Sunn O)))'s Greg Anderson.

The second part featured a look at the 'true doom' community, doom labels, funeral doom/drone, oral histories from Candlemass's Leif Edling, Trouble's Eric Wagner, Saint Vitus' Dave Chandler and Cathedral's Lee Dorian. The issue also looked at stoner/sludge, doom artwork, the impact that doom had on the music world at large and posters of Electric Wizard and My Dying Bride.

Part three opened with a look at the doom scene in Maryland, Virginia and DC, themes in doom, concepts of sin and suffering in doom, forgotten doom, oral histories from Solitude's John Perez, Pentagram's Victor Griffin, My Dying Bride's Aaron Stainthorpe, and Sunn O)))/Khanate's Stephen O'Malley. Ending with a doom metal top ten for each of the main subgenres.

Death Metal Special (#148, #149, #150 & #151, 2006)

The Death Metal Special has been the largest special to date, spanning four issues. The first, with a Deicide cover, contains an extensive history of the genre, a look at the scene in Florida and Stockholm, a double-sided Morbid Angel and Deicide poster, a look at progressive death metal and oral histories from Cannibal Corpse's Alex Webster and The Haunted/At the Gates' Anders Björler.

The second part opened with an interview with Albert Mudrian, author of *Choosing Death: The Improbable History of Death Metal and Grindcore*, a Gothenburg scene report, an article on death metal artwork and the over-the-top sounds of Anal Cunt and Lawnmower Deth. Also included were oral histories from Immolation's Ross Dolan and Nile's Karl Sanders. The third part, the issue also including a feature on Napalm Death and a tribute to Napalm Death/Terrorizer's Jesse Pintado who died August 24, launched with a look at the role tape-trading played in the growth of the genre, death metal in Eastern Europe (in particular, Vader, Decapitated and Behemoth), and in the UK (Carcass, Bolt Thrower, Napalm Death and Akercocke), as well as oral histories from Deicide's Glen Benton and Incantation's John McEntee before closing with an examination of the death/grind crossover.

Part four may have contained less death metal specific content than the first part, but it finished the series with an eighteen track covermount compilation CD, part sponsored by UK satellite channel Redemption TV. The CD featured a broad history of the genre, including tracks by Carcass, Repulsion, Autopsy, Morbid Angel, Deicide, Bolt Thrower, Cannibal Corpse, Entombed, Atheist, Obituary, Malevolent Creation, Nile, Suffocation, At the Gates, Cryptopsy, Dying Fetus, Hate Eternal and Behemoth. Due to licensing problems incurred by the death of Combat Records, Death and Possessed were noticeably absent. The rest of the magazine contained oral histories from Morbid Angel's Trey Azagthoth, Obituary's John Tardy and Cryptopsy's Flo Mounier, a roundtable discussion with the participating bands of the Swedish Masters of Death Tour (Dismember, Unleashed, Grave and Entombed), a look at the death metal scene in Canada, the labels that were involved in the genre's genesis and finally a death metal top 40.

Prog Special (The Return of Prog) (#161, #162 & #163 2007)

Although covered previously in 2002, then News Editor Joseph Stannard felt that progressive rock needed another go, kick-starting a three part Prog Special. Issue 161, to date the best selling issue of the magazine, featured Rush, Sean Malone, a feature on Prog into Metal, Oral Histories with Voivod's Away, Van der Graaf Generator's Peter Hammill, Jethro Tull's Ian Anderson, Zombi's AE Paterra and Genesis's Steve Hackett. Issue 162 contained an interview with Aghora, a feature on progressive rock art and a top ten album sleeves, Oral Histories with Dream Theater's Mike Portnoy and James Labrie, Akercocke's Jason Mendoca and The Nice's Davy O'List. Bringing up the rear was an article on progressive hardcore and forgotten classics of prog. Issue 163 concluded the special with Oral Histories from Jesu's Justin Broadrick and former Yes man Rick Wakeman, features on krautrock, Lee Dorrian's sizeable record collection, the Satanic prog of Coven and others, as well as "Twenty Essential '70s Prog Albums". Positive feedback for the special was registered both in the letters page and in a later feature conducted with Opeth's Mikael Åkerfeldt.[5]

3.7.3 Terrorizer Online

Launched in the autumn of 2007, *Terrorizer Online* is a weekly ezine characterised by a more personal and irreverent tone, frequently introduced by various members of the editorial team directly. In addition to this, the newsletter features exclusive content, ranging from reviews to alternative versions of lead features such as Down, Apocalyptica, Today Is the Day, Dam, Testament, Cannibal Corpse, Pestilence and completely original interviews with Massacre, Finntroll, The Locust, Sepultura, Bad Brains, Wintersun and Iced Earth.

3.7.4 John Peel

British radio DJ John Peel, famously a champion of death metal and grindcore, revealed himself to be a fan of the magazine in an episode of *Home Truths* on BBC Radio 4.

"...I took several copies of a music magazine called 'Terrorizer' out of my luggage before leaving for New Zealand via Los Angeles in 2002 and given the hostility of the officials we encountered in California I'd say we did the right thing..."[6]

3.7.5 Writers

Terrorizer 's pool of writers includes former Stampin' Ground bassist Ian Glasper, who has also written three books on UK punk, *Burning Britain: The History of UK Punk, 1980–1984*, *The Day the Country Died: A History of Anarcho Punk 1980–1984* and *Trapped in a Scene: UK Hardcore 1985–1989*, former Cradle of Filth keyboard player Damien (aka Greg Moffitt), comedy writer and Moss drummer Chris Chantler and guest columns from Fenriz, Today Is the Day's Steve Austin, Amon Amarth's Johan Hegg, Brutal Truth's Kevin Sharp and The Haunted's Peter Dolving.

3.7.6 References

[1] Yardley, Miranda: *Who We Are*, 19 April 2010, accessed on 20 April 2013.

[2] Andy R. Brown (2007). ""Everything Louder than Everything Else"". *Journalism Studies* **8** (4). Retrieved 10 November 2015.

[3] "The Age of Extremity", *Terrorizer #100*.

[4] "May the Source Be with You", *Terrorizer #149*.

[5] "Progressive Revelation", *Terrorizer #164*.

[6] "John Peel (1939–2004)", *Terrorizer #126*.

3.7.7 External links

- The *Terrorizer* website
- The official *Terrorizer* profile on Myspace
- The *Terrorizer* forum

3.8 Zero Tolerance (magazine)

Zero Tolerance Magazine is an extreme music magazine published by Obdurate Ltd. in the United Kingdom. Published bi-monthly, it can be found on newsstands in the UK, Europe and North America - and is available (with some delay) on newsstands in Australia and specialist retailers in New Zealand and Taiwan. The magazine features a covermount CD.

It was launched in 2004 by Lisa Macey (formerly publisher of *Terrorizer Magazine*) and Leon Macey (of experimental UK extreme metal band Mithras). The magazine is edited by Nathan T.Birk. Previous editors are Calum Harvie and Lee du-Caine.

Zero Tolerance Magazine gives coverage to both established extreme music artists and underground artists without the balance of coverage tipping in favour of the most obvious artists. ZT is especially notable for seeking out obscure artists in experimental noise music and power electronics - a 4 page section entitled Power Lines is curated by the magazine's resident noise "expert" Scott McKeating and features every issue. With Nathan T. Birk curating the Underground Black Metal (UGBM) section and the recent introduction of the Cormac O'Síocháin curated Anger Burning section - dedicated to crust, d-beat, rawpunk, hardcore-punk and dis-core - the magazine covers metal as well as similar genres.

Industry features with visual artists, directors, music producers and the like have been regular in *Zero Tolerance Magazine* since its launch in 2004 and the magazine has been home to interviews with the likes of HR Giger, Dan Seagrave, John Carpenter and Andy Sneap.

Contributors, referred to as "The Panel", hail from the UK, North America, continental Europe, and Australia. Notable regular contributors include Chris Kee, Alan Averill aka Nemtheanga of Primordial, Cormac O'Síocháin, Scott McKeating, John Norby, Liz Ciavarella, Callum Brownson-Smith and MetalGeorge.

[1] [2] [3] [4] [5]

[1] Zero Tolerance Magazine, print-based magazine

[2] http://www.ztmag.com

[3] https://www.facebook.com/zerotolerancemagazine

[4] Brown, Mark. *The Guardian Newspaper*, 2006

[5] Various contributors. *Zero Tolerance Magazine*, 2004-2011

3.8.1 External links

- *Zero Tolerance* Magazine
- *Zero Tolerance* Facebook
- *Zero Tolerance* Magazine MySpace

Chapter 4

Text and image sources, contributors, and licenses

4.1 Text

- **New Wave of British Heavy Metal** *Source:* https://en.wikipedia.org/wiki/New_Wave_of_British_Heavy_Metal?oldid=690833180 *Contributors:* The Anome, Amillar, SimonP, Edward, Lexor, TUF-KAT, Jonik, Morwen, Toreau, Pigsonthewing, Iam, Sbisolo, Sam Spade, MikeCapone, Gwalla, Mintleaf~enwiki, Wiki Wikardo, Golbez, R. fiend, SURIV, Child of Bodom, Phil Sandifer, Bumm13, Vim Fuego, MementoVivere, RevRagnarok, An Siarach, Necromancer~enwiki, Clawed, Reeeno, Auto movil, Xezbeth, Martpol, Bender235, Jaberwocky6669, CanisRufus, Shanes, BarkingFish, Nicke Lilltroll~enwiki, Na2rboy, Petdance, Gargaj, Joost~enwiki, Iothiania, Ashley Pomeroy, Dkikizas, CloudNine, Wadems, Kevinskogg, Red dwarf, Blufive, Firsfron, Jackel, Kzollman, Mestesso, GregorB, Graham87, Qwertyus, Rjwilmsi, Tim!, Salix alba, Fish and karate, FlaBot, Margosbot~enwiki, YurikBot, RobotE, Foxxygirltamara, C777, CambridgeBayWeather, Cryptic, Wiki alf, Veledan, ONEder Boy, Anetode, Zwobot, Preziuiwf, Bota47, Wknight94, E tac, Mitchell k dwyer, Little Savage, Nae'blis, Meegs, WesleyDodds, Sardanaphalus, KnightRider~enwiki, SmackBot, Zazaban, Hatto, PJM, Mr Pyles, Pasajero, Kakun, Yamaguchi??, Portillo, GeorgeBuchanan, Chris the speller, Mokwella, Jprg1966, Thumperward, MalafayaBot, Colonies Chris, VirtualSteve, Chipsy, Daddy Kindsoul, Racklever, Gohst, Anarchodin, Crispin Giles, Mwtoews, COLUFAN1, Bretonbanquet, Deepred6502, TullFan2000, Vildricianus, Thesmothete, RedArrow21, Gusiman, Robofish, Butko, Draco Ignis, Majorclanger, SQGibbon, Mr Stephen, Kseferovic, Dl2000, Ryouga, BranStark, OnBeyondZebrax, Spark, Alygator, Anger22, CmdrObot, WeggeBot, URORIN, Womble bee, Itsgotbigteeth69, Sparkiplasma, AKnot, Fair Deal, Gogo Dodo, Blackmetalbaz, Fonetikli, DumbBOT, Inhumer, Andyschism, PamD, Thijs!bot, Luminifer, Hervegirod, Marek69, GirlWithBlackEye, Okki, Mr. Brain, Ddude87, Siggis, Gary cumberland, Prolog, I'll bring the food, JAnDbot, Deflective, Matthew Fennell, MegX, Amaccormack, VoABot II, DFS, Jamo.au, JNW, Twsx, Kameejl, Clear air turbulence, Spellmaster, Grinder0-0, Squidward247, FMAFan1990, Garret Beaumain, Sleeper141, NewEnglandYankee, JSellers0, Imagi-King, MaxThonder, Gordlogan, Smiling Bob117, Jaguar83, Gothbag, Stranger4001, Cbj77, AlnoktaBOT, Asarlaí, Magnius, Papa Ul, Headmess, Nihiliststar, Anna Lincoln, IllaZilla, Jotsko, Abdullais4u, UnitedStatesian, Yaakov Pinus, Gibson Flying V, Maxim, Dirty Hoghead, Metalion SOS, IL7Soulhunter, Zifirl, Rock Soldier, AlleborgoBot, Funeral, Logical Defense, Anarchist92, Kirazoglu, Gus, Peter Fleet, SieBot, Scarian, N-HH, Da Joe, Gordomebix, Rplant1961, Nigel C. Fortune, Mustangs0098, Nite-Sirk, Meman1234567890, Klippdass, Aspects, Debil13, TallShip108, Navnløs, Bospo, Axelriv, Fishnet37222, Florentyna, Metaldetector, Cibomatto, Impmope, ClueBot, Broadbandmink, Cagedfish, Binksternet, Hesky10, Albert Mond, Mezigue, Skeeball93, Niceguyedc, Bardin, Deathbringer from the Sky, Nymf, Eignatus, Eeekster, RCBobEdwards, Vbhargava, Wiki libs, Ostalocutanje, AN OLD MAN, Cantor, Indopug, DumZiBoT, Themetalicaruz, Gnowor, Poyumat, SilvonenBot, Alexius08, Addbot, Malconfort, RandySavageFTW, Fieldday-sunday, TPainRoxx, Thefinn666, The Shadow-Fighter, Nickin, Getting Hotter, Angry Shoplifter, Tassedethe, Travelling Tragition, Spacefan75, PlankBot, Yobot, Ptbotgourou, Wailer, Guy1890, Nallimbot, Camcdonalduk, AnomieBOT, Choij, Galoubet, Materialscientist, Mista13, ArthurBot, Xqbot, Wether B, Axelsegen, TheWeakWilled, Zerst, 3family6, FilthMerchant, Aussie Ausborn, Omnipaedista, RibotBOT. Sabrebd, Infanteriesoldat, GripTheHusk, Harkowl, Brianbek, Serbianboy, Wikiandbas, Magne62, Colchester121891, Riccy52, TheStrayCat, Rockgenre, RojizoMaster, Fozforus, Tbhotch, Lassewikman, DARTH SIDIOUS 2, Ripchip Bot, NwObHm1980, Ajraddatz, Lewismaster, ITshnik, Mashaunix, GoingBatty, Buccaneers123, Portgowerboy, ABC paulista, 1998metalhead1, Dawntrader, DeeAngel, Ian Gillmore, NicholasJr7, Tinalee32, Rocketrod1960, ClueBot NG, CactusBot, Maison Dijon, Razzman50, Nerdtrap, Martimsaintive, Curb Chain, BG19bot, ThrashingHeavy, Cyberpower678, 30 hertz, Jap17274, Tubesmer, Brayness, Myxomatosis57, Khazar2, Esszet, Movario, Brutalfrank, Bwaren, ClaytonLovesJesus, Epping232, Batamamma, Thrashmaniac99, Yilku1, Pubdomino, Synthwave.94, JudasPriestFanatic, Noyster, Bringerofmetal, Carlos Rojas77, Abbotttracey, Peter33p, 101blacksun, Sj666 and Anonymous: 597

- **A II Z** *Source:* https://en.wikipedia.org/wiki/A_II_Z?oldid=686812985 *Contributors:* Mushroom, RJFJR, Woohookitty, Jemiller226, Rjwilmsi, Isotope23, NawlinWiki, Thiseye, Rmky87, Peter, SmackBot, Elonka, Bluebot, Daddy Kindsoul, Greenshed, Headshaker, BrownHairedGirl, Siva1979, Dl2000, The Haunted Angel, J Milburn, CmdrObot, Pit-yacker, Katherine Tredwell, Andyjsmith, Gay Cdn, BeastmasterGeneral, TAnthony, MegX, .anacondabot, Grinder0-0, Horstvonludwig, Stranger4001, WOSlinker, Barkeep, James25402, Florentyna, Arjayay, Addbot, LaaknorBot, Lightbot, Yobot, Marauder09, Xqbot, RjwilmsiBot, Lewismaster, Bryce Carmony, CactusBot, Amroknian, Sabbatino, KasparBot and Anonymous: 10

- **Angel Witch** *Source:* https://en.wikipedia.org/wiki/Angel_Witch?oldid=686810680 *Contributors:* Andrewman327, Floydian, Pigsonthewing, Postdlf, Naufana, Alvestrand, Bumm13, Xezbeth, Sn0wflake, Aranel, CanisRufus, Warpozio, Cmcrjameson, Giraffedata, Kamyar~enwiki,

Walter Görlitz, Selena von Eichendorf, MrSomeone, Rjwilmsi, Florian Huber, YurikBot, Cryptic, Lu3ke, SmackBot, Mr Pyles, Thumperward, ShogunMaximus, Marcus Brute, Dl2000, Cydebot, Fair Deal, Blackmetalbaz, BeastmasterGeneral, MegX, Markoff Chaney, Serge ZZ, Imagi-King, Bogartotron, Lorddragyn, Headmess, Inx272, Ecgecg, Gus, Lordofgore, James25402, Cyfal, Martarius, De728631, Simon Villeneuve, Blackless, Tuzapicabit, Mr Larrington, Jax 0677, XLinkBot, TheSickBehemoth, Addbot, LaaknorBot, Kigconker1, Lightbot, PlankBot, Yobot, Arch stanton1138, Piano non troppo, Ant smusher, Marauder09, SAULGNRFAN, WikiWikingerX, DefaultsortBot, Josexamf, RedBot, Pikiwyn, Hemert, Swork21, Dayvog, EmausBot, Nebelmond, Lewismaster, GoingBatty, Bollyjeff, L1A1 FAL, Olderthantimeitself, Amroknian, Noclassfanzine, DokkenRocker100, Danroush, Tatask89, Calebbro, KasparBot and Anonymous: 72

- **Atomkraft** *Source:* https://en.wikipedia.org/wiki/Atomkraft?oldid=686810978 *Contributors:* SimonP, Postdlf, Ravn, Pmsyyz, CanisRufus, Art LaPella, Megan1967, Exxolon, Mandarax, Rjwilmsi, FlaBot, RobinH~enwiki, RussBot, The Obfuscator, ZhaoHong, Pasajero, Zytsef, Bluebot, Derek R Bullamore, Angryxpeh, Dl2000, Asatruer, ShelfSkewed, Womble bee, Cydebot, Chubbles, Memset, MegX, CCS81, Imagi-King, VolkovBot, Rei-bot, Vinyl999, Oxymoron83, Martarius, LoserJoke, Carriearchdale, XLinkBot, Addbot, Iberesfo, Angry Shoplifter, Yobot, Amirobot, Marauder09, ArthurBot, DefaultsortBot, Lewismaster, Burbridge92, ClueBot NG, Hrossharsgrani, Gabriel Redon, KasparBot and Anonymous: 27

- **Avenger (British band)** *Source:* https://en.wikipedia.org/wiki/Avenger_(British_band)?oldid=676039458 *Contributors:* Violetriga, The JPS, Woohookitty, Rjwilmsi, RussBot, Colonies Chris, Dl2000, CmdrObot, Cydebot, Chubbles, Imagi-King, VolkovBot, Themetalicaruz, XLinkBot, Hetfield81, Ct1976 da, Addbot, Download, Tassedethe, Yobot, J Milburn Bot, AnomieBOT, Marauder09, Thehuntersmetal, DefaultsortBot, EmausBot, Lewismaster, Jenks24, Burbridge92, CactusBot, Jelmerdw, Ruby Murray, Wordsalad1 and Anonymous: 17

- **Baby Tuckoo** *Source:* https://en.wikipedia.org/wiki/Baby_Tuckoo?oldid=676044360 *Contributors:* Derek R Bullamore, Dl2000, Ilion2, Odd-MNilsen, The Thing That Should Not Be, UnCatBot, LilHelpa, Lewismaster, Cotefarm, Killmeister, Melonkelon and Anonymous: 7

- **Battleaxe (band)** *Source:* https://en.wikipedia.org/wiki/Battleaxe_(band)?oldid=679242321 *Contributors:* Eugene van der Pijll, Lowellian, Oberiko, Bedders, CanisRufus, 119, Dismas, The JPS, Jpers36, Rjwilmsi, Windchaser, Bgwhite, DanMS, SmackBot, Chris the speller, Shadowlynk, BillFlis, Dl2000, Karenjc, Cydebot, Gonzo fan2007, Eugenespeed, VoABot II, Feidb, Somearemoreequal, Lady Mondegreen, MartinBot, Keith D, Don Cuan, Rei-bot, James25402, Dlrohrer2003, Sun Creator, GFHandel, XLinkBot, Addbot, Angry Shoplifter, PlankBot, Luckas-bot, Yobot, Ant smusher, Marauder09, Methcub, DefaultsortBot, John of Reading, Lewismaster, Burbridge92, FytTigersharq, FTRM, Makecat-bot, KasparBot and Anonymous: 30

- **Black Rose (UK band)** *Source:* https://en.wikipedia.org/wiki/Black_Rose_(UK_band)?oldid=676045365 *Contributors:* Bearcat, Woohookitty, BD2412, McGeddon, Dl2000, Cydebot, JaGa, CommonsDelinker, Logan, LoserJoke, Icarusgeek, Sun Creator, XLinkBot, Ben Ben, Yobot, AnomieBOT, FrescoBot, I dream of horses, John of Reading, Lewismaster, GoingBatty, Razzman50, BG19bot, Amroknian, Cyberbot II and Anonymous: 5

- **Blitzkrieg (band)** *Source:* https://en.wikipedia.org/wiki/Blitzkrieg_(band)?oldid=681710863 *Contributors:* Andres, Bumm13, Fls, Rich Farmbrough, Spearhead, Cecil, Jeff3000, Exxolon, Bruce1ee, Maverick Leonhart, BOT-Superzerocool, SmackBot, Knightmare, LuciferMorgan, Carbonrodney, AWeenieMan, Cobain, OrphanBot, The Elfoid, Guroadrunner, Dl2000, UncleDouggie, JohnCD, Skeletor2112, WeggeBot, Cydebot, AdmiralvonAxehaufen, Blackmetalbaz, Fisherjs, Ilion2, Dark Devil, MetsBot, MiltonT, OddMNilsen, Fleebo, Electriccarz, Labalius, MysteryCereal, Zifirl, AlleborgoBot, Scarian, Khvalamde, Binksternet, Deathbringer from the Sky, Sicbot, Brett dixon metallica, XLinkBot, Jcinicola, Dark Mage, TheSickBehemoth, Cochese516, SlubGlub, Addbot, Download, Nickin, Lightbot, Luckas-bot, Yobot, Themfromspace, Legobot II, Arch stanton1138, Materialscientist, Marauder09, GrouchoBot, LucienBOT, DefaultsortBot, Lewismaster, ZéroBot, Guitarist0407, Franckverre, Burbridge92, ClueBot NG, Gareth Griffith-Jones, Derpguy101, Nerfhurrdurr, Meatsgains, Blitzkrieginfo, KasparBot and Anonymous: 40

- **Bronz** *Source:* https://en.wikipedia.org/wiki/Bronz?oldid=676045620 *Contributors:* Bearcat, Daelin, SMC, AllyD, Huw Powell, Bondegezou, SmackBot, LuciferMorgan, Bluebot, Colonies Chris, Derek R Bullamore, BNutzer, TenPoundHammer, Bronz~enwiki, CmdrObot, Neodammerung, Ken Gallagher, Cydebot, Nick Number, Dark Gravity, Appraiser, Imagi-King, GrahamHardy, The Thing That Should Not Be, Mr. Laser Beam, Wiki libs, Tassedethe, Infanteriesoldat, HJ Mitchell, DefaultsortBot, Alan Pront, Cgmp, Lewismaster, Slurpee242, Eestimaa, Dipankan001, Khazar2, IanBaker2903 and Anonymous: 41

- **Budgie (band)** *Source:* https://en.wikipedia.org/wiki/Budgie_(band)?oldid=686274172 *Contributors:* Kpjas, Zoe, Quercusrobur, Bagpuss, TUF-KAT, Michael, Milkfish, Jimregan, DJ Clayworth, Saltine, Iam, RedWolf, Djinn112, Kusunose, Ingman, Bjorn1101, Justin Foote, Rich Farmbrough, Ahkond, Xezbeth, Hapsiainen, Spearhead, Func, Sun King, Someoneinmyheadbutit'snotme, Japanese Searobin, Bjones, Jdcooper, Rjwilmsi, FlaBot, RussBot, Welsh, Recordco, Patrick Neylan, PeepP, Prezuiwf, Shyam, WesleyDodds, Zanoni, SmackBot, Mr Pyles, Squibman, Greenshed, Derek R Bullamore, John, GilbertoSilvaFan, E-Kartoffel, HisSpaceResearch, NickS, Malcolmvxx, Anger22, CmdrObot, Speedking90, Bonás, Random name, ShelfSkewed, Cydebot, Fair Deal, Blackmetalbaz, Thijs!bot, Kubanczyk, Luminifer, Rrose Selavy, Mr. Brain, JustAGal, Andrzejbanas, Mclaren jk, Canadiana, BeastmasterGeneral, MegX, Bongwarrior, Cal42, Markoff Chaney, Al66, BoozBro, Farbowski, Welshleprechaun, Bloodyroots, Johnpacklambert, DandyDan2007, FruitMonkey, Bohemianroots, Doomsdayer520, Satani, Pwimageglow, Slysplace, ^demonBot2, Inx272, GlassFET, Pgroen, EndlessWires, Nite-Sirk, G00labek, Gumdropgas, Martarius, LoserJoke, PipepBot, Fyyer, Drmies, TheSpunkyLobster, Arjayay, Two Hearted River, DumZiBoT, TheSickBehemoth, WikHead, Addbot, RandySavageFTW, Nohomers48, DutchDevil, Daicaregos, Angry Shoplifter, Tassedethe, Kickboxer20008, PlankBot, Luckas-bot, Yobot, SAULGNRFAN, Thehuntersmetal, Archiveng, Bogustopping, GripTheHusk, FrescoBot, Misiekuk, FotoPhest, Citation bot 1, DefaultsortBot, Roupheinos, Evangp, Discographer, Rockgenre, John of Reading, Terry cubberley, Burbridge92, Knotrice, Capnwhit, Budgiefan, SSDGFCTCT9, CactusBot, Helpful Pixie Bot, Drblooter99, BG19bot, Justinius1, Glacialfox, FishFlower, Cyberbot II, Esszet, Bloomgloom, Svengali Rising, CJAllbee, Shallowmead077, Linuslimpansandberg, Synthwave.94, Kblogg777, KasparBot and Anonymous: 147

- **Chateaux (band)** *Source:* https://en.wikipedia.org/wiki/Chateaux_(band)?oldid=690911672 *Contributors:* Karst, Chris the speller, Dl2000, Blackmetalbaz, Lewismaster, Amroknian, H. 217.83, I call the big one bitey and Anonymous: 1

- **Chrome Molly** *Source:* https://en.wikipedia.org/wiki/Chrome_Molly?oldid=676045912 *Contributors:* Dl2000, Michig, Gongshow, FrescoBot, Lewismaster, Dewritech, Godfrey63, Sol1, Synthwave.94, 7Sidz, KasparBot and Anonymous: 2

- **Cloven Hoof (band)** *Source:* https://en.wikipedia.org/wiki/Cloven_Hoof_(band)?oldid=681388077 *Contributors:* Woohookitty, BD2412, Rjwilmsi, SmackBot, Bazonka, DéRahier, Derek R Bullamore, Dl2000, Radagast1983, Cydebot, BeastmasterGeneral, MetsBot, Kraftlos, Fingerpuppet, James25402, Martarius, Drmies, Cledus99, DumZiBoT, XLinkBot, Calakmul2003, Addbot, RandySavageFTW, Tassedethe, 2hats,

4.1. TEXT

Lightbot, Yobot, Spada2, Marauder09, SAULGNRFAN, Thehuntersmetal, Infanteriesoldat, LucienBOT, DefaultsortBot, Tim1357, Don Quixote is awesome, Lewismaster, Rogermsw, Amroknian, Khazar2, Dexbot, Stormriderritual, Theashcooper, KasparBot and Anonymous: 50

- **Dedringer** *Source:* https://en.wikipedia.org/wiki/Dedringer?oldid=676046376 *Contributors:* David Gerard, Woohookitty, DI2000, Blackmetalbaz, Tassedethe, Hiddenstranger, Lewismaster, Helpful Pixie Bot, BG19bot, Northamerica1000, Second Skin and Anonymous: 2

- **Def Leppard** *Source:* https://en.wikipedia.org/wiki/Def_Leppard?oldid=691119697 *Contributors:* Mav, Camembert, Mbecker, Tim Starling, Sannse, TUF-KAT, TUF-KAT, Jacquerie27, Cherkash, Hauser, Invalid username 12583~enwiki, RickK, FixerMX, JohnCastle, Alexina, Jni, Dale Arnett, Iam, RedWolf, Romanm, Merovingian, SchmuckyTheCat, Phthoggos, Mushroom, Dina, Angmering, Peruvianllama, Everyking, Gamaliel, Rick Block, Niteowlneils, Wronkiew, CryptoDerk, Gscshoyru, Nickptar, TJSwoboda, Jh51681, Sonett72, Esperant, Mike Rosoft, Freakofnurture, Discospinster, Bneely, Notinasnaid, CanisRufus, PhilHibbs, Mike Garcia, Longhair, Cmdrjameson, GTubio, Davidbix, Feduciary, DCEdwards1966, Hooperbloob, Stephen Bain, Storm Rider, Alansohn, Walter Görlitz, Phitzdisco, Derumi, Marianocecowski, Ebz123, Mad Hatter, LFaraone, Ndteegarden, Ianblair23, Someoneinmyheadbutit'snotme, SteinbDJ, Patito, Dopefish, Woohookitty, Vorash, JetsLuvver, AtomicMass, WadeSimMiser, Exxolon, Miwasatoshi, Floydgeo, Mizzou1307, BD2412, BorgHunter, Jdcooper, Bivariate-correlator, Koavf, Jweiss11, FutureNJGov, XLerate, Ligulem, Mcauburn, Dar-Ape, Elmtailye, FlaBot, Gringo300, Ian Pitchford, SchuminWeb, MacRusgail, RexNL, Redwolf24, Jay-W, JonathanFreed, Chobot, Xtfer, Gwernol, Cornellrockey, UkPaolo, YurikBot, Senafran, Tommyt, Extraordinary Machine, Karnak, Mr Frosty, RussBot, Hede2000, Ericorbit, Foxxygirltamara, Pauly0, Shell Kinney, MrAmazing8270, CambridgeBayWeather, Rsrikanth05, Stassats, Draeco, NawlinWiki, Armagod, Joel7687, Qirex, Justin Eiler, Harrow, Irishguy, Cholmes75, El Pollo Diablo, Bota47, Phantompong, BassPlyr23, Canuckguy, Mrbluesky, Orioane, Teiladnam, MadMoonchild, SMcCandlish, Little Savage, Kreinsch, Katieh5584, Meegs, Kingboyk, WesleyDodds, SmackBot, Brian1979, Ratarsed, Hux, 1dragon, Royalguard11, Pgk, LanceManion1973, C.Fred, Grandmaster, Hatto, KocjoBot~enwiki, Weatherman90, IainP, Lsommerer, Jab843, Mr Pyles, Provelt, DizietSma, Dither, Cavie78, Chris the speller, Bluebot, Scottboy79, Thanissaro, SweetP112, Thumperward, BabuBhatt, Miquonranger03, Spidremonkey, Ataricodfish, Kungming2, DHNbot~enwiki, Gracenotes, Yanksox, Thief12, Daddy Kindsoul, Can't sleep, clown will eat me, Multiman dan, Erayman64, OrphanBot, S ellinson, The Elfoid, Tdl1060, Jmlk17, Krich, Mmathu, Khukri, Nakon, Valenciano, Derek R Bullamore, Mtlcrue, Richard0612, Bretonbanquet, Curefreak, Ohconfucius, Thejerm, Spiritia, Mouse Nightshirt, Jqlr, Kuru, John, Babaroga, Aljullu, Breno, This user has left wikipedia, Werdan7, Cory pratt, SQGibbon, Monni95, Flibble, Jim McGowan, DI2000, Amitch, Ryouga, Wallstreethotrod, Scanz851, OnBeyondZebrax, Iridescent, Abog, DefLeppardVanHalen, Beno1000, Hedpeguyuk, Dirtydeeds7, Anger22, Rekoil, Sportsnut, RattleandHum, Alpha Ursae Minoris, Used1, The Prince of Darkness, CmdrObot, Evilasiangenius, TheMongoose, The ed17, Neelix, Irishninja1980, Eposty, Sopoforic, Cydebot, Fnlayson, Warhorus, Fair Deal, Gogo Dodo, TicketMan, Jcon91, Littlebadger, Dancter, Strom, BeachJediSC, HK51, RottweilerCS, MeWiseMagic, Vanished User jdksfajlasd, East 99 187killum, Krylonblue83, Mattisse, Thijs!bot, Epbr123, Thedarxide, Thellkid, Sry85, Mojo Hand, JSmith5150, 803290, Clay70, Mr. Brain, JustAGal, E. Ripley, Rasimkilic, Stupid cow5566, Michael A. White, Sliderjr2, Tombest, Jdodonnell, AntiVandalBot, Prolog, Dr. Blofeld, 3-14159, DarkAudit, 17Drew, The Phantom Blot, Roundhouse0, MikeLynch, Xnux, Husond, Sanchom, Roleplayer, MegX, DefDazz, Mr. Metalhead, The Equaliser, Y2kcrazyjoker4, LittleOldMe, JamieFoster, Bongwarrior, VoABot II, Todeskaefer, EMario, Gabe1972, Blabbone, Baccyak4H, Majestic Lizard, Theroadislong, Kameejl, Heywoodg, Ciaccona, Allstarecho, DerHexer, Philg88, Mokgamen, Anterdvizer, FisherQueen, Smaunsell, MartinBot, Ace900, D@ve, Sthrndixiecwgrl, Keith D, CommonsDelinker, Squidward247, FMAFan1990, J.delanoy, Kb1, Pharaoh of the Wizards, Scoopla1, Ali, Bogey97, 12dstring, Patricks110, Wrathteen, The Wiki Priest, Katalaveno, McSly, Andy Johnston, Crimson667, Mozzarella stick, BreakerLOLZ, Metallicker, Carewser, JSellers0, Prozapxxx, ArleneElizabeth, Kechie, Rookie66, David Whitton, Jwmmorley, Xiahou, Maniaphobic, ICE77, Jeff G., Mrsyetidooscreecher, JuneGloom07, Mks22690, Dwmr, Ronan5557, Kww, KevinTR, Frog47, Chyken, GcSwRhIc, Joseph.tobin, Qxz, Clarince63, Corvus cornix, Brettpam, Ortega orang tegal asli~enwiki, LeaveSleaves, Electrokinesis, Argcar5199, Metal80s, DShiznit, Hippiepeece, DLL25, Kaiketsu, Theanimelink, Stupid cow5567, Purgatory Fubar, Vchimpanzee, Rock Soldier, Funeral, I-High Football Rules, DarkShattenjager, RHendrickson, Hippieal, Peter Fleet, Scottocaster, Radioinfoguy, SieBot, AvailibleLight21, Sposato, Mark753, Scarian, Hchrishicks, Winchelsea, Bigd 28, Rajiv6900, Alterego269, Flyer22 Reborn, O.clark, Qst, Keaneau, Frogstyn, Klippdass, Fencejumper, Stewgunn, Batbag12, AngelOfSadness, Kubrickrules, Hobartimus, Gunmetal Angel, Perfectapproach, Navnløs, Mygerardromance, TubularWorld, Escape Orbit, Bassist 100, Troy 07, Robmark23, Mario Žamić, Martarius, Superwarrior25, ClueBot, NeoExDeath123, The Thing That Should Not Be, Kreynolds6931, GrimReaper39614, Wysprgr2005, Secrets100, Delta40, Hystericalgirl, Dave2107, JimboV1, Uncle Milty, EverybodyHurts, DShiznit3, Metal Head 4 life, CounterVandalismBot, Skeeball93, Niceguyedc, Dunderhizzle, Blanchardb, Rockythewocky, Scholarmusician, Trivialist, Moonpie08, Turkum, Kfrharris, DragonBot, Deathbringer from the Sky, Gnome de plume, Yellowxander, Metal Head Dave, Natt the Hatt, RaineSnake, A Powerful Weakness, Domestic Correction, Foshizzleediter, Roches2, Colourdance, Rhododendrites, Wiki libs, Jorddeano, Two Hearted River, Ostalocutanje, Razorflame, AN OLD MAN, Nestor12a, Maine12329, Thehelpfulone, C628, Thingg, Acabashi, Die for your government, PCHS-NJROTC, Canihaveacookie, Party, DumZiBoT, XLinkBot, Robrob5, Pheonex, Jovianeye, Terminaator, DCMoose48, Electric Japan, WikHead, Rhonnyuk, PL290, Paragon of Arctic Winter Nights, 43matej43, LiveWireNews, Thatguyflint, SlubGlub, Count of Tuscany, Kbdankbot, HexaChord, Angryapathy, Addbot, RandySavageFTW, Wolfywiki, Guoguo12, Rayvee2, Rickholler, DougsTech, Ronhjones, Frankensite, Sharkey2011, Noozgroop, Kellydawn83, Vidovich96, Theartsvault, Matthewshiflett, Mrushton24, Debresser, 5 albert square, Chazella, Angry Shoplifter, Tassedethe, Seeker alpha806, Äppelmos~enwiki, Lightbot, OlEnglish, Picknose, Gail, Rodericksilly, Luckas-bot, ZX81, Yobot, Greg D. Barnes, ArchonMagnus, See Below, Filastin, Motherjoe, Eric-Wester, Radiopathy, Zwillmaster, Orion11M87, AnomieBOT, 732SOUTHPAW, 1exec1, Choij, Emoponyboy, Piano non troppo, Ipatrol, Chuckiesdad, Ulric1313, Materialscientist, RadioBroadcast, ArthurBot, Quebec99, LilHelpa, Xqbot, Slugmaster31, Jake10663, Defleppardrox, Wether B, Degree9, Superchicken781, Dutchluck, Live Light, Grim23, Ched, Mlpearc, Maloo2147, LostLikeTearsInRain, Aussie Ausborn, J04n, GrouchoBot, Mutante96, Journey84, Sabrebd, Doulos Christos, EpicRock, Smallman12q, Jhs student, Nicksharpe, GripTheHusk, FrescoBot, Surv1v4l1st, LucienBOT, FateForger, FotoPhest, A vision of it, Ranchloopseven, N0obcakez, Jamamamo, GKBrown, Elfast, Sweetmarie123, DivineAlpha, HamburgerRadio, MrIpodz, DrilBot, I dream of horses. Tinton5, JackShestak, Jschnur, MondalorBot, DefMaiden, Thatblueford, Sidevar, Poppedmypoop, Classicrock655, TobeBot, Tough Thickpan, Rockgenre, Sublimefan97, Deafleopardsucks, Bryceskotnicki, Tigger-ibby, MrX, 777sms, Defender of torch, Crispyman01, Brakerestbrake, Reach Out to the Truth, Pinkchicken221, Willdow, RjwilmsiBot, NameIsRon, Sbrianhicks, Loudrocksurfer, John of Reading, Avenue X at Cicero, Tristis Oris, Ajraddatz, Lewismaster, Arqui1992, Racerx11, GoingBatty, Maronlovel, Shovelheaded, Dishcmds, Tommy2010, Thecheesykid, Evanh2008, ZéroBot, Cupidvogel, Historyhermann, Chryed, Helper12, Mab987, KiwiJeff, Metalegacy, Magsky2009, EWikist, Confession0791, Nigel tempest, Burbridge92, Mcmatter, Tolly4bolly, Faketodd, L1A1 FAL, Kekkofranco~enwiki, Evilcasper, Kranix, Tableclothes, RyanTaylor1987, Defrock81, Eknirb, JodieCox200, Shearlined, ChuispastonBot, NicholasJr7, Danny oldsen, Visvambhar, Riley delong, ClueBot NG, Therein8383, CactusBot, Gareth Griffith-Jones, Bob4141, MelbourneStar, This lousy T-shirt, MusoForde, Njg929, Jesse Striewski, Joefromrandb, Rockerforlife96, Widr, Zmaher, Dtman74, Nobycane74, Jamcad01, Superatomico, Helpful Pixie Bot, Whipped91, Calabe1992, Wbm1058, Wings68, BG19bot, Blackrabbitgirl, Oscarmannenberghe, TheWiselyStupidOne, Queen Zeppelin Metallica Floyd, Beachdude42, Wiki13, Laurend23, MusikAnimal, Christine:pnatalie, ValkyrianMusic, Banzai-chan, Beast8446, SilverBullitt, Smileguy91, Waycool86, Cyberbot II, Chie one, ChrisGualtieri, Myxomatosis57, YFdyh-bot, Tx rnel, Rthn, Mogism, Fretsurfer12, Lone boatman, Mlpearc Phone, NoeG2012, ROBLOXfan123, Retrohead, JustAMuggle, Politsi, Matt.Sharp98, Chartbot, NottNott, Synthwave.94, MetalDiablo666, Goodyntox, Morettiv2, Hystericalpyromaniac8783, Fran1996, Jakewhyland, Olliebear93, DannyMusicEditor, Fatal Disease, DLManiac, Carlos Rojas77, John Ozyer-Key, Kutter harrison, Makeitrock, Macbwill, AmyJoStout, RobertBDurham, AugustusLarch, Scottiwkt, BDR77777, Pwood33, EternalFloette, Estra1974, Jussimer209, Ledzeppinkfloyd, BuddyRedBow, Sbranti5, Minnesotaraised, RyanTQuinn, Swca1001, Dndbdbdh, RobW1991, Gittoid, Sammy f g, SouthHillEditor, Rycheskull69, Rafał Abako2, TheKirby64, Popcornsztop, Cade1234567890, Prazm021, KasparBot, Tiger 5647, Evereveronward, WisconsinPat, Theoneasdf, Ashneve, Tyler Hayward1 and Anonymous: 1460

- **Demon (band)** *Source:* https://en.wikipedia.org/wiki/Demon_(band)?oldid=685068462 *Contributors:* RobinCarmody, Cnwb, BVZM, Shanes, Woohookitty, Derek R Bullamore, Headshaker, Regan123, E-Kartoffel, Dl2000, Cydebot, Blackmetalbaz, GlynJames7, J.delanoy, Imagi-King, Codeispoetry, Martarius, Mhockey, Addbot, Atethnekos, Nomed1, Yobot, Themfromspace, Arch stanton1138, Screwfacexxx, Marauder09, GrouchoBot, FrescoBot, DefaultsortBot, John of Reading, Lewismaster, Franckverre, Abzr, Lashuto, Tronkmeister, DokkenRocker100, RandomLittleHelper, KasparBot and Anonymous: 36

- **Diamond Head (band)** *Source:* https://en.wikipedia.org/wiki/Diamond_Head_(band)?oldid=690245632 *Contributors:* SimonP, Ewen, Delirium, CatherineMunro, JASpencer, Steinsky, Bearcat, Cholling, Mushroom, Michael Devore, AlistairMcMillan, Guillaumito, Child of Bodom, Bumm13, Ukexpat, Mecanismo, Florian Blaschke, CanisRufus, Mike Garcia, Alansohn, Someoneinmyheadbutit'snotme, Starblind, Muya, Jeff3000, Thebogusman, TheEvilBlueberryCouncil, BD2412, Jclemens, Jdcooper, Rjwilmsi, Jamie Kitson, Linuxbeak, Bruce1ee, FlaBot, Stormwatch, YurikBot, RussBot, Hede2000, Heavynash, C777, Rsrikanth05, Cryptic, Welsh, Epa101, DeadEyeArrow, Engineer Bob, Whitejay251, Illuminus, Jogers, WesleyDodds, Crystallina, SmackBot, SubsonicViper, Rhys 100, Hmains, Msignor, Colonies Chris, Kanabekobaton, Kittybrewster, Derek R Bullamore, JonathanWakely, Marcus Brute, Harryurz, Dakedake, Dl2000, Iridescent, Eastlaw, Karenlesley29, Mattbr, Mika1h, ShelfSkewed, Cydebot, Fair Deal, Travelbird, AdmiralvonAxehaufen, PamD, JamesAM, Thijs!bot, Jedibob5, RobDe68, JustAGal, Trencacloscas, Kbthompson, IrishPete, Kauczuk, Andrzejbanas, Exclaim, Bongwarrior, Kameejl, MetsBot, CCS81, CommonsDelinker, Johnpacklambert, Squidward247, Eybot~enwiki, Arnvidr, Endobiont, Jaygtee, Russelwilkins, Sxuk, Heresbubba53190, Wrathteen, LordAnubisBOT, Katharineamy, Sleeper141, Aervanath, Imagi-King, Doomsdayer520, Andrewself, Fingerpuppet, Nitrofest, MyTemple, Dij88, AlleborgoBot, Moira N, Gus, WereSpielChequers, WRK, Adabow, PolarBot, Wight-Boy, PhilMacD, Fratrep, Atonefornothing, Martarius, Niceguyedc, Gwguffey, Wiki libs, SchreiberBike, Mhockey, DumZiBoT, Rror, Solino, TheSickBehemoth, Addbot, RandySavageFTW, Queenmomcat, Laaknor-Bot, Metalhead of the East, Angry Shoplifter, Lightbot, Алый Король, BrianTatler, Spacefan75, Luckas-bot, Yobot, Dethmyname, Molepatrol, Arch stanton1138, Marauder09, Martinreed, Ximmerman, Aussie Ausborn, Dunc0029, FrescoBot, Frehley72, David Coverdale's White Snake, JIK1975, Elockid, DefaultsortBot, Porky metal 666, MrX, EmausBot, SuperVirtual, John of Reading, Lewismaster, Racerx11, Whitewhaleholygrail, GoingBatty, Rocker.1986, Burbridge92, May Cause Dizziness, 1998metalhead1, BrandonsLe, ClueBot NG, CactusBot, Delusion23, Niriop, Hanyaisthesex, BG19bot, Cyr-henry, Gomollk, DenseFog, Ksio.amaral89, ChrisGualtieri, Esszet, Mogism, UselessToRemain, Svengali Rising, Thusz, 1916Walker987, NickKrammes, GTXiki, Heavybassist, Permafrost46, SoldierHead, EternalFloette, Mario64325, Tianthegreat, KasparBot and Anonymous: 162

- **Dumpy's Rusty Nuts** *Source:* https://en.wikipedia.org/wiki/Dumpy'{}s_Rusty_Nuts?oldid=676046961 *Contributors:* Verloren, William Avery, RobinCarmody, Bonalaw, Dave.Dunford, Graham87, Foxxygirltamara, Joel7687, SmackBot, McGeddon, CHawke, Miquonranger03, D-Rock, Ritchie333, Robofish, Dl2000, Iridescent, Cydebot, Blackmetalbaz, MarshBot, JeffDeHart, Nouse4aname, Cyfal, Soft shepherd, Mezigue, Anon126, XLinkBot, Texasrv, Addbot, Matt.T, Yobot, AnomieBOT, Marauder09, Lewismaster, Peaceray, Triggerthcat, KasparBot and Anonymous: 8

- **E. F. Band** *Source:* https://en.wikipedia.org/wiki/E._F._Band?oldid=676047143 *Contributors:* Bumm13, Bruce1ee, Ttwaring, FlaBot, GeeJo, Fair Deal, Wordbuilder, GrahamHardy, Horstvonludwig, McM.bot, Doger, Mungo Kitsch, Addbot, Aranyos, Lightbot, DefaultsortBot, Lewismaster and Anonymous: 4

- **Elixir (band)** *Source:* https://en.wikipedia.org/wiki/Elixir_(band)?oldid=679747073 *Contributors:* Andrewman327, Woohookitty, Rjwilmsi, Sherool, Cryptic, SmackBot, Bluebot, O keyes, AWeenieMan, X-Flare-x, Derek R Bullamore, Dl2000, Cydebot, Rip Claw, NovaSTL, IllaZilla, James25402, Aspects, ImageRemovalBot, MystBot, Addbot, Tassedethe, Lightbot, Yobot, Babypengy, Leefeni,de Karik, AnomieBOT, Marauder09, DefaultsortBot, Tim1357, Lewismaster, Kidneyman, KasparBot and Anonymous: 11

- **Eric Bell** *Source:* https://en.wikipedia.org/wiki/Eric_Bell?oldid=676110488 *Contributors:* Gsl, Michael Hardy, Mattworld, Ferganim, D6, Ardfern, GregorB, BD2412, Mayumashu, Koavf, Smiddy67, FlaBot, Snappy, Pigman, Tony1, Mike Selinker, Rms125a@hotmail.com, TBadger, SmackBot, Folajimi, Can't sleep, clown will eat me, Derek R Bullamore, Evlekis, Bretonbanquet, John, Syrcatbot, Dl2000, Jetman, Anger22, CmdrObot, ShelfSkewed, Cydebot, Jon C., OrenBochman, Waacstats, JaGa, IceDragon64, Avy, Leahtwosaints, Чръный человек, Addbot, Leszek Jańczuk, Macaedha, Zorrobot, Luckas-bot, Yobot, Filastin, LilHelpa, Obersachsebot, Tuesdaily, Martin IIIa, Marek Koudelka, ZéroBot, Τασουλα, BattyBot, Stevenbfg, VIAFbot, Synthwave.94, Jimfitz23, KasparBot and Anonymous: 30

- **Ethel the Frog (band)** *Source:* https://en.wikipedia.org/wiki/Ethel_the_Frog_(band)?oldid=687499423 *Contributors:* Silvonen, Asparagus, Warpozio, Woohookitty, JIP, Rjwilmsi, RussBot, Crystallina, SmackBot, Derek R Bullamore, Headshaker, Dl2000, AndrewHowse, Cydebot, Thijs!bot, Xeno, Keith D, Johnpacklambert, Bogartotron, Nouse4aname, James25402, Florentyna, Sheppola, CohesionBot, Addbot, Angry Shoplifter, Legobot, KamikazeBot, AnomieBOT, Marauder09, DefaultsortBot, PaulMacnamara, Updatehelper, STATicVapor, Lewismaster, Cyberbot II, Alphacross99, SalemUK, KasparBot and Anonymous: 10

- **Fist (band)** *Source:* https://en.wikipedia.org/wiki/Fist_(band)?oldid=676049181 *Contributors:* Rjwilmsi, RadioFan, Rigadoun, Dl2000, Neonblak, Cbj77, Gus, Martarius, ClueBot, Drmies, Niceguyedc, Muhandes, Malconfort, Yobot, DemocraticLuntz, Freshfighter9, Marauder09, Erik9bot, Ibradleys, In ictu oculi, Hiddenstranger, John of Reading, Lewismaster, Bollyjeff, ClueBot NG, CactusBot, Handsomedude43, XMelirunex, Monkbot, KasparBot and Anonymous: 4

- **Geoff Barton** *Source:* https://en.wikipedia.org/wiki/Geoff_Barton?oldid=667907726 *Contributors:* Rjwilmsi, Racklever, Ser Amantio di Nicolao, Waacstats, WazzaMan, Martarius, Mr Larrington, PlankBot, Yobot, RjwilmsiBot, Lewismaster, KasparBot and Anonymous: 8

4.1. TEXT

- **Girl (band)** *Source:* https://en.wikipedia.org/wiki/Girl_(band)?oldid=676049636 *Contributors:* Zanimum, Rl, Charles Matthews, Steinsky, Rdsmith4, Aranel, RoyBoy, Pablo X, Bobo192, Georgia guy, Canadian Paul, Rjwilmsi, Bruce1ee, Gringo300, Cjmarsicano, SmackBot, Fuhghettaboutit, Derek R Bullamore, Dl2000, Cydebot, JustAGal, Michig, MetsBot, Smaunsell, Tiptoety, ImageRemovalBot, Martarius, Mickeyde, Addbot, Binary TSO, Tassedethe, Drpickem, Yobot, FotoPhest, Ywmpq205, DefaultsortBot, Swellhead, Lewismaster, Retserrof84, Tigercompanion25, KasparBot and Anonymous: 27

- **Girlschool** *Source:* https://en.wikipedia.org/wiki/Girlschool?oldid=690491807 *Contributors:* Kevinbasil, David Gerard, DocWatson42, Gargaj, Ynhockey, Thryduulf, Woohookitty, Uncle G, Robwingfield, Roda~enwiki, BD2412, Bruce1ee, FlaBot, Pinkville, YurikBot, RussBot, RadioFan, Nicke L, Fnorp, Jamesgibbon, Grange85, Asarelah, Wknight94, SmackBot, Chris Keating, Onorem, The Elfoid, Anarchodin, Headshaker, Evlekis, Ohconfucius, JHunterJ, E-Kartoffel, Dl2000, OnBeyondZebrax, Hndsmepete, J Milburn, JForget, Vega84, Cydebot, Thijs!bot, SummerPhD, White Devil, Michig, MegX, Tirolion, Delage, Twsx, Bubba hotep, Kameejl, Starrycupz, Alan Burridge, BetBot~enwiki, Northmetpit, Evb-wiki, Drwhawkfan, ViccoLizcano, TXiKiBoT, Headmess, Scarian, BotMultichill, Mungo Kitsch, Klippdass, Aspects, Grim-Gym, Lottalava, Navnløs, Cyfal, ImageRemovalBot, Martarius, Dinahenid, Spxmet, Keraunoscopia, Mild Bill Hiccup, Skeeball93, Trivialist, Aryavib, SchreiberBike, Indopug, WikHead, MystBot, Addbot, Trs bigjim, LaaknorBot, Drummergirlno1, Favonian, Angry Shoplifter, Tassedethe, Lightbot, Matěj Grabovský, Emotion666, Ben Ben, Spacefan75, PlankBot, Yobot, RockfangBot, Gongshow, AmeliorationBot, 1exec1, Reverter15, Tranztek, W1K9, Screwfacexxx, Freshfighter9, Marauder09, J04n, CalmCalamity, Super lenton, FrescoBot, MrX, Cowlibob, RjwilmsiBot, In ictu oculi, John of Reading, GA bot, Lewismaster, Jordanasdf, H3llBot, Piantanida31, Sugar-Baby-Love, ChuispastonBot, CactusBot, This lousy T-shirt, Joefromrandb, Helpful Pixie Bot, BattyBot, Cyberbot II, DokkenRocker100, Meadow Gate, Falconet8, Sol1, Synthwave.94, Igirlschool, Monkbot, KasparBot, Morriellomusic and Anonymous: 100

- **Grim Reaper (band)** *Source:* https://en.wikipedia.org/wiki/Grim_Reaper_(band)?oldid=689758047 *Contributors:* Sannse, Rl, Steinsky, Robbot, Bumm13, Gscshoyru, Klemen Kocjancic, Sn0wflake, CanisRufus, King nothing, Alansohn, Youngamerican, Jdcooper, Rjwilmsi, Biederman, Bruce1ee, Www.jpfo.org, Niz, Muchness, Prezuiwf, Nikkimaria, Dposse, SmackBot, Bluebot, Derek R Bullamore, Majorclanger, IronGargoyle, Dl2000, Mika1h, Tim Long, HalJor, Cydebot, AdmiralvonAxehaufen, .anacondabot, Imagi-King, Clownempire, JKlehr, JukoFF, James25402, Aspects, Rlest, ImageRemovalBot, WimTaymans, Martarius, ClueBot, Regibox, TheSickBehemoth, SilvonenBot, Tim010987, Addbot, Tassedethe, Zorrobot, Luckas-bot, Yobot, TaBOT-zerem, Groucho NL, JackieBot, The Great Duck, Marauder09, GrouchoBot, Pejoe68, DefaultsortBot, Ericbourland, Eustanacio IV, In ictu oculi, Mk5384, Lewismaster, ClueBot NG, CactusBot, BG19bot, MusikAnimal, Rockastansky, I call the big one bitey, Alzantir, Threesidesofthecoin, KasparBot, BU Rob13, FortyFiveAuto and Anonymous: 95

- **Haze (band)** *Source:* https://en.wikipedia.org/wiki/Haze_(band)?oldid=660334855 *Contributors:* Bearcat, Pigsonthewing, Michael Devore, Jdcooper, Bruce1ee, SmackBot, Bluebot, GoodDay, Derek R Bullamore, Cydebot, IrishPete, Oculi, Arjayay, Snailb, Gabadon, Lightbot, DefaultsortBot, Lewismaster, PigsOTWing, Ruud NL, KasparBot and Anonymous: 6

- **Hell (band)** *Source:* https://en.wikipedia.org/wiki/Hell_(band)?oldid=676060031 *Contributors:* LindsayH, Woohookitty, Cuchullain, Kolbasz, RussBot, Cpc464, Derek R Bullamore, Dl2000, Markoff Chaney, Dbiel, Omegastar, Dabomb87, Niceguyedc, Boleyn, XLinkBot, MystBot, Addbot, Malconfort, Vio2112, Spacefan75, Yobot, Spada2, Dizzydalek, The Banner, FrescoBot, MrX, Lewismaster, Starcheerspeaksnewslostwars, K.eight.a, Erpert, SkywalkerPL, MauchoEagle, M60dk, ChrisGualtieri, Sipsftw, SteenthIWbot, MetalS-W, MarkusvonDeaseton, Rocknroll94, CryogenicDead, Sam mclaughlin, MetalicMadness, KasparBot and Anonymous: 54

- **HellsBelles** *Source:* https://en.wikipedia.org/wiki/HellsBelles?oldid=680459563 *Contributors:* Rjwilmsi, Korny O'Near, Chris the speller, X-Flare-x, Derek R Bullamore, Dl2000, AndrewHowse, Blackmetalbaz, Interested2, Nick Number, DuncanHill, MegX, Gjhdiver, Niceguyedc, Rockfang, XLinkBot, WikHead, Tassedethe, PlankBot, Yobot, ScarTissueBloodBlister, FrescoBot, Lewismaster, BG19bot, BattyBot, City boy 123, The Quixotic Potato and Anonymous: 11

- **Hollow Ground (band)** *Source:* https://en.wikipedia.org/wiki/Hollow_Ground_(band)?oldid=689164762 *Contributors:* Bobo192, GVOLTT, RussBot, Crystallina, SmackBot, Dl2000, Dlohcierekim, John kirk, BeastmasterGeneral, FatDrummer, Imagi-King, Metalion SOS, Gillyweed, Gus, James25402, Oculi, Florentyna, Yobot, Marauder09, Mfwitten, DARTH SIDIOUS 2, Lewismaster, CactusBot, Jeremy112233, ChrisGualtieri, Alzantir and Anonymous: 12

- **Holocaust (band)** *Source:* https://en.wikipedia.org/wiki/Holocaust_(band)?oldid=680594473 *Contributors:* Jfdwolff, Child of Bodom, Bumm13, Ary29, Twthmoses, Allen3, Bruce1ee, FlaBot, Bgwhite, SmackBot, Derek R Bullamore, Dl2000, Iridescent, WeggeBot, Cydebot, Odie5533, RottweilerCS, Escarbot, Kevinmon, Ascraeus~enwiki, CommonsDelinker, Bogartotron, Munci, Gus, Mungo Kitsch, FreeFragSGS, Johnanth, TubularWorld, Niceguyedc, PixelBot, Wiki libs, TroubleWithin, Addbot, Blashyrkh66, Lightbot, Luckas-bot, Yobot, Arch stanton1138, Materialscientist, Marauder09, AlanZhan, GrouchoBot, JIK1975, DefaultsortBot, Thrashcanman16, Fixer88, Don Quixote is awesome, Tashivana, John of Reading, Nima1024, Lewismaster, Burbridge92, JGM Edinburgh, Witm777, MrJohnMayer, Graham Edmund Hall, Holocaust Band, Atreides54798, KasparBot and Anonymous: 36

- **Iron Maiden** *Source:* https://en.wikipedia.org/wiki/Iron_Maiden?oldid=690630480 *Contributors:* Kpjas, Eloquence, The Anome, Deb, William Avery, Zoe, Hephaestos, Olivier, Nevilley, Nightfall, Edward, Infrogmation, Llywrch, Kidburla, Vera Cruz, Ixfd64, Graue, Zanimum, Sannse, Dori, Ahoerstemeier, KAMiKAZOW, CatherineMunro, TUF-KAT, Angela, Kingturtle, Uri~enwiki, Rl, Conti, Hashar, Htaccess, Charles Matthews, Timwi, Twister, Unbanned User, Timc, Tpbradbury, Morwen, Tempshill, Toreau, Raul654, Eugene van der Pijll, RadicalBender, Sjorford, Klehti, Sander123, Fredrik, Korath, RedWolf, Altenmann, Modulatum, Postdlf, Academic Challenger, SchmuckyTheCat, Tony The Tiger, Hadal, JesseW, Wereon, Mushroom, Lupo, TPK, Cecropia, Cordell, Carnildo, Radagast, Gershom, LittleBrother, DocWatson42, Peoplesyak, Peruvianllama, Nunoalves, Everyking, Alison, Beardo, Mboverload, Jackol, Bobblewik, Chowbok, Utcursch, SoWhy, Antandrus, Demonslave, JoJan, MisfitToys, Child of Bodom, Mamizou, Djhipflask, Kesac, CJCurrie, Wikster E, Secfan, Martin Wisse, Ary29, Icairns, MRSC, Ingman, Coburnpharr04, Kurek, Ukexpat, Valproate, Andreas Kaufmann, Mike Rosoft, Mernen, Alkivar, D6, Bloodless, Mormegil, Imroy, Rcog, Chris j wood, Discospinster, Rich Farmbrough, C12H22O11, Andrewferrier, EliasAlucard, Djce, LindsayH, Samboy, Sn0wflake, Mani1, Pavel Vozenilek, Martpol, Paul August, Bo Lindbergh, Stbalbach, Snow steed~enwiki, Violetriga, CanisRufus, Adrianward, Illumynite, Chairboy, Shanes, Spearhead, C1k3, Sietse Snel, Triona, Bookofjude, Mqduck, Logger~enwiki, Warpozio, Mike Garcia, Sole Soul, Bobo192, Circeus, Func, Wisdom89, GTubio, Texas.veggie, Dungodung, Pokrajac, Giraffedata, Darwinek, VBGFscJUn3, Alphax, Thewayforward, King nothing, Ire and curses, Mr. Brownstone, Bloduly, Ral315, Nsaa, Ranveig, Jumbuck, PrimEviL, Woohoo5241, Alansohn, Eixo, Gargaj, PopUpPirate, Rd232, Jeltz, Jtalledo, ABCD, Ashley Pomeroy, Cherryblack, Bz2, MarkGallagher, Robert Mercer, Jackliddle, Mailer diablo, TomH, EdwardTheGreat~enwiki, Nowoco, Idont Havaname, Snowolf, Wtmitchell, Bucephalus, Mad Hatter, Garzo, Evil Monkey, RainbowOfLight, Drat,

Kober, Kestral~enwiki, Ndteegarden, Vanish3, CinnamonCinder, Versageek, Sleigh, Alai, Geographer, Djsasso, Adrian.benko, RyanGerbil10, Blufive, Sars~enwiki, Woohookitty, Mindmatrix, RHaworth, Craighennessey, Vorash, SusanLarson, EvilCheeseWedge, Myleslong, Kzollman, Mazca, Bratsche, TheoClarke, Ardfern, Exxolon, Tedneeman, Twthmoses, Clemmy, Easyas12c, JRHorse, Pasteler0, Vanished895703, Jon Harald Søby, Supersonic^, Dalkaen, Prashanthns, DarkBard, Moleskiner, Lovro, Turnstep, Joe Roe, Dysepsion, Mandarax, Jcuk, Magister Mathematicae, Taestell, Cuchullain, BD2412, Jclemens, Josh Parris, Jdcooper, Sjö, Lhademmor, Rjwilmsi, JVz, Koavf, Jake Wartenberg, MordredKLB, Panoptical, Equinox137, Boccobrock, Matt Schley, DoubleBlue, GeorgeBills, Dar-Ape, Hermione1980, Jamdav86, Sango123, FuriousFreddy, Yamamoto Ichiro, Fish and karate, Tommy Kronkvist, FlaBot, Maitch, Gringo300, Tokus, RobertG, Doc glasgow, Djrobgordon, Nihiltres, Gtmo, Brianreading, Fandango`, RexNL, Gurch, RobyWayne, GreyCat, Bashe, Imnotminkus, Jfiling, Chunkyasparagus, Hatch68, Visor, DVdm, Igordebraga, Bgwhite, Gwernol, Cornellrockey, Flcelloguy, RandyRhoadsRonnieDio, Wasted Time R, Sus scrofa, YurikBot, Tommyt, Sceptre, Blightsoot, MMuzammils, RussBot, Edward Wakelin, Jtkiefer, Wilbus, Pigman, Piet Delport, DanMS, Rapomon, Foxxygirltamara, C777, Gaius Cornelius, Theelf29, Rsrikanth05, Pseudomonas, Wimt, Gustavb, Shanel, Wiki alf, Daemon8666, Joshdboz, Grafen, NickBush24, Wolfmoon, Nightmare X, Joelr31, Atheistrabbi, PedroV1, Robdurbar, Cool Z, Banes, Cholmes75, Passive, Ruhrfisch, Aaron Schulz, BOT-Superzerocool, Gadget850, Ccoll, Brat32, DeadEyeArrow, Bota47, Kendricken, Tekana, Mrbluesky, Slicing, E tac, FF2010, Kronocide, Zzuuzz, Lt-wiki-bot, TheMadBaron, OMenda~enwiki, Bayerischermann, Closedmouth, Great Cthulhu, Pb30, Grmagne, Spinboy 11, Jogers, Ward99, Tom walker, Sarefo, MikeMetaled, JuJube, Acctorp, GraemeL, Voievod, Red Jay, Alias Flood, Ekeb, Mais oui!, ArielGold, CapPixel, Jud, Chris93, Katieh5584, Snaxe920, Meegs, NeilN, Kingboyk, GrinBot~enwiki, Dkasak, Perulovesyou, One, WesleyDodds, Vanka5, SmackBot, Moeron, Prodego, Hydrogen Iodide, Umph, Bjelleklang, Unyoyega, Pgk, C.Fred, Grandmaster, Blue520, Hatto, Garchy, IainP, Chairman S., Delldot, LuciferMorgan, MindlessXD, Ilikeeatingwaffles, ZS, HalfShadow, Evanreyes, Szobi~enwiki, Gilliam, Betacommand, Skizzik, GoneAwayNowAndRetired, Chris the speller, Zouf, Andrea colombian, Kurykh, SSJ 5, MrDrBob, Catchpole, Anullst-God, Leyasu, Master of Puppets, SchfiftyThree, Droll, Bazonka, No-Bullet, Nalyd357~enwiki, Wikipediatrix, Derekjhunt, Rob77, KingAlanI, Rama's Arrow, Daddy Kindsoul, Gsp8181, Royboycrashfan, Alex 101, Salmar, Can't sleep, clown will eat me, David Morón, MadameArsenic, Shalom Yechiel, Axl182, Alphathon, AP1787, Chlewbot, OrphanBot, Onorem, Racklever, GBobly, TheKMan, VinTheMetalhed, Doh286, Rsm99833, Samguana, Greenshed, 168pin, The Elfoid, Jmlk17, Flyguy649, The Moving Finger Writes, Rufus Sarsaparilla, X-Flare-x, Shrine of Fire, Nakon, New Rock Star, RJN, Faz90, Dreadstar, RandomP, Stephcra, 4hodmt, Leonardi, Sbluen, Mwtoews, MetalHeadBanger, Metamagician3000, In Flames, Isaac Benaron, Asics, UVnet, Marcus Brute, Ligulembot, Bretonbanquet, Pilotguy, ReToOcS, Ceoil, Ohconfucius, Nomoretears, SashatoBot, ArglebargleIV, Geach, Rklawton, AidanPryde, John, Ergative rlt, Euchiasmus, METALGOD42088, Markdr, Kuyku, Ocee, Cardinal Wurzel, NJZombie, Bjankuloski06en~enwiki, Madris, Mark Lungo, CyrilB, Climhazzard999, Skeev, Slakr, Stwalkerster, George The Dragon, SQGibbon, Rock4arolla, Darz Mol~enwiki, SandyGeorgia, Ravenloft, Mets501, E-Kartoffel, Peppermint Wardrobe, Andy5190, Insomniacsdream, Squirepants101, Jkaharper, Johnson542, Amitch, ZaidAhmed, Ryouga, SimonD, Deaþe gecweald, BananaFiend, Iridescent, Spark, Sasaki, Mikehelms, Adriatikus, Shoeofdeath, Bahamut-, Halifax corey, PhilC., Ouzo~enwiki, Tony Fox, MGlosenger, Prahladv, Marysunshine, Courcelles, Thesexualityofbereavement, Audiosmurf, Anger22, Hindsmepete, Painjoiker, Hmas, Tawkerbot2, Daniel5127, Rattleand-Hum, IronChris, Chetfarmer, Jknobull, Ldshfsklahfdjkla, Codemastercb, Mr. Metal Head, JForget, Vega84, Fache, Ohthelameness, InvisibleK, CmdrObot, Sarcastic Avenger, Seal Clubber, Mattbr, Blondu99, Speedking90, Hucz, Cyrus XIII, Brucethegreat, CBM, Machchunk, Drinibot, Skeletor2112, Matthew Auger, Steve355, OMGsplosion, ShelfSkewed, Casper2k3, Angelo.paz, Cheesysam, John Skywalker, Cydebot, Fnlayson, Steph11, Fl, Fair Deal, Michaelas10, Gogo Dodo, Travelbird, WillBeardmore, Flowerpotman, Corpx, Matt d84, ST47, Inertia77~enwiki, Blackmetalbaz, ChrisGuy, GurTheFred, Kakamuro, Annakaycanada, Littlebadger, Shotmenot, Tkynerd, Manuelggg, Dancter, Strom, Odie5533, Jameboy, Tawkerbot4, Anger222, HK51, Sgt-D, DumbBOT, Chrislk02, Phydend, Rickyadnett, RottweilerCS, Mikepope, Prodigenous Zee, Btharper1221, Omicronpersei8, Vanished User jdksfajlasd, Gimmetrow, Rocket000, Kenox, Sabbre, JamesAM, Kingbotk, Thijs!bot, Epbr123, Chu333222, Demon.fish, Kohran, Dasani, Cain Mosni, MaulYoda, Luke poa, Padgett22, Mojo Hand, Cris Spiegel, Headbomb, Fluxbot, Deep Shadow, John254, Barakitty, Doctorjbeam, Danowest, James086, Clay70, Uther pendragon, Yettie0711, Mr. Brain, Sivazh, Inner Earth, JustA-Gal, DavidJJJ, Kbenhelli, NigelR, Grayshi, Andy Rosenthal, Sectornine, Sean William, DannyQuack, Sherick, Trencacloscas, Hole in the wall, Eddiewrathchild, Millagorilla, Cactusjack11, Afcb4ever, AntiVandalBot, Tookery, Luna Santin, Opelio, Tiger Trek, Quintote, Prolog, Kbthompson, Strappingthesource, JimboB, Jhsounds, G Rose, Maladroit2, White Devil, XtoF, Z-vap, Jimeree, Myanw, Andrzejbanas, Bigjimr, JAnDbot, Dan D. Ric, Luds, Leuko, Kaobear, DuncanHill, MER-C, EvilUnderFoot, Bigar, Areaseven, Fetchcomms, Timkovski, Db099221, BeastmasterGeneral, East718, Gavia immer, MegX, Abyssobrotula, Roman Dog Bird, SEGA, Kirrages, JimCubb, Kerotan, Y2kcrazyjoker4, LittleOldMe, .anacondabot, Acroterion, Willisx90, Casmith 789, Sloopy2, KrissiMaidenn, 75pickup, Acdc51502112, Bongwarrior, VoABot II, Jamo.au, Will231982, Davidjk, CattleGirl, Feeeshboy, Stephenhammett, Tedickey, Saurabhzutshi, Miketm, Lamentingvampire09, RobF, Vegheadjones, Adil Ghanty, Duffcub, Cerpin taxt, Bubba hotep, Le Saint, The Purple Nazz, Arabigo, Xiola06, 28421u2232nfenfcenc, Mike Searson, Zagmac, Rui.franco, Taylor2k, Paris By Night, Noonand, Jasonipod2, Pepe alas, Glen, DerHexer, CCS81, Hbent, Kan-os, Patstuart, Dotcanada, Leon Sword, DeathDude, Thompson.matthew, Harachte, Varsindarkin, Ajmo, FisherQueen, JakeRiddoch, Jjaazz, MartinBot, M3tal H3ad, BAMEXP, PowerSane, Rrv1988, Rettetast, Zouavman Le Zouave, Progohio, Smoke xxx, CommonsDelinker, Admc2006, Cathar maiden, Batman123456, Cornerbock, Grblundell, FMAFan1990, Arighboke, J.delanoy, Nev1, Iaberis, Veritas Blue, Trusilver, GreenRunner0, Rgoodermote, Marlinspike, Ali, Wacky walrus, Numbo3, Uncle Dick, SlightlyInsane, Nickx33, WarthogDemon, Darth Mike, Ijustam, Wrathteen, The Copper 17, Mr Rookles, DarkFalls, Doc Gloom, McSly, Willie the Walrein, Loftf, Dskluz, Yellowtruck, Nitrogem, Anti-SpamBot, IanBishop, Dasegad, SJP, MissLadle, Mufka, Imagi-King, Lathilde, Shroopliss, Jackaranga, KylieTastic, Cometstyles, Ardius01, Doomsdayer520, Jc4p, Jeff robertson, Jamesontai, Leladax, Ajeje, I0ngunn3r~enwiki, Tinkiewinkie, Redrocket, Gtg204y, Mightyrearranger, S, Icecold7, Jman 69, ThePointblank, CardinalDan, Idioma-bot, Spellcast, Lordnyra, ACSE, Deor, Jbruyndonckx, Fire.Tree, VolkovBot, Demonic One, Thisisborin9, Enders shadow89, Jeff G., LethalSRX, WOSlinker, Barbiebrutal, MyTemple, Philip Trueman, TXiKiBoT, Zidonuke, Cosmic Latte, Danorama, Vipinhari, Platonnc, Assassinoc714, Names and Numbers, Anonymous Dissident, Headmess, Qxz, Someguy1221, Plam, Chausean, Lradrama, IllaZilla, Dendodge, Leafyplant, Bocky7, Krispy k, Dado-w, Abdullais4u, Eatabullet, Jackfork, LeaveSleaves, Scchipli, Electrokinesis, Robert Newbould, ProfEraser, Krauser415, Wcudmore, Defunct Lies, Metal80s, MrMaiden, Paco55, Jsderwin, Pgw123, Karunkarri, Inx272, Gustav Lindwall, Lollercopter, Feudonym, Matt newlands, Kornman230, DamageIncM, Joelasaurus, Jakk6, Bottlecap-Warrior, 2ulus, Tinyclaw, Falcon8765, Djkuula, Morthis, Darthrya, Symo-EFC, Rock Soldier, WyntonM, Psychicdj13, Insanity Incarnate, Entirelybs, Somguy3, HiDrNick, AlleborgoBot, Kehrbykid, Funeral, X-cort, Kalivd, Iamtheblackwizards, HitokiriGaijin, The Rabbit42, JimmydaWorm, Metal Michelle, Yellowtail, Atilladrjb, Peter Fleet, Thw1309, Burningclean, Barkeep, Eksbg, Tibullus, SieBot, Maurauth, Gorpik, Madman, Maidenmaniac1, Sposato, Mark753, Tresiden, Pro Game Master87, Tiddly Tom, Moonriddengirl, Work permit, Scarian, CircafuciX, Weelijimmy, Ori, Clamticore, Corrupt toolbox, Wikimaiden, Pidgeathemel, RJaguar3, ChickenDumplings, Cheeselor1, Bud99999, Smsarmad, PenalOwnage, Ludivine, Alterego269, Paranoidis, Nite-Sirk, Zanders5k, Scorcha101, Undertaker39614, Cracktyrone, The Evil Spar-

4.1. TEXT

tan, JD554, Arbor to SJ, Elpiggo, DEATHLEADER, Jimsorenson, Eneskilic, Wombatcat, Samuelken, Kobrakai 1986, Oxymoron83, Antonio Lopez, Faradayplank, AngelOfSadness, RedSectorZ, Kosack, Lightmouse, ClayBay, ToBeBetween2, Techman224, FloydFred, Emogirlhelena, Slaves290, JonathanDaby, Harout72, RJL Hartmans, Ian Hampson, Fratrep, Gunmetal Angel, Flyinghigh82, Reginmund, Navnløs, Khodium, Veldin963, Voiceofcrube, TheStrip, Vanished User 8902317830, Louis-rules-okay, Dabomb87, Michaelkenney, −.SLDHSK.-, Drummer-AKAJordan, Zii XFS, Kriss22, Fezmar9, REDYVA, Fanniel, Prowler239, Peoplesrepublican, Falcor1984, Loren.wilton, Martarius, Rurik16, De728631, Elassint, SuzeOlbrich, ClueBot, Avenged Eightfold, Binksternet, Heavymetal4ever, Flatline686, Snigbrook, The Thing That Should Not Be, Matdrodes, Jackgordon6, Plastikspork, Ndenison, Keraunoscopia, MAVIII, Eldom20, Taroaldo, Venusdoom, Heavymetalis4ever, Dr-mies, AlasdairGreen27, Cube lurker, JimboV1, Jonathan Wash, Hipermegacuanticus, Pen.isman123, Mezigue, Parkesey666, Ymmusic, Leod-macleod, Anti-Cena, R n R High, Peanut4, Mattkyu, Blanchardb, Stylteralmaldo, Dimitrakopulos, Makavelijames~enwiki, Vrfour, Cholmes77, PMDrive1061, LukeTheSpook, Metalheadro, Artswatch, Nolimitownass, Matiashs~enwiki, Deathbringer from the Sky, Jsmith3393, Johnathon Duff, Excirial, Leo4313660, Megastrike14, Nymf, KnightsofCydonia, Crywalt, Erebus Morgaine, A Powerful Weakness, Nickeldiva, Kel-lydj14, Iamtheonewhoeats, RCBobEdwards, Brooksyakathemovieman, Concubined, Luigi 91, Grey Matter, Lurulu, Akashu, Wiki libs, Kmas-ter, DMan142, Bondbrotherz, WillRun, Hooks21101, LackOvComprehension, Maiden101, The x reaper, Dekisugi, Scullion2k7, Audaciter, 101cheese101, Twojawas, Powerdaze, Polly, BOTarate, Thehelpfulone, La Pianista, C628, Fight the Foo, Nesersert, Thingg, Svcroller, Aitias, Ertemplin, Versus22, Blackless, Almosthonest06, Kokoro20, Johnnyknocker, WriterGrrl, Rockk3r, DumZiBoT, Uscalldaway, Nestor16, Belchey, Heironymous Rowe, Matt Schwarz, BarretB, Cooltrainer Hugh, XLinkBot, Banffsurf, Hotcrocodile, Gnowor, Albinostorm, Pheonex, Ynot4tony, Dark Mage, SlayerXT, Guitarplayeraustin, Archereon, DaL33T, TheSickBehemoth, Officeone, HMFS, Nestor1980, Facts707, Wik-Head, Alexius08, Renoarctica, Yuvn86, HIPERAKNOSTIKUS, Gazimoff, Aussiedude007, Michaelmadden, Kaustubh.sapru, Ictaros, Javatyk, Kbdankbot, HexaChord, CalumH93, Andrem37, Le Rusecue, Kiloi6, Addbot, Proofreader77, Cxz111, Ryryz666, Malconfort, Kemrin45, Nose-bleed180, Heep13, RandySavageFTW, Shithead245, Guoguo12, Nightmareishere, Hot200245, Stalls standing, DougsTech, Mystical-bunny, Ronhjones, Ironmaiden123, Mases26, Fieldday-sunday, HFGR, Connorr1919, Nvte, 20p, CanadianLinuxUser, Fluffernutter, Reptoid34, Blue Square Thing, Cst17, Paucostacos, GTAtrivium76, Download, Protonk, LaaknorBot, Chamal N, PranksterTurtle, The Shadow-Fighter, Pro-vokedsumo, DFS454, Z. Patterson, Davidrurik, AndersBot, Chzz, XRK, Favonian, Tjwhittles, Kyle1278, Koppas, LinkFA-Bot, VMJE, Nicky Stake, Guffydrawers, Strat0master14, Angry Shoplifter, Buc Nasty95, Tassedethe, Fredrik001, Seilacei, Trendlists, Jbrockfan, DubaiTermina-tor, Tide rolls, Danjo5588, Lozer69, Lightbot, OlEnglish, Dellstein, Ranaldo, Krano, Brothir, Luckas Blade, Teles, Hatto0467, Poketfulashelz, Trotter, Ironmaiden01, LuK3, Scarffo, Lucy Pinder, Ironwaiden, Frehley, Ynot4tony2, Ben Ben, Legobot, Spacefan75, Luckas-bot, Yobot, Deathmagnetic08, RockaRollaRocky, 2D, LP Sérgio LP, MaidenfansUS, Be Black Hole Sun, Madridista92, PWWII, Rancidpete, Giusex27sc, MAIDEN SINCE I WAS 5, 46tits, Arch stanton1138, Knownot, ByM4k5, TestEditBot, AlexLevyOne, Tempodivalse, Radiopathy, Maiden-rich, N1RK4UDSK714, Juliancolton Alternative, Yogartm4n, Clarkie2008, AnomieBOT, Srobak, Cliffordburton, RGWarrior9001, Nael615, Ciphers, 1exec1, ZZeBaH Punk, The Parting Glass, LeifEriksson62, Jay-Jay215, L doddrell, Jim1138, IRP, Uptheironsnc, Piano non troppo, Di-noZon, Merube 89, Krem12, RandomAct, GetMKWearMKFly, Materialscientist, Soulfulbohemian, BlackSabbath16, Riotsquad83, Citation bot, Frous, Ih8ironmaiden, Marauder09, Drax113, Shallow Bloody Treason, Tanner9461, ArthurBot, Connor272, Sachora Infinite, Xqbot, Tomas tobar, Azuos~enwiki, Klstew1, Rafaldluzynski, Mfybht, Capricorn42, Wether B, Lepercon123, 4twenty42o, Ka'Jong, Metand.azv, Arollins, Ratman9513, Veggie40, Oogabooha1, Nascarfan1964, Mlpearc, Omar Maiden, LostLikeTearsInRain, Xenath, Immergradeous, Anonymous from the 21st century, Aussie Ausborn, J04n, Aidant666, Mutante96, Bynhola, Corruptcopper, Iron16timesmaiden, Jezhotwells, Metalhead616, FireCrystal, RibotBOT, Mattg82, Juan maiden, Dry valleys, Defjams776, Supernino, SPKirsch, Jkspawn, Moxy, Guatiao, Shadowjams, Cru-ento, SchnitzelMannGreek, Erik9, Fmnn100, Ryan1546, CallMeAndrew, Leon666a, GripTheHusk, Davidthrossell, Bassshredder95, Omfgi-likecheese, FrescoBot, Dustin4444, Surv1v4l1st, Xenmorpha, Griffey0511, Threeocs, Sky Attacker, FotoPhest, Lmxdoomguyx, Dhfkjsaehglkjn, A vision of it, Ranchloopseven, Recognizance, Cheesemanmonkeyhead, Arkclown, Serbianboy, Fquaid, BulsaraAndDeacon, Elfast, Tetraedy-cal, Nich43, NobbyR, HamburgerRadio, Talalz 94, Javert, Careful with That Axe, Eugene, MrIpodz, DrilBot, Whitewarrior251, Biker Biker, Killerangelhate, SpacemanSpiff, Pinethicket, I dream of horses, Mrix1985, Deathie~enwiki, Usaf72, Tomcat7, Xididthepopex, Xfansd, Solid State Survivor, Kentpilot, Porky metal 666, Mullac2580, Piandcompany, Wlwhyte1, NeoTarget, LairepoNite, Dessypoo, Wayward crumbs, Reconsider the static, Legodino, Utility Monster, Tim1357, IronMaidenMax, Lordnecronus, Discographer, Gunakibomb182, ToBeBot, MC-Standen, Colchester121891, Welkhazen, DixonDBot, Yunshui, Intruder2110, Rockgenre, Lotje, Lakiluki, Me310392, MrX, Bsignori, Wanky-wank, Specs112, Fastilysock, Suffusion of Yellow, Jd Tendril, Gabe19, Gleebies74, Stroppolo, Reach Out to the Truth, RobertMfromLI, Maxxsteel, Pugpitbullduck, Mrbattleman, DARTH SIDIOUS 2, Oscarberghe, Hockey39boy39, Mean as custard, The Utahraptor, Rjwilmsi-Bot, Clawzx, Oscar.dm, Aaqibahsan, Mr. Floyd kjøyrar motorsykkel, Bossanoven, RichieMurray, HrZ, Lopifalko, Ciru86, Noommos, Ptd619, Ironpriestdeth, Slon02, Lxcainxl, Laduron61, Bryman117, TajiMatsuki, Rob Ruiz Anderson, Eddster, Nima1024, WikitanvirBot, GA bot, Re-alsniper, Dakota Pauls, Madlamp, STATicVapor, Ragowit, Lewismaster, Oscar776, Super48paul, Lespaulonfire, Eduardofoxx13, Racerx11, GoingBatty, Samcaffery, Goose.johnson99, Britni ignoranceisnotbliss, Dreamlift, Transekvoten, Tommy2010, Winner 42, Rusty1111, Jay-dark123, Maidenfinalfrontier1, Anirudh Emani, Bob566, HMRok, Atari2, ThatRockMetalGuy, ReflectionDivine, Chrisbfmv, Libertariandude, Oasis1994-, Whathexup, Ida Shaw, Swallowing gum, A scary mansion, There is a dead ghost, Shuipzv3, Mcg182m, Monkeyface101, Ela-tionAviation, Topper46231, Saurabhshinoda, Mab987, H3llBot, Yousuck248, Unreal7, S trinitrotoluene, Acdcisawesome, Burbridge92, May Cause Dizziness, Colby stearns, Kevon100, L1A1 FAL, Ranzua, JoeSperrazza, Cohanlon95, Novascotia101, Τασουλα, Metalfreak121, Ba-maman14, Intothatdarkness, Donner60, Maiden66six, IronMaidenFan1810, Metalvayne, 2tuntony, Vsdhfiwehfvnvow, Bobbyd2u, Theabomb, Iamcool74, ChuispastonBot, NicholasJr7, Horways, Todpower, PsychoticChimp, Sven Manguard, DASHBotAV, Square1style, Adgadg3, Mjbm-rbot, 220livres, Red904blue, XLAxMetallica, Universal599gto, Mhiji, ClueBot NG, Aces888, Therein8383, Hepulis, CactusBot, Joefromrandb, Shylocksboy, Pc335, Parvaaz, Bright Darkness, Delusion23, Lpshorty, Keogruteras, Djodjo666, Slepone14, Zemand, DEFINEMETAL, Widr, Siddino7, Judaispriest, SnakeRambo, FaustPOLSKA, Nerdtrap, DayKey, Mishukdero, O7VS, HMSSolent, Corn2003, Strike Eagle, Calabe1992, Avengednightmario, Tom-1674, BG19bot, Oscarmannenberghe, Matěj Suchánek, Einstein294, Tylewhite, Northamerica1000, Uzielis, Kobas96, Eternities, AMadJester, MusikAnimal, RandomHeroTribute, Slothen74, Fukhhkbg2457854, Russell.360, DoktorWerther, Rm1271, Laliwil, Dangerzone77, Metalhead918579, Zeke, the Mad Horrorist, Der Naturfreund, Wishshadow, LondonER19, Unyum, Mouzourides, Thomas West-ermann, Fr bck, Brymzanthony, The1337gamer, Ilovebeards, Brayness, Al12179, Megajaja, Anmáistir, Vanspua, Arr4, Geekkid123, S4suraj, STKS91, Chie one, Myxomatosis57, Surajiron, Khazar2, Amb1997, Killmeister, Chizcw, Tfjellsoy, Chef Ramsey666, Dexbot, TwoTwoHello, GuitarGeek, Jetpack66, Nikoloco, Metalheadmitchyj, DanielTom, BeanZull, Camdof1, Epicgenius, Clashfan2, Kk1712, Haarryj, Rattlehead93, Riddb79, Emod Morales, SeaOfSmiles, Chartbot, Krisfrosz133, LancasterBomber1, Tenrag the Scot, 2beg90s1g, 1080STEVEHARRIS, Chris-tianJosephAllbee, Ginsuloft, SNUGGUMS, Goodyntox, Rambotje, Captainchaos123, Jakewhyland, Monkbot, Filedelinkerbot, Number-fidler, Asser.memo, Dylberry98, Dankthrone420, DRNSTR666, Chudmyster, Gina workman, Bschifman, ChamithN, RyanTQuinn, DangerousJXD,

PaulYtaak, Metalgvrv, Solkreig Aiereus, RALFFPL, Lacy3345, Johnirish755, Malcolmirish722, Pranavtherocker35, Crackstack22, Kirito Kazzuha, KasparBot, ICommandeth, Charliewonder7, Rasbin thapa, MetalMetalMetalMania, Johncmarcia, Fatmikey, Sparkysilverfish, Siraj bista, Rambo66966, Craigcarson92, DonZwicker and Anonymous: 3639

- **Jaguar (band)** Source: https://en.wikipedia.org/wiki/Jaguar_(band)?oldid=690667550 Contributors: Asparagus, DocWatson42, Recury, Woohookitty, Fnorp, Crystallina, SmackBot, Derek R Bullamore, Headshaker, Dl2000, Cydebot, Fabrictramp, Bhippel, CommonsDelinker, Wilhelm meis, Acakewouldbenice, Steven J. Anderson, Vinyl999, Undead warrior, WereSpielChequers, James25402, Florentyna, ImageRemovalBot, Arjayay, Llb9977, Addbot, Yobot, Marauder09, FrescoBot, Georg Rehm, DefaultsortBot, Orenburg1, Bristoliensis, EmausBot, Lewismaster, GoingBatty, Xrsj, MelbourneStar, Jeffreyalancox, Jodosma, Dragonlady9, Jaguarnwobhm, Anotherbandmember6, Thisragingsilence, KasparBot, Jaguarnwobhmband and Anonymous: 18

- **Jameson Raid (band)** Source: https://en.wikipedia.org/wiki/Jameson_Raid_(band)?oldid=676100566 Contributors: MBisanz, Woohookitty, SmackBot, Derek R Bullamore, Dl2000, CmdrObot, Cydebot, Nick Number, L0b0t, OddMNilsen, Imagi-King, Nite-Sirk, Dravecky, Wiki libs, Duffbeerforme, Yobot, SAHBfan, Marauder09, SAULGNRFAN, FreeRangeFrog, Lewismaster, Finflix, BG19bot, Amroknian, Jimbo2371, Alzantir, KasparBot and Anonymous: 14

- **John McCoy (musician)** Source: https://en.wikipedia.org/wiki/John_McCoy_(musician)?oldid=686879102 Contributors: Bearcat, David Gerard, Quadell, ESkog, Ogg, Woohookitty, GraemeLeggett, Mandarax, Koavf, Gffghgfhkghfk44323, SmackBot, Derek R Bullamore, E-Kartoffel, Dl2000, Fsotrain09, Waacstats, Twsx, Hekerui, Keith D, WOSlinker, Grodvin, Technopat, Klippdass, Martarius, Ostalocutanje, Jax 0677, Addbot, Tassedethe, Lightbot, Yobot, Gazebo81, Francodamned, FrescoBot, HRoestBot, Angel Snap, Hoalong, RjwilmsiBot, Beyond My Ken, WikitanvirBot, Marek Koudelka, Mvdejong, Toppsud, Khazar2, Dobie80, KasparBot and Anonymous: 21

- **Judas Priest** Source: https://en.wikipedia.org/wiki/Judas_Priest?oldid=690265653 Contributors: Malcolm Farmer, AlexWasFirst, Camembert, Olivier, Stevertigo, Delirium, Tregoweth, Ellywa, DropDeadGorgias, LittleDan, Andres, Conti, Mulad, Kroum, Toreau, Aqualung, Elwoz, Stormie, UninvitedCompany, PuzzletChung, Pigsonthewing, RedWolf, Nurg, Naddy, Bertie, Tobycat, Hadal, UtherSRG, Dehumanizer, Arm, Leonig Mig, Djinn112, Gtrmp, Ferkelparade, Ds13, Mboverload, Gadfium, Child of Bodom, Ellsworth, Borameer, Karl-Henner, Tromatic, Deleteme42, Freakofnurture, EugeneZelenko, Discospinster, Eel, Rich Farmbrough, Cfailde, BVZM, Narsil, Sn0wflake, Edgarde, CanisRufus, Illumynite, Spearhead, Keno, Mike Garcia, Adambro, Bobo192, Mrbicrevise, Nicke Lilltroll~enwiki, MARQUIS111, King nothing, Helix84, Pearle, Jumbuck, Alansohn, Gargaj, Edgriebel, Andrewpmk, Hyperlink~enwiki, Keepsleeping, TenOfAllTrades, Someoneinmyheadbutit'snotme, Dopefish, Metamorf, Woohookitty, Mindmatrix, Vorash, Rechlin, FPAtl, Muya, The Wordsmith, Exxolon, Twthmoses, Roda~enwiki, Metal man123, Paxsimius, Graham87, BD2412, Jclemens, Dennypayne, Rjwilmsi, Nightscream, MordredKLB, Elwyn5150, FutureNJGov, Vegaswikian, MarnetteD, Fish and karate, Leithp, FlaBot, Gringo300, Tokus, Gtmo, Eatpie75, Flowerparty, RexNL, Redwolf24, Neofelis Nebulosa~enwiki, Avador, D.brodale, Www.jpfo.org, Walter Moar, Chobot, DVdm, Gwernol, YurikBot, RobotE, Blightsoot, Lawnboy1977, Hede2000, Piet Delport, Kerowren, Gaius Cornelius, Cryptic, NawlinWiki, Irk, Wiki alf, Spike Wilbury, Welsh, Ondenc, Cleared as filed, Shinmawa, Cholmes75, Keithlard, MakeChooChooGoNow, Cerejota, Samir, JdwNYC, Nlu, E tac, Mitchell k dwyer, David orlovic, Lt-wiki-bot, Omdfg, De Administrando Imperio, Smurrayinchester, A Doon, Garion96, Banus, Meegs, GrinBot~enwiki, WesleyDodds, Dposse, SmackBot, Avengerx, Moeron, Simon Beavis, Slashme, Unyoyega, Hatto, IainP, Stifle, Mr Pyles, Daddycruel, Ppntori, Kearby, Chris the speller, Artoftransformation, Pietaster, Faded, Postoak, Bazonka, SamirKagadkar, CSWarren, Wikipediatrix, Jfsamper, Colonies Chris, Daddy Kindsoul, Scwlong, Alex 101, Sgt Pinback, Dumpendebat, Bonze50, AdamjVogt, Egglord, Doh286, Darwin's Bulldog, Steelbeard1, The Elfoid, Pushit, Nakon, Oanabay04, RafaelG, Derek R Bullamore, MetalHeadBanger, Metamagician3000, In Flames, Marcus Brute, Bretonbanquet, CallumJenkins2, Ohconfucius, Vasiliy Faronov, Nomoretears, Technocratic, RedArrow21, AlanD, Gsmuk, BadgerBader, SilkTork, J.Fries, CenozoicEra, Soumyasch, GizmoKSX, Ckatz, Beetstra, Monni95, Redeagle688, AHTNF, The Damaja, Dl2000, KJS77, Ryouga, OnBeyondZebrax, Iridescent, Spark, Ollie the Magic Skater, DefLeppardVanHalen, Bassman156, Izaakb, Tony Fox, Bombs Away, Wwallacee, Dunne409, Courcelles, Anger22, Tawkerbot2, RattleandHum, Jknobull, Mr. Metal Head, CmdrObot, Deon, Seal Clubber, Addict 2006, THINMAN, LotR, Drinibot, CWY2190, Tony lion, Franck Drake, Tim Long, DanielRigal, Cumulus Clouds, ShelfSkewed, Corporal clegg48, URORIN, Icarus of old, Cydebot, KingGohma, Boundless One, Fair Deal, GalenKnighthawke, Damifb, BeachJediSC, Dickinson~enwiki, Christian75, Sgt-D, RottweilerCS, NorthernThunder, Cscott530, Gimmetrow, Epbr123, A Sniper, Thedarxide, Luminifer, GentlemanGhost, Rebekah13192, Orchestral, Serpent-A, Padgett22, Headbomb, Fluxbot, Zeeny79, Java13690, Mr. Brain, DavidJJJ, RFerreira, Jbl1975, Bethpage89, Nick Number, Classic rocker, Sectornine, Sherick, Millagorilla, RetiredUser124642196, AntiVandalBot, Antique Rose, Prolog, LinaMishima, Daniel Villalobos, Marat75, Sadchild, Darklilac, Spencer, NESFreak, White Devil, Mattleek12, 1mickh1, Abeyi76, Rohanpais89, Andrzejbanas, Kaobear, MER-C, Egoc, Janejellyroll, Areaseven, Tohru Honda13, Durandal1717, TomGibb, MegX, The panson, SEGA, Y2kcrazyjoker4, LittleOldMe, Pedro, Bongwarrior, VoABot II, Fusionmix, TheEsb, Normandoe, Twsx, Markoff Chaney, PenguinJockey, Rodparkes, Kameejl, Simonxag, Andi d, Romancer, Grinder0-0, Woknam66, DerHexer, Totophi, Wi-king, JPNo1Fan, Robfrules, Varsindarkin, SwankRock3000, Furyo Mori, Conquerist, MartinBot, BetBot~enwiki, Helltopay27, Perón, Sinister13, Keith D, T-Prime85, Supe~enwiki, Deansaliba, Cyberface, FMAFan1990, J.delanoy, Nev1, DandyDan2007, Ali, Herbythyme, Howa0082, Mutehero, Eliz81, Crimsontider, George415, Wrathteen, The Copper 17, The Wiki Priest, I teh yuh, AntiSpamBot, Nwbeeson, Chanakaj, Imagi-King, Jrcla2, FGT2, David Whitton, Mercury93, Izno, Adreamer323, Dagoh, Signalhead, Bigger Boss, ACSE, Jrugordon, Bovineboy2008, Highcouncil, Tmohr, LethalSRX, Hapori Tohu, TXiKiBoT, BoBrandt, Danorama, Devilxhlywood, Technopat, A4bot, GDonato, Mosmof, Riles has styles, Dadsnagem, Bookkeeperoftheoccult, Lvivske, Qxz, IllaZilla, Yilloslime, Melsaran, Moju123, HHH-DX, Electrokinesis, ^demonBot2, BotKung, Zolireds, Inx272, Damooster, Joelasaurus, Tinyclaw, Falcon8765, Robothefreak, Symo-EFC, NinjaRobotPirate, Jochim Schiller, Rock Soldier, Entirelybs, HiDrNick, Apmetal, Quantpole, Funeral, AllJudasPriest, Stay Dead, Anarchist92, CrimsonOmega, Differentbreed, King005~enwiki, Shyte, Metal Michelle, HomerRamone, Peter Fleet, Burningclean, Dog Man311, SieBot, Gorpik, YonaBot, Scarian, CircafuciX, Clamticore, Mungo Kitsch, Diskwiped, Alterego269, Nite-Sirk, Domonicrini, Happysailor, B33Jaysrfun, Brozozo, OneLove1977, Dtmy, Le Pied-bot~enwiki, Klippdass, B.C.Schmerker, Antonio Lopez, Nuttycoconut, Earendil11, Benea, Lightmouse, JudasAngel, V(g), Lebe.alan, Ilikeeggs1, Mkeranat, Gunmetal Angel, CC-best, TallShip108, Navnløs, Cyfal, W.e whatever, J.D.myface, Judassab, Willy, your mate, Joseutu, Tkreuz, Atonefornothing, ImageRemovalBot, Libertarian92, Martarius, ClueBot, Tomlupton, Sennen goroshi, Binksternet, Snigbrook, Dobermanji, Witchwooder, Keraunoscopia, Horsdumonde, SomeGuy11112, Gunrbotter2, TheOldJacobite, Mezigue, Evermore2, NNtw22, Deathbringer from the Sky, Nymf, KnightsofCydonia, Yellowxander, Metal Head Dave, A Powerful Weakness, Adyacdcrock88, Iamtheonewhoeats, Muhandes, Michaelsmith81, Wiki libs, Hydrofujita, Basilo12, Asa Cloud, C628, Thingg, Shooty668, Anarkangel, Caper454, Rockin dead, Qwfp, SoxBot III, Indopug, Rockk3r, Vanished User 1004, Phantomwiki, DumZiBoT, Crazy Boris with a red beard, Terr-E, XLinkBot, Zakkman, Wiseleo, Pheonex, Electric Japan, Blääköb, Solino, TheSickBehemoth, WikHead, Alexius08, Yuvn86, Karl47, MystBot, Kbdankbot, Addbot, Malconfort, RandySavageFTW, Ma0zz3d, Dan56, Laughingman78, Sibuachu, Sfgasefg, AllTriumph,

4.1. TEXT

IbLeo, Haxxiy, Fieldday-sunday, Canedil~enwiki, Leszek Jańczuk, Aryder779, Gerryforbes, Jyoo25, Cst17, Download, LaaknorBot, Glane23, Nickin, Vio2112, LinkFA-Bot, 5 albert square, Beast from da East, Angry Shoplifter, Tassedethe, Moshpot101, Äppelmos~enwiki, Jbrockfan, OlEnglish, Zorrobot, Megaman en m, Ynot4tony2, PlankBot, Luckas-bot, Yobot, Deathmagnetic08, Tdl185, Legobot II, Carrot98, Roger Workman, IW.HG, Bsterbakov, Redjedia, AnomieBOT, Clintschaff, 1exec1, Koffe113, Piano non troppo, Judas91, The Great Duck, TParis, Krem12, GetMKWearMKFly, Cutmynoseofftospitemyface, Jeff Muscato, Materialscientist, BlackSabbath16, Aff123a, Citation bot, Makele-90, Judas Priest is effin awsome, ArthurBot, Llauzonvt, Ximmerman, Tomhornstra, Melkortheevil, The Banner, Capricorn42, Wether B, Resident Wiki, Axelsegen, Danebramage8020, KingRatedRIV, Wrightstuff1111, Davedj, Mlpearc, Inferno, Lord of Penguins, LostLikeTearsInRain, Aussie Ausborn, J04n, Genghis spawn, Smartperson45, Minerazo, Dear cobain, Polargeo, Motorpunk, Spongefrog, Nicksharpe, GripTheHusk, Nixón, FrescoBot, Imhazzardelf, Jexic, Poopmaster98, Michael93555, A vision of it, Ranchloopseven, Singh is cool, Pellestar, Jukka Tarvonen, Wikimoocow2, Nuppiz, MrIpodz, Dpepper73, DPCDD, Slam3, Fixer88, Île flottante, K.tikadar, Duskb, Erlandinho, Mathnor, Eddie666bm, Lordnecronus, TobeBot, Colchester121891, Mickle Elden Snott, Ironmaidenfan800, Rockgenre, Exagon, Bigjohn johnson, Ewines, Xvix56, Tigger-ibby, Dinamik-bot, SeoMac, BC Rocky, Scottrc44, Matiasmoritz, Rationem, Pilmccartney, Tbhotch, Drakebell260, Thebeerman12oz, Woogee, Axl kg, Nahyan007, HrZ, Lucazeppelin, EmausBot, Nima1024, Mzilikazi1939, STATicVapor, Oscar776, Katherine, Eduardofoxx13, Dewritech, LeperMessiah117, Mra10, Starcheerspeaksnewslostwars, GoingBatty, Thomasionus, Hamidmushtaq, Martyleehi, SomeGuyWhoNeedsAnAccount, Sepguilherme, Nehankun, Leandro Drudo, Troika ness, Kingsofrocknroll, Jpl928329, Ted Phelan, Jefftemple, Lateg, Mab987, Bass Genius69, Edit3rnchief, Syny6, Burbridge92, Wayne Slam, Tiganusi, L1A1 FAL, L Kensington, Colinwriter, JohnnyangelNIU, 100loves, VLN1025, MajorHawke, ChuispastonBot, Poster Nutbag, SSDGFCTCT9, Mjbmrbot, ClueBot NG, Mansmokingacigar, CactusBot, Johnlor, Aamoth, Rock&RollSuicide, MelbourneStar, TheRyk, Joefromrandb, Painkiller220, Revelationer, Syns123456789, Judaispriest, Jamcad01, Anupmehra, Helpful Pixie Bot, RageGuy, Gojira95666, Afifanno1, Lowercase sigmabot, Thor cherubim, Evilqueen620, BG19bot, Island Monkey, Oscarmannenberghe, Duality67, Morradierman, Intervallic, Thatemooverthere, XxTyrant17xX, The Macabre Milkman, Robocoop80498, Rockcenter, DrKilleMoff, The1337gamer, Metalhead321658, Cyberbot II, Chie one, Calu2000, NitRav, Thefateshavewarned, BenS1978, JYBot, Killmeister, FreddyHalford, Dexbot, VanNatteris, Webclient101, I call the big one bitey, Mogism, Jamiri, UselessToRemain, Old Time Music Fan, Lugia2453, Loki-zer0, SFK2, Herve Reex, ChakaKong, Ilikepeanutbutter1000, Retrohead, Queenfanuriah, Awesomejones, Howicus, Bjgluv, T72sim1, RealMetal, Gasmaskboi19371945, 2beg90s1g, Vycl1994, Shewire, Synthwave.94, MrLinkinPark333, Chanhmatt, Captain Magma Quack, Epic Failure, Sabbatino, Fruitloop11, Carlos Rojas77, Bryemycaz, Esmost, JohnnyJohnsonJohn, Filedelinkerbot, Twyfan714, Hissler, Lukejordan02, Tonysentinel, ZyklonicHD, EternalFloette, DissidentAggressor, Johnny338, DarkPsalms, Wajenkins, YesPretense, Deity Hunter, MoJo3161981, MetallicaLightning, Cheezemunkey, Hate This Ernie, JohnnyToxxxic and Anonymous: 1439

- **Lionheart (band)** *Source:* https://en.wikipedia.org/wiki/Lionheart_(band)?oldid=689326979 *Contributors:* Bearcat, Pascal666, Woohookitty, Rjwilmsi, Gringo300, Malcolma, Steelbeard1, Derek R Bullamore, Cydebot, Furyo Mori, J.delanoy, Standingfish, Weakmassive, Tiptoety, Martarius, Crossfire365, Natt the Hatt, Yobot, Materialscientist, Marauder09, SAULGNRFAN, WikiWikingerX, Crackmagazine, Cowlibob, EmausBot, John of Reading, Lewismaster, ZéroBot, ClueBot NG, Kingevz, Mark Arsten, Flyingvivaldi, Jesuspoochrist, KasparBot, Billyhatcher18 and Anonymous: 4

- **List of New Wave of British Heavy Metal bands** *Source:* https://en.wikipedia.org/wiki/List_of_New_Wave_of_British_Heavy_Metal_bands?oldid=690161996 *Contributors:* Nigel C. Fortune, Dthomsen8, Lewismaster, Sj666 and Anonymous: 3

- **Magnum (band)** *Source:* https://en.wikipedia.org/wiki/Magnum_(band)?oldid=690187041 *Contributors:* Robbot, Pigsonthewing, Alsotop, Xezbeth, Mairi, Mattbrundage, Saxifrage, Japanese Searobin, Mahanga, Exxolon, Jdcooper, Rjwilmsi, Koavf, Bruce1ee, Mark83, Brooza, WpediaIsNotPaper, PGPirate, SmackBot, Chris the speller, Derek R Bullamore, Mikejstevenson, Bydand, AB, Monni95, Dl2000, Jaksmata, Bearingbreaker92, CmdrObot, Krushsister, Cydebot, Ebyabe, Thijs!bot, Fisherjs, Magnumaniac1958, Lee Gregz, MegX, Magioladitis, Miketm, Rich257, Twsx, Zagmac, Bazaray, Jdh1971, OohBunnies!, Andrewself, Dom Kaos, WOSlinker, Butseriouslyfolks, TXiKiBoT, Reeferboy, Andrew Wild, AlleborgoBot, Charlescrawley, Derekjc, Xarr, Theoldgoat, James25402, MisterVodka, Aspects, Cyfal, Escape Orbit, Eetwartti, Smcleish, MAVIII, Yellowxander, Moonriddengirl2, DumZiBoT, Kbdankbot, addbot, Tassedethe, Rafwuk, Lightbot, Rodericksilly, Luckas-bot, Yobot, Ptbotgourou, AnomieBOT, The Great Duck, Mcoupal, KeyDroyd, Infanteriesoldat, B3t, Mrix1985, DefaultsortBot, RjwilmsiBot, EmausBot, John of Reading, Lewismaster, Kjoh2010, GoingBatty, Ben10Joshua, Marek Koudelka, Dogsbody56, Burbridge92, Michael13111983, Soleymourning, MauchoEagle, KLBot2, BG19bot, Mr Rabbit8, Glevum, Highlander58, Khazar2, Mogism, Materasi, Rover85, Metadox, KasparBot and Anonymous: 94

- **Mama's Boys** *Source:* https://en.wikipedia.org/wiki/Mama'{}s_Boys?oldid=685490154 *Contributors:* Delpino, Jpgordon, NeoChaosX, Ardfern, Metropolitan90, Million Little Gods, RealWingus, JulesH, Irishrocker, Jogers, Bluebot, Derek R Bullamore, BNutzer, Monni95, Skinsmoke, Dl2000, CmdrObot, Cydebot, Nick Number, Dougm1970, OddMNilsen, Muddylives, AlleborgoBot, Tataryn, DiamondDave84, Aspects, Gazzaguitar, HentaimanXT, Caper454, SlayerXT, Addbot, Lightbot, PlankBot, Yobot, Harveybear, Marauder09, Costj, Scabichav, Lewismaster, CactusBot, Conor O'Neill, Murry1975, Amroknian, LibraryListings, Alzantir, KasparBot and Anonymous: 24

- **Marseille (band)** *Source:* https://en.wikipedia.org/wiki/Marseille_(band)?oldid=676477579 *Contributors:* Bearcat, Bgwhite, ZaphodBeeblebrox, SmackBot, Chris the speller, Thumperward, Racklever, Dl2000, Elbeonore, CmdrObot, Cydebot, Bakilas, Dbuckley, Johnpacklambert, Sally Anne, Uncle Dick, Imagi-King, Nouse4aname, Rustedinpeace502, Sheled Umlal, DumZiBoT, Addbot, Ironholds, Yobot, Triquetra, Marauder09, FrescoBot, DefaultsortBot, IvyLeed, Thedeanjones, Hiddenstranger, Lewismaster, GoingBatty, Ianzarquon, Rockhead666, Gallifreyjack, Marseillenige, Amroknian, Horrido1954, Dilly29, CatCat, Alzantir, KasparBot and Anonymous: 26

- **Mirage (metal band)** *Source:* https://en.wikipedia.org/wiki/Mirage_(metal_band)?oldid=654406914 *Contributors:* Bearcat, Ritchie333, CommonsDelinker, KylieTastic, Niceguyedc, BG19bot, Cyberbot I, StewdioMACK, Artie Fuftkin and Anonymous: 2

- **More (British band)** *Source:* https://en.wikipedia.org/wiki/More_(British_band)?oldid=687061627 *Contributors:* Warofdreams, Tabletop, Derek R Bullamore, Dl2000, Dsalazar23491, Cydebot, Lugnuts, Thijs!bot, Businessman332211, Anna Lincoln, IllaZilla, Undead warrior, James25402, MystBot, Addbot, Yobot, Marauder09, Erik9, MrX, EmausBot, Lewismaster, KasparBot and Anonymous: 31

- **Motörhead** *Source:* https://en.wikipedia.org/wiki/Mot%C3%B6rhead?oldid=690915948 *Contributors:* WojPob, The Anome, Berek, Olivier, Mrwojo, Liftarn, Darkwind, Lancevortex, Charles Matthews, Tpbradbury, TheChin!, Aqualung, SD6-Agent, Donarreiskoffer, Bearcat, Jmabel, Nurg, Naddy, Ukuk~enwiki, Hippietrail, Delpino, David Edgar, GreatWhiteNortherner, David Gerard, Xyzzyva, DocWatson42, Gtrmp, BenFrantzDale, Ferkelparade, Michael Devore, Ezhiki, Node ue, Bobblewik, Alexf, Child of Bodom, Paulley, Joyous!, Mike Rosoft, Freakofnurture, MattKingston, Bornintheguz, Discospinster, Rich Farmbrough, Guanabot, NrDg, Abelson, Michael Zimmermann, BjarteSorensen, DS1953,

Kwamikagami, Shanes, Spearhead, Art LaPella, Pablo X, Mike Garcia, Mactenchi, Alphax, Nev, Almightybooblikon, Libertas Gentis~enwiki, Pearle, Methegreat, Frodet, Alansohn, Marnen, Tayal01, Ozzyslovechild, Snowolf, SidP, Henry W. Schmitt, Someoneinmyheadbutit'snotme, Gene Nygaard, Mattbrundage, Chrysaor, Red dwarf, Megan1967, Stemonitis, Woohookitty, John Cardinal, Tabletop, Al E., GregorB, Roda~enwiki, SeventyThree, BD2412, Qwertyus, David Levy, Kbdank71, JIP, Jdcooper, Rjwilmsi, Koavf, Teklund, Trlovejoy, Vegaswikian, Brighterorange, Bensin, Ucucha, Sango123, FlaBot, RobertG, McPhail, Vclaw, Flowerparty, Gurch, OpenToppedBus, NoseNuggets, Windharp, Mcy919, Hahnchen, YurikBot, Tommyt, NTBot~enwiki, RussBot, Epolk, Foxxygirltamara, Hydrargyrum, Gaius Cornelius, Cambridge-BayWeather, Rbrtplnt777, Fnorp, NawlinWiki, Wiki alf, Aeusoes1, Jaxl, Moe Epsilon, Oakster, Bota47, Spute, Elf ideas, Rosc0, Teiladnam, Closedmouth, KGasso, Jeemag, Steveweiser, JoanneB, Kingboyk, WesleyDodds, SmackBot, Jaseparlo, LochNess, Zazaban, Ze miguel, Hatto, Delldot, LuciferMorgan, Mr Pyles, AnOddName, Geoff B, Dustmites, Gaff, Yamaguchi??, UnqstnableTruth, Gannon 13, Algont, Ghosts&empties, Carl.bunderson, Bluebot, Dark Apostrophe, Colonies Chris, Emurphy42, Daddy Kindsoul, Chlewbot, OrphanBot, KevM, Rrburke, TKD, Rsm99833, Greenshed, Whpq, The Elfoid, Ritchie333, Fuhghettaboutit, X-Flare-x, RJN, Derek R Bullamore, Metamagician3000, Pen of bushido, Curly Turkey, Kukini, ReToOcS, Zappafan33, Ceoil, SashatoBot, Robomaeyhem, GoogleMe~enwiki, Awesimo, Gobonobo, Butko, Mark Lungo, JHunterJ, Fuzzy510, E-Kartoffel, Manifestation, Scorpion0422, DabMachine, Fasach Nua, Ryouga, ISD, OnBeyondZebrax, Slash99, Iridescent, Sasaki, Shoeofdeath, CanuckGod, The Secretary of Funk, Courcelles, Anger22, Sportsnut, Vampain, Dlohcierekim, J Milburn, Mr. Metal Head, The Prince of Darkness, FunPika, CBM, Drinibot, Tim Long, Yarnalgo, Ferdiaob, ShelfSkewed, Jedudedek, Aaru Bui, AndrewHowse, Valf~enwiki, Cydebot, Warhorus, Fair Deal, Vanished user vjhsduheuiui4t5hjri, Crocodileman, Jameboy, HK51, RottweilerCS, AndTheCrowdGoesWild, Xx vampireheart xx, Brad101, A7x, BetacommandBot, Epbr123, Luminifer, PEJL, Tobz1000, PanAndScan, Fluxbot, Hayabusax1, Dawnseeker2000, Tiger Trek, Prolog, Paste, IrishPete, RobJ1981, Nadim Scolris, Hoponpop69, Jessiejames, G Rose, White Devil, Myanw, Ghmyrtle, Leuqarte, Abeyi76, Sprcp, Andrzejbanas, JAnDbot, Xnux, Deflective, Kaobear, MER-C, Greyo, Endlessdan, Reign of Toads, East718, MegX, Y2kcrazyjoker4, Magioladitis, PacificBoy, 75pickup, Bongwarrior, VoABot II, Auburn-Pilot, JamesBWatson, Delage, Bubba hotep, Sticks66, Kameejl, Lemmy the lurch, Fhb3, Horsequit, Lost tourist, Alan Burridge, Smaunsell, Mr Shark, Davepoth, Fonoq35, Keith D, Mschel, R'n'B, CommonsDelinker, Raonisousa, Lilac Soul, FMAFan1990, Sklirada, J.delanoy, Pharaoh of the Wizards, DrKay, Trusilver, DandyDan2007, Tikiwont, SteveLamacq43, Hip-Hop and Rock, Dispenser, Pletet, Aar, Simon Curtis, Cometstyles, Nikki311, Drwhawkfan, SmallPotatoes, Mimr, Useight, Izno, VolkovBot, Thedjatclubrock, Meaningful Username, Stranger4001, Dij88, Antongandon, ArnoldPettybone, TXiKiBoT, Tricky Victoria, Bdb484, Xr 1, Jay95, Papa Ul, Someguy1221, IllaZilla, MarkMarek, LeaveSleaves, Electrokinesis, Mrbeasty, Andres gnr, McMe 3:!6, Bashereyre, Gustav Lindwall, Enigmaman, Bothorth, IL7Soulhunter, Acacia70, Eeecccwww, Number87, Falcon8765, Insane-Contrast, Symo-EFC, Rock Soldier, Schweinehund, Quantpole, Funeral, Anarchist92, EmxBot, Peter Fleet, Balthazar, Moonriddengirl, Scarian, Ktulu6, Saltywood, Gerakibot, Clamticore, Nite-Sirk, Domonicrini, Flyer22 Reborn, Arbor to SJ, Yerpo, JSpung, Lightmouse, Seth Whales, Techman224, Fopply didlo, Fratrep, Gunmetal Angel, Thundermaster, Arundhati lejeune, Navnløs, Maxi64, Ferrer.jorge, Dabomb87, Jza84, Bbefilms, Escape Orbit, GrimReaper75, Dodopie, WWEFanatic14, Mario Žamić, Cincinnati135, Martarius, Mike Tv 2007, Leahtwosaints, ClueBot, Binksternet, Bristolrover, The Thing That Should Not Be, Zaka1980, Jkerl8, Pmitas, Drmies, Qsaw, Niceguyedc, Swiss toni69, Bardin, Rockfang, Deathbringer from the Sky, Nymf, A Powerful Weakness, Lartoven, Ykhwong, Thejasonboy, Lurulu, NiciVampireHeart, Wiki libs, Arjayay, Titan50, Wkharrisjr, Thingg, Jonr2112, DudeatBish, Dana boomer, MelonBot, Indopug, Rockk3r, Myspace69, Billus 4, Mr Larrington, Hotcrocodile, TheSickBehemoth, Fred the Oyster, WikHead, Jkolak, SilvonenBot, Tim010987, Count of Tuscany, Kbdankbot, Scramble94, Tealdon, Kiloi6, Addbot, Malconfort, ScaryhairyOriginal, RandySavageFTW, DOI bot, Friginator, Willsied8, Elderhead, Kezza59, TutterMouse, Leszek Jańczuk, I feel like a tourist, LaaknorBot, Cambalachero, DFS454, Glane23, DARRK99, MF-Boris, SuperSilver901, Kyle1278, AtheWeatherman, LinkFA-Bot, Crasherisntmydogsname, Iluvmetal28, Kisbesbot, Angry Shoplifter, Behemoth91, Tassedethe, Numbo3-bot, Seilacei, Tide rolls, Backhander66613, Zorrobot, Khayyinn, Frehley, Legobot, Luckas-bot, Yobot, JJARichardson, Ptbotgourou, Guy1890, Jordaneus, Roger Workman, Matrix8110, IW.HG, AlexLevyOne, Radiopathy, AnomieBOT, Floquenbeam, Rubinbot, 1exec1, Jim1138, Galoubet, Pyrrhus16, Bringme1369, Kingpin13, RandomAct, Bluerasberry, Jeff Muscato, Materialscientist, Sofajockey, AnthonyPaul0209, Fschriner, Citation bot, Tanner9461, LilHelpa, Ximmerman, Jkdfhgkhd, MauritsBot, Xqbot, TheP1990, HellrazEr214, Wether B, Mlpearc, LostLikeTearsInRain, Aussie Ausborn, Djmichaelray, J04n, GrouchoBot, NightmareSnake, Abce2, ProfAuthorityFigure, Mutante96, Billyrobshaw, Jon742, Ricardobq666, Prunesqualer, RibotBOT, Motorhead69, Amaury, BlackMath77, Richard BB, GripTheHusk, Het zel, FrescoBot, LucienBOT, SHDFEBJohey, Jascol0140, A vision of it, Edge3, RandomGuy666, Giratina55, Riu Zuchi, Eddie Wall, Fart in your face!, Jiggaboo132, Bercowich, Citation bot 1, Arctic Night, LittleWink, Lukétis =D, W2446797, RedBot, Île flottante, Porky metal 666, Motorizer, User456, Erlandinho, Legodino, Mondozilla, Drugyourlove, Tim1357, Jãoraimunds, TobeBot, Colchester121891, Mr. Colomy, Argolin, Rockgenre, MrX, Panel Guy, Andymcgrath, Syxxpackid420, Paulandersonmusic, Cowlibob, Studnotia, DiehardinRI, Anbu XD, Mean as custard, RjwilmsiBot, TjBot, Alph Bot, Ripchip Bot, HrZ, Rlholden, FairlyOddgodLOL, Danieljo2013, Cooksontrains, Slon02, DASHBot, EmausBot, Orphan Wiki, Scc83, Mk5384, Lewismaster, Oscar776, Dyl Man21, Pkimmich, ITshnik, Eduardofoxx13, Mashaunix, GoingBatty, Prenigmamann, Wikiturrican, SlackG, Tommy2010, Drumkid13, Martyleehi, ThatRockMetalGuy, Werieth, ZéroBot, SpennyT, John Cline, Nick6917, Alpha Quadrant (alt), H3llBot, Burbridge92, Proximawest, May Cause Dizziness, L1A1 FAL, Steelkeeper, Metalvayne, Viniguimas, WikiCopter, Orange Suede Sofa, ChuispastonBot, Brutalhovno, NLinpublic, Blackadder1234, Harrywiki45, ClueBot NG, Dwc89, Cactus-Bot, Gareth Griffith-Jones, Flathead49, GianlucaCaniglia, Sagi nair14, Joefromrandb, Rosso1990, Tresla1408, Blaguymonkey, Widr, Nerdtrap, Tomseattle, Helpful Pixie Bot, Bonifacio Dunkel, Goodgrief957, BG19bot, Southernrocker75, Oscarmannenberghe, Vagobot, Sleazemetal, Ich901, Claptonn, Metricopolus, RockNRollDog, Renegade Al, Joe Kaniini, Herbolzheim, TheMetallican, Matt Mohandas Gandhi, MisterMorton, H.morrison 98, Intensity254, BattyBot, Justincheng12345-bot, Cyberbot II, Chie one, ZappaOMati, Cristianho19, Khazar2, JYBot, Concerttour, Dexbot, Disturbedasylum, Metalheadmitchyj, Bloomgloom, Retrohead, HurluGumene, Roberto191, Shallowmead077, Rattlehead93, DavidLeighEllis, Berengaria, Rhietala, Ugog Nizdast, SparklyDeathKitten, Synthwave.94, Originalchampion, Sam Sailor, SNUGGUMS, MetalDiablo666, Tyadasm2006, Olliebear93, Teh Thrasher, Monkbot, Pepón Lleixà, Chloemuzza, DrewieStewie, Dwinchester267, Kolpos, ClassicOnAStick, DarkPsalms, RyanTQuinn, RALFFPL, Olivermetallica, JCW555, Calebbro, KasparBot, Farissxp, Metal ozzy, Joangupe.6, Disturbedkorea, Oldpeculiar65 and Anonymous: 1101

- **Nicky Moore** Source: https://en.wikipedia.org/wiki/Nicky_Moore?oldid=676237257 Contributors: Hmains, Derek R Bullamore, Waacstats, StAnselm, Martarius, Jax 0677, XLinkBot, Addbot, Tassedethe, Yobot, BlackBoneTorso~enwiki, SassoBot, Lewismaster, ClueBot NG, Chris-Gualtieri, Hmainsbot1, KasparBot and Anonymous: 18

- **Nightwing (band)** Source: https://en.wikipedia.org/wiki/Nightwing_(band)?oldid=686006214 Contributors: Discospinster, Florian Blaschke, Woohookitty, RussBot, Gilliganfanatic, Derek R Bullamore, Dl2000, Cydebot, Rpeh, Steve bartley, Niceguyedc, Darkerdizzy, XLinkBot, Tassedethe, Yobot, Marauder09, Mlpearc, Wiseowl10, John of Reading, Lewismaster, Gerbear70, BG19bot, Mozaika2, KasparBot and Anony-

4.1. TEXT

mous: 13

- **Pagan Altar** *Source:* https://en.wikipedia.org/wiki/Pagan_Altar?oldid=676237683 *Contributors:* Postdlf, Rjwilmsi, RussBot, Piet Delport, Onorem, Derek R Bullamore, DI2000, Cydebot, Lugnuts, Seaphoto, BeastmasterGeneral, Nothingagainst, Imagi-King, Asarlaí, Technopat, Zifirl, Mungo Kitsch, James25402, Nite-Sirk, Danio, Bibliophylax, Bulgakoff, Lau Kar-Yung, Blackless, Addbot, Queenmomcat, Yobot, Marauder09, TonyHagale, FrescoBot, Lewismaster, Bollyjeff, ClueBot NG, North Atlanticist Usonian, Helpful Pixie Bot, Jeraphine Gryphon, Scopecreep, CaSJer, DannyMusicEditor, You'reNotMyBrain, KasparBot and Anonymous: 70

- **Paul Di'Anno** *Source:* https://en.wikipedia.org/wiki/Paul_Di'Anno?oldid=685355917 *Contributors:* Shoaler, Habj, Toreau, Kulkuri, Pigsonthewing, RedWolf, SchmuckyTheCat, Carnildo, Niteowlneils, D6, Sn0wflake, Bumhoolery, Martpol, Bender235, Fatphil, Gargaj, PopUpPirate, Tainter, Stemonitis, GVOLTT, Commander Keane, Exxolon, Graham87, Dennypayne, Rjwilmsi, Koavf, Gringo300, Gtmo, Stormwatch, David91, DVdm, YurikBot, RussBot, C777, Cryptic, Howcheng, Harro, Tony1, Bota47, OMenda~enwiki, Mike Selinker, CapPixel, Kingboyk, SmackBot, Hux, LuciferMorgan, PJM, Mr Pyles, Ohnoitsjamie, Bluebot, Bazonka, Doubting thomas, Can't sleep, clown will eat me, OrphanBot, The Elfoid, HannuMakinen, Derek R Bullamore, Mwtoews, Bretonbanquet, Kristenq, Nomoretears, Euchiasmus, GizmoKSX, Tuspm, The Damaja, DI2000, Radman 99 1999, GiantSnowman, CmdrObot, Mattbr, CBM, ShelfSkewed, WeggeBot, RockMaster, Cydebot, Steph11, Springfinger, Trident13, RottweilerCS, Prodigenous Zee, After Midnight, NMChico24, Thijs!bot, Kohran, Nick Number, MichaelMaggs, Stevvvv4444, MrMarmite, Duh Svemira, IrishPete, Eddyspeeder, DShamen, Areaseven, PhilKnight, MegX, SEGA, Acroterion, Magioladitis, Litpho, Limelight05, Evilonline, PenguinJockey, Rechta, Horsequit, Radio gaga~enwiki, Furyo Mori, Jasonater, Seacow12222, Thaskalos, FruitMonkey, Stranger4001, Rivazza, Gune, Kww, Snowbot, Cheesebox, BigJoeRockHead, EmxBot, Scarian, Born Again 83, SE7, Geoff sebesta, Klippdass, CutOffTies, Aspects, Maquesta, Macy, Vanished User 8902317830, Mr. Granger, Martarius, Leahtwosaints, Dobermanji, Mild Bill Hiccup, Crywalt, A Powerful Weakness, Alejandrocaro35, Arjayay, 1ForTheMoney, Dozysplot, Jax 0677, XLinkBot, SlayerXT, TFOWR, WikHead, SilvonenBot, Bazj, Addbot, Otterathome, Yasharx, Opus88888, DougsTech, DutchDevil, Rojelio, Ferroequus, Angry Shoplifter, Tassedethe, Lightbot, Teles, Zorrobot, AndreyA, Count druckula, Yobot, Hambone9119, Jamesdjharrod, Leefeni,de Karik, AnomieBOT, Srinivas, Nofixedaddress, Czeitnewdewek, J04n, Eric Blatant, Off2riorob, Joey8030, Moxy, Edgar Grey, Outback the koala, MrIpodz, VitriolicHate, Mrix1985, Xfansd, Colchester121891, VaXo, Hoalong, RjwilmsiBot, EmausBot, SuperVirtual, John of Reading, Lewismaster, Eduardofoxx13, GoingBatty, Kimiko20, Txcal69, John of Lancaster, Ida Shaw, Unreal7, Puffin, DASHBotAV, ClueBot NG, Svenne J, Joefromrandb, Shylocksboy, Matthewrwarnock, Nerdtrap, Zimen88, Finncowboy, Der Naturfreund, BorrisTheCat, Brayness, ChrisGualtieri, Khazar2, VIAFbot, Batiste Igienice, Andrelol3, Three2Ski, Wikismasha, KasparBot, Quackriot and Anonymous: 259

- **Persian Risk** *Source:* https://en.wikipedia.org/wiki/Persian_Risk?oldid=683063612 *Contributors:* Mboverload, Bumm13, Oknazevad, Forbsey, Bjones, Leithp, RussBot, Wiki alf, La Pizza11, Derek R Bullamore, Bretonbanquet, DI2000, Maestlin, Cydebot, Standingfish, Vinyl999, James25402, Klippdass, Martarius, Niceguyedc, Bbb2007, Addbot, Binary TSO, Tassedethe, Yobot, Marauder09, SAULGNRFAN, Omnipaedista, WikiWikingerX, Cowlibob, WikitanvirBot, Lewismaster, GoingBatty, Joefromrandb, Amroknian, Babitaarora, Alzantir, BethNaught and Anonymous: 17

- **Pet Hate** *Source:* https://en.wikipedia.org/wiki/Pet_Hate?oldid=676238063 *Contributors:* Bearcat, Woohookitty, Jeff3000, Lewis R, Paul Erik, Crystallina, SmackBot, Chris the speller, HisSpaceResearch, Cydebot, Gene93k, Boleyn, Fluffernutter, PaddyGoo, Tide rolls, Surv1v4l1st, MenoBot II, Lewismaster, Starcheerspeaksnewslostwars, ClueBot NG, Rainbow Shifter, Robevans123 and Anonymous: 6

- **Praying Mantis (band)** *Source:* https://en.wikipedia.org/wiki/Praying_Mantis_(band)?oldid=690271822 *Contributors:* Kpjas, Liftarn, Asparagus, Bumm13, RJFJR, Ketiltrout, FlaBot, RussBot, SmackBot, PDD, Tsca.bot, Derek R Bullamore, Headshaker, Hoodinski, E-Kartoffel, DI2000, CmdrObot, Cydebot, Blackmetalbaz, Furyo Mori, Imagi-King, James25402, Florentyna, Chris fardon, Martarius, Unbuttered Parsnip, Jax 0677, XLinkBot, Addbot, Favonian, Tassedethe, Lightbot, Count druckula, Luckas-bot, Yobot, Marauder09, FrescoBot, DrilBot, MrX, John of Reading, Stryn, Lewismaster, SporkBot, Fsantos222, Lashuto, Turboyogi, AORmaniac13, Materasi, Sabbatino, Wolpat, Titancards, KasparBot, Esonkcid and Anonymous: 34

- **Quartz (metal band)** *Source:* https://en.wikipedia.org/wiki/Quartz_(metal_band)?oldid=676238565 *Contributors:* Bearcat, Bumm13, Woohookitty, Jeff3000, Hmains, Derek R Bullamore, DI2000, ERAGON, Cydebot, TenthEagle, Thijs!bot, BeastmasterGeneral, MegX, Appraiser, Twsx, Imagi-King, James25402, Aspects, Florentyna, BOTarate, Londonclanger, XLinkBot, Чръный человек, Addbot, Luckas-bot, Yobot, Arch stanton1138, Marauder09, FrescoBot, Frehley72, DefaultsortBot, TheEvilSop, Lewismaster, ClueBot NG, Turboyogi, ChrisGualtieri, Ozzie5catrugbyrugby, 1dazj and Anonymous: 9

- **Rainbow (rock band)** *Source:* https://en.wikipedia.org/wiki/Rainbow_(rock_band)?oldid=690971791 *Contributors:* Tarquin, Amillar, Rmhermen, Camembert, Ewen, Wapcaplet, Delirium, TUF-KAT, TUF-KAT, Michael, Tpbradbury, David Shay, Nv8200pa, Stormie, Robbot, Moriori, Sbisolo, Naddy, Jeronim, Auric, Wereon, Seano1, Cyrius, Alan Liefting, Capitalistroadster, Gamaliel, Gyrofrog, Bonalaw, Sysy, Silence, Mike Garcia, Slugguitar, Nk, Willerror, Linuxlad, Mike65, Skuld, Someoneinmyheadbutit'snotme, Tainter, Bastin, Megan1967, Woohookitty, Linnea, Neanderthalprimadonna, Palica, Marudubshinki, Jcuk, Cuchullain, BD2412, Kbdank71, Jclemens, Dpv, Lhademmor, Koavf, Teklund, Drench, FlaBot, Gringo300, Gtmo, RexNL, Neofelis Nebulosa~enwiki, Terrx, Chobot, DVdm, RandyRhoadsRonnieDio, YurikBot, Borgx, RobotE, Kinneyboy90, Mr Frosty, Ikar.us, Gaius Cornelius, ONEder Boy, Bleck, Tony1, Dissolve, E tac, Mitchell k dwyer, WesleyDodds, That Guy, From That Show!, SmackBot, TomGreen, Buf7579, Cubs Fan, Umph, Mr Pyles, Kintetsubuffalo, Gilliam, Bluebot, KaragouniS, No-Bullet, Lazyern, Neo139, OrphanBot, Greenshed, The Elfoid, Grover cleveland, Madman2001, M3TALL1CA2000, Ritchie333, Dan1216, Derek R Bullamore, Headshaker, Marcus Brute, Ohconfucius, GoogleMe~enwiki, Megamanic, Harryurz, InedibleHulk, E-Kartoffel, DI2000, Jona2112, Ryouga, Impy4ever, Spark, Hyukan, Malice1982, Anger22, AnotherBrickInTheWall~enwiki, Tawkerbot2, IronChris, Vazor20X6, The Haunted Angel, ShelfSkewed, CDarklock, Neelix, Cydebot, Fair Deal, Andre666, AdmiralvonAxehaufen, RottweilerCS, Thijs!bot, Mr. Brain, Rosencrantz1, Dgies, Sectornine, Escarbot, AntiVandalBot, MrMarmite, Soheil b, Ktappe, MECU, J'onn J'onzz, Xnux, Wpiehgdfpiahbpsi, Barek, .anacondabot, 75pickup, Zdeněk Zikán, Shanealun, Limelight05, Soulbot, Usien6, Kroberts, Talltim, Richard Lionheart, Clear air turbulence, Zagmac, JMyrleFuller, Rroldgit, Rif Winfield, Vytal, DannyRay, FisherQueen, Bradroenfeldt, Connacht~enwiki, FMAFan1990, Carre, Yonidebot, Kenwoodrd1982, Andy5421, Skier Dude, Garret Beaumain, Vegan4Life, STBotD, David Whitton, Idioma-bot, Hammersoft, Jeffreybh, TXiKiBoT, Dan ad nauseam, Hammard, Muro de Aguas, Lvivske, Martin451, Broadbot, BotKung, Symo-EFC, Rock Soldier, Arachrah, AlleborgoBot, AdRock, Peter Fleet, WereSpielChequers, BotMultichill, ToePeu.bot, Tripscale, Showninner, Ludivine, Vobor, EwanSmoggie, Oculi, Fratrep, Crash3021, Martyn gryphon, M4, Frazier, Avy, ClueBot, Binksternet, Purple74, Howenstein115, D10, Testu, Drmies, Pete Ridges, Nymf, Mynameisnotpj, Yellowxander, Retne, Wiki libs, Bbedn, MBTP Editor, DumZiBoT, Johan Rachmaninov, XLinkBot, Чръный человек, Helwik, SilvonenBot, Addbot, Dk pdx, Adeli, RandySavageFTW, Bitthebeast, CanadianLinuxUser, Fluffernutter, Mac Dreamstate, Download, The Shadow-Fighter, Favonian, LinkFA-Bot, Mercury87, Tassedethe, Seilacei, Trendlists, Krenakarore, Drpickem, Yobot, PaulWalter, MSClaudiu, Arch stanton1138, AnomieBOT, Spada2, Materialscientist, Minervauk, Krobertj, Didaktron, Jesie, ArthurBot, Britte, Xqbot, Wether B, Tomflaherty, Mlpearc, Aussie Ausborn, J04n, Armbrust, Wizardist, Classickid7, Sabrebd, Someone963852, Richard BB, Eugeneelgato, GripTheHusk, FrescoBot, Ranchloopseven, MrIpodz, David Coverdale's White Snake, DefaultsortBot, Ver-bot, JPGR69, Jorgicio, Impala2009, Gurnemanz12, Evangp, Magical Girl Fan, Sapphirewhirlwind, MrPanyGoff, Rockgenre, MrX, BC Rocky, Muttdog, Cattrall, Braghis, Hiddenstranger, Warmride, EmausBot, Nima1024, WikitanvirBot, Lewismaster, Starcheerspeaksnewslostwars, GoingBatty, Ykraps, ZéroBot, Kingsofrocknroll, Anir1uph, Sd31263, Burbridge92, L1A1 FAL, Pefp, Bill Hicks Jr., VLN1025, Valkyrietod, Aramil Meliamne, CactusBot, Bk81, CeeBee52, SnakeRambo, Jamcad01, Helpful Pixie Bot, Pinkd, Murry1975, TryfanUK, Vagobot, EpicHeavyMetalRoadie, Hallows AG, Vlattenham, SilverBullitt, Bluesisblood31, ToaTPM, Kubelsky, RockNWrite82, BattyBot, ChrisGualtieri, Amb1997, Winkelvi, Killmeister, Kanghuitari, Dexbot, Uriahdan, Donjohns, MetalS-W, Awesomebriks, Edvpj, French Achilles Last Stand, Ynot0207, DavidLeighEllis, MetalDiablo666, Rambotje, Nstockley, Fran1996, DLManiac, Carlos Rojas77, Monkbot, Bziggy1995, DelayTalk, John g Antonson, Nippleface43, KasparBot, Dunphyesque, Ze Marsh-mellow, JuggaloProghead, Hansyeropuer, LouSklarIsrael and Anonymous: 384

- **Raven (British band)** *Source:* https://en.wikipedia.org/wiki/Raven_(British_band)?oldid=686842928 *Contributors:* Bumm13, Ary29, Graeme-Leggett, Bruce1ee, YurikBot, Yrithinnd, Wknight94, Jogers, Rehevkor, Quadpus, KnightRider~enwiki, SmackBot, Elonka, Chris the speller, OrphanBot, Racklever, X-Flare-x, Derek R Bullamore, Dl2000, Diediemydarling, Ken Gallager, Cydebot, AdmiralvonAxehaufen, Thijs!bot, Majin GeoDooD, LeaHazel, Kameejl, Furyo Mori, ACSE, Nouse4aname, Malcolmxl5, James25402, Martarius, Ctlr, Drmies, HentaimanXT, Alexbot, Wiki libs, Drterror666, Llb9977, DumZiBoT, Jax 0677, XLinkBot, TheSickBehemoth, SilvonenBot, Sparksmedia, Addbot, RandySavageFTW, Angry Shoplifter, Tassedethe, Zorrobot, Luckas-bot, Yobot, Babypengy, Arch stanton1138, AnomieBOT, Marauder09, Eumolpo, FrescoBot, KrzysM99, DefaultsortBot, MrX, In ictu oculi, John of Reading, Mk5384, Lewismaster, Burbridge92, Black60dragon, CactusBot, Joefromrandb, Mogism, Ganspare, KasparBot and Anonymous: 48

- **Rock Goddess** *Source:* https://en.wikipedia.org/wiki/Rock_Goddess?oldid=678961131 *Contributors:* DragonflySixtyseven, Willerror, Woohookitty, Rjwilmsi, Feydey, David91, Derek R Bullamore, Headshaker, ABoerma, Tehw1k1, Dl2000, DabMachine, Cydebot, A Softer Answer, MER-C, Tirolion, Keith D, Steven J. Anderson, James25402, Aspects, Sfan00 IMG, Arjayay, Muro Bot, Addbot, Lightbot, Yobot, Marauder09, LilHelpa, Xqbot, MrX, Lord of the Pit, Lewismaster, ZéroBot, CactusBot, Joefromrandb, Shirudo, Peter1209, Geezer987, Frisson Art, KasparBot, Huhu Uet and Anonymous: 21

- **Rogue Male (band)** *Source:* https://en.wikipedia.org/wiki/Rogue_Male_(band)?oldid=677829200 *Contributors:* Michael Devore, Rjwilmsi, Wiki alf, Mike Selinker, Caiaffa, Iridescent, CmdrObot, Puppybarf, Appraiser, Zepromz, Sapphic, Fratrep, Grogm, TheRedPenOfDoom, Tassedethe, AnomieBOT, Materialscientist, Roguesreview, Cullen328, John of Reading, Lewismaster, Snotbot, Khazar2, Jim "The Rogue" Lyttle, KasparBot and Anonymous: 15

- **Ronnie James Dio** *Source:* https://en.wikipedia.org/wiki/Ronnie_James_Dio?oldid=691082854 *Contributors:* Deb, Camembert, Michael Hardy, Stephen C. Carlson, Miciah, DavidWBrooks, Pudreaux, Dcoetzee, ZeWrestler, Bearcat, Nufy8, Moriori, RedWolf, Goethean, Pillsbur, Timrollpickering, UtherSRG, Qwm~enwiki, ScudLee, Curps, Varlaam, Beardo, Naufana, BigHaz, Guillaumito, Mamizou, Llewdor, Rdsmith4, Secfan, Gscshoyru, TiMike, Joyous!, TJSwoboda, Ratiocinate, Bloodless, Haruo, Discospinster, Rich Farmbrough, MeltBanana, Harriv, Edgarde, Bender235, CanisRufus, Spearhead, Jpgordon, Adambro, Bobo192, Elipongo, Mr. Brownstone, Hagerman, Petdance, Tra, Storm Rider, Alansohn, Gargaj, CyberSkull, Snowolf, Aka, Dave.Dunford, Ndteegarden, BlastOButter42, Mattbrundage, Kouban, Kazvorpal, RPIRED, Dopefish, Woohookitty, Fingers-of-Pyrex, Klander Brigade, Pol098, DavidFarmbrough, Stefanomione, Pepsi90919, Darren Jowalsen, MassGalactusUniversum, Magister Mathematicae, Kbdank71, Pjetter, Koavf, Chadbryant, Matt Deres, FlaBot, Gringo300, Gurch, Str1977, TeaDrinker, 6~enwiki, Trankin, Chobot, Kirloo, DVdm, Bgwhite, Spinecraft, Jason.cinema, RandyRhoadsRonnieDio, The Rambling Man, YurikBot, RobotE, PowerGamer6, Kinneyboy90, RussBot, Sanjosanjo, Torinir, C777, Reluctantpopstar, Athox, Spike Wilbury, Robertvan1, Tedsrecords, SirWoland, Retired username, Bleck, Tony1, Dissolve, Asarelah, Scope creep, Fallout boy, E tac, Theda, Mike Selinker, E Wing, AchimP, JLaTondre, Mzzl, Katieh5584, Tim1965, Meegs, SkerHawx, Amberrock, Kf4bdy, Dlainhart, Knowledgeum, That Guy, From That Show!, IslandHopper973, SmackBot, Helga76, Skudrafan1, Elonka, TomGreen, Cubs Fan, Moeron, Umph, MarshallStack, Eskimbot, Hardyplants, Doc Strange, Mr Pyles, HalfShadow, Master Deusoma, Rmosler2100, Tv316, Bluebot, Fishhead2100, Emurphy42, Hellfire81, Dethme0w, Neo139, OrphanBot, Onorem, Death2, Malmsteen Maiden, Patons02, Darwin's Bulldog, Siege72, The Elfoid, Ritchie333, Downwards, DantheCowMan, Leonard Dickens, Invincible Ninja, IrisKawling, Derek R Bullamore, Melkor., Wybot, Wizardman, Hairmetal4ever, Metamagician3000, Evlekis, Milchama, Lambiam, Nishkid64, Rory096, Ser Amantio di Nicolao, Molerat, John, Kuyku, Shadowoftime, Majorclanger, Soxfan6978, Shimmera, Cory pratt, Viifog, Optakeover, Dr.K., Malomeat, Bolt Vanderhuge, The Damaja, Ragusino, Shoeofdeath, Courcelles, Thesexualityofbereavement, Anger22, Pathosbot, Enwilson, Tawkerbot2, RattleandHum, Kevin Murray, Geezerbill, IronChris, Eastlaw, Vazor20X6, The Haunted Angel, Jknobull, ERAGON, DJ BatWave, Athanasius Soter, Stockdiver, Speedking90, KyraVixen, Musikxpert, Mika1h, Schrmty, Wonduhbread, Gingerdave, Neelix, Ken Gallager, Chicheley, Cydebot, MC10, Jack O'Lantern, Gogo Dodo, Anonymi, Meltdownrock, Gbondy, DavidRavenMoon, Tawkerbot4, Akaisuisei, DumbBOT, Eneville, RottweilerCS, ThylekShran, Alienpmk, Thijs!bot, A Sniper, Thedarxide, Signify, Dasani, Irishmonk, Kronos, Serpent-A, N5iln, Andyjsmith, Headbomb, Marek69, Revrant, Java13690, Rosencrantz1, Joe Capricorn, Dgies, Nick Number, AntiVandalBot, MrMarmite, Antique Rose, Readro, Gdo01, Mutt Lunker, G Rose, White Devil, Kprobst, Andrzejbanas, ScotClayton, Gregorydebonis, Xnux, KerryKing666, TigerK 69, Smiddle, Kissfaq, Sitethief, Hobson, MegX, SEGA, Jarkeld, Y2kcrazyjoker4, 75pickup, Bongwarrior, VoABot II, DFS, TheAllSeeingEye, SYLFan74, Cadsuane Melaidhrin, Limelight05, UnaLaguna, Vegetaman, ElDandy22, Bubba hotep, PenguinJockey, KirinX, Pierreboro, Loonymonkey, XMog, Dio4president, Rpgaddict2005, AndoDoug, MiTfan3, Belsen, Jasonater, MartinBot, Bradnomfeldt, Guido Gonzato, Anaxial, CommonsDelinker, Bobo92, FMAFan1990, J.delanoy, Dandy-Dan2007, Rgoodermote, Cocoaguy, Scott Free, Andy5421, DragonDance, DarkFalls, Ryan Postlethwaite, Ron Stowmarket, Garret Beaumain, AntiSpamBot, SJP, TurtleofXanth, Doomsdayer520, Lisagosselin, Pdcook, Oedipalwreck, Avitohol, WWGB, TheSeventhOne, Gothbag, The Mob Rules, One Night In Hackney, DOHC Holiday, Sti571, Jeff G., Sir Baka Jones, Cliffiv, Nunoni, Soliloquial, Tenacious D Fan, Philip Trueman, TheInterviewArchives, Oshwah, Gueneverey, Fxhomie, IommiRocks, Walor, Eternity is within85, Sillyputty1, Anna Lincoln, Slysplace, LeaveSleaves, Snowbot, Maxim, B5Erik, Magpiecat, Inx272, Feudonym, TortheViolator, Jeddiebyrd, Mrdehate, Rock Soldier, Insanity Incarnate, Polylepis, Funeral, Anarchist92, Brandon97, Vince989, Pickles27, Peter Fleet, Frazail, SieBot, Sposato, Moonriddengirl, Euryalus, Corrupt toolbox, Davidlagreca, Kamilpejas, Ludivine, Nite-Sirk, Happysailor, Diarmaidc, Arbor to SJ, Sohelpme, MisterVodka, Bobashotmace, Oxymoron83, Cyk036, Navnløs, Witchkraut, Tommi Ronkainen, Dabomb87, Lukehatton, Precious Roy, 7valleyguy, ImageRemovalBot, Martarius, ClueBot, C xong, Danielspencer91, Ndgp, Binksternet, Snigbrook, All Hallow's Wraith, Mattgirling, Andranikpasha, Joao Xavier, Malikbek,

Pfw, Kenmgj, Puchiko, Luke4545, Metalgodfan, Excirial, Nymf, Jusdafax, Metal Head Dave, Bryanbent666, A Powerful Weakness, Metalgodlover, Urbanchampion, Wiki libs, Timorose, Peter.C, The Red, Holzman-tweed, BOTarate, Clemo pcl, Johnnydeppishawt, TheDarkSavant, Alvareo, GFHandel, Thingg, Caper454, Astrostl, Contains Mild Peril, Vanished user uih38riiw4hjlsd, Unkalapukkala, Jskryp, Ohrbe, TheSickBehemoth, Slasherphenom, Nat Miller, TheBillyFag, Paper45tee, Addbot, Mighty warrior of metal, Willking1979, RandySavageFTW, Some jerk on the Internet, Socheid, Dan56, Major slb, OmegaXmutantX, Jwfarmer10, Ronhjones, Groundsquirrel13, Mac Dreamstate, Alucard010, Cst17, Download, Favonian, 5 albert square, Tassedethe, Aorjoe, Tide rolls, Lightbot, Zorrobot, Legobot, Luckas-bot, Yobot, Edguy420, Senator Palpatine, Andrewandwow, DisillusionedBitterAndKnackered, Kbeartx, Mmxx, AnomieBOT, Momoricks, SlayerXTT, Tucoxn, Piano non troppo, The Great Duck, Materialscientist, Drummike46, E2eamon, Bjohanson, Krobertj, ArthurBot, Spidermanizdabest, Xqbot, Capricorn42, Wisems, Opjeshke, Mlpearc, CatholicW, Sir Stanley, J04n, Berserkur, Wizardist, Wilsonchas, RibotBOT, Ivan Shmakov, Dear cobain, Earshear34, Sesu Prime, Cekli829, GripTheHusk, Saturn-78, FrescoBot, Frehley72, Rozzlyn31, Masterknighted, HJ Mitchell, Covenman, Elfast, Citation bot 1, Gdje je nestala duša svijeta, SuperJew, David Coverdale's White Snake, DrilBot, DefaultsortBot, LittleWink, PrincessofLlyr, Byu14, Tinton5, Dead Hypocricy is painful, Xididthepopex, Headhold, Evenrød, Aardvarkzz, Drugyourlove, BlackSwann1, MrPanyGoff, TobeBot, Edshaft, Vrenator, Singlemaltscotch, Crusty Crouton, NovakFan76, Lkjhgfdsa 0, Hoalong, Nascar1996, Reach Out to the Truth, Pugpitbullduck, Pitpug, Jackass2009, Onel5969, Ramloser, CaptainAmerica2, RjwilmsiBot, RepliCarter, HrZ, DASHBot, EmausBot, Nima1024, Tjhiggin, Mk5384, Oscar776, Ozzyisbetta, MK121, Giobaski, Firesword bg, Starcheerspeaksnewslostwars, GoingBatty, RA0808, Mrmannyman2, Torturella, SSBDelphiki, Jim Michael, John of Lancaster, The Blade of the Northern Lights, ResidentsFan, Erpert, Realxsalo, ThatRockMetalGuy, IBoy2G, Derp555, ZéroBot, Traxs7, Francesco Malipiero, Dffgd, Speekr, Disneybird, Unholydiver31, Killgor789, H3llBot, Cots777, EWikist, Azrael Moros, Core703, Anoldtreeok, Moomoopashoo, Putofag619, L1A1 FAL, Diamana, Jay-Sebastos, Shamonaheehee123, Ilovejesus525, Umbr3on!!, Oiyoudonthavethisname, VLN1025, 1wutthebleep1, Inflatablevajayjay, Valkyrietod, ClueBot NG, RJD324, Angelanamraka, Danissimo.bg, MelbourneStar, Darshan84, Vukajlija121, Erreicher, Floatjon, Atom22, Letstryhonesty, Trekman1701d, Chriscatton12, SnakeRambo, Darkrai21, Tobystewart, PineappleFTW, Arcade8787, Helpful Pixie Bot, O7VS, Mcc0022, Nusacc, PunkRock1313, BG19bot, Northamerica1000, Platinum Maze, EpicHeavyMetalRoadie, Hallows AG, PsyberWizzard, BizarreLoveTriangle, Cdog2012, The Uncyclopedian, Cyberbot II, Myxomatosis57, EuroCarGT, JefferyTheGambler, Moskea, Laiho1995, Dexbot, Ciarantolan, Mlpearc Phone, Kierpf, Old Time Music Fan, ScottyDio, Everything Is Numbers, VIAFbot, Passaroo90125, ChakaKong, Plant's Strider, YLCC23, Scottchetock, Gabby Merger, Donjohns, IAmAxew, Machinhead666, UW Dawgs, I am One of Many, Sabbathbloodness, Qwerkysteve, Edvpj, Ynot0207, DavidLeighEllis, ArmbrustBot, EmiliustheGreat, YosemiteDan, Adolf Hipster, I'm An American With This Username, Pauuuvicious, Da Cow 2.7, Monkbot, JamKaftan, Eloy1073, Hissler, JezTwyning, Justiepoo, Keirtheweird, Dragonballs41, DarkPsalms, Tina MHN, Anonloser, An0nl00zer, Diometalgod, KasparBot, Helpmewriteit and Anonymous: 986

- **Salem (UK band)** *Source:* https://en.wikipedia.org/wiki/Salem_(UK_band)?oldid=687495266 *Contributors:* Wouterhagens, Bender235, Woohookitty, Bgwhite, Derek R Bullamore, Ohconfucius, Cydebot, Keith D, CommonsDelinker, Tesscass, Cindamuse, Mungo Kitsch, ImageRemovalBot, XLinkBot, Yobot, Gilo1969, Erik9bot, FrescoBot, LittleWink, PaulMacnamara, MrX, John of Reading, Lewismaster, GoingBatty, BG19bot, Iseesky, SalemUK, KasparBot and Anonymous: 13

- **Samson (band)** *Source:* https://en.wikipedia.org/wiki/Samson_(band)?oldid=682807429 *Contributors:* Andre Engels, Steinsky, Mushroom, Martpol, Bugo, Someoneinmyheadbutit'snotme, Exxolon, Koavf, Vegaswikian, Gringo300, MacRusgail, YurikBot, OMenda~enwiki, Meegs, Kingboyk, Dposse, SmackBot, Mr Pyles, Hmains, Cyberninja49, HannuMakinen, Derek R Bullamore, Hoodinski, Dl2000, J Milburn, Thijs!bot, Kohran, Headbomb, Trockya, Cooldude3310, Areaseven, .anacondabot, Xiola06, MetsBot, Dakki78, LordAnubisBOT, Imagi-King, Ardius01, Kvdveer, VolkovBot, Harfarhs, Headmess, IllaZilla, JhsBot, James25402, Nite-Sirk, Flyer22 Reborn, Tiptoety, Aspects, KyoufuNoDaiou, Voiceofcrube, StigBot, PixelBot, Wiki libs, JamieS93, BOTarate, Rockk3r, Life of Riley, Jax 0677, Cnoguera, XLinkBot, Addbot, Malconfort, Tassedethe, PlankBot, Yobot, AnomieBOT, Feral-wedgE, GrouchoBot, RibotBOT, WikiWikingerX, DefaultsortBot, Rockgenre, MrX, EmausBot, Lewismaster, Burbridge92, JohnnyangelNIU, ChuispastonBot, CactusBot, Joefromrandb, PaulSamsonArchive, BattyBot, Panther Pictures, ChrisGualtieri, KasparBot and Anonymous: 61

- **Satan (band)** *Source:* https://en.wikipedia.org/wiki/Satan_(band)?oldid=689400799 *Contributors:* TJSwoboda, The JPS, Woohookitty, Rjwilmsi, IainP, BNutzer, Llamadog903, Angryxpeh, Dl2000, Mika1h, Cydebot, Conquistador2k6, Blackmetalbaz, Alaibot, PamD, Thijs!bot, Manuelle Magnus, Imagi-King, VolkovBot, Stranger4001, Rivazza, Cbj77, Philip Trueman, Undead warrior, Matthew Yeager, Nite-Sirk, Martarius, ClueBot, Fishyhoracio, XLinkBot, WikHead, Addbot, LaaknorBot, Lightbot, Luckas-bot, Yobot, Mission Fleg, AnomieBOT, Ant smusher, Michalisphyl, The Banner, GrouchoBot, Tigerarmy73, DefaultsortBot, EmausBot, Lewismaster, Jenks24, ClueBot NG, Daveceil, BG19bot, Senke666, The1337gamer, BattyBot, ChrisGualtieri, The True Reality Returns, Mogism, Stainedclasssinner, Mustache sax man, WitchCrosS, KasparBot, Radiphus and Anonymous: 36

- **Savage (band)** *Source:* https://en.wikipedia.org/wiki/Savage_(band)?oldid=676254751 *Contributors:* DCEdwards1966, SmackBot, Chris the speller, Eastlaw, Little Professor, Conorcosgrave, Elizium23, Addbot, Costafinkel, Yobot, Amirobot, LilHelpa, Omnipaedista, I dream of horses, RichieMurray, Satan's Wizard, Hiddenstranger, John of Reading, Lewismaster, Postwar, Rmw73, ClueBot NG, Savageuk, Mavngoose, BG19bot, Dcolt13, Alzantir and Anonymous: 13

- **Saxon (band)** *Source:* https://en.wikipedia.org/wiki/Saxon_(band)?oldid=691120252 *Contributors:* Lancevortex, Ec5618, Jrdioko, Utcursch, Child of Bodom, Bumm13, Bonalaw, Imroy, AgentSteel, ESkog, Nabla, Lankiveil, Rje, Helix84, AnnaP, Woohookitty, Skyraider, Tabletop, Selena von Eichendorf, Palica, Jcuk, Jclemens, Jdcooper, Rjwilmsi, Demian12358, Ian Dunster, Tbone, FlaBot, Ian Pitchford, Ground Zero, MacRusgail, 6~enwiki, BrianFG, Flcelloguy, YurikBot, Koffieyahoo, Wiki alf, Qirex, Zottmann, Slicing, Rfsmit, WVH, Nosyteikm, Amalthea, SmackBot, Cubs Fan, Zonder, Eskimbot, LuciferMorgan, Mr Pyles, Betacommand, Vain, Bluebot, MrDrBob, Bazonka, Wikipediatrix, Egsan Bacon, Cobain, OrphanBot, Racklever, The Elfoid, PaulBaldowski, Eyeball kid, Derek R Bullamore, Marcus Brute, Arabwel, Bretonbanquet, Zofar, Euchiasmus, Orion Polaris, JHunterJ, Martinp23, Cory pratt, GilbertoSilvaFan, AHTNF, Dl2000, Radagast1983, Anger22, Marcus Bowen, Mr. Metal Head, CmdrObot, Speedking90, Toby.e.hawkins, Saxon747, Cydebot, Fair Deal, AdmiralvonAxehaufen, UA-Justice, RottweilerCS, PKT, Thijs!bot, Mr. Brain, JustAGal, Big Bird, Dawnseeker2000, Jay Firestorm, AntiVandalBot, Mad Pierrot, JAnDbot, MER-C, Robvanspunkmeyer, Magioladitis, The-flea, BigDukeSix, Delage, Twsx, Antmusic, Zagmac, TheLetterM, Grinder0-0, Vonrohr, Lost tourist, Furyo Mori, BetBot~enwiki, MiltonT, Keith D, The Crying Orc, Gorgutz, Kandy Talbot, KylieTastic, Vanished user 39948282, Kimberley at, Funandtrvl, Malik Shabazz, Jbruyndonckx, Dfisek, Haggarman, Dij88, Seb26, Moutane, Inx272, Entirelybs, AlleborgoBot, Derekjc, SieBot, Mikemoral, AS, James25402, Aspects, TheRealNomad, Navnløs, Martarius, Leahtwosaints, Lethemania~enwiki, EoGuy, Nymf, Yellowxander, Sun Creator, Wiki libs, Arjayay, C628, Electric Wizard17, Markydolphin46, Mr Larrington, Cnoguera, TheSickBehemoth, Kbdankbot, Addbot,

Hitsemptyoy, SpBot, West.andrew.g, Guffydrawers, Angry Shoplifter, Äppelmos~enwiki, Delta 51, Luckas-bot, Yobot, Amirobot, Arch stanton1138, AnomieBOT, GetMKWearMKFly, Makele-90, Arnef, Axelsegen, Nasnema, Aussie Ausborn, GrouchoBot, Mattmel, Eugene-elgato, Solonoob., FotoPhest, A vision of it, Kwiki, MrIpodz, DefaultsortBot, Knallis, Porky metal 666, Full-date unlinking bot, Cnwilliams, Truenwobhm, Onel5969, GabeMc, EmausBot, John of Reading, Lewismaster, Austinrok, Fæ, Josve05a, Dogsbody56, Chroncrue, H3llBot, The Fall of Rasputin, Burbridge92, L1A1 FAL, Mentibot, SkywalkerPL, Lord Gorbachev, ClueBot NG, Adville, Joefromrandb, Snotbot, Delusion23, Rezabot, SnakeRambo, Helpful Pixie Bot, BG19bot, Rijinatwiki, Amroknian, Aciolilaureano, Poolishh, CulturalSnow, Naimbrain, Lardmonkey123, Cyberbot II, Chie one, Mattmetallica, Mogism, Heavymetalthunder100, MetalS-W, Stainedclasssinner, DavidLeighEllis, JaconaFrere, Paul Might, Fatal Disease, DLManiac, Coventry76, RobertBDurham, WitchCrosS, EternalFloette, DarkPsalms, KasparBot, Goodnews15 and Anonymous: 239

- **Shy (band)** *Source:* https://en.wikipedia.org/wiki/Shy_(band)?oldid=676263256 *Contributors:* Paul A, Bjarki S, Asparagus, Bkonrad, Goldom, Jeff3000, BD2412, Ketiltrout, Rjwilmsi, Erebus555, Aphasia83, MoRsE, Fnorp, Derek R Bullamore, Retromaniac, Ollie the Magic Skater, CmdrObot, Cydebot, Tkynerd, Alaibot, Comeinfromtherain, Thijs!bot, Dragonforce~enwiki, GurchBot, MetsBot, Jbasketts, Magnet For Knowledge, TXiKiBoT, Hisnibbs, Clairekelly12, Addbot, Yobot, Gongshow, LilHelpa, Pensativa, Richyaorock, EmausBot, Lewismaster, ZéroBot, Uzma Gamal, Joefromrandb, AORmaniac13, LoudandReal, RealAndLoud, KasparBot and Anonymous: 39

- **Spider (British band)** *Source:* https://en.wikipedia.org/wiki/Spider_(British_band)?oldid=676265878 *Contributors:* Bearcat, Woohookitty, SmackBot, Hmains, Derek R Bullamore, QuiteUnusual, Werldwayd, Explicit, Addbot, Tassedethe, Yobot, John of Reading, Lewismaster, Peaceray, Tinalee32, Khazar2, Hikersguide42 and Anonymous: 10

- **Stampede (band)** *Source:* https://en.wikipedia.org/wiki/Stampede_(band)?oldid=676362340 *Contributors:* Bearcat, Klemen Kocjancic, Malcolma, SmackBot, Chris the speller, Derek R Bullamore, Dl2000, EoGuy, Favonian, Yobot, John of Reading, Lewismaster, GoingBatty, Crosskeys62, BG19bot, Amroknian, KasparBot and Anonymous: 3

- **Starfighters (band)** *Source:* https://en.wikipedia.org/wiki/Starfighters_(band)?oldid=676655300 *Contributors:* Asparagus, Bender235, Wipe, Rjwilmsi, Kingboyk, Crystallina, Derek R Bullamore, Headshaker, Dl2000, Fdssdf, CmdrObot, Aia94, Euromark, James25402, Florentyna, Sebleouf, Angry Shoplifter, DefaultsortBot, John of Reading, Lewismaster, Yoooz, MarkDesmo, Cody McQuail, Enklaste, KasparBot and Anonymous: 10

- **Stratus (English band)** *Source:* https://en.wikipedia.org/wiki/Stratus_(English_band)?oldid=679746761 *Contributors:* Bearcat, Stormwatch, Derek R Bullamore, Dl2000, NossB, Yobot, Fama Clamosa, Lewismaster, Starcheerspeaksnewslostwars, ClueBot NG, Xlakra, Synthwave.94, KasparBot and Anonymous: 2

- **Sweet Savage** *Source:* https://en.wikipedia.org/wiki/Sweet_Savage?oldid=690550280 *Contributors:* Karada, Ericl234, Bruce1ee, FlaBot, Gringo300, Grafen, Renata3, Tony1, SmackBot, Folajimi, OrphanBot, BrownHairedGirl, Dl2000, Eastlaw, ShelfSkewed, Dover 5, Cydebot, Tirkfl, CharlotteWebb, MegX, FMAFan1990, TXiKiBoT, Electriccarz, Gus, Sposato, Theroadandthesky, Martarius, Rustedinpeace502, Iohannes Animosus, XLinkBot, CrackerJack7891, MystBot, Addbot, RandySavageFTW, Metalmp, Twosidesofif, Angry Shoplifter, Yobot, MasterExploder123, Nbah92, J04n, JIK1975, Robcasscaveproductions, Whisky drinker, EmausBot, John of Reading, Lewismaster, Starcheerspeaksnewslostwars, Jumpinthefire83, ZéroBot, LeaMichelle12, The New New New, 2sidesofif, CactusBot, Stevefireland, INeedAHero2247, Mr. Guye, Alzantir, Irishmetalman, KasparBot and Anonymous: 63

- **Tank (band)** *Source:* https://en.wikipedia.org/wiki/Tank_(band)?oldid=690572048 *Contributors:* Ary29, Petdance, GraemeLeggett, Mandarax, Rjwilmsi, Retired username, Dsreyn, SB Johnny, Huon, Derek R Bullamore, Dl2000, Himenow, Mika1h, Cydebot, AdmiralvonAxehaufen, Taschenrechner~enwiki, Andyschism, Thijs!bot, Escarbot, BeastmasterGeneral, Magioladitis, JamesBWatson, Faizhaider, MetsBot, The Wiki Priest, Imagi-King, Eksosrock, VolkovBot, Stranger4001, Cbj77, Mrsyetidooscreecher, Godozo, Bashereyre, Tankfilthhounds, Arveragus, Undead warrior, James25402, Martarius, Soft shepherd, Yellowxander, Llb9977, DumZiBoT, Johan Rachmaninov, Jax 0677, XLinkBot, Jcinicola, TheSickBehemoth, Addbot, FluffyWhiteCat, Favonian, Yobot, Ptbotgourou, Ikespirit, JoniFili, Ant smusher, Marauder09, SAULGNRFAN, Xqbot, J04n, GrouchoBot, RibotBOT, Progenie of the great apocalypse, Bohemiaroad, I dream of horses, DefaultsortBot. Eustanacio IV, Lewismaster, GoingBatty, SporkBot, L1A1 FAL, CactusBot, Rollingdell, BG19bot, Myxomatosis57, Killmeister, Jamesx12345, Epicgenius, 17A Africa, Sabbatino, DLManiac, Writers Bond, Calebbro, KasparBot and Anonymous: 47

- **Terraplane (band)** *Source:* https://en.wikipedia.org/wiki/Terraplane_(band)?oldid=687100353 *Contributors:* Bearcat, Giraffedata, Jdcooper, Bruce1ee, Tony1, Derek R Bullamore, Bawtyshouse, Mondo one, Scchipli, Leahtwosaints, Lightbot, DefaultsortBot, Lewismaster, Wikipelli, Mancyboy, Laodah, Suejaynebunnies, KasparBot and Anonymous: 11

- **The Handsome Beasts** *Source:* https://en.wikipedia.org/wiki/The_Handsome_Beasts?oldid=676050824 *Contributors:* Thane, Racklever, Dl2000, Steel1943, Sparklism, MrX, Lewismaster, Jimbo2371 and Anonymous: 2

- **Thin Lizzy** *Source:* https://en.wikipedia.org/wiki/Thin_Lizzy?oldid=688349182 *Contributors:* TUF-KAT, Jschwa1, MyallR, JohnCastle, Gutsul, Toreau, Fvw, Stormie, Bearcat, Pigsonthewing, Modulatum, Postdlf, Merovingian, Meelar, Beardo, Jason Quinn, Jackol, Neilc, CGorman~enwiki, Deleteme42, Guppyfinsoup, Duja, Bender235, Violetriga, CanisRufus, Nk, DCEdwards1966, Brianboru, Gargaj, Spangineer, ProhibitOnions, Dmccabe, Amorymeltzer, Someoneinmyheadbutit'snotme, Tfz, Firsfron, Woohookitty, Myeslong, Ardfern, Tabletop, Mizzou1307, BD2412, Koavf, Jamdav86, FlaBot, Yopohari~enwiki, YurikBot, RobotE, RussBot, Resonance, Red Slash, Equalpants, CambridgeBayWeather, Cryptic, Wiki alf, Bachrach44, Ad Nauseam, Tony1, Merosonox, CorbieVreccan, Fenian Swine, E tac, Bakkster Man, SilentC, Veteran dj, Jogers, AlfredG, Meegs, DearPrudence, Algae, Mathew1905, SmackBot, TomGreen, Dashwortley, NantucketNoon, Pgk, Hatto, Setanta747 (locked), Deelnemer8, Iantnm, Gilliam, Portillo, Gruggor80, Bjmullan, Sirex98, Arvatov, Rcleere, Cobain, Ww2censor, The Elfoid, Invincible Ninja, Derek R Bullamore, James Mohr, Marcus Brute, Evlekis, Bretonbanquet, Alcuin, Catalpa, Ohconfucius, SashatoBot, John, NewTestLeper79, Catapult, Gnevin, Mark Lungo, E-Kartoffel, Cbuckley, Wwagner, DabMachine, Ryouga, Jimmyeightysix, Ripleyy, Evanoquigley, Twas Now, Jonbecker03, Hyukan, Gil Gamesh, Anger22, RattleandHum, MarkTB, Mr. Metal Head, The Prince of Darkness, Lord Dracula, Eric, Beeflin, ShelfSkewed, Cydebot, Fair Deal, Andre666, **dave**, Flowerpotman, Sk8punk3d288, RottweilerCS, Asenine, After Midnight, Omicronpersei8, Ezenden, Thijs!bot, Callmarcus, Srsrsr, Mr. Brain, Nhl4hamilton, Jimmybob32, Mentifisto, AntiVandalBot, Jayron32, Klapi, Hoponpop69, JAnDbot, Michig, MegX, Y2kcrazyjoker4, PloKoon13, Unused0029, 75pickup, Bongwarrior, VoABot II, BertieBasset, Kameejl, Paladin91, CCS81, Samwise 06, JediLofty, Wikiart~enwiki, MartinBot, AkankshaG, Cyberface, FMAFan1990, Sam Golden, J.delanoy, Captain panda,

Rafaelblock, SteveLamacq43, Spoonman.au, Russell McBride, Agadant, Eivindgh, Perssonja, TheBigOneUpFront, Cometstyles, STBotD, Halmstad, Highfields, Signalhead, Izzy007, Egghead06, Trcjt, VolkovBot, DOHC Holiday, WOSlinker, Kaghup6, Broadbot, Keres~enwiki, Josh Allain, Smithie ie, Walkinmyshadow, Bobo1130, Falcon8765, Alaniaris, Raphaelaarchon, Funeral, Logan, Cosprings, Peter Fleet, Silver Hammer Man, OlliffeObscurity, James25402, Yintan, Crash Underride, CombatCraig, Editore99, Satyrical lyrics, Klippdass, Agbomuzeli, Gunmetal Angel, Ital Congo, AllHailZeppelin, Avy, Hifihitman, Martarius, Leahtwosaints, ClueBot, Binksternet, Revolutionaryluddite, Howenstein115, RashersTierney, Gu1dry, Kage109, Black wolf010, Gtstricky, Sun Creator, Phil O, Wiki libs, Juice07, Brosandi~enwiki, Indopug, Phantomwiki, DumZiBoT, Jonesy79, Rock 'n' roller boy, Jameselmo, LHMike, XLinkBot, Fattylikecake, Чръный человек, Johnny1976, WikHead, PrideOrPunishment, MPalangio, Kbdankbot, Kodster, Addbot, Malconfort, RandySavageFTW, Joe0495, Lizzyfan86, SDolphyn, BecauseWhy?, Diddylevine, GTAtrivium76, Freemasonx, Favonian, Angry Shoplifter, Tassedethe, Seilacei, PlankBot, Luckas-bot, Yobot, Chipthief00, Best O Fortuna, Be Black Hole Sun, Davidkt, AnomieBOT, Funzi159, Piano non troppo, E2eamon, ArthurBot, Obersachsebot, Xqbot, Asatvolca, Wether B, Rocknroll47, Utilizer, Avizisa, Chunk9590, Aussie Ausborn, J04n, Eric Blatant, GrouchoBot, Mutante96, Jezhotwells, Frankbarber, Sabrebd, Wildonelynott, Trafford09, A Quest For Knowledge, Supernino, Middle 8, GripTheHusk, Racula, FrescoBot, FotoPhest, Michael93555, A vision of it, Teekayd25, David Coverdale's White Snake, DarthKrait, Maroon25, JPGR69, Kbr1656, Grunge jam, Throwaway85, MrX, Canuckian89, HrZ, John of Reading, Bondiolo, GA bot, Altalbal, Deogratias5, GoingBatty, Lolgasm9000, Peaceray, Tommy2010, ZéroBot, John Cline, Utar, H3llBot, Burbridge92, Hugo McGuinness, Nexxoxx, Noel C Taylor, Thinlizzyfans, Revilal90, TakomAni, Maxiguy, Mhiji, ClueBot NG, CactusBot, Osario~enwiki, DrDrake100, BarrelProof, Jesse Striewski, Widr, SnakeRambo, QWERTY123, Calabe1992, TheLoverofLove, Amroknian, Yoda956, MossChops99, Leigh Burne, Glutamine.sr, SilverBullitt, Mythpiano, Charlie1761, BattyBot, Carmine1216, Deadboy9, Cyberbot II, Kronosgreen, Dexbot, GuitarGeek, Robbgoblin, Rotlink, Retrohead, UW Dawgs, Dobbyelf62, Shallowmead077, GeezerB, Chartbot, Dustin V. S., Rattlingrabbit, Hc30001, Bängg, Synthwave.94, Teh Thrasher, Lukejordan02, Peter33p, NiborNoslen, Willissucks, Wmifflin, KasparBot, Panzer, CelticBrain and Anonymous: 534

- **Thunderstick** *Source:* https://en.wikipedia.org/wiki/Thunderstick?oldid=676538056 *Contributors:* Gtrmp, Abu badali, Bumm13, TJSwoboda, Philroy, Rjwilmsi, FlaBot, Foxxygirltamara, Gaius Cornelius, Mike Selinker, Chris93, SmackBot, Moeron, Umph, LuciferMorgan, Bluebot, Siorse, OrphanBot, The Elfoid, HannuMakinen, Nomoretears, Dl2000, Iridescent, Steph11, Prodigenous Zee, PamD, Padgett22, Sunhawk, Kauczuk, SEGA, Waacstats, Jasonater, Fbifriday, Snowbot, Rock Soldier, SieBot, Finley, Tankaman, Jax 0677, Чръный человек, Addbot, LaaknorBot, Tassedethe, Lightbot, Luckas-bot, Yobot, Xqbot, J04n, Ver-bot, Egntiger, MrX, Miracle Pen, RjwilmsiBot, Lewismaster, Burbridge92, ClueBot NG, CactusBot, Gareth Griffith-Jones, Nerdtrap, KLBot2, PaulSamsonArchive, KasparBot and Anonymous: 54

- **Tobruk (band)** *Source:* https://en.wikipedia.org/wiki/Tobruk_(band)?oldid=676540176 *Contributors:* Rich Farmbrough, Rjwilmsi, Wavelength, Chris Capoccia, Jed, Mr.Atoz, Iohannes Animosus, Addbot, RandySavageFTW, Favonian, Yobot, Ajono, LilHelpa, Evangp, Menino617, Lewismaster, H3llBot, ChrisGualtieri, Alzantir, Monkbot, Neddy Trubshaw, KasparBot and Anonymous: 7

- **Tokyo Blade** *Source:* https://en.wikipedia.org/wiki/Tokyo_Blade?oldid=688204655 *Contributors:* GreatWhiteNortherner, Alvestrand, Rich Farmbrough, Woohookitty, Rjwilmsi, FlaBot, Gringo300, Avalon, SmackBot, Derek R Bullamore, Khazar, Dl2000, Iridescent, Prophaniti, ShelfSkewed, Limbonic, ST47, Smallfortunebas, Imagi-King, KylieTastic, Funeral, Klippdass, Martarius, Binksternet, Arjayay, Saintrico, XLinkBot, MystBot, Addbot, Download, Tassedethe, Yobot, Ant smusher, Marauder09, LilHelpa, SAULGNRFAN, J04n, FrescoBot, Kellerwilliamslarchmont, Ace1011, Cowlibob, Dick van Aggelen, Tokyobladefan, SpyderSilico, In ictu oculi, Lewismaster, GoingBatty, ZéroBot, BG19bot, Dethbro, Amroknian, Stripmallarchitecture, Lilahdog568, Rkancho, RuzzChra, KasparBot and Anonymous: 35

- **Tredegar (band)** *Source:* https://en.wikipedia.org/wiki/Tredegar_(band)?oldid=676540917 *Contributors:* Rjwilmsi, Bretonbanquet, Whytecypress, Martarius, XLinkBot, Yobot, LilHelpa, SAULGNRFAN, Thehuntersmetal, DefenseSupportParty, Locobot, Misiekuk, Monolung, WikiWikingerX, Lewismaster, Brincken, KasparBot and Anonymous: 5

- **Trespass (band)** *Source:* https://en.wikipedia.org/wiki/Trespass_(band)?oldid=676541286 *Contributors:* Bearcat, Chowbok, Rjwilmsi, Fair Deal, Imagi-King, Clarince63, Gus, Ttonyb1, Yobot, Erik9bot, Lewismaster, Strike Eagle, BG19bot, Sguyclarke, 17A Africa, TechnoTim2011 and Anonymous: 7

- **Tygers of Pan Tang** *Source:* https://en.wikipedia.org/wiki/Tygers_of_Pan_Tang?oldid=679912317 *Contributors:* Mushroom, Gastronaut, Bumm13, Cmdrjameson, Geschichte, Graham87, Gringo300, Thozza, YurikBot, Epolk, Mitchell k dwyer, Allium, SmackBot, Eskimbot, Quackslikeaduck, The Elfoid, Derek R Bullamore, Monni95, Angryxpeh, Dl2000, Maestlin, IronChris, J Milburn, Mika1h, Cydebot, AdmiralvonAxehaufen, JustAGal, SeventhSon777, Jj137, Bubba hotep, Wiki Raja, OddMNilsen, LordAnubisBOT, Imagi-King, Kaji13, ClinIrwin, Inx272, Finngall, Clin Hoolihan, Phe-bot, James25402, Fratrep, Florentyna, Martarius, Sennen goroshi, Drmies, Nymf, Johnmc2, Saxonufo, DumZiBoT, Jax 0677, TheSickBehemoth, JBse, MystBot, Addbot, Malconfort, Jon Wisbey, LaaknorBot, Tassedethe, Tyger rocker, Lightbot, Zorrobot, Luckas-bot, Yobot, Ant smusher, Marauder09, SAULGNRFAN, TRAFICANTE, Monkberry, Chaheel Riens, FrescoBot, MrX, Yehia.tawfik, Lewismaster, Saigonshakes, L1A1 FAL, ClueBot NG, CactusBot, Delusion23, Helpful Pixie Bot, Amroknian, Turboyogi, Leigh Burne, DokkenRocker100, Gav Gray, Stainedclasssinner, DavidLeighEllis, KasparBot and Anonymous: 75

- **Tytan** *Source:* https://en.wikipedia.org/wiki/Tytan?oldid=689919863 *Contributors:* Pigsonthewing, Rich Farmbrough, Woohookitty, Rjwilmsi, Derek R Bullamore, Dl2000, Cydebot, Addbot, Yobot, Bunnyhop11, JackieBot, Jezhotwells, WikiWikingerX, Lewismaster, Amroknian, Gorobay, Khazar2, Flyingvivaldi, Joolsnwobhm and Anonymous: 8

- **UFO (band)** *Source:* https://en.wikipedia.org/wiki/UFO_(band)?oldid=689394203 *Contributors:* Hephaestos, Quercusrobur, Mbecker, Infrogmation, JohnOwens, MartinHarper, TUF-KAT, Michael, Jar Jar Binks, Maximus Rex, Gutsul, Ray from texas, David Gerard, Www.dave-wood.org, Dbenbenn, Matthäus Wander, Ocon, Mindspillage, Noisy, Edgarde, Sloppy, Fee mercury moon, Mike Garcia, Nicke Lilltroll~enwiki, Giraffedata, Pearle, PopUpPirate, Walter Görlitz, Evil Monkey, Someoneinmyheadbutit'snotme, Tainter, Woohookitty, Exxolon, BD2412, Kbdank71, Jdcooper, Koavf, MordredKLB, HappyCamper, Krash, Gringo300, Eubot, Gtmo, Igordebraga, YurikBot, Patrick Neylan, Cholmes75, Zwobot, Ospalh, Jogers, Shyam, Allens, Katieh5584, Zanoni, Scolaire, SmackBot, Mr Pyles, Gilliam, Bluebot, Jkortsch, T-borg, DantheCowMan, Derek R Bullamore, Victor Lopes, AngelTears~enwiki, BrownHairedGirl, John, Tktktk, Megamanic, E-Kartoffel, Dl2000, Smenzel, Jonbecker03, Anger22, Vazor20X6, Karenlesley29, Mr. Metal Head, Athanasius Soter, Cydebot, Alucard (Dr.), Jameboy, HK51, RottweilerCS, GentlemanGhost, Iccohen, Gary cumberland, Sgtpppr84, Spartaz, J'onn J'onzz, Chiefgango, Xnux, Txomin, MegX, PloKoon13, Dekimasu, Richard Lionheart, Xiola06, VictorLaszlo, Vulk, Smjwalsh, Contra10, Sagqs, Anaxial, Zouavman Le Zouave, Squidward247, FMAFan1990, DandyDan2007, Tikiwont, Tristangreatrex, Bohemianroots, Andrewself, Meiskam, VolkovBot, Cowboy Rocco, Garyms1963, Headmess, Steven J. Anderson, IllaZilla, Scchipli, BotKung, Josephabradshaw, Rondo66, Pomerol1963, Funeral, Finnrind, Peter Fleet, Marshallgourley, Radioinfoguy, SieBot, TJRC, Proscript, Born Again 83, Nite-Sirk, Klippdass, AMCKen, Hdxstunts1, KyoufuNoDaiou, Veldin963, ImageRemovalBot,

Martarius, ClueBot, Snigbrook, The Thing That Should Not Be, Theseven7, Drmies, Alexbot, Yellowxander, Wiki libs, Dementia13, DumZi-BoT, XLinkBot, TheSickBehemoth, Addbot, Adeli, Aimulti, Sp nz, Leszek Jańczuk, Chzz, RetroS1mone, Tassedethe, Numbo3-bot, Seilacei, Lightbot, Legobot, PlankBot, Luckas-bot, Yobot, Arch stanton1138, Body-Head, JackieBot, Ant smusher, DirlBot, Ally OBE, Ologr, J04n, Superastig, Sushiflinger, KX33, FrescoBot, LucienBOT, FotoPhest, A vision of it, JPEriksson, Tiegron, Manonthemoon999, Mfaiiazi, Hasenläufer, TobeBot, MrX, CobraBot, BrightBlackHeaven, NES Wii, RjwilmsiBot, Hiddenstranger, EmausBot, Paranoialevel5, Jang66, Lewismaster, GoingBatty, Chocopopcorn, JamesMohr, Moonslide, Burbridge92, ClueBot NG, CactusBot, This lousy T-shirt, Visnusen, Nerdtrap, BG19bot, Vagobot, Amroknian, Анна Волкова, Christiangeorges, RockNWrite82, Cyberbot II, Yamayamada, Killmeister, Rushfan21, Uriahdan, DavidLeighEllis, Jdesousa, Zolque2000, MetalDiablo666, Goodytox, Metaljim1, DLManiac, Joseph2302, KasparBot, Huhu Uet, Dingus magee and Anonymous: 272

- **Urchin (band)** *Source:* https://en.wikipedia.org/wiki/Urchin_(band)?oldid=684587343 *Contributors:* Bender235, Smalljim, Woohookitty, Tabletop, BD2412, Rjwilmsi, FlaBot, Gringo300, The Rambling Man, YurikBot, RussBot, Avalon, SmackBot, ZS, Derek R Bullamore, Hoodinski, Dl2000, Brucethegreat, Livingston7, Prodigenous Zee, JustAGal, MegX, Grayor, Nono64, Standingfish, Ardius01, Mokgen, Signalhead, VolkovBot, JukoFF, James25402, Tiptoety, Aspects, ImageRemovalBot, Martarius, ClueBot, Sennen goroshi, EoGuy, Addbot, Lightbot, WikiDreamer Bot, Luckas-bot, Yobot, Drwiddly, Johnhoye1, Hoyehoye123, Kendy Van Halen, Baztac, FoxBot, Lewismaster, Burbridge92, Hattara, Nerdtrap, Chip996, KasparBot and Anonymous: 16

- **Vardis** *Source:* https://en.wikipedia.org/wiki/Vardis?oldid=688670182 *Contributors:* Angela, Lupin, Bobblewik, Child of Bodom, Bumm13, Spearhead, Beyondthislife, Lkinkade, Woohookitty, Mazca, Twthmoses, Bruce1ee, FlaBot, Isotope23, Joshdboz, Ospalh, SmackBot, Derek R Bullamore, Bretonbanquet, Dungeoneer, Dl2000, CmdrObot, Bakanov, Cydebot, GirlWithBlackEye, Okki, Evilonline, Skumarla, R'n'B, James25402, Aspects, Navnløs, Martarius, ZaZam, Mild Bill Hiccup, Misterpomp, Deathbringer from the Sky, XLinkBot, Grebbsy, Addbot, Jimi197O, Lightbot, AndreyA, Yobot, Gongshow, AnomieBOT, Johnnyfr, LilHelpa, Orenburg1, MrX, Jahughes3, Hiddenstranger, Lewismaster, Bollocks ca, Quoguy, Peaceray, Ghoti666, 999-SLF, Mirror horse, ChrisGualtieri, Faizan, MetalManiaxe, VardisRocks, EternalFloette, Paulparkerlastmarker, KasparBot and Anonymous: 58

- **Venom (band)** *Source:* https://en.wikipedia.org/wiki/Venom_(band)?oldid=689139738 *Contributors:* Lancevortex, RickK, Kaare, Wilbern Cobb~enwiki, HarryHenryGebel, Stormie, Jeffq, Robbot, Astronautics~enwiki, Iam, Meelar, Mushroom, Child of Bodom, Borameer, Ary29, Xadai~enwiki, Canterbury Tail, Mindspillage, EugeneZelenko, Eel, Martpol, Spearhead, C1k3, Longhair, Wisdom89, Nicke Lilltroll~enwiki, Redf0x, Zachlipton, Gargaj, Macho, Walter Görlitz, Lightdarkness, Wtmitchell, Mad Hatter, Jobe6, Someoneinmyheadbutit'snotme, Ceyockey, Sjv27~enwiki, The JPS, Woohookitty, MrDarcy, Twthmoses, Roda~enwiki, GraemeLeggett, BD2412, Jclemens, Rjwilmsi, Darkday, Fish and karate, FlaBot, Frenrir1, Margosbot~enwiki, Barnolde, Rift14, Chaos333~enwiki, RussBot, Edward Wakelin, Splash, Piet Delport, Rsrikanth05, Stassats, Wiki alf, Lowe4091, Bwaquin, MakeChooChooGoNow, Terryc, Jogers, LeonardoRob0t, Meegs, WesleyDodds, SmackBot, Moeron, Delldot, Cacuija, Mr Pyles, Pasajero, Dark Prime, Gilliam, Jagerbreath, JRSP, Leyasu, MalafayaBot, Daddy Kindsoul, Can't sleep, clown will eat me, Rsm99833, Davard, The Elfoid, Nickcarr, ReToOcS, Ceoil, TenPoundHammer, JanderVK, GoogleMe~enwiki, Asemoasyourmom, Catapult, JHunterJ, AHTNF, Angryxpeh, Guitar01, Dl2000, DabMachine, Ryouga, Radagast1983, Anger22, Eastlaw, The Haunted Angel, CmdrObot, The Librarian, Bobfrombrockley, Dougdougy, Cyrus XIII, StarScream1007, Skeletor2112, Cydebot, Reywas92, Lunar eclipse, Anonymi, AdmiralvonAxehaufen, -Lemmy-, Lugnuts, Blackmetalbaz, Wikipediarules2221, Dcach, RottweilerCS, After Midnight, Thedarxide, Saaskis, Eugenespeed, Marek69, Erg0, Dezidor, Sherick, AntiVandalBot, Mnsc, Andrzejbanas, JAnDbot, Waitsian, Bocharoff, Kenmorton, Twsx, Cic, Adamravenscroft, Bubba hotep, Kameejl, JaGa, CCS81, Danleary25, BetBot~enwiki, Raed Gadjee, Helltopay27, Squidward247, DreamtheaterVIII, FMAFan1990, Jmm6f488, Tazzaler, Jlcrss9, Brazilian Man, Biglovinb, Cronoz, Gothbag, Antonio97b, Asarlaí, GDonato, Xr 1, Headmess, Blackmetal101, IllaZilla, Sexecutioner, Inx272, Falcon8765, Stalaggh1, AlleborgoBot, Sjluk, Funeral, Logical Defense, Vinyl999, AdRock, Undead warrior, Peter Fleet, SieBot, Maurauth, Scarian, WereSpielChequers, BotMultichill, Born Again 83, Mungo Kitsch, Nite-Sirk, Domonicrini, Hxhbot, GuitarMike123, HamadaFanFFSM, BeerPunkOiOiOi, Fratrep, Gunmetal Angel, Thundermaster, Landoftheliving, Arundhati lejeune, Navnløs, Wuhwuzdat, Ken123BOT, Atonefornothing, Hanter, Hell-Bull, Libertarian92, Okram 09, MenoBot, Martarius, LoserJoke, ClueBot, Tomlupton, Binksternet, Ian Rockwell, The Thing That Should Not Be, ZaZam, Ndenison, Albert Mond, Conorcosgrave, Dominguito, Nymf, Eeekster, Wiki libs, Darthrul, Blackless, Cucumberjohn, Vanished User 1004, DumZiBoT, Dmacewen, SlayerXT, Hawks10, TheSickBehemoth, Tim010987, Texplosion, Kbdankbot, Addbot, Malconfort, RandySavageFTW, Bloodfall, Landon1980, Niderbib, Jackmantas, Rostere, Nickin, Sepulwiki, Beast from da East, Angry Shoplifter, Tassedethe, SuperDamian, Spacefan75, Luckas-bot, Yobot, Amirobot, KamikazeBot, CombatMarshmallow, Suntag, Radiopathy, AnomieBOT, Darolew, Rokermen, Marauder09, LilHelpa, Ximmerman, Xqbot, DSisyphBot, Fallengrademen, Mlpearc, Aussie Ausborn, GrouchoBot, BlackMath77, Freakyllama, Richard BB, Viper076, GripTheHusk, Bercowich, Morbid Fairy, RedBot, MastiBot, Fixer88, Porky metal 666, Erlandinho, VanPunker, Colchester121891, DixonDBot, Rockgenre, MrX, Aurongurdian, Lolnoobslol, Hoalong, Axl kg, Nahyan007, Ripchip Bot, Cruzifixus, EmausBot, John of Reading, Lewismaster, ITshnik, Citation not needed anymore, Strawberry Slugs, VLN1025, Bigfloyydonkey678, Bassplayrcl, GRyaRya, Lihi Laszlo, ClueBot NG, CactusBot, Outaouaisrock, Halloween burns, Joefromrandb, ETFFAN123, Keogruteras, Helpful Pixie Bot, Electriccatfish2, Gavslater, BG19bot, Antton666, Reddogsix, City of Tragedy, Altaïr, Jesuslovesyou666, Soulstaticsound, VEZZLA, H. 217.83, Intensity254, Myxomatosis57, Esszet, GuitarChief, Paokaraforlife, Webclient101, Mogism, Nasmith1234, Ojalvar, Metalheadmitchyj, Ilikepeanutbutter1000, Kevin12xd, Retrohead, Eyesnore, Jamiebee03, Asrith7, GravRidr, Jamiebird000111, JudasPriestFanatic, MetalDiablo666, Ravahe, Teh Thrasher, Monkbot, Lukejordan02, ArmandoBecker, GREYBOYY, Georgieboy666, Laughingpig, Egb2, KasparBot, Kekkofranco, TheHeavyMetalThunder, J6vi91, Palagius, Le Phantomlord and Anonymous: 448

- **White Spirit (band)** *Source:* https://en.wikipedia.org/wiki/White_Spirit_(band)?oldid=676561383 *Contributors:* Stephan Schulz, MacGyverMagic, Bumm13, BD2412, Rjwilmsi, FlaBot, Gringo300, Pegship, SmackBot, LuciferMorgan, Bluebot, Derek R Bullamore, Gobonobo, Dl2000, Clarityfiend, ShelfSkewed, Helldhaz, Darklilac, DuncanHill, Michig, Waacstats, Neverstar, Clnaveen, Imagi-King, Kyo5656, Evb-wiki, Eksosrock, James25402, Nite-Sirk, Tiptoety, FloydFred, Martarius, Laticsdave, Avoided, Addbot, Gripweed, Mikespaldin, Tassedethe, Lightbot, Luckas-bot, Yobot, Ptbotgourou, Michaeljackson215, Krem12, PFR63400, Frehley72, WikiWikingerX, Bobby bobstone, MrX, RjwilmsiBot, Lewismaster, GoingBatty, ZéroBot, Alpha Quadrant, Ego White Tray, ClueBot NG, CactusBot, Amroknian and Anonymous: 17

- **Whitesnake** *Source:* https://en.wikipedia.org/wiki/Whitesnake?oldid=691024882 *Contributors:* D, Wapcaplet, TUF-KAT, FlinkBaum, Fvw, Bearcat, Robbot, Iam, Postdlf, TimR, DocWatson42, Mintleaf~enwiki, Ido50, Foot, Bonalaw, Cfailde, CanisRufus, Spearhead, Mike Garcia, John Vandenberg, Giraffedata, Alansohn, Hu, Snowolf, ProhibitOnions, Arag0rn, Someoneinmyheadbutit'snotme, Don G., Kazvorpal, Kamezuki, Dismas, Sjv27~enwiki, Woohookitty, JetsLuvver, Exxolon, MrDarcy, Tabletop, Mhoulden, Grace Note, GregorB, Neanderthalprimadonna, Palica, Mandarax, Jcuk, Tslocum, Irishrichy, Graham87, BD2412, Kbdank71, Jclemens, Ketiltrout, Rjwilmsi, Koavf, Stevekeiretsu,

Ian Dunster, FlaBot, Gringo300, WillC, CarolGray, Butros, DVdm, Mhking, Jpfagerback, YurikBot, Blightsoot, RussBot, Foxxygirltamara, Wimt, Wiki alf, Grafen, ONEder Boy, DrHydeous, Zwobot, Ospalh, Vlad, DeadEyeArrow, Zzuuzz, De Administrando Imperio, Out-of-focus, Archola, Kingboyk, WesleyDodds, Luk, SmackBot, Lashiec, Grandmaster, CWD, Delldot, Jongpil Yun, Peloneous, Mr Pyles, ProveIt, Jory, Daysleeper47, Icemuon, Chris the speller, SSJ 5, MalafayaBot, Fishhead2100, Thief12, Daddy Kindsoul, DéRahier, The Elfoid, RandomP, IrisKawling, Derek R Bullamore, Adamriggio, Bretonbanquet, Kukini, Spiritia, SashatoBot, Swatjester, Harryboyles, John, IzzyVanHalen, Euchiasmus, Ckatz, Timmeh, Cory pratt, SQGibbon, Monni95, Dl2000, Spark, Torsir, Anger22, Kamikazelover, CmdrObot, ShelfSkewed, Shizane, Neelix, Rgavz, Jac16888, Cydebot, Fair Deal, Andre666, ST47, Charolastra charolo, HK51, DumbBOT, After Midnight, Thijs!bot, Jurqeti, Robsinden, Kronos, Yvonnefitz, PEJL, MaulYoda, N5iln, Roger Pearse, Z00ropean, Childeric~enwiki, Mr. Brain, JustAGal, Grayshi, Nick Number, Sectornine, Hmrox, Martyn Smith, Dr. Blofeld, Lekkerweertje, LordArakis, Necromancer539, Darklilac, Spartaz, Qwerty Binary, Abeyi76, Dybdal~enwiki, TrueGrit, Piegas, MER-C, Bahar, David Coverdale, MB1972, Matthew Husdon, MegX, VoABot II, TheAllSeeing-Eye, Telxon04, Christo jones, POKETNRJSH, Woknam66, Mokgamen, Purslane, Lecomte99, Keith D, R'n'B, Dukewisdom, LedgendGamer, FMAFan1990, RockMFR, N4nojohn, Sam Golden, J.delanoy, Arnvidr, Calamity-Ace, Igli, (jarbarf), PMBO, NinjaIsMe, Obrez, Tiggerjay, DH85868993, Donmike10, Chris516~enwiki, The Little Internet Kitty, Geosultan4, Saint rik, 28bytes, VolkovBot, Dogame, Nburden, RRParry, Kara kutu, Philip Trueman, TXiKiBoT, Nsoranzo, TempeBrennan, Broadbot, ^demonBot2, Magpiecat, Thunderbuck ram, Mistercutts, Pomerol1963, Symo-EFC, Rock Soldier, LordEniac, Logan, Metal Michelle, Peter Fleet, SieBot, TJRC, BotMultichill, Mungo Kitsch, Nite-Sirk, Domonicrini, MisterVodka, AngelOfSadness, KirbyMaster14, StaticGull, Martyn gryphon, KyoufuNoDaiou, Altzinn, Wpac5, Dp67, Martarius, Beeblebrox, Leahtwosaints, Afnecors, ClueBot, Binksternet, Howenstein115, JimboV1, TheOldJacobite, Skeeball93, Mr. Laser Beam, Acciostarbucks, Jmp003, Nymf, ToNToNi, MiladyLane, Darkhelmet322, PixelBot, Eirik Solum~enwiki, Sun Creator, MacedonianBoy, Wiki libs, Arjayay, Ostalocutanje, Soccer girl51, Mikaey, Jimmy Fleischer, Amsaim, C628, BalkanFever, Rockk3r, DumZiBoT, XLinkBot, Robrob5, Tarheel95, Fattylikecake, Чръный человек, SlayerXT, Leia, Mark 88 turbo, TheSickBehemoth, WikHead, JBse, Kbdankbot, HexaChord, Addbot, Cupivistine Noscere?, Blethering Scot, Darwin-rover, CanadianLinuxUser, Snakehead2, Download, Drmotley, Digichannel, Favonian, Kyle1278, Guffydrawers, Tassedethe, Lightbot, Funsuka017, Samboob, Beyond-The-Dark-Life, Legobot, Luckas-bot, Yobot, Deschamps33, Gongshow, QueenCake, Radiopathy, EgbertMcDunk, AnomieBOT, SlayerXTT, AaRH, Jim1138, Martinbr66, Sigshane, Hopscotch23, The Great Duck, Flewis, Marauder09, ArthurBot, Xqbot, Psolley, Capricorn42, David Glyn, Wether B, Axelsegen, Deaths Angles, Live Light, Opjeshke, Seedyswimmer, Mlpearc, Ubcule, Aussie Ausborn, J04n, Tunebroker, Moxy, Nietzsche 2, Shadowjams, Infanteriesoldat, PM800, DeathByMetal666, GripTheHusk, FrescoBot, Sammy Samhain, Metallbanez, Gritssandwhichesforbreakfast, FotoPhest, A vision of it, Ranchloopseven, Pellestar, Jukka Tarvonen, Reckless Eric, HamburgerRadio, David Coverdale's White Snake, Pinethicket, Mrix1985, KirillM, JackShestak, Remsrock, Gwladys24, Dspencer9, Stoneroll, Rockgenre, Adamjackson77, Retrowarrior, MrX, Andymcgrath, Reaper Eternal, Marbod Egerius, Axl kg, John of Reading, MATHEUS HS, Lewismaster, Andrei Cvhdsee Brazil, Starcheerspeaksnewslostwars, GoingBatty, Jim Michael, Tompaine1009, ThatRockMetalGuy, Evanh2008, ZéroBot, Leandro Drudo, Lekermode, Mrmatiko, SchwartzPadre, Superhippie, Mike in Aus, Gajer, Strutter72, L1A1 FAL, Kekkofranco~enwiki, Duphmeister, The Country Girl, ChuispastonBot, ThatRockGuy, Aleksion, Metallicaya!, Cgt, Kwesiidun91, ClueBot NG, CactusBot, BarrelProof, Jesse Striewski, Dafidbrtlt, Kasirbot, Whipped91, SheridanCNV, Lowercase sigmabot, BG19bot, Marin 100 Stoikov, Ditto51, CityOfSilver, Blazeallday, Leigh Burne, Evilemperorzorg, Beast8446, LondonER19, The1337gamer, Ilovebeards, Brayness, BattyBot, Cyberbot II, Harrison 1979, Chie one, Nadeemsshaikh, Robertsklavins, Khazar2, Dokken-Rocker100, AlchemistOfJoy, Planetofjelly, Killmeister, GuitarChief, FreddyHalford, Hinton1994, Mogism, Makecat-bot, Mlpearc Phone, Whitesnakerocks, Herve Reex, Patricktandrews, Heavymetalthunder100, Thelastcanadian, Edwar77, DavidLeighEllis, Supertrill99, MrLinkinPark333, Bdaljev, Fran1996, Kitesailor73, DLManiac, Carlos Rojas77, Filedelinkerbot, Calenter2003, Ivo minchev, DangerousJXD, Mebetgna, Wajenkins, KasparBot, Knife-in-the-drawer, Bigc198387 and Anonymous: 684

- **Wild Horses (British band)** *Source:* https://en.wikipedia.org/wiki/Wild_Horses_(British_band)?oldid=676561888 *Contributors:* Woohookitty, Rjwilmsi, Gringo300, Sverre, ▯▯▯▯ robot, Derek R Bullamore, Marcus Brute, Bretonbanquet, TenPoundHammer, Dl2000, Cydebot, JustAGal, Serpent's Choice, VictorLaszlo, Standingfish, Knutsvendsen, Cyfal, Binksternet, Gibsonboy4, XLinkBot, Чръный человек, Favonian, Jillybo, Yobot, SAULGNRFAN, WikiWikingerX, Hiddenstranger, Lewismaster, Burbridge92, CactusBot, Ling.Nut2, Azealia911 and Anonymous: 12

- **Witchfinder General (band)** *Source:* https://en.wikipedia.org/wiki/Witchfinder_General_(band)?oldid=676562001 *Contributors:* Postdlf, Cfailde, Spearhead, Draconiszeta, Joost~enwiki, MrSomeone, FlaBot, Mr Pyles, Mika1h, Soul Crusher, WeggeBot, Dave.T, Knightfever17, Cydebot, Lugnuts, Thijs!bot, Paliosun, BeastmasterGeneral, CommonsDelinker, Thazandril, Asarlaí, IllaZilla, George bennett, Lordofgore, James25402, Rainlen, Deathbringer from the Sky, PasabaPorAqui, Nymf, PixelBot, XLinkBot, Addbot, Angry Shoplifter, Zorrobot, Luckas-bot, Yobot, Arch stanton1138, Piano non troppo, Marauder09, Arch satan, DanFord2, Space harrier, Murrarie, Dancewithme2, EmausBot, Lewismaster, ZéroBot, ClueBot NG, FWDoom, Amroknian, MikeL1289, KasparBot and Anonymous: 38

- **Witchfynde** *Source:* https://en.wikipedia.org/wiki/Witchfynde?oldid=676038810 *Contributors:* Stormie, Bumm13, Exxolon, Rjwilmsi, Kinu, Bruce1ee, FlaBot, Welsh, Derek R Bullamore, Khazar, Metao, Dl2000, Eastlaw, J Milburn, ShelfSkewed, Blackmetalbaz, Kristmace, Magioladitis, VoABot II, Imagi-King, GaryPaddles, VolkovBot, Gus, James25402, Keilana, Versetechnu, Arjayay, Grebbsy, Addbot, Angry Shoplifter, Yobot, Arch stanton1138, Screwfacexxx, John of Reading, Lewismaster, Postwar, KevinCFH, CactusBot, Rollingdell, Helpful Pixie Bot, Thrashgod500, BG19bot, Khazar2, Materasi, Overdriveontherun, KasparBot and Anonymous: 18

- **Wrathchild** *Source:* https://en.wikipedia.org/wiki/Wrathchild?oldid=676564027 *Contributors:* Ary29, Zenohockey, Lankiveil, Alansohn, Walter Görlitz, Jeff3000, Exxolon, Rjwilmsi, Stormbay, C777, Zzuuzz, Carlosguitar, Crystallina, DazB, Daddy Kindsoul, Derek R Bullamore, Dl2000, BSI, CmdrObot, JPilborough, Cydebot, TylerThorne, Thijs!bot, IrishPete, RebelRobot, Mokgamen, MiltonT, FMAFan1990, Kudpung, Glamster, Steel1943, IllaZilla, Andres gnr, Dick Shane, Fratrep, Navnløs, WikipedianMarlith, Martarius, ClueBot, Qsaw, Love2live9, Dunktattoo, Wiki libs, Wprlh, SchreiberBike, C628, Fotiu, XLinkBot, Plingsby, WikHead, NellieBly, Dynamitegirl, Kbdankbot, Addbot, Tofusando, Angry Shoplifter, Tassedethe, Bfigura's puppy, Lightbot, Zorrobot, Yobot, AnomieBOT, Utan Vax, LilHelpa, A vision of it, Jamescrofts, Kidnuke, XxTimberlakexx, Pvcpsycho, Caspian Rehbinder, JackGoMad, MrX, Pasteit1, Wrathchilduk, Hiddenstranger, Lewismaster, Shearonink, Werieth, AvicAWB, Snotbot, Braincricket, Amroknian, Floating Boat, Wildsideriot, Aisteco, AORmaniac13, Cyberbot II, Mogism, Jossriot, Retrohead, Riccardo.arrigoni, Sleazemetal84, Alzantir, Yellowcagoule, Dimedag, KasparBot and Anonymous: 57

- **Heavy metal fashion** *Source:* https://en.wikipedia.org/wiki/Heavy_metal_fashion?oldid=661504402 *Contributors:* The Anome, William Avery, Ahoerstemeier, TUF-KAT, Johnleemk, RedWolf, Sam Spade, Steeev, Hadal, Arm, Michael2, Akadruid, Lupin, Everyking, Naufana, BigHaz, Phil Sandifer, Ary29, RevRagnarok, Mindspillage, MeltBanana, Erolos, Jaberwocky6669, Brian0918, CanisRufus, Spearhead, Sietse Snel, Bobo192, Burbster, R7, Joost~enwiki, Riana, Fritz Saalfeld, Malber, TenOfAllTrades, Alai, Geographer, Dennis Bratland, Woohookitty,

Kzollman, Xiong Chiamiov, Josh Parris, Lhademmor, Rjwilmsi, Dimitrii, NatusRoma, KharBevNor, Asterism, Sanbeg, Paul foord, DesdinovaUK, BradBeattie, Visor, Mustard29, Piet Delport, Gaius Cornelius, Spike Wilbury, Badagnani, Seegoon, Rbarreira, Cheeser1, Mysid, Wknight94, DNAku, FF2010, Closedmouth, MadMoonchild, De Administrando Imperio, Ladysway1985, Brianlucas, Rotten Bastard~enwiki, SmackBot, SoulSlayer, Swed Simon, Zazaban, Leyasu, Weltanschaunng, CSWarren, OrphanBot, Rrburke, Cyhatch, M2K 2, Sepulcher1443, Rory096, AThing, Kuru, PANDA(PersonAmendingNumerousDefectiveApostrophes), ZaidAhmed, HisSpaceResearch, ILovePlankton, Alygator, Anger22, Tawkerbot2, IronChris, Pink Fae, Ethii, J Milburn, CmdrObot, TheEditrix, Skeletor2112, Kung Foo, Parrot love, ShelfSkewed, Michaelas10, Spylab, Krator, Tawkerbot4, Omicronpersei8, Barticus88, Barek, MegX, Wuji~enwiki, Bongwarrior, Dpmath, Freezing the mainstream, STBot, Zouavman Le Zouave, R'n'B, Wiki Raja, J.delanoy, GreenRunner0, Outlawed Heroine, Anincent, Being blunt, Randydeluxe, Jeff G., Marskuzz, Yaakov Pinus, Corvus coronoides, AtTheGatesOfBodom, HamstaDance, Funeral, Bloody Pierrot, SheaRua, Maurauth, Euryalus, Revenant42, Jay316, Mungo Kitsch, BlueAzure, MisterVodka, Avnjay, Voltagemada, Gunmetal Angel, Smilo Don, Gabriel Texidor, Navnløs, Vanished User 8902317830, Dabomb87, ClueBot, Connor.carey, Mezigue, Niceguyedc, Deprimenthia, Narcie, Urbanchampion, Wiki libs, Zomno, Jumanji656, XLinkBot, Paragon of Arctic Winter Nights, Lemons&Limes, Addbot, JackorKnave, Piemonkey, OlEnglish, Luckas-bot, Bass of the, Eduen, Xqbot, Capricorn42, Veritatem1212, Metalindustrien, FrescoBot, LittleWink, Locutus1966, Orenburg1, Chrolls, ITshnik, ClueBot NG, SicFREAK, Cntras, MerlIwBot, StuGeiger, Dzumaya, IRON MAIDEN1337, Thatemooverthere, ChrisGualtieri, ArmandoBecker, Sstreella and Anonymous: 265

- **Heavy metal subculture** *Source:* https://en.wikipedia.org/wiki/Heavy_metal_subculture?oldid=687243302 *Contributors:* William Avery, SimonP, Fuzheado, Maximus Rex, Steeev, Smjg, Tom harrison, Gzornenplatz, Andycjp, JoJan, Eel, Rich Farmbrough, Kevin Jones, ESkog, Spearhead, Thu, Burbster, InShaneee, SidP, Fourthords, Defacto, Woohookitty, Sonake, Barrylb, BillC, Radiant!, Tslocum, MassGalactusUniversum, Graham87, FlyingCoyote, Boccobrock, Naraht, RexNL, BrianFG, Rell Canis, TheSun, WhyBeNormal, Lightsup55, Mustard29, YurikBot, RussBot, Gardar Rurak, Asa~enwiki, Stephenb, Gaius Cornelius, Wiki alf, Aeusoes1, Badagnani, CecilWard, Eulogy, Bucketsofg, DNAku, 7Munkys, Pegship, Moonrat506, Druff, PTSE, TheMadBaron, Sugar Bear, Selmo, SmackBot, Nihonjoe, Pmppk, Judasandmegadeth, Reedy, Jagged 85, SigmaX54, SkiBumMSP, Hardyplants, Evanreyes, Commander Keane bot, Portillo, The monkeyhate, Persian Poet Gal, Leyasu, Fluri, CSWarren, Mladifilozof, Daddy Kindsoul, Kotra, David Morón, KrutoOn, Mrwuggs, OrphanBot, Rrburke, Berzerker~enwiki, Cyhatch, Fuhghettaboutit, X-Flare-x, Jake Lancaster, Derek R Bullamore, EdGl, Salamurai, Usernamefortonyd, Ceoil, Dbtfz, John, Cat Parade, Hrududu, Perfectblue97, IronGargoyle, Hanii Puppy, TheDecayTheyFear, Kirbytime, Cory pratt, Vanished User 03, Johnson542, OnBeyondZebrax, JoeBot, Aeternus, Halifax corey, Igoldste, Anger22, Tawkerbot2, Iddqd iddqd, Fdssdf, IronChris, ChrisCork, The Haunted Angel, Switchercat, Traitorfish, Sjmcfarland, Random name, Heatsketch, Keredan, VladB, Michaelas10, Gogo Dodo, Corpx, Inhumer, Arcayne, Omicronpersei8, Barticus88, GentlemanGhost, Marek69, Dayn, Nick Number, Hugo Zorilla, AntiVandalBot, Seaphoto, Benjaburns, Prolog, Likeloftoflies, Renaissance rainbow, MegX, Incassiana, .anacondabot, VoABot II, Hugotheboss, Dace59, Twsx, KConWiki, ForestAngel, Ours18, DerHexer, JPNo1Fan, Jowe27, RIII, Hdt83, Zouavman Le Zouave, PrestonH, Yonidebot, FSG, AquamarineOnion, Happy8, Garret Beaumain, Zeldaninja, STBotD, Zara1709, Idioma-bot, VolkovBot, Overt Ninja, Marskuzz, Cloud3514, Pwnage8, Ripeugenedebs, Fulltilt420, Slysplace, Jackfork, Madhero88, Metalion SOS, Andrewaskew, AtTheGatesOfBodom, Malfestance, Necris, Funeral, SieBot, Nelly4, Maurauth, Caulde, BrunoAssis, Mungo Kitsch, Slaytanicslaughter, D616g, Xe7al, ThePaintedOne, Mezmerizer, Dezzrek, Gunmetal Angel, Zyrkh, Tyr Odinsson, Navnløs, Sardaukar Blackfang, DeepQuasar, TubularWorld, Escape Orbit, Angelo De La Paz, Musicaindustrial, Martarius, ClueBot, VictimofDeception, Jshpik1, Arakunem, Darth Spase Peepole, Niceguyedc, Blanchardb, Megadetha~enwiki, Thobe, Cirt, Bardin, Puchiko, Nick19thind, Brewcrewer, Eeekster, TheEmpiricalGuy, NuclearWarfare, Wiki libs, Kmaster, Iohannes Animosus, ReBeL94, The Red, Powerdaze, Warlordring, DumZiBoT, Sgusaman, Zakkman, Little Mountain 5, JCDenton2052, Saxonthedog, Sec 1971, Addbot, RandySavageFTW, GargoyleBot, Fieldday-sunday, BrutalHeavyMETAL, Tassedethe, Tide rolls, Lightbot, Krano, Dimebag Dan, PlankBot, Yobot, Legobot II, Killing3, SwisterTwister, AnomieBOT, Jamie-is-koolie, Madjoe5, IRP, Piano non troppo, KieranO653, LilHelpa, Xqbot, 4twenty42o, Runnable, GrouchoBot, Veritatem1212, Mister M00n, Amqui, FireCrystal, CalmCalamity, A7xandquantumtheory, Saumil.shrivastava, XxTimberlakexx, Squid661, Daw42, RedBot, Iron Aden, Bgpaulus, Drakoe29x, Deinonychosauria, AndyJones233333, ElectricWizard 0, TjBot, EmausBot, Lewismaster, Burnberrytree, Gudtonoyah, Ajstov, Mjbmrbot, Prove you're robot, ClueBot NG, Helpful Pixie Bot, Wbm1058, BG19bot, Ihavenoideawhatiamdoing, H. 217.83, Wisehelp, Khazar2, Ozarth, Racer Omega, Richard Kuklinski, Turdice, Thrasher513, Peter33p, DangerousJXD and Anonymous: 498

- **Kerrang!** *Source:* https://en.wikipedia.org/wiki/Kerrang!?oldid=689963966 *Contributors:* Olivier, Morwen, Johnleemk, MrWeeble, Riddley, Bearcat, Acegikmo1, Everyking, Varlaam, Pne, Isidore, Barneyboo, RobinCarmody, Sam Hocevar, Mike Rosoft, Freakofnurture, Rich Farmbrough, Loganberry, Bumhoolery, CanisRufus, Kiand, Bobo192, The KZA, Alansohn, Gary, PopUpPirate, Ashley Pomeroy, Ronark, Mikeo, Redvers, Woohookitty, Mazca, WadeSimMiser, Exxolon, Bartash, Tabletop, RomeW, MrSomeone, Rjwilmsi, Tim!, Tarnas, Davelong, The wub, Jamdav86, FlaBot, Chris is me, Sharkface217, YurikBot, RussBot, Hede2000, Stephenb, C777, Grafen, Irishguy, Malcolma, BOT-Superzerocool, Closedmouth, D'Agosta, Omdfg, Jogers, RockyMM, Spliffy, Kingboyk, Felisse, SmackBot, Elonka, JAB, Midway, Jab843, 13-days, Canderra, Evanreyes, Gilliam, Portillo, Cabe6403, Sirex98, Thumperward, Cbh, Daniellane, Daddy Kindsoul, Zsinj, Factorylad, TheGerm, Racklever, Wine Guy, Tkosullivan, RJN, SlaughterOfTheSoul, Manboobies, Ohconfucius, WTH, John, Dudo2, Minna Sora no Shita, IronGargoyle, Jxb311, DanielMrakic~enwiki, Mr Stephen, AxG, DabMachine, −5-, HisSpaceResearch, DJ HEAVEN, RekishiEJ, Gophergun, Marcus Bowen, Superscribe, Neelix, Ren0, Pit-yacker, Beastmouth, YesMapRadio, Gpmuscillo, Doug Weller, Phydend, BetacommandBot, Epbr123, Peter Znamenskiy, Nessuna, Z10x, JustAGal, DavidJJJ, ZachWhitchurch, Hackstar18, Hmrox, AntiVandalBot, Gioto, Mike1326, Darklilac, DCman, Chriscornwell982, Claire323uk, Kaobear, Dsp13, Timkovski, Endlessdan, Noface1, MegX, Bencherlite, Magioladitis, Poiuytre, VoABot II, Jamo.au, BlueEvo2, Twsx, Smith666, Red Sismey, Beelzebloke, Ashrock76, JediLofty, B. Wolterding, MartinBot, STBot, Zouavman Le Zouave, CommonsDelinker, Smokizzy, J.delanoy, Truncated, Jkneon, Smiley~enwiki, Tikiwont, Neon white, OohBunnies!, Redl@nds597198, Beerslayer, MyChemical, Doomsday28, STBotD, Tbone762, MyChemicalRomance13, VolkovBot, Shortride, ErleGrey, Smnyng, Raziqrauf, EmeraldLita, Pwnage8, Planetary Chaos, Lolomgwtfbbq, Pmedema, Anna Lincoln, Clarince63, Megadeth186, Seb26, Mongloid, Thesonglessbird, Falcon8765, Geanixx, Hmmyeshmmyes, Nouse4aname, Cronos12390, BeepBoopBop, Scarian, WereSpielChequers, Technocracy, Winchelsea, Joebalo, Conor55, Sticky bandits1, Aspects, Crisis, Gunmetal Angel, Graeme Mullins, Svick, Escape Orbit, ImageRemovalBot, Martarius, ClueBot, The Thing That Should Not Be, Cokeandaroll, Clinton Baptiste, Caroline72, Bradka, Scrouge, MurderedInTheMosh, CounterVandalismBot, Jasper the Friendly Punk, Bardin, Oreos-and-converse, Megastrike14, PixelBot, Tgmonkeyman, Arain321, Grey Matter, Wiki libs, Hungrywoods, Basketball110, Rylann, Flibblesan, Hiko88, Shadow Snatcher, Josh Heza, QuintusPetillius, Avoided, Skarebo, RyanCross, Bazj, Addbot, HellektroNaz, Loudrocksurfing, Chzz, LiirAndTrismForever, Taopman, Tassedethe, Lightbot, Rodericksilly, Drpickem, Luckas-bot, Wooblz!, Yobot, Elvisvsjesus, Lawrence Biancardi, Gongshow, AmazinglyAwesome, Jim1138, JackieBot, Materialscien-

- **Metal Forces** *Source:* https://en.wikipedia.org/wiki/Metal_Forces?oldid=671343141 *Contributors:* Bearcat, Alba, Rich Farmbrough, Woohookitty, Tim!, Bruce1ee, Pigman, Stephenb, Grafen, Malcolma, LuciferMorgan, Thornstrom, Chris the speller, Bluebot, TenPoundHammer, ShelfSkewed, Neelix, Blackmetalbaz, Bobblehead, Jayron32, Dsp13, Moonriddengirl, Metaldetector, Plastikspork, TheRedPenOfDoom, Yobot, AnomieBOT, Zoident, FrescoBot, Lewismaster, Helpful Pixie Bot, Metal121, Tigercompanion25 and Anonymous: 6

- **Metal Hammer** *Source:* https://en.wikipedia.org/wiki/Metal_Hammer?oldid=688923916 *Contributors:* Ahoerstemeier, Bearcat, Esperant, Fizzyfifi, D6, Rich Farmbrough, Cfailde, Dennis Brown, Pearle, Gargaj, Jackliddle, Zsero, Danhash, GVOLTT, Mandarax, Tim!, Davelong, FlaBot, Who, Neofelis Nebulosa~enwiki, GreyCat, Visor, RussBot, Hede2000, Piet Delport, Stephenb, Huangcjz, Meegs, Hirudo, SmackBot, LuciferMorgan, Carbonix, Thumperward, O keyes, Can't sleep, clown will eat me, Cobain, François Renner, Derek R Bullamore, WTH, BrownHairedGirl, John, Bagel7, Osbus, DabMachine, Nelson ImI, Marysunshine, CmdrObot, Lugnuts, Bigwhiteyeti, Dog fun, ArchitectREX, Thijs!bot, Tommyudo, BabylonAD, MegX, Poiuytre, -the-muffin-man-, Watwat~enwiki, Skweetis, Frank Renner, VolkovBot, Managerpants, Shortride, Headmess, Amog, Chris9086, Kornman230, AlleborgoBot, Lightmouse, Gunmetal Angel, Martarius, De728631, Niceguyedc, Bardin, 718 Bot, Muhandes, Kmaster, Arjayay, Ostalocutanje, Addbot, Yobot, Ptbotgourou, THEN WHO WAS PHONE?, Rachmaninoff, AnomieBOT, Saimon91, Materialscientist, GrouchoBot, Motsm, Cnwilliams, BaldBoris, Lotje, KristofferAG, Human Rights Believer, Lewismaster, LeftFootRight, SporkBot, WikiMan225, SkywalkerPL, ClueBot NG, Beaver991, 149AFK, Dominoid747, BG19bot, Krazyklod, VampireKilla, LordRapture, BattyBot, Bilalokms, Egeymi, Lu0490, Bugsy101, I call the big one bitey, DissidentAggressor, Willydat, Hutzre and Anonymous: 72

- **Raw Power (TV series)** *Source:* https://en.wikipedia.org/wiki/Raw_Power_(TV_series)?oldid=667975017 *Contributors:* Sjorford, HaeB, Tim!, RussBot, SmackBot, Stuart P. Bentley, Azumanga1, Dl2000, CmdrObot, Mattbr, Razdan1974, JediLofty, R'n'B, Musicbox24, Fuddle, Gwynrwilliams, Niceguyedc, Jjeeffuuqa, Barutazaru, Nibi, 120selrahc, Alvin Seville, MikeAllen, Lewismaster, RenamedUser01302013, Khazar2 and Anonymous: 5

- **Terrorizer (magazine)** *Source:* https://en.wikipedia.org/wiki/Terrorizer_(magazine)?oldid=689963616 *Contributors:* Stormie, Bearcat, Rich Farmbrough, Spearhead, Ire and curses, SteinbDJ, Woohookitty, BD2412, Rjwilmsi, Tim!, FlaBot, RussBot, Willirennen, Jogers, Lyrl, Dsreyn, SmackBot, Xombie, Bluebot, Hibernian, Colonies Chris, Klacquement, Mark in wiki, Andrew c, Twas Now, CmdrObot, ShelfSkewed, Khatru2, Blackmetalbaz, Spylab, Inhumer, After Midnight, Maziotis, PKT, Nick Number, Hole in the wall, Prolog, Robina Fox, MegX, Tenniselbow, Magioladitis, Appraiser, JaGa, R'n'B, Jimmy christ, Technogoat, Speighticus, ItReallyDoes, Jack Merridew, Nite-Sirk, Android Mouse Bot 3, ImageRemovalBot, Martarius, Bardin, Alexa.mcgov, Choosingdeath, Northern Hammer, Openjiffybag, Addbot, EGibb, LaaknorBot, Tassedethe, Luckas-bot, Yobot, LilHelpa, Tiller54, GrouchoBot, Metalindustrien, Lotje, ZéroBot, Myxomatosis57, Egeymi, Tigercompanion25, Questionofpower and Anonymous: 35

- **Zero Tolerance (magazine)** *Source:* https://en.wikipedia.org/wiki/Zero_Tolerance_(magazine)?oldid=675858953 *Contributors:* Bender235, CloudNine, Tim!, Jak123, Hall Monitor, Dialectric, Aelfthrytha, Salamurai, IronGargoyle, MikeWazowski, JohnCD, Lucidacurve, Tango Alpha Foxtrot, Havoc21, Torchpratt, Formyanger, Lisa zt, Theadelph, Aphex456, SardonicRick, Cacolantern, Geena Hall, Dpmuk, Lisabel345, Od Mishehu AWB, Alexa.mcgov, Mfan666, XLinkBot, Malconfort, Dawynn, Tassedethe, AnomieBOT, Creotine, BG19bot, Zerotolerancemagazine, Lisamaceyzt, BattyBot, ChrisGualtieri, Synthwave.94 and Anonymous: 8

4.2 Images

- **File:Ace_of_Spades_tour_booklet.jpg** *Source:* https://upload.wikimedia.org/wikipedia/en/e/e5/Ace_of_Spades_tour_booklet.jpg *License:* ? *Contributors:*
  Photograph of User:Wiki alf's tour booklet *Original artist:* ?

- **File:Ambox_important.svg** *Source:* https://upload.wikimedia.org/wikipedia/commons/b/b4/Ambox_important.svg *License:* Public domain *Contributors:* Own work, based off of Image:Ambox scales.svg *Original artist:* Dsmurat (talk · contribs)

- **File:Angel_Witch_Hellfest.jpg** *Source:* https://upload.wikimedia.org/wikipedia/commons/2/2b/Angel_Witch_Hellfest.jpg *License:* CC BY 2.0 *Contributors:* http://www.flickr.com/photos/psych0mantum/5876520672/sizes/l/in/photostream/ *Original artist:* psych0mantum

- **File:Angel_Witch_live_2010.jpg** *Source:* https://upload.wikimedia.org/wikipedia/commons/a/ac/Angel_Witch_live_2010.jpg *License:* CC BY-SA 3.0 *Contributors:* Own work *Original artist:* Lewismaster

- **File:Blitzkrieg_-_Jalometalli_2008_-_11.JPG** *Source:* https://upload.wikimedia.org/wikipedia/commons/8/83/Blitzkrieg_-_Jalometalli_2008_-_11.JPG *License:* CC BY-SA 3.0 *Contributors:* Own work *Original artist:* Cecil

- **File:Blitzkrieg_-_Jalometalli_2008_-_13.JPG** *Source:* https://upload.wikimedia.org/wikipedia/commons/7/7b/Blitzkrieg_-_Jalometalli_2008_-_13.JPG *License:* CC BY-SA 3.0 *Contributors:* Own work *Original artist:* Cecil

- **File:Blitzkrieg_2012.jpg** *Source:* https://upload.wikimedia.org/wikipedia/commons/d/d1/Blitzkrieg_2012.jpg *License:* CC BY-SA 3.0 *Contributors:* outdoor band photoshoot
  Previously published: used on blitzkrieg official website which i run and on blitzkrieg facebook page *Original artist:* Blitzkrieginfo

- **File:Brian_Robertson_in_2011.jpg** *Source:* https://upload.wikimedia.org/wikipedia/commons/7/7d/Brian_Robertson_in_2011.jpg *License:* CC BY-SA 2.0 *Contributors:* http://www.flickr.com/photos/bluetit/5328231149/in/faves-24788065@N02/ *Original artist:* Daragh Owens

- **File:Bruce_Dickinson_and_Eddie_30nov2006.jpg** *Source:* https://upload.wikimedia.org/wikipedia/commons/4/42/Bruce_Dickinson_and_Eddie_30nov2006.jpg *License:* CC-BY-SA-3.0 *Contributors:* Own work *Original artist:* Darz Mol
- **File:Burke_Shelley_of_Budgie,_1981.jpg** *Source:* https://upload.wikimedia.org/wikipedia/commons/c/ce/Burke_Shelley_of_Budgie%2C_1981.jpg *License:* CC BY-SA 2.0 *Contributors:* http://www.flickr.com/photos/watt_dabney/2327467972/ *Original artist:* Andrew King
- **File:CampbellDef.JPG** *Source:* https://upload.wikimedia.org/wikipedia/commons/d/d3/CampbellDef.JPG *License:* Public domain *Contributors:* Originally from en.wikipedia; description page is/was here. *Original artist:* Original uploader and author was Weatherman90 at en.wikipedia
- **File:Cardiff_Bay_WMC.jpg** *Source:* https://upload.wikimedia.org/wikipedia/commons/1/1f/Cardiff_Bay_WMC.jpg *License:* CC BY-SA 2.0 *Contributors:* Flickr original image *Original artist:* grahamwell / Graham profile at Flickr website
- **File:Cartandhorses.jpg** *Source:* https://upload.wikimedia.org/wikipedia/commons/0/08/Cartandhorses.jpg *License:* CC BY-SA 3.0 *Contributors:* Own work *Original artist:* Freddysbg
- **File:Collen2.jpg** *Source:* https://upload.wikimedia.org/wikipedia/commons/3/33/Collen2.jpg *License:* Public domain *Contributors:* Originally from en.wikipedia; description page is/was here. *Original artist:* The original uploader was Blofeld of SPECTRE at English Wikipedia
- **File:Commons-logo.svg** *Source:* https://upload.wikimedia.org/wikipedia/en/4/4a/Commons-logo.svg *License:* ? *Contributors:* ? *Original artist:* ?
- **File:DavidCoverdale1983.jpg** *Source:* https://upload.wikimedia.org/wikipedia/commons/5/58/DavidCoverdale1983.jpg *License:* CC BY 2.0 *Contributors:* Whitesnake - Donnington *Original artist:* Cathy Griffiths from Odiham, England
- **File:David_Coverdale,_Manchester_Apollo,_2011.JPG** *Source:* https://upload.wikimedia.org/wikipedia/commons/7/79/David_Coverdale%2C_Manchester_Apollo%2C_2011.JPG *License:* CC BY-SA 3.0 *Contributors:* Own work *Original artist:* Hinton1994
- **File:DefLeppard1.JPG** *Source:* https://upload.wikimedia.org/wikipedia/commons/7/7b/DefLeppard1.JPG *License:* CC-BY-SA-3.0 *Contributors:* http://en.wikipedia.org/wiki/Image:DefLeppard1.JPG *Original artist:* wikipedia user Weatherman90
- **File:Def_Leppard_Allstate_Arena_7-19-12.JPG** *Source:* https://upload.wikimedia.org/wikipedia/commons/6/6d/Def_Leppard_Allstate_Arena_7-19-12.JPG *License:* CC BY-SA 3.0 *Contributors:* Own work *Original artist:* AngryApathy
- **File:Def_Leppard_Sweden_Rock_2008.jpg** *Source:* https://upload.wikimedia.org/wikipedia/commons/d/dc/Def_Leppard_Sweden_Rock_2008.jpg *License:* CC BY 3.0 *Contributors:* Own work *Original artist:* Äppelmos
- **File:Demon_live_2010.jpg** *Source:* https://upload.wikimedia.org/wikipedia/commons/7/72/Demon_live_2010.jpg *License:* CC BY-SA 3.0 *Contributors:* Own work *Original artist:* Lewismaster
- **File:DiAnno.jpg** *Source:* https://upload.wikimedia.org/wikipedia/commons/e/e8/DiAnno.jpg *License:* CC BY-SA 2.0 *Contributors:* http://www.flickr.com/photos/viradacultural2008/2445490937/sizes/l/in/set-72157604780366164/ *Original artist:* Silvio Tanaka - Expansão Cultural
- **File:Diamond_Head_–_Headbangers_Open_Air_2014_01.jpg** *Source:* https://upload.wikimedia.org/wikipedia/commons/f/fd/Diamond_Head_%E2%80%93_Headbangers_Open_Air_2014_01.jpg *License:* CC BY-SA 3.0 *Contributors:* Own work *Original artist:* Frank Schwichtenberg
- **File:Dio.JPG** *Source:* https://upload.wikimedia.org/wikipedia/commons/4/4e/Dio.JPG *License:* CC-BY-SA-3.0 *Contributors:* No machine-readable source provided. Own work assumed (based on copyright claims). *Original artist:* No machine-readable author provided. Jacob2106~commonswiki assumed (based on copyright claims).
- **File:Dio_monument.jpeg** *Source:* https://upload.wikimedia.org/wikipedia/commons/2/2b/Dio_monument.jpeg *License:* CC BY 3.0 *Contributors:* http://www.vesti.bg/index.phtml?tid=40&oid=3351211 *Original artist:* Unknown
- **File:Dio_throwing_Horns.jpg** *Source:* https://upload.wikimedia.org/wikipedia/commons/2/22/Dio_throwing_Horns.jpg *License:* CC BY 2.0 *Contributors:* Heaven And Hell img_7339.jpg *Original artist:* rjforster from Worcester, UK
- **File:Doogiewhite.jpeg** *Source:* https://upload.wikimedia.org/wikipedia/en/e/e6/Doogiewhite.jpeg *License:* CC-BY-3.0 *Contributors:* ? *Original artist:* ?
- **File:Doug_Scarratt_performing_in_2011.jpg** *Source:* https://upload.wikimedia.org/wikipedia/commons/0/08/Doug_Scarratt_performing_in_2011.jpg *License:* CC BY-SA 3.0 *Contributors:* Own work *Original artist:* Mattmetallica
- **File:Dumpy85.jpg** *Source:* https://upload.wikimedia.org/wikipedia/en/9/92/Dumpy85.jpg *License:* PD *Contributors:* ? *Original artist:* ?
- **File:Edit-clear.svg** *Source:* https://upload.wikimedia.org/wikipedia/en/f/f2/Edit-clear.svg *License:* Public domain *Contributors:* The *Tango! Desktop Project*. *Original artist:*

    The people from the Tango! project. And according to the meta-data in the file, specifically: "Andreas Nilsson, and Jakub Steiner (although minimally)."
- **File:Elixir_live_2010.jpg** *Source:* https://upload.wikimedia.org/wikipedia/commons/3/34/Elixir_live_2010.jpg *License:* CC BY-SA 3.0 *Contributors:* Own work *Original artist:* Lewismaster
- **File:Eric_Bell_&_Bo_Diddley_by_Zoran_Veselinovic.jpg** *Source:* https://upload.wikimedia.org/wikipedia/commons/7/73/Eric_Bell_%26_Bo_Diddley_by_Zoran_Veselinovic.jpg *License:* CC BY-SA 2.0 *Contributors:* http://www.flickr.com/photos/56492970@N07/5601402049/ *Original artist:* Zoran Veselinovic
- **File:Eric_Bell_1972.jpg** *Source:* https://upload.wikimedia.org/wikipedia/commons/4/47/Eric_Bell_1972.jpg *License:* CC BY-SA 2.0 *Contributors:* http://www.flickr.com/photos/khiltscher/3141138463/in/faves-24788065@N02/ *Original artist:* Klaus Hiltscher
- **File:Flag_of_the_United_Kingdom.svg** *Source:* https://upload.wikimedia.org/wikipedia/en/a/ae/Flag_of_the_United_Kingdom.svg *License:* PD *Contributors:* ? *Original artist:* ?
- **File:Folder_Hexagonal_Icon.svg** *Source:* https://upload.wikimedia.org/wikipedia/en/4/48/Folder_Hexagonal_Icon.svg *License:* Cc-by-sa-3.0 *Contributors:* ? *Original artist:* ?

4.2. IMAGES

- **File:Front_Thin_Lizzy.jpg** *Source:* https://upload.wikimedia.org/wikipedia/commons/4/46/Front_Thin_Lizzy.jpg *License:* CC BY-SA 2.0 *Contributors:* http://www.flickr.com/photos/watt_dabney/2326629305/ *Original artist:* Andrew King
- **File:Girlschool_Jackie_Chambers.jpg** *Source:* https://upload.wikimedia.org/wikipedia/commons/e/e9/Girlschool_Jackie_Chambers.jpg *License:* CC BY-SA 2.0 *Contributors:*
- Girlschool_band_2009_Jackie.jpg *Original artist:* Girlschool_band_2009_Jackie.jpg: Edward Burke
- **File:Girlschool_Kim_McAuliffe.jpg** *Source:* https://upload.wikimedia.org/wikipedia/commons/1/1b/Girlschool_Kim_McAuliffe.jpg *License:* CC BY-SA 2.0 *Contributors:*
- Girlschool_band_2009.jpg *Original artist:* Girlschool_band_2009.jpg: Edward Burke
- **File:Girlschool_band_1981.jpg** *Source:* https://upload.wikimedia.org/wikipedia/commons/1/1f/Girlschool_band_1981.jpg *License:* CC BY-SA 2.0 *Contributors:* http://www.flickr.com/photos/watt_dabney/2329355695/ *Original artist:* Watt Dabney
- **File:Girlschool_enid_and_lemmy-2.jpg** *Source:* https://upload.wikimedia.org/wikipedia/commons/1/13/Girlschool_enid_and_lemmy-2.jpg *License:* CC BY-SA 2.0 *Contributors:*
- Girlschool_enid_and_lemmy.jpg *Original artist:* Girlschool_enid_and_lemmy.jpg: Gastr0naut
- **File:Girlschool_live_2009-2.jpg** *Source:* https://upload.wikimedia.org/wikipedia/commons/6/61/Girlschool_live_2009-2.jpg *License:* CC BY-SA 2.0 *Contributors:*
- Girlschool_live_2009.jpg *Original artist:* Girlschool_live_2009.jpg: Gastr0naut
- **File:Girlschool_poster84.jpg** *Source:* https://upload.wikimedia.org/wikipedia/en/a/a2/Girlschool_poster84.jpg *License:* Fair use *Contributors:* photo of the original poster
  Original artist: ?
- **File:Gnome-mime-sound-openclipart.svg** *Source:* https://upload.wikimedia.org/wikipedia/commons/8/87/Gnome-mime-sound-openclipart.svg *License:* Public domain *Contributors:* Own work. Based on File:Gnome-mime-audio-openclipart.svg, which is public domain. *Original artist:* User:Eubulides
- **File:Graham_Bonnet.JPG** *Source:* https://upload.wikimedia.org/wikipedia/commons/9/96/Graham_Bonnet.JPG *License:* Public domain *Contributors:* Own work *Original artist:* Eetwartti
- **File:Grim_Reaper_live_2010.jpg** *Source:* https://upload.wikimedia.org/wikipedia/commons/3/3a/Grim_Reaper_live_2010.jpg *License:* CC BY-SA 3.0 *Contributors:* Own work *Original artist:* Lewismaster
- **File:Harris_1.jpg** *Source:* https://upload.wikimedia.org/wikipedia/commons/8/89/Harris_1.jpg *License:* CC BY-SA 3.0 *Contributors:* Own work *Original artist:* Metalheart
- **File:Headgirl_please_dont_touch.ogg** *Source:* https://upload.wikimedia.org/wikipedia/en/b/b0/Headgirl_please_dont_touch.ogg *License:* Fair use *Contributors:* ? *Original artist:* ?
- **File:HeavyMetalJckt.jpg** *Source:* https://upload.wikimedia.org/wikipedia/commons/e/e0/HeavyMetalJckt.jpg *License:* Public domain *Contributors:* Own work (Original text: *self-made*) *Original artist:* A metalhead in Boston
- **File:IRON_MAIDEN_-_Manchester_Apollo_-_1980.jpg** *Source:* https://upload.wikimedia.org/wikipedia/commons/d/d4/IRON_MAIDEN_-_Manchester_Apollo_-_1980.jpg *License:* CC BY-SA 2.0 *Contributors:* Flickr: IRON MAIDEN - Manchester Apollo - 1980 *Original artist:* Harry (Howard) Potts
- **File:IronMaidenBNW.ogg** *Source:* https://upload.wikimedia.org/wikipedia/en/4/41/IronMaidenBNW.ogg *License:* Fair use *Contributors:* ? *Original artist:* ?
- **File:IronMaidenCSIT.ogg** *Source:* https://upload.wikimedia.org/wikipedia/en/2/25/IronMaidenCSIT.ogg *License:* Fair use *Contributors:* ? *Original artist:* ?
- **File:IronMaidenRTTH.ogg** *Source:* https://upload.wikimedia.org/wikipedia/en/c/c0/IronMaidenRTTH.ogg *License:* Fair use *Contributors:* ? *Original artist:* ?
- **File:IronMaidencollage2.jpg** *Source:* https://upload.wikimedia.org/wikipedia/commons/e/ed/IronMaidencollage2.jpg *License:* CC BY-SA 2.0 *Contributors:*
- File:Steve Harris 521.jpg *Original artist:* File:Steve Harris 521.jpg: adels
- **File:Iron_Maiden'{}s_Eddie1.jpg** *Source:* https://upload.wikimedia.org/wikipedia/commons/c/c4/Iron_Maiden%27s_Eddie1.jpg *License:* CC BY-SA 3.0 *Contributors:*
- Iron_Maiden's_Eddie.jpg *Original artist:* Iron_Maiden's_Eddie.jpg: Metalheart
- **File:Iron_Maiden_-_The_Number_Of_The_Beast.jpg** *Source:* https://upload.wikimedia.org/wikipedia/en/1/1f/Iron_Maiden_-_The_Number_Of_The_Beast.jpg *License:* Fair use *Contributors:*
  Derived from a scan of the album cover (creator of this digital version is irrelevant as the copyright in all equivalent images is still held by the same party). Copyright held by the record company or the artist. Claimed as fair use regardless.
  Original artist: ?
- **File:Iron_Maiden_-_bass_and_guitars_30nov2006.jpg** *Source:* https://upload.wikimedia.org/wikipedia/commons/e/eb/Iron_Maiden_-_bass_and_guitars_30nov2006.jpg *License:* CC-BY-SA-3.0 *Contributors:* Own work *Original artist:* Darz Mol
- **File:Iron_Maiden_086.jpg** *Source:* https://upload.wikimedia.org/wikipedia/commons/1/14/Iron_Maiden_086.jpg *License:* CC BY-SA 3.0 *Contributors:* Own work *Original artist:* De-fexxx666

- **File:Iron_Maiden_en_Costa_Rica.jpg** *Source:* https://upload.wikimedia.org/wikipedia/commons/9/96/Iron_Maiden_en_Costa_Rica.jpg *License:* CC BY 2.0 *Contributors:* originally posted to **Flickr** as Iron Maiden en Costa Rica *Original artist:* adels
- **File:JoeElliott.JPG** *Source:* https://upload.wikimedia.org/wikipedia/commons/1/1e/JoeElliott.JPG *License:* CC BY 3.0 *Contributors:* ? *Original artist:* ?
- **File:Joe_Lynn_Turner_in_2008.jpg** *Source:* https://upload.wikimedia.org/wikipedia/commons/1/11/Joe_Lynn_Turner_in_2008.jpg *License:* GFDL *Contributors:* photo taken by my friend *Original artist:* deerstop
- **File:John_Sykes_1984.jpg** *Source:* https://upload.wikimedia.org/wikipedia/commons/7/7f/John_Sykes_1984.jpg *License:* CC BY-SA 2.0 *Contributors:* http://www.flickr.com/photos/odonata22/909872905/in/faves-24788065@N02/ *Original artist:* odonata22 (Dana Wullenwaber)
- **File:JudasPriest.jpg** *Source:* https://upload.wikimedia.org/wikipedia/commons/0/09/JudasPriest.jpg *License:* CC BY-SA 2.0 *Contributors:* Judas Priest *Original artist:* Zach Petersen from Cedar Rapids, Iowa, USA
- **File:Judas_Priest,_päälava,_Sauna_Open_Air_2011,_Tampere,_11.6.2011_(38).JPG** *Source:* https://upload.wikimedia.org/wikipedia/commons/f/fc/Judas_Priest%2C_p%C3%A4%C3%A4lava%2C_Sauna_Open_Air_2011%2C_Tampere%2C_11.6.2011_%2838%29.JPG *License:* CC BY-SA 3.0 *Contributors:* Own work *Original artist:* Makele-90
- **File:Judas_Priest_-_Redeemer_of_Souls_-_9th_Oct_2014_-_Barclay_Center,_Brooklyn_,_New_York.jpg** *Source:* https://upload.wikimedia.org/wikipedia/commons/0/0c/Judas_Priest_-_Redeemer_of_Souls_-_9th_Oct_2014_-_Barclay_Center%2C_Brooklyn_%2C_New_York.jpg *License:* CC BY-SA 4.0 *Contributors:* Own work *Original artist:* Sibuachu
- **File:Judas_Priest_K.K._Downing_Glenn_Tipton,_1984.jpg** *Source:* https://upload.wikimedia.org/wikipedia/commons/5/56/Judas_Priest_K.K._Downing_Glenn_Tipton%2C_1984.jpg *License:* CC BY 2.0 *Contributors:* http://www.flickr.com/photos/fcatalina/2904786833/ *Original artist:* Fernando Catalina Landa
- **File:Judas_Priest_Retribution_2005_Tour.jpg** *Source:* https://upload.wikimedia.org/wikipedia/commons/d/d3/Judas_Priest_Retribution_2005_Tour.jpg *License:* CC BY-SA 2.0 *Contributors:* ? *Original artist:* ?
- **File:Judas_Priest_Sweden_Rock_2008.jpg** *Source:* https://upload.wikimedia.org/wikipedia/commons/b/bc/Judas_Priest_Sweden_Rock_2008.jpg *License:* CC BY 3.0 *Contributors:* Own work *Original artist:* Äppelmos
- **File:Judas_Priest_dal_viy_a_Cardiff_in_dal_1981.jpg** *Source:* https://upload.wikimedia.org/wikipedia/commons/2/2b/Judas_Priest_dal_vi%E1%B9%BF_a_Cardiff_in_dal_1981.jpg *License:* CC BY-SA 2.0 *Contributors:* http://www.flickr.com/photos/watt_dabney/5090994178/ *Original artist:* Watt Dabney
- **File:Kerrang!_Magazine_Cover.jpg** *Source:* https://upload.wikimedia.org/wikipedia/en/3/3b/Kerrang%21_Magazine_Cover.jpg *License:* Fair use *Contributors:*

  From the magazines Online Editor John Longbottom

  Original artist: ?
- **File:Lemmy-taylor-clarke.JPG** *Source:* https://upload.wikimedia.org/wikipedia/en/e/e7/Lemmy-taylor-clarke.JPG *License:* ? *Contributors:* originally a promotional picture, re-used in various DVDs of the band, in the interview sections

  Original artist: ?
- **File:Lemmy_Kilmister.jpg** *Source:* https://upload.wikimedia.org/wikipedia/commons/5/55/Lemmy_Kilmister.jpg *License:* CC BY 2.0 *Contributors:* Flickr http://www.flickr.com/photos/molcatron/183779592/in/set-72157594190255782/ *Original artist:* Alejandro Páez (Molcatron on Flickr)
- **File:Lemmy_St._Albans_1982.jpg** *Source:* https://upload.wikimedia.org/wikipedia/commons/c/c5/Lemmy_St._Albans_1982.jpg *License:* CC BY 2.0 *Contributors:* https://www.flickr.com/photos/parkstreetparrot/11002796195/sizes/o/ *Original artist:* PSParrot
- **File:Loosenlethal.jpg** *Source:* https://upload.wikimedia.org/wikipedia/en/f/f4/Loosenlethal.jpg *License:* Fair use *Contributors:*

  The cover art can be obtained from the record label.

  Original artist: ?
- **File:Magazine.svg** *Source:* https://upload.wikimedia.org/wikipedia/commons/7/7d/Magazine.svg *License:* Public domain *Contributors:* modification of Booyabazooka's Image:Newspaper.svg, which in turn was based on open clipart Image:News.svg *Original artist:* Halibutt, Booyabazooka
- **File:Masters_of_Rock_2007_-_Motörhead_-_6.jpg** *Source:* https://upload.wikimedia.org/wikipedia/commons/1/1f/Masters_of_Rock_2007_-_Mot%C3%B6rhead_-_6.jpg *License:* CC BY-SA 2.5 *Contributors:* Own work *Original artist:*
- commons: KaJaNa
- **File:Metal'{}s_not_dead.jpg** *Source:* https://upload.wikimedia.org/wikipedia/commons/e/e1/Metal%27s_not_dead.jpg *License:* CC BY 2.0 *Contributors:* http://www.flickr.com/photos/timparkinson/2361285833/ *Original artist:* http://www.flickr.com/photos/timparkinson/
- **File:MetalHammer_logo.png** *Source:* https://upload.wikimedia.org/wikipedia/en/e/ea/MetalHammer_logo.png *License:* Fair use *Contributors:*

  http://www.metalhammer.co.uk/ *Original artist:* ?
- **File:MetalKutte.jpg** *Source:* https://upload.wikimedia.org/wikipedia/commons/2/2c/MetalKutte.jpg *License:* CC BY-SA 2.0 *Contributors:* originally posted to **Flickr** as Metal kutte *Original artist:* liftarn
- **File:Metallica_-_Am_i_Evil.ogg** *Source:* https://upload.wikimedia.org/wikipedia/en/9/99/Metallica_-_Am_i_Evil.ogg *License:* Fair use *Contributors:*

  The song "Am I Evil?" by Metallica

  Original artist: ?

4.2. IMAGES

- **File:Miners_strike_rally_London_1984.jpg** *Source:* https://upload.wikimedia.org/wikipedia/commons/d/da/Miners_strike_rally_London_1984.jpg *License:* CC BY 2.0 *Contributors:* Miners' Strike rally, 1984 *Original artist:* Nick from Bristol, UK
- **File:Motorhead-01.jpg** *Source:* https://upload.wikimedia.org/wikipedia/commons/a/af/Motorhead-01.jpg *License:* CC-BY-SA-3.0 *Contributors:* Own work *Original artist:* Mark Marek

Mark Marek

- **File:Motorhead-03.jpg** *Source:* https://upload.wikimedia.org/wikipedia/commons/0/0c/Motorhead-03.jpg *License:* CC-BY-SA-3.0 *Contributors:* Own work *Original artist:* Mark Marek

Mark Marek

- **File:Motorhead-04.jpg** *Source:* https://upload.wikimedia.org/wikipedia/commons/2/29/Motorhead-04.jpg *License:* CC-BY-SA-3.0 *Contributors:* Own work *Original artist:* Mark Marek

Mark Marek

- **File:Motorhead-Live-Norway_Rock_2010.jpg** *Source:* https://upload.wikimedia.org/wikipedia/commons/9/9e/Motorhead-Live-Norway_Rock_2010.jpg *License:* CC BY 3.0 *Contributors:* Transferred from en.wikipedia; transferred to Commons by User:Kafuffle using CommonsHelper.
  Original artist: Dark Apostrophe (talk). Original uploader was Dark Apostrophe at en.wikipedia
- **File:Motorhead-johngullo-photograph-sofajockey-com.jpg** *Source:* https://upload.wikimedia.org/wikipedia/commons/4/4c/Motorhead-johngullo-photograph-sofajockey-com.jpg *License:* CC BY 1.0 *Contributors:* Own work *Original artist:* John Gullo
- **File:Motorhead_25th_Anniversary_Concert_Ticket.jpg** *Source:* https://upload.wikimedia.org/wikipedia/en/2/2a/Motorhead_25th_Anniversary_Concert_Ticket.jpg *License:* Cc-by-sa-3.0 *Contributors:* ? *Original artist:* ?
- **File:Motorhead_Port_Talbot_1982.jpg** *Source:* https://upload.wikimedia.org/wikipedia/commons/6/64/Motorhead_Port_Talbot_1982.jpg *License:* CC BY-SA 2.0 *Contributors:* Flickr: Motorhead Port Talbot 1982 *Original artist:* Andrew King
- **File:Motorhead_Snaggletooth_Belt_Buckle.jpg** *Source:* https://upload.wikimedia.org/wikipedia/commons/9/96/Motorhead_Snaggletooth_Belt_Buckle.jpg *License:* CC BY-SA 3.0 *Contributors:* Own work/selbst fotografiert *Original artist:* Frank Behnsen. Snaggletooth design by Joe Petagno/Lemmy Kilmister
- **File:Motorheadselftitled.jpg** *Source:* https://upload.wikimedia.org/wikipedia/en/f/f2/Motorheadselftitled.jpg *License:* Fair use *Contributors:* not known - available on multiple music sites such as AllMusic *Original artist:* ?
- **File:Motörhead.ogg** *Source:* https://upload.wikimedia.org/wikipedia/en/3/3c/Mot%C3%B6rhead.ogg *License:* Fair use *Contributors:* originally downloaded from the band's official site at http://www.imotorhead.com/discography/albums1.htm *Original artist:* ?
- **File:Musical_notes.svg** *Source:* https://upload.wikimedia.org/wikipedia/commons/a/ac/Musical_notes.svg *License:* Public domain *Contributors:* ? *Original artist:* ?
- **File:MusicalnotesSweden.svg** *Source:* https://upload.wikimedia.org/wikipedia/commons/2/29/MusicalnotesSweden.svg *License:* CC BY-SA 3.0 *Contributors:* Based on Musical notes.svg and Flag of Sweden.svg. *Original artist:* Albin Olsson
- **File:MusicalnotesUK.svg** *Source:* https://upload.wikimedia.org/wikipedia/commons/3/38/MusicalnotesUK.svg *License:* Public domain *Contributors:* Own work *Original artist:* Wereon
- **File:Nibbs_Carter_performing_at_Download_2012.jpg** *Source:* https://upload.wikimedia.org/wikipedia/en/c/cf/Nibbs_Carter_performing_at_Download_2012.jpg *License:* CC-BY-SA-3.0 *Contributors:*
  Own work
  Original artist:
  Mattmetallica
- **File:Nick_Tart.jpg** *Source:* https://upload.wikimedia.org/wikipedia/commons/6/61/Nick_Tart.jpg *License:* CC BY-SA 3.0 *Contributors:* Transferred from en.wikipedia; transferred to Commons by User:Kafuffle using CommonsHelper. *Original artist:* Original uploader was Sleeper141 at en.wikipedia
- **File:Nicko_McBrain_2.jpg** *Source:* https://upload.wikimedia.org/wikipedia/commons/a/a9/Nicko_McBrain_2.jpg *License:* CC BY 2.0 *Contributors:* originally posted to **Flickr** as Iron Maiden en Costa Rica *Original artist:* adels
- **File:Office-book.svg** *Source:* https://upload.wikimedia.org/wikipedia/commons/a/a8/Office-book.svg *License:* Public domain *Contributors:* This and myself. *Original artist:* Chris Down/Tango project
- **File:Phil-Lynott_Thin_Lizzy.jpg** *Source:* https://upload.wikimedia.org/wikipedia/commons/e/e4/Phil-Lynott_Thin_Lizzy.jpg *License:* CC BY-SA 2.0 *Contributors:* http://www.flickr.com/photos/rmarchewka/2833867753/in/faves-24788065@N02/ *Original artist:* Richard Marchewka
- **File:Portal-puzzle.svg** *Source:* https://upload.wikimedia.org/wikipedia/en/f/fd/Portal-puzzle.svg *License:* Public domain *Contributors:* ? *Original artist:* ?
- **File:PrayingMantisSRF2010.jpg** *Source:* https://upload.wikimedia.org/wikipedia/commons/8/83/PrayingMantisSRF2010.jpg *License:* CC BY-SA 2.0 *Contributors:* originally posted to **Flickr** as Praying Mantis *Original artist:* liftarn

- **File:PriestScorpionsNEC_017_Halford.jpg** *Source:* https://upload.wikimedia.org/wikipedia/commons/5/53/PriestScorpionsNEC_017_Halford.jpg *License:* Public domain *Contributors:* Originally from en.wikipedia; description page is/was here. This is a cropped version of another image, also originally from en.wikipedia, of which The original description page was here. All following user names refer to en.wikipedia. *Original artist:* Cropped version uploaded by Naufana; original uploader was Christopher Dale at en.wikipedia

- **File:Question_book-new.svg** *Source:* https://upload.wikimedia.org/wikipedia/en/9/99/Question_book-new.svg *License:* Cc-by-sa-3.0 *Contributors:*

  Created from scratch in Adobe Illustrator. Based on Image:Question book.png created by User:Equazcion *Original artist:* Tkgd2007

- **File:Rainbow_27091977_02_500b.jpg** *Source:* https://upload.wikimedia.org/wikipedia/commons/b/b0/Rainbow_27091977_02_500b.jpg *License:* CC BY 3.0 *Contributors:* Own work *Original artist:* Helge Øverås

- **File:Rainbowonstage.jpg** *Source:* https://upload.wikimedia.org/wikipedia/en/7/72/Rainbowonstage.jpg *License:* ? *Contributors:*

  Rainbow Live in Munich 1977

  Original artist: ?

- **File:Raventheband_(1).jpg** *Source:* https://upload.wikimedia.org/wikipedia/en/a/a4/Raventheband_%281%29.jpg *License:* PD *Contributors:* self-made, self taken

  Original artist:

  Llb9977 (talk)LLB9977

- **File:Reading-81-poster.jpg** *Source:* https://upload.wikimedia.org/wikipedia/en/4/42/Reading-81-poster.jpg *License:* Fair use *Contributors:* http://www.ukrockfestivals.com/reading-81.html *Original artist:* ?

- **File:RickAllen.JPG** *Source:* https://upload.wikimedia.org/wikipedia/commons/2/2e/RickAllen.JPG *License:* CC BY 3.0 *Contributors:* Transferred from en.wikipedia to Commons. *Original artist:* Weatherman90 at English Wikipedia

- **File:Rick_Savage.jpg** *Source:* https://upload.wikimedia.org/wikipedia/commons/3/3a/Rick_Savage.jpg *License:* Public domain *Contributors:* Originally from en.wikipedia; description page is/was here. *Original artist:* Original uploader and author was Weatherman90 at en.wikipedia

- **File:Ricky_Warwick,_June_2011,_Download_Festival.jpg** *Source:* https://upload.wikimedia.org/wikipedia/commons/d/d5/Ricky_Warwick%2C_June_2011%2C_Download_Festival.jpg *License:* CC BY 2.0 *Contributors:* http://www.flickr.com/photos/sezzles/6047522860/sizes/l/in/photostream/ *Original artist:* Sezzle

- **File:Rob_Halford_Motorbike_1988.jpg** *Source:* https://upload.wikimedia.org/wikipedia/commons/b/bc/Rob_Halford_Motorbike_1988.jpg *License:* CC BY-SA 3.0 *Contributors:* http://everyrecordtellsastory.com/2012/05/25/judas-priest-live-at-hammersmith/ *Original artist:* Every Record Tells a Story

- **File:Ronnie_James_Dio_HAH_Katowice.jpg** *Source:* https://upload.wikimedia.org/wikipedia/commons/0/06/Ronnie_James_Dio_HAH_Katowice.jpg *License:* CC-BY-SA-3.0 *Contributors:* za zgodą Maross - Marek Krajcer *Original artist:* Maross

- **File:Ronnie_James_Dio_Tomb.JPG** *Source:* https://upload.wikimedia.org/wikipedia/commons/4/43/Ronnie_James_Dio_Tomb.JPG *License:* CC BY-SA 3.0 *Contributors:* Own work *Original artist:* Floatjon

- **File:Salem_1983.png** *Source:* https://upload.wikimedia.org/wikipedia/commons/a/a9/Salem_1983.png *License:* CC BY-SA 4.0 *Contributors:* Own work *Original artist:* SalemUK

- **File:Salem_2014.jpg** *Source:* https://upload.wikimedia.org/wikipedia/commons/4/47/Salem_2014.jpg *License:* CC BY-SA 3.0 *Contributors:* Own work *Original artist:* SalemUK

- **File:Satan_band.jpg** *Source:* https://upload.wikimedia.org/wikipedia/commons/e/e0/Satan_band.jpg *License:* CC BY-SA 3.0 *Contributors:* Own work *Original artist:* Lewismaster

- **File:Saxon_-_Denim_and_Leather.ogg** *Source:* https://upload.wikimedia.org/wikipedia/en/a/a1/Saxon_-_Denim_and_Leather.ogg *License:* Fair use *Contributors:* ? *Original artist:* ?

- **File:Saxon_Sweden_Rock_2008.jpg** *Source:* https://upload.wikimedia.org/wikipedia/commons/9/98/Saxon_Sweden_Rock_2008.jpg *License:* CC BY 3.0 *Contributors:* Own work *Original artist:* Äppelmos

- **File:Saxon_performing_at_Leeds_O2_Academy_2011.jpg** *Source:* https://upload.wikimedia.org/wikipedia/commons/7/75/Saxon_performing_at_Leeds_O2_Academy_2011.jpg *License:* CC BY-SA 3.0 *Contributors:* Leeds O2 Academy *Original artist:* Mattmetallica

- **File:Seventh_Son_Eddie_2013.jpg** *Source:* https://upload.wikimedia.org/wikipedia/commons/3/3b/Seventh_Son_Eddie_2013.jpg *License:* CC BY-SA 2.0 *Contributors:* Flickr: Eddie *Original artist:* dr_zoidberg

- **File:Spike_band.JPG** *Source:* https://upload.wikimedia.org/wikipedia/commons/f/f4/Spike_band.JPG *License:* Public domain *Contributors:* Own work *Original artist:* Orlovic

- **File:Steve_Clark.jpeg** *Source:* https://upload.wikimedia.org/wikipedia/commons/8/8c/Steve_Clark.jpeg *License:* CC-BY-SA-3.0 *Contributors:* http://image.wetpaint.com/image/1/ZKuoc-MGMUFddwDAX55PLA36924/GW281H426 *Original artist:* Thuddy

- **File:Symbol_book_class2.svg** *Source:* https://upload.wikimedia.org/wikipedia/commons/8/89/Symbol_book_class2.svg *License:* CC BY-SA 2.5 *Contributors:* Mad by Lokal_Profil by combining: *Original artist:* Lokal_Profil

- **File:Tank_1982.jpg** *Source:* https://upload.wikimedia.org/wikipedia/commons/d/de/Tank_1982.jpg *License:* CC BY-SA 3.0 *Contributors:* Own work *Original artist:* Rollingdell

- **File:Terrorizerlogo.JPG** *Source:* https://upload.wikimedia.org/wikipedia/en/8/82/Terrorizerlogo.JPG *License:* Fair use *Contributors:*

  The logo is from the http://www.terrorizer.com/ website. [1] *Original artist:* ?

4.3. CONTENT LICENSE

- **File:Text_document_with_red_question_mark.svg** *Source:* https://upload.wikimedia.org/wikipedia/commons/a/a4/Text_document_with_red_question_mark.svg *License:* Public domain *Contributors:* Created by bdesham with Inkscape; based upon Text-x-generic.svg from the Tango project. *Original artist:* Benjamin D. Esham (bdesham)
- **File:Thin_Lizzy_(20).JPG** *Source:* https://upload.wikimedia.org/wikipedia/commons/f/f8/Thin_Lizzy_%2820%29.JPG *License:* Public domain *Contributors:* Immagine personale *Original artist:* HeavyMezza89
- **File:Thin_Lizzy_-1983.jpg** *Source:* https://upload.wikimedia.org/wikipedia/commons/9/95/Thin_Lizzy_-1983.jpg *License:* CC BY-SA 2.0 *Contributors:* http://www.flickr.com/photos/harrypotts/4630747797/in/faves-24788065@N02/ *Original artist:* Harry Potts
- **File:Thin_Lizzy_-_Manchester_Apollo_-_1983_(2).jpg** *Source:* https://upload.wikimedia.org/wikipedia/commons/9/90/Thin_Lizzy_-_Manchester_Apollo_-_1983_%282%29.jpg *License:* CC BY-SA 2.0 *Contributors:* THIN LIZZY - Manchester Apollo - 1983 *Original artist:* Harry (Howard) Potts
- **File:Thin_Lizzy_-_TopPop_1974_1.png** *Source:* https://upload.wikimedia.org/wikipedia/commons/f/f1/Thin_Lizzy_-_TopPop_1974_1.png *License:* CC BY-SA 3.0 *Contributors:* Beeld En Geluid Wiki - Gallerie: Toppop 1974 *Original artist:* AVRO
- **File:Thin_Lizzy_1978-Live_and_Dangerous_lineup.jpg** *Source:* https://upload.wikimedia.org/wikipedia/commons/1/1e/Thin_Lizzy_1978-Live_and_Dangerous_lineup.jpg *License:* CC BY-SA 2.0 *Contributors:* http://www.flickr.com/photos/chris_hakkens/5110137560/in/set-72157625104139417/ *Original artist:* Chris Hakkens
- **File:Thin_lizzy_08081977_04_800.jpg** *Source:* https://upload.wikimedia.org/wikipedia/commons/9/93/Thin_lizzy_08081977_04_800.jpg *License:* CC BY 2.5 *Contributors:* Own work *Original artist:* Helge Øverås
- **File:Tygers_of_Pan_Tang_–_Headbangers_Open_Air_2014_04.jpg** *Source:* https://upload.wikimedia.org/wikipedia/commons/a/a3/Tygers_of_Pan_Tang_%E2%80%93_Headbangers_Open_Air_2014_04.jpg *License:* CC BY-SA 3.0 *Contributors:* Own work *Original artist:* Frank Schwichtenberg
- **File:UFO_-_Hamburger_Harley_Days_2015_04.jpg** *Source:* https://upload.wikimedia.org/wikipedia/commons/6/68/UFO_%E2%80%93_Hamburger_Harley_Days_2015_04.jpg *License:* CC BY-SA 3.0 *Contributors:* Own work *Original artist:* Frank Schwichtenberg
- **File:Venom,_Conrad_„Cronos"_Lant_at_Party.San_Metal_Open_Air_2013_12.jpg** *Source:* https://upload.wikimedia.org/wikipedia/commons/c/c2/Venom%2C_Conrad_%E2%80%9ECronos%E2%80%9C_Lant_at_Party.San_Metal_Open_Air_2013_12.jpg *License:* CC BY-SA 3.0 *Contributors:* Own work *Original artist:* Jonas Rogowski
- **File:Venom_live_at_hellfest.jpg** *Source:* https://upload.wikimedia.org/wikipedia/commons/1/12/Venom_live_at_hellfest.jpg *License:* CC BY-SA 2.0 *Contributors:* http://www.flickr.com/photos/rinmedwithfire/2621132858/ *Original artist:* mithrandir3
- **File:Vivian_Campbell_&_Brian_Downey_by_Alec_MacKellaig.jpg** *Source:* https://upload.wikimedia.org/wikipedia/commons/b/b3/Vivian_Campbell_%26_Brian_Downey_by_Alec_MacKellaig.jpg *License:* CC BY 2.0 *Contributors:* http://www.flickr.com/photos/amks_photos/5333839342/in/faves-24788065@N02/ *Original artist:* Alec MacKellaig
- **File:Whitesnake-1980.jpg** *Source:* https://upload.wikimedia.org/wikipedia/commons/7/78/Whitesnake-1980.jpg *License:* CC BY-SA 2.0 *Contributors:* http://www.flickr.com/photos/watt_dabney/2973862537/ *Original artist:* Andrew King
- **File:Whitesnake.jpg** *Source:* https://upload.wikimedia.org/wikipedia/commons/0/00/Whitesnake.jpg *License:* CC BY-SA 4.0 *Contributors:* Own work *Original artist:* Thelastcanadian
- **File:Whitesnake1983.jpg** *Source:* https://upload.wikimedia.org/wikipedia/commons/4/4b/Whitesnake1983.jpg *License:* CC BY-SA 2.0 *Contributors:* http://www.flickr.com/photos/watt_dabney/5165535102/ *Original artist:* Andrew King
- **File:Whitesnake_Hammersmith_Odeon_1981.jpg** *Source:* https://upload.wikimedia.org/wikipedia/commons/1/19/Whitesnake_Hammersmith_Odeon_1981.jpg *License:* CC BY-SA 2.0 *Contributors:* Whitesnake Hammersmith Odeon 1981 *Original artist:* Andrew King
- **File:Wiki_letter_w_cropped.svg** *Source:* https://upload.wikimedia.org/wikipedia/commons/1/1c/Wiki_letter_w_cropped.svg *License:* CC-BY-SA-3.0 *Contributors:*
- Wiki_letter_w.svg *Original artist:* Wiki_letter_w.svg: Jarkko Piiroinen
- **File:Wikidata-logo.svg** *Source:* https://upload.wikimedia.org/wikipedia/commons/f/ff/Wikidata-logo.svg *License:* Public domain *Contributors:* Own work *Original artist:* User:Planemad
- **File:Wikiquote-logo.svg** *Source:* https://upload.wikimedia.org/wikipedia/commons/f/fa/Wikiquote-logo.svg *License:* Public domain *Contributors:* ? *Original artist:* ?
- **File:Zero_Tolerance_magazine_(first_issue_cover).jpg** *Source:* https://upload.wikimedia.org/wikipedia/en/c/c4/Zero_Tolerance_magazine_%28first_issue_cover%29.jpg *License:* Fair use *Contributors:*
  May be found at the following website: ztmag.com/archives *Original artist:* ?

4.3 Content license

- Creative Commons Attribution-Share Alike 3.0

Made in the USA
Middletown, DE
07 March 2019